THE LETTERS OF LINCOLN STEFFENS

by the same author

THE SHAME OF THE CITIES (1904)

THE STRUGGLE FOR SELF-GOVERNMENT (1906)

UPBUILDERS (1909)

THE LEAST OF THESE (1910)

OUT OF THE MUCK (1913)

JOHN REED: UNDER THE KREMLIN (1920)

MOSES IN RED (1926)

THE AUTOBIOGRAPHY OF LINCOLN STEFFENS (1931)

BOY ON HORSEBACK (1935)

LINCOLN STEFFENS SPEAKING (1936)

THE LETTERS OF LINCOLN STEFFENS (1938)

THE LETTERS OF
LINCOLN STEFFENS

VOLUME II: 1920-1936

EDITED WITH INTRODUCTORY NOTES BY
ELLA WINTER AND GRANVILLE HICKS
WITH A MEMORANDUM BY CARL SANDBURG

hb

HARCOURT, BRACE AND COMPANY, NEW YORK

Designed by Robert Josephy
PRINTED IN THE UNITED STATES OF AMERICA

CONTENTS

ILLUSTRATIONS

BOOK TWO

BOOK TWO

1920-1936

VII

MAYBE, PERHAPS—BUT
(1920-1923)

IN JANUARY, 1920, leaving G. in Paris, Steffens went to Copenhagen with George Lansbury, Labor M.P. and editor of the London *Daily Herald*. They talked with Maxim Litvinov at the time Assistant Commissar for Foreign Affairs in the Soviet Government. The conversations finished, Steffens again visited Berlin. On his return to Paris, he found that G. had left, and he followed her to Monte Carlo. The possibility of revolution in Italy awakened once more his passionate curiosity about the processes of change, and they went to Rome. G. returned to America in June, and Steffens went to Vienna and Prague with E. A. Filene. After a brief stay in Germany, he sailed for New York.

He was trying to understand all that had happened to him and the world during his absence from America. When he started out for the peace conference, he had written Laura that he might be back so soon there would be no time for letters. He had stayed two years. He had observed the conference and later peace meetings; he had looked at defeated Germany, insurgent Italy, and revolutionary Russia. And even in the autumn of 1920 he was loath to leave Europe.

That he was learning all the time he did not doubt, but he could not say what. Writing came hard. He was thinking, not very precisely, of a book on the two cultures, the dying culture of his era and the culture of the future. But he was not writing it. At times he was depressed: "If I can't write any more," he said in February, 1920, "I ought to know it and turn definitely to other things." And again, a fortnight later: "My stuff does not of itself take a form and so help write itself. This scares me a little. Form is the essence of the creative faculty, and I may have lost that." But in more confident moments he knew he was right in waiting: "My writing is not important, and finding out things is very important."

At times he felt that his function was to modify the excesses of the revolutionaries. "There must be liberalism," he wrote. "The Socialists haven't it at all, and they will need it most of all, as Russia shows." Yet what he most consistently preached was the need for absolute intellectual honesty and the scientific method, qualities that he seldom found in the liberals of his acquaintance. "My chief interest," he decided, "is to open up criticism of Socialism from the Left and point to errors in that philosophy which have appeared under its initial applications. A third philosophy is evolving, and I think I have some leads for it."

"A man can," he wrote, "now and then get out of his grooves of thought, be free, and see the world anew." That was what he wanted to do. "I have to reconsider everything in the light of my experience in the war and the revolutions." Everything! It was not an easy nor an altogether pleasant process, but he was ready for it, and he did not despair. "I would like," he said, "to spend the evening of my life watching the morning of the new world."

In the autumn of 1920 he lectured his way across the continent, telling large audiences, sometimes enthusiastic, sometimes shocked, what he had learned. It was an uncommonly tentative lecture that he gave, and hence disturbing. After a brief visit with his sisters, he went for the third time to Mexico, and then tried, unsuccessfully, to enter famine-smitten Russia with Jo Davidson, the sculptor. On his return he lectured and worked for Russian famine relief, and began once more his campaign for amnesty for political prisoners. At first, as always at first, he was in high spirits. "Think of all the hopeless fellows saved. . . . And don't forget my old promise to the McNamaras *kept,* at last!" He carried the fight from Postmaster General Hays to Secretary Hoover to President Harding. Debs was released, and that was all. "So,—I fell down once more."

And instantly a new idea: "I want to go to India, and see and talk with Gandhi." But the British Government would not grant him a visa. Indeed, until the autumn of 1923 he was barred from all parts of the Empire. The explanation, he later heard, was that Lloyd George, who with Wilson had authorized the Bullitt mission to Russia, now feared to have his part in that expedition revealed. Steffens, ignorant of all this in 1921, thought the visa was only temporarily delayed, and went to California with the expectation of sailing for India. When opposition persisted, he returned to Washington to press his case, and finally went to Europe.

In May, 1922, he took the place of Karl von Wiegand, correspondent of Hearst's Universal Service, at Genoa. He was at Bad Pyrmont in June, at Sorrento with G. in the summer, in Paris in the autumn. He spent a few days at the Lausanne conference, and in January, 1923, he sailed for New York. He picked up some of the old threads, and visited his sisters once more, but in June he was off again for Europe. After another summer in Italy, he made his last trip to Soviet Russia, this time with Senator La Follette, his son, Robert M. La Follette, Jr., Jo Davidson, and others whom he had long desired to show "the Future." On his return to Paris, he found that England had lifted the four-year ban against him, and he went to London.

After Versailles Steffens had felt that he was about to make discoveries of fundamental importance. He had said that enough facts had been gathered, and that the important thing was to draw conclusions from them. But the generalizations had eluded him, and he had gone on gathering facts. In August, 1923, he stated to Dr. Suggett some of the questions he was trying to answer. "I am really puzzled," he went on, "really interested. I may discover something, something I don't know." Probably, when his generalizations were stated, they would turn out to be commonplace. ("Damn these universities, all of them. They have made my life one of unlearning literally, and all my discoveries are of well-known, well-kept secrets.") But he must draw conclusions if he could, and toward that end he went on gathering facts.

Meanwhile, except for his occasional journalistic jobs, he wrote little. Letters he wrote in abundance, more than can be published, but the book on the two cultures would not take shape. He did write a number of fables, polished little stories that said part of what he wanted to say. Many years before he had learned that men would often accept the ironical statement of truths they would otherwise reject. Now, with his vivid sense of the two cultures, paradox and parable became natural forms for him to adopt. He began a longer fable, which later became *Moses in Red,* and meditated on a life of Jesus, which would also have been a parable. And he thought, now and then, of writing his autobiography, "My Hard Life" or "My Life of Unlearning."

The personal problem looked as though it had solved itself, though not without distressing moments, and he and G. looked forward to spending the remainder of their lives together. He was still interested in Ella Winter, but, he told himself, objectively. Yet, when he had his visa and wrote Laura that he was going to England to see his old friends, he knew, and Laura knew too—for she understood her brother—that he was thinking of the girl he called Peter.

To All at Home in Calif.

Hotel Chatham, Paris,
Jan. 4, 1920

Dear Laura, Allen, Dot, Jim:

I may go to Kiev, Russia. G. will tell you if I do. It is for the Ukrainians, really. They want to make peace with the Bolsheviks. But they fought with Denikin; they are a bit ashamed to make their advances. They want a liaison. They appealed to Lansbury, and he suggested and they accepted me.

Things are moving fast here, faster than the news makes clear. The victory of the Red Russians is extraordinary. England sees the East all exposed, her East: Afghanistan, Persia,—India. It is a crisis "abroad." And "at home" in England the Labor forces are marching steadily on and on. . . .

The Italians here tell me that they think that they can have a bloodless revolution; and soon. Do you wonder I want to go south? But peace in the Baltics is more pressing, and I can be back here in a month or six weeks. And I may not go, of course.

Love to all,
Len.

To Ella Winter

Paris [Jan., 1920]

Dear Peter:

. . . Did you read my first article on the French and the International? How they were withdrawing from the Second and not going to be accepted by the Third, but were considering with the English a Fourth International or,—none? Well, that's my predicament, personal. She knows about Us. I didn't tell her at first; she was too ill. But, Lord, I can't conceal anything like that, and she's a woman.

There was something the matter. She felt it, of course; said nothing for a few days, and then asked. I told her the story. She took it as you said she would and as I knew she would. And now she wants to be my friend. Like you. So I'm going to be a lover completely surrounded by friends! That is justice, you will say; as she does, but I hate justice. I believe in mercy, and love, and so,—well, I warn you, as I have her, I'm going to look around for a Fourth International to join. Me and the French. Absurd, G. L. says, but a Fourth is better than none.

I'm going to destroy all your letters, Peter, before I leave here, wherever I go. It will hurt, they are lovely letters, but it is best to do away with them and you have a right to know that they do not exist. For, while it is all right to commit crimes, it is a mistake to leave a record of them.

You see, I can laugh yet; even at so serious a subject as myself. But I don't mean to pretend that there has not been some anguish,—all around. There has been nothing ugly in it, however; not from any angle. Some day we must all three meet, we good friends of

Stef.

To Laura Suggett

The Daily Herald,
London, E.C.4,
January 11, 1920

Dear Laura:—

This is a Sunday. I came over from Paris yesterday to see about that trip to Kiev. I have just had lunch with the men who want me to go, and they saw right away that my idea for the approach was better than theirs. They wanted to go via Holland and Warsaw. I held for Copenhagen and Berlin, where I can determine to my satisfaction whether it is worth while going farther.

It was, it is hard on G. She is really not well. And, then, to make matters worse for her, she suspected and I had to tell her all about that little, passing fancy of mine for the young girl here. She counts it as more important than I do, now. She may write you about it; she said she wished to be the first to tell you, and you will not let her know I ever said a word. But I also want early to say to you that I did, and I do, like E. W. very much, but it is her young genius that attracts me, and that's all. She has had a scientific training, which is good, and science may be her field, but I think she can do imaginative work and I am influencing her to try some visualizing writing: fiction or an essay. I should not have told G. anything about it, but I can't conceal much and, of course, once having mentioned it, I couldn't keep it in perspective. G. wanted to release me at once, and go home, but I objected to that. It is right that I go away myself. But I'll go back to G. and I'll return with a fresh sense of the true nobility that is in her. I hope you will write to her and, when you do, show her some affection. She not only loves me, she is a very true friend of mine and,—ours; inexpressive, but deep and good, very, very good. . . .

Love to Doctor, Nellie, Frenzy and,—the Dots, but don't send this letter on.

Len.

To Ella Winter

Hotel Kongen af Danmark,
Kobenhavn,
20 January '20

The Channel was smooth, Peter, and the air was balmy. It was a fair crossing. I spent the time peacefully reading Chinese poetry; talking to George [1] about the things that are on his mind to say here and do; and watching a blond, young American drummer playing poker in the smoking room. A handsome boy he is, and gay; good, too. He didn't even look at the blonde girls on the boat. . . .

Yesterday, the first day here, was full of light. We had two hours with L. [1] in the forenoon, and G. L. [1] got and filed two interviews or, rather, one statement and one long interview. There was no mail out till tonight. We talked blockade-lifting, and the consequences; Third International; conditions inside; and,—everything. . . .

We dined last night here with L. and Mrs. L., sitting it out till midnight. Awfully interesting. G. L. and L. discussed the theme of my book; not purposely, but accidentally, and I steered just enough to see the difference between the thinkers of evolution and of revolution. Tonight we have the evening with one of the Small Nations: mine. But George has one, too, and we'll call on that today.

I'll write again before I leave here, probably Friday, and then not

[1] L. and Mrs. L. refer to Litvinov, Assistant Commissar for Foreign Affairs, and Mrs. Litvinov, and G. L. or George to George Lansbury. At this time it was dangerous to use people's full names because letters were liable to be opened.

till Berlin. I wish I could go into particulars. It has been rich, and promises more, much more. But I'll have to leave it for talk. All I'll say now is that I wasn't altogether right in the impression I gave of the plans of the Future; and where I was wrong, the truth is interesting, very. The Future is uncompromising; hard, but not because of military successes. No, it is our old friend Economic Determinism,— which is ruling the minds in there: Fate; a Certainty which is startling. There will be no easing up for the Second International, for example. The Third will be driven ruthlessly through, the Left backed everywhere and the Right and Centre sacrificed,—pitilessly. Persons don't count, only forces. This cannot be the final truth, of course, but it's the fact. . . .

Write me at the Hotel Adlon. I'll be there till about February 1, Peter dear; her

Stef.

To Allen H. Suggett

Berlin, Jan. 30, 1920

Dear Allen:

. . . Germany is depressing. It is worse than it was when I was here last fall. Bankers and business men are saying to the reporters that confessed bankruptcy is the only way out. This may be propaganda. But it is an expression in financial terms of the real feeling of many of the little people I meet and talk to. Despair is the note struck everywhere. . . . All one can be certain of now is that something has got to happen in Germany. The sense of this is that it is bringing the French and others to talk of letting up a little on the Germans. You get that. The French papers have shown it plainly; said it straight out. It is the beginning of wisdom, but as usual on our side, it is late. We should have tackled the peace itself from the start as a world problem, and as such settled it; not as a punitive or graft thing. I wish our statesmen could grasp the fact that their folly is the best card counted upon by the Bolsheviks, who predict our every turn, announce it in advance and so win prestige throughout their part of the world, eastern Europe and Asia. I feel the effect of it in my talks with the small nations. They know they have to watch and talk to and hear both sides, and their wonder at the Russian foresight, definiteness, open diplomacy and prowess grows apace.

When I was in London, the English Government was under some

pressure from business men to settle with the Soviet Government. The Scandinavian Governments felt the same thing, and now here in Germany the correspondents are about to write stories about how the German Foreign Office talks of the urging it gets from German business men. We are hearing of "conservative Bolshevism." The explanation I offer is that the men Soviet Russia is sending out to talk business are quiet, business-like, well-dressed fellows who really understand business and set forth a plan for big trading which gets around the difficulties of exchange. They have hides and flax to trade for made-leather and steel: so much stuff for so much stuff: no money involved. And Russia gives the credit! That is to say, Russia is willing to deliver the hides and other raw material, let the buyer make it into useful articles and wait for Russia's agreed-upon share of the finished goods. This is a way out, and it naturally attracts the business mind. A business man I talked with about this met my suggestion that it was propaganda for Bolshevism by saying simply that it "wasn't propaganda; it would work, and I see nothing else proposed that will do that."

The secret of the Bolshevik strength at home and abroad lies right in there: that they have a plan for the solution of the problem both at home and abroad. . . .

Len.

Paris, Feb. 10, 1920

Dear Allen:

This is Tuesday. I got back here Sunday morning. G. was gone. She went south, to Monte Carlo, and I shall follow as soon as I can get a place on one of those crowded trains. She was ill here. It was a terrible thing I did to her: bringing her over here to be made well, then putting her up against a half-explained situation which hit her fluttering heart and,—leaving her to think, to feel it almost alone. Am I a blankety-blank? I don't know. But certainly I can do fierce things to those that love me. I wonder why I have imagination for a Small Nation, and none for a friend. I could have gone to Kiev for the Ukraine. But I could not lay over a few days to clear up a dark place for G.! I am really puzzled to understand myself. But I guess that is because I don't want to see myself so straight as, for example, you may be able to do.

Your picture and Laura's of Carmel and the future is lovely, and it

pulls me hard. I get awfully homesick. But I mustn't quit this yet.
It is opening up a clear vision of the future, the next stage of human
development. I feel sometimes that I can see how it is going to be. I
can see that it is to be a Socialist state, better, much better than ours,
but not perfect, and the imperfections are going to be the result of
our bad thinking in this stage, the fighting ideas resulting from the
class-war, which is war; and they in perfection are going to be in-
tolerable. Labor is not ready to take over society, but Labor is going
to do it anyhow; and it must. And afterwards Labor is going to have
to learn to be fit for the job. . . . It is the next stage after Socialism
which would interest me. For, of course, I am not a Socialist and I am,
—something else.

To Ella Winter

Hotel de la Terrasse,
Monte Carlo, Feb. 19, 1920

Dear Peter:—

Your nice long serial letter in several moods got here yesterday, and
I'll answer part of it. Not the personal part. That's too painful to me.
You didn't guess half the truth, but you used the right method. You
took yourself as the key to me, and that will open anybody to you;
some day; when you have sunk lower in human degradation and
know it. I was jealous. That's what I didn't mean to say. I had
imagined something, vividly, and, though there were other elements
in my misery; the thought of the things you needed to know; the
big, black core of the pain was envy (which is what jealousy is, at
bottom). And when I reflected that I wanted you to find a lover, and
marry him, even if he were the wrong one and the marriage were a
mistake and had to be undone and done over,—when I saw that my
feeling was against my better wishes, and mean and selfish and not
really in your interest, I knew that I had something besides love in
my heart, and that I had to dig it up, look at it straight, and chuck
it out. And I did. I had to hurt my image of you a bit, to help myself;
as you had to hurt mine to get you over a bad place once. But I restored you, Peter. When I was all cleaned up, I found I could be
a good friend again. So that's that.

Now about the writing, which you want to do and don't do. I can
help you there. I have been that way, and I know others, of all ages,
who have been that way. I could tell you very amusing stories of

writers whose names you know, who have worried as you do. I read last night a preface by George Moore to his novel, *Lewis Seymour,* which touched on the problem and the solution. He was trying to rewrite his "Lover" story,[1] and couldn't,—so long as he had only the desire to. But one day in the bath, the old story came to him in a new form: scenes, dialogues and all, and he rushed to write. He couldn't wait to dress; he dried himself, threw on a robe and dashed in to his stenographer and,—dictated, fast, 2,000 words a day for three months till the thing was done. . . .

You can write. Believe me, you *do* write. As your letters to me show. I tried to get you to turn your general desire upon some one story; I tried, but not hard enough. You distracted me. I fell in love with you, and love is more selfish than friendship or, if you prefer (as I do) my love of myself got in the way of my love for you. I must do better now; I'd rather talk than write this, but you have called and I must respond. How can you concentrate your general longing to write?

First, you can do as I suggested before: Take some little story,— any one you really know, understand and like, and work at it. Write it to me. Tell me a story.—But you didn't do that, and that may mean that there is none that is ripe yet; no story ready to take form. All right, then.

Second. Think of your thesis (or the report) in chapters. Note them; write at least one heading. Raise the question to be answered in it, and, as you get your facts, let it, encourage it to take form. This means to take on phrases, sentences, paragraphs; it means bringing your impressions and ideas to a head.

The trouble with both these suggestions is that they are based on my psychology and therefore are the method by which I can work through to the writing stage. If we were conversing, I might detect in your answers, a difference in your mind and its processes, and so much more exactly your needs. But we are not talking, I am writing and so all I can say is that what I think you need is to bring your thoughts to such a state of form that you will not only wish generally to write but be forced by the distinctness of your images to grab paper and pencil and put them down in the words which should occur to you.

One foolish question I can dispose of, if you haven't yourself already answered it. You are neither too young nor too old to write, and

[1] *A Modern Lover* (1883), revised as *Lewis Seymour and Some Women* (1917).

you never will be. But, before you are thirty, it would be well to get
your mind in the habit of thinking things through into actual words,
phrases, sentences and,—form. You can help yourself to do this by
practicing it in conversation. Don't argue much, but express. State a
thing in one form and, if it doesn't go, say it again in another form,
putting more perception into it; a forced, clearer grasp. And, of course,
this means that you don't care at all about convincing your hearers.
You are only playing with them. With yourself, you are working.
Superficially light and careless, deeply sincere. Which makes good conversation, by the way, tending rather to wit than to debate.

And you must not doubt yourself, Peter. At least that much you
can take from Stef and from all your other lovers. You have genius.
I can't classify it yet. I don't know just what art form it requires for
its own expression, but that's only one evidence that you have it; that
you are different. I can tell you that, however,—you lovely Thing,—
that when I'm away from you, here, where your personality and your
person can't affect me, I do what I did at first: I appreciate your
genius; your gift to grasp and to do. That is clear: that is your true
beauty. Graham Wallas said that "maybe" your genius was not to
write, but to do; that "maybe" you were an executive, and he remarked
also that that was a form of greatness and a very rare and useful one.
And it is. And in a woman it needs to be doubly great, since men
have seized all the executive jobs and, though they can't fill them, they
do instinctively keep women out of them.

But the world is changing, and there are some men, like me, that
want things done and care not whether they are done by a male or a
female. Indeed, I'd like to see a great woman do a great job; and I'd
like to have men see her do it; and get the full significance of it. . . .

Stef.

To Jack Hollister

Monte Carlo, Feb. 21, 1920

Dear Jack:

I have but just received your letter of Dec. 6. . . . Europe isn't doing
very well. . . . It is illiterate peoples, the Russians and the Mexicans,
who alone are making experiments in scientific government and trying
to abolish poverty, vice and war. All the governors of men that I
watched fumbling the ball at Paris were afraid of anything new. They
thought it enough to have good intentions and mean well. Well, most

men mean well. But Lenin, about whom you ask, is not trying to be good. He wants to be wise, and as a matter of fact, he is cautiously applying to the social life of Russia the best we know of the science of government. Moreover, he is making a go of it. The stuff you read in the papers about him and about Soviet Russia is mostly lies. It isn't believed by the men who write it, as I know; nor by the European editors who print it, as some of them have admitted to me; and the truth, as I saw it in Russia, is known to men high up in the governments that are fighting and starving Russia, the Balkan states, and holding Germany down.

I tell you, Jack, my generation is too dishonest and too unscientific to solve the social problem. Labor, with its new culture, may do the job. The lower classes at least SEE the problem and the upper classes, in their blindness, don't, and are gradually forcing the workers to tackle their own problem. Meanwhile both sides in the class war, which is on over here, are knocking out the Liberals, bidding all neutral and evolutionary minds to "shinny on their own side." It looks bad for Liberalism, and the great Liberals I know are disheartened. But there must be liberalism. The English have it in its finest form. The Socialists haven't it at all, and they will need it most of all, as Russia shows. So that is the line of development for you young fellows. Try to find out while you are in college what the books can tell you of the sicknesses of society, read up yourselves all the proposed remedies and, without deciding upon one till you know and can experiment with all, go out into this superstitious world and help it. Work with and in it as your father does on his ranch. He reads up or listens to the scholars in agriculture, then he experiments for himself, and he has done some things the books say can't be done. . . .

Work hard on languages, history and geography. I haven't nearly enough tongues for the day's work. But then I haven't enough of anything. I'd like to go to school again.

To Allen H. Suggett

Monte Carlo, March 26, 1920

Dear Allen:

I haven't written you for a long time, and the news as I see it will interest you. It is a revolution in Germany,—almost, and it happened in a very typical, interesting way. The Reactionaries started it. One of my generalizations about revolutions is that they never are started by revolutionists, but always by the Government or the "interests."

When I was in Berlin the first time, last fall, the leader of the Independents, the Left Socialists, Dr.—What's his name [1]—who was assassinated a few days later,—well, anyhow, he told me that I must be back by March if I wanted to see the revolution. That was his idea of the time when he and his crowd would set the ball rolling.

The last time I was there, a few weeks ago, I dipped into that crowd and I could not find that they had any plans, hopes or vigor. My conclusion was that I need not be in Berlin this spring. But I did not, of course, get into the monarchist circle and so heard nothing of *their* plans, except rumors which came from foreigners. All that looked dangerous was the general psychology of all the upper class and probably of everybody in Germany, yes, and everywhere else, I guess. Everyone is trying, more or less unconsciously, to wiggle or work or plot himself back to where he was before the war. This makes a surface movement backward and seems to justify those observations which call this a reactionary period.

But the world cannot go back: never. It can fall or sink as Greece and Rome did, but it cannot get just where it was before, take up again the line of development and proceed as if the war had not been. Evolution is on, as ever, and so you have the deep forward movement which paralyzes the static thinkers, the minds that think of things as fixed, like buildings, sculpture and,—not like constitutions. That onward urge is pressing all the time, but it isn't led by radicals and so they cannot guide or time its acts. But the reactionaries can. They don't want to, of course, but they conspire to get back. If they were wise, they would, in Germany for example, have stood by the conservative Socialist government they had and still have. They can hold what they possess of wrong, and so work out in an evolutionary way, gradually, but it must move forward. But, no, they plot to bring back the military party, and ultimately a kaiser. The wisest of them were only waiting, we learn now, till their plans were better drawn and their forces better organized.

Ludendorff, who is the arch-monarchist leader, was not in this movement. He was planning, we hear now, for June. But the monarchists have their Lefts too, and so Kapp and the rest would not wait. They marched in, threw out the Right Socialists, who were harmless, and,— they don't get what they wanted, they don't take power and, holding it, turn the world back. No, they start the revolution. They bring on

[1] Hugo Haase.

just what they don't want. They release the Red forces and the discontent, and they break down the only government that can suppress the Spartacists.

I take no stock in the reports that the monarchists were playing with the Reds, for the Kaiser or a Lenin, the old order or Bolshevism. I don't believe the monarchists are intelligent and modern enough to play any such game. And I know that the Reds would not play with the Monarchists. I think I see at the moment a scared union of all the conservatives to get behind even a Socialist government to hold what they all had before the coup of von Kapp. The question is whether they can. I doubt it. As I say, the world cannot go back. It has slipped, we don't yet know how far. I'll go and see later. But I think now that the combination has got a hold on things again, will beat off the Spartacists, who are Bolshevik, and will arrange a settlement with organized labor. That will cost capital something, but the system may be saved.

I am watching Italy. There is a railroad strike on for April 1. The Government has had time to settle with labor, but it won't. There also is that same tendency, not to accept what has happened and fix it fast, but to get back, which is impossible. The Government, instead of meeting and settling with organized labor, its best friend, is preparing to run the railroads and the country with the army. They may start the revolution in Italy. The radical leaders there are the most intellectual in the world. They know and they tell me that they can't start the revolution; but they declare that the Government and the employers will. We shall see, you as well as I. I shall sit here in sunshine and comfort putting my money, not on the red and black at the Casino, nor on the Reds of politics, but on the white old guard of Italy, and France, and the U. S. It is the men who want it least that are making the revolutions of the world. Another proof of the humor of God.

I have been tempted to go to Rome, but the period of street fighting is barren for me. Nobody has time to think or report, and the little they tell me then is news only to the lovers of force. I am handy. I shall go south when a decision is reached and one can know whether the revolution is on, or,—only a strike. But Italy is more interesting than Germany to me, and maybe to you. Love to all.

Len.

To Laura Suggett

Monte Carlo, March 29, 1920

Dear Laura:

. . . Germany still is fighting its civil war and will soon be very interesting to me. I shall want to go there by and by. But since I am here, right at Italy's door, I think it wise to wait and see what the Italians do. And the significance of the Italian movement is that it is what we have never seen outside of Russia, and there only after years of revolution: the Italian labor movement is a united movement. The Left, the Right and the Middle Socialists, organized labor, unorganized labor, the Peasants' Union and the cooperative movement are all together, agreed even as to political action and direct, and how much of each. There too the connection is closest with the Russian Communists (Bolshevik); the communication is most constant and the study and application of the lessons of the war, revolutions and post-war strikes is most up to date. The Italian crisis as it is brought on by the strike may be the most educative of all, not excepting that of Russia. Only the Italian character and temperament are against that view.

Dr. said in his letter that Fremont was asking about my philosophy as it is in the becoming. An interesting question, even to me. I would like to know it myself. And I think I shall have a line on it when I get farther on with my book. Writing always was necessary to form my thinking and make it definite, and I find that especially so now. As I write along it interests and somewhat surprises me to see what I have been thinking. I don't like to attempt to write any of it briefly, in a letter, but I have three chapters almost in shape to typewrite and I am going to send it to you as I copy it, in small batches, and you will let Fremont read it when you have enough to see that it is not all or merely a bit of humorous writing.

For one thing I have got out of all this experience is the comedy of the conflict between the dying culture and our living conduct. I recognize that it is a tragedy: none more than I. But I have been to Moscow and, like everybody else that has seen that, I am sure of the future. My chief interest is to open up criticism of Socialism from the Left and point to the errors in that philosophy which have appeared under its initial applications. A third philosophy is evolving, and I think I have some leads for it. But this third philosophy has to get rid of the capitalist ideas of force, democracy, etc., and it will proceed not by fighting Communism, but by evolving it out into what it will be disposed of itself to be: a less organized, less certain and righteous, not at all a moral thing, but genially experimental and always growing and playing. Life is not so serious as the Russians see it; it is not so materialistic as the European Socialists plan it. It is, and so I think it will become, a comedy of errors and not a tragedy of sins.

G. is better, much better. She is well. I feel that she is strong enough to be abandoned and otherwise wronged, if need be. She sleeps. She is busy mornings with her own unimportant business and afternoons she attends with me to my most important affair: taking a walk somewhere, getting exercise, taking in air and scenery, and having some fun.

Len.

Pension Boos,
Rome, May 2, 1920

Dear Laura:

May 1 was yesterday, and it was amusing. It still is. There is cavalry in the court under our window. There have been troops all over the city. And nothing to do. The radicals had no plans for action. They avoid days on which they know the Government expects and prepares for trouble. But the Government represents the middle and upper classes, and these have a real terror for labor. Living in that atmosphere, I can feel, and G. with her Italian hears of it from the people themselves. It is pathetic, it is like everything else over here, comical. The troops are necessary to calm the fears of the bourgeoisie. So there they are out there, loafing, smoking, exercising their horses and passing the time, with good measure: two days of guard duty, protecting the people from the people.

Stuck on my book, temporarily, I wanted to let it cool so as to go at it again afresh. I began therefore a story that has been growing in me: a story about the French and Wilson. It is the story of a peasant girl in a laundry of Paris who believed in and stood up for Wilson against the pressure of the unions, saw the President arrive, hoping he would end wars, and then learned that the organization was right. One man could not make such a peace; only the people can do that job. The title is "Madeleine Loved Veelson." [1] It is a story, not a satire;

---

[1] Never published.

it is the story of the best part of France, and it will contain, if I can work it out, my conception of Wilson's work.

To Allen H. Suggett

Rome, May 2, 1920

Dear Allen:

. . . Rome carries the mind back to history. No one could resist backward thinking here, certainly not if he went sight-seeing. I get it hard. A guide the other day, talking about the persecutions of the early Christians, and the visit to the Catacombs where the followers of Christ were run underground, brought up the I.W.W. and the Bolsheviki. The Christians today are doing to others all that was done to them, and for the same reason, with the same excuses and the same end: the utter failure of force to beat out ideas.

But the guide himself was interesting. He had great sympathy for the early Christians. He hated the Socialists. He hissed at some workingmen we passed near the labor headquarters. He saw no parallel. And he saw not at all his own story, which he unconsciously told us. He pointed with pride to his name on an ancient stone. It commemorated some ancestor, he said, and I believe it. And I thought how his famous ancestor probably justified the system of those days, as his offspring does ours of today: he wanted the chance to provide for his children and therefore stood for privilege and property. The guide did, thinking of *his* children. But his ancestor never foresaw that one of his descendants would make his living showing people around over the stones of old Rome. I wonder what some Morgan would think if he could foresee that some of his children will, in the future, be guides in New York to some rich Bolshevik from Russia and the rest of them wine-sellers, boarding-house runners and beggars.

I wonder what men would do if they could visualize the future, as one has to do here. For when I say that Rome makes me think of the past I really mean that it reminds me of the future. The Italians are the future of Rome. They are the future of all other people too. Is this depressing to think of? It need not be. The lower class culture, which my book is about, is full of the consciousness of history. I think sometimes that one of the ways of saying what is happening in the world today is to repeat that Man is becoming conscious. In other words, Man is being born. Anyhow Labor is reading history for use: to keep it from repeating itself. The soldiers, fired into by the mob the other night, shot back, under orders, and aimed into the air. It was near the Coliseum.

To Laura Suggett

Rome, May 8, 1920

Dear Laura:

I have just this minute finished the first part of the story I had to start, about Wilson and the French. A copy of it is enclosed for you to read and keep. I take the other to work over and to guide me in the rest, which is not all planned out yet. She is to meet an American, good type, as near to Wilson himself as I can make the man. And her relations with him are to be parallel with those of Wilson with France. He goes away leaving the child, as Wilson left the peace, and,—Jacques takes the burden over, Jacques the radical. That is in general my plan. I may change it. But my idea is by this story to tell the Wilson story, from my own and from the several French points of view. *Le Feu* will see it all, as Clemenceau does; Jacques, as the Left sees it. The problem will be to hold it true to the characters and yet show the bigger story in the little one. But I shall not go right on with it now. I shall turn back to the book, revise the first chapter and write the second. I am in the mood for work.

I get letters from my friends in New York urging me to come home. I don't want to. They say there are many things to do in "the States," but I am not interested now in the things they are doing. Teaching isn't in it with learning, giving opinions isn't as fascinating as changing them. I am very *"content"* here, as the French say. Seeing old Rome with G. has been a rich and suggestive experience for me, coming as it does into my absorption in the new. It has broadened me, made me more patient and "philosophic" than I was. I wish Older, of all men, could have a season of all this, both the old and the new. Most of my friends need it, but it would comfort Older, do him good deep down. There is progress; it is plain here in Rome. And some things are permanent.

Len.

To Allen H. Suggett

Rome, May 15, 1920

Dear Allen:

This Government, like all that I have peeked into, is really sabotaging nature, unintentionally, of course, in innocent ignorance and meaning well. It is fierce, the lack of culture among the educated. They are living from hand to mouth, hanging on, preparing to suppress uprisings no one is plotting, and organizing the counter-revolution long before the revolution is even thought of.

I was taken to the Parliament, and it happened to be the day Nitti was beaten and resigned. The Socialists did not ask to be heard upon the new ministry, and they were not consulted because everybody, from the King down to the humblest voter, knows that the Socialists, who could make any ministry go, will join none. So it looks today as if Nitti might have to remake his own government. No other party seems able to, and the Socialists who beat him are willing to see him try again. They are saying every day that he, or some one of the old parties that made the war, should first tackle the difficulties left by their own war. The patience, the faith in economic forces, the definiteness of the forward policy,—these all are wonderful exhibitions to me, and they give me a sense of certainty about the future. Nature is to have some chance here in Italy. And all the while the leaders are not brash, not sure. They consult together, ask advice, go far to get it, and watch other countries for ideas on tactics. They are the most modest of leaders.

Those that I met are going next week to Germany on their way to Russia. They are going there, not to inspect and judge, but to consult, to take advice. It is amazing. Most men who go to Moscow want to tell the Russians something, alter their policy here or there. Not so these Italians. They are going there to take up with the experienced leaders of Russia the international problems, and they told me that their own course of procedure, even here in Italy, may be determined in very large measure by what they learn there, in distant Russia. It is a sign of their strength, both as to numbers and as to character and morale, that the Italian Government not only gives them leave to go, but cars to travel in as far as Königsberg where they transship for Reval! I have got a deep respect for the movement in Italy and the wisdom of its leaders. And I remember that the French Socialists had that same feeling. . . .

I want to do that book, finish this story and start another which I have long had in mind: the story of Moses.[1] My title for that suggests the idea: Moses; divine justice. It will be the story of the Revolutionists who do not go through, who don't like the Promised Land. Moses

[1] *Moses in Red,* published in 1926.

was spared their tragedy. But I am sure I have talked this to you. And then there is the Christ story, upon which I did some work the last time I was in Germany.

Mexico calls. But not very loud. That is all right, as it is going. Obregon is a good man, as good as Carranza, though in a different way, and Alvarado, who is named among the leaders of the new Revolution, is a better man,—from the Left point of view. So long as we Americans, and the other foreigners, keep out, I am content to watch from a distance the development of Mexico by the Mexicans.

I am more satisfied than ever, you observe, merely to watch social processes. I have not the old ache to butt in. A great time is coming, but not so much of achievement as of learning.

To Daniel Kiefer

Paris, June 21, 1920

Dear Dan:

Here I am again, just back and I find your letter, with some others from other friends and critics, who seem to think I should go 'way back and be home. My plan is other than that. I am watching the fronts of the movement, you see, while you fellows keep your eyes on the rear. Both are interesting, both important, and I cannot for the life of me understand what difference it makes just where in the procession a man marches. I don't think that what I am doing is the most essential thing in the world; it only interests me the most, and seems to be generally worth while.

Frank Stephens, Fred Howe and others I owe letters to, I shall pay in time. Give them my love and say so. I may do some more letter writing this week, though I am eager to get out and find out what the French have learned in the last four months. The Italians say the French don't learn at all, but they do, slowly, and what they do they can tell. So I can learn new things even from them. And the English are learning; and leading, too. Lenin taught them something, and they heard what he said and reported it faithfully. He said that they and the pacifists and all reformers were really bourgeoisie, living and thinking and feeling and reacting like "capitalists." And they are. And most of us are. And it is not necessary that we should be. I believe that a man can now and then get out of his groove of thought, be free, and see the world anew. It is hard to do, but it is possible. I know it is possible, for I, who am typical, have done it a lot over here. I have thought along lines of reasoning with men with whom I disagree, and it was like crossing a continent by a new route: I saw some very beautiful scenery. A locomotive engineer cannot do it, of course, because he is bound to take his trains over fixed routes. But I find that even some locomotive engineers have enough romance left in them to be interested in an account of what I see on another line. 2,500 French engineers, by the way, are applying here now for passports to go to Russia to work; they are being "locked out" at home.

I wish Henry George were over here and could see all this. He was ready to get the meaning of it, and write a rich philosophy. But then, when he wrote it, a lot of fellows would take it whole, and when the next flood of facts burst upon us, he would have to come on again and write another book, which, etc. Human planets become fixed stars so easily.

I see that John Clayton, a correspondent of the Chicago *Tribune*, says that Emma Goldman doesn't like Bolshevism in action, and wants to get back to free America. She is right. I had that feeling about Moscow and I came back to Paris, which I like. But I can see that it isn't important whether Emma and I get liberty. The important thing is that Bolshevik Russia shall go through its tyranny patiently and arrive at liberty for the whole Russian people and perhaps for the world; not me and Emma and you and McGill alone. Lenin isn't getting results; he is laying foundations, and what he and Russia need is criticism of some of his foundations, as such. It's no use telling him Russia is uncomfortable, illiberal and state socialism. What he wants to know is how he can change some of his foundations so as to be surer of ultimate liberty and general happiness. The Single Taxers could help the Socialists, if they would accept the coming of Socialism and make suggestions where the Socialists are looking for them; for a solution of the land question which the peasants could understand and would accept. But we won't. Like Emma, we will fight state capitalism directly, talk peace and liberty and,—results. I wish somebody would write a revision of George's philosophy in the light of the war and revolutions. That is what Lenin thinks some Socialist should do for Marx. I believe the Socialist will do it first. Single Taxers have learned the least from current history, less even than the business man. They have changed their minds less, I mean. Or am I wrong?

Steffens

To Ella Winter

Paris, June 26, 1920

Dear Peter:

Among my friends is a man, a gentle man, whom I used to expose in all his naked goodness. Whenever I or some other among his acquaintances neglected him, failed to call upon him or write, I found that he explained it to himself and always to the credit of the unde-serving. I made other people notice this. I would tell of some neglect, tell what the real cause thereof was and guess what my friend would have said, then I would take the witness up to this remarkable case and ask him how he had explained the matter. And always he would have had a gentle interpretation of it all.

I think you will stand this test. I haven't been writing to you, but you have written now and then to me. That was something. But there was more. I watched what you did write with acute interest. There was such a good chance for misunderstanding, for resentment. If there had been a trace of yellow in you, it would certainly have shown it-self. And there was no sign of color! Not a trace. Once you said some-thing which was not pure white, but I happened to know that that was the effect of an old wound. And I answered that. I couldn't let you think that! And it did not appear again.

I offer you my compliments, Peter. And some day I shall offer you an explanation, which you do not ask for, do not need, but, in justice to myself and as a flower to you, you should have. Not now, however; not this way.

It's a story, and I want to tell it you, watching you all the while.

And now will you tell me what you are doing? You have finished your job with the committee. How did you do it? What did you find out?

My plans are better drawn than usual, more definite, and yet not fixed. I expect to go to Vienna before the middle of July, thence to Prague and on to Berlin, where I may stay a while, if it is as "good" as it looks. Then back here, and Italy again.

You will write me, won't you? And then, some day I will tell you how it is on the Amazon. Not that you need to be told. You know two other rivers, and all rivers are alike, but,—they are all interest-ing, each in its own funny way, and you are young still, aren't you?

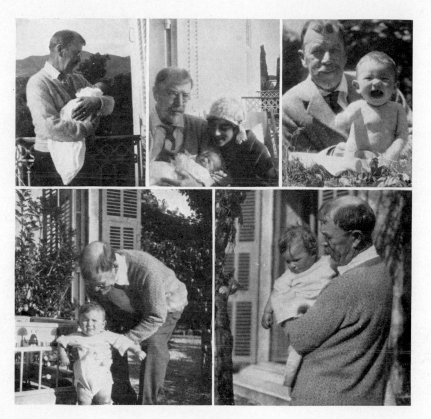

ITALY

upper left: LINCOLN STEFFENS WITH HIS SON, PETE, AGED NINE
DAYS. *upper center:* PETE STEFFENS, AGED THREE WEEKS, AND
HIS PARENTS, SAN REMO. *upper right:* LINCOLN STEFFENS AND
PETE, AGED SEVEN MONTHS, ST. CERGUE, SWITZERLAND.
lower: LINCOLN STEFFENS AND PETE AT ALASSIO, 1925.

If you know where Jack Reed [1] is, I wish you would tell me. I asked Ewer, and he wrote that, since I wasn't answering letters, he wouldn't write me. Which was strange, since I did answer all his letters, did what I could for his blooming friends. He wouldn't stand the test you flew over like a bird.

You are an extraordinary person, Peter. I have been right on that from the start. That was not the mistake. You are pure gold, and I not only admire, I am deeply grateful to you, as I may have a chance to show you some day,—after I have shown you some other things.

Stef.

Hotel Bristol, Wien,
Aug. 1st, 1920

Hello, Peter:—

This is what I wanted this sheet of paper for: one sheet when you gave me two. I wanted only enough to say "Hello, Peter." And so I say:

Hello, Peter.

But seriously, life is like that, all comings and goings, meetings and partings,[2] and yet it is good, so good. Maybe that's why. Maybe that's why marriage is so often a failure. I dunno. And you don't.

But seriously, do you realize what a false impression I have of Vienna? Think what I'll see when I think of Vienna now; how I'll feel about it, how I can't really be moved to help a city which is so happy—

I think I'll let E. A. have and help Vienna for his work. I'll take Prague or Karlsbad. I'll see and feel the misery there.

I wonder where we'll meet for the next chapter.

Pstef—

To the Family

Hotel Palace Passage,
Prague, August 2, 1920

Dear G. and Laura and Allen and Dot and—

Prague, where I arrived today from Wien, is a striking sight or sense. It's a city also. The people in it are alive. They move, in great

---

[1] John Reed, after spending three months in prison, had just been released, and had returned to Russia.

[2] Ella Winter went to Vienna to work with the Friends' Relief Mission in July, and Steffens, travelling with E. A. Filene, spent a week in the same city.

numbers, with a quick step. They smile. They wear good shoes, and new clothes, cheap, but made this year apparently, for this summer season. They don't stop and look at food in the windows of shops. They seem to have had enough food. They don't swallow nervously when you pay them money, and they don't reach for more. The little children in the back streets have straight legs; no blue lines under their eyes. Nobody tells you and so you have no sense all the time that people are dying of starvation. And tonight for dinner, up on the hill overlooking the beautiful city and the river, we had goose, *Gänsebraten,* like in the old German days.

My background for Prague is Vienna, and Wien, old, proud, aristocratic, merry Wien, is a dead city. It's the end of a state. It's the final product of the capitalist system, and as such I saw it. For E. A. was there to see, with that thought in mind, what could and must be done by the world, either the Entente, the League of Nations or (as I interpolated) the Third International. I suggested that he ask the captains of industry, diplomacy and states what plans they had to save Wien. They had none. We had all the "great men" of the Government, party leaders, Reparation Commissions, Relief, banks, factories and business, —and Labor,—conservative labor (organized) to lunches and dinners. And I was there. I wouldn't let them escape. I quoted Lenin: "I'll beat them all because," he said, "I have a plan, and they haven't. My plan may not be the best possible; it may not work in the long run, but,—I have a plan. And they have none." They didn't want Bolshevism. E. A., a business man, told them they couldn't have the old capitalist system back. A middle way must be found. Who saw one? No one.

And it's hell there. We saw the tenements, the hospitals, the children's barracks— We saw Wien, and it is hell. And as the bankers and industrialists counted it out on paper; even if they get coal and food and credit, they cannot, at our prices and their exchange, market their stuff in competition with the world!

And they can't, they don't blame labor. The employers of Wien boast that their workers are highly skilled, educated, honest workers, and that they listened to the Bolshevik propaganda and rejected it. And their leaders said to us: We had the leaders from all over Europe at our table, as well as the Viennese leaders; all Second International, and they said they wanted to work under the capitalist system until, at least, their children could eat. They didn't want a revolution. No.

Capital has "good" labor in Wien, and they are together. It is the system that has failed. The war and the peace, too, but the war and "the" peace are fruits and flowers of the capitalist system of which Wien is but the logical conclusion.

It's going the way of Rome, Greece, old Rome. And I met a Philadelphia reformer there who asked me in a daze what it meant. I said he was seeing what would happen to Philadelphia too some day. And the Bolsheviks are approaching Warsaw, and we hear today that Zittau in Saxony, Germany, is going to them; that Serrati has his answer from Moscow to Italy and,—there is a God.

We'll be here three days, then Karlsbad for two weeks, and I'm going to take the cure. . . . I like Europe. Love to all.

Len.

To Ella Winter

Prague, Aug. 2, '20

Prague, Peter, is a sudden city. You are told you will reach it at 4, so after lunch on the border you all lie down and sleep. With the perfect faith of death you sleep till,—somewhere around two,—people rush in seizing vacant seats and demanding others, yours among them. You ask questions; you get the answer: "Ja, Prag ist es!" You pick out your things from among the new baggage, chuck it out of the window and break the glass. That is Prague. And, with Vienna in mind, you feel a city alive. It's quite striking. In the late afternoon, we drove around to see the sights: The Tower, the old Huss church with the shops up against it (English; not the American phrase); the old, old Jewish cemetery where (you say) our ancestors are really beautifully buried; and then up on the hill to a restaurant upon the edge of it, with a great, calm sweep of a city strung on a river,— another river.

But there's something lacking here. I can't make out what it is. I don't care much for it; I don't care if it is alive. I miss something. Now in Wien,—ah, yes, I know what it is.

E. A. sent out by a messenger all his letters of introduction, doubting the etiquette but backed by my disregard of the conventions, and so he says we must all be up betimes tomorrow. The callers may begin to come at 9. I thought they wouldn't hurry so, but I did not say they might not all come at all. No, I didn't. And I was warm, too, and hot, and,—something else.

Peter.

But, no, I'll not say that.

There's music in the court outside my window, and good music. It has just started up. But, yes, it is good music. I don't miss Wien so much as I did. There was music in Wien or what is like it: harmony.

Stef.

Prague, Aug. 5, 1920

Dear Peter:

I am writing so much to you for two reasons. One is that you asked me to. You said you liked to have lots of letters "at first," meaning immediately, after a separation. I understand that. And I would have liked to have some from you here. It's my fault. I didn't know and so I did not give you my hotel.

It's fun making the acquaintance of cities. They have distinct personalities; hard to describe but recognizable. I used to notice this when I was doing cities as a muckraker in the U. S. Chicago was big, bluff, busy and careless, but open-minded; willing to learn or teach; indeed to give anyone a chance,—once. I felt it was like a "tough" or a rough, successful, good-natured drummer. New Orleans was effeminate, indolent, soft, smiling but a bit too ready to stab. And so on. And it's so over here. Just as I feel at different times that I'd like to be with different people, so I find myself writing for Florence or Berlin or London for the mood they mean to me. Someone should write the story of a city in this personal way, telling the way it came to be what it is.

Prague is a good example. It is very old; it was founded by the Jews and it bears the marks of them, clearly. Other races flowed in, and out; and various rulers came and went. It is beautiful, aged, somber, but what strikes me about it so far is that the people here now dominant seem to have no relation to it. They are here, but they don't belong here. They are like the Italians in Rome. They are not Romans, not the makers and masters of Prague. They are a young, crude, healthy folk who have inherited the splendid city of some other people. The Soviet in the Czar's mistresses' palace at Petrograd. It is odd, but it is not to be regretted. It is too interesting. Only sometimes it may seem to me to be sad; the city, I mean, the spirit of early old Jewish Prague.

And yet it's only one scene, one little chapter of the history of our race, the most complete, most tragic and significant story of a people in human history.

But, as I was saying, dear, the other reason why I am writing so much to you "at first" is because I like to. There we get back, as always, to your very, very selfish

Stef.

But I have not been writing so much or so often; not every minute; not even every day, and not as frequently as I wanted to.

This reminds me of a chapter in a book Hutch published. It was about me as a newspaper editor, and he wrote it after he had resigned or I had "fired" him; I forget which. It was called "An Interesting Failure," and was a genial account of the experiences of our staff in an effort to put art (and life) into a news service. It was so good that Hutch, the artist, couldn't change it, even after he had changed his mind about it and me. So he printed it, just as he wrote it originally, and simply added a footnote at the bottom of the last page, saying that what he wrote was not right; that the experiment was a success and that the editor he referred to was a success also.

"Am I inconsistent?" said Walt Whitman in reply to his critics. "If I am, then I am inconsistent."

Sweet Peter—

To Daniel Kiefer

Karlsbad, August 20, 1920

Dear Dan:

Please tell Frank Garrison that I shall seek a conversation with him on non-resistance. He is too logical. I think with him, but I have seen some things and talked with men who agree with us, about facts which pull the light out of a straight line, as Einstein discovered the sun drew the light of a star. Lenin is one of the men I mean. The Red Terror of Russia was started by the attempt to assassinate Lenin, while he was in the hospital helpless. That brought on the use of force. But he says, and I begin to see, that violence develops out of the endless conspiracies and outrages of the counter-revolutionists. You see it in Ireland where the leaders whom I have talked intimately with are dead set against force. It breaks out like boils on a sick system, and that is what Lenin means when he points out to British labor that, whether they intend to have a bloody revolution or a gradual bloodless evolution, Winston Churchill and his crowd will, by the use of force, cause the force of resistance. This is not understood in England.

They think Lenin demands that it declare for a bloody revolution; all he is trying to say is that the experience of Russia and Hungary show that whatever the radicals propose, the reactionaries will force the issue to battle and that, therefore, the radicals should, working for non-resistance, be ready to fight if they must.

It's all a part of my perception that, before we can practice a generous, just and gentle theory, we have to destroy somehow the force, often organized, and set up the economic, social and psychological conditions which make the beautiful possible. If we had the eloquence to convince more men of our ideal, we could get a big majority to drop their ideas and settle upon ours, work for it, and we could establish the right with non-resistance. But, Dan, a minority alone will do the trick, and that means one more short, sharp battle or war,—a war to knock out our present system of violence and lay the foundation for evolution, democracy and liberty, all three of which are impossible now either as aims or as methods. Ask Garrison to think it over, so that we can all discuss it. I want to learn, too, but I have now to reconsider everything in the light of my experience in the war and the revolutions, Russian and Mexican.

I dread my old convictions in my good friends; I shy at principles, "logic," "reason," and all systems. I have seen the steadiest mariner of all the ages in this man, Lenin, steer out of his course for rocks and storms, and the pitiful wailings of the crew. He has the substitute for consistency of action; he thinks straight: when he goes off the course, he knows it, notes it in the log and always, always has a plan to get back, always, except where the experience has taught his cool, scientific mind that there was an error in the course; that man did not know it all. Now you understand what I said yesterday; that the socialist program hereafter will be nearer what Lenin did than what Marx thought and wrote, and so will the Single Taxers and Henry George.

Affectionately,
Stef.

To Ella Winter

Hotel Adlon, Berlin, Aug. 28, 1920

Dear Peter:

I have just been reminded of you, and thinking of you (and your long, double-barrelled rebuke) made me think of me; which recalled a bull-pup I had once. He was a good-natured, mischievous, understanding little devil. His favorite sport was to go over into a neighbor's place, call out all his (17 or so) dogs and start a general fight. It was always a perfectly general fight; not only against him, but each one for himself against the whole pack. It was all right as fun, but my pup always came back cut up, bleeding and dirty. So I beat him. I laughed, but I did my duty and cuffed and kicked him: not hard, but— And he understood. He laughed too. He would come back, obviously expecting a licking; he would rush up to me as if to say: "Hurry up and beat me; get it over with." And I obeyed, and he? He would shake himself, back off, bark and laugh at me, and whirl about in a sort of ecstasy of joy. And what he said of that licking as plain as human speech was that "it was worth it," meaning that the fun he had had and the result he had achieved and left behind him on the neighbor's place was worth the licking.

Of course I got the deuce from Peter, but she gave me what I wanted: the assurance that she would tell me when *he* did turn up. And I want that because I am really deeply concerned. That's what you miss *or* don't understand. I wish he would come along soon. I told Felix [1] so. He said there was no hurry. I say there is. So I'm interested and eager, but,—he's got to be some man, as we say in American: young, big, intelligent, quiet-minded and a good wife. I explained to Felix what I mean by that. Your man must be big enough to let you fly high and far. He must be to you what a good wife is to a man. As a feminist, I can't see why a great woman like you should not be backed by a man who won't be jealous of your greatness. I'd love to see you blossom myself, and we've got to find a young man who will be as willing as I to have greatness in the family, even if it is not his, but his wife's.

Affectionately,
Stef.

To Mrs. J. James Hollister

Carlton Hotel, Pall Mall, London,
September 19, 1920

Dear Dot:—

Laura will have told you that I am going home for a while, and that I want to visit you, Jim and Bolitas. I have just written Jack

[1] Felix Frankfurter, of the Harvard Law School, whose secretary Ella Winter was at the Peace Conference.

warning him that I shall be calling soon on Groton. My plans are not fixed, of course. I am preparing a lecture trip to the Pacific Coast; I have to do it that way to pay my expenses, and I hear that the prices are fierce in the United States. But I hope to get about and, if possible, even to Mexico, and yet return here by February or March. It is interesting here. Germany is sinking slowly into bankruptcy; France is holding up in false hope of American aid (cancellation of debts) after our election; Italy is sliding left; England here is yielding step by step; and the rest of Europe is fighting, waiting, starving. I have seen hell. But I see light too; the dawn, and would like to spend the evening of my life watching the morning of the new world.

I'll not write more now. Writing is hard and talking is easy, and it will soon be time for the train from San Francisco to,—Dot's place. Love to all.

Affectionately,
Len.

To Laura Suggett

The Players, New York,
October 5, 1920

Dear Laura:—

Paul Reynolds said over the telephone yesterday that he had not yet been able to sell the Armenian article.[1] He had offered it to several magazines and had got back only polite refusals, except from the *New Republic,* which said they had printed articles "on the other side, and therefore—" I had Lowell Mellett, the new managing editor of *Collier's,* to lunch with me here. He is an old friend of mine, a man I gave lots of news to on Mexico in Washington and on the Peace Conference at Paris. He would do all he could for me (and also for my ideas) but he said he was up "against the System in his own office." He would sound them on me, and telephone, but he had no hope.

John S. Phillips, the old editor of *McClure's* and the head of our old group on the *American,* is now on the New York *Evening Post.* He said he'd try the *Post.* Howard Wheeler, ex-editor of *Everybody's,* wants me to tie up to nothing till I see his crowd on the Federated Press, an international syndicate. I'll see others today. It's amusing. I'm not a bit discouraged or depressed. I have some news, real news,

[1] "Armenians Are Impossible," finally published in *The Outlook,* Oct. 14, 1931.

and I'll put it over somehow. You'll see. And the prepossession against me is nothing but the price I have to pay for my independence and straight reporting. . . .

Affectionately,
Len.

To Upton Sinclair

The Players, October 18, 1920

Dear Upton:

Your letter of October 12 caught me here. I came home,—for a visit, —two weeks ago, and I heard of some of your doings: books, editings, etc. It is bully the way your vigor works its wonders. *The Brass Check* has been lent to me all along the line from Vienna, to Berlin, London and here. But I haven't read it yet. I think I'll not have to, since everybody tells me what it says. But if you will write your name, and my name, in a copy and send it to 850 Francisco Street, San Francisco, I'll read it there and put it in my little library of books of my real friends. For I'll be West this winter, and I'll see you, of course. I must. There are things you have to know: ideas you shall consider. For revolutionary Europe is finding out, Upton, that some of our theories, yours and mine, won't work.

Love to those you love.

Affectionately,
Lincoln Steffens

To Col. E. M. House

The Players, Oct. 28, 1920

Dear Colonel House:

May I come to see you pretty soon? I really need a talk with you; not for information, but for some sort of comfort. And I can tell you how things are going in Europe,—in my field.

Yours sincerely,
Lincoln Steffens

To Laura Suggett

The Players, October 28, 1920

Dear Laura:

Very little news. I'm writing, and the article goes along pretty well. No hitches so far.

Bullitt got into town last night, and has a flat right near the club here. He has been breeding dogs, and apples, but the dogs are not bulls; they are mere police dogs. He's going to write some, then next year he's to try China, Japan and the Far East.

I saw a political parade tonight. It made me sick.

I told you, didn't I, that I wrote the President last Sunday, briefly, but sincerely. He's pretty low, they say, and the election may kill him. And then he'll be a god again. Which will be also wrong. Oh, gee!

I'm seeing lots of people, and I'm telling them fairy tales, folk lore I picked up in Europe. They are lovely, and they seem to surprise everybody, coming from me. But beauty, mere beauty, is the only antidote for all this hideousness.

I've written Shaw, Colby's secretary, for another appointment. I want the amnesty for political prisoners; and a let-up on war practices generally. We must have some liberalism.

Good night. Love to all.

Affectionately,
Len.

To Allen H. Suggett

The Players, November 18, 1920

Dear Allen:—

Your letter of November 10 was here when I got back from Washington this morning. I was two days there, seeing, among others, Palmer and Colby and Tumulty.

Palmer was glad to explain or state his view of his policy. He felt aggrieved. I urged a general amnesty. He gave technical reasons why that could not be, but individual pardons, releases, etc., are under way. To my objection that this was a loss of opportunity to show a change of policy and arouse a change of feeling, he came back with the inquiry as to how otherwise we could get that. I suggested a conspicuous case.

"Which one?" he asked.

"Debs'," I said.

"Ah, yes," he answered impatiently, "everybody comes to the Debs case. But that's hard. Debs doesn't ask for a pardon; he is contumacious. He defies the Government and the Constitution, hates our institutions—"

"That makes it a good case for the purpose," I said.

I think, from his gestures and expressions, that he will act on Debs. But he sprang at an obscure case I offered, of a Bulgarian I.W.W. boy, convicted with the 200 in Chicago and out now on $20,000 bail, pending appeal, who wants to go to Bulgaria to see his mother who has gone insane. Palmer didn't say what he would do, but I suggested it as a difficult case to be acted on openly and generously and he asked, with a sigh, for a memorandum. . . . The trouble with Colby, as I told him, is that he is not a principal; he's an agent, and other men decide for him. I don't know what he'll do. He wanted to be afraid of me, and I wouldn't let him.

"I suppose you'll go and roast me," he said.

"I've never used my pen for a personal purpose," I said.

That relieved him, but someone had been telling him things.

"You're dangerous," he said once. "You are all soft-spoken, you radicals, but you go out and you—you're a menace."

I laughed. I appealed for Mexico, and what I said hit him hard. I explained Russia, and that scared him. It was a funny interview, and pathetic, too.

Hotel Seneca,
Rochester, N. Y.,
[ca. Dec. 1, 1920]

Dear Allen:—

Just before I left N. Y. Friday evening, I got your good, long letter, and I had it to read on the train. It was like having a companion with me; like being at home. For it was mostly about 850.

I hope Frenzy can last till I see him once more. I'll have to meet him quietly, without rejoicing, and I suppose he and I can't play bugaboo-man any more. It will be hard to lose him, but it will be worth the pain to have had him. And you have certainly given him a good life.

I saw Creel before I left N. Y. and I have him again at lunch Wednesday. He told me his story, from the time Doheny fooled him on to now. And he's still on the job of getting recognition. And he thinks his demands on Mexico are fair. I don't. But I haven't said a word so far, I let George talk and only listened. I'll hear some more on Wednesday, and then I'll say my say. It's no use, but I think I can show Creel (if not the President) that the attaching of *any* conditions to such a recognition is an assertion of super-sovereignty, of our right to tell Mexico what to do and what to omit. It's imperialism. It's the case of Cuba over again.

The President is too sick and sore to be moved at all. He is finished. What a story!

I had a great meeting last night in Toronto. It was a mixed crowd of about 1,800; upper class and labor, university men (professors and students) and Socialists, with blocks of Communist-Bolsheviki. I didn't tell my story as well as I have been doing it of late, but it went. The audience not only applauded, as my audiences do not usually do; it cheered. It broke into cheers sometimes while I was talking, and when I finished it was embarrassing. It was a demonstration, really.

The incident that pleased me most was after it was all over; as I left the stage entrance a lot of Russians met me and an old, white-haired woman spoke for them. She said they had to thank me, and only in the cold, American-Canadian way: in words. "If we were in Russia," she said, "we would carry you to your carriage. As it is, we will kneel down if you'll let us, and you can walk on us to the car." They feel expressed and they have been long suppressed. Also I really think I speak much better than I used to. Everybody says that.

Affectionately,
Len.

To Laura Suggett

The Hollenden,
Cleveland,
December 10, 1920

Dear Laura:

My lecture grows clearer, firmer, redder as I repeat it, adding more and more facts and thoughts and recollections. And it arouses more and more resistance. Maybe it is because I am moving westward; maybe it is because the talk is better. I don't know. But at Johnstown last night, one-third of my audience was visibly shocked. I hold them while I talk; and they take it while I am giving it to them. The moment I cease, however, and they begin to think and talk it over with one another they ask me questions which sound very like exclamations. And out in the street afterwards, they gathered to discuss it and to feel it.

And it is pretty new, and unexpected. It challenges majority rule, "morality," explains how harmless a dictatorship can be when the sources of evil are closed up; and laughs at industrial democracy in the shops after the owners and stockholders and banks are driven out. The psychology and the uses of the Terror are stated scientifically, which is worse than a literary description. It's an adventure every time I talk. And apparently I am to talk every night, except tonight, and one week from Christmas to New Year, until I land in San Francisco or jail.

Len.

The Players,
New York,
Jan. 2, 1921

Dear Laura:—

We got back yesterday, and I found your Christmas card here this morning. It was from Carmel. Pretty place. You suggest a week-end there in February. All right, only I'll not be so eager to get away from 850; not in the short time I'm there. And I ought to go down and see Dot and Jim. However, plan as you please. It will all please me. And I'm not so sure of my movements as I was.

The Soviet Medical Relief is breaking up. Martens'[1] deportation is the chief cause. They will not want me to speak for them therefore. But the Chicago committee, which was well organized, is for changing the name and going right on. They would make it a Children's Relief Campaign, and have asked me to go on with my lectures. And I may. If I don't, I may either go right away to California or run off and get Mexico done, going to California after that.

I've been sending you a few pamphlets on Soviet Russia, and I'll have more for you. I thought of them as the beginning or middle of a little reference library on Bolshevism. Small as they are, some of them are important, especially Lenin's.

G. wrote to you from Atlantic City, and she let me read what she said. I had to laugh. It answered your letter to me, though I did not let her see that. My future happiness depends so much upon how you and she hit it off that I keep out of it all I can. G. is sensitive, too sensitive for me, but she is used to me now and I can settle down and feel at home more with her than with anybody I know. I never have

---

[1] Martens, who was unrecognized by the State Department as the representative of the Soviet Government, left the country just as the wire for his deportation was cancelled.

to play up to any expectations. No use. She knows me and she accepts me as I am. So it's all good for me.

Love to all.

Affectionately,
Len.

To Allen H. Suggett

Hotel Baltimore, Kansas City, Mo.,
Tuesday, Jan. 25, 1921

Dear Allen:—

. . . Laura's word of the end of Frenzy hit me harder even than I thought it would. I find I had hoped to see him once more. I had even planned how I'd meet him without exciting him. I do wish I had had one more look into his big, brown eyes. But I realize also that you miss him most, all the time. I'll get that when I am at 850.

Hotel Rainbow, Great Falls, Mont.,
Feb. 1, 1921

Dear Allen:—

This trip of mine is under the management of the Red Star League, a new organization ambitious to do for revolutions and strikes, the class war generally, what the Red Cross does for war. The representative of it with me is Irwin St. John Tucker, an Episcopal clergyman, who is a poet. And a good poet too. But he's a Socialist and with Berger and the rest was under sentence by Judge Landis to 20 years in the penitentiary. Yesterday he read in the local paper that the Supreme Court had upheld his (and Berger's) appeal; Landis was reversed and Tucker is free. He cried a bit; he was elated, and last night he spoke well.

There is, of course, a split in the Labor and radical ranks over the Red Star. There always is a jurisdictional fight in any Socialist or labor enterprise. That has hurt us some. It prevented a meeting being arranged in Seattle. I shall speak there alone, under other auspices.

Love to Laura: a greeting to Nellie (as affectionate as she will permit) and,—I wish I could add something to Frenzy. I feel and think a lot about that little old friend of mine.

Your brother,
Len.

To E. A. Filene

850 Francisco Street,
San Francisco,
February 16, 1921

Dear E. A.

A card of yours left at The Players was forwarded to me here. It showed me how little you understand me; how progressive I am; how I am ever on the move; never stand pat, even physically. I have lectured clear across the continent, been forbidden to speak by two mayors and allowed to do so by one court (which enjoined the mayor). And about done now. I shall go on as planned, to Mexico, for a month.

I have also a clipping giving parts of the speech of yours at Boston on Russia. Very good. Only I had to laugh at your statement that the Russians are not yet ready for communism. They are just emerging from communism and not yet ready for capitalism. You know that. Why do you say the other?

Affectionately,
L. Steffens

To Laura and Allen Suggett

The University Club,
Mexico City,
March 9, 1921

Dear Laura and Allen:—

I got here this morning on time (6:30 A.M.), one day late. And a long, hard, dusty trip it was, too. It's three days, you know, to San Anton', over the desert two days; and it's two days and nights from S. Anton' via Laredo to Mexico City.

There was some amusement on the way. A bull fighter group got on at Nuevo Laredo. It was Sunday; they had fought that day, and been almost mobbed because the bulls were no good. But they were cheerful. After discussing the day's work, with gestures and passion, they settled down to drink and play. Their berths were over, opposite and next to mine, so that I felt the full effect of their play, drinks, flirtations. I didn't mind. Life is for joy. They had it, and I got it by proxy, without much effort.

Mexico is full of life now. It is Mexican life; not active, but populous, and the old costumes are back in use. With the soldiers, peons and

Indians all out, it was a sight all the way. Indeed it got better and better as we came south, till, in Mexico here, I saw, for the first time, a backward metropolis, donkeys, automobiles, street cars, busses,—all in full swing, with all the shops open, the hotels full. It was a new city to me.

I eat, work, visit, and write letters in the club. I find some old friends, and all the oil men. I hear the same kicks. I am not sure that Obregon is all right yet, but it is hopeful that the Americans are down on him. I wish that they were more bitter. He evidently is not a "strong man," either way.

But I have seen no Mexicans yet. I landed here dirty, had to go see my room, get breakfast here, then go to the bank for Mexican gold and then it was a bath: ordered, hot, good, oh, so good. I may not be a lost soul, but my body is certainly lost. It can't stand dirt. In the afternoon I slept, came back here to meet the members who gather at teatime (for cocktails) and get the gossip. I felt the oil men draw back from me. It's very flattering, and they sent the A.P. man to ask me if I was going to write up Mexico. I said I didn't know whether it was up or down or write or talk. It makes me think of Paris in peace-making days: all oil, and business and everything but peace. But I said little; smiled and,—waited. But it is disgusting. The Mexicans have no friends amongst us. . . .

Len.

To Allen H. Suggett

Mexico City,
March 11, 1921

Dear Allen:—

It's been a busy three-four days. De Negri is here. I found him with Saenz, the Sub-Secretary of State, when I called to present to Saenz my letter of introduction from De Negri. We had a good talk, and I went the same day to see Pane, the Secretary of Foreign Affairs, whom I knew as head of the national railroads and as Minister to France in Paris. He's about the only Carranzista left in this Government.

The Mexicans are not going to take back anything in their Constitution for us; not going to bargain for recognition. They are scared at what may happen to them, but they are going to fight for their own.

I've met (Mr. and Mrs.) Turner,[1] the author of *Barbarous Mexico,* who is at the Iturbide. He lives at Carmel. Haberman,[2] whom I knew in N. Y., an East Side radical, in the government here, telephoned that he will call this A.M. I'm waiting for him now.

Of course I see the Right Americans here at the Club. They stop talking when I approach, as they did before when I was here. They'll get over their caution by and by. But already I have the sense of their hopes, and the plan or objective upon which they have agreed. They want to put Mexico where Cuba is: under us economically, and politically,—"free." It's Paris all over again. Much talk of peace, all thought upon oil and gold and lands; and preparedness for war.

When they asked me what I was chasing around all over the earth for, and not writing, I told them I was seeking stuff for my own private purpose: to go off somewhere, retire, remember what I had seen and so,—laugh myself to death.

Len.

To Laura Suggett

Mexico City,
March 16, 1921

Dear Laura:—

I thought I told Col. Wood [3] I was going. He forgot. But you ought to keep him on your small list. He's a remarkable proof that a human can survive the system. He was the son of a Navy doctor, graduated himself from West Point; served long in the Army; practised law; became a corporation attorney, a leading citizen and yet,—he's a straight-seeing radical and a poet. . . .

I'm getting into this thing down here; and I can see it will take more time than I thought. They get me just right: that I'm not a friend of Mexico, but only an interested inquirer into all reforms and revolutions. So there's no bunk. I say to each of them that they haven't abolished the system, as Lenin did; that it is bound to get them in time; and then I ask how it got Carranza. They can tell me what happened to Carranza. Some of them tell it with bitterness, but

[1] John Kenneth Turner's series on "Barbarous Mexico" (1909), dealing with the Diaz administration, appeared in the *American Magazine* till suddenly stopped.

[2] Roberto Haberman.

[3] Charles Erskine Scott Wood, author of *Heavenly Discourse, The Poet in the Desert,* and other books, one of Steffens's oldest friends.

when I remind them that it is not his character nor theirs that interests me, but the forces which work against C. and O. and all of us, they become more careful, less personal and bitter, and very much more scientific and thoughtful. I can see that the form of the interview acts as a sort of warning to them of what they are up against. So they get *that* out of it, and I am gradually getting a very clear and statable picture of what ends revolutions,—in failure.

Another thing I have done is to clear up the confusion here among the Reds (high and low) on Russia. I had twenty of the heads of organized labor together night before last; and a good interpreter. I gave them my Russian story. Sentence by sentence they took it. I had to cut some. It took two hours and a half. But I could cut anything to fit it to them. And it was the crowd, remember, which joined with Gompers. When I got through, they asked some very thoughtful, penetrating questions; all very practical. At the end, their spokesman said that, for the first time, he and his colleagues felt that they understood Russia, Third International and all. What is more, I could see that they got it; and today I heard echoes of it showing that they did.

To Mrs. J. James Hollister

Mexico City,
March 16, 1921

Dear Dot:—

. . . I wrote an article (now out seeking an editor) on the Armenians. They are a mean, trading, highly intelligent, but utterly unproductive, sharp-grafting race. I pointed out that all the races left around the Mediterranean by the rise and fall of the several civilizations located there: the Assyrians, Egyptians, Greeks, Romans, Turks, etc., are like that. They are all what we call "Jews." But the Armenians beat them all: Greeks, Turks, Italians, Jews. "The Armenians," as I said, "are Jews and Christians, too!" In other words they are the final development of the commercial culture which is the only one we have ever had,—so far. They show what our culture does to Man.

Now then, Jim is active in the early, rising stage of that culture as it is established in America. He is fighting its processes in detail. Let him fight, and let Jack come along and carry on the fight. Don't bother them with ideas too much. But once in a while, let's all sit down and compare our ideas with their facts. Let me ask Jim and

Jack to step back and look at men as they look at fruit, vegetables, grain or chickens; ask what kind of men our conditions seem bound to breed; consider what conditions of soil and law would make better men.

What Jim is doing is politics; real politics; it is statesmanship. Jack will follow in his father's footsteps. I'm thinking that maybe a real statesman may come out of Las Bolitas. We certainly need one from somewhere.

But do you remember that a man cannot act and think at the same time. I have learned that, and you, a psychologist, know it to be true. A period of reflection, then a period of action.

I joked Rudolph Spreckels once for being so certain of something, and I reminded him that the year before he was certain of something else which did not happen. He asked me what of it? I said: "Well, I think you should not be so positive of anything as you are of everything. You should doubt some."

He put his hand on my knees, and said:

"Oh, Stef, don't make me doubt. If I were not certain, I could not act."

So I understood that I, the man of thought, was hearing the true cry of the practical man. I was the "intellectual" up against the man of action. It was my job to doubt; his to do. One is not better than the other. We are merely different. And it's only now and then that we should consult together, listen to each other and, so, really, trade and learn.

I didn't mean to do this when I sat down here. I meant to tell you about Mexico. Your letter did it.

Len.

To Ella Winter

The Players, New York,
June 21, 1921.

You must write to me, Peter, and tell me about your father. I care too much to be left where your letter, dated May 11, leaves me. . . .

Your letter had started to be long and interesting. I would have liked to hear more. But it stopped, and then there was that brief dark note. I wish I had had it before. I was over there. I went to Stockholm to get in touch with Russia, learned a little there and then came on down to Berlin, where I saw Krassin, Lomonosoff and others who had just come out. They told me just what I wanted to know, and asked me not to persist in my plan to go in. It was too bad. Jo Davidson was with me, and when we quit, he was more disappointed than I was, because he is a sculptor and can see only with his eyes. He was depressed, troubled, so I came on down to Paris to spend a week with him, then sailed back home. I got here yesterday.

I'll go West now for the summer, then to your side again. This time I'll visit England. But again I'll not be long, since I want to be in Mexico next February-March. *That* revolution has found out some things the Russian will uncover before long. The Mexicans failed, but they are going at the objective now in another way. Which also will fail, no doubt. And no matter. It isn't success we are after yet. It's the cause of all these failures.

That's enough for now. You'll write, and I'll be wondering and wondering unpleasantly, till I hear,—good news, I hope.

Stef.

To *Allen H. Suggett*

The Players, June 23, 1921

Dear Allen:—

. . . I have a formal invitation to take the editorship of the Seattle *Union-Record*. There was an awful row among the owners, organized labor, of this paper; an investigation, a report and a decision. They say they need an outsider to allay the conflict still on among them, and they ask me to state the terms on which I'd take the job. I may go up around that way to see them all. But I do *not* want that job.

I'm having some clothes made, a lot. My old ones were pretty bad. I had to get one new suit in Paris to come home in, and I've about made up my mind to pay what it costs, get a good wardrobe and keep it up. Love.

Len.

To *Mrs. J. James Hollister*

850 Francisco St.,
Saturday, August 6, 1921.

Dear Dot:—

Your letter to Laura arrived yesterday, but so did the Rolls-Royce and you didn't get much attention. We read your letter, but it certainly was unimportant, comparatively. We read it and then shot out to try the car. Doctor isn't sure of himself in it yet. He drives as if it were made of cut glass. And that's the way it looks. And that's the way people look at it. I think Doctor will make what it cost him in advertising and, if there is any margin, it will be covered by his satisfaction in the perfection of the thing. As for me, it makes me want a Ford. I hate to be careful.

I am going downtown now to see Secretary Fall. He is at the St. Francis and he is refusing to see anybody. But Stephen Mather, the Director of National Parks, called me up last night to say the Secretary would like to have an exchange with me on Mexico. Mather said he said that he would regard a talk with me, not as work, but as a recreation. He knows we differ, you know; and how; and there is no chance of an agreement. But I can get the policy of the Administration out of him and he can have from me, he thinks, the plans of the Mexican Reds. That's what he told Mather. And he is right.

That's all. I like your letters, Dot. They always make a picture of the family at Las Bolitas. And, of course, I would like to be remembered to Jack, Joe, Clinton and the nicest girl in the world, and their father and their mother and the Chinaman,—when they are not too busy.

To Ella Winter

San Francisco,
August 16, 1921

Dear Peter:

Thanks for this good letter, which has just come: the one telling me your father had recovered. What little you said about his condition made me think that,—well, that the next letter would not be so good. Which helped me imagine the full meaning of what you did write in this amazing letter. For, you know, I liked your father.

And you still are in doubt which way to go, which job to take. I have no advice to offer, Peter. It matters what you do, but I am afraid you will not be allowed to choose. Some job will choose you.

You were leaning toward the college in your letter, inclined to go back to teaching. Why not? You will have lots of time for other things. You will have as a teacher to formulate what you think into definite shape. I think I would like to hear that you were teaching. I would rather hear that you were in love and that some splendid man was in love with you. And that is sure to happen some day. But that is sure to happen whether you are a professor or merely a learner.

I never read *Main Street*. I heard so much about it that I thought I need not actually read the book, so I urged others who live on Main Street to do the work for me, while I took it all in secondary form. A good way to get it. For it is, as you say, as dull as Main Street. Upon that point all readers agree. But I am wondering how that subject could be put over otherwise than by endless repetitions.

Your question about Single Taxers is one I often ask. But they are what they are only because they are so sure they are right and that no one else is. I have my trouble with them. They think they have a claim on me, and they are always remonstrating with me for my interest in other subjects and especially in my practice of talking or writing with tolerance and even some understanding of the Russians or revolutions. I answered one in New York one day last summer. He very politely, but firmly, remarked to me that "we Single Taxers, who know better, should not give countenance to what was going on in Russia these days." "Why not?" I asked. "Russia is very important. It has shown me what the hell of the Single Taxers is to be." That interested him; he asked what the S. T. hell was, and I told him it was a place where all that Henry George wanted to see done was accomplished, but not by the Single Tax or the Single Taxers.

No, Peter, don't ever be like the Single Taxers, and the only way to avoid that is to be never too sure that you are right. You are sure to be wrong if you are, for certainly certainty is,—error, human error. The experience of the Socialists in Russia is showing that the solution of the land problem is not the Socialist theory. This suggests trying another. The S. T. is a well thought out other way, and I would like to see it tried. And if it worked out and did the job, then I would be for trying it everywhere. I might then be a regular, hopeless, single-minded Single Taxer, but not before. Up to now I am an awfully doubting listener to all theories; theories, I say; and there is nothing else in so-called human knowledge except theories. Is there?

The next time I go abroad will be to Mexico, but the next to the next, I think, will include England and that means, of course, Peter. My best feeling goes this time to your father. I hope he not only got well, but that he got rid of whatever it was that was ailing him, so that his life may be long in the land.

Affectionately,
Stef.

To Jo Davidson

San Francisco,
Sept. 3, 1921

Dear Jo:

You have an awful nerve. You never write a letter, and yet you trouble my conscience when I don't write to you. It makes me tired. I suppose you think that you can speak only in marble or bronze or mud. Bunk. You have got to write to me or I am going to make an herculean effort and forget you; and all yours too. For you are not the only one with nerve; there are others that don't write too. . . .

I came out here, and then went to Lake Tahoe. G. joined us, and we played around for three weeks. That is to say, they did: G., Suggett and my sister. I worked. Yes, I did. I wrote a story and an essay up there. And when we drove back here, I did a fable; another essay, not quite finished; and a movie. The movie is that Dutch legend: "Why Misery Never Dies." And it turned out to be a bully theme for a photo-play. I am not sure of the form, but it is written in something like the form I have seen and, anyhow, it is ready for an expert to take it and, I suppose, ruin it. Meanwhile I was asked to take the editorship of a labor paper; escaped, but I have to go to Seattle soon to help it out of a hole and prescribe for a busted Labor movement. Then I shall lecture my way east to New York, visit Washington and, in February, go to Yucatan to steer an experiment in government under a radical Governor who is afraid of the U. S., as he damned well ought to be. After that I kinda think I'd kinda like to go to Europe; maybe France, but France proper, not Paris. Paris is France improper, and there are some people there I think I may be wanting to forget. We'll see. Love to all, a little; about all that's left.

Stef.

To Laura Suggett

New York, September 24, 1921

Dear Laura:

. . . I went to Washington with a small committee of Reds, called there by Hoover, who wanted to ask them to leave off fighting him to get together for Russian relief. He had asked me to come along, so did the Reds, and the Quakers, who don't like or trust Hoover, also had sent for me. It makes me laugh. These people who so often denounce me for my connections with the Left are glad I am there sometimes and reach out to use my relationship with the Reds. Well, I am willing to be used. Before the conference, I had lined all sides up on an agreement to work separately for Russia, each in its own way, and Hoover accepted that solution. He wouldn't have done it two weeks ago, but he felt the effect of the Red fight and he was glad to plan for coordination. He suggested that I act as liaison, and so covered me with suspicion, I fear, though I haven't seen the committee since. Hoover asked me to remain after they left and so added to the impression that he and I were friends. When I came out the others had gone to their train. I shall see them all tomorrow.

Hoover tried to show us that his chief, his sole concern was for the helpless sufferers in Russia; that he had no political purpose and no personal end in view. We told him that it was not the Red leaders who were spreading suspicion, but his own men, who in the past had played politics. The chief reference, direct, was to Captain Gregory's story [1] of his own conduct and Hoover's and the Entente's in Hungary. He said Gregory had not told the exact truth. Max Eastman asked him, Hoover, to state it his way. Hoover didn't want to, and we passed on, but we soon got back to it, and finally Hoover gave his version, which was merely not complete or clear. Max thought it worth his, Hoover's, while to write carefully a full account of that incident, marking out just where he and Gregory differed. Hoover didn't say he would; he looked merely annoyed. He appealed to me once, to state the thing as I knew it from the Paris end, and I did, and it supported Gregory, not Hoover, but my appeal was that he accept the suspicion as unavoidable and work along with us in a way to prove by this experience that he and his men could give charity without playing politics. And I showed that most of such politics was unconscious, not deliberate. It was a two hours' talk, and it ended well. We are all to work along parallel lines, communicating information, results and plans.

I stayed another day in Washington: to fix up my fences, see the new men, form personal relations, now, before I want anything. It

[1] Capt. T. T. C. Gregory, representative of the American Relief Administration in Hungary, had written an article in *World's Work*, June, 1921, stating that America's relief activities in Europe under the direction of Hoover were for the purpose of "fighting Bolshevism." Captain Gregory claimed to have assisted, through his work, in the overthrow of the Soviet regime in Hungary in the summer of 1919.

was an interesting day, including visits with the press to Hughes and the President. But I shall not stop to tell it all now. I went to Philadelphia yesterday to report to and agree with the Quakers, whom I am urging to withdraw from their present subordination under Hoover, and to go on alone. I certainly like the Friends.

After them I saw and spent the night with Dan, going over our reviving lecture plans. He has about a thousand dollars' worth in sight, and that is enough. I am to give most of my time to the Russians for nothing or expenses. Before I left here last week, I had seen Bullitt about the movie and Glenn Frank [1] about the fable. I think I told you or Doctor what Bullitt said about Death and the Beggar: that it was one hundred per cent impossible. And he went on to recount how, in every one of the big movie concerns, there are men who keep trying to put on something fine and true, but they all fail. Even some that I thought had succeeded Bullitt said had lost money. *The Blue Bird,* for example. The movie people, whom they call Boobery, could not get it. They looked dumbly at it, went out and told their friends it was "no good," thus killing it.

Frank was delighted with the fable, and brought in his art editor to talk over the illustrations for it. He said he had given the story to Cesare, the cartoonist, to do and he was on it now. I am to see his work before it is used, but Frank said that he didn't care how much it cost. He would pay Cesare for his work and then not use it if we didn't think it was good. As for me, he offered me the highest price he ever had paid, viz.: the same rate he had just paid Galsworthy for a five-page story, but I asked him not to start me off at a rate which might hinder him from taking more things. He laughed, but he saw the point; he has to justify to the company whatever he pays me.

He said he would think it over and "see." I shall be content with two or three hundred. He wants another fable. I told him the one about organization, and he ordered it at once. I shall do it pretty soon, and it will be easy, because I have told it so often that I could dictate it to a stenographer, though he does ask that I make it a bit plainer to those readers who don't already realize the danger of organization. He did not like the essay and when I took it home, I didn't care for it either. It must be done another way. The story I

---

[1] Glenn Frank was at this time editor of the *Century* magazine.

have not had time even to go and get, to say nothing of sending it out to an editor.

Love to Doctor and, by the way, how about the Rolls-Royce? We mustn't forget that in all our other troubles. And Nellie? Is she back? If she is, remember me to her and very, very cordially too. I'm for Nellie.

Lin.

To Allen H. Suggett

The Players, Oct. 2, 1921

Dear Doctor:—

. . . Laura sent me a fine, wrong letter from my fine, old anarchist friend, W. C. Owen, now in England and an editor of *Freedom*. He tried to make an Anarchist of me in S. F. when I was preparing for Berkeley; and he fought for his ideas against Carranza, et al., all through the Mexican Revolution. He fights Lenin now. It is sad, but it is interesting.

Roberto Haberman, the man I got to go on the Mexican mission, learned that Calles, the chief of Obregon's cabinet, and the leader of the Left, is in this country. Haberman went to see him and wires that Calles accepted our idea and plan; will come here this week to see me and then go home and put it over. The Russians are delighted. They want me to go on lobbying and propose that I live in Washington, D. C., till my lectures begin out in the Middle West. I would like to be in Washington. I think I will try for a general amnesty for all Labor and "political" prisoners.

The night before last I dined alone with Mrs. Wm. Astor Chanler. I met her on the steamship last spring. Our deck chairs and dining chairs were next. She evidently took a shine to me, for I have learned from others that she has been standing up strong for me in her set. She wants her Allied Relief (now out of a job) to do what I say as to Russia, and that's what we were talking about at the dinner. She says her set ask her if she is my "manager." She's a determined little woman, with a lot of power. And I didn't realize on the boat that she was an Astor. She was listed as Mrs. W. A. Chanler. Very amusing, and not useless. I am warning her that I am and am likely to appear radical, and that she must not misrepresent me as a mere liberal. Such people have a way of going back on one,—hard.

To Ella Winter

The Players, Oct. 28, 1921

Dear Peter:

Your letter and a half (and the half the better third) came in this morning, with H. G. Wells and a lot of other great people, come here to make peace. They'll make war. No matter. There still is Peter. I'll give all my attention to her, for a moment. I must. I leave here this afternoon,—for the West again; on business.

I have a job, too. When the Famine came to Russia, the Russians and the friends of Russia; labor and capital rose up to answer: to send food. And they began, first, to quarrel. I was in San Francisco, a beautiful place to be. Telegrams came from the fighting groups, asking me to come here, and I came, and we have united all the Radical and Labor groups under a committee of which I'm executive secretary. . . .

I knew the Black Forest well, once. We "did" it, often, as students from Heidelberg, pleasantly, carelessly, cheaply, and it was fun. I think of it fondly; too fondly to wish to repeat. That Black Forest is filled with me and I with it. Nothing so well done, so happily done, should be done again. If I ever do a forest again, it will be some other forest. The Black one is perfect. And I like to think that you have that in your memory. I'll hear the story some day, hear it and edit it, —gently. I care less and less to edit. God writes and tells things, Man does the editing.

Yes, I'm glad you are teaching economics. You will be sure to learn it then. And you will grow on *that,* as you would in anything else. Not that it doesn't matter what you feed on. I mean only that you are so vital that you are bound to grow, anyhow, for a long while.

One warning: What you say about the Future makes me think you are not getting it. Be careful. That experiment is not yet finished. It has done wonders. It will do more. I wish I could take the time to write you 5,000 words on what Russia has proven to be "bunk" and what it has shown to be possible.

As to your articles on Germany, smile, Peter; just smile. You are a young writer. The editors can do to you what they used to do to Wells, but cannot any more. Your friends may be hurt now, but they'll forget.

Read a book by John Dos Passos called *Three Soldiers* for an example: how to write superficial observations so as to make them reveal the fundamental and profound. It's a great piece of writing, and I know the boy who did it. Some day you may cross his path. But I suggest the book because it has the art of telling in bits only what the eye sees: a string of hardly related incidents in such a way as to, well, make the Army and the Law and the State and the Press howl with rage at the exposure of "our Army and the War." Young observers should always tell things somewhat in this way: thoughtless observation. I hear there's another book by Youth that does the same thing: it's called *This Side of Paradise*. And this one is awful. Men of my generation say they can hardly read it, and that they cannot understand or believe it.

There, now, I must go. I've said enough. The World is all right; it's coming along. And so is Peter all right; she's coming along.

Stef.

To Allen H. Suggett

Chicago, Nov. 1, 1921

Dear Allen:—

In your last to me you said you had made a short speech without writing it and that it went so well that you were going to repeat it. I am sure that is right. It cost me dear to learn that. When I went out, some years ago, on my first lecture trip, it was as a writer and I wrote my lecture. Then I committed it to memory. My memory is bad. The consequence was that I was trying all the time I was talking to remember. My attention was backward, upon what I had written; not forward, not on my thought. It was a passable failure, that trip, and what saved it was that I so often forgot my written speech and had so often to go ahead on my own thoughts, that parts of every lecture were extemporaneous.

After that I wrote no more; I made notes, sometimes in great detail, but I never used my notes on the platform. I tried to once or twice, and the result was so disastrous (I couldn't find what I wanted and got confused) that I chucked notes. I made them out, but only to help me think through a theme. That done, say, an hour ahead of the talk, I would destroy a packet and forget what I had written.

Now I know that a speech is a combination of the forces of the speaker and the audience. The speaker has the ideas and some feeling about them; he has a line-out of them: a track laid, an ordered, thought-through, more or less logical statement. Mine is usually a narrative, founded on chronology. But as I look over an audience, I get their status, mood, etc. Unconsciously I feel that. It crosses with mine, and off we start. As I go on, I see the audience laugh, frown, smile, shake their heads, applaud: signs of how they like it, how they feel, and I literally rise on that. I extend a statement to clear off a frown, I shorten a statement, when I see they have got it. I feel my way.

Repeating a talk is great practice. It's a form of editing. This shortening, lengthening, changing, improving,—really, in time, will form a lecture or a speech, and, in some cases, as in my "Mexico," I got me finally as perfect a statement of the case as my hundreds of hearers and I together could make.

Talking is an entirely different art from writing, and it's the better art. The writer aims to write as one talks, and it's hard to do. Few learn to. It's absurd then to try to learn to talk as one would write, especially if one is not an expert writer.

To Allen and Laura Suggett

Chicago, Nov. 12, 1921

Dear Laura and Doctor:—

My letter [1] certainly seems to have landed on Hays. We have been corresponding by wire to arrange a meeting in Washington. Evidently he is in earnest. He could have said it was out of his department; and it is. But, no, he wants to do something, and I shall show that nothing but the whole, big thing will do the business. No little gesture will count. My letter puts it as it is. From other sources I have heard that it was proposed once to let Debs go, and there was a kick. The American Legion especially raised the deuce. Harding told a friend of mine that the A. Legion gave him "a panning." Well, I'll offer, if they will list the individuals they are afraid of, to go and "get" any one, two or three,—enough to show it can be done. And, as for the Governor, I shall ask him to attend to Stephens; and not only to get to California, but to make sure my friends in prison there are not forgotten.

Of course it's an awful lot to get actually done, this amnesty, but won't it be great if it is done! Think of all the hopeless fellows saved! And the good will we'll have to work with in the people and the Administration. And don't forget my old promise to the McNamaras

[1] See Appendix IV, p. 1041.

kept, at last. Why, I'll be square with everybody in the world; all debts cancelled; a clear slate to start a new life on. My part will be secret, of course, but I'll *know* and *some* of the convicts shall know.

To Allen H. Suggett

Chicago, Nov. 28, 1921

Dear Allen:—

. . . No news. I made a harsh speech at Valparaiso Saturday night where I wanted to do well. It was for James H. McGill, a great, great friend of mine; a well-to-do manufacturer who is really radical and who contributes to anything I say. He wanted me to win his club, a lot of the leading citizens of Valparaiso: bankers, lawyers, professors at the University, etc. And I wanted to. But, as I talked I saw Main Street in them: opposition, prejudice,—everything I detest, and so,— well, I gave them Bolshevism in the spirit of the Bolsheviki. I wrote an apology yesterday.

But the experience, and the remorse, fixed me for last night here, so that I did my very best and got the whole crowd.

Talking is always an adventure.

Love to Laura.

Len.

New York Central Lines,
Monday, Dec. 5, 1921.

Dear Allen:—

You and Laura will be relieved, as I was Friday night, when I got a wire from Hays to meet him Sunday at the Blackstone (Chicago) Hotel. I did. He said my letter made a (mild) sensation. It hit him so hard that he took it to a cabinet meeting, and read it. The President asked for it. He called it "that letter," and he speaks of it always as "that letter." And the cabinet was for doing what it suggested. "There was really no opposition," Hays told me. But, he said, as they talked it over, they began to realize that it meant to pardon, not only "political prisoners," but men who had committed crimes: killed persons and destroyed property. So the retreat began.

"And so," said Hays, "we are going at Christmas time to pardon the men who—" And he tried to describe "men like Debs, who did no harm, but only talked," etc.

"But you," I said, "why don't you stand up for our purpose?"

"I did," he answered, "but I couldn't. They had it on me. They said that no one expected anything like that."

"Well," I said, "you were missing the whole point. It is precisely the unexpected that should be done. You are thinking of pardoning a few men. I am asking you to break the hate; and the war psychology; do the free, uncalled-for, magnificent Thing. I'm talking politics, you justice."

"I know," he said. "I love the way you speak of politics. I love that. But, see here, I can't get them to see that; not even the President. You'll have to do that yourself."

"I will," I said, "if you'll get me the chance I'll talk to the President."

He thought a moment. "He's awfully busy, you know," he said. "The Conference and all. But,—you'll get in on this. Yes, I'll fix it. Don't you ask to see him, I'll ask him to. I'll tell him he must send for you and make you talk about this and,—all those other things you've been telling me." (I had told him about the Bolsheviks and Europe; Labor and—)

There was a lot more. I offered, if he would make a list of them, to go and "get" the captains of industry and the governors who might kick at all this. He jumped at that. And I said I'd see Debs and ask him not to come out and talk hate, but "only to go about appealing for food for Russia." "Fine!" he said. "Just what we want. I'll see that you get to Atlanta."

So it's arranged. He'll be in Chicago all Thursday. Then I'm to meet him in Washington. I go on, then, to see Debs, and either before that or after, I have a quiet hour with Harding. If I win him, Hays is to give me the list of opponents they're afraid of and of governors; and I'm to see them. *And,*—and we are to try to put off the Christmas gift to God till we have arranged for all and everything. "No hurry," I said. "No hurry," he said. So here I am keeping 'Gene Debs in jail! And I'll have to tell him, and he'll be glad.

To G.

Hotel Bellevue, Washington,
Dec. 11, 1921

Dear G.:—

My business goes pretty well. Hays wasn't back Friday, so I went about getting permission to visit Debs and I was going at it very openly till I learned at the Attorney General's office that it was "impossible." That made me cautious. I sounded around and soon learned that the head of Federal Prisons was the husband of Pres. Harding's favorite sister. He is a retired missionary. I called and we talked missions, China and Christianity till we became good friends, then I stated my business and he said it was hard to manage; that both the Warden at Atlanta and the prisoner had to ask me to call. I suggested a letter, and the good man wrote it that way. This was Friday afternoon, and it is 19 hours to Atlanta. I might expect to hear Monday, tomorrow. I called up today, and the answer was there: a cordial invitation to come on down. I shall go tomorrow afternoon, after I have seen Hays. I should be back here Thursday, possibly Wednesday night.

Hays came in Friday night, but didn't turn up at his office Saturday. I found him today, but he was "out." I think he was. I am afraid the story that he is to be president of all the movies is true. I am afraid because I learn that some members of the cabinet are not so human as Hays, and if he goes out soon I might be left alone and would have no access to Power. I am feeling for substitutes, and the Prison Director may be just the one. He is back-stairs, but what do I care? I would stoop to get in the back way.

When I wasn't working on my own job I joined with the workers for peace, especially the correspondents. I made the rounds with them, attended the "conference" with Hughes and the President, saw the places where the delegates work and generally entered into the spirit of the whole thing. I met lots of friends. It is just like Paris; I kept thinking of the Crillon. Most of the correspondents and many of the statesmen who were there are here. It was a real pleasure to get into it again. Of course they all guyed me, asking what I was doing there or why I hadn't been there before. I told them I had trusted them to make a mess of it and so waited till they had done that. I had come there now at last to find out where the next war or revolution was to be. That got them guessing, and it was rich to see how they believed there would be other wars and possibly a revolution. They are a cynical lot. They don't so write, but they are, and they don't know why. Just a hunch or, as you would say, intuition.

I had lunch with S. S. McClure's man, who is helping the old man remake *McClure's Magazine*. I was able to give him some good tips. I would like to boost S. S. but I would not care to work for him

PETE'S FIRST BIRTHDAY. ALASSIO, ITALY, NOVEMBER 21, 1925.

again. That period is over for me. I dined with Wm. G. Shepherd
and Bickel. The first is the correspondent I went to Russia with the
first time, the father who made me godfather to his son, Bill. The
second the editor of the United Press. We reviewed the world from
the inside, held a reception at the Shoreham and, then, late that night,
I got a Mrs. Something, and we called at the Mexican Embassy to
learn the Latin view of these goings-on. That was good. I can make
an article out of it. I breakfasted at the Melletts'[1] with Elmer Dover,
Mark Hanna's secretary of the Republican National Committee, and,
to my surprise, learned that he had been in Mexico for Harding, had
represented Obregon here and was urging recognition. He told us his
whole story and it dove-tailed in with the Mexican Embassy story.
I am to see more of Dover. His narrative shows that Hughes is misled on Mexico by Fletcher, the former American Ambassador to
Mexico, whom they now are trying to have promoted out of harm's
way to the American Embassy at Brussels. At noon today Gov. Folk
of Missouri came and took me home to dinner and to see his wife,
who is one of my oldest and best friends. Folk represents, as attorney, Peru and Egypt, and is interesting on international law. That's
all.

I have just had a call from the Universal Service, asking me to
write something soon and offering facilities. Sorry, I had to put them
off. The Amnesty comes first. But I have to go over and see him,
the manager, and so cannot write the letter I meant to, to Laura; and
I can't tomorrow or, come to think of it, for several days. I wish you
would send this on to her as soon as you have read it. I got a nice,
long letter from her today and there are things in it to answer, but,
—I can't; not now.

Len.

To Allen and Laura Suggett

Cosmos Club,
Washington, D. C.,
Friday, Dec. 16, 1921.

Dear Laura and Doctor:—
My interview with the President is at 1 P.M. tomorrow, and that will
settle it, I think; and I fear, now. Hays is sick. He had to quit and go
away. And he is needed on this job. But he had to leave it to his

---

[1] Lowell Mellett, Washington newspaperman.

secretary to carry out his end: to have the President send for me. And that's done.

But the President will not decide. He'll consult, and that's where Hays would come in. I have been looking for a substitute, and I picked Hoover. He listened, but, as the full import of my proposal dawned upon him, he said:

"But you are proposing to let go fellows that blew up buildings, killed people and,—all that."

"I am," I said.

We were in his closed car, driving from the White House to his (Hoover's) department. He looked at me, and a bad expression flushed his face.

"Why," he said, "I'd see those fellows rot in jail—"

"Don't say that, Mr. Secretary," I said, and he halted. "That is the very spirit that you condemn. That is the feeling of hate and revenge which you express in words, which my friends, who can't talk, put into the form of explosions and murder."

The car had arrived at his door; the man opened the door, but Hoover sat there; I think he was "getting" what I said. He stared, and I let him; it must have been a minute. Then I put my hand on his knee, and I said, very quietly,

"You all are using fear too much,—too much fear."

He sprang out of the car, and was running (his way) into the building. I got slowly out of the car. And he turned.

"Don't you want to stay in the car? It will take you anywhere you want to go."

"No," I said, "I'll walk and,—think."

I think I made a dent. Anyhow I'll follow it up. I told some of his staff about it, and said I'd hold them responsible for what Hoover did. And I'll suggest that the President talk to Hoover. I'm avoiding the Attorney General.

But what I started to say was that, if the President turns me down hard and cold, I'll quit and go to New York. If he accepts or says he'll consider, I'll stay here and work. And he may accept my offer to go and see governors and captains of industry for him on the proposition.

The interview with Debs was good. The Warden left me two hours alone with him, and I spent it trying to get Debs to understand (and not to judge) Russia. He saw it all. He said so; he showed it in his questions; and he was delighted. He agreed that the thing for him to do was to go out with or after me to plead for bread for Russia, —to be sent to the Soviet Government direct. He hadn't been clear on the dictatorship, minority rule, the red terror, etc. I just told him the story, showing how some things happen that we don't expect.

He's a Man—

There's an awful lot to tell, but I can't write it. There's so much more to get. I love to go around with the reporters on the peace-making. They tell so much more than they write; and the truth.

To Allen and Laura Suggett and Nellie [1]

Hotel New Southern, Chicago,
Dec. 20, 1921

Dear Laura, Allen and Nellie:—

I know. I haven't been very good, but I have been awfully busy. And I can't be very explicit now. I shall have things to do. But—

I failed in Washington. Hays fell ill. . . . I saw the President Saturday noon. He said: "No." I laid it all out, and he had the impulse; I saw that, but,—"No." He liked me, he said; he didn't expect to, but he did. He wished I'd call often; and make more such suggestions, but, no, he wouldn't do often what I wanted him to do. That, too, he could see. We could never agree or, seldom.

I got the list broadened a little, and I think I knocked over a condition. I certainly jumped hard upon it. He said he knew I would, but he read it to me. It was from the Attorney General suggesting that all but Debs be asked to swear allegiance anew, and say they were sorry, etc.

"Oh, no," I said. "No, no. That's a bargain. That's business. And no man who'd say that is fit to come out and breed children."

He chucked it on his desk, and repeated: "I thought you'd object to that."

Only those will come out who merely said things. Those that did anything stay in. So,—I fell down once more. . . .

To Allen and Laura Suggett

Chicago, Dec. 23, 1921

Dear Laura and Allen:—

I want to go to India, and see and talk with Gandhi. The head of the revolting party in Washington begged me to go; he said he'd give

[1] Nellie was the Suggetts' Irish housekeeper.

me a card that would open everything to me, and he told me how to work it. I said "No" to him; it was too far and I had other engagements: Mexico and Russia. But he said things that stuck in my head and grew. I begin to want to cut everything, and see that other sort of a revolution: the non-resistant type. If I went, I'd go West just the same, do those lectures, meet on the ranch business with you-all, and get my teeth put in final order. Then I'd shoot off, either from S. F. direct or from N. Y. via London. If I am quick and lucky, I might be back in time to go to Russia, later; not in the spring, but in the summer early, and cover Europe before the fall, when I'd come back with something to say; some things to compare. I might even have some wisdom at last.

We got a wire yesterday that Debs was "out"; it was not for publication till this morning, and no doubt the papers have it today. I am glad, very glad, and I know now that he is clear on Russia. I told you, didn't I, how I told him the whole story and repeated till he got it.

The other thing is that I'm sending through the Coopers (the charming man and wife, who run the Walden Book Shop) a book on Stinnes. It's not a good book; tells very little of the new Captain of Industry, who may be the business Kaiser of Germany and more. But I want to get you interested and curious about Stinnes and what he represents, because,—it is possible that his way is the way out. It isn't my way, or Doctor's or yours; it's the capitalist, the business way, and I don't believe it can work to a finish. But it will interest you and be good for your heads to read this short, light book with the thought in mind that: maybe Lenin is wrong and Stinnes right.

Len.

To Mrs. J. James Hollister

"850" [Feb., 1922]

Dear Dot:

I would like also to talk to you. Your attitude toward Jim and his present interest isn't quite fair. It isn't bad, it is good for a man to get an interest like this of Jim's. And he ought to be sure of a sympathetic interest in it and in him among his friends. I don't believe you understand that, if the farmers of this country do not get together and fight, the financial powers will eat them up. There will be not even a living in farming. I received the other day a statement showing that the increase of tenant farmers has been greater than ever of late, and when I was in the Northwest, some banker friends of mine were explaining to me why they did not close mortgages and take the farms. They could have done it. They thought of doing it. I have no doubt it will be done some day. The farmers by uniting and defining a clear policy may beat Nature; I think they can only postpone the day when the land, like labor, is capitalized. Some schools of theorists believe this should be done; that it will hasten the day of final settlement with the financiers. I don't make any guess on that, but I do know that Jim is getting into the world war at a point of great advantage to himself and his education; and his children's. You might go into it too, along with Jim, helping him all you can. When your sons come home from college they are going to have to follow you in,—unless they prefer to take up the bankers' end. And even then it is well for them to learn what Jim is finding out right now.

I have about decided to go East. I'll buy my ticket today, probably for next Monday, which will give me a day in Chicago and land me in New York at the end of next week. I have business there, and I have a lot to do in Washington. N. Hapgood writes that Geddes, the British Ambassador, told him that when he consulted our State Department about letting me go to India, someone there knocked me. I must see about that. But I shall soon be sailing for Europe, either Germany, Sweden (Russia) or England. I must work out that India business in London too. For while you and Jim are pottering around with the farmers' solution of the farm business, I have to watch the Reds tackle the whole social problem, which, I think, will have to be done before the farmers can do theirs. I don't know; I only think this. It seems to me that in a capitalist system the capitalist is bound to win. I dunno. I am guessing.

Anyhow: my love to you and Jim, and one bit of advice: band together, you two farmers anyway. The Bolsheviki say that a solid minority, no matter how small, if it is united, courageous and free from bunk, can lead the majority always.

To Laura Suggett

The Players, New York, March 17, 1922

Dear Laura:

. . . I told you, I think, that Jo Davidson is here; to have an exhibition of his work. He brought my bust to show and there is one of Anatole France.

I am now in touch with some British ex-Foreign Office people who are to help me pull out my visa for India. They tell me it was somebody in our own State Department that knocked me, and I have to see about that. I'll go to Washington next week. Genoa is still in the air for me, but I think that it will happen and that I will go.

I sat for Cesare the cartoonist who did my "Tale of Tails." [1] He is to illustrate the organization fable.

Jo told me last night a pretty fact for a fable. A friend of ours, a talented man, but a bore who used to buttonhole us and then talk, talk, talk, is deaf. A psycho-analyst told him he became deaf because he did not want to hear. Isn't that a great story? Or fable? The fellow would give all he's got now to hear. And he can't. Gee! Justice is fierce!

Affectionately,
Len.

To Col. E. M. House

New York, April 4, 1922

Dear Colonel House:

After my conversation yesterday morning, I heard from Washington that my passport had been passed, so that is all right.

There remains only the refusal of the British Foreign Office to grant me a visa. You may be able to help me there.

The facts are as follows:

My original intention was to go to India, and my interest was to learn as much as I could of the British plans for the solution of this, one of its most difficult imperial problems. That is why it would have done me no good to go without their cordial consent. The Indian story of the Indians isn't one half of the story that I want.

When I applied in New York for the visas I was told that my application would have to be referred to London. I went West to wait, not doubting that I would get them, but they wired me very courteously that my application had been refused. And in my application was not only India, but Egypt, and other British ports, and England itself. Thus I stood debarred from the whole of the British Empire.

When I came back to New York I asked the British Consul here to ask London if that was intended. He cabled that I asked at least to

---

[1] *Century*, Feb., 1922. The organization fable was "The Devil's Own Way," *Century*, June, 1922.

be allowed to go to London to see if I couldn't straighten my record with the Foreign Office. That also was declined, and so it stands.

Some English friends of mine here inquired as to the reason for all this, and the answer they brought to me was that it was somebody in the American State Department who was reporting against me.

Mr. Frank Polk said he didn't believe it, and advised me to see Mr. Leland Harrison, at Washington. Mr. Harrison, who is the secretary to the Secretary of State, said that it was not true; that the department had granted me a passport; and that no one could go behind that. I am sure Mr. Harrison believed what he said, but I still think there is someone in the State Department who, unofficially, is working against me. I shall do what I can about that, but I think that you might help me if you would take the trouble to explain to someone in authority among the British that I worked during the war and the Armistice with you in the radical field; that the book I am preparing is to be on this field; that I do not conspire; and that you, for example, have found me not untrustworthy. At any rate, you can say that I will do just what I promise.

If you can get the British to lift their blockade against me, I wish you would let me know of it at Genoa, care the American Express Company. Then I shall make application again and go from there or Paris to London, and myself clear up the situation. I have some friends there who will help me.

Thanking you for what you may do, I beg to remain,

Yours very sincerely,

Lincoln Steffens

To Laura and Allen Suggett

Berlin, May 6, 1922

Dear Laura and Allen:

What my work is to be I haven't decided yet, but I have a hunch it will be my life: "A Hard Life." The *Century,* as you know, wants that, asked for it and offered me seven hundred and fifty dollars a chapter. Wasn't that the price? I have forgotten, but I told you at the time. Anyhow it doesn't matter. The point is that they propose to run it as a serial and afterwards make of it a book. A very good proposition. It didn't hit me at the time Glenn Frank asked for it, and I didn't know I had been chewing it over. But evidently I have been considering it, for I find myself actually organizing the thing and it is so uppermost in my under-mind that I am guessing that when I do sit me down to write, that is what I shall find myself doing. No telling, however; not for sure. And again I say: no matter. If not that, then something else.

The most interesting people I have met here are Kenneth Macgowan and Robert Jones. The first is the dramatic critic of the *Globe,* the second is the boldest and the greatest play-setter on the American stage. They are over here making a book about the stage in continental Europe, and they have been taking me to some of the plays which, for one reason or another, they have been studying here. I knew both of them when they came out of Harvard, about Jack Reed's time. Macgowan started fast, but got tuberculosis and had to lay off to cure. This he did, and resumed his career, which has been worth while and a success professionally. Bobbie Jones, as we called him, was a queer-looking, queer-doing youth, whom I remember as playing with toys of his own making. He said he was playing plays. He was making stage scenery, dressing puppets and generally creating plays without words. It struck one as silly, but he got his first chance with an amateur performance and he made such a hit that the regular stage took him up and has used him ever since. "The trouble with playwrights," he said the other day, "is that they think of it as,—this" and he made a pantomime of a man writing on a typewriter. In other words, he would say that play-writing isn't writing; it is making scenes, presenting persons, showing situations and producing emotions. There is insight in that speech, and Bobbie's genius is in color. He wants playmakers, however, to use all the arts: painting, music, sculpture and poetry, and the something else besides.

But I must stop this nonsense and go out, partly for food.

Dear Laura and Dr.,   Genoa, May, 1922

The arrangements here are good. There was an officer at the station where we were received and provided for. The town is crowded; hotels are commandeered by the Government, but there is one for the correspondents. It's a new apartment house overlooking the harbor; called for the present Hotel *Albergo dei Journalisti.*[1] A guy drove us out there, and we got a big double room temporarily. I get a separate

---

[1] Steffens frequently spelled foreign languages, as well as his own, phonetically.

room today. The prices are all fixed by the Government and cheap: 1.50 each.

We have very little time for the room, however. The crisis of the Russo-German treaty was coming to an end. We met correspondents everywhere. They live at our hotel and,—elsewhere; and we run into them there, on the street, but mostly here, at the Press Club: *Casa de Stampa.* We came here, got our credentials (with photo) and hurried off to lunch. We had to get through in time for Lloyd George's conference with the reporters, and lunch takes time; not for eating, but to greet acquaintances and trade news and rumors.

It is just like old times at Paris. I'll not name now all the men I found. We were in the current of the news-getters, and we floated along, up and down the beautiful old city full of police, soldiers and foreigners. But at three we got to the St. George's Hall where Wilson spoke and where now Ll. George was to talk to us about the treaty crisis. We couldn't help getting the story of it; each man we met told us his bit, so we were prepared for the interview. It was well ordered. Tables and chairs laid out in squares, columns, series. We grabbed what we thought were the best and watched the crowd gather: more old acquaintances, some of whom I had forgotten. They joshed me on being late, but,—George came. He was applauded as he entered, made his way to the presidium and, after a few nervous movements, rose and spoke, briefly, but with humor and good humor. Then he asked for questions to be written. And he answered with great tact. Each answer was translated by the interpreters, first into Italian, second into French: I was surprised to find I understood the Italian better than I did the French version. The George conference lasted an hour. It was "news": the crisis was over, the incident "closed." "Peace will be made." Fine.

So we broke up and Jo and I went with some of the Reds to the Russian peace room where we met Rakovsky and Ruff. The latter was the Russo-Soviet ambassador to Berlin during the war. A good talk there, then off to the formal "conference" of the Russians at the University. Rakovsky conducted it. He takes a classroom, one of those small halls where the professor stands at the bottom and talks and looks up at the hill of hearers before him. I was amazed to see it crowded: see the correspondents come, even ours. Even the reactionary correspondents of the *Times, World,* A.P. were there, and Rakovsky explained the Russian position and policy to them; and not only as to the treaty; he taught Communism, the philosophy of the history of revolution. He fascinated the French reporters with his light on the French Revolution. And then he too answered questions, quietly, firmly, with knowledge both of current facts and history; with humor—all in the most perfect French. Out again, into the court or patio of the University; lovely. Then back to the *Casa de Stampa,* where we traded views of the day's developments. I saw Von Wiegand from Berlin, the regular Hearst correspondent. We came to an understanding in no time, how we are to divide the work. Then dinner with him, Jo, Max Eastman, and the Labor *Herald* correspondent: Slocombe. Some of these dressed and went to a formal reception by the City after dinner. I didn't. I went to bed, tired, and I slept ten hours.

Len.

To Laura Suggett

Grand Hotel de Gênes, Genova,
May 16, 1922

Dear Laura:

It's all over. There's the plenary session tomorrow; early, at nine A.M., then we send our last cables: then there's a lunch by the British press for the Italian press, and then,—rush for the trains. I shan't leave till Saturday,—today is Thursday,—and I go straight to Berlin. And I am going there to be ready to travel with the Russian delegation here to Moscow. My Russian permission to come is arrived. I lack American permission, but the U. S. Ambassador here advises me not to apply, but to go and take chances of being sent home from Riga.

Jo lost 21,000 lire to a group of the correspondents at baccarat the other night. He can't pay, so he's giving them a dinner tonight, as he leaves for Paris at midnight. He comes to Berlin later to join the party going to Moscow. I go direct to Berlin, and since the Russians stay here till Monday and then plan five days in Berlin, there is time to do things.

But I must stop this. I am tired and relaxed with the thought of the end. I'll go home after supper and sleep. Jo will wake me up when he comes for his baggage, but not for long. I shall resume and be up for the early meeting of the Powers. What a farce! Especially these plenary sessions!

To Dan Kiefer

Hotel Esplanade, Berlin,
May 23, 1922

Well, Dan:

How do you like my neglect? I certainly gave you a free chance to think things out for yourself, and I'll bet you are all wrong on everything again. Sorry, I couldn't help it. I was loafing along my philosophic way at Genoa, when von Wiegand, the Hearst correspondent, had to rush away to get the Kaiser's book for his papers. He asked me to do his cable a day for him, and I did it. It was work. I didn't like the hustle of it as I used to, when I was your age; it wore me out. And worst of all, in expanding my cables, they made me say little of what I wrote and a lot that I never even thought.

No matter, however, it forced me to know all that was doing, and I saw this conference close up. Not a pretty sight. I shall write some articles around it for Hearst's magazine or his papers. In fact I did one this morning and I started another yesterday, which I shall finish before I go East. If I go. I have the Russian permission, but I am seeing so much of the Russians here, as at Genoa, that I doubt if I need go to Moscow. There is only Lenin there to see, and he is out in the country for his health. I hear that no one is allowed to visit him. I'm in doubt therefore, but we'll see. . . .

Germany is still a dependent country, defeated and waiting the conclusions of other countries that fix her fate. Exchange goes up and down on news from Genoa, London and Paris. Just now she is counting on J. P. Morgan, which is tough. I wouldn't like to have my future hang on the word of an American. We are just! The French are bad enough, but,—there is worse. The conference was, of course, a failure, as the others were; as the Hague will be. They talk about the Bolsheviki, but they don't do as well. And nobody asks why. No, they do as you did during the war. They vent their indignation on a man or a nation; it's Lloyd George or the French, as it used to be Wilson; and so they miss the trail to the truth. See?

But I must quit this nonsense and go out to dinner. One lives well here. It costs a lot of marks, but not much money, and an American with a lecture manager like mine can outbid a German nobleman, unless he has gone into the money-broking business. And even then we are neck and neck. It's pleasant to live in a country where one is rich; it's a malicious sort of pleasure, but a wicked person like me can be amused by wicked littlenesses. . . .

To Ella Winter

> Bad Pyrmont, Germany,
> June 13, 1922

Dear Peter:

    . . . I do want to take some things out of your mind. There is one conception you do not grasp, or not sufficiently. We have talked about it before. You accept it but you don't hold it all the time. It is, in brief, that we are not to judge but *explain* events and men. Just now everybody is blaming the French instead of asking why they balk at all our plans. There is a cause for their conduct; they themselves give reasons and your writers answer with counter-arguments. If you come here, I will show you that the French have all the reason on their side. They are holding the world back but,—there's a cause; not a reason, but a cause. And what is true of the French is true of us all. The course of the Russian Revolution is due, not to the misconduct of the Bolsheviki, but to the laws which govern all revolutions.

    I have just been talking with Emma Goldman about that, and she won't take it. She admits that the Russian Revolution has followed the curve of the French Revolution, and I show her that the Mexican Revolution moved along the very same road, but she still denounces the Communists and so will not draw inferences which are necessary to prevent the next revolution from being like,—all the others. You see, my theory is that, if we will study events we can avoid the repetitions of history. And we can't study events, if we pause to judge the men. Lloyd George is another example. I watched him at Genoa and he doesn't do what I would have him do, but I could see that he cannot; and that the criticism wasted on him is needed to get at the forces which keep him from doing what terribly demands to be done. Really, Peter, I have something to give you along that line; and you are ripe to take it. You probably think you have it already, but you haven't it as a mental habit. The scientific attitude isn't instinctive yet; it isn't a constant. And you must have it in your business. Come and get it.

> Stef.

To Allen and Laura Suggett

Haus Sievers, Pyrmont,
Germany, June 17, 1922

Dear Laura and Dr.:

This is a pleasant, pretty place, and it has done me good; and I can work as well as cure in it. I rewrote that short story, "Pull," [1] and sent it off to Miss Ford to copy. Then I got out that Moses, which grows on me. I can't finish it because I have no English Bible here, but I can't let it alone either, so I edited and typewrote the part I had in bad-penciled copy in my bag, and I shall send it to you or to Miss Ford before I leave here. Meanwhile I went at the new part: the actual story of Moses, and I am having fun with it. It *is* a good story. I do wish I had a Bible. I am so in the mood for the thing that I could reel it right off. Maybe I shall write it through and put in things out of the Book of Moses later. I am thinking some of doing it thus without details to send to Frank. However, you will see when it comes to you, that it is in three parts: The lead about the Russian who was going to Russia and his friends, the revolutionists, who had been there and were broken-hearted. I know more of that story now; I saw Emma Goldman in Berlin and heard her talk. It is a sad story, but I don't know whether it is a tragedy or a comedy. This first part leads up to the story of Moses which I am playing with. And that leads up to the third part, all done: the conclusion from the experience of the Russians that it was just or merciful of God to put Moses to death before he went over into the Land of Promise.

Whenever this week I have been sensible and realized how silly it was to make bricks without straw and to write the Moses story without his book, I have turned to the fable about the Japs: [2] Why they are so bad; why they imitate what we westerners do instead of listening to what we say. I am putting the explanation into the mouth of a Chinese, a wise old humorous diplomat. He says, you remember, that the Japs who went forth to study Christian civilization did not really understand our western languages; they seemed to because they are so polite, but they didn't get a word we said and so assumed that we believed in what we did. This should be finished before I leave here. And I may stay on till July and do more.

[1] *Survey-Graphic,* Mar. 1, 1927.
[2] "The Pallor of the Yellow Peril," *Century,* Oct., 1924.

Bad Pyrmont is a celebrated old Kurort, not used much by foreigners. One gets up betimes, goes out and slowly drinks warm water, walks, gossips and after an hour returns to a light breakfast. I work till noon, then out again to join the idiots who walk up and down drinking water before dinner. This washes out the stomach and develops an appetite. I have eaten heartily ever since I have been here. After dinner, everybody takes a nap; which spoils that sport. The fun of sleeping after noon is partly in the sleepy thought that everybody else has to work. However, I sleep for an hour, get up, dress in white shoes, breeches, etc., and meander down among the trees to the Kur Park, where there is a concert twice a day: afternoons and evenings. When the afternoon concert is over, at six, we all wash out our tummies again, read the newspapers and change for dinner. No, no full dress; only warmer clothes for the evening, which is usually cool. Supper is a lighter meal and the drinking is over for the day, so that about eight o'clock we go to the concert and take coffee and dessert. By ten it's all over. Bed; study Italian; sleep. How is that for a day's work? . . .

I see that the reporters, especially the Americans, are making a row at the Hague because they are kept out of the sessions. Sauerwein, the famous French correspondent of the *Matin,* says that the Dutch are afraid the Americans will find out about the part oil is playing in all these conferences. We got hold of that at Genoa, you remember. My papers killed it out of my despatches, but I encouraged the *World* men [1] to push it and they did. It broke out in fine shape and nearly busted up the conference. The oil men from everywhere rushed to Genoa and kicked up an awful row. And the chief offender was the Dutch Shell Company, which had made a tentative contract with the Bolsheviki after it had been agreed, apparently, that none of them was to make any separate treaties with the Communists. The Hague may bring on the bust-up among the capitalist states which the Russians hope for and, it is said, are playing for. This last I could not detect, but I can believe it. They are desperate and they understand the capitalist game and psychology. . . .

A long letter, what? Well, read it gradually, and take revenge upon me. I can stand it. I could read a mile from you two any time now. Goodbye.

Len.

[1] Especially Sam Spewack; see *Autobiography,* 809.

Hotel Regina, Paris,
July 10, 1922

Dear Laura and Dr.:

I am not working today, only writing letters. I had to. I have let my correspondence go too long and too much. I have done a stack of replies, so I might as well make a correspondence day of it by doing one letter for fun alone. . . .

Germany shows signs of bucking. The French financiers think the Germans are going to buck right away, and it is not bad that they so err. It renders them abnormally reasonable. But I know that the Left had no plans when I was there; the assassination of Rathenau and the anger of the people at it, laid off the Right. So I am betting, as you know, on no immediate break in Germany; not till the fall. In other words, I intend to go to Italy unless I hear new news this week. I may. A German Communist, who knows the situation from the inside, is to meet me in Paris in a day or two, and he can send me to Germany. Otherwise,—

. . . E. A. Filene is here. He wants to go with me to Russia. So does Max Epstein, the Chicago rich man, who is at Baden-Baden, Germany, now, and is contriving to meet me in Italy to settle details. I am asking him to go home, see my list of applicants for the Russian trip, and arrange the American end of the scheme. He will, I think. Meanwhile I am getting E. A. to go up to the Hague to see Krassin, whom I fixed for this plan at Genoa. The reasons I am for this are two: first, it might help the Russians and they like it; second, such a group could afford to hire a special train, equipped with food and water to bathe in. If we could travel and live on a train, there would be little discomfort and no danger of typhus or cholera. This may sound more sensible than heroic, and it is so meant and confessed. I have some sense of romance left, but I am no hero. I know that my old folks at home are a little like that.

I have been seeing old friends and acquaintances here, Americans and French, which is pleasant but distracting. I must go away and be alone. With G., who can be nobody, as Dr. knows well, too well. He doesn't like it, but it is a great gift sometimes. I know nobody that has it except G., certainly not to her extent.

E. A., by the way, who is an organizer, who, his friend Justice Brandeis says, is "forever organizing Chambers of Commerce, Boston, Massachusetts, National and finally International, yes and many, many more such well-meant institutions that the enemy takes away from him and uses against us,"—E. A. has just been dropped from the Directorate of the International Chamber of Commerce, his place being given to a reactionary of the Rightest type! He told me last night and I laughed till I cried with joy, and he with rage. E. A. and Dan fill a very real want of mine: idiots that one can enjoy. I like 'em, and I love the damn-fool things they do; and though they may seem to do enough, I wish they would do more. All they need is more time, but I would willingly give them some of my time so that they could keep me fuller of joy. You should have seen E. A. as he told me that. You would have thought it unnatural and unexpected to fire him from the Thing he had spent years founding, building and moulding to the uses of democracy; the International Chamber of Commerce. Yes, Chamber of Commerce.

I don't understand why people are so prejudiced against damn-fools. Laura, frinstance, you get mad at them. Oh, yes, you do; I have seen you. It's a defect in your make-up; it's as if you were color-blind or deaf in one ear. It's as if you liked flowers, but drew the line at vegetables. . . .

I have made some mashes on girls, but,—don't worry,—they are pure, they are purely literary, but they are nice girls. One is Mrs. Child, the wife of our Ambassador at Rome, another is Janet Scudder, the American sculptress, and a third is Gertrude Stein, the cubist writer. Miss Scudder has just cut out sculpture "forever." She says it is too hard to do. She is painting now. That is easy. "There is nothing to know about painting. Don't let anybody tell you anything. They will talk values and,—all that rot. Don't listen, just go and buy the materials and then, paint. It's great. But sculpture? No, that is awful. Why, it takes twenty-five years to learn enough about sculpture to know there is something you have to know, and then you know you can't learn to know it." I told her she should stick to painting for twenty-five years at least, and she asked me, "Why twenty-five?" Kind o' nice, ain't it? Goodbye.

Len.

To E. A. Filene

Dear E. A.:   Sept. 2-3, 1922

Walking along the Seine the other day with a girl of mine who knows you, not well, but badly, and yet sends a greeting, cordially, she says, we saw some Frenchmen fishing, three of them, and they were getting bites. So I said:

"Let's stand here and see one of them catch a fish. I would like to wire E. A. that I had seen (with a witness to prove it), actually myself seen, a French fisherman catch a fish."

So we stood there a long while. The spirit of contradiction held me to the job. It would have been a bully joke on you to have seen such a thing and wired you of it. The trouble was that none of those fishermen got his fish. Some day I will get you though.

But that isn't what I am writing this letter to say. I don't waste time on silly letters. With all the statesmen in the world and all the business men, with all the conservatives like you, doing their best to make a revolution in Germany, Austria, Portugal or,—somewhere, I feel the soberness of life and I like to reflect it in all I write, even when doing a letter to a man like you. What I wonder about is why your class at home are arresting "reds," who can't do a thing, when they ought to be arresting one another. And the chief of police hurrying back from America to Germany just for a few riots.

But that isn't what I set out to say. This letter reads like a speech by you. The leading thought is constantly being postponed by some other passing idea which gets on the track and throws the mind into a ditch. Why don't you correct that fault, E. A.? I suppose it is for the same reason I can't get over polishing and changing what I write. And we are made so, are we?

But that isn't what I wanted to say. What I wanted to say is that I received your letter advising me to go to Vienna, and I may. And I'll be glad for a few letters. Also I could use a reference to a cheap hotel; not the kind you frequent. But I cannot go to Austria unless they prevent the people of Germany from starving in a disorderly fashion. I may have to go there. And I still think I may try again for Russia. Why won't they have you? You are not a radical. I'll be here long enough to hear again from you, if you will be prompt in your reply to this very urgent letter. . . .

To Laura Suggett

Paris, Sept. 9, 1922

Dear Laura:

I am sick abed again, but only in my pleasant way: and not of my own will this time. . . . I went to call on August F. Jaccacci, the art editor of the old *McClure's Magazine*. He is the man who discovered me and engineered my appointment as managing editor. And he was a help to me there and a friend always. He is a queer fellow. No one knows whence he came. The best guess is Arabia. He speaks all modern languages and all with an accent. And he likes all his friends, but all with an accent; he sees through you. His present job is being good to his friends, mostly the French and especially the sick children of French soldiers lost in the war. Well, Jac, as we call him, saw I had some fever. He was glad of it. He took command, he gave me a treatment, which consisted of several pills, and a room filled solid with eucalyptus fumes, after which he sent me home with orders to go to bed. That is something I like to do anyhow, so I obeyed. He said I would be well in the morning, but I wasn't; so I got up at eight o'clock only long enough to go downstairs, meet Williams, when he drove up his car, and tell him I could not go. Then I returned to bed and read and thought all day. Yes, I slept some, but mostly I thought. And among other things I thought about whether to go to Russia or to the south of France; which is to say: whether to go on getting news or sit down and write what I have. I didn't decide, not that I know of, but I think I felt that what I ought to do and what I would really prefer to do is to write.

Dull letter, isn't it? I'll hold it a day and see if I cannot add to it an interesting word.

Sunday: I don't find the above a dull letter. It simply wasn't written for you; it was for me. I am better today, so I see clearer. I see what I meant when I said "dull." Being a bit sick, I was homesick too. When I am homesick I am apt to think of home, and home to me means not a place but persons, you, G., Dr. Well, I can relieve myself by writing anything or nothing to you, to 850 or to G. For while I am writing I feel together with you. So a letter like this may be an imposition, but,—dull is not the word.

Yvonne called this morning, about noon,—Jo Davidson's wife. I like her. She is French. And just now Edouard Dolléans [1] was in; he is French too. They illustrate what French means to me. It means taste, reason, loyalty of a very dignified sort, controlled by a grave respect for you, the friend. They are thrifty, and not mean, sensible and polite, but self-respecting. There are things they won't do for you or any-

---

[1] Professor of History at Dijon University, later Secretary of the International Chamber of Commerce.

body. Dolléans wouldn't go with a party of us to the Ambassador's one night, and he told me afterwards that he would have gone with me alone or with two of the Frenchmen in the group. He refused because it developed in the conversation that two of the Americans were going to see the naked women in the show. There were naked women on the stage but they were a very beautiful picture. That picture Dolléans would have appreciated, but he didn't want to be with people who would see only the nakedness.

In a word, I know a few French people who keep me thinking of the French always as decent, above all other people clean. I think I told you once of the audience at a show that applauded the climax of a piling up of women like a pyramid till at the top a nude appeared, a very beautiful woman at the peak of a very beautiful spectacle. But the applause was so hearty, that the curtain lifted again and the nude bowed. The audience hissed her, and rightly. By her movement, she had changed a posed nude figure into a naked woman and so spoiled the picture. She had done an inartistic thing. But this happened right after the treaty-making, when there were no foreigners in Paris, when the French were left by themselves; and it is we foreigners that demand and get the things in Paris called "French."

Len.

To Ella Winter

Hotel Regina, Paris,
Sept. 10, 1922

Yes, Peter, I am back and I have been back here for some ten days, and I didn't write you. I dunno why. I saw Margaret and Lucien Wolf, and they reproached me for not telling you. But I didn't know what I was going to do or where I was going, and I am all up in the air even yet. But what I am writing to say is:

What are you going to do? Where are you going? You were in some doubt in your last letter. You spoke of America. I suppose America means something far away and romantic to you. I hadn't thought before of that. I think of the States, which I know, as I think of Australia, which I never saw, as prosaic and matter of fact. It's hard to see why anyone should want to go there. But to you the States are a glamour. If so, you should go there; and not to reduce the illusion, no, but to have the romance. I ought also to go home, but I will not do my duty. I stay here if I can. Unless the call for me becomes very much louder I remain here where is romance for me.

This letter is an example to you. Write me one just like it, telling me what you think you should do, what you would like to do, and then what you think you will do. I am in a state of mind to understand you at your worst.

Stef.

To Laura and Allen Suggett

Paris, September 23, 1922

Dear Laura and Doctor:

We have been sitting on the edge of war here for several days; and nobody seems to mind. I get scared, I go around for comfort to other people who prefer peace expecting to canvass with them the chances of escape. They are glad to see me; they want to talk over the new office they are about to take or the baby's health. They know as well as I do the chances Lloyd George is taking. A rash act by some wild Turkish officer or a British subaltern, and over we would go into the next war. We are wondering whether the French, British and Italian statesmen meeting here this week can get together. We know how they differ, how they hate each other. I think myself that we shall get by. But I realize also that governments have more power than they think they have; they regard public opinion more than they need to. Everybody I know in Paris was leaving the question of war or peace absolutely to the premiers. And by "absolutely" I mean that they left it out of their minds, the people did; they went right on about their own daily business upon which and upon which alone they were thinking. Sound them and you found them aware of the crisis, but only as they were aware of the weather. Democracy!

The trouble down there in Asia Minor is oil; "petrol" as the French call it, and other concessions. The British jumped in while the war was on and nobody looking, and they copped off all the good things they could see. To protect them, they seized Gallipoli, the Gibraltar of the Straits, and other points giving them control of the freedom of the Straits. The French woke up late to what had happened; they were awfully busy, you remember, fighting Germany. The war was over before they realized that their friend and ally had gone in behind their back and gobbled up a lot of good things from among the weaker nations and so extended the Empire during the war against empire.

The French, having kicked in their private way in vain, were told to go on down there and get what was left. They did; the French-Russian treaty of Angora is the result. But all the while the French were at it, the British were having the French accused of imperialism and militarism! And the French were denying the charge!

Talk about comedy! The farce goes right on. Lloyd George was working to get all the rest of us to disarm, and he worked us all right. He worked us so well that he had us reproaching the French for not giving up force and turning to reason. He was getting the League of Nations to drive on for general disarmament and his plan was to go and complete the triumph by making himself a speech for general disarmament. He was through fighting for a while, he thought. He had the Greeks fighting the Turks for him, but nobody said so, the world didn't notice. The governments that knew and could prove it were being gentlemen,—and silent. George's speech was written, I hear, and all was ready when the unspeakable Turks turned in and licked the Greeks. France laughed and was gay. The British got mad, Winston Churchill and the British Imperialists said: "Well, but we have the French and Italians with us down there, let's force them to stand with us and block the Turks."

So they put out their note declaring that the Turks should stop where they were. The French stopped laughing, the Italians got scared at the prospect of another war, and the French withdrew their few troops from Asia back to Europe. They talked justice and common sense. What they were thinking of was their new concessions just got from Kemal Pasha. They are pro-Turk, they are anti-British. But the French had to think of Germany, reparations and the debt of Germany to them. They couldn't break with England, not quite. The British showed them what might happen. Their bankers agreed to trust the Germans for eighteen months, as the Germans asked. The Bank of England will pay Belgium in six months and let the German Reichsbank pay the Bank of England in a year and a half. In a word, the British gave the Germans what the Entente had refused,—a moratorium. And the German banker who negotiated this deal said in his private report that the British were moved in all this business solely by "political considerations."

Now this, in brief, is the comic but possibly tragic situation upon which the ridiculous but powerful statesmen of England, France and Italy are sitting this very day, free to make a war of it or a "peace."

And nobody is much worried. The people here treat it as none of their business.

We had a summer day yesterday, the first for months and, if today is a true sign, the last. It is dark and cold again. . . .

I begin to want to go out and hear what news the reporters are getting about the—war.

                                                                    Lin.

To Allen H. Suggett

                                              Paris, September 27, 1922

Dear Allen:

No news here. We are waiting for the decision: war at Constantinople or peace at Venice. I am for peace at Venice. It's warmer there and, then, I think, they might really make a peace this time and I would like to see peace made once.

E. A. Filene got here Sunday, and when I called, he showed me two tickets to the Carpentier-Siki fight and insisted that I go with him. I did. It was my first. When I was at police headquarters and afterwards a city editor, I received complimentary tickets to every fight that happened, and I never went. I thought a prize fight was nothing but an exhibition of brutality. And it is brutal, but that isn't all it is. The Carpentier-Siki fight was a story, a good play, half comedy, half tragedy, and I could see why men like such shows. It is a contest of man against man in which everything counts; strength of body and of mind and of character, all in the nude. Anybody could understand it.

The comment around me was in French, English and American, and it all showed that everybody realized that a fortune was at stake: millions of money and world fame and glory. Carpentier was the hero: a great fighter, a fine man, powerful but gentle, strong and graceful, skillful, an artist. Siki was nothing but a black, undeveloped man, fresh from the jungle. He had no chance against Carpentier; it was thought not quite sportsmanlike for the king of the ring to refuse to meet his equals and take on a "nigger" he could so easily beat. And yet, the "nigger" MIGHT win; and, if he did,—Gee, he would achieve riches and three titles, all in an hour.

The "nigger" came on first, smiling, embarrassed, awkward and pale. He was afraid. Our seats were close up; I could see Siki swallow; and his legs shook. Carpentier came down a bit late, but he came

bowing, proud, sure, but kindly. But he wasn't in very good shape.
He hadn't even had a hair cut. He sprang up on the platform and
genially, very cordially shook hands with his opponent. He stayed to
say something pleasant to Siki, holding his hand. It was as if he wished
to put the humble darky at his ease. Then Carpentier walked to each
of the four sides of the ring and bowed to the crowd, which cheered.
All the sports liked the champion.

When the bell rang, Carpentier stepped out to meet the Negro and
he did not strike; he smiled. The "nigger" was so obviously scared.
And Carpentier, amused, feinted, with his eyes only for the crowd, and
sure enough, Siki ducked and covered his face with his gloves. "Ah,
it's a sell," said someone near me. "Money back," said an American.
And it got worse. Carpentier tapped Siki, here, there, where he pleased,
and Siki in sheer fright, dropped to his knees. It was as if he had
thought that he was going to fight with the greatest fighter in the
world; that the greatest fighter would lick him, of course. He had
thought this many, many times, every night alone in his bed he had
seen himself knocked out by Carpentier, the mighty Carpentier, the
greatest man in his world, and he had imagined, too, how the blow
that landed him might kill him. He was afraid. The moment had
come. Carpentier, the God, was hitting him. Yes, Carpentier hit Siki,
right, left, to face, to body, but lightly, for the fun of it. It was amusing to the crowd, and then, there was the cinema business. He had to
make a long enough picture to be worth a fortune. Carpentier stepped
around, came back and struck! Siki dropped to his knee, feeling himself to see if he was dead. The referee had to caution Siki that he must
fight. Siki respected the referee. He had to obey the judge. He couldn't
drop any more, so he clinched. He hung as close to Carpentier as he
could hug. And Carpentier laughed and let him, only jabbing him
here and there to show that he could. And then the bell rang.

Siki rushed for his corner. Safe. One round and he wasn't dead. Gee!
He grinned. His seconds said things to him, and he smiled, nodded;
he was happy. But the time between rounds is short. The bell rang,
and Siki rose, yes, but he was not happy. Carpentier would land him
this time. Where? Would it be very terrible? But Carpentier was upon
him. Carpentier hit him, and hard too; and again. Siki struck back,
hard, but missed; Carpentier was graceful, quick; it was easy to dodge
the dazed, the awe-struck Negro. He dodged and he landed blow on
blow, hard, quick, and Siki clinched or covered. Sometimes he covered

his face so long that the crowd yelled at him or laughed. And while he was covered thus, he could not see and Carpentier could have knocked him out to body or chin, where he did hit him; to say nothing of body blows. But Carpentier was still playing cat and mouse. When the gong sounded.

Siki, back in his safe, cosy corner, felt himself over. He wasn't dead; he wasn't even hurt. Maybe his seconds told him, maybe he thought of it himself. Maybe I am imagining too much. Anyhow it seemed to me I could see that black face saying that it had stayed two rounds with the greatest fighter in the world, and that maybe he could stay a lot more. In a word, he gained confidence, courage.

He went willingly to the next round. He struck out, and he landed. Carpentier may have felt the difference. He hit harder, faster. The "nigger" also hit harder, and the "nigger" is a formidable animal. But he still wasn't a man. Some blows he got must have been almost up to his dreams, for he covered again and getting no respite now, he clinched. And it was in a clinch in this round that, I think, the tragedy happened. Carpentier had been very fine to Siki. Once, when Siki hit a bit low, the referee said something about a foul, and Siki started back in alarm. He knew well what a foul was; and he evidently had not meant to foul. He said, "No, no," and Carpentier also said, "No." And he took and he shook both the "nigger's" hands. It was a fine gesture, and Siki appreciated it; he grinned and nodded to Carpentier. But the fight went on, and it was so hard and fast and clever that Siki grabbed Carpentier and they both went down into the ropes, Carpentier under. And Siki returned the fine courtesy of the white man. He lifted Carpentier bodily up to his feet and, aware of his chivalry, Siki grinned and nodded. Thus off his guard, Carpentier hit him, and he hit him so hard that Siki staggered. But Siki's jungle level was reached. Hurt by the blow and by the unexpected return for what he thought a kindness, he swung with his right fist; a wild swing it was and hardly aimed, but it was a terrible swipe and it landed. It seemed to me to take Carpentier on the jaw. Anyway, the champion dropped and Siki stood over him, amazed apparently. He had landed the greatest man in the world, he had hit him and he was down. Descamps said the next day that that was the crucial moment. He said that Carpentier was stunned and needed time; he should have waited for the count to nine. But, no, Georges, the great, the champion, could not stay down before the crowd and the cinema; he rose at three or four, and looked around to show that no chance blow from an amateur could knock him. He had slipped; and to show that he had only slipped, he slipped again, and again. But he was sick; he was hurt; he was not in condition to go on, so he dodged and HE clinched till,—the bell. This time it was Carpentier who rushed to his corner.

The next two rounds were a fight. Some of the veterans near me said this whole fight was the greatest they had ever seen, but I think they must have meant the second half. The Negro had lost his awe; he had a lot of respect left for the champion, and some fear for himself. But Carpentier was alarmed; he fought as if he realized that he had to do quick whatever he was to do. For, you understand, at just about the same moment when Siki seemed to be saying to himself: "I have a chance to win; to WIN. I am not to be killed, I may be the champion of the world and rich and,—everything," Carpentier seemed to say to himself: "God, I may lose. I am sick now, and weak. I may be licked by this gorilla and lose,—everything." So they fought, the champion in despair, the "nigger" in hope, a faint, an impossible hope, but,—hope. Carpentier had the advantage in spirit; the Negro still could not believe his luck. He did not see how much stronger he was than the wounded man before him. But he fought; he had to. Carpentier was attacking, and fiercely too; unfairly. His character had been ground down to where the gentleman disappeared and the brute was laid bare. He butted Siki twice. The first time Siki protested, not the second. He wasn't so astonished the second time that the finest man in his world could be unfair. It was a fight, he knew then. And some of Carpentier's friends point out that Georges probably did not know what he was doing. His right face was skinned, raw, and both eyes were closed so that he could not see well, if at all: and he behaved like a blind man. He hunted and did not always find Siki, who still ran in and out, bold and afraid by turns. But when Carpentier did find Siki, in the fourth round, he hit him and clinched. And in the fifth, he only clinched. And in the sixth, he didn't even clinch; he did what Siki did in the first rounds. Carpentier covered his face and hung his head.

And in the sixth, Siki, told he was winning, trying to believe he was winning, would rush at Carpentier, pound him,—it was awful,—and, having pounded him on the head, on the body, he would start back. He seemed to back off to see why Carpentier did not strike him. And Carpentier didn't; he dodged around with his head covered, groping for Siki to hang onto him, close, close. Siki shook himself free or the referee would break them, and Siki rushed in again, raining blows, fearful, fast, hammering blows. But always he stopped, himself, stepped back,—to see if it was true. And it was. Siki drove Carpentier into Carpentier's corner and when he hit him there, and Carpentier clinched, Siki jerked loose and as he broke, hit the falling champion who lay with one leg held high to guard against the fear of the gaping, wonder-struck champion.

Thus ended the sport, and as usual, Business butted in. It had all been fixed for Carpentier to win, of course. I don't say that Siki had been instructed to lose. I am sure he wasn't; that was not regarded as necessary. But all the cinema interests and all the business men of the ring, all the betting was for the champion to win. And the referee knew that. And the referee had to, and he did do his business best. He gave the fight to Carpentier on a foul by Siki. Siki threw up his hands in astonishment. They said he tripped Carpentier as he fell the last time and the slow cinema shows that the two had their legs tangled. No doubt Siki's jerk out of the clinch jerked Carpentier's leg. But I doubt that Siki knew or intended the trip. And I am sure it wasn't necessary. Carpentier was defeated before he fell; he was a licked man long before that last clinch. And the crowd knew that. They rose to their feet in protest at the decision. There was danger. A few fellows jumped into the ring and lifted Siki into the air, to proclaim him victor. The referee left it to the judges, and they very soon decided that Siki won and that Carpentier quit.

Why am I telling you all this? You are not interested. Well, I am. I saw very plainly what I saw in that fight, and what I saw was not pugilism. It is what I have been seeing all my life, in games at college, in business, reform and politics, in arctic exploration,—Man put to the test, and almost always failing. I am seeing it here at these peace conferences. Man is not up to his job yet; he is not fully developed. But in this fist fight I saw it plainer, when I saw Carpentier fail,— in character. For, of course, Siki did not win, except under the rules of the game. In truth Carpentier defeated himself.

Just put these notes away for me. I may want them some time. I may want to show what a great thing it would be if some of our financial and political champions could be put to an obvious test like pugilists are. Watch Siki when Montmartre and his friends and the girls and the wine and the vanity and the glory have had a few rounds with him.

All's well with me. My cold is better. I could travel, and I may soon.

Love to all,

Lin.

To Laura Suggett

Paris, Oct. 12, 1922

Dear Laura:

. . . Col. Arthur Woods, Police Commissioner of New York, with whom I got that experiment made in Free Speech, is here. He came in yesterday and last night we dined together. He has been asked by the Rockefellers to be president and manager of another of their great funds: four millions a year to spend, and Woods doesn't know just what to spend it on. He asked my advice, and I laid out a scheme which he liked. It is to finance a thoroughgoing inquiry by scientific men into "What causes war; not who, but what?" When I got him really enthusiastic, I warned him that one of the causes was oil, but he didn't balk. He was for finding out,—whatever the truth was.

He sounded me as to whether I would work on the thing with him, and I said I would help pick investigators; I would do whatever I could do over here, but I would not take any work that required me to stay in the U. S. or any one spot. That was all. Woods is a fine man, conscientious and broad. He married one of the Morgans and through her is rich, but he has not much money himself and I think takes none of hers. At any rate he lives simply; is economical and tries hard to make the crowd he is thrown in with see something beyond society and money and business. He has won young Rockefeller's confidence; Hughes (Sec. of State),—everybody likes him. He is one of the men I got to work the State Department for my passport, and he has helped me a lot there.

His report last night of what he had accomplished shows that he had done more than I realized, for he got a promise from Harrison, the First Secretary (permanent), which I shall call some day. If you have any suggestion for the use of four millions a year, tell me and I will write it to Woods; he sails for New York next week. . . .

Love to Dr. & all.

Len.

To Allen H. Suggett

Paris, October 17, 1922

Dear Allen:

. . . I have been reading a book which I recommend, certainly to all writers and with reserves to all wishers to know and understand men. *Ulysses,* by James Joyce. It is an attempt to run along through a story of what some people did and said during twenty-two hours,— a line of their thinking or cerebrations. It is done. The events are utterly unimportant, I see as yet no "plot," but there is a narrative interest, however subordinated, and there is a sense of character, sometimes sharp, oftener vague. Also there are chapters of satire of other writers. The book is long, as long as your telephone directory, and it wanders at will over all fields of thought. Streaks of it are obscene. Of course they are, being the unconscious or suppressed glimpses of the brain at work under a conversation, for example. No doubt, the author used his own mind as his key to others and is assuming that his self-knowledge is knowledge of others. He may go wrong on some people.

But I was struck by the recognition I had of the confused and scrappy and often irrelevant thinkings of my mind when not concentrated. He thinks a lot like me. The last chapter is the thoughts of a woman just before getting up in the morning. They are pretty fierce, but I asked a woman who had read the book if they were true or typical, and she replied that she had seen her mind like that when she was warm and sexually discontented. To do this, the book has to say things and to use words never printed. As someone put it, there are words written in this book never written except on back fences. So *Ulysses* is condemned; it is not in general circulation and it is hard to get, except here in Paris where it was published. But the library should have it, and writers should be able to borrow it. For the value of it, as I see it, is in the unperfected form Joyce has found to do in a book what the Greek chorus did on the stage, give also the thinkings of characters before, during and after their acts and speeches.

The form Joyce uses is imperfect, I think, because it is often hard reading, obscure, and affectedly so. He could make it simpler by mechanical devices which he scorns: quotes, italics, etc. Some day this will be done. Joyce has said the first, not the last word, in the artistic handling of the subconscious. He makes a lot of old writing look void, but he has not made his stuff look clear. Colonel Wood should see

Ulysses. Maybe he has; maybe he could help get you a copy; maybe I can, if Laura says the library will take it. It costs a big price here; I don't know just how much. . . .

Paris, Nov. 7, 1922

Dear Allen:

Your letter, with the clippings from the *Call* of the fight, also letters from Older and Laura, are here, and I haven't time just now to reply severally to you; I must say it to you and let you tell whomsoever it concerns.

It was all right to print it and, in general, I won't mind you and Older deciding for me. If I had had any idea Older or anybody would want to publish the fight, I would have reread what I type-wrote you and made it better. As it was, some good fellow of Older's did touch it up here and there. Thank that man for me. Whoever he was, he is an editor. The thing was awfully well dressed. And your thought to copyright, yours and Older's, was well meant. But in future, don't do that unless I ask it. My feeling is that, whenever anything of mine is to be published it should be spread as far as possible. In a word, when once you two had decided to print it, then you might have let anybody and everybody have it.

I showed the story to Mason, the International News man here, and he said that, when he heard me tell it, before I wrote it; when his reporter and some others who had seen the fight, when each of us was giving his version,—Mason says he thought of cabling Pew [1] to let him order me to write it. "But," he said, "I was afraid Pew would wonder why I was getting you so far out of your field and would answer, No." They all here like the story published better than they did my verbal narrative. Pew wired Mason to have me cover that next Siki fight in London and I said I would, if I was in London or near there. I think I shall be in Lausanne then. The Turk peace conference is tentatively set for Nov. 25 now; that would mean being there till late in December. But the conference may be put off even later.

Thank Older for his interest in the fight story, for the bully way he handled it and for his praise which I like quite outside of our good old friendship. For Older reacts with mathematical accuracy on any written word.

[1] Marlen Pew, of International News Service, later editor of *Editor and Publisher.*

To Ella Winter

Paris, Nov. 19, 1922

Peter dear:

I can't go to England, not yet. I have seen the proper official here at the British consulate, and he is very friendly and he is amused too, as I am, as everybody that knows about it is. It is really funny, you know. It is very flattering likewise: the idea that I might break up or block or injure the mighty British Empire. I love to tell people about it. I can see their esteem for me increase. So it has its compensations. But I still can't go, Peter. Not to Britain and therefore not to you.

But I am going to Lausanne. I leave here tomorrow evening and I may stay there a long time. For I think the peace-makers will be there a long time, unless the war starts soon and interrupts them. When I get back, I shall try again to go to old England and I may ask a friend or two at Lausanne to help me. But I am almost persuaded that I must confine my movements to those parts of the world where you are not subject and I may have to find a girl friend of some other color. Yes, and if it keeps up this way, I may be compelled to oppose the Empire. They don't think of that; they may make me dangerous. . . .

Affectionately,
Stef.

To Allen H. Suggett

Hotel Beau-Sejour, Lausanne,
November 25, 1922

Dear Doctor:

I sent off to Pew, of the International News, a descriptive interview with Mussolini two days ago, and I told Pew that, if he didn't care to use and pay for it, to forward it to you so that you could let Older steal it. But I think there is no doubt about his using it; it may be out in the *Call* before you get this, unless Pew holds it for the morning paper service as a Sunday feature. Even the youngest of the correspondents here like this Mussolini story; those who also wrote it admit mine is the best.

You are a by-word here among the correspondents. They know the story of the Siki article, often ask me if I am writing something to my brother-in-law, and the other day when the British Press man asked me for what service I was working this time, one of the British correspondents spoke up before I could answer, saying: "Oh, Steffens; he writes for his brother-in-law." Having no knowledge of how fine and appreciative a brother-in-law can be, they cannot understand why I "waste good stuff" on mine.

The peace conference is moving along, attending to business. Literally, I mean. They are doing little about peace, so little that Lord Curzon, who presides, cautioned the delegates yesterday to speak more of peace. He said that they must not forget that that was the purpose of the conference, and he advised that they mention at least the word in every speech they make. Of course the reason Curzon said that is that he is just now under the influence of Coué, the mental curist, who makes all his patients say twenty times each day: "I am better today in every way than I was yesterday," but the advice really shows the state of affairs at this conference.

The city of Lausanne gave the correspondents an excursion today, Sunday, up into the snow mountains. I got into a bully Italian car with a driver who has been a racer. He raced all right. We started out seventh in the morning and passed them all. Coming back this evening, we got away second, passed the first in a mile and never again saw anybody. The trip was straight up into the high mountains, some seventy miles back, up to the peaks; a banquet; then down another way to the head of the lake and so past all the famous places on Lake Geneva. It was a glorious trip. Smith, the A.P. man in our car, was reminded of his trip this summer to Yosemite. I thought of that, and of Tahoe. I would enjoy having you see some of the great auto trips over on this side.

Well, this isn't much, but it must be all for today. I find I am drowsy, the effect of so many hours in the open air and the Alpine cold. I shall sleep deep and wake up early for a good day. And it will be interesting. Ambassador Child has been under criticism by the American reporters, who complain that they have to depend for all their news on the British; they can get nothing from our "observers," Child, Bristol and our Minister to Switzerland, Mr. Grew. Child talked to me about it last night and finally asked me to let him tell me everything that happens tomorrow,—confidential and all,—so that I can indicate what is news and advise as to what he can, under the official restrictions, give out. That is to say, trusting me as a friend (as he did at Genoa), he will be guided by me as a newspaper man. It's an experiment. I think it will work out. We'll see. . . .

Good night, lots of love,

Lin.

To Ella Winter

Lausanne, Nov. 30, 1922

. . . This conference is clear enough to me. I see through it. I don't care for the details, the daily news. So long as I have the key to it, have seen it at work, I can visualize and correct the newspaper reports. I am free to leave, therefore, and my intention was to go to the south of France. And I may still do that or stay in Paris. But there are several calls to New York, not irresistible; errands I could do nicely now, so I have half a mind to respond and go, returning early in January.

What do you say? I said I would see you before I went home again; I meant for good. But I may be able to swing off the straight path west or south, if you wish. It would be fine to have a good, long talk with you about the world and you and me and us. I'm pretty clear about us, clearer than I am about you and me. It doesn't matter, however. There will be a moon somewhere on a river or if no moon, then the street lights, and if no river then the sea. Just answer promptly and to Paris. I may still be here. I am waiting only for a talk with Chicherin, who was expected next Sunday, but gets here now tonight. I may see him tomorrow. And then I shall be in Paris by Monday.

Stef.

To Laura Suggett

Hotel Richepanse, Paris, December 12, 1922

Dear Laura:

Your letter suggesting the talk with Coué got here just about the time that Jo Davidson arrived at my hotel to beg me to go with him to Nancy,—on almost the same errand,—to see the man. Only Jo is to make a bust, not to interview him, and he wants me to talk to him while he, Jo, busts him. I said I'd do it, but for you, not for him, and he declared he didn't care. . . .

And by the way, Jo and I are invited to a tea this afternoon to meet James Joyce, the author of *Ulysses*. I hear that Joyce is an empty man.

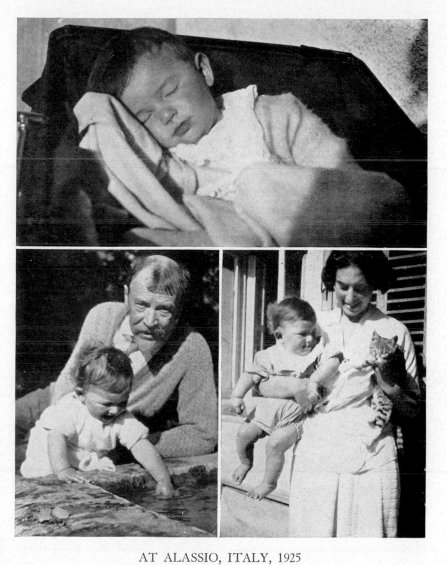

AT ALASSIO, ITALY, 1925

upper: PETE ASLEEP ON THE TERRACE. *lower left:* AT THE POOL.
lower right: PETE AND HIS MOTHER, ELLA WINTER.

He put all he had into that book, spent ten years on it and now talks only of his ills: he is almost blind, has other troubles and they so interest him that he talks of nothing else. As somebody said, Nature used him, used him up and has cast him aside empty. But we'll see. Everybody isn't a very good reporter.

The news here is pretty warm. The French are saying today they will seize part of Germany. The situation, as I see it, is that the English at Lausanne are holding the French in line for an anti-Russian treaty with the Turks, who are afraid of the Bolshevik influence. "If," said a Turk delegate to me, "if we stand out with the Russians and resist the Allies, it may mean war, which is bad enough, but the war would throw us completely into the hands of the Russians and so arouse among our people and the people of Asia the Bolshevik hopes of big changes. We prefer to side with the English, who are making us fair offers and may bring the Allies to a reasonable treatment of us." Tchitcherin wagged his head sorrowfully when I remarked that it looked to me as if his ally, Turkey, was leaning classward. "Timid," he said. "Afraid of the enemy, afraid of us, afraid of their own people."

To G.

Paris, December 17, 1922

Dear G.:

Just back from Nancy, where I went with Jo who was to do a bust of Coué, and I find, by the way, that during my absence, some bodies have got into my room, cleaned my typewriter, put in a new ribbon (which doesn't ink very well so far), filled a vase with holly and left me a book I have been wanting. I shall trace the typewriter work to Frank Mason, the book to Guy Hickok, but the holly I dunno. Some one of my wives, I guess. Having no wife of my own, I have been making love to "all the wives of correspondents here who are happily married." I will tell you about it some day. It's a joke around our crowd, the outsiders jeering at me because I play so safe and because both the women and the husbands trust me. The rounders say that is a disgrace to me, that it shows I am not dangerous. However,—

Laura suggested first that I see Coué, and she wanted me to ask him some questions for you as well as for her and Dr. I had the chance. I was with Jo all the time he was at work, we had Coué alone and twice at his conferences or cures. Indeed, we both took the treatment, and we played around with his disciples and favorite patients.

We got him all right, and I think I will sit down tomorrow and write a descriptive interview covering the two days and half, with the pictures we took of the man and of Jo's bust. The Inter. News would take it, I think. But this letter is for you and, when you have read it, for Laura. It is the gist of the matter for your cases, the essence of the doctrine.

When you go to sleep, you can say to yourself that you will waken at seven o'clock and you can do it. Why cannot you say then that you want to go to sleep at eleven? Coué's answer is that your wish to rise in the morning is addressed to the subconscious, to the mechanical part of you, which is accurate and reliable. Your wish to sleep, however, is expressed by you awake to your mind, and your mind is an undeveloped organ, erratic and weak. So he concludes that the thing for you to do when you want to go to sleep is to talk to the subconscious, to the machine underneath the brain. Hence you mutter, "*Ça passe,*" or "I am going to sleep" as fast, as thoughtlessly, as mechanically as you can,—twenty or more times. And so with everything else. If it's a stomachache or any other kind of an ache or ailment, you say swiftly,—he himself says it so fast that you can't catch the words "*ça passe, ç'passe,*" and it passes if you believe it will pass. And the reason you say it so fast and so thoughtlessly, is to keep from thinking that it won't pass. The Catholic Church, with its mutter litany in Latin, has long had the practice, if not the idea.

Coué performs miracles thus; we met some of them. He recently cured a man who, shot in the war, had a piece of broken bone pressing on a part of his brain in such a way as to cause paralysis. The man did not believe. But he was an educated man, an engineer, and he stuck through weeks of failure because he declared that Coué was right on his mechanics. So he repeated the formula till he could say it without a thought as to what he was saying (and hence no doubt, no fear, no—nothing) and he got well. His theory was that, without removing the foreign matter from his brain, the organ had found a way around the obstacle; it had developed what Coué himself calls "compensations." This goes to mean that, in some cases, one can get around a surgical operation by inducing the subconscious to find a track around the trouble. . . .

I may think later of some more points and write again about this. All I will add now is that the method does really work in a great many cases. Jo got it, for example. There was nothing the matter with him, but we both took the treatment at both the conferences we attended. I was a failure, but Jo said, and he showed, that it had done him good. And in my case, I did not, I felt I could not, obey Coué. He made each of us fold our hands gradually, hard, harder, tight, and then suggested that we think we could not open. It was hypnotism. I did not think I could not open. I thought: "This is interesting. I will see if I can open," and of course I could and did. But, as Coué remarked, I proved his theory as well as Jo. Jo did think he could not open, so he couldn't, while I, thinking I could, did. One night at the time my bowels often move, I felt no movement, so, just for fun, I said, jokingly, thoughtlessly, "*Ça passe, ça pass', ç'pass',*" and Jo nearly died because I had to go to the closet. Coué says he did that to a constipated man once, and the fellow had to tear out of the room. But, then, Coué hypnotises. He really puts himself over on a crowd, and he never works except in a crowd. . . .

To Laura Suggett

Paris, Jan. 23, 1923

Dear Laura:

I sail a week from tomorrow, on the *Olympic,* due in New York on Feb. 7th-8th. . . . I shall soon be with you. Yes, and I will work. The fact that I haven't is in all G.'s letters lately. She has almost nagged me, a thing she never did, and the Dr. has kept dropping hints. You speak of it sometimes. And my conscience talks about it all the time. I must do something. I will go straight to you, and we'll have our visit. But pretty soon after I get there, I mean to move in to some hotel or pension and settle down to the daily grind. It is hard; it is a grind. But I must either do it or agree with myself not to do it; to stop talking about what I do. I reckon that I should get to San Francisco around March first.

Dr. and Older will be pleased to hear that the official report of the French *Boxe* Association gave a story of the Siki-Carpentier fight, which pointed out the very incidents I mentioned to make my story, and this report is the only one except mine that did see those incidents. I guess I still can report, still see with my eyes. Some of the young fellows here have noticed the confirmation, and spoke of it.

Len.

To Arthur Woods

850 Francisco Street,
San Francisco,
March 23, 1923

Dear Col. Woods:

The letter enclosed came from Dr. Scott [1] yesterday. Will you kindly read it and then return it to me? . . .

The proposal, as I see it, has two purposes; to really begin the search for the causes of war and, second, to give an example of the application of the scientific method to a social problem. Consequently, no witness should be allowed to try to make propaganda or to fix the blame upon persons or corporations or even classes. The question is: What,—not who,—are the causes of war? In relating incidents that led to a war or that might have brought on a war, it may be necessary to name persons and companies, but the examiner, by his questions, would be able easily to bring out the common denominator,—the economic forces,—which alone are the "villains." At any rate, my experience as a muckraker convinced me that we are wrong whenever we punish persons, that all the evils in the world can be traced back to our misunderstanding of natural forces and that the scientific method will demonstrate this.

Mr. Root [2] is here just now. He is visiting his family or branches of it, and is refusing therefore to commit any public act. He may not care to do any business. He might not wish to see me on our matter. But I put into my wire to Dr. Scott the fact of Mr. Root's presence here and I am telling it to you, as a hint that, if you think Mr. Root would welcome me, I would be glad to call on him at his hotel and I feel that I could interest him. I am willing to do any service in my line toward our end, as you know well. I would not like to cut my visit home here to go to New York, but I would if you and Dr. Scott asked me to.

To Jo Davidson

San Francisco, April 9, 1923

Dear Jo:

There is a letter from you today, and it fits in with the weather. It is raining. This is a land of sunshine, and we have had a lot of it.

[1] Dr. James Brown Scott, secretary of the Carnegie Endowment for International Peace.
[2] Elihu Root.

I ran into the spring-like summer of California out of a freezing East, a blizzard-blown Middle West, a desert of ice. It was fierce; my train was twelve hours late, and so it was a wonder to puff up the Sierras of snow and darkness, dive into the snow-sheds and bang out upon a California with the valleys flooded with a hot sun, a dazzling light that hurt and all a-budding with the blossoms of the orchard and the fields. And the heat and the light lasted for weeks. I rejoiced in it down to my very bones. But the farmers kicked; they swore around, clamoring for rain, and the churches prayed. And lo and behold, it began to rain, kept it up for days, and with one day off,—yesterday,— has been at it ever since it started. Seven days of it. . . .

But you are a darned stinker not to tell me the gossip of the crowd. You say I get that from the gossips themselves. Wrong. I don't. They write, some of them, but they don't tell me the news. They also say I get that from the others. What an unimaginative, un-self-knowing, bum lot you all are. But I have imagination, so, while I get no news, I can see you at your trivial occupations, all of you, all wanting something you can't have, all suffering in the midst of abundance (of things you would want if you didn't have them), all needing a good, long look at Jo Davidson's bust of Miss Stein. That suggests philosophy and repose, understanding, a sense of proportion and applied knowledge, which is wisdom.

And besides, I have other friends out here. A great crowd. As warm and good as our gang in Paris, and much older in my friendship (some of them) and better tested. I mean that I have seen them put through all the paces, felt them suffer, cave or stand up, so I accept them more absolutely than I do the Paris gang. I still expect something of Paris. But from San Francisco I expect nothing; I know what they will do because I know how they have behaved. We here never judge at all at all. It is very good. There is Andy Furuseth, for example,—the old labor leader, the head of the International Seamen's Union,—the man with the head we all want you to do in mud and rock,—remember? Well, old Andy is out here to fight for the control of his organization against the Bolsheviki, who want it for the uses of the revolution for which Andy has prayed and worked all his life. God, how he has suffered for the great revolt. We all know all this, we are dead against Andy's purpose now; he is "wrong" we say. But he's "all right" too. He knows how we feel, he has heard us talk, but he comes rejoicing "home" to our table and we rise as one man to receive and embrace him. And we all love him. We don't expect him to be right or reasonable; we know damned well he won't; and he knows all about us and has no expectations of us in this, his great emergency. No. There is nothing but love and respect, just as there is sunshine and rain. And it is beautiful so.

They have given me a dinner, and they have sat and listened to me. They have lent me their minds along with their ears. They have let me change some of our conclusions; not many, not much; but what they wanted most to hear, and, having heard, rejoice over, is that I have not changed. They did not think I would, but they are glad now to know it for a certainty. I wish you knew Older and Andy, C. E. S. Wood and Sara, Mary and Lem,[1] my sister and her—my brother-in-law, et al., et al. And there are always some new folk that fit in, a poet or an ex-convict, an editorial writer or a crooked lawyer,—anybody that is "wise." You would belong here as well as in Paris; better, I really think. You have no gang in Paris, you haven't; nobody but acquaintances. And that is one thing the matter with you. We ought to build a crowd in Paris. But then,—a crowd such as I mean is not a matter of form; it cannot be built; it can't be formed. . . .

Give my love to Yvonne and recall me respectfully to the good boys and their bad companions when you write to any of them.

Stef.

To Laura Suggett

The Players,
New York,
May 10, 1923

Dear Laura:—

It's an awful rush,—to get ready and go, but it has one good feature: it makes me hustle and I'm making things fly.

I took the manuscript[2] to Glenn Frank yesterday after I wrote you, and he was to read it last night and meet me for a talk at luncheon here today. I am awaiting him now. But he wants me to do my story, the Life, and he is very persuasive. Maybe that is the way to tell what I don't know. I shall listen to him today, and we'll see. And I shall report the results. Indeed, I'll report almost every day till we sail.

---

[1] Mary Field, short-story writer and sister of Sara Bard Field, and Lemuel F. Parton, newspaperman.
[2] "Moses: A Miracle of Mercy," *Century,* Dec., 1923.

I talked over the 'phone with Mrs. Villard's secretary today, about that meeting on how to fight war. It's to be Monday evening, and only the heads of all the peace societies, etc., are to be there. None but executives and not only women. It's not to be reported; which is my request. I can open up, and I am sure I can make them see that they must see and fight,—causes.

That's all today. I don't see G. till tomorrow. We both have too much to attend to to meet for fun. Life is not for happiness. Business before pleasure. Any copy-book will give you the rest.

Love
Len.

To Allen H. Suggett

Hotel Cocumella,
Sorrento,
June 7, 1923

Dear Allen:

. . . McClatchy's [1] poison didn't touch me. It's serious. He and the *Bee* have a strong pull in the whole Sacramento Valley, and that counts. It could spoil some plans I might have. And he's not well. He writes like a fixed mind, and a fixed mind is indeed fixed. Nothing could change him except a personal talk, and he would avoid that. The instinct that makes me seek out a person that thinks differently from me would keep a fixed mind off. C. K. would shun me, feeling that I might change him; as he should,—to save his soul. For he would soon feel that I'm just what he dreads, just as he is just the man I'm after in all I'm saying nowadays. . . .

Older should know that there was a reason for Burns's willingness to do something for me. I saw that he was the moment I walked into his office, but I didn't know why. I sounded around, as I put my questions, and at last I had it. He used, when he saw or telephoned me, to call me "Sam," meaning Gompers and implying that I was a friend of the old crooked Labor boss. But this time, when William J. bragged that he was onto the fact that the Reds were against Gompers,

---

[1] C. K. McClatchy, editor and owner of the Sacramento *Bee* and other California papers had written on May 10 a bitter attack on Steffens for his role in the McNamara case: "Lincoln Steffens is at it again. . . . Lincoln Steffens is a Radical and a Red of the deepest dye. . . . The proper place for Lincoln Steffens is in jail. . . ."

I said: "Yes, but, Burns, that's old, old news, and you should have known it long ago. And you didn't. I know that, because you used to call me Sam. You didn't know that I and my sort were more down on Sam than you were."

"Oh, hell, yes," he said. "I know now. I knew you were onto the whole thing from the very start. But fellows like you and Older, you are always about 1,000 years ahead of all of us."

In brief, he has learned to respect "fellows like Older and me." And he wonders, and he asked me why I didn't laugh in his face when he called me a friend of Sam. I said, "Older and I have learned to do our laughing all in our sleeve."

I'm going soon to write to Mussolini for an interview. Glenn Frank wants me to follow up my last article (for July or August), using it as an introduction to three articles or four: one on Italy, one on France, the third on Germany and the last on Russia. It's the French I'm working on now; I have that all in my head. I have to get more on the Fascists and I'd like another look in on Germany and Russia.

To Laura Suggett

Hotel de la Ville,
Rome, July 27, 1923

Dear Laura:

We have been in Rome now for about five days, but they have been busy, hot days for both of us. Mussolini refused, through his secretary, to give me an interview, but I saw Child, our Ambassador, the day I got here, and he gave me a card to a man who is friendly to us, and I discovered also that this man and Mussolini's friends are so eager to save M. from interruptions that they will talk in his stead. Well, that suits me. My letter to Mussolini was misunderstood. I said I wanted one for my own information, not to quote; what I sought was light on the Fascist program. I can get that from anyone who knows it and, as Child said, there are several men who can talk better about that than Mussolini. I shall see them. . . .

We made some bully excursions, two in the big power boat which the Cocumella uses for handling freight and baggage for the hotel. With this one day we visited the islands and peninsulas across the Bay of Naples and liking it so much, a bigger part, took the boat for a run to Paestum. This last was two days. We crept around close in ashore on the mainland to about Amalfi,—where we landed at night and were driven up to Ravello, where there are fine hotels. Amalfi at night looks a little like the commanding city it once was. And Ravello in the morning looks worthy of its fame for beauty. The second day we sailed along the shore again till we came to Capri, which we went out and circumnavigated, stopping to visit the grottoes not usually seen by tourists. We got home in time for a swim before dinner, and so completed a tour such as I would like to make to many points on the Mediterranean and, for that matter, the Adriatic. Boating is the way. I would be glad to do the Greek Isles on a yacht.

I shan't know what I am to do till I reach Paris, see my mail and friends. My disposition now is not to go home this fall, not to lecture, but to stay over here and go on writing. G. backs me up in that, but, when I feel like lecturing, she is for that. I am onto her. She wants me to do whatever I feel like doing so long as it is work, and I love her for that. But it is no use writing about this now. The next letter from Paris will carry the decision.

Affectionately,
Len.

To E. A. Filene

Paris, Aug. 9, 1923

Dear E. A.:

. . . I shall stick around Paris till about August 24; then, I think now, I may go to Berlin to see where the wealth of a country goes when it goes out of its money. I would like to know who has the public and private riches of the Germans. From Germany I may run over into the Future for a short spell, but I am not sure of this. Jo wants to do Mussolini's head, and his sittings would be a fine chance for an interview with the man who represents American ideals so literally, and so truly European conditions. I expect to stay over here somewhere for six months at least. I like it. It gets better all the time for my purposes. Read an article of mine in the *Century* of August on "How Europe Can Help America," and you see at last what I mean. I would like to be understood by you.

It must be a relief to you to have a New Englander once more in the Presidency, and such a representative one, too. I should think you would want to go home and show him what you see. He might help Europe and the League of Nations, though I think myself he will do more for the Third International; for which everybody is working so hard now. . . .

Yours affectionately,
L. Steffens

To Mrs. Daniel Kiefer

Paris, August 21, 1923

Dear Mrs. Kiefer:

Your cable reached me this forenoon, and I wired immediately to Henry,[1] who is in the country. He went there to paint out of doors for a month. I told him you wished him not to return and that I was leaving here tomorrow night for Berlin to join La Follette, who may be going into Russia.

Dan is the best friend I ever had; he is yet. For I have him all as he was in my memory, and always shall have. You and I can bring him up to us whenever we are together. And we shall be together often, I hope. You don't know now what you will do, I know. But by and by you will live again, and you may come to see about Henry; and maybe to look after me a bit. I should like that. We wouldn't have to say much.

G. was with me when I got your cable, and her eyes filled with tears. We went to lunch. We didn't talk. But by and by she hit upon what was hurting me: some of those letters I used to write to Dan. I don't like to think of them now, but surely Dan knew I was more than half joking and all loving. He knew I loved him, didn't he? He knew those were love letters, he must have; and, even if he didn't, you knew and you told him. You will answer this, won't you?

I wrote Dan Sunday and this very morning I wrote to you a letter answering one from Dan, the one in which he suggested how ill you all thought him. I do not recall exactly, but I think that both of those letters from me to you and to him were all right. I would not like to pain you. I would like to do something for you. If there is a chance you will let me, won't you? I owe Dan much. I could never have paid him in any way, but I might you a little. He would like that.

I must stop now. I could not say any more, not quietly. Love from us both.

Affectionately,
Lincoln Steffens

[1] Henry Kiefer, son of Daniel Kiefer.

To Allen H. Suggett

Dear Dr.:   Paris, August 28, 1923

. . . The news here is amazing. The governing statesmen express and they evidently realize the danger of the situation, but they will not, cannot, handle the problem. Is the human mind so helpless or are the men with their old ideas helpless? The *Century* article puts it up to our culture, our logic, our right-and-wrong theories, and you might expect me to rejoice in the verification of my interpretation. But that is too complete. It goes my way so altogether that I can hardly believe it, and I am trying to get a bit closer to hear what they say, off duty, and see if there are not other elements in the problem.

The French are going to stick it out, we hear; the Germans are encouraged to fight to the finish; and they get their encouragement from the attitude of the British, which seems to be positively inimical to the French and almost friendly to the Germans. All that is clear is that each one is acting according to the Marxian theory of economic interest, in the near and narrow sense. But why cannot they see that the interest of each, if carried out to its logical end, will smash the system? Or, if they do see that,—and they say they do,—what is it that prevents them from handling the problem as a whole? In a word, what, technically, is "economic interest"? I am really puzzled, really interested.

I may discover something, something I don't know. Something, however, which when I express it will turn out to have been known for centuries. I wish I had had an education, so that I could have really started with what was known and so gone on to the news. Damn these universities, all of them. They have made my life one of unlearning literally, and all my discoveries are of well-known, well-kept secrets.

I met James Joyce last night, and his wife and daughter. He was at dinner with Ezra Pound, and I went over and had a short talk. He has been treated for his eyes and other ailments and looks very much better than when I saw him last winter; and he talked with some life. He will be doing something else now, and that is good news.

To Laura and Allen Suggett

Dear Laura and Allen: Berlin, Aug. 30, 1923

We leave here tomorrow at 8 A.M. for Russia. We are Senator La Follette, Mrs. La Follette, Robert M. La Follette, Jr., Basil and Mrs.

Manley, Jo Davidson and I. Ike MacBride may join us, but inde-
pendently. The 7 are a party in diplomatic visas. Our route is Stettin
tomorrow noon; German boat to Petrograd direct, where we are due
Monday morning. A day or two there and we'll go on (12 hours) to
Moscow for most of our time. Bob wants to make one trip into the
country, but we are to be gone only 3 weeks or a month, so we'll
concentrate on Moscow.

Things will be happening here while we are gone. They are happening now, for that matter, but they start slow and will develop
slowly. The big change may have occurred when we get back, but
I doubt it. I think we'll be back here in time to see it. And I think it
will be Italy all over again: a Right dictatorship, for which plans are
making right now.

To G.

Moscow, September 11, 1923

Senator La F. and his original party are leaving here tomorrow for
Warsaw–Berlin. Jo and I remain for a while; not long. I meant to go
with the Senator, but we have been here only four or five days and
that is not enough. La F. got what he wanted to know and so have I,
but I'd like more details.

The big points are that the Bolsheviki have yielded nothing. They
are on their course, proceeding as they began and they intend to see
it through ruthlessly. That's the first good news. And the second is
that their policy is working. Conditions are amazingly improved and
their state machine of federated industries is pulling out of the hole
of war, famine and corruption. All that I said about this is true, still
true. I had begun to doubt myself, but I needn't have doubted. But I
must make this short. Bobby La F. will take it out, mail it from
Berlin. . . .

We were well received here, put up in their best guest-house: the
old sugar king's palace, like the one the Bullitt mission had. I found
friends a-plenty, Jo made a hit and of course the Senator was taken
care of, as he wished. Jo is to have a studio and sitters. He begins with
Lunacharsky, head of education, tomorrow afternoon and is to have
another at night. For he and I are to go in two weeks. I am to see his
sitters and meet and talk with anyone I wish, and they ask me to see
the heads of opposition parties. But what they have suggested for me

to do is to write some stories. "No books," Nuorteva[1] said. "We are fed up with books. Do a story or two to illustrate the life." I objected that fiction required more knowledge than a book of facts, and they knew that. "We'll put you up against men with real stories to tell, and we'll show you the background too." I'd like to do that. I have heard one story I'd like to get and do. It would tell the whole story. But the time is short and I must not stay. Germany is sinking and,—it's cold here.

There are lots of people here I know: Max Eastman, Bill Haywood, Anna Louise Strong and her father, Williams, etc. All glad to see me. We had the news. Coming direct from Paris and Berlin, we could tell them what they didn't know and our reports made them want to get out.

Love to all. . . .

To Laura Suggett

Paris, October 1, 1923

Dear Laura:

Jo and I got back here yesterday at 2:40 P.M. Yvonne met us at the station, and she had planned to take us home and have a Sunday dinner, but I declined. I had been sick on the train, I was sick at the station and I asked to be dropped at my hotel, where I went to bed and slept: I slept from 4 o'clock in the afternoon till six this morning, I must have been worn out; I was tired. It has been a terrible trip, six weeks on the go, but it was worth it. There is really something new in the world. There is a powerful, intelligent government in Russia, which owns and means to control all those economic interests which own and control every other government in the world. And our trip began with Germany, where the old culture is driving on to its just but awful destiny, and ended in France, where the old culture is being driven to its logical conclusion. It is a story worth the time to tell, but it is too long for a letter.

Russia is strong. All I have ever said about it is true, and more also. The Bolsheviki have not retreated, they have not yielded, they don't mean to surrender. They understand with bare brains what they have achieved, what they are up against; they know what it has cost and what it will cost to hold on; but they have turned the corner, they are succeeding, things are improving, they are sure they can win

[1] Chief of Anglo-American Department of the Soviet Foreign Office.

and they will fight on to the end. They are bringing up the youth to fight and die. You see these youth on the street, audacious, dapper, ready for the next war, which they are taught is to come, the final great war, in which they are to die, these boys. And they walk by you with heads up, thinking you are what they call N.E.P. men,—business men produced by the New Economic Policy, profiteers, money-makers. They despise business men, these boys; all the New Russians despise business men and seekers after individual success. They give such no votes, no respect, no hope. They tolerate them as we do prostitutes, because they cannot abolish them yet. It is awful to be a business man in Russia. I met some, and they are tragedies.

"They treat us like dogs," said one. "They let us operate, but they leave us out of everything, they disfranchise us, they look down on us, but worst of all, they take our children away from us. I mean," he corrected, "I mean that our children leave us and join the Communist party, which is the fashion, the religion of the youth of Russia today."

We went from here to Berlin through the occupied district: the Rhine Provinces, the Ruhr, passing alternately time after time the French and the German inspectors. It was idiotic, a bore, but amusing. Berlin was dead; sore, whipped, tired, sick. Stresemann had just come into power, and there was a ray of hope, but we, foreigners,—we learned that Stresemann knew he had to yield. The Germans did not know that. Germany was done in,—like Austria a year, two years ago. The mark was at a million for a dollar. We stayed a week, a long sufficient week, in that country where everything is going down, and the mark went down to eight and twelve millions to a dollar, before we left. And we left with La Follette and his party,—all pro-German, —for Stettin, where we took ship for Petrograd.

But the Baltic, a shallow sea, was rough, as ever; everybody but the Senator and I were sick, so we quit the boat at Reval, Esthonia, and went on by a bum train to Petrograd. There were old-fashioned sleepers on the train, and we had the best, but there were no beds, no bedding. We sat up and shivered in the cold, empty cars. We were three days in Petrograd, led about by the officials, who, friends of mine, showed us, as they did at Moscow, everything, both good and bad. And they know what is bad. In Russia they have the only government I ever ran into that does not lie to itself and likes to show you the rotten side; they do not lie to you either.

But what I saw was a city come to life. I had seen it dead in 1919, in 1923 I saw it recovering: a resurrection. We went to Moscow on a perfect train of Pullmans, with every comfort, in cleanliness and on time. We were met at the station by Nuorteva, an old friend of mine whom I knew in his disgrace in America, and he told the Senator (and me) that he had a hotel for us, a good one, and guides whom we could use or not, as we chose; who would show us anything we asked to see, rotten or fine. We went to his hotel, a palace run for distinguished guests at $5 a day for room alone, and the Senator rightly took it, but Jo and I soon quit and got into the Savoy, also a Soviet house (all hotels, most houses belong to the state or city) where the correspondents and the concession-seekers live, where they have news and some fun. It was cheaper there, better, more gossipy.

Jo began doing busts of the leaders, I set about inquiring; we went to the theater, concerts, operas, ballets. We met our friends, American, English, German and Russian. I soon got what I wanted to know, but Jo was busy and wanted to stay a while, so we let the Senator go out alone and we hung on till Jo had to leave to make his appointments in New York. I was invited by Nuorteva to go with him to the Crimea, which is their Riviera, Florida, California,—a sunny shore with oranges, palms, sea bathing, and I'd have gone if I had been sure I could return via Constantinople, Greece and Italy. But I was afraid to come back late in the cold fall through Moscow, Petrograd and Warsaw or Germany. I came home with Jo. We left Moscow a Tuesday afternoon via Minsk, Brest-Litovsk, Warsaw, Vienna and Switzerland, five days of it, with double inspections at seven borders and many changes of trains, languages and moneys,—a slow, nervous, wearing journey, arriving in Paris the following Sunday,—tired out, as I said. But sure of the future, which is here. . . .

Love,
Lin.

Paris, October 4, 1923

Dear Laura:

Ezra Pound and Hueffer, the English master of prose, are to have a monthly magazine to be published here.[1] I had tea with Pound yesterday and left with Hueffer, who took me home with him. His idea is to use the thing as a playground for the younger writers now

[1] *Transatlantic Review.*

working in silence and the dark. I know some of them; they are good; he says he knows several more, and he is very enthusiastic about them. He thinks an English magazine in Paris will be free and may be fine. Hueffer is the man who taught Conrad to write and signed with him some of Conrad's early stories. He certainly can handle the technique of our language.

My particular friends here are away, the Hickoks,[1] the Birds, the Hemingways, and others you never heard of, but there are others. I like Paris. But I want soon to go to London, get some clothes and see my friends over there. By that time the Woodses should be coming along and we shall plan the next few months. The Hutch Hapgoods, who are here, have taken an apartment for three months.

That sick weariness with which I got back here is all over. It took three days and nights of long sleep to do it, but it is done and I am all right.

To Fremont Older

Paris, Oct. 5, 1923

Dear Fremont:

Since I last wrote to you, I have made a trip through Germany and Esthonia to Petrograd and Moscow and back via Poland and Austria to Paris. I wrote to Laura a bit about it and asked Dr. to repeat parts of what I had to say to you. I want you to get the good news I find. You seem to need it. And Europe is all to the good, as I see it. The rotten system you are up against there, in S. F., and cannot reform, is going down under its own weight in Germany, and it will surely carry other countries with it. And in Russia, the alternative, the new system, is rising with all the strength of youth and courage, hope and a fresh grasp on life and the facts. There is no doubt in my mind about the vigor of Russia. There had been no surrender there, and there will not be for two generations. For the older generation, the fellows that carried on the revolution, are as ruthless, arrogant, hardboiled, as prisons, torture, suffering and failures can make men. They are terrible in their determination to stick it out. And to this will to go on, there is added now the sense of victory. They have not only beaten the human enemy, they have won out in the civil war, in the foreign wars, in diplomacy; they have won over the peasants, they

[1] Guy Hickok of the Brooklyn *Eagle,* William Bird and Ernest Hemingway.

have got labor to work, they have brought about enough planting so that the famine is defied. They will have grain to export. They have money now to repair, paint, order and build. And they know it. Moscow is booming. Russia is beginning to live bravely and smile. But the surest light ahead is the youth of Russia, the boys and girls from sixteen to twenty-eight. They are the proudest human beings you ever saw. THEY fear nothing, neither the foreign foe, nor their own police; not even the Soviet Government can cow them. As one of these young devils said to me: "There may be another revolution in Russia, but it will be of the Communist youth against the Old Communists for Communism." They want to go farther to the left, and they mean to. And there is nothing to prevent them. They have no property, cannot own anything; they can only serve, and their religious ideal is efficiency. When they come out into the street and march, everybody stands back in awe. For they are it.

You who don't believe in human nature should get this, Fremont. The first leaders of the revolution found that they could not hold communism because the old generation of the peasants and workers were accustomed to the old ways. These could not stand the new. Lenin let them slip back, saying, however, that as they, the old slaves, had been made by slavery, so the children could be made heroes by liberty and education. So they gave the kids liberty and they gave them schooling in the army and in the schools and at mass meetings. No one else had liberty, only the children. They were not punished, they were spoiled; that was their liberty. But they were led to worship self-discipline and hard service for the cause. That was their education. And hasty as it was, unorganized, it proved,—this is what I want you to get,—Russia proved that you can change human nature sufficiently in one generation,—nay, in nine years, to fill your cities, country, army and political party with Reds that make the old reds blush visibly. You ask if they will hold it, and I answer that they have also taken away from these children the surroundings and the possessions and the hope of gains which among us spoil our children and make business men of them. These kids despise a business man. They point at them in the street, cruelly, and laugh. Service for a profit is a shame, but service of the state for communism is a glory, especially if it is the slow building of an organization to produce something useful. I think the children of Russia are a guarantee of its Red future and, if they have been produced in ten years, what will the schools and the army and the factories which they make do to the new children in two or three generations? And give the new conditions a few hundred years and I believe they will make a race, the meanest of which will be as noble as the best men of our day. And you must realize that the best human being is a living proof of human possibility. You know some pretty fine men, Fremont, fine in spite of our mean conditions. What would they have been in a fine, generous world?

Coming out of Russia with such thoughts, such facts in my eye, I saw Poland and Vienna with their people and their children, who recalled Germany. No. The world is all right. The rotten old Things are falling, the brave new Thing is here. They may have to fight, but, —we saw something of the Red army. The New will win. You can go up on the ranch and watch the sun rise tomorrow morning, and you can make a face at it. For I tell you that the human sunrise I have been seeing is beautiful, colorful, sure as that of the daily Light. And I begin to see that that is what nature has made the dawn so lovely for: as a prophecy to us, to say to you, even Fremont Older, "So is it to be with your kind. There will be millions as good as you."

I wired today to Bradford Merrill offering two articles along this line, but I wanted you to get it pure, without any details; not in the facts but in my vision of the truth,—for your good health, Fremont. I have always felt ashamed that I could not give you the best I had; only some stories, incidents, little amusing tips. This time I am trying to hand you something simpler and much more amusing, man to man, with love.

Affectionately,
Lincoln Steffens

▄▄

VIII

THAT LONDON GIRL
(1923-1924)

LINCOLN STEFFENS'S stay in London was prolonged for three months, and the cause was Ella Winter. Steffens was well aware of the objections that, in view of the difference in ages, would be raised to a marriage, and he was acutely conscious of his disloyalty to G. He did not want the marriage to be generally known until he had told G. about it in his own way. When, however, he found that he was to have what "in my bones, all my life, I have wanted—a baby," his joy made him unwilling further to delay announcement. He set out to win the approval of his wife's family and to hold the love of his own.

Two years later, when he was working on his *Autobiography*, G. asked him not to mention her. "I promised," he wrote Laura, "but it's too bad. What I really am is shown by that story better than any other. The whole will be hurt by the omission." "It belongs," he said later; "it shows,—not to me; I don't understand,—but it must reveal to others what is the matter with me." And to Dot he wrote, "If I tell only the professional tale of my life I shall be more of a hero than, for example, G. knows me to be or my sisters."

Since it was his own wish to tell the story, it is told in his letters. The regret that he felt for the injury he had done G. was intense, and, so far as reparation could be made, he made it. But the happiness in his life, the new confidence that he felt in his writing, and the eagerness with which he looked forward to the birth of his child overcame both bewilderment and self-condemnation.

After the departure from England, the year was spent in Italy, with a brief interlude in Paris. Steffens did several more fables, wrote one or two articles, and completed his *Moses in Red*. His theories underwent some modifications, but they were still tentative, and he was quite content that they should remain so. He had begun another extended fable, the story of Satan, but the conviction was growing that he could best say what he wanted to say by recounting his own life. This was the project that he was considering when, in September, he and Ella Winter went to San Remo to await the birth of the baby.

To Laura Suggett

London, October 29, 1923

Dear Laura:

I came over here last Friday (this is Monday) with Fred O'Brien ("White Shadows in the South Seas"), who sails Friday for New York and Sausalito. He promises to call at 850 and report: and he's a good reporter and a bully fellow. But I have a long letter from you to answer. It came on from Paris today; with a note from Allen enclosed.

I understand how you feel about shooting letters into the air, when you can't see where I am. I have the same sense of falling to earth, I know not where.

The library affair [1] is distressing, and I see how it makes you tremble for the Russian experiment. It is liable to percussion and block. But Lenin foresaw this danger and he organized as well as he could against it. He put the future in the hands of the oligarchy, the older men of which have younger understudies, who succeed to power. Then he instructed and warned the Young Communist Party to watch and suspect the Old Communists; and he told them just what to look out for. I think Lenin fixed his experiment for two and a half generations. But I think that you may yet have your day. It may come late, after one more administration, but I think it will come. You'll laugh: another optimist. But optimism may be right. Anyhow pessimism is too easy to offer me any comfort.

I'll not see your professor of the Russian language *this* winter. I might go to China, but Europe is too interesting to quit at this stage. London is a very good place to see it from after Paris, Berlin, Moscow (which has a visa) and Paris again. The English are anti-French.

I rejoice to see how Poincaré hangs on to his logic. He may blast

---

[1] Laura Suggett was librarian at the Sutro Library in San Francisco; "politics" were threatening her plan for enlarging its functions as they were her constructive ideas for the California County Library system.

reason once for all in his field, and I hope he does. His answer yesterday to the new proposition for a world conference was unyielding and I enjoyed the way it flabbergasted the British.

I am getting two suits of clothes, both dark, and for the rest, I'll see some men I know about China and some men who know the Bible about Moses. I'll go back to Paris in about two weeks.

Doctor writes about the reactionary conduct of the American Federation of Labor. Tell him Organized Labor in France, England, Germany, Austria and Italy is almost as bad, showing that some natural force or law is at work. . . .

I have an article almost done for the Hearst papers on Russia,— short, sharp and authoritative. The *Examiner* will have it in San Francisco.[1] I'll mail it this week from here.

Len.

To Allen H. Suggett

London, November 1, 1923

Dear Doctor:

I'm going to Cambridge tomorrow to be near a library and some scholars who know Bible texts and Old Testament lore and theories. It is for my Moses, which I'll finish this winter, and I'll be away a week or ten days.

The talk here is of the new conference proposed with the United States in, but it's the point of view that interests me and that's the same on all subjects. There's not a bit of science in it. . . . It was a relief to talk with men in Russia. They see it scientifically and big. They know what is the matter and they know what is to be done. It's only on details and the colonies, lesser facts of the Western world, that they go wrong, and their lack of current facts is due to their inability to get the news. But, even in there, with La Follette around, the vision was unclear. He was against them; "Marx is not the way to do it," he said. And he really believes he is on the way. But what he and Mrs. La Follette said merely was that they did not want our civilization to be destroyed in order to correct its evils. I said and I say, I can't see why everybody is so anxious to save this rotten civilization of ours. It won't be destroyed. It can't be. The Russians have only altered our culture, replacing it with the beginnings of a new one. But, taking

[1] Dec. 2 and 9, 1923.

what the Poor Fish say and think they mean, why would they preserve what does not work, what causes the very terrors that make them wish to reform,—the railroads or the banks,—a little?

Laura finds that the darned thing won't let even her quiet, little reform go through. Nothing good can go clear through to a fine finish. As a matter of fact, not even an evil thing can go through logically, as the French are learning with their Versailles Treaty. . . .

Frederick O'Brien, who has been living and travelling with me for the last three or four weeks, is sailing day after tomorrow on the "Paris." I have enjoyed his easy, humorous, romantic attitude toward life. He got something out of the Pacific Ocean that keeps a light shining in his eyes. Even London can't douse it. He says he has to go away, but I believe he could stay here and shine. He'd have to drink to do it, but he'd do it. Everybody drinks in London, all but myself. I don't mind it so much as that.

Len.

To Mrs. Daniel Kiefer

Alfredston, England,
November 13, 1923

Dear Mrs. Kiefer:—

The letter you wrote in Philadelphia on October 28 has just caught up with me here, a lovely country place near the sea in Suffolk. They call it the Downs; I'd call it the ups and downs, for it is both: all little hills and little valleys. It's a part of England I never saw before. As someone here said: "This is England," meaning that London isn't and the Lake Country isn't. Suffolk is just the pleasant average.

You ask me why I went to so many countries on the Russian trip. A map would show you that I had to go to or cross all the countries I named, and I was glad of the chance to see in sharp contrast the condition and the state of mind in the old civilization and the new. Russia is a great sight to see all by itself. But to go to it from Germany and to leave it by Poland and Austria is like rolling from the desert of Nevada over the Sierra Nevadas down into Golden California and come out on the Pacific Ocean. Russia is an oasis now of hope in a world of despair. I wish I could tell Dan how close they are to his and our idea of the solution of the problem. I think they have it. Of course I did tell him the Good News. But I did not tell it him so that he really got it. And that's the regret I reproach myself with: that I wrote him lightly or humorously things he needed to hear seriously and seriously accept and believe. But, never mind. My self-reproach is the sense we always have when we think of friends we can't see again. We almost always wish we had been different, more expressive, more kind. And I can and I want to believe that, as you suggest, Dan liked me and my letters to him as we were. He must have known the love that wrote them, however they were expressed. Yes, he did. He used to say so, and Dan always meant what he said. But we'll have our talk about him, we two, who both feel, I am sure, that he is with us, alive, in our hearts. And I mean alive. I do not think of him at all as gone away. I know that, because the other day when I spoke of him to a stranger I smiled to myself. No. Dan is an active influence on me and it will be good to meet you and sit down and talk together with him there with us.

I haven't seen Henry, of course, since I left Paris, but he is in full vigor, working, happy, sure. Men blossom, you know: open, like flowers, and bear buds. So Henry now. I wish you could see him in his new environment, with his girl, who loves him as a Western woman does a man and adores and serves him as the Eastern women do. She may spoil him, but only as a mother does; and that's nice, I think. Only wives suffer from spoiled men, and she is guilty of whatever harm she does. So we can smile and let her do her best or worst.

I like the news about the family: new homes, little girls coming along. Thanks for a dear, kind letter.

Affectionately,
Lincoln Steffens

To Ella Winter

Hotel Rubens,
London, Dec. 8, 1923

Peter, my dear,

Your diary of yesterday, with the song of Chaliapin, the Greek for loveliness forever and the chilblain, slipped under my door like a whisper at nine o'clock this morning. I got up and read it, and my breakfast over and the verses sent off to Bill Bullitt, I can sit me down and write to my girl the answer to her essay on fifteen guineas.

If the roses, my Peter, were to become intellectual and reason like you, they would refuse to bloom because the fruit trees in the orchard had been smitten by the frost.

We have rather agreed, I believe, that sex should not be separated from love. We might go on and see together that mind should not be set off against matter, thought separated from sentiment, and action cannot be cut off from emotion. There is something to be done about Germany, and when an intelligent spirit feels as the German students made you feel, it should think, with the kind of emotion that inspires mind and will, of that thing which ought to be done. Not of charity, not of useless self-denial, not of fifteen guineas. If I saw a chance to help Germany, really, I would give her more money than fifteen guineas and more of me than the mood of a day. I offered up two years of my life once to stab the world with an idea, and in vain; and at the climax I made myself as beautiful as I could. I slept long the night before, swam far out in the Pacific before breakfast, rubbed my body till it shone, dressed like a dude and braced my nerves to a readiness and a courage and a clearness that,—counted for my idea. Beauty is a power, Peter, and women will do whatever they do as women; not as human beings, but like men, as man to man, man to woman, woman to woman and woman to man. Each in his part, perfectly.

A woman candidate for Parliament said the other day that, if she were elected, she would wear her loveliest gowns, her diamonds, all her jewels, and she meant all her womanly charms, in the House of Commons. Right-o. I wish we men would see the simple truth and mighty power of that and do it. The flowers do it, the animals. The world is striving, not toward the truth; that's but a means to the end. The end is beauty.

I rewrote the half of the Messiah-Chief yesterday. I'll finish it today, and may get it typewritten and into the mail. Also I received and answered some more letters, mostly from Paris, one from Billy and Sally,[1] a married letter, written together at one table and read by each and answered by the other, an amusing epistle. Not so deep-reading as yours, Peter dear.

S.

To Laura Suggett

Dear Laura: London, December 28, 1923

I have been in Cambridge getting at books and men who tell me what is known about Moses. I came back here Tuesday afternoon, just

[1] William and Sally Bird.

in time to get my mail and my room here, then I went to bed, knocked out by bronchitis and by a sharp return of my stomach trouble. I must have needed a rest. I went to bed at 4 P.M. and slept till 10 A.M. Christmas Day. Staying in bed, I ate nothing but a glass of warm milk till 4 P.M. Invited to a big American Christmas dinner at 5, I got up, bathed and went to Queen's Gate, to the apartment of an old, Red New York friend, Helen Augur and her husband, Warren Vinton. There was a Miss Anthony there who is doing a life of Catherine II for the *Century* and had been all summer in Moscow. Later came Crystal Eastman and her husband, Walter Fuller; Charles and Mrs. Hallinan, he an old reformer and one-time organizer for La Follette, she a prominent Votes for Women leader,—nice people; Norman and Mrs. Ewer, he the foreign editor, she the dramatic critic, of the *Herald;* and last, the author of *Main Street,* Sinclair Lewis, and his wife. Well, we ate (and I mean that I ate too) a big turkey dinner with all the fixings: cocktails, two wines, liqueurs, soup, oysters, meat, stuffing, sweet potatoes, plum pudding and,—*and* nothing happened. From that time I began to improve and today I'm better. . . .

Tell Doctor not to worry over the rows in the Communist Party in Russia. It's weakening, but it is history. It has occurred, therefore it will occur, and either they must solve the trouble or leave it to the next revolution to avoid. Outside, the drift toward recognition is very powerful from many sides. Italy started, but as Mussolini cools off, the British Labor Party gets warmer. Only, remember, the British Labor Party is not radical; it is only about 10 per cent socialist and 50 per cent labor. There are Liberals more radical than the Labor Left. MacDonald is more anti-Bolshevik than he is pro. And even in the Party's attitude toward the European mess, there is more of pro-German and anti-French than there is of internationalism in the true sense. . . .

To Allen H. Suggett

London, Jan. 21, 1924

Dear Doctor:—

Col. Wedgwood, M.P., had me at dinner one night last week, with his lovely, deaf wife. Theirs is a love story, and I love love stories. And one scene of it is in the sand lots out near the ocean in San Francisco where the heroine lived for months alone in a wagon. She has promised, when she comes to San Francisco, to let you two and me take her out there so that she can show us where she had her caravan till the cable came from Wedgwood telling her to meet him in Washington. Now they are living happy ever after, as, I find, so many people do.

After dinner they took me to Lady Astor's reception to the new members of Parliament, and there Wedgwood went off on his own, leaving me with Mrs. Wedgwood on my arm. She likes me because I'm not afraid to use her trumpet, and since she is beautiful, we had a reception of our own. She introduced me to the English, I her to the Americans, and whomever I talked to, I spoke over the trumpet. I found it an effective way to talk. For example, once I was greeted joyously out of a group of women M.P.'s by one of them who remembered me at Paris during the armistice. I had forgotten, but she recalled: it was at the Crillon, and Bullitt and Polk and others were present. She said we were trying to guess what would happen to Wilson and his 14 points. I repeated this into the trumpet. Mrs. Wedgwood nodded and asked if we had guessed right. The lady M.P. said we had. And I, telling Mrs. Wedgwood this, said:

"We could see what would happen to Wilson, and so we can see what will happen to Ramsay MacDonald."

The group, all Labor M.P.'s, caught fire. They couldn't see. "What will happen?" they asked. And, out loud into the trumpet, I explained: "They can't see that MacDonald also will fail. And so, when he and they fail, they won't know why they failed. And so, the next Labor Government also will fail. It's a pity. For if they could see why, it might not happen; they might be able to prevent a repetition of history. What do you think is the matter?"

Before Mrs. Wedgwood could answer, my M.P. friend flew up and said:

"The matter with Wilson was that he hadn't the character and courage,—" I cut in on the trumpet, and said very clearly: "The matter is that so many of us think that character and courage,—"

"Well, but what do you think is the matter?" asked the M.P.

I repeated her question into the trumpet and said:

"And I have just said that I think what the matter is is the way the Labor M.P.'s think that it's MacDonald's character and courage that are the matter."

That caused consternation because, of course, they think that MacDonald and they themselves have the character and courage that Wilson lacked. And I so explained to Mrs. Wedgwood, who knows and understands my theory. We had been talking it at dinner, her husband being with us. But the increased crowd was demanding to know what I thought would balk and beat MacDonald, so I answered into the trumpet:

"The same Things that beat Wilson will beat MacDonald unless he and his crowd know what those Things are and beat them."

"Oh, you with your history and parallels!" said the M.P. that knew me and, laughing, she kicked off and took her crowd with her, while I laughingly explained the difference between their morality and scientific economics to Mrs. Wedgwood whose eyes sparkled with her understanding that I was really only talking at our friends' backs.

That's all, Allen. In that incident, I have told you all about the Labor Government, which already, under the guise of "caution," "political wisdom," "evolution," "safety" and "just compromise," are selling out, just as all governments,—ministries do. And they not in office yet. It's clear it's our culture that's wrong. Not nature and not human nature, but the good forces of life that we do not yet know how to use for instead of against us.

Love,

Len.

To Laura Suggett

London, January 28, 1924

Dear Laura:—

You don't talk enough. I've just been reading your "Equal Opportunity vs. Extension" and "The Sutro Library Association," and after puzzling over them, especially the first, I've come to the conclusion that there is one sentence missing. Just what it is, I don't know. If you talked more, you would learn under the pressure of conversation, to sum up a thought in one sentence. It was this that I taught Walter Lippmann and my other disciples. It used to anger them. When Lippman showed me a paragraph, I'd say: "Good, but just what did you want to say?" He said he meant to say what the paragraph said, but I'd shake my head and wonder, till in a rage he would plunk it all out in one good clean sentence. Then I'd say, let's put that sentence into the paragraph, and,—well, he learned to do it and it is a noted element of his style.

The new *Transatlantic Review,* No. 2, has my monologue on "NEP's." Haven't seen it myself yet.[1]

Love to Doctor et al.

Paris, Feb. 26, 1924

Dear Laura:

It seems long since I last wrote you, but I have had no letter from you meanwhile, so it can't be so very bad. And I have done some work. I expect to have the whole of Moses done within a month. Then I shall turn to something else, for I am in a working mood.

Personal things have interested me, too. Louise Bryant Bullitt has been having a baby. They were married a year ago, telling nobody but me and Clive Weed, a cartoonist who is over here trying to learn to paint. While I was in London Louise kept writing that I must come home; she couldn't have the baby without me, and Billy wanted me there too. And the baby was due. Well, I lingered and yet when I did come, the baby didn't, and it was only last Sunday night that it was born. And it is my baby theoretically. Billy wanted a boy, so did Louise; I preferred a girl. They said that if it was a boy, they would keep it, if it was a girl, I should have it. When the labor pains began, Billy phoned and I went up there. That was Sunday forenoon. I left at three in the afternoon, and it was not till the next morning that Billy reported that the baby was born fifteen minutes before midnight. And it was a girl. Billy told the hotel to tell me I had a daughter, and they did tell me in a most puzzled way. Billy said on the phone that it was not merely a girl; it was a terrible, dominant female. It came out kicking Louise, it made a mad, bawling face at Billy, grabbed the doctor's instrument and threw it on the floor.

"I shall have nothing to do with it," said Billy. "I am afraid of it. All I ask of you, as parent, is to keep it off the streets. But I doubt that you can do even that. It will do whatever it wants to do. I can't give it to you because it isn't mine. That baby belongs to itself. Even Louise feels that it is an utter stranger, self-reliant, aggressive, cold." I saw it next day, and it is a pretty child, a bit red yet, but handsomer than any new-born baby I have seen; and I have seen some in the last few years, since my friends have begun to pay dividends on their marriages.

Owen D. Young told me ten days ago that he thought he and

[1] "N. E. P.'s," *Transatlantic Review,* Feb., 1924.

Dawes had an acceptable settlement; that the Germans had agreed to it and that the French knew they had to. It is a sort of U. S. & Cuban arrangement: an International Bank of *Emission* is to absorb all the great German banks and all the sources of money and credit, and so guarantee France all that Germany can pay; and no more. Today the news is that both Germany and France are kicking. I told Young that my, the red theory, is that neither he nor any other capitalist can solve the problem; that our culture of good and evil does not contain a solution, cannot even visualize the problem; which is economic and not moral. I was sure this last effort to make peace would fail like all the others. He listened, and he said he would give me the plan before it was published, as soon as it was mapped out, and two nights ago he said he would be ready soon to talk. I shall see him tonight. I want to spend next week in the country on Moses. If I get the scheme, I may write it to Dr. But it is strange, isn't it, how, with my positive theory that they can't make peace, I keep thinking maybe they will; and I can listen to their hopes without impatience or cynicism. Maybe,—I am really a liberal, I guess; an optimist, a learner who can listen. . . .

Tell Dr. that it looks as if they would get Poincaré at the next general election in France. The surest sign is that so many people who don't vote are registering. Even some friends of mine who don't believe in voting have taken out the papers and declare they are going to vote. "For whom?" I ask, and they say, "For nobody, anybody,—against Poincaré."

Ospedaletti, Italy,
April 6, 1924

Dear Laura:

We were alone in your last letter. Dr. was gone to Kansas City, the maid was on vacation, so to speak, leaving us in an empty house. It was sad, but there was something nice about it too. Dr. is back now, and our regular routine is running us, which also is comfortable, pleasant. Life seems to be pretty near right, from our narrow family point of view.

This is my birthday, I recall. I celebrated it by finishing my article for Frank on the oil scandal.[1] That is to say, it is written through and

[1] An article, never published, on the Teapot Dome scandal in the Harding administration.

typed. I shall sleep on it and reread it in the morning. No doubt I shall edit it a great deal, enough to make it dirty "copy," and in anticipation of this effect I have written Frank an enclosing letter, asking him to have Miss Ford copy it,—if there is time. And there should be time. I had two weeks, according to his cable, and it is now ten days. The article is about three thousand words.

In my letter to him, I suggested that Frank get someone to answer my argument and so open the way to a thorough discussion of the subject. I tried but I could not think of the right writer. Nicholas Murray Butler with a sense of humour would be a good description of the man I would wish for. Bernard Shaw is another kind of man that would see the uses of such a debate and help it perplex the reader. My article really needs amplification and, hoping for a chance to explain further, I have left tempting holes for a controversialist to walk into. There are some assertions in it that some people will think impossible of justification. Dr. will see them and smile; you will hardly notice them at all, I think. Dr. could fill them, you will do it almost unconsciously. I hope Frank will see them enough to feel that they should be dealt with. . . .

Monday morning: I must close this. It is a lovely day, and I have reread the "Apology for Oil": it will do, but I must clear the typewriter and copy the last page, which I had to rewrite again once more. You, as an author now, know what that means.

Love to Dr., Dot, Jim and Older; he will like this article, since it is against the man-hunt.

Len.

Ospedaletti, April 16, 1924

Dear Laura:—

Please read this letter, first, to yourself alone. Afterwards you may let the Doctor see it or you may tell him what is in it; as you think best. He must know, of course, and soon, but I would like to feel that I am telling you first, and second, G. And I don't know when or how I can tell her.

It's a story that goes back four years to the time I was seeing a good deal of "that London girl," as you called her. I liked her then, more than you know. I liked her so much that G. felt it before she read, by chance, a letter that told it all, and said it would better be over. And I believed it was all over. I couldn't then turn from G.

She was in Paris; she was tired and ill, looking forward to a happy, restful summer with me. To get myself in hand, I went away north to Denmark and Germany and, when I returned to Paris, G. was gone to Monte Carlo. I was settled, sure in my mind, so I followed, and there on the Riviera we made it up and had a quiet, happy time. And it has been all well with us since, except that G. said she felt a change in me and often reproached me, asking what the matter was. I said there was nothing. Sometimes I said it impatiently. For I verily believed there was nothing wrong; that that other was over and she and I were as of old.

But last summer, when I observed myself a difference and sometimes half admitted it, I had no idea what it was. I thought it was merely the natural decline of love,—I really did. Only once in a while, when (at rare intervals) I heard from London, I had a pang which surprised me and set me wondering. I didn't go; I couldn't, you remember. I didn't get a visa till last fall and then I went not for any conscious personal purpose. I saw her, of course, and the old story revived and continued. She was working at Cambridge on a psychological experiment; I saw her there a lot. It went on. We had very many common interests and friends.

She finished her Cambridge *Arbeit* before I started back to Paris, and I asked her to come along. She did. She had excuses enough to go, to explain it to her family, to us. She lived at the Richepanse, met my friends. We lived together the same life in Paris and we came away down here together, she to finish the translation of a scientific book out of the German and to start a novel, I to work. And we have worked, steadily, fast, well. . . .

If it were not for G. I would be deep down glad; I feel I am anyhow. I have to write to G. I don't see how I can; nor what I can say. It's the second time I have done this to her! All I know is that I cannot tell her how I feel about it and about her. I can't tell her, but I can say to you that one of the deepest secret desires of my life is about to be fulfilled. If it were not for G., I'd be inexpressibly happy. As it is I am,—all mixed up. . . .

It is late at night. I am sitting up alone to write this, which I shall lay aside to send a few days later, as I said. And I don't want to wait, because I want to hear from you. How I would like to have a talk with you, Laura.

Ospedaletti, April 17, 1924

Dear Laura:—

Since the enclosed was written last night, a letter is come from you today: the one about your having learned to drive a car; Doctor's decision never to retire at all at all, but to hang on till he does more harm than good; *and* about coming to China and not to Italy. Oh, yes, and you thought maybe Filene (or somebody) might give $10,000 a year to your cause. I'll answer this last first.

Every rich man has a pet cause of his own. He won't give to others' causes, not even other rich men's causes. And Filene will not give unless there is some réclame, advertisement, even, to his own cause. No. That's a wrong tree to bark up. The only way for you to raise money for a cause like yours is to ask a lot of people to pay a little each, and $10,000 a year is impossible,—I think. And I'd rather put it into politics, if I had it, and go and "get" a governor,—before he is elected; before he is nominated, and then come in with him and yourself for what you want to have done.

I'd like to ride with you. I am a brave man, having no fear of death and it isn't *my* car. Doctor is nervous for that reason. He is not in the least afraid for his life. He simply hates to think of his precious R-R running up a tree and getting knocked. If you were a really loving wife, you'd buy you a Ford or something and learn on that. Poor Doctor. I said I'd like to ride with you in his car, and I would, but not with Doctor beside or behind or in front of me.

I wish you would come over here or wherever I am. I'm homesick for you two, and it isn't sure now that I'll go to China. I meant anyhow to go east from here, but I don't know what I'll do or where I'll go. I can't decide alone. I'd give a lot for a few quiet hours of consultation with you. And, to get the next best thing: a letter from you. I am tempted to send off tomorrow morning the one I wrote you last night. If I do, it must be thought a confidential communication till I write again. And of course there's a lot more to write.

Frank (of the *Century*) says he hasn't read the Moses yet; he's waiting to see it all! That's disappointing because I needed a word of encouragement from the editor to go on working. I'll write him again, and kick. But he is all for the oil (which he wrote himself about), though he hasn't my article yet or hadn't when he wrote.

I went down the shore an hour and a half today, to find a place to

upper: VILLA MONTAGU, ALASSIO. *lower left:* PETE, AGED
EIGHTEEN MONTHS, AND HIS PRAM. *lower right:* PETE AND HIS
"GRANDMA," MRS. A. WINTER.

live. This hotel closes about May 1. I found what I want and shall move me and my family in a few days. I shall not let it interrupt the writing except for the one day of moving. . . .

Ospedaletti, April 19, 1924

Dear Laura:

I sent off "the" letter to you today. I must hear from you, for better or worse. And I wrote just now to G., but not about that. I have written asking about her health, upon which everything hangs. If she is well, I shall tell her what I told you. But, if she is ill again, what can I do then? You understand, don't you, that our last summer closed badly. I was saying, and believing, it was nothing but a bit of weariness, but what happened in London showed that she was right and I wrong: there was a change. I can write if she is all right, but if she is ill, I'll have to go to New York and see and gradually, carefully, tell her everything.

I hope you don't think I am nervous or worried. I am humbled and sorry, but I am all there: thoughtful and thinking and ready. It's a relief to write to you, but I am not laying any burdens off upon you. I'm asking advice, but I'll make all the decisions and take all the responsibility.

. . . You should cultivate more people like Doctor Morrell, people of means and power, who can be influenced to do fine things. You and I can win some kinds of men and women, and we do not do it enough. We neglect our job, waste our power. I do, anyhow, and I suspect you.

But I have no heart to write of such things now. One thought, one problem, engrosses me, and I fear you also may not care to hear from me on anything else. Well, you'll hear about that: all that happens, all that is thought, unless your answer is a refusal to hear anything. If you judge, it will be, but I think you will not do that; not to me.

Easter Day at night [1924]

Dear Laura:—

We leave here Tuesday for Alassio, where I engaged rooms last week, so the physician is coming tomorrow morning to give his final diagnosis. . . .

You know a little about her: "that London girl." She wrote to you once. She's a clever, vital young woman, born in Australia, brought up in London, where she graduated with first-class honors at the London School of Economics. They kept her on there as lecturer and assistant professor for a year, but she wanted to do some more in psychology, so she undertook an experiment at Cambridge. Meanwhile she had organized the University Branch of the Labor Party, managed H. G. Wells' campaign for Parliament and translated from the German into English the story of Otto Braun, the young poetic and philosophic genius of Germany who was killed in the war; his letters and poems. Now she is translating another German book. A couple of German psychologists, caught on Teneriffe during the war, made an intensive, experimental study of chimpanzees, and made a report, a tome, called "Intelligence in Anthropoid Apes,"—a great book.[1] But her preoccupation is a novel, of which she has done three chapters, which I call good; very good, and quite new in form.

She has sense and poise. She is impulsive, but knows it and so has control. . . . We have been together about every minute for three months, and still don't like to part, not for an hour or two. Her father died last August. Her mother and a brother, a metallurgist, and a sister, both unmarried, live in London, well-to-do, but far from rich. She is prominent and popular and useful in the Labor Party, but now she cares nothing for all that; only for what is going on within herself: a curiously absorbing sort of vegetation, without qualms, almost without thought. . . .

To E. A. Filene

Alassio, April 30, 1924

My dear E. A.:

Your card is here, the small one with the many, searching questions, which I proceed herewith to answer:

(1) Yes, I still love you. I don't care at all about anyone else; it matters not at all even if no other person gives you his or her heart. Mine you have. But why did you ask?

(2) Yes, your persistence in well-doing does strike me as marvellous and, if not noble, it is at any rate obstinate. And I think it fine that you keep it up regardless of success and failure, heedless of whether

---

[1] By Wolfgang Köhler. Published as *The Mentality of Apes* (1924).

mankind wants to be helped or no. But why did you doubt my approval? And why did you ask for it?

(3) No. I did at first think I might compete for your European prize for a way to make peace, but I took my scientific ideas in hand and read in the light of them the list of judges. I decided then to stay out of the running with you yourself. Why did you wish me to enter the race? You don't really want to know how really to get peace, do you? You only want, as I do, to make men think; and I have thought too much for my day and age.

(4) I can't tell at this distance whether you are more comely than of yore, but why should you wish me to think you are? It doesn't matter what I call handsome, does it? Even if it is you; especially if it is you.

(5) My plans are, as you say, very vague. I am moving along through Italy, observing the good effects of the white terror and how the whites like it. I may return to France, though I don't like the exchange rates there. But then I have no doubt they will be better by the time I want to go back. By that time this last peace-making will prove to be no peace either; don't you think? As for work, I have been doing my *Moses*. I have no thought of returning home to work for Coolidge, none at all. But I might, if the Democrats should put up a man I would like to see get into the White House. I am sure I could help such a man by making a stump tour for the President, with the true reasons for reëlecting him.

And now, my dear E. A., let me pose for you the following questions, all but one of which my efficient secretary, with a sense of humor, could answer to my complete satisfaction, even if not to yours. And we should not expect, you and I, both to be pleased with the same answers to any question; should we?

I subscribe myself, with sincerity,

Yours affectionately,

Lincoln Steffens

?
?
?
?
?
?
?

To Laura Suggett

Alassio, May 23, '24

Dear Laura:—

Your letter of May 2, the answer to my "news," is here, and it is about what I looked for. I don't see how anybody that knows G., and G. and me, can feel otherwise. I myself am suffering on that side. I don't seem to care how miserable I am or may be; what hurts so is that I am hurting other people: you and G. and our friends, who never will understand. How can they, when I don't? And yet, maybe G. will. I got a letter from her this morning: a long, firm, kind and yet very proud letter. All she knew at the time she wrote it was that "something" had happened which cut us apart. She accepts without question, but she asks for time, one month together this summer, for a talk out of which she can adjust herself. I answered at once: that we would have that month. . . .

It is a long complicated story which only a wise novelist could write and only a wise reader would not judge. I can't write it. If she were there to illustrate, I might tell it; her youth and clean goodness, her vivid being and her quick interests might make convincing a tale that told how a man, loving one woman, could love also another. And I love them both; in different ways, but both truly, genuinely. . . . How can this be? I don't know. My meagre philosophy does not go that far, and my knowledge of myself seems nil. . . .

Sometimes I think that I am in a phase: a creative phase, out of which is coming work done and the child. I seem to be able to do anything. I sent you a post card two days ago, reporting another fable, and I said I'd now do a story. I didn't start the story. Looking through my papers, I found the sketched beginning of still another fable and I took it and yesterday and today I finished it before the mail arrived at 11 A.M. today. This will have been my most productive year, I verily believe, and I think that the good and the miserable of it are all out of one source. . . .

To Allen H. Suggett

Hotel Florence, Bellagio, Italy,
[July, 1924]

Dear Dr.:

If you will glance at a map, you will see that the auto trip we have just taken was a long one, a pretty good test of that kind of travel

in Europe. And it was all easy and pleasant. We drove out of Alassio
about nine-thirty one morning and ran into a typical rain, light and
short, hardly enough to lay the dust. Their summers are much like
ours in California. The road was good. We could have made time if
we had wished, but I had told the chauffeur Peter's condition and, a
careful driver anyhow, he went very slowly and picked his track well.
The road skirts the sea all the way, leaving the shore only to get
through towns and cities, and now and then to tunnel a promontory.
The towns are old, their great days having been in the Middle Ages
when they had to fend off the Moors, Saracens and other pirates.
Hence the walls and forts, with lookouts.

The ride to Genoa is a beautiful stretch of the Italian Riviera, which
extends from Ventimiglia to Pisa. We crept through Genoa, having
had lunch before it. I stopped only to get some money changed at a
good market rate. Then we drove along one of the most famous roads
in all Europe, the Napoleon Road to Rapallo. It threads a string of
old towns and cities for about thirty miles, with the intervals of
villa and farm lands widening between, until by and by it is all hills,
vines, olives. We didn't go on to Rapallo that afternoon as we intended. Turning off to a peak or *Kulm,* the view was so big, the air
so cool and the hotel there so kind, that we got out, washed, dined,
sat out in starlight and,—in short, spent the night. The next day
brought us to Rapallo and to Santa Margherita (where the Russians
stayed during the Genoa Peace Conference); we ran out to Portofino
and back, and then went on slowly to Genoa, through it and on the
other side struck the road inland to Milan.

We stopped at a small inn in a small place before Milano, saw and
heard and smelt the cattle market there, and the next morning drove
to Milano, where we revisited the *Dom* and the "Last Supper," did
an errand and had lunch, before we lit out on our last flight to Como,
the town.

Now the Lombardy Valley through which we had been travelling
from Genoa on is a flat, elevated plain between mountain tops. It is
very lovely, but very different from the seashore of the day before,—
two days before. It was a pleasant change, and it lasted till Como.
There we took the mountain road to Bellagio, and it was so different
again, so charming that even the chauffeur was struck into speech.
He has a girl to whom he is engaged, a maid at our hotel in Alassio.
She wants to come with us to San Remo as maid, and I think we will

take her. The question is whether she will be married to the chauffeur before or afterward. When we ran in among the trees and the half-hidden villas of the mountain road that skirts the Lake of Como, the chauffeur turned and said he thought that, when he did marry, he would bring his girl for that ride as a honeymoon. It took us an hour and a half to make the distance from Como to Bellagio,— twenty miles of narrow road among hamlets and woods, flowers and flashes of lake.

Some day you must tour some of this country, and this would be a varied and fascinating drive as you could choose. And the roads are good. The streets of all the cities and towns are awful, as with us, but you have to slow up anyhow, since they are as narrow as alleys and infested with business and kids. Outside of the towns, however, there was but one stretch of bad road, from Genoa up the grade to the Lombardy Valley. And, as everywhere in Europe, there are many and pleasant stopping places. Bellagio is a "sight" for tourists, and they are coming and going all the time. But we pay no attention to them. We go on with our work and when they talk about marvellous views from this peak or that in easy reach, we smile and,—go on with our work. We went swimming in the lake yesterday; not very good, after the sea at Alassio; about like Tahoe, but it was a cool pleasure for a hot day. We may make some trips from here, but not many and not for the views; only for a change and rest.

' . . . My address till September will remain Paris, care American Express. The Fascisti are getting up a public indignation on account of their crimes which may break them in two and throw them out of power. And the crimes have been by their more violent hangers-on, high up in the councils; the representatives of Business. I would not have believed this myself had I not been here to get it straight. Our business men have not got down to murder yet. But the Matteotti assassination was by the politicians for the oil men and bankers. He was about to expose some of their steals with evidence, which he had. I hear Sinclair's name mentioned, but I have seen no facts to connect him with it. I suppose it was his Italian partners who had it done and that he is guilty only as Mussolini is of bad associates. He would not have asked for a murder, and such a clumsy one, sure to cause a scandal. . . .

Affectionately,
Len.

Bellagio, July 13, 1924

Dear Doctor:—

. . . A few evenings ago, when we were sitting in the lake front garden restaurant, a face I knew greeted me and I sat down opposite it, beginning to frame it into a place. The man it belonged to had been travelling in Spain, in Italy and was bound via Switzerland, Paris, London, home. It took me half an hour to find out that home was S. F. and that the man was Robert Porter. He has travelled well. He was fine on Spain, which he liked; and good, but not so good on Italy, which he did not like. He described Spain; he judged Italy. He described Spain as a unit: city and country related; scenery, interest and people all one thing. No sense of the past in the life. In Italy the Italians, so to speak, are a people living on, not in, a country that *was:* Rome or the Middle Age republics. He is keen on the beautiful, rather than ideas, and he gave his mother the credit for that. He did this very beautifully, after telling me how beautifully she had died. His, the esthetic mind, is very unlike us, the intellectuals: sees differently different things. No wonder we can't communicate. He heard nothing that I said, so I gave up and listened. Which was worth while for me. He met my wife, but casually. The introduction made no news impression on him, so far as I could see, and yet he may speak of it to you or to others.

The Fascists are up against a growing opposition. The papers are angered by the strict censorship set up to meet the indignation at the Matteotti murder. But they are careful, these papers; they speak of it as a general movement: to get back to normalcy. And that's the drift still everywhere. Coolidge and Davis at home; both normal; and La Follette not actually running! It's just as well for me to be staying here, writing Satan; nothing doing elsewhere. . . .

This is Sunday. The place, Bellagio, is off the railroad on Lake Como and it is quiet six days of the week, when only tourists come and go in silent little steamboats. But Saturday night and Sunday, when the Italians are free to rest from labor, they come in autos, on motor-cycles, in busses and boats with bands, and the noise is like that of our 4th of July. It is fierce, and all the more racking because of the contrast with the week of silence and the serenity of the water and the mountains. I don't work Sundays. I write letters, row on the lake or walk in the woods, leaving Italy to the soul of the people which can be expressed only by noise. Hence this and several other uncalled-for letters,—letters I mean that are not answers to letters received.

Love to Laura.

Affectionately,
Len.

To E. A. Filene

Bellagio, July 21, 1924

Dear E. A.

. . . No. I don't want a thing; not even peace in Europe. I accept the world as it is and leave all vain attempts to change it to you practical business men. You lie so close to the cause that I am convinced you, and you alone, can correct things; and won't; and that God will have to do the job in his slow, sure method of killing off the old and saving as many of the youth as He can from the damnation of an education at the hands of the old men and women who mean so well.

I see you are following your own, old tracks: London, Paris, Berlin, Vienna, and that the only new stop for you is Italy: a big place for a small man. But Italy interests me, personally. It is not that I am there now, but that I am likely to be here in September; at San Remo. . . . This winter I intend to write my own Life. You business men might buy me off from this dire purpose; it would be worth a good deal to you to stop it, for I am going to convince you, finally, at last. I suggest that you take it up at the International Chamber of Commerce and, just between you and me, I will give you a small commission for any price you may get that is big enough to buy me off. If you don't, well,—a warning is enough, and you are a wise man; more lovable than wise, but yet,—wise, in a way.

Lincoln Steffens

To Laura Suggett

Bellagio, July 22, 1924

Dear Laura:

. . . I have had not a line for about two weeks. A hitch somewhere. This morning everything poured in together. You will be interested to hear that Frank writes, June 30, that "the fables are glorious,"— his word,—"as usual." Then he says: "I am sorry for the blundering way in which I have handled your oil article. I have scheduled it and pulled it out, again and again. I have been unable to get a permanently satisfactory feeling about it. I know from innumerable conversations with you the point which lies back of it, but I cannot feel that the article makes that point. I have read it to a dozen open-minded people who have not had my advantage of knowing what is in your mind and that point, the point on which the article depends, does not get over to them." He asks me to write an additional paragraph or two on the one point of the compulsion which is on business to control government. "We will then use it at a strategic point during the campaign," he says. I have written him that I will do that today and tomorrow: and I will.

He evidently had not received, when he wrote this, my letter asking him for a repetition of his offer to run in the magazine twelve chapters of the Life and then publish it in book form. I have told Frank about it, but I said I would not offer it to him, since he had enough of mine. I don't know where to place Satan. *Life* or *Judge* might take it, if they had enough humor, but the thing sounds serious and I might fool them. I may send you for safekeeping a copy of the three or four chapters I feel are done; I shall hold copies here for my use. But as you read these chapters written so far you may not yet realize that I am making a search for the root of all evil and that the whole will be an essay in my philosophy. The form is that of a detective story without adventurous adventures, with no melodrama, but a narrative interest. . . .

This leaves out what you especially asked for; what I am thinking about. But I am thinking mostly these days about my work. It is not necessary, I find, to go off and drink one's self to death when in trouble. One can drown it in work. But I am referring here to my conscience as to G. The other is well and more richly human than you have any idea of; much wiser and sweeter and more devoted. Like so much else in life, like the lessons of my life and philosophy, this cannot be cloven into clean-cut parts, the good and the evil. It is all mixed up, and the tragedy of it is that I, the only villain, I get the best of it: it is the innocent that suffer.

Love to Dr.

Affectionately,
Lin.

Paris, Aug. 4, '24

Dear Laura:—

. . . Peter, as I call "that other," is gone to Erlangen, Bavaria, to revise with the author her translation of the book on animal psychology. He was to be there five days, so she expected to be back here on the sixth day. It's a free interval in which to see G. without having her conscious that I was going from her to be with someone else. When she comes back, P. will have to work out the changes she has noted and she can stay here or, if G. is in Paris, go into the country.

. . . Jo Davidson is back. He has done his head of John D. Rockefeller and it is frightening: a terrible face. It is Jo's masterpiece in portraiture, I guess, and the Rockefellers liked it! ! ! When you see it, you will understand my amazement. It's an exposure, a caricature, a fearful insight into Man. It gives away more than Miss Tarbell did in her whole book. I'll be glad to hear from Doctor.

Love,
Len.

To Ella Winter

Paris, Aug. 4, '24

Dear Peter:

It's eight o'clock in the evening; the close of a hot, busy day and I'm a bit fagged, but I'm not hungry, not for food. And I am hungry for an hour with you. So I'll write. That brings you very close, sweetheart. . . .

The Masons [1] won't have me at their house till you come back. Bullitt has asked me to dine at his house tomorrow evening with the Masons and Streit, the correspondent from Constantinople, and his wife. Billy says we'll dine again when you come. They're all for you, Peter. I wonder why.

Harris [2] has interesting business in Italy. He's to finance a return to the German owners of a big group of factories in Italy. The Italians want to sell them back and, since the Germans can't pay cash, they want Harris to issue a loan.

Later: I found G. After I had written as above, I felt hungry and

[1] Frank and Ellen Mason. He was correspondent for International News Service.

[2] Hayden B. Harris of the Harris Trust Company, Chicago, was connected with the Treasury Department for a short time.

I went out to get something to eat. Then I walked down to the Regina on the chance that Jo was right, and in she came. We did not stay in the lobby. We walked in the gardens and we talked. She did, I mean, and she had it all pretty much as it is. Her accusations are true; I admitted them, and it really did her good. The truth is healing. Of course it was distressing; it is, but she was fine. I certainly do respect G.; her mind and her character. All I seemed to be acute in was to protect you. It would be some relief to clear me and put it all on you, but I couldn't stand that. And I was right. There was other relief and it lay in the facts as they are. I'll see her again tomorrow and she shall pour it all out, every bit.

But I must go to bed. I'm tired. I was done up this evening when I sat down with you; now I am utterly worn out. I wish you'd come home, and yet it is fortunate you are not here for a day or two. I'll spend hours with her tomorrow and maybe get her quiet and smoothed out. I am capable of friendship with a woman. I have a genuine affection for G., respect, fondness, a liking that is warm and frank, without love. I wish you could know her, and that you two could be friends. They say it isn't possible; I say it is. I'd like to keep G. as a dear friend always. But she'd have to take you in, too; you and little Pete.

Good night, Pete and Peter.

Petest.

To Laura Suggett

Paris, Aug. 5, '24

Dear Laura:—

I've found G. Last night I walked down to the Regina on the chance that she might be there. And in she came, looking very tidy and well. She'll tell you about it, and maybe she will tell you she was mad,—at herself. She smiled. I took her arm and we walked out of the hotel together as of old, went in the gardens across the street and sat on a bench. I was to tell her everything, but I didn't have to; she talked. She had to to keep back the tears, so she tore along zig-zag, and once when she nearly broke, I got her up and we walked on, arm in arm, I holding her hand as we used. She didn't notice it for a long while, then she withdrew her hand as if I were not to notice it. We sat or paced up and down in the gardens till midnight, and G. summed it up pretty well toward the end.

"My," she said. "I haven't done a thing as I had planned it. You took me by surprise. I had staged our meeting and decided just what to say and how, and it hasn't gone that way at all. I've said anything that came into my head. I've said first things I meant to keep till the last; I've said things I didn't mean to say; and I haven't said things I meant to say."

I suggested that she go home and tomorrow when I come back, she can have rearranged her speech and so deliver it as we speakers do, sometimes, as we outline it. She laughed. To her amazement and horror, she laughed several times, and she didn't cry once. What broke her up more was that I didn't defend myself. She had her indictments all drawn and she presented them one by one, out of order, but in some of the telling phrases she had polished in the watches of the night, and I didn't deny them. She denounced my character and I improved the terms thereof: and so she laughed.

But also she said things that showed me that she has been accusing herself. She didn't intend to reveal that secret, but it was good that she did. For I did defend her, and she was relieved. She said so several times, and I could see her face clear gradually and feel her nerves quiet down. . . .

Len.

To Ella Winter

Paris, Aug. 8, '24

Dear, dear Peter:

Outraged by the bad housekeeping I live under, and desperate, I went out and bought some letter paper and envelopes today, so I can answer you. And your mother; and Ogden,[1] for that matter. I read them first: there's a bit of easy psychology for you. With your letter in my hand, I stood up and read first Ogden, then Mrs. Winter, and then I brushed my teeth and undressed.—I did all my chores first, then (and not till then) I lay down on my bed and read your letter, —last. Can you explain that? I can. . . .

Your brief summary of Köhler's objectivity is dramatic,—metaphysically. I want you to mention Einstein to him; try, first, a mere naming of his name: Einstein. If that doesn't draw him, remark that Einstein is just taking us back to Kant, even Berkeley and the idealists. He is, you know. When the two parties of observers of the

---

[1] C. K. Ogden, editor of the series in which *The Mentality of Apes* appeared.

last eclipse reported, the one that Einstein was only a few thousandths too high, the other a few thousandths too low, he did not rejoice that his theory had been amazingly confirmed. He said: "So! Well, they have erred,—a few thousandths each." See? He is so sure that the mathematical laws of mind are right that he believes the observers erred in not confirming them to the dot. And he's the greatest mind that the public knows about. But here comes K., holding that the observer and the observation are all of it, the mind and the idea nothing. If he sees the metaphysical drama of two great, contemporary minds flying apart to the very poles of the philosophic world, he should scorn or denounce or get angry at the mere mention of Einstein's name. If he doesn't, he should have contempt for Einstein's conclusion: that, not the *Ding an sich,* but our *idea* of it, is all we know.

If you can get an expression of that or of any emotion about Einstein, we shall have a great story. Try it out. What you say about his rejection of all such words as "idea," "mind," "thought," etc., is thrilling to me. It shows that the new reaction to (philosophic) idealism is not to be complete. The scientists will differ, in a big way, AND, if they fight, they will succumb to Satan, my Satan, and miss the track again. For, believe me, they both are right or neither; I don't know which. And you must not. It is death to decide; it is life to,—wonder and watch and wait. Age must take a side. Youth alone can see both ways to the end. Hence, by the way: it is because I can see and say this that I know I am young. I'll bet K. has decided, Einstein has and, I suspect, Peter dear, that you are talking to the peer, the opposite, but the equal of Einstein, the general, the prophet of the reformed church, the protestant. Don't miss the fun of it. Draw K. out; draw him into metaphysics. Talk about the scientific method, mathematics *vs.* observation. You'll get your reward in this world, and the sign of success will be: some emotion, anger, contempt, impatience, perhaps eloquence. And don't forget that when he first read your translation, he thrashed the floor with his bedding [1] in the direction of Ogden and you, the enemy out of reach. He's only an evolved ape, too. . . .

If I had thought you could and would have gone to Russia with

[1] This gesture was an expression of anger with the apes.

me, I believe I would have taken Harris up. It's too late now. I told
H. off. But don't regret it, Peter. We'll have other like chances. . . .

Stef.

To Allen H. Suggett

Paris, August 12, '24

Dear Allen:—

I haven't written to either of you for the last four or five days. G.
and I have been together every day, usually all day, had both lunch
and dinner together and the evenings, all but one. She feels, I think
now, that her visit has been worth while. I'm sure it has done her
good. She got expressed most of the things she had on her mind to
say: all that she could think of, she said last night. And she has
"drawn out" of me, she declares now, all that she wanted to know.
She understands the story, me, the other girl,—all. She says so, and
I do think she has it clearer than I have. She's very intelligent, you
know. She is much less bitter; her face actually shines. But she wants
our meetings to stop now. Her reason seems to be that Peter gets back
this afternoon. That need make little difference, and I noticed when
I said at parting last night, that I would be getting my mail at the
American Express today at noon, she laughed and I know she will
be happening to be getting hers at about that same time. . . .

All I can't understand about the presidential situation is why La
Follette is so strong, why they treat him with such respect. He must
be a real menace and, if he is, then my estimate of American darkness
is too dark. Whence came the light?

That's all, I think. I'll write soon to Laura, who is getting to be a
sort of Supreme Court of Final Appeal for us all. Only, the funny
thing is that we all love her: G., I and even "that other," who says
she is the rightest Right she ever heard of.

To Ella Winter

Paris, Monday evening,
[Aug. 26, 1924]

No, the evenings are not the worst. They are the best. Now for
example. I have been out all day seeing people, all day alone with
people, and I come home early,—it's 9:30,—and here there is nobody
but Peter. . . .

You are not the little girl that ran away with me. You're a

woman, a person and, back of you, is a gang; and a good gang: Yvonne and Jo and Edouard, the Woodses and the Birds, the Hicków, the Bullitts, the maids and the men at Bellagio, Alassio, Italy and Paris. It's hard on a family to get that; it hurts. It should not hurt, but it does and *their* love is checked, not raised by respect. We must learn the lesson early. I'm sure I shall. I respect little Pete, now, as I respect you. And that's what you love about my love; as our baby will love and,—dear,—respect it. He shall be our little chum and we'll be three,—three individuals, a small gang with a big gang back of us. You'll see. . . .

One's youthful friends are accidents. Your new friends are your own choice. I wish you could have heard Sally tell Billy and me today about you. . . . Sally likes and she respects you, and so does Billy. You are taking exactly the position I wanted you to,—exactly. And it's your own. My only part in it is to set the pace. I speak of you in a certain way and they all catch the tone. I never call you my wife and I never say "the baby." It's Peter or Ella Winter and Little Pete. And the one who is onto me and approves is Yvonne. The rest only feel it. . . . But, Peter, that's partly Paris. London would never get it, and back of that is the reason I don't like to go to London and do like to work on my *Satan*.

This brings me to the last, bad word in your Sunday letter: "Friday." But it's all right, Peter. Stay if you must, only, if you do, stay cheerfully. I want you to be happy all the time and I want our dear little girl to be born,—happy.

I haven't said anything about my day, but it doesn't matter. . . . A weary day of wanting, Peter, wanting. What is wanting? It's an ache. For you are lacking, you world. Yes, you are my world.

To Marie Howe

> Villetta Margherita,
> Strada Privata Hope,
> San Remo, Italy
> September 17, 1924

Dear Marie:

It's too late, and it's too bad. I would have liked to see you, but when I wrote Fred, asking you-all to come way from Genoa, he answered that he couldn't; that you and he could not agree on routes, and I inferred that you did not want to see me. I'm sorry. I wanted to seek you out in Paris when I was there in August, but didn't: thinking you preferred not. And now,—on Sept. 8, we,—there's three of us or two and a half,—came down here, where I had rented this lovely little villetta. I can't go back to Paris. But if you come down to the Riviera, you can come here and see me. I'll introduce to you my wife, whom you will like; Ella Winter, and, if it's after Dec. 1 (about) I'm pretty sure I can introduce you to a baby. I wish you would come, Marie. Ella Winter is a young thing and babies are usually young, but I'm an old thing myself and I like the old things you mention, all of them; especially old friends. . . .

Yours affectionately,
Steffens

To Jo Davidson

San Remo, Thursday, Sept. 18, 1924

Dear Jo:

It's a hard life and I can understand why it has to be lived down. We got here tired out, weary of the blue sea, the sunshine, the travel. The agent of the real estate man met us at the station, ordered our baggage to be sent to us unexamined and himself drove us home to this villa on the hill back of the town. There were the usual troubles. The regular cook was at the door to receive us, but she had a bad arm, could not work and so had to present to us a substitute. The substitute took our orders, rushed to town and got us food, which she soon had cooked,—well,—for a substitute. We had to unpack; you know what that is, and Peter in her enthusiasm worked late. Yes, and the next day she worked overtime, happy, but silly, one eye on the garden, one at sea, and both on the house, which, she complained, was so clean that she did not feel like a housewife.

But there was no maid when we arrived the first night. We asked the cook if she knew of one. She did, and when we were at breakfast in the garden under the trees the next morning, she came up with a pretty girl who was sure she could please us. The nerve. She was in her work clothes, sure and ready, and poor Peter had no chance to deal with the servant problem at all. That maid just stayed; she picked up the dishes, cleared the table and she went upstairs and cleaned up everything in a jiffy. We were going like an old institution by noon. No experience at all at all. As Peter said, bitterly, What is it that women talk so much about, the problem of servants and the troubles of housekeeping? We are missing something.

In two days,—lovely, warm, sunny days of deep contentment and fun,—we were settled into a routine; breakfast under the trees at eight, both at work there by nine,—lunch there at one, a nap upstairs and an afternoon of shopping; dinner at seven-thirty; reading all evening till ten, then slowly to bed, tired out. Peter is working a lot in the garden with the gardener for exercise and doing her article on the apes. I am swinging along with *Satan,*—fast and good. We are arranging for the birth, which is going to be easy, clean and right. We have now and apparently we are to have for nine months nothing but this same hard life. Come down and see and share it, Jo. Really. You have work to do for the moment. Do it, get fed up and, when you are willing to loaf and talk and walk a bit, come down here and make us happier still. It's a little paradise. Peter wants to get it going still better before others come, but she doesn't mind you. She says, "Jo can come any time." . . .

Stef.

To Laura Suggett

San Remo, October 2, 1924

Dear Laura:

. . . I've read Wells' *History of the World,* and been helped to a comprehensive grip on the story of man. I wish all great writers and thinkers, as well as all historians, would write that story, over and over, as the Middle Age painters used to paint the Madonna over and over.

Also I have read,—finished it last night,—Shaw's *Back to Methuselah.* That's Shaw's philosophy and his religion. A big thing. But it's his limit too. It shows his boundaries, beyond which he cannot see. He scorns all that he doesn't believe in. He throws out cause and effect to lift up Will. Why can't one see both? They are both elements in the problems, both powers we can use. I am afraid that critics will see in my *Moses* and the *Satan* imitations of Shaw, but I can't help it and I don't care much. I would be willing to imitate; I didn't, so I wouldn't like to have it said that I did. I wonder why. . . .

Affectionately,
Len.

To E. A. Filene

San Remo, Sept. 21, 1924

Dear E. A.

I received this Sunday morning your question marks from Paris. Why? I wrote you some two weeks ago at Morgan, Harjes, Place Vendôme, explaining all your questions and telling you my recent transactions with life and my plans for the near future. You must have turned upon me before you fetched your mail. However, I will repeat a little.

I have come down here to take for nine months this lovely villetta for the purpose of having a baby. The mother thereof is Ella Winter, whom I married in Paris last February. You know her; she was in Vienna once when you and I were there and I nominated her to you for a secretary. Fortunately you preferred someone else, so I had a chance to get her and I did. We were rather too happy in Paris for the comfort of our friends, so we left there and sneaked off here to hide our bliss and spare the green streaks in human nature, as we know it. We wouldn't mind having you with us; nobody minds how an old settled bachelor suffers, and the baby isn't big enough to be spoiled yet; it is only some seven months old and its first birthday is estimated to be about November 28. Its sex is decided, but not yet known; all we know is that it is to be the greatest baby on earth and is to be brought up dead onto business and statesmen, or both in one. Not much chance for you, E. A. And it is not to be a muckraker either.

But this will only bore you. If it doesn't and you want to know more, ask Dolléans about us, or Jo Davidson (whose bust of Rockefeller you *must* see) or Yvonne. And, seriously, E. A., when you return to the peace of Europe, do come along this way and see how simple and lovely life can be,—if the livers are wise.

When you go home this week, as you predict, back La Follette. That will make the winners of the election respect you. They know, the worst of them. And, if you cannot afford to risk the peace of Europe to save your own country just now, wait till Bob is defeated and then help him pay the debts of his courageous, hopeless attempt to do what has some day to be done. Nobody likes to pay for dead dogs, but that is the noblest sort of campaign contribution I know of. And it is the most appreciated. You won't? All right with me. You are far beyond good and evil with me. I love you no matter how wrong you are.

Affiectionately,
Lincoln Steffens

To Laura Suggett

San Remo, October 12, 1924

Laura Dear:

. . . I find that my mind of itself is brooding over the *Life* and already it wants to know some things I do not remember. When did we move from San Francisco to Sacramento, from Second Street to between Sixth and Seventh, from there to K at Sixteenth? When did I get my pony, when the colt from Col. Carter, when did I go to St. Matthew's School? Can you answer these few starting questions? They are not essential. I want only to know about how old I was when these things happened. I am not going to make much play of dates, but there are a few that would help me, and there will surely be other points I would have to get from you. Dr. foresaw this. He asked if I had all the data I would require. It will be some job, and not for me alone. My sister will have to work too. . . .

. . . This is a bully place to do work in; . . . it is quiet; the neighborhood is "good,"—our two neighbors are titled widows; there is no traffic near us, except the deliveries which are always by boys or girls on foot. A wheel on the road is an event; it has happened but twice in the six weeks we have been here. . . .

I suppose I shall do what I have always planned: go from here to China and live there a while, for my last active chapter, finishing off my education with a glimpse into Chinese culture.

Affectionately,
Len.

To Fremont Older

San Remo, Oct. 15, 1924

Dear Fremont:

It was worth getting married to draw a letter from you, and such a warm one. You always do write love letters. You are reaching the point of development where love is about the only motive you can act upon. Even your *Call* is a love newspaper, you know. You print things you WANT people to read and "get." Darrow's speech is but one example. You love Darrow, you love his speech and you love to have all your readers feel it so. So the letter to me is but an item in the Older "policy," if one can give a conscious name to an unconscious procedure. Well, anyhow, I "got" the love in the letter and in the *Call*. And I return it, Fremont; not herewith, but I do give it back.

And Darrow's letter, enclosed in yours. Funny you both should have gone on to the same theme: "Grow old along with me." I will, I am aging, but I offer you both the next line: "The best is yet to be." No, this is not a matter of my recent marriage. I have always been so. Perhaps it is a gland I have over you or the lack of a gland, or something. But I do enjoy life, more and more; it grows richer and more significant. I see, for instance, that Darrow applied to this terrible murder case [1] the philosophy of modern science, and put it over upon the law. That is a step ahead. And you printed it, later; not as news; and it lifted your sales for that day. The public took it. That is a step.

Of course, as I get older, I look more sharply for the signs of the future, but I do not fool myself, do I? I can see it is not going my way. I have been wrong, but that helps, it does not hinder me from seeing aright. It has taught me not to expect the right, nor to care if I am wrong, so long as I can learn to see straight. And I saw Russia, when many a radical missed it. So I think I can see now that Business is to be more powerful, more concentrated, more trustified over here than ever. It is business men that are making the peace; not politicians. They are crossing the national boundaries to settle their common troubles and to own. International business trust. That makes some old radicals want to die. But look, now, at Russia: the Reds there are not practising the spirit of Christianity or even that of socialism. They are doing business. They have had to do business, and the whole of their effort is to keep the one business monopoly they had to create and see to it that it is not broken to pieces again.

What does that mean? I think their compulsion and their purpose is the same as Stinnes'. It is to shut out the petty competition of little business, hold the monopoly of all business till men have learned to work under a new system, noncompetitive and for service. The Bolsheviki want the State to take, hold and own business; Stinnes, who despised government, willed that the business monopoly should take, hold and include the State. What is the difference? In both cases, as

[1] The Loeb-Leopold case.

you can see in Russia and will soon see in Germany, the State goes under and the economic machine becomes all there is of government. I can go home either westward via New York or eastward via Pekin. I always have taken the westward route, but I am inclined in my growing age to take the Dollar Line east next time. I shall get there just the same; only I may see new peoples and new ways of living wisely or foolishly. But I don't think it matters how my friends go. I am for Russia. Also I am for the Stinnes Line in Central Europe. I can see around the world either way.

And, by the way, Weismann did get some facts. He increased our positive knowledge of biology. But he did not deny and he did not explain the changes that occur with the growth all about us. He taught the biologists caution; he blocked one road, but he opened others, and you and Darrow would do well for your peace of mind to have a talk with some thinking biologists about the problems they are working on now; and their significance, however solved. The growth and the power ahead will make us look like monkeys, and our pessimism sound like superstition. In this book my wife has been translating, the cold German experimenter learned that the apes could not learn by imitation or by the force of punishment; they made no progress by "trial and error." They had insight, and they learned to solve their problems by understanding and by their own will. And they did learn in the course of his years with them; they increased their intelligence. . . .

Maslin would "get" the monkey book. It is hard reading, with its inhibition of interpretation, but with the article and, possibly, a few tips from one of us here, he will see that the experimenter was proving something all the time, and what. The cave man is perfectly accounted for, the honest one, I mean; and the lyncher; and the party man.

Glad to hear what George West is doing. I think the best department of a newspaper for propaganda, of the right sort, is the sporting column, but the dramatic criticism is almost as good. The trouble is that the young fellows don't see what they can do except in departments where they have seen it already done. Sport is so wide open with chances because it is sport, fun, games, play,—the loveliest thing in life; and the ethics of it are theoretically our very best morality. But art is the noblest pursuit, and dramatic art is art, even when it is bad. Nay, when it is bad, as in the movies, for example, a slow process of cultural criticism, aimed, not at the producer, but at the public (sympathetically) would gradually raise the stage and with it, the public, not only in the drama, but in life.

Do write me when you feel depressed, Older. I am so happily situated down here on the side of a hill of olives and roses with an eye of the sea always upon me, winking, smiling, joshing, that it is a pleasure to hear how blessed I am among my friends; how I have escaped justice and beaten hell by anticipating,—the other place. I wish Darrow would come over here and cheer me up,—in that way. You won't, I know. If you would, I'd show you my child, due about Dec. 1st.

Greet Barry [1] for me, too, and, if you see them, the good fellows at San Quentin. I think the constancy of Barry, in temper, in faith, yes, and in practice, is marvellous. He represents the love policy most serenely, most literally and naturally. What you all must have done to San Francisco is not measurable, but I'll bet that you have raised that old city, say, at least a tenth of an inch. And yet they say we cannot, by taking thought, raise our stature.

To Marie Howe

San Remo, October 18, 1924

Dear Marie:

. . . I started this letter yesterday, meaning to answer your question about what I am living into. It occurred to me that, if I tried to tell you, I might find out for myself. I was interrupted. We had to go up the road to call at the nurses' home and arrange for a nurse. I am off that now and besides it will be more fun to talk than to write about that. Writing is a definite art. And you will be coming down here, sooner than you think, I think. Paris is the best of cities, but one does get tired of it and its shadows. Remember that here there is always sunshine, sea, country and some people.

We have been trying out our near neighbors and they are "not so bad," as the Italians say; they are not young, they are mostly titled folk, but there are personalities among them. I am surprised at some of these people, our next door neighbor, for example. She stood out on the road, listening to us talking one day, then came up in her old straw hat and garden gown, all dirt. "I'm your neighbor. Maybe you

[1] John D. Barry, one of "Older's men," and a well-known West Coast newspaperman.

don't care or don't want to be spoken to. If so, say so. I would. I listened to hear what language you spoke. It was English. If it was anything else, I wouldn't have said a word. I like to stick my nose into other people's affairs, but only if they are not too foreign." So began the Contessa Maggiolini, and yesterday, speaking of babies, she observed: "It is funny, but I notice that babies nowadays are born about three to five months older than they used to be. My children's heads drooped when they came out. THEIR children come out head up and sassy. We used to have to feed our weaklings every two hours; now they go three and four." She went on to give other differences, and I was interested because I have never read or heard of this before; it is in line with the recent observations of biology that evolution shows thus in birth: maturity is developed in the women. And she said it was generally true of all the children she knew, English and Italian, but she knew a lot of these two races. She is a Scotch or English widow of an Italian nobleman. A character.

Anyhow there are some people hereabouts, outside of us, as well as climate and loveliness, and you will remember that. And you will come. Meanwhile, write again. No, no clippings, unless they are gossip. News is awful. It isn't news any more to me. The papers don't tell me what I want to know. But anything that interests you would interest me, if I remember right.

Yours affectionately,
Lincoln Steffens

To Laura Suggett

San Remo, October 18, 1924

Dear Laura:

. . . E. W. is not what you picture her. She is not the "intellectual type" and she is not the "radical youth" either. She is not radical enough for me in her economics, but I don't care. That has nothing to do with personal relationship. I never cared that G. shared few of my opinions. G. complained in Paris last summer that I didn't mind enough. Her theory was that I liked the radicalism of E. W. and that, if I had devoted more attention to her, G.'s, education in such things she would not have been at a disadvantage. I told her and I repeat, perhaps in vain, that that has nothing to do with it. I don't love opinions, not even my own; they change too readily and too often.

Personality is the thing in personal relations. I love G. I love E. W.

I love Dr. I love you. I love Older. I love Yvonne Davidson, and Jo. I love lots of people and I mean *love*. There are differences, of course, but the biggest is not sex; not with me; and this is no sex adventure, this with E. W. She is a charming, sensitive, understanding person. Everybody that meets her feels right away an affection for her. You will get that from Wood and Sara. Indeed, I tremble when I think of them talking to you about E. W. lest you think, from their enthusiasm, that they are propaganding. They will not be. They don't know enough of the situation to propagand, and that means that they don't know enough to avoid the appearance of it. They saw a great deal of E. W. in Florence where she was happy among the pictures and the scenes of the Middle Ages, happy over the baby that was coming and with me, and she is always joyous. She likes things, she is always full of vigor and life and she gives herself freely.

She is not calculating. One of her faults is thoughtlessness. She was writing a novel, so to speak (a simple narrative of her own childhood in Australia), when the baby gave signs. The novel disappeared, she took up the making of baby things, and ever since then she has been a narrow specialist; a mother. It is lovely to see. Certainly it is nothing to hurt her and turn upon. She will get back upon her job some day. Thinking it good for the child to have its mother work some, I tempted her to go on with the translation and, that done, to write an article to clear her own mind on the theory of that book. She did it. She has will power, and she went off to Germany, saw the author, finished the translation and now she has written and rewritten her article: it has gone to the editor who asked for it. But in the meanwhile her mind and her hand kept going all her work for the present passion, the coming child. And I can tell you it is a beautiful thing to be living with and taking care of the woman who is thus occupied. It is as beautiful as my Chinaman; [1] it helped my Chinaman be wise and kind, even though he was seeing and pointing our folly. . . .

You say she is "young," meaning callow. She is not. She went through that at college. Her experiences at the Peace Conference cured her of it. She "got" the import of that tragic failure, so that now one feels in her a woman, child-like in her wonder at things, unsure of her opinions but eager to learn more and more. She is brilliant, but she doesn't know it. It doesn't occur to her. She is too heedless, too thought-

[1] In "The Pallor of the Yellow Peril," *Century,* Oct., 1924.

less for that, and too worried about what she does not yet know even of what is known. And she has had clear glimpses of what the biologists and psychologists and the rest are trying to find out; that keeps her intellectual attention upon the unknown.

She and G. are both beautiful women. You should not only admit that into your thinking, you should really "get" it. It might not affect your judgment of me to know that E. W. also is a gracious, generous, sensitive creature, but it would alter a bit your grasp of the situation.

However this turns out, E. W. is in my life and yours and G.'s. She is not to be hated, not pitied, nor misjudged. She is not even to be judged. She also is to be understood, she and her point of view and her relationship with me. And I would like to add that the unborn baby is not to be rejected either, not pitied, nor judged. Welcome to me, I am not concerned that she (or he) shall be great, but I do mean to teach or let her love and be loved. I think I want most that it shall be a laughing baby, laughing with and finally at me, as I still can myself. And as friends and equals, there are lots of babies coming along now among my friends who will always be about the same age as mine. And even if she does not see her Aunt Laura I am going to tell her about you; and Dr. will have to straighten her teeth.

Lin.

To Marie Howe
San Remo, November 15, 1924

Dear Marie:

. . . It still is lovely here, like California. We are having what they call bad weather, a cold snap, and sometimes the sun is clouded over for several hours at a stretch. But the flowers don't take any stock in the depression; out in hundreds, they keep a-coming, and there are bees at work every day. I love it, but the old residents, humans, say this is nothing. "Wait," they tell us. The flowers come later! . . .

I am interested in politics; I have had a personal feeling about La Follette's campaign, and know how the results must hurt. But also I know how the swath he cut in the anxieties of Wall Street and the old gangs will encourage La Follette to hold to his religion. And I think his religion has been blown up. It was mine too. And there is something humanly fine in the way La Follette fights on for the good old church. It is like the way the noblest and best of the Southerners stood fast for their cause after the North had licked them and wiped out slavery and state rights and all that. I still can respect character and love a friend. But there has been a war, a revolution, many peace-makings and they were sad and costly failures. They knocked out a part of the race and most of our lives and convictions. I don't see how any mind could have sat by and seen all these things happen and not learned,—enough to change our conception of political conduct. And they were La Follette's methods and creed that were blown up, not only Lloyd George's. The statesmen and the reformers have gone right on along their old courses since the débâcle, though you and I can see that their (our) errors made the war, prevented the peace and went to the bat and defeat in Russia. The only modern statesman that has taken to himself any of the lessons thereof is Mussolini. And so far as I can make out, the only reformer to have been really reformed by our current schooling in blood and tears is myself. Democracy cannot be achieved by democratic methods.

It is a long talk we need, Marie; or a book, not a letter. But for the present I will answer your question: whether I am not interested in the election and Bob's gallant fight, by saying that I am, but in much the same way that I am interested in the ants, bees and spiders in our garden. I make experiments upon them: wipe out a procession of hundreds of ants, for example; thinking of man and his war, and I observe that those that were not killed follow on along the same trail to the same end. Then, I read the books and I learn of ants also that the only way to change their fixed ideas is to proceed as a dictator, get back to their queens, get onto the laws of their beings and alter the circumstances so that they have to modify their conduct; and then, as you know of the bees, they evolve, change, rise to the new conditions.

It seems to me that there are enough facts lying scattered around us to indicate a new and perhaps a better way to proceed to do what La Follette so loyally and so hopelessly is trying to do. He and I talked this all out on our trip to Russia; we had Germany and Poland between us; Russia before us; and, behind us, the U. S. A. and the rest. For a modern illustration, there was Italy. What we need is someone to collect and sort our scattered information, and present it in good order for the scattered brains of man. I can't do it. I have no organizing power, no sense of literary order. I know because I have attempted to lay it all out before Bob and others; all in vain. All I have written about it is a book on the life of Moses, showing from that (and from the war, peace and the revolution) how God showed Moses that the slaves of Egypt could not learn His new ideas of law and conduct, nor take and hold and create the Land of Promise. God told Moses to lead the People of Israel around in the wilderness until all the adults had died, and only the children that had not learned the ethics of slavery but the fresh morals of the desert, could go over into the Land of Promise. And I pointed out that God included among the uselessly conservative all the liberals and radicals, all but three of all the leaders. He put Moses to death on the last hill before the crossing of the Jordan.

And I mean that he would have in our day to put La Follette and,— me out of the way to save mankind, because we also were reared,—in opposition, but none the less,—in Egypt.

Yes, and I see that you would have to be removed, like Miriam, "the sister of Aaron," who thought that she also could prophesy. You say, "All the things he (Bob) stood for were so reasonable." The women of England and the U. S. got nothing by being reasonable, nor did the Labor Party of England, nor will Herriot in France. You women and the Russians got something by,—taking it. Biology says that all you get by evolution is the development of the species; variations come by force, out of explosions. And variations are what we want: revolution.

I am trying to set forth this lesson in my Satan, who stands for morality, reason, the maintenance of the species; and resists, as evil, all progress, change, variation from the species. Of course, then, his followers and worshippers and tools are the Good, not the Bad folk. And that explains why so many of us found that we could be comfortable with the bosses and other honest crooks and loathed the righteous. Don't laugh and call me conceited, but believe me: you need a talk with me. You are sound, Marie, but you must learn, not only to admire and be sorry for, but to *enjoy* La Follette; even his defeats, and so also the spectacle of Europe, which is an immense, mysterious complicated ant heap, but understandable and corrigible; but not by the insects themselves. We used to think wrong in Tom's day. I often imagine him looking on here and "getting it." I really believe he would have seen it clearly and himself too.

I am delighted with the way you are taking to Peter. So is she to you, for she feels you, and her heart has gone out to meet you. Don't get her wrong. She may have been well-dressed, but Yvonne and I did that; and she always looks fresh and alight, which is a kind of beauty, but her mind is not at all on being a beautiful, well-dressed woman. That is all with her left hand. Her charm is her abundant life and her wonder and working interest in life. She is at an age where she is a little girl just turning into a woman, an intellectual college graduate putting her good, young mind on to her job, or jobs, for they change. Just now she is having a baby, and it is a delight to watch her do it with all her intelligence as well as all her heart, and yet laughingly knowing how important and how unimportant it all is. A wise, kind adult playing with a child's doll, with respect and yet also for fun: that is what she is. I say this because I lay store by your liking her and I don't want you to be disappointed; I don't want you to be even surprised. You may find her a child laboring earnestly, with deep concentration and joy, with a real doll that opens and shuts its eyes, and not only wears clothes but pulls on them. And, by the way, don't give the baby clothes. Peter and her mother, her sister and,—everybody have built up a room full of things for it to wear. Why not help her to be born with a silver spoon in her mouth, something she can keep forever? A cup is guaranteed, but a spoon will be needed, and I would like to have her have that from you. It is to be a girl, you know; if our prayers are answered, a girl that is to have every chance that boys get now; and then some.

Affectionately,
Lincoln Steffens

IX

A BABY AND A BOOK
(1924-1927)

PETE STANLEY STEFFENS was born November 21, 1924, and at once his father began writing letters about him. He studied Pete with the eagerness with which he had studied the social systems of the world, and he wrote about him not only with joy and affection but also with precision, humor, and a kind of humility. Though he was concerned with Pete in all his letters, he found Ella Winter's mother the best audience for his account of the day-to-day progress of the baby, and the supposed correspondence of Pete to his Grandma became voluminous.

Pete's first winter was spent in San Remo and his first summer in St. Cergue-sur-Nyon in Switzerland. His first birthday found him, after a trip to Paris and London, in Alassio. The next summer he again went to London with his mother, and then joined his father in Carlsbad, whence they all proceeded to Salzburg. The winter he was two he lived in Jo Davidson's old manor-house, Bêcheron, in Touraine.

Wherever he was, Pete grew, and his growth continued to fascinate Lincoln Steffens. But Pete shared his father's interest with the *Autobiography*. The two preoccupations seemed often to merge into one. As Steffens watched his son's progress, his thoughts went vividly back to his own childhood, and the first chapters of the *Life* readily took shape.

But there was another reason why work on the *Autobiography* fitted into the mood of those years. As he so often said, the Russian Revolution had changed the whole course of his thinking. "When you see the Russian Revolution," he wrote Gilbert Roe, "you observe that it goes against your theories and mine, wherefore you give it up. . . . I, having seen two revolutions, the Mexican and the Russian, got from their perverse course the notion that, not the revolutions, but my theories were somehow wrong. . . . I cast out, not the revolution, but my old manner of thinking, ceased to be a liberal and have since been watching events as if they were divine (or natural) revelations."

He was content now to watch from a distance. ("I don't miss reporting any more. I find that I do not have to go, for example, to the British General Strike; I can 'get' it out of the papers with what I know from other experiences of the sort.") But he was watching closely. And he was not going to commit himself prematurely. Perhaps, he thought, big business men like Stinnes would be the instruments of change. Perhaps fascism was one more "event" that, even though it failed to fit his theories, served nature's purposes. Liberalism was bankrupt; that he knew; but he would not attempt to prescribe for the new era. He would wait and watch, and in the meantime he would review his own life.

As the *Autobiography* grew, he sent chapters to his friends, and was delighted with their praise. Marie Howe, for example, was one of those whose advice he asked, and, as she read and criticized the *Autobiography,* he read and criticized her *George Sand.* Soon publishers, many of them, were asking to see *The Life of Unlearning,* and inquiring about other books. "It looks," he wrote Laura, "as if the *Life* may get publishers for the fables, for the Boss stories and—for all my 'works.' "

Pete and the *Autobiography,* the baby and the book, the book and the baby, these are the themes, not only of most of the letters in this chapter but also of many other letters and parts of letters that have been omitted. And finally the book and the baby pointed to another topic,—America. For a long time Steffens had lived abroad, partly for financial reasons, partly because he wanted to watch Europe. Now he began to be homesick. His friend, E. A. Filene, was talking about muckraking articles, and the idea of muckraking from his new point of view piqued Steffens. Clarence Darrow wanted him to try again to secure pardons for J. B. McNamara and Matt Schmidt, and for that cause he would readily have traveled twice the distance. But most of all he was thinking of rounding out his life, of renewing his contact with his own country for the sake of the *Autobiography,* and of giving his son American roots. Lincoln Steffens, with Peter and Pete, sailed for New York March 17, 1927.

To Allen H. Suggett

San Remo, November 21, 1924

Dear Allen:—

The baby was born this morning, a boy, small: six ½ pounds. He came very easily, after only 3¾ hours of labor, with hardly any pain and no evil effects. Of course, one cannot see or say anything much of such a young baby. Eyes, hair and shape of head all change. But there is lots of space between the eyes; that is permanent, they say; and he has not a long upper lip. He will not be righteous, therefore. As to the rest, he is active, strong, and has a powerful voice with (I judge) no ear for music. . . .

Len.

To Frederic C. Howe

San Remo, November 24, 1924

Dear Freddie:

I begin to understand you. There is a letter from you this morning, a bully one; and my Peter has one from Marie which I have not read yet. (Peter always insists on seeing her own letters first, especially when they are from Marie.) But your letter clinched an idea I have felt growing up in my head about you for some time past. I see now what you are up to, over here also, and you must not do it. Not yet. I want to have a voice in this scheme.

You are a founder, Freddie. I think you don't care much what you found; a home or a farm, a colony or an Athenian summer school; and, if I am right, you are perfectly unscrupulous where you found your foundations. 'Sconset or Sicily are all the same to you, since it is an instinct, not a conscious, intelligent matter with you. So as to Europe, you speak of a seashore, but the truth is that you want to found something in Europe only because you happen to be in Europe, and wherever you accidentally stay a while, you will begin to found. Which is all very well. I don't want to interfere with your submarine nature. I would not want to try to stop a fish from spawning or a spider from swallowing her lover and pouring out baby spiders.

I even let Peter have a baby, though I had no use for one myself. My attitude toward this child of mine is refreshingly sane and sensible. Most fathers make themselves ridiculous by thinking out loud that their baby is the greatest baby on earth. I have no patience with any such bunk. I don't think that; I know it. That is why the other fathers have been so silly while I am so calm and rational. So, you see I would not butt in and spoil your funny impulses to do idiotic things. On the contrary, if you are going to set up or lay down a colony over here, I will help you with the same philosophic sobriety that I help my girl have a baby and bring it up the way it wants to go. As you say, I have become a very different person from the one you used to know.

I will help you make a place for all of us to live and not work, to think and not act, but, though it shall be exactly as you wish, I insist that it be on the seashore, that we introduce there the California bungalow, which is peculiarly suited to the only kind of climate you should choose: a warm, sunny, indolent climate, and that, therefore, you should resist your instinct to found wherever you are found yourself, and that you hear me out on the progress I have made in my lifelong search for the most perfect place in the world. I have seen some strong candidates along this shore, spots overlooked; I know some farther south on this sea, and I am on the trail of some on the Adriatic, both sides, which we must inspect before you settle and begin to function. See? I am not interfering, not at all. But I think we should divide up the job of searching and while I do China, whose coast is unexplored except by oil men, and the Hawaiian Islands, you run around the southern hemisphere. Marie might be drawn into the search,—if we could make her sure it was useless and foolish (and it is). Oh, there is a lot to say about this vision, but let's say it in February, not in letters now.

Now I must go upstairs and read Marie's letter, for I shall have to answer it,—if it is to be answered. The nurse won't let Peter do letters for a while. Not that there is anything weak or broken or even wounded about her. It is merely the latest idea in bringing up a mother from the depths of childbirth. And, by the way, Fred, women have bunked us on that, saying it was so hard that only a woman could do it. It is easy. It is so easy that any ordinary male could do it, and, as for men like you and me,—I think now that we really might attend to all that ourselves, and I am convinced from my studies of ants and spiders that we should, if we are to preserve the male at all.

I must write to Bob.[1] HE is all right. His plans and his party make me tired, but he, the uncurable, unreformable Bob, is wonderful. I

---

[1] Senator Robert M. La Follette.

upper left: LINCOLN STEFFENS AND ELLA WINTER WITH SIN-
CLAIR LEWIS, SAN REMO, 1925. *upper right*: WITH JANE B. HOL-
LISTER AT KARLSBAD, SUMMER OF 1926. *center*: MANOIR DE
BECHERON, TOURAINE, FRANCE. *lower*: WITH YVONNE, JO, AND
JACQUES DAVIDSON IN THE GARDEN AT BECHERON.

would go farther than you would apparently with him; I would give him the United States to play with if he wanted it. I would even enjoy seeing him go wrong. The seat I would like to have to watch the show from is Wall Street or any high-up labor union presidency.

My love to Marie.

Affectionately,
Lincoln Steffens

To Jo Davidson

San Remo, November 26, 1924

Dear Jo:

Your letter (Yvonne's too), referring to the fact that a baby has been born, has just been handed in, and I must reply at once. I owe you an apology. In a letter I posted this noon to Yvonne I spoke slightingly of you as my former friend. I take it all back. Now that I have got a letter out of you,—or my son has,—I am willing to forget and forgive both you and your neglect.

But even yet I am not satisfied. You have not told me about your Owen D. Young sittings. That is one count. And the other is the tone of this letter of today. It is light, just such an one as you might have sent me before. I want you to understand that those old, frivolous days of mine are over; I don't care to be reminded of the times I ran around the world with you wasting precious hours that should go into hard labor. I find that paternity has a sobering effect upon one. It is the child, I think. As he lies there so fresh from God, bred in the spirit in which we all are evidently meant to live; quiet, dignified, absorbed in whatever he is doing; as he lies on his side and devotes every thought and every grunt to the serious art of digestion,—I tell you, Jo,—I am ashamed of the way I throw in my food and forget it. Life is real, life is earnest. I can see now that that is true, and that most of my habits have been unworthy, wasteful, wanton and adultish. I mean to be more childish hereafter. I propose, since I cannot set Peter's baby an example, to let him set one to me.

And again, Jo, I feel in your letter a disposition to cotton up close to me, on a basis almost of equality, on the ground, forsooth, that you have had a boy too,—two in fact. That doesn't go. You might have had ten boys. You might have had more than that. But I want to rub it into you that numbers don't count. In the matter of boys we don't go by any quantitative standard. It is quality that counts, and quality alone.

And speaking of quality, I feel bound to suggest that there is not and there never was such a boy as Pete. He is almost a girl. I wanted a girl, Peter wanted a girl, we prayed for a girl and lastly, all the clothes we got are for a girl. Therefore,—if you get me,—just as any one little girl is above all the boys that ever were born, so Pete, having come so near to being a girl and YET BEING A BOY must logically be greater and more wonderful than all the boys AND all the girls in the world.

No doubt other men will be thinking themselves in my class because they have a boy. I mean to put a stop to it. Hemingway, for example,— I got a letter from him today, in many respects a very good letter (considering that he is a young writer not yet respectably published), but he has a boy and he spoke of his boy in the same breath with mine. I am going to call him down too. But as for you and your boys! Why, for one thing your boys are almost grown up. In the second place they have grown up, not under ideal personal environment and influences, but part of the time under yours. I will not go on. I think my point is clear. If it isn't, let me say to you that I mean to bring up this boy myself, me-an'-Peter.

That is all for today. The rest of your letter is pleasant and calls for a pleasant response, which I am in no mood to make. But I must add this: First, I don't believe you are coming down here. In the second, if you do, you will be received into open arms, and not by Peter alone. As for the bust of the baby, if you do it life-size, bring along half a brick and be prepared to knock off the corners. That will be about all, thank you.

Stef.

To Laura Suggett

San Remo, November 26, 1924

Dear Laura:—

Two letters from you, one good. You say you have achieved optimism. How did you do it? I have never, except momentarily, been a pessimist. . . .

. . . The Doctor's disappointments came of watching the election returns; and watching them with wishes in his mind. That's hell, of course. If he had the talk with La Follette that I had in Russia last year, he would not have cared so much about his election or even his progress. He is a conservative; a real one. He would do Wall Street and business good, if he were in and could have his way. He's against nothing but graft, and he isn't as *liberal* as the English Labor Government.

The only conservatives who understand the advantage of radicalism of that sort are those of Italy, who, having had a taste of it, play in with Mussolini now. The wise Liberal (crooked) leaders have a hard time holding down the fools in their camp who would like to take the offices and serve themselves. These do not realize that they cannot make labor work the way Mussolini can. Any false labor leader (false to labor) is better for capital than any capitalist leader can be.

But all this has nothing to do with optimism and progress. That is coming out of the laboratories and the conditions. Read young Haldane, and Julian Huxley; they, this younger generation of British science, are thinking and saying things,—things they get out of their scientific work in their laboratories. And the Germans are getting close to it and reporting it. Or, watch the German and the French captains of industry forming international trusts. These are all signs of real progress. There must be something like it in the U. S., only we don't see it. It isn't reported,—or, if it is, only the scientific bodies are getting the news.

Tell Older to send a good reporter (West, for example) to the universities, Berkeley and Stanford, and to Burbank; and ask each in person what he is doing and thinking that is new. Offer to suppress names. He'll see and he'll get a fine series of articles,—unless there is with us nothing like what is going on in Europe,—everywhere.

To Mrs. A. Winter

San Remo, December 20, 1924

Dear Mrs. Winter:—

Last night at this time I had just about decided that only grandmothers should have babies; mothers are too much like children themselves. The reason was that I had gone upstairs after writing to you and I found the baby crying and his mother in bed, almost asleep. And so sleepy was she, so dead tired out that the best she could do was to tell me, like one a-dreaming, to do what I was already doing. And she beat the baby into unconsciousness. The last sentence sounds dubious: it means that, in a fair race for unconsciousness between child and mother, the mother won. It does not mean that the mother got up and beat the child with a stick or anything like that.

Peter's exhaustion was due, of course, to the reaction from the departure of the nurse, the work of succession and her nervousness at complete responsibility. The baby cried the whole evening through, after its feeding, and there was pain. That much we could understand. We surrendered, therefore, to the new regime. Peter hesitated. The nurse's last words to her were, "Don't give up the four-hour feeds." And the nurse's influence hangs over, you know. But, anyhow, we fed at nine-thirty instead of at ten. Pete whimpered a bit (that is when Peter gave up and slept). But he soon quieted down and he slept,— we all slept till about four. When he woke, he cried and it was the hunger cry. We got up, gave him all the trick remedies, water, dill-water, a turn-over, etc., in vain. He wanted milk.

Now you must remember the story up to now. He used to waken to hunger at two, then three, then three-thirty, then four and finally five. Four was a bit of a set-back, but it still showed a gain which we were loth to lose. So we huddled together, Peter and I, and let the little fellow storm at us till,—not six, but five-thirty, theoretically; maybe it was five-twenty or, one watch said, five-fifteen. In brief, it was a compromise. And compromise leads to peace even in a home. Little Pete slept,—we all slept till Giannina, the cheat, called us late, at nearly nine. Little Pete slept on during our breakfast and we had to wake him for his bath. (It is fun waking a baby. He acts so like a big boy or a loafer of a man, stretching and dropping off again, promising to get up and then lying down on his word, yawning, making faces and sighing. I like that job. Anyone with the slightest trace of cruelty would.)

After Pete's bath, the doctor came and gave us some advice, along your line; but also he said it was absurd to worry at all about a baby so well, with such clear eyes, clean skin and altogether so robust as Pete. The only thing is the weight, which, he said, *must* begin now to increase. And so it did. He weighed over seven after his six o'clock feed tonight. But I am getting ahead of my story. We were ready to shorten the interval of feeding at noon but Pete was so busy out on his hot veranda that it would have been a shame to wake him. . . .

Peter is again tired out. "It's the hardest work I ever did," she said once today. She is good at it, does it swiftly and neatly, and she certainly seems to me to take it all easily, with never a loss of her sweetness and cheer. But she is putting herself into it. "I think I will not try to write," she says, "not for a while." She doesn't exactly worry, but she does think about it and she feels Pete's calls. Wind in his stomach is a storm in our Peter's. I see her sometimes sitting and staring at him wondering or wishing or,—something. I suppose every mother does that. But it goes through my heart to see this little girl look at her baby with such longing. And Pete looks back, with much the same longing or wishing, like a wise, old man. I guess they are about equal, these two. You are going to be very proud of your daughter, Mrs. Winter. You love her, of course; you will find out down here why we all respect her also, everybody. Peter is a great Person, great and lovely. AND her baby has gained in weight; he is going to go on gaining now. He will take you to the opera some night and take good care of you. But I am glad you are coming soon.

Good night, and, I reckon, goodbye. No more letters are sure to reach you, are they? Next time we communicate it will be directly at Ventimiglia. You may expect a pretty drive in the dusk between the sea and the hills up to a nice little nest in a dark garden, where a welcome awaits you from all.

Merry Christmas to Rosa and Rudi; and, also, to the cook.

Stef.

To Laura Suggett

San Remo, January 1, 1925

Dear Laura:

. . . Tell Dr. things are or may be happening here in Italy. I can't explain them yet. Mussolini has given notice of a new election law, which does not suit either extreme of his own party and angers the opposition. I suppose he is shifting his ground; seeking new alliances and new foundations for his throne. He must be moving to the right, if my theories are true; that all governments must move backward, never forward,—after the first short chapter of power. The conservatives, called the constitutionalists, are after him. Their pretense is that they want to return to constitutional, parliamentary government, and he may have made secret terms with them. That is indicated by the exposures of him and his part in the assassinations, etc., by members of his own Fascist bloc, and by the adherence to him of Giolitti and the "liberal" ministers taken into his council at the last crisis. Mussolini is a political genius; he may slip through; he is taking a bold course. But anything may happen in Italy this next year,—anything. It is a good place to be, though Italian papers do not print the news. Their service is editorial. The news leaks out; it becomes known in

Rome and in the bourses, and we, the newspaper readers, get it, first, in the editorial comments upon what is assumed to be known.

There is trouble, too, in Germany. Europe is not so settled as the settlers think it to be.

Affectionately,
Len.

San Remo, January 5, 1925

Dear Laura:—

There is a lovely letter here from you tonight, all about your busyness and telling me the Doctor is sending me a book and you a shawl of mother's. The shawl warmed me. It is meant, no doubt, for the baby, and it will not be here for a week or two. No matter. It has done its service. And I am sure mother would like to know that. And I think she would like to see it around her grandson. Maybe she will, for it certainly will wrap him round.

I wrote to Clinton yesterday, asking him to have Peter Stanley Stef registered at Groton School. And I told Clint about his cousin, who really looks as Clinton did when I brought him East one year. It is strange that Pete, as we call him, resembles our side more than his mother's. He has my eyes, and not in color alone, my nose, my homely upper lip, and he has a wide space between the eyes, wider even than mine. I suppose all babies are solemn; the nurse said so; but this little fellow has a funny way of staring long, quietly, steadily at one, ending often in a lifting of the brow, as if in puzzlement. His sobriety is amusing; it looks as if he were thinking or wondering, and then giving it all up.

He never sucks his thumb or fingers. He does like a mouthful of cotton-wool; and, by the way, I wish the Doctor would advise me what to give him to chew on that will not displace his jaw. It is only for after meals, when I smoke. He seems to be comforted by something to chew on or suck for half an hour; I imagine it keeps the saliva going to help his digestion, which is not perfect. The nurse gave him a doubled strip of cloth about an inch wide with a little water soaked in it. He mouths it a while, then drops it and stares around till he goes to sleep. He is what they call a good baby, crying very little and always for cause. I would like to have him have the one luxury he cares for and, since it cannot be the condemned rubber ring, etc., I would like to know what the orthodontists advise.

You were going to Washington on your business, the Doctor accompanying you. Good. It will be a change for you and I am guessing that you are going to find out that you are a natural lobbyist. Don't expect to be perfect; you cannot win everyone. My experience is that each of us gets only our own, only those who happen to speak our language. You lose patience easily, I think, and are prone to chuck up a side job if you begin with failures. Good lobbyists are good losers; they win by very patiently sticking to it. Col. House, for example, is at his job yet. He works out of the limelight exactly as he worked in it, and here he is, in Paris now, after having been all around Europe seeing the Germans, the English, the Italians and the French. Nobody may hear of it, but House will have some votes to swing. He will help some; he will win out some day, if victory is possible under natural laws. Time is your ally, not your enemy. It is the enemy only of impatient people. . . .

I think you will find that several of Older's staff, now and formerly, are rare fellows. Such men drift naturally to Older and he uses and saves and develops them. There are some of Older's boys, now men, on the Eastern weeklies and dailies. I used to have a staff like that, from which men were graduated to other jobs which mine prepared them for, deep down. Yes, Older knows very well.

Affectionately,

Len.

To Allen H. Suggett

San Remo, January 9, 1925

Dear Doctor:

. . . I don't want to see the people look to Congress rather than to the presidency. That is a democrat's wish, a liberal hope. Liberalism is dead over here. The war killed it. It may recover, but there is no hope in that. Mussolini gave it the answer. He returned to the dictatorship. He did not do anything with it; he did not intend to, I think, but he and Lenin showed the way; you will take power, first, use it to change the circumstances of life, and then, maybe, you may breed men fit for self-government, if they want to govern themselves. But Mussolini says they don't; and he has come pretty near to proving it. Italy was glad to have him do it all for them. He didn't, but Lenin did for Russia. I think we know why the one did and the other didn't.

But anyhow, here lately, when public opinion in Italy seemed to demand a return to constitutional forms of parliamentary government, Mussolini yielded and would have gone through, but the timidity, the stupidity, the cupidity of his CONGRESS, made him sick and he told it to its face the other day to go to hell. It was amazing the way the parliamentarians took it, lying down. Mussolini has gone back to his despotism; he had to carry on. Nothing can be done by or with a legislature,—without a boss or a lobby, and,—even then,—Italy is back to the dictatorship. There will be a fight. That is another matter.

It is a risk to prophesy so close to an event, but I expect to see Mussolini shot out of office. He told the parliament that he would assume all responsibility for all that had been done by the Fascisti,—ALL, you understand; and Rome understood that he meant assassinations, mobs, castor oil, everything. And he pointed to the law for impeachment, bidding them try it. They voted for his motion like cowards; they fear, they respect, they can work under a dictatorship, and not otherwise. No, your wise man is a wise man, but he will be still wiser some day. Ask Older. Consider La Follette and his vote. The job can be done, but not by democratic methods.

I have a very illuminating letter from Russia, which I am using for an article. When I have done with it, I shall send it you or my article or both. It is about the Trotzky row and in brief says that Trotzky is down and out,—certainly for a long time: years; no check will result to the Soviet Government, since the opposition of Trotzky is silent on his part and has no following at all. The dispute was about the theory of the revolution, a theoretical, not a practical difference. There is an orthodoxy in Russia, you know, and Trotzky is not orthodox. . . .

Well, you and Laura are going,—you probably will have been,—to Washington by the time this reaches 850. I shall be interested to hear what each of you separately is struck by there. I hope you will have seen Brandeis and La Follette. You should seek out others also, Andy Furuseth, for example; but it is too late to advise you now. The most interesting spectacle is the Senate in session. I have watched it for hours and I never wearied of the forms of it; they are so good, so well adapted to the purpose of them and so handily used by the old members. The House is nothing in comparison, but one sight of it makes the Senate appreciated. . . .

Affectionately,
Len.

To Laura Suggett

San Remo, January 26, 1925

Dear Laura:

. . . Maybe Dot is showing you my letters to her. I hope so. Lest she keep them from you, I want to repeat in other terms something I have said to her. She warned me that, having a child myself, I would soon begin to tend to the Right. I admitted to her that, since that happened to others, it might to me. But I find that it does not work that way. I am more radical than ever and precisely because I have a child. I will tell you what I did not tell Dot: that this experience of a strengthening of my radicalism makes me think that maybe I can really carry out in the education of a child my ideas of preparation to live and serve and enjoy it without falling into despair at the repetition of failures. I certainly can prevent a child from getting or holding long the unscientific bunk that now passes for knowledge. I may even put into a young head the substitute for morality.

At any rate I am intensely interested, more than as if I were a young careerist, in the mind of the child, which I find begins early to unfold. I snatched a nipple out of his mouth the other day in fun, and he smiled; a sense of humor or, at any rate, of fun. With that for a starter anything is possible; and it is his first sign of brains. I am going on the theory, pronounced so often, that the telling time in the life of a baby is the first few years. I intend to work hard early; even now. . . .

I have said more than I meant to, more than you want to hear. No matter. I can't write so much as I do to you and not give some sign of the most intense interest in my life. Especially when I have no news, like today.

To Brand Whitlock

San Remo, January 28, 1925

. . . The experimental method in politics is as difficult to apply as in astronomy, but no more so. We cannot take Marx, for example, into a laboratory, set up Socialism and try it out. The old-time colonies left out the influences of natural passion. The success of them would have meant no more than their failure meant. But the astronomers wait for an eclipse and, taking that as an experiment, observe it and,—so test their theories. Thus must we study politics, I think. When the hardest Marxians in the world seized control of revolutionary Russia and started out to try Marx to the bitter end, it may have been hard for the Russians, but it was, it is, a chance to watch the experiment with interest, without prejudgment, willing to learn just what Socialism is practicable and what not. The great trouble is that statesmen don't know and don't stick to main issues. Lenin put it well once when I was talking with him. "In the long run of history it will have been better for us to have tried out Marx to a finish than to have made a mixed success."

It was reports in this spirit that interested Wilson and made him do what he did for me. And he did me some service. Once, after the Bullitt incident, when all the secret services were pestering me in Paris and the papers were hot after me, Wilson stepped out of the group of premiers at the Crillon and, with a crowd looking on in astonishment, put his arm over my shoulder and whispered in my ear,—nothing. He meant to rebuke the detectives and reporters, and he certainly did it. He took my view of Mexico and acted upon it and I think he might have done the same on Russia. He definitely did not, but he let me know that he was treating the peace-making as his job, sacrificing everything to that, even the revolution. I think I understand Wilson and what happened to him. But so does Clemenceau, who is scientific, really. It has made Clemenceau cynical; and cynicism is not scientific. But then he, like Wilson, had to act. They could not go around openheaded as I could. The most scientific scientist in the position of a statesman would have to act unscientifically in crises. All we can complain of in a man like Wilson is that he does not KNOW that he is subject himself to the forces he studies, but goes on giving reasons for acts that have no reasons but only causes. Lenin never erred here.

Artists take another way out. They avoid knowledge of the crafts they practice. My contention is that they also must, first, become conscious of their art (and their artfulness) and then,—and still be able to execute with the subconscious. They say, no; that to be aware of their technique hurts their painting. Writers survive knowledge. Conrad knew exactly what and how and why; and yet did it masterfully. But the painters and sculptors I know are like the statesmen I know; they are opportunists, have no policy, no conscious art, no philosophy. (They are afraid to know.)

Mussolini has a theory. I would like to tell you about him. This letter I see is growing, and I must stop it. But I will close my thought. Mussolini has no worth-while purpose that makes his policy an experiment in politics; but he did watch the Russian Revolution, as I would have such things watched, drew some conclusions scientifically and, acting upon them, confirmed some theories of Lenin as to political method. In a word there is in the news of the day a basis for a science of politics, not complete perhaps, but introductory and fruitful, if we could but drop ALL our theories long enough to see frankly that some other theories, not ours, are in the laboratory.

That may give you an idea of what I am thinking, if not doing. I am de-educated. I am disillusioned, but I am working along in a leisurely, unimportant way, upon my discovery that whenever I lose an illusion I can find in the facts that destroyed it a better, or at any rate another,—illusion. And that is the path that has led the physical sciences so far. The human sciences and arts can go just as far along that trail, and it is a pleasant, a most dramatic road to tramp on, provided one carries not too much luggage. And I don't. There is the baby now, but, as the poor girl said when she had one without a husband: "Yes, but it is such a little one."

If I go north, Brand, I will call on you. If you come south,—and I would like to feel again the feeling I used to have when I was with Nell. Let's meet. You may have heard that I am an agitator. Don't you believe it. I have changed as little as you have, really. I am as indolent as you are serene. And as un-exigent.

To Mrs. A. Winter

San Remo, February 15, 1925

Dear Grandma:

I slept from ten o'clock last night till seven this morning, and I feel bully. "Bully" is a crude Americanism which you English would not use; and I may drop it sometimes as my mama drops spoons, stockings and,—people, when she thinks of something else all at once. But today it expresses the way I am. That is why I did not cry even when I did wake up. I lay there listening to mama snore waiting for her to come to. And then when she looked over into my cot I smiled and,—she is very intelligent,—she said that I must be hungry and so,—she is very executive,—she fed me.

But then I have been well now for several days, and that was lucky, for there has been no sun for at least five days. On the contrary there has been rain and wind, darkness and cold. Mama has a cold, which I am thinking of getting and trying. I have to try everything, you know. But I do wish the sun would come out and warm things up and spread some cheer around. Of course, Rocco and the peasants are glad. Rocco doesn't have to water the garden and the peasants and the flowers and the water company are all rejoicing; they had begun to think there would be a water shortage. So the rain is good for such common things as theirs. But we aristocrats, we want sun all the time.

. . . I heard mama and papa talking together the other day, wondering why I cry myself to sleep sometimes. "He is obviously sleepy; and yet he fights as for his life against sleep." Now I can't tell them anything; but you are humble like me, so I will tell you why all us babies cry before we go to sleep. I know it from my own psychology. I cry because I am afraid I am going to die. That's why. They have lived a long time and so they are pretty sure when they fall asleep that they will wake up. But I am very small; I have not waked up often enough to be sure I always will. My hold on life is slight; and I do like living. Well, and so you see, when I feel myself slipping off somewhere into what you know is sleep and I know is unconsciousness, I feel as if I were really FALLING into the darkness of death. And so I holler. And when my papa comes around and grins at my struggles, it seems cruel to me because I think I am in a life and death struggle. I am terrified. I don't think that that is sympathetic and fine, do you? And then, still not understanding, he wonders why it is now that I smile when I wake up. I smile with surprise and joy, for it is just like being born, except that waking doesn't hurt the way being born does. . . .

I wrote you a letter the other day, but papa forgot to post it. It got torn; you won't mind piecing it together, will you?

P. Stan Stef.

To Allen H. Suggett

San Remo, February 17, 1925

Dear Doctor:

There have been no letters from 850 lately; not for a fortnight or more, it seems, but the shawl came day before yesterday. It looked absurdly large when it was laid out for the baby. He is such a tiny little fellow. I have been thinking of bringing him up as a jockey, only he is intelligent enough for something better. He is good enough to be a horse.

Anyway when I laid him on that great, warm shawl it made me laugh, but I wrapped it about him and then I saw what it was for. It turns out to be just the thing, and he does not mind having it against his face as he does other such garments and coverings. He resents a blanket, for example. But this,—I have seen him bury his face purposely into it and when it is cold or blowing it can be put right over his face and,—he breathes through it. It is the most constant thing in his equipment now, a most useful thing. And I love it for what it was and what it means. I wish mother were alive so that I might have someone to whom I could write about Little Pete. I have to talk to him, and I do. . . .

I put some money into the stock market when your friend Cal was elected on the theory that the crooks had really been scared by La Follette and would rejoice and go dotty when the sure result was announced of the election. I did not risk much, only enough to carry two hundred shares. I have had some good profits, some of which I have taken and the rest of which I shall soon call in, though I think this bull market will go on for a year or so. I shall not wait for the top. I never did and I certainly shall not now. I wanted to pay for the baby, and that I have already done several times over. . . .

Len.

To Mrs. A. Winter

San Remo, [Mar., 1925]

Dear Grandma:

My mama told me she's going to write you today and she was going to tell you my news, but I said I wanted to tell you myself, so she said all right I might.

Well, it's this. I've begun earning money for the family. You know how everyone envied Jackie Coogan's parents because they didn't have to work any more but could live on him; well, and he only started at 5 years and now I have at 3 months. It was like this. One day there was a loud knock at the door, and my mama brought in a funny yellow envelope and it was addressed to my papa but my mama opened it and read it to him. I didn't know 'zackly what it meant but I went downstairs in the night when my mama and papa was asleep and I got it out of papa's desk and I'll copy it for you: "If you'd do frank 3,000 word article 'most wonderful thing in the world a baby' and what it means to philosopher traveller your age feel sure *Cosmopolitan* would like it. Must be Steffens talking from his heart."

Well, I understood some of it. My papa said at once, "I won't do it," but my mama, who is sometimes quite wise about my papa, said a lot of things, and the one I noticed was, "*You* needn't do that sentimental stuff they expect, Stef; why shouldn't you write it in your own way as you feel it? You know you love writing about the baby. Why, the letters you wrote to Mother would make fascinating reading for all the people who've had babies. And *I* know how original your attitude to the baby is,—and how people would roar over it if you wrote just like you wrote those letters." Well, I didn't see why people should laugh at me, but I did see a chance to be economically independent right off my own bat alone now, early, so I chimed in and said, "Do, papa; I'll help." My papa he looked at me and said, "All right, Pete, you and me, we'll roast mama," and ever since, my papa sits every morning at his desk and he an' me have a fine time roasting mama. Well, the magazine that sent the funny yellow envelope sent another yesterday and said that they wanted it very much and would pay a thousand dollars. My papa says perhaps they won't be so anxious when they've seen it, but my mama said something about their not being able to resist it, and I like it myself, specially the part where my papa says that he knew and loved me long before my mama did because for a long while I was only a sick tummy to my mama and all that time I was my papa's son. I never liked being just a sick tummy, it is rather humiliating when you've just come a long way and left all the other boys playing up there, just to please my mama and papa, isn't it?

Please don't get to love all those other babies my mama told me about, too much, because I want you to love me more-'n any other baby in the world. You won't, will you? You will be true to me as I am to you?

Pete

San Remo, Marzo 21, 1925

Dear Grandma:

I have a important question to ast you today. My papa and I, we have been playing pirates and I want to know if it is fair for me to be always the fellow that walks the plank. My papa says it is. I say that since I am the littlest member of the gang, I ought to get some consideration and a chance once in a while to be the one-eyed captain that rules the seas and buries the treasures in the ground. He says not so, that it is just because I am the smallest and weakest that I got to be the prisoner and, when the sun rises every morning, walk blindfolded off the plank into the sea. I say it isn't right, and he admits that, but he argues that that is the way of life the way grown-ups have arranged things and that I got to learn it and learn it young. I want to appeal to you or,—to somebody that would naturally side with me. Have I got to walk off into the sea every morning? Can't I ever be even the mate or the cutthroat devil of a sailor that always has a knife in his mouth?

My papa says that the only way out is for me to grow big and strong. But he said that weeks ago, when I was a little bit of a fellow. I have grown since. I am going on eight and a half and I can kick and knock around so terrible now that even my papa runs. I think then that the next morning I can make him walk the plank, but no,— Every morning when mama is asleep (and she always neglects me then, the sleepy-head) my papa wakes up. It is awful the way he looks over at me with his one good eye, over the bed clothes,—he looks at me, grabs me, sneaks me off my ship over to his and, there without a hearing or any kind of a trial, condemns me to death. It's terrible not to know where you are going, when you are so young. My papa says no grown-up ever knows where he is going and that I got to get used to being blindfolded, that I will make a good soldier and a better voter if I am brought up that way. I admit I kindo like the thrill of it; I have to laugh a little and I will confess I would rather die the way I do than not be pirates at all. But that plunge, that sudden drop from the plank into the cold water,—there must be some way for me to get out of it. . . .

My papa says you are a practical grandma and not interested in matters of the soul and spirit. But I can't believe that. I hear him talk about mother-in-laws in a tone of voice that shows he is as unfair to you as he is to me. So goodbye, Grandma. Do your best for your own, only, dear

Little
Pete

San Remo, April 2, 1925

Dear Grandma:

I should not write to you, because you don't answer my letters. You have not paid the least attention to my last one. You always write to my mama, who swanks it over me till I get almost green somewheres, where I oughtn't to. But I have a complaint to register or, anyhow, a very searching question to ask of you, whom alone I feel I can trust. But first I must tell you some news.

I weigh nine pounds plus 2 ounces. I don't feel any difference, but I notice that the other day, when I had to have an outing, it was my papa, not my mama, who carried me down town. Mama did not go at all, and when we got home, my papa told my mama that, for the first time in years, all the women turned around to look at him. Mama used one of my words: "Blah," she said, "that was because Pete has on Grandma's new cap." Which does make me look pretty sweet, I admit.

But I think the girls stared at us on account of the way my papa carried me. He stuck me under his arm, as if I were a bundle of books, and that is not the position in which my mama bears me. I like papa's way, however, since it leaves me room to kick back; and I have learned to kick. I can kick with each hand, with one hand and one foot, with one foot and both hands and, sometimes, when I get a good start and somebody is watching so as to make it worthwhile to do my best, I can work all four things together and almost shake the roof off. . . .

And this brings me to my complaint. I was having a lot of fun with my papa, and some with my mama, till about three days ago, they received some advice from somebody,—I haven't caught the name yet, —but some spoil-sport who cautioned them against playing with me. This Person must be one of those people who are afraid of the growing intelligence of Man. His, or her, line of reasoning was that a child's brain can take it out of the body and nerves by developing too fast. And I can see that that might be so in an ordinary baby. If an ordinary child of ordinary parents developed his head too rapidly and too much, it might either drive him crazy or produce common people that would become politically intelligent. And that would hurt business. But, you can see,—you were the first to see that I am no ordinary child. Genius and other exceptional traits do skip a generation. But anyway you have from the very first recognised that I must be treated in a special way. So I have to ask you whether you approve of this idea of bringing me up in the way other children are brought down,—to where they are,—well,—look at the people all about us. Would you have me one of them? Don't you think that I should be handled the opposite from the ruck of kids? Don't you think that this Person's advice should be countered? Well, if you do, I wish you would write, for once, to my mama and say so. . . .

My best love goes to my Grandma, who is always on my side, even, I trust, in the matter of brains.

Pete

Nursery Note:

Pete laughed out loud today. The most beautiful music I ever heard. Three notes three times . . . I nearly cried. Stef.

San Remo, April 6, 1925

Dear Grandma:

I am home again, and my return was a triumphal tour, like your English Prince is having. My mama came for me, early. I imagine she and papa and the servants missed and needed me. She came all pink and lovely, as she always is when she is eager, and she just grabbed me, as if I had been lost or something. But I was all right. I was taken around visiting. And everybody seemed to like me, even one I laughed at. She was an old lady, who was dressed funnily, not like my mama at all, and I just had to laugh out loud. The old lady was hurt a bit. "Why," she said, "I don't look so absurd as all that, do I?" But it wasn't just that. I laughed partly because I felt so well.

And when I left the hospital, everybody saw me off; the doctors (I had two), nurses and patients all was for me, Pete. Even the driver of my carriage was nice and careful. And then as I got home, Giannina ran up and she kissed me, Giulia laughed and was glad and my papa jumped on me and took me away from mama. He carried me upstairs, where he and mama (principally mama, you understand, my papa is all very well to play with, but my mama is the One that does things for me) put me into my little cot, which came home with me. I would have liked to go around and see things, but, no, my mama said that, because I had slept on the way home in the carriage, I had to go to bed and stay there. And so it happens, that while my mama isn't looking I can write to you, my first and best spoiler.

And I can tell you that I am a proud boy. I have had an operation, I have learned to laugh, I can talk just like a grown-up (nothing to say, but talking just the same and all the time) and, best of all, hardest to get, I have a letter from you; and such a witty one. My papa said he was surprised, delighted and might be mistaken about you. He said that maybe I was right. He does not like to be wrong about anything, I notice; he isn't humble like you and me and my mama; he wants to be right all the time, and so he consulted my mama about you and whether you were not also, like mama, an intellectual, and I was awful interested in what my mama would answer. But she didn't answer. She just laughed.

You see, my papa and mama are funny people, not like the nurses at the hospital and in the streets when I pass by; they don't converse. A conversation, as I understand it, is where everybody talks, sometimes all at once, sometimes all in between arguing. But my papa and mama, they take turns, first she talks,—a blue streak, then he monologues. They don't answer each other, not at the time. It is more like a parliament, I think; first one has the floor and talks till exhausted, then the other rises and goes at it till tired out.

But I am getting sleepy, my eyelids are dropping over my eyes so— so—that—I don't want to go, but I—I feel—I feel just like as—well— as if the whole world were sinking and, me too,—all falling, falling— falling—asleep.

Dear Mother-in-law:

I'm sorry but Pete couldn't finish and sign this letter. He struggled, his hands grabbed for a line or a straw, but there was none. He fell. He is sound sound asleep, but he's smiling in his sleep, dreaming, no doubt, of his grandma. A beautiful baby, ten times more beautiful and precious than before he went away. He was away all night, you understand. All night long we all slept, all four of us, in an absolutely empty house. But he is back. I don't think now that he can go to see you. He leaves, when he leaves,—he leaves nothing for us behind, —not a thing. No, you'll have to come to us.

Pete's Papa

To Gilbert E. Roe

San Remo, April 16, 1925

Dear Gil:

. . . My view now is that we all have to make a sharp distinction between our thinking and our conduct. As I have been saying to you, we should oppose tyrannies, graft, dictatorships, but only as leads to the causes of these so-called evils. Fight as Bob fights, but not so certainly as he does that he is up against the fundamental evil. It seems hard to get this division. I agree with you that a dictatorship like Mussolini's is bad, but it is neither backward nor forward. It happens that we get a dictator whenever there is a crisis. The thing to do then is not to judge it, not to say it is good or bad, but, foreseeing that it will occur, be ready to use or to be it. And so I would like to show that a revolution does actually pass through certain well-marked stages with certain ever-recurring evils, which need not perturb us therefore, because being known and understood they can be discounted and, when we really know enough about them, obviated,—perhaps.

. . . I think that you and all liberals have, as I had, certain theories of right and wrong. When you see the Russian Revolution you observe that it goes against your theories and mine, wherefore you "give it up"; it is all wrong. Emma [1] did that. I, having seen two revolutions, the Mexican and the Russian, got from their perverse courses the notion that, not the revolutions, but my theories were somehow wrong. I read up other revolutions. I found that they all took the same course. I inferred thence that a revolution, like a storm, is subject to natural laws and forces, which produce always the same effects.

And upon this conviction I cast out, not the revolution, but my old manner of thinking, ceased to be a liberal and have since been watching events as if they were divine (or natural) revelations. I act pretty much as I did before. I feel with the fellows, like you and Bob, who go to the front and fight the battles that make in the right direction, but more now like a navigator than a sailor. The book I have just finished is the story of Moses, told in the light of the Revolution, as a classic example of how a revolt of a people goes. Jehovah symbolizes Nature; Moses, the reformer, and leader; Pharaoh the King or the employer-capitalist; Aaron the orator and the Jews as the people. The parallel with the Russian or any other revolution is striking. But so is any other revolution like a classic revolution, so is one reform like another, one city like all the others, as all states and all nations. There is under all this a basis for a science, but it will not be a liberal science, and the liberals are becoming its chief opponents.

We had a creed, Gil, and I think we are in danger of standing with the legions of darkness against the light, which comes out of historical events, no matter how bloody they are, no matter how tyrannical. Wars, revolutions, reforms, elections,—all show us what can be, and it's up to us not to resist these, but to understand and undermine them.

. . . My love to the family which does indeed seem to have grown up behind my back. I wonder if my baby upstairs there will ever grow

[1] Emma Goldman.

up and go off to school and college and,—all that. How I would like to have a talk now with Mrs. Roe. It's the wisdom of women I need now, not that of wise men, however wise.

Affectionately,
Lincoln Steffens

To James H. McGill

Dear McGill: San Remo, May 4, 1925

Here is a photo of my boy Pete taken as I was telling him about what you and George Briggs wrote about yourselves and your boys. He apologizes for his mirth, but he pleads that he could not help it. He asked me where you fathers got the idea that "us kids," as he put it, would rise way above their source. He asked me if I had any thought that he, Pete, was going to do my unfinished work, "because," he warned me, "I ain't, you know. I am going to live my own life, choose my own work (which will not be labor), and be altogether a separate person." I have been telling him about a lot of my friends, and he says he can't "get" grown-ups at all at all.

When I described Darrow, for example, and quoted his question, "Is life worth living?" he had such a fit of laughter that his mother wanted to call in the doctor. Pete cannot get pessimism. He says he came here with no expectations possible of disappointment and he has pledged me not to make an idealist of him. I am to tell him the little I know of what is what, indicate to him as best I can the meagre possibilities of improvement of the human race and the civilization such adults have naturally built up, and let him choose whether to try to better things or just enjoy them.

And I have promised him all he asks. He can be a lounge-lizard if he likes. All I am against is that he shall work, especially for a living. He can work for fun, if he likes, the way the artists do, but never from a sense of duty.

He is getting self-control now. The other day he put his finger in his mouth, a thing he seldom does. I jerked it out. He gave me a cold, hard look and stuck it back. I jerked it out. He studied me a moment, seemed to decide it was a fight and slowly, deliberately, he put his whole fist into his big mouth. I drew it out and I smiled. "Oh," he seemed to say, "it is a joke, not a fight!" and he left his hand at his side. He was willing not to suck his thumb, but he was not willing to have another will put over upon his.

Well, life is a game, education is a game. And why can't I teach him that it is all a crooked, silly game, but that one has to play it, so the thing to do is to pretend to play it, and, since it is easy, to play it well, but never to take it seriously, never as work, always with a laugh, such a laugh as that which you called forth upon his wise little face? Meanwhile he can see straight and he can think straight. Pete is never to be, or to be called, a "good boy." He is never to have any duties. He is not to know about thrift or honesty or "service" or "liberty," except as funny notions of the old generation that made the war and the peace.

I read what you all write, I see your troubles but I am not afraid. I think my boy Pete will bring me and his mother up as we should go. I dunno. Of course you will say "Wait." And I shall always listen for more and more of what you have to tell me. But just the same I rejoice that I have Pete on my hands and I think of his bringing-up with pleasure.

To Mrs. A. Winter

San Remo, May 18, 1925

Dear Grandma:

Your last letter is so nice that I must answer it at once. Do not be sorry. I suppose you thought when you had got it off that you were through with me for a while and it is really ungracious of me to come again. But you need not reply to this one. I shall be well *content,* as the French say, to have you let two or three of my letters accumulate before your sense of duty drives you to clean up your desk.

I just have to tell you, however, that I have struck a new note. I found it by accident one day last week when my papa was away. I used to speak, you know, in a treble, like a girl or a baby, and I envied my papa's deep male voice. I did not expect ever to rise to that height, —not till I was grown up,—I thought I would have to go on talking like mama throughout my childhood till the time came when a boy's voice breaks. But on the memorable day I am recalling so proudly, I happened to be talking to myself at the same time that I was feeling something wrong way down in my tummy and all of a sudden I struck a deep, base note. I was delighted. I was afraid too. I feared that I might lose it, so I set about practising it, and I really got it: a round, full, baritone sound. I was afraid to go to sleep, but I had to, at last. My mama had heard me, she picked me up, kissed me, laughing, and then laid me away so clean that I fell. But when I woke up, I got it again; and now another day is here and yet when I tried it this morning, there was my voice, big, deep, grown-up and male. My mama says I may be a singer, but my papa says no, that with my brains I am sure to be better than the opera; he says if I am diligent and cautious I may become the man in uniform who calls the numbers of the carriages outside the opera at night. Won't that be great? . . .

The garden is lush with flowers; all are out, and the house too is filled with them. My mama by the way is happy over her success as a journalist and keeps putting off her novel to do an article on Housekeeping in Italy or Children in Italy. She is becoming almost a professional housekeeper and child expert. Funny, is it not, how people change? My papa says that if we work together, I and he, we can really get mama down where wives and mothers ought to be got,— right down in the ground. But I bet on my mama. I think her mind will survive even her happiness. It is my papa I worry over. He would rather change my diapers than write about it or anything else. The only reason he can't be downed is because he is already down, and I think he knows it. But all this is between you and me. . . .

I am using my judgment just as I am my new register for the voice. I have dictated this whole letter in that tone, as you may have noticed, a deep, sincere, masculine voice. The only part in the old note is the signature.

Pete

To Allen H. Suggett

San Remo, May 26, 1925

Dear Doctor:

. . . For next year, I had thought of trying France, but one trip of inquiry was enough. The prices are high and the houses businesslike; made to rent. Here in Italy there are houses for rent that the owners have to live in themselves and the terms in lire are lower for eight months than they are in francs in France for four, five or six months. St. Cergue is in the French Alps, so we can practice our French there for three or four months, and then come back to, I think, Alassio, an hour and a half from here. . . .

You have seen that Glenn Frank, the editor of the *Century,* is appointed President of Wisconsin University. My one and only last editor gone! Not very good for me, but I know that Frank will try to do something real at Wisconsin, and that state needs it; and that university. But the job of it! I saw Bobby La Follette here a few days ago; the Senator's son and manager, a young fellow about thirty years old, and he was grieving over the University. It lacked a president, he said, and they could find no one. I bade him get me the job and I told him what I would do. He asked me if I would really take it; I said I would. A college presidency is about the only price I have left. But, as I wrote to Frank, I am glad I have not got it; I am glad he has it. For it will be a fierce undertaking to go up against the half-reformed politics and condition of that state. Frank knows all that. We have talked education a lot together. Now we'll see what he can do. He is young, strong, tactful, and he has some ideas; some; he is not deep, but he is ambitious. And he was assistant once to an old college president who let him run things pretty much as he liked. An expert, therefore. Worth watching. . . .

To Marie Howe

San Remo, June 2, 1925

Dear Marie:

. . . I like immensely Heywood Broun's column, but I could not do one like that every day,—not by a long shot. I would write and re-write and write it again. No. It is an attractive form, but I remember once doing a column a week at a thousand dollars a week; and I was glad to quit at the end of ten weeks. The editors who were paying for it rose then *en masse;* I was doing politics from Washington and they bawled me out,—to my relief.

I think my job is just being a father and, on occasion, a friend,—if not in need. You know.

Yours,
Steffens

To Mrs. A. Winter

San Remo, June 2, 1925

Dear Gran'ma:

These are boresome days for me. I have nothing to do but lie around on the bed watching other people packing. . . . It is my mama that is doing the packing so far. She starts right in after my bath in the morning and she just does it. My papa says it will be his turn next. I don't know about that. I see my mama taking out his clothes and dusting them, hanging them out in the sun and folding them away, while my papa sits down in his library and writes letters all the morning. And this afternoon, he dressed all up and when the battle of the trunks was at its height, he betakes himself downtown where (he said) he was awful busy arranging for a villa if the one at Alassio fails us. But—

I sat there on the bed and watched my mama work. She didn't pay any attention to me. She was all for baggage and she had the room strewn with things till you would not recognize it as the sacred room where I was borned. It was a sight. I suffered some. It was very hot and I asked her to reduce the temperature; she can do anything, my mama can, and I know she can cool off the sun the way she does my mouth when it is warm; but, no, she would not listen to me. She let it be hot. And by and by a baby breeze blew up, it came in at the French window, danced across the bed and kept kissing me all over. I liked that, so I lay there till by and by my mama sat down near me to drink some tea our Giulia brought up to her. Then I laughed at her. Mama did not know what I was laughing at. She looked up surprised and I laughed again. At last she laughed too. It is hard sometimes to make grown-ups laugh, but she did laugh at last. And then she and I, we both laughed. And she said I was a darling for being so patient!

I have some progress to report. You remember my feet. You noticed them once, and I wondered because you seemed to identify them with me. Well, I have found them and now I know what they are for. I used them at first to wave around in the air and they still are useful for that. And for kicking at the ceiling, which, however, I have not yet been able to touch. Some day I will. But that is not what feet are made for. I got hold of them one day, not long ago, one hand on each foot and I found I could roll and hold myself in almost a circle thus. And I do that a lot. But my ambition now is to get them into my mouth. I can't yet. My tummy or something is in the way. But I know now that that is what feet are for and I shall soon have them where they belong,—both in my mouth at the same time. How old were you when you first did that? And how old was my mama when she could do it?

The servants asked mama and papa for recommendations the other day and my papa did them some that made them laugh. But he would not give them up till Giulia and Giannina had promised to write a "recommend" for us. They promised and they delivered them today, very good things for us to show to other Italian servants. I am not mentioned, but, as my papa says, I am implied. So it is all right.

Packing will soon be over. Tomorrow comes papa's packing; which I really am curious to see; and then Saturday, when we are to start off to see the world. The last time I saw it I was inside my mama and the view was not so clear as it will be this time.

Your affectionate grandson
Pete

Hotel Auberson,
St. Cergue-sur-Nyon,
Switzerland,
June 8, 1925

My dear Mother-in-law:

In compliance with the terms of our implied agreement, I beg to report to you that we arrived here yesterday in good condition and feel this lovely morning that life is not so hard as some people seem to think or say all the time.

Our parting from the villa was sad. Peter was quite moved, Giulia broke into tears and ran into the kitchen, and even his lordship the gardener was unusually kind-eyed and haughty of demeanor. I felt it a bit. Pete alone was untouched. The car was piled high with baggage, most of it on the top; we drove slow and had an easy, pleasant ride over the now familiar road along the old shore. Everybody helped us at Ventimiglia because of Pete; for travelling I recommend a baby by way of a passport, lacking a French visa; better than bribery. . . .

Our baggage was all there at the frontier, the examination was easy and swift, and we arrived at Geneva at noon. And there was Yvonne with a car. We piled everything, except the trunk, into the car and off we went through Geneva in the sunshine with a fine fresh breeze blowing, up along the lake shore some thirty kilometers, till, all of a sudden we turned off into the country for ten kilometers,—all beautiful. Then we began to climb up a road that twisted around among the freshest of fresh woods which we drank in the green of to sate the thirst of dry, yellow Italy. We were hearing from Yvonne all about St. Cergue, the hotel, the village, the people and also about Yvonne and her business. She is almost completely recovered, as she knew she would be with weeks of this mountain air. We could believe it. It was bracing us all up. I held Pete high in the air to get the wind in his face and he laughed and laughed. We and Yvonne are the only guests so far, so we get all the attention of the whole staff.

Pete and I slept the afternoon away, Peter and Yvonne talked and unpacked and talked and walked and talked and had tea. After my nap I had a bath, which was like a revolution, and then we had a pleasant dinner, with a walk up the hill afterwards to the big hotel which is empty and its full view of Lake Geneva lying like a colored map far away and below us.

Pete is now lying outside on the veranda of my room bawling his head off while I am writing to his grandma. He was good all the way on the trip here, but was spoiled for plain living. He was with us all the time, received much attention and was held in the arms whenever he asked to be taken. The result is that now he is lonely. We have to break him in again; as soon as that is done, he says, he will write you all about it: some complaints of his parents, but in general good news.

Your son-in-law
L. Steffens

To Mrs. Robert M. La Follette

St. Cergue, June 20, 1925

Dear Mrs. La Follette:

The news struck up at me out of a tiny paragraph of two lines in a provincial French paper. It hit me hard. But the feeling I had was not so much sorrow as triumph. Bob is a victor, one of the very few. His life is a success. In an age when most "successful men" are the most tragic (or comic) failures, our Bob proved to us that a man can succeed,—in himself. And that is a triumph, because it is well-nigh impossible. Bob knew. You know. All the conditions of social living are against the development of beauty of character and the virtues we are taught to prize. It is foolish to be honest, it is dangerous to be loyal, it is called cowardly to be brave, it is patriotic to sell out your country, it is demagogic to serve the people: it is a disgrace to be such a hero as Bob was every minute of his fighting life, fighting for the American people whom he trusted as no other leader has ever trusted them. And he won his fight. He won it every minute; not as a battle or a charge, but foot by foot all the time.

But he did not win the people's fight. That remains to be fought, especially in America, where there is no people; but only farmers and workers, bankers and special interests. We differed, Bob and I, on how long the war of the people has to be carried on. But we did not differ in the faith that the war must and will be carried on, and I believe Bob will go on leading it. A man like yours does not die. In the first place, he has left two sons who cannot help carrying on, and I believe that the people who know what their father was will believe in his sons; even as you and I do. Young Bob and good old Phil are both La Follettes and certainly the people of Wisconsin know it. And then there is Bob himself. He lives in Wisconsin, his spirit is in his state as the spirit of the state was in him. That spirit will go right on growing there and spreading everywhere with the obstinacy and courage of "the" Senator who would not surrender and so cannot die. In a word: Robert M. La Follette is immortal.

But, Mrs. La Follette, I do grieve. I feel what you feel, the personal loss of his going, I sympathise with you and the family; but also I feel that you feel with me the grim triumph of the life you have lived with your life-long lover and partner. I would like to be with you and the boys and the girl, yes, and the little grandson, who are the personification now of the man I loved too.

Affectionately yours,
L. S.

To E. A. Filene

St. Cergue-sur-Nyon,
June 27, 1925

My dear E. A.:

. . . It is cold here now, almost down to freezing, but it has been warm,—in the mountain sense: sunny and comfortable, but invigorating. I don't like it, preferring warm climates like that of Italy, but it is supposed to be good for the baby boy, who (quite by the way) is as brown and hardy as a nut and more fun than anything I ever had to do with. He is much more fun than my bull pup was and develops faster than my history of Satan or even than my own wisdom. I want you to see Pete, who needs some spoiling. His mother is rather firm with him so that all the foolishness he gets is from me when she is not looking. He can't wink yet, but he can laugh, and his smile is corrupting. He learns fast; I have taught him already to pee in a pot; but I had to threaten him to make him do it. I tell him that if he can learn not to do it in his pants, we will send him to Harvard; if not, he goes to Oxford or Cambridge. We are very ambitious for him of course. He can be anything he pleases except a business man; he is to be absolutely free, but we prefer to have him become a lounge-lizard, preferably at the American hotels in Paris. A lounge-lizard makes lots of money very easily, and develops such a good opinion of himself that he must be happy, and parents (I now understand why) want their children to be happy.

But Pete himself has shown so far no clearly defined tendencies toward any calling. He says he is going to consult with you and some other of my friends before deciding upon his career. I advise him rather to look you over, not to consult but study you, and he may do that. If you see him look at you very hard, say nothing; you may feel comfortable in the knowledge that he is sizing you up.

I write at length, E. A., because I know you are a very busy man and you know how I feel that every minute I can distract a busy business man from business is so much saving to the world. I don't want Pete to do it. I want him to be wise. And I am foolish, like you, hopelessly so; we try to save the world because that is easier than saving ourselves. I still have not seen a French fisherman catch a fish.

Now you may go back to your work, E. A. I'll go and have a chat with Pete, who is doing nor good nor harm in the world. Yes, you must see and do try to learn from him how to get to heaven.

With the compliments of his mother, I remain,

Yours affectionately,

Lincoln Steffens

To Laura Suggett

St. Cergue-sur-Nyon,
July 23, 1925

Dear Laura:

Jane [1] was here the day before yesterday and I was delighted with her. She is so intelligent, and so quiet and natural about it. No bunk at all. It took her but a minute or two to accept me, and she opened right up; we had the beginning of a talk she had need of. It is about her. All these young people seem to want to know what they are good for. Isn't it amazing that our educational system drives no probe there, neither inquires nor leads the student to ask scientifically what

---

[1] Jane Hollister, Steffens's niece.

he or she is made for. Jane has gifts, she has general desires, but she neither knows nor knows how to find out just what sort of a life-work would satisfy that side of her nature. It is so of Ella Winter too, talents but no sense of her best "lay." But she has experimented enough to tell Jane how to experiment, quickly, and I could lead Jane to see into herself a little more boldly. I did it by opening up an irreverent insight into the profession she leans to. I got this out of it: that Little Pete shall be studied acutely for his gifts, sent to school with such a sense of what we don't know that he will be curious enough to study and learn and, I hope, with some idea as to how to get onto himself and determine what he can and would REALLY like to do. . . .

I have signed and returned today the lease for the Casa Montagu at Alassio; it runs from October 8th till June 1st. I am well satisfied; I have wanted to live in that villa from the day I saw it, two years ago.

The article I wrote on cable order for the *Cosmopolitan* is definitely rejected.[1] There seems to have been some strong difference of opinion among the editors; that caused the delay, but the decision came while Janey was here. I don't care much. I have made enough on Wall Street to make life comfortable for the present. . . .

To Allen H. Suggett

St. Cergue-sur-Nyon,
August 7, 1925

Dear Allen:

. . . You express a preference for Peter over Pete and Stanley over Peter. Right. My theory of names is that Pete himself some day will have and exercise some such preference. I gave him the two names, so different, in order that, if he becomes (as he may) a roughneck, he can be Pete; if he turns up a high-brow he can drop Pete and be Mr. Stanley Stef. I notice that people who see Pete, from Janey down, all take to the roughneck name; partly because he is so distinctly not a roughneck. He responds to it, knows it is his and tries himself to say it. He watches my lips when I pronounce it to him slowly; he moves his lips and then, when the word will not come, laughs aloud. I am afraid, for your sake, that Pete will stick: Pete, not Peter. Indeed, I rather think you will use it when you see Pete. There are lots of babies here and many nice people, but Pete is the most popular person

---

[1] "Radiant Fatherhood," first published in English in *Lincoln Steffens Speaking* in 1936.

at St. Cergue this year; he is known as Pete, and we, his mother and father, are spoken of as "the Petes." . . .

. . . Laura likes your interest in all the children; mine has been increased by Pete, who, contrary to Dot's prediction, makes me more, not less, radical and general in my ideas. When I think that some day "they" may be wanting Pete to go to the front for some oil concession, I get a very vivid picture of what war is for all children. . . .

We took Pete, who was especially invited, to visit Jane's friends [1] at the Château Rougemont. We got there in the afternoon, all went down to tea, and I suppose some trouble was expected from Pete. But he was perfect. "The baby that has no nurse," as they describe him, sat up, smiled at the pretty girls and laughed at the men, and then went off dry to be held out. All the girls went along and he performed according to expectations. Mrs. Breckinridge had never seen so small a baby so well trained. We all had a pleasant dinner and evening of conversation, and the next morning a sight of the old castle, which has been beautifully modernized. They drove us to the next station, where we lunched with Peter's mother and came home the same afternoon. . . .

To Laura Suggett

St. Cergue-sur-Nyon,
August 19, 1925

Dear Laura:—

There is no mail from home, no letter to answer, but I feel like writing to you. And I have nothing to say. A nice, a significant feeling, this; like that which makes one sit down to write a love letter; like going to call on someone we need and then sitting together saying nothing. I think you have it about me. I was thinking of it the other day, when I was trying to say to myself what my sentiment was for Little Pete. It was so like my feeling for you. Unlike my feeling for Peter or for G. I want something back from them. From Pete I get nothing back, nothing in kind. And then I thought of you, and how I wanted nothing back from you; it is enough to give. There is an exchange, a trade in "love,"—the love between a man and his woman, —but between the love of a father and that of a child, there is no such traffic. I don't mean that I get nothing back from you; I get as much as I give. What I am trying to say is that that is not necessary. And

[1] Mr. and Mrs. George Breckinridge and their children.

I rather think that along that line of thinking is the way to the conclusion of Chinese wisdom which sets up "friendship" in the place we westerners put love. Only the Chinese,—at any rate in California,—do not call it either friendship or love. I remember that the Chinese we knew used to speak of their cousin. A child they liked was their cousin; I was the cousin of the cook at the Zete House. Our servants used to say they wanted to go see a cousin, when they meant only a friend or a chum, in Chinatown. Well, Little Pete is my cousin, Jane is my cousin, you are my cousin, in this sense; and the point is that cousinship is deep down, enduring, unrelated to deserts or service or return; it is surer and solider than love. It is a nice thing, this irrelative relationship.

Jane is a person, not a mere niece; she and I would not have to be blood relations to be friends. She may think of me as her uncle, but she felt and she liked it that I took her in on the level. I liked the way she thought about things; she liked the way I talked about things. She expressed it when she asked me (and Peter) if I always talked with young people as if they were just people. And I do, I find. I do it with Pete. He fell over yesterday, bumped his head a bit,—his first fall, and surprised and hurt, he looked up to see whether to cry or,— what. And I laughed. So he laughed. Since I joke most of the time with him, he is becoming a jolly little fellow. He smiles at everybody and at most things he laughs; and his laugh is heartier than any laugh I ever had myself. I never learned to laugh, not all over the way Pete does. If he keeps it up he will enjoy life, seeing the humour of it where others see only the tragedy. A university could not hurt him if I can so prepare him for it that he will go through his courses laughing at his instructors and their instruction; and I think I can. He gives many signs of having a good natural intelligence. Of course I hardly know yet what or how to teach him, but whatever I do attempt he catches on to very soon. . . .

. . . The culture of orthodontia, to my way of thinking, is its teaching that men and women do not have to be all their lives as they are born or bred. Doctor can change and perfect the functioning and the form of their mouths and even of their faces, including looks, digestion, breathing and, yes, their temperament; for ease of breathing, etc., must affect the disposition. I would show Jack or Jo that Doctor's practise will rub it in: that man can complete, if he cannot imitate, creation; and having oneself got that into one's system, one can teach it.

But there is culture in every job. Farming, if scientifically learned and practised, teaches what can be done by breeding and conditions; painting teaches us that we can (and that we really have to) learn to see; running a library teaches all that governing might teach. What we lack is preachers to develop the knowledge men have into philosophies, applied and to be applied.

I must stop now. We leave here about the end of the month, partly to meet Jane in Paris. She wants help in her shopping, and I am good at that. I know where to get things. During the month in Paris, Peter will run over with Pete for a few days in London. After that,—Alassio for a solid winter of work.

Affectionately,
Len.

To Mrs. A. Winter
St. Cergue, August 19, 1925

Dear Grandma:

It's an age since I have written to you, centuries in the development of a man. My papa says I have passed through several geological and many more biological periods, and I feel it is so. And I am so glad that I have to tell you about it, though my papa says you won't be happy about it. But I sprinkle salt on his opinion and go right on believing in and thinking of and loving my only grandma. And I can trust him to report me right, for, with all his faults, he is a reporter and an American reporter, none of your English interpreters of the news for your *Daily Mail* or *London Times* readers, who can't be trusted to take facts raw.

But I have physical progress also to report. Not only in weight. My mama has told you how I have gained till now I am almost normal. But has she told you that I have found out what my hands are for? They are not to eat, as I used to think; they are to reach out with and pull to me things to eat. My soul is still in my tummy. But when I found out that I could grab things on the table or wherever I was, I was so glad. My papa and mama weren't, not exactly. My papa said he shared my pride but not my indiscriminate grasp; and things did fall on the floor. Yes, and jam did get all over my face, clothes and friends. But that was because I was not able, at first, to aim my hands right. I would shoot for something, miss it or, if I hit it, could not so

upper: LINCOLN STEFFENS WITH ANTON JOHANNSEN (Pete on his lap), ELLA WINTER, THERON AND NETTA COOPER, MAR-GARET JOHANNSEN (on arm of chair), CHICAGO, 1927. *lower:* 850 FRANCISCO STREET, SAN FRANCISCO, HOME OF ALLEN AND LAURA SUGGETT (house on right).

coördinate my movements that I could bring the tablecloth straight from the table to my mouth. But I am learning that now. It takes study, patience, persistence and great skill, but I shall get it; I am sure I shall soon be able to lift the breakfast table from where it stands so uselessly and put it into my mouth, which meanwhile I am enlarging as fast as I can. It seems affected the way grown-ups pick up each particular thing from the table and so one by one eat all they want. My papa says I am preparing for the wholesale business, and that is true, only why does he laugh? Why should one go slow in eating when he wants to go fast?

. . . Why do grown-ups grow up? And why, with all my clear perception of their bunk, why do I aspire to grow up? However, I will not annoy you with questions even my papa can't answer. I will proceed with my letter of love and boasting.

Socially I have progressed as much as I have intellectually. I know everybody here, which is more than my papa and mama can say; and more people know me than know them. I was toasted separately last night when they were giving out the prizes for the tennis tournament. The speaker of the evening held up his glass of champagne and said: "And here's to Little Pete." And everybody drank to me, just like that.

I am sorry to think that I am getting independent of my papa's services as a nurse. It is his fault. He shoves me off in my pram either outside the hotel or in the back garden, leaving me there alone to practice talking and wig-wagging with my feet and hands or, as he says, to learn to think; and I get pretty bored and wet.

But I am teaching my friends to beat this game. They used to stop on their way to poke me in the ribs or make faces (already sufficiently made ugly). Now I am teaching them to serve me more practically. There are some nice American girls here who at first would sit down by me to be entertained. I used to ask them to change me; in vain. So I cried one day. My papa came down to me and he scolded the girl that was there. He said rude things about the modern girl and what she did not know, and then he held me out and changed me. The girl brought the other girls and they all took a lesson in changing a boy baby. At first they were awfully careful about it, washed their hands after each change and otherwise were too dainty for words. As they got used to it, however, they liked it; there are now three girls who, to the envy of many more, can be counted upon to change me, certainly often enough, and I think too frequently. The result is, as I said above, that I am almost independent of my papa-nurse during the day. At night when my mama falls asleep and won't wake up, I still am dependent on him. But in the daytime I am free; . . . and I am and always shall be,

Your tough but darling little
Pete

To Ella Winter

Paris, Saturday afternoon, [Sept., 1925]

Dear Peter:—

  . . . I came downtown to the Continental, had a talk with E. A. till Delaisi[1] arrived. I left him to the mercy of E. A., whom I am to dine with tonight. Lunch I had with Jac at Victor's. There I heard all about Pete, whose friend, the headwaiter, was very attentive to me. Jac had another guest, a Mr. Frazier, who used to be first secretary of the U. S. Embassy here and now lives in the South of France. Jac and the headwaiter told him all about your call with Pete, and they praised Pete so extravagantly that Mr. Frazier, who has a baby himself, really inquired of Jac whether my baby was so wonderful. And Jac said he was, the waiter said he was, and I could see that they meant it. I guess it's so; that Pete is an unusual boy,—so far. Then they talked about you, Pete's mother, and I lost interest. It sounded as if I had nothing to do with Pete's wonderfulness.

  I have a letter from a fellow in the U. S. who says he saw a photo of Pete, liked it, and then he saw Louise Bryant, who showed him two photos of Pete. One was inscribed: "Pete hearing about the Peace Conference." He says he demanded to keep that, and Louise surrendered it. So Louise is carrying about pictures of Pete.

  Peter, dear, I'm afraid Pete is going to knock us out, put us in the background and leave us nothing but parents: Mr. and Mrs. Pete. Perhaps you'd better leave him in London. The English will reduce him to standard and give us a chance. But, then, perhaps you'd better not leave him. No, I'll take him back at any cost.

  Be sure I know what train to meet.

Stef.

[1] Francis Delaisi, author of *Oil*.

To Pete Stanley Steffens

Paris,
Tuesday, September 29, 1925

Dear Pete:

I have your letter, your very first, and by way of response to it, I command you to come right straight home. Sunshine in England! I know, my son, that you will have to learn some day to lie. You may go into business, you may be a politician, a diplomat, a lawyer; you may even become a gentleman and have to have good manners. But I am rather hoping you will be a writer of fiction or of plays, a painter or a sculptor, and you must not acquire the habits of success and polite society until we have given up all hope of your entering the arts or science. And in your letter you speak with pride of gathering crowds around you and winning them with your smiles. Oh, Pete! And you could not see that it was your smile that made the English think and tell you that the sun was shining; and in London, you said; every day!

I don't mind a certain amount of swanking. That is inevitable; you have got that weakness from your mother. It is legitimate, therefore, and harmless in young people. But you must understand that it is swanking, which is mere vanity, and by watching me, gradually overcome it. I did not run off to London when we had exhausted the power of Paris to admire us. No, vanity can be developed into a virtue akin to pride. . . .

The sun does not shine in England. It is against the law. It would be indecent to pour light upon the English. They are a respectable people; respectability is their one virtue. I don't know whether they are thus because of the mist and smoke that have always covered them over or whether the mist and smoke and rain and cold darkness have been sent by Nature to shield their shame. But I do know that the full light of the sun shining upon that blooming island would show them up in such a way that the world would be shamed by the scandal. No, my son, I can believe that the English mistook your bonny Italian radiance for sunshine, but I cannot forgive you for letting your grandma put the false notion over upon your sensitive young mind. You, an Italian, born and brought up in sunshine, should not be fooled ever,—not on that subject. . . .

I blame your grandma most of all. Evidently you trust your grandma! Don't. Please remember that she is also my mother-in-law, an institution which you will find literature clear and sound upon.

The seers have nothing but warnings against mothers-in-law. But she will be telling you that she is not your mother-in-law, but only mine, and she may add some remarks about sons-in-law and plead that she loves you. So I am bound to warn you that while she may love you as a grandchild, she does not love you like a son, I mean that she does not love you the way she did her own children. She is not so careful of you as she was of them. She took no chances with her own children, but she does with you. With her own children, she was correct in every detail, she did not indulge herself for a moment, she made a sacred duty of her devotion and would have felt it a sin to enjoy them as she does you. I must ask you, upon receipt of this,— unless you have already yourself felt the danger and left London for good,—I am bound to command you to pack up your nappies and bring your mother back to Paris and me at once.

Your fear-full father,
Stef.

I note that you sign yourself Peter Stanley. That's all right, if you want to. But don't let your grandma influence you. Tell your mama I got her Channel post-card this morning.

To Mrs. A. Winter

Villa Montagu, Alassio, Italy,
Friday, Oct. 9, 1925

Dear Grandma:

Ever since I got back to Paris from London, I have wanted to write you. I told my papa, so he took all the fun out of it. He said, "Sure, you ought to write your bread-and-butter letter. It is your duty." I had thought of it before with pleasure, as a natural way of tying up the sweetness of our visit together with the life I was living in Paris and this here. After my papa said that about "duty" and "what's done," my impulse changed and I had no heart in it at all. There were pleasant things to do, not duties, and when my papa saw how I felt he just grinned. "That is the way we grown-ups take the joy out of life," he said. "You might as well learn the game." I wish you would explain some of the life problems to me, Grandma.

Another thing, my papa said we were going back where I came from, to Italy, and I expected to get up and go. But no, one evening I was all dressed up, put down with a lot of bags in a box and papa called a taxi; we all sat perfectly still and then when Mrs. Yvonne and the other kind faces said au revoir and goodbye, the whole city of Paris started up and it went,—Paris, not we, went by,—to what people call a station. There was my Auntie Rosa. She helped me up into another box on what they call a train, and she also said goodbye; and that we were going to Italy. Well, I watched and again we did not move, not we. It was all France that moved, fast; it flew all night, all day till the next night when, about seven o'clock, Italy met us, Italy and the Italians, smiling as usual, kind, helpful. They did not bother about baggage. One of them held me to let my mama unlock a trunk, just one trunk, and when that was half opened, they said it was all all right,—they boosted us on a train for Alassio, and again I watched, and this time the Mediterranean flew by us to Alassio. I felt as if I had gone some, but I had not; not a step, and anyway there we were, and I for one was tired. Oh, I showed off in my bath; I didn't want to much, but there was a crowd watching, so I had to; but after I went to bed I fell asleep, a deep, very deep and long sleep.

And another thing, the next morning in the hotel where my papa says I used to live I was sick, my mama called it. But it wasn't me at all. I woke up all right and I smiled at my papa, but he looked at my sick stomach and the smile died on my face. I tried my mama, she was not the same. I picked up a toy, one with ducks in it that swim, and I had got interested in licking it up, turning it over and over first in one hand, then in the other; I had got so that I could almost handle it and meant to master the thing this winter in Italy. But, now this morning I not only could not hold it, I didn't want to. Everything had become all of a sudden a duty. The world was sick, not I, and yet They said I was sick. They had a doctor to back them up and so I appeal to you. What is sick? And who is sick when the milk is bad, when your own hand tastes tasteless and your parents are an irritation and a disappointment?

My papa stayed with me all the day. My mama was busy. She was absorbed in her unpacking. My papa stood by, let his unpacking go and just sat there, almost crying himself, listening to my mother digging out her things, putting them away and talking to herself about how good life is, how romantic this villa is and how she was blessed with a good husband and a *sage* baby boy! *Sage!* And there I lay and whimpered; I was so wretched and I had nobody to love me but my papa. And he was no use. He did absolutely all he could both physically and psychologically, gave me hot water and pity, but it was so that I discovered that I do not need a papa, I need a mama.

The proof of it came at the end of that terrible day,—a day I shall remember for several hours, I am sure. When the dusk was closing in and mama was discovering that many lights would not light and the house was feeling lonely and neglected like your poor little Pete, my papa got mad and said, "Pete, holler, holler as you never have hollered, holler long and loud; put gasps into it and sighs; try screams, and let's see if we can't make her come to us." So I did. My papa said I didn't do much, not half as well as he had heard other kids bawl, but I did not have to. My mama began to holler back to pick me up, cork me up, shut me up, and my papa did pick me up but privately in my ear, he told me to keep it up. And I did. I settled down into a regular cry which taught me what most babies know at birth: the efficiency of tears. My mama came. She did not feed me right away, though it was an hour after time and I had been fasting under the doctor's orders. She bathed me first and slowly; and I yelled bloody murder. And when she begged me to stop, my papa stood by me and said, "No, Pete, you holler your head off; it is the only way to get the attention of a modern mother."

I obeyed papa, who is all right intellectually, but what's the use of brains? When at last I had won and mama took me to her heart, fed me, wrapped me up and laid me away in my cot, I had for the first time that day a lovely sense of relief from pain and fear, and such a delicious sense of comfort that I rolled off the hill into the ocean of deep sleep. And the next morning, today, I appreciate my mama. I am aware I cannot ask too much from her; she has a lot to do and she says I have to learn to take care of myself, even to cure my own miseries and the great world-sickness which weighs so heavily upon my weak little tummy. My papa I can have at any time, and he is all right as another good-natured dub, but really he is as helpless in an emergency as I am. No. I hear him talk about fathers and the father-complex, but between you and me, one's mother and the mother-complex is the thing, the real thing, especially in families where it is the father that is busy and neglects the children. When my mother has time for me, she can do anything in the world, even to curing a belly-ache; and my father can't do a darn thing even when he puts in the whole day and his whole heart on the job. . . .

Pete

To Laura Suggett

Alassio, October 13, 1925

Dear Laura:

Two days we have been here, two days of unpacking, ordering and, —sickness. Pete was ill, for his very first time, and, for the first time, he was just a little baby. We took his temperature: 104. I sent for a doctor, who did not come till night, so all day long I sat there with the baby; not Pete, but a weak, suffering, little baby, who could not eat and slept only for an hour at a time. There were things to do, the house to see, a fight to make with the wretched landlady, who is really a Lady: the Hon. Mrs. Bruce, titled in her own right and the wife of the famous royal Scotch house of the Bruces. Well, I like that. I would like to tell about this British Lady in a story or an article. She would do nothing. There was no kitchenware in her "furnished house," no tableware, lights that would not light, stoves that would not cook or heat, repairs that were obvious, howling to be done; this on the surface and underneath,—awful. And all she wanted was her rent.

I did not care. The two servants that the agent, who hates Mrs. Bruce and likes me, had for us were good, as good as the old ones at San Remo, so after two days at the hotel I decided to move and in we came with the Little Pete still sick. The doctor ordered no food for one day more. He said it was nothing serious, and he was right. But,—I guess I am no good for a father,—I did nothing but sit with Pete. Peter said he should be left alone, that I would spoil him by answering every cry, every sigh, but I could not help it. When his mouth puckered, it seemed to me that it was not the physical pain he minded, but he was afraid to be left. Anyhow, I stayed right with him all day. And so the next day, when he got well and today when he is just as before, he cries whenever I leave him; he wants me or somebody all the time. I suppose we shall have to break him in again to be self-sufficient, and I am for that; it was wonderful to see him so independent. But what about the next time he is ill? The only solution I see is to keep him absolutely well all the time.

And that should be possible here. . . .

The Casa Montagu was built years ago, the garden is one of the oldest, but it is one of the highest villas here. There is no dust, therefore, the air is always fresh, clear, whether it comes salt off the sea or down along the coast and, facing south, the house has the sun all day; and, like all the Riviera places that know why they exist, both the house and the town are protected perfectly from the north whence the winds and weather from the high Alps come, the cold that makes Genoa and Florence hard winter climates. For you understand that this hill is the first of the foothills of the Alps. Pete has his own room wide open at night; there he sleeps alone in the dark at night.

We have set out to get back to the old routine, which was so good for him. We leave him a lot alone; he cries a while, then settles down to sleep or play. It looks and it certainly sounds hard, but it works. Yesterday afternoon, for example, we took him in his buggy downtown, and while Peter shopped, Pete and I watched the waves. He was fascinated for an hour, and he liked rolling through the queer old street; some village boys helped push him back up the hill, and that amused him. He had a good time and got nice and tired. But once back home and left to himself he kicked. He was allowed to kick till his bath hour, then he was bathed; he kicked on; then he was fed, and started out again to demand attendance. He was looked over carefully, seen to be all right and, when we went down for supper, Pete was shoved off into a dark room alone. I thought his heart would break, but Peter insisted and, sure enough, after no more than five minutes, there was silence.

I can see that there is a lot to learn about bringing up children and that one's sentiment and emotions are not sure guides. The hold Little Pete has on me is the most violent force that has ever gripped me. It could weaken me and be not good for him; I am afraid I would indulge too much. But Peter is firm with him, careful, thorough, but not a bit sentimental; the contrast, as the child must feel it, is clear, and yet he prefers his mother. Dressing him in the morning is always a scrap between them and I rather sympathise with Pete, who hates clothes, but when it is over and we both offer to take and play with him, he chooses his mother, who gives him a few minutes, much less than I give, and then slams him into his cot or buggy to fend for himself. I don't quite get it.

I have,—I am writing this in a room on the roof, which is tiled and fenced like a great veranda. It commands the widest view of sea and hills. . . . The only question is what I am to write. I don't know myself. I feel like a story; I have the lost chapters of *Satan* to rewrite and always there is the *Life*. I suppose that, deep down in my bones there is a decision, but I shan't know what it is till I sit at the table with paper and ink before me. Surely, however, I should produce something good this winter. Eight months of quiet, warmth and comfort; and beauty. There are drawbacks. The bath is a slow, hard problem of separate heating with no certainty of success; the equipment of kitchen, dining room and,—the whole house is rotten, and, as for the Landlady, she is a story all by herself. But the house is large, roomy, giving a sense of space and cool quiet, and the garden is a thing of loveliness, flowers and walks, pools and shade-trees. And then there is always the sea, the deep, still Mediterranean, blue ad infinitum. No, it is good; especially with Little Pete there to play with and watch make his discoveries, which are daily surprises to him and to me.

I wish I could hear from or about G. I know that she has adopted a policy and she will stick to it, but what is the use of taking a course in such a matter as this of ours? It may be all right with a child, like Pete, but among grown-ups sentiment can be trusted a little. It is the brains that spoil everything. I can help G., I could ease any pain she suffers alone and we shall always be friends. Why behave like strangers?

Len.

To Mrs. A. Winter

Alassio, November 18, 1925

Dear Grandma:

I have gone to bed myself. I had to; I got so tired playing with my blocks and my boxes that I had to leave them, drop into my Philomena's arms and be carried off to bed. I have never in my whole life been so worn out, physically and mentally. But I have told my papa what to say to you and he has promised not to change a word of it. Moreover I shall re-edit myself in the morning and see; and sign it.

I have to thank you for your birthday presents; yours and Uncle Rudi's and my nice Aunt Rosa's. They are lovely things. At first I did not realize that they were for me. My mama said, when the parcel was handed in, that it was Pete's; they discussed whether to open them now or wait for my birthday; and my papa said to wait. But my mama couldn't wait and I think my papa only wanted to annoy my mama. Anyhow he grinned and winked at me when my mama got the knife and ripped open the package. But when it fell apart I observed that he and the cook and Philomena formed with my mama a human wall between me and my presents from you. I did not get a look in. I heard the shouts and the rejoicing, the approval and the

irrelevant agreements about your good taste, but I was left sitting up
at the table in our chair, yours and mine, sucking a crust of bread
unable to see what it was all about.

I can wait, as you know. I have learned patience. I have had to. My
two parents go off and leave me to myself for hours at a time. They
quite forget me. I used to holler, but they never heard,—so what was
the use? I hear people say lots of times that Pete is a good baby, but
I can tell you that Pete's goodness is a matter of necessity, like most
good people's goodness. It certainly is not inborn. You can infer that
from your knowledge of my ancestors. I am good because my parents
are not good, as such. That's why.

However, they did finally remember that after all it was my birthday, that most of the things were, not theirs, but mine, and that I really
should have a sight of them. So they brought me in from the dining
room, sat me on the floor and dumped the whole load around me. You
can picture my amazement when my papa (for of course he had to
butt in) pulled out of one small box a lot of boxes which he piled up
till they were over his head. Then before I could get that through my
head, he takes a lot of blocks and piles them up over my head, though
I was sitting up on the pot with the frozen rim at the moment. Before I could make out what it was all about, my mama, who is forever putting on or taking clothes off me, got busy putting on the coat
you sent with the two pockets, the one from Aunt Rosa, and, to save
it, laid down the rubber sheets from some most foresightful friend.
They were waving a plate for me to eat or eat off of; it looks sweet
enough to be eaten, I think. I was lost in confusion till at last they
got tired, as grown-ups do of a sport, and left me to myself.

Then I made a study of Uncle Rudi's blocks and boxes, and I found
out what he likes such things for. I took each box out one by one till
I got down to the last one, then I put the blocks one by one into the
box and then one by one I took out the blocks and then by that time
it was night time for me and I had to go off to bed to rest up for
tomorrow when I shall renew my hard labor upon my birthday gifts
from my English relations in dear old London town.

But I dictated this letter on the way and in between and I want to
tell you that I have loved my chair and my pen. When they were
opened up I was allowed to be present and I saw them disentangled.
They were so beautiful that I thought they were parts of the scenery

and not of any use, but when I was sat up in the one so that I could eat on a level with the whole family and then, presto change, I was sat down low in it for coffee in the *saletto* [little salon], I was delighted. The pen too has a use. I have my carpet in that and I can play in it in my room, on the veranda or in the garden. I tell you, grandma, I am grateful. I think I am a lucky child, for while my parents are below the average, what my papa sums up as his wife's fambly is so far above that I feel I can look any kid straight in the eye and challenge him on breed and the weakness of my grandmother and her spoiled children.

My fourth tooth is out. There is not much debate about it any more. My papa still laughs at it, as if it weren't much to brag about, but my mama, she sticks up for it and I myself can feel it. Of course the other older teeth, they look down on the baby tooth, but let 'em wait. I myself, the whole of me, did not amount to much at first; and now look at me. I think my fourth nobbler will be a front-rank tooth,—some day. . . .

With love to my Aunt Rosa and my Uncle Rudi I remain

Your own grandson,

Pete

Pete's House,
Pete's Day,
[Nov. 21, 1925]

Dear Grandma:

Yes, I know. I wrote you only a day or two ago, but this is my birthday. You might not have known, except for the Christmas-look of my room, that it was. You might, had you been here, you might have inferred that it was the grown-ups' birthday, my papa acted as if it was his, my mama as if it was hers, and as for the O'Briens, I am sure they had the false impression that it was theirs. Mr. Fred, he did give me a toast with his old cocktail, but he never gave me a drink. And when my pop held up his champagne, he did remember me with a word, but not a drop, not one. However, I got the feel of a birthday, somebody's, and I had been told it was mine, so, when the table grew happy with the food and the drink and the talk, I hollered as I have never hollered before. Nobody would listen to me, but I did express myself and the spirit of the day; I did; I laughed and yelled so that finally my mama made my Philomena carry me into the next room where she choked me into silence with a bottle,—of milk.

After dinner those noisy grown-ups walked off around the garden and I played with my blocks and boxes and a duck that I can bring to me with a string, to the infantile delight of my proud mother, who says I am almost as intelligent as a chimpanzee. She sat me on my pot in the *saletto* where they all were, but she stuck me out of sight behind the door. I can shove my pot across the floor now, so I began to move out into the sun; that's all. But grown-ups don't understand much. When I hove into view they laughed. I thought they admired the way I could hitch the pot along the floor. Apparently that was not the point, for as I moved up into the room and then around and around they said things I couldn't understand either. I got so mixed up that I forgot to p and my papa had to take me out in the garden, hold me tight and explain that, after all, business is business, and I know what business means. It means do it and do it now. So I did, and Fred O'Brien says: "Well, I'll be darned; Pete knows that, eh?" As if I hadn't known that ever since I was a baby. . . .

Your affectionate grandson,

Pete

To Edward A. Filene

Alassio, November 25, 1925

Dear E. A.

. . . I have started my autobiography and it goes so easily that I have not rewritten a single chapter, hardly a paragraph, and I have done four chapters. I shall have a dandy chapter on you, a story all by itself, a story I have clean-cut in my mind. So I don't feel so much like writing your life. Just the same it ought to be done and you should do it yourself, with me for editor; not Frank. He wouldn't make you tell it; he also is discreet and not frank. The only way to tell your story is to tell it. However, you shall do as you like; I shall have the cream of it in mine, which I think, at the present rate, I may finish this winter. I would like to do your chapter now in advance so that you can see it, but I don't want you to kick about it. One of your fatal faults, one of the reasons for some of your failures, is your caution; you have never been a man that *They* had to reckon with; They could set you aside, as in the International Chamber, knowing you would not cry out, knowing you still would work for them. It is time for

you to make a mistake and maybe the only way is for me, irrespon-
sible anyhow, to make it for you. No one would blame you for an
indiscretion of mine, especially in a book full of indiscretions. My story
will be true. And yet you will find beauty and kindness and understanding in its truth, in its facts, in its muck. . . .

Lincoln Steffens

To Mrs. A. Winter

Pete's House and Garden,
November 29, 1925

Dear Grandma:

You remember those teeth that dug their way out of my tender little
gums. Well, and you remember that they hurt and that I came through
it all well and alive. Sure, you have not forgotten that. But I have to
tell you that there must be some more like those coming; I don't see
why. I can eat with those I have. I can bite off hunks of apple and
chew them till they suck down into my tummy like milk, almost. But
here come these other useless teeth; what for? My papa says they are
to develop my character which is built entirely on suffering. But I
never can tell what my papa means; can't trust him at all. Tonight, for
example, I was awakened by those new teeth; I was frightened, it
seemed to me they were going to chew me up, so badly did they hurt.
So I cried, and my mama and papa came running up to me. I thought
I would be comforted and my mama did grab me warmly in her arms,
but then she put me on my pot, which wasn't what I wanted at all.
And so, while I was saying so out loud, my papa came in and,—and,—
now you wouldn't believe this, if you did not know him as you always
told me you did,—he came in and he laughed, and laughed. And he
said that you, we all of us have teeth. He admitted that they were not
much use to a boy like me, but that it was the fashion to have teeth;
it wasn't done not to have them. I said that they hurt, but he said
that grown-ups all have things that hurt and that still are kind of nice
to have. I don't know what to say or think. So I ask you to put me
and my question down on your list: Do we all have to have things
that give us trouble and yet are nice or good form to have? . . .

I beg to remain, my dear Grandma,

Your loving grandson,
Pete

To Marie Howe

Alassio, November 29, 1925

Dear Marie:

Your letter, with all its suggestive questions,—it is all for my book, I know. Not to be answered now and here. But I can tell you that I can answer them very definitely, most of them, and it will interest me to do so. You are helping, as you meant to help. You are a good girl, almost as good as Fred is a boy. And that Fred is good even that stupid review that you sent us sees and reports. Maybe my prediction will come literally true. Fred's book [1] may make him president or something.

And, as for me and my book; ditto. I am midway in my boyhood story, but I can tell you already and Peter will back me up: Fred is a sour, hard-headed, bitter pill compared with me,—for sweetness. My long, curly locks and my darling innocence will move you, if not the world. The only hint of trouble, the only problem so far is my sad talk of how I was always being loved without loving back. But that prophetic note is not clear and sharp yet. No, the story up to now is tender, so tender that Peter cries whenever I read it aloud. Of course, as you can see, I am giving much more of my childhood than Fred did.

But what moves me, myself, to tears (of joy) in this work is, thanks to you and to Peter, I am not rewriting; I go straight on. The other day when I read two chapters aloud I could not stand certain passages, so I did rewrite them, and the whole thing will have to be written, really written some day. But I think I shall have these first, sweet chapters copied and sent to you to read just as soon as I can get at it. You are willing to edit and help; I am going to let you do it. Maybe I can make you let sleeping authors lie hereafter. . . .

Stand by to comfort Freddie as the reviews come in. His book is a great chance for all the wise guys to write as if they understand all about the world as we muckrakers exposed it before we did our work. They will not lose the opportunity he gives them to look down upon his (and my) innocence, our childlike faith and girlish ignorance. I felt like insulting or beating up the Strunsky ass, who does not even now know what Fred shows he found out. He says that his ideas are the same as ever; he never changed his mind. I believe that and I can imagine the dirty state of his head after all these years of no washing up and no new underwear. THAT man is the kind of dub that made

---

[1] *Confessions of a Reformer.*

reform impossible, that used to patronize me till I told them off. The intelligentsia! They shoot 'em in Russia; and I know why; they have to be shot every time the world moves, shot or crushed. I shall put him in my book, him and his crowd; all the ignoramuses that are so sure that THEY know. No, gimme the crooks or the honest men who are honest up to their brows, like Fred. And me, the sweet little boy that did get his hair cut finally and so went forth and took the world as he found it; not as it seems, but as it is.

Ask me some more questions, Marie. Love to Fred and you from all of us, all.

Stef Steffens

To Frederic C. Howe

Alassio, Dec. 6, '25

Dear Freddie:

There are letters from you and Marie to answer, correct or contradict: and, since I'm in bed (with a touch of pleurisy), I'll attend to them. And, since I can't very well typewrite, I'll have to pen it all. Maybe only Marie can read it.

First, about your book. It's no wonder to me that it is selling. It's an honest man's story, honestly told, and I think that they have had enough of personal (psychological, sex) confessions and are relieved to find an autobiography which reveals the world; not the author, except as a hero. Most of our recent confessions have made the hero a villain. Yours shows a (near) saint up against the wicked world. And, believe me, you do expose the world.

I think I shall imitate you in my *Life,* showing up the world and not me. And not only shall I spare myself, I shall also try to make myself out to be an innocent sufferer. My danger is overdoing it. You were, apparently, so unconscious of what you were doing that nobody (but me) gets onto you. I, having read your book, and tumbled to its cunning, I'm afraid that I shall seem (as I am) quite conscious. If we both are run for the presidency at the same time, you'll beat me. You'll get the popular vote: I'll get Wall Street's, who will think that they can do business with a slick guy like me.

. . . One question I'd like to ask you: Shall I say anything about my wives? I can see that if one does bring them in, truly, one cannot be a hero, unless one lies a little. That is bad enough when a fellow has but one wife to confess. But I have three to own up to the mistreatment of. I don't see how I can ever mention them. Do you? My wives had no part in the development of my discovery of the world. They are not essential to the story. It's all a mere matter of courtesy. You got out of it by dedicating your book to Marie. I can't dedicate it to any one wife. I evade that issue by dedicating it to Pete, my son, who made my book possible and purposeful.

Marie asks about the title for mine. I thought you all knew; it was chosen years ago: "A Life of Unlearning." But I'll listen to advice on that. If your title helped your book, I might make mine, "The Confessions of a Muck-Raker," or, even, "A Muck-Raker's Plea of Guilty," "A Muck-Raker's Apology," "My Apologies to the Muck-Makers," or "A Book for Marie and Peter," "A Warning to Little Pete,"—anything that will sell the book will do. I'm indifferent just now to anything but the fun of writing this story. . . .

Affectionately,

L. Stef.

To Marie Howe

Alassio, Dec. 23, 1925

Dear Marie:

Two inimitable letters from you yesterday, one for each of us; and one for me from Fred. And my answer, prompt and complete is this, the only copy of my first chapter, the angelic period. You are to treat it, not as a thing by itself, but as a sample of the tone, taste and content of the whole book. Of course you must praise it; since you have set out to make me do my *Life,* you and Peter, you cannot discourage me and yet you cannot let me get off on the wrong track. Some problem for you. The only solution I see is for you both to praise me to beat the band, but always sincerely, wisely, truly. In a word you must boost and I must produce work deserving of your inflation.

Don't you worry about my wives. I shall put them in as they bear upon my development outside. Josephine comes in exactly as you indicate by your questions. And her diary which she wrote, partly for me, I think, was certainly an epoch-making revelation of me to me. Maybe I never told you about that; it is almost a story by itself, one case where a man got his, really saw himself done to a turn. My remark about leaving out my wives was a subconscious expression of my sense that mine is not an inside but an outside story; the interest in it is in what one nice little boy, willing to learn and determined in his bones to find beauty, discovered of the world and life. But everything you say about it, Marie, is a help to me, a reminder and a push, just as all that you write to Peter is creative. We rejoice in your letters and when they are thick we call out the good news: "And a big one."

The best news in both your letters, yours and Fred's, is that you are back upon George Sand. Fred said you were writing again. You say you are assembling notes and that you are rather appalled at the detail and the work to be done. You might not feel that way if you would think of your story of her, not as a complete thing requiring a dutiful handling, but as a phase or a case, so that you can do little or much as you please. My sister Laura, who is an industrious woman who never idles and yet hates conscience and all labor, put our philosophy into a sentence once when she and some girls were putting over the hard work of a pleasant job in their state library service. One of the girls, tired out, complained of the work. My sister sent her home at once. "Why work," she said, "I never work, I always play." And indeed she does. She does what the children do. She plays a job is play and then she,—plays; until she tires, then she waits till it is play again. George Sand for you should be what my *Life* is to me: a great joke, a sport, a play. It is the first thing I have done for years for fun. George Sand, as you say, is an Old Girl who got up against the New Girl's problem. It was more impossible in her day than in ours and yet she solved it. The Old Boys of her day did not understand her and never did "get" her solution. Hence all their accounts of her are one-sided, unfair. They think of her as selfish and false to her selfish, false lovers. But today all the New Girls can understand this Old Girl's way out and, as for the Old Boys of our day, *they have got to*. See? Do it like that and you will not have to work at George Sand. . . .

Lincoln Steff Steffens

Alassio, Jan. 8, 1926

Dear Marie:

We wish you and Fred a new year of happiness and some work.

Your two letters are here, with the ms. of the first chapter of my *Life* safely enclosed. Thanks. Really. You are helping me. Your criticisms are encouraging and I feel that so far they are sincere. Best of all, though, are your questions, Marie. They are pertinent, searching and very suggestive. Indeed these in this last letter (with the first chapter) make me want to answer them here in this answer. I have to remember that you don't want the answer now and here, but in the story, and they will have to be inserted there.

My grandfather, for example, had that habit of brooding thought which I have and which my father had to such an extreme that it worried my mother often. With me it is a kind of thinking that is inexpressible in words. It is rapid, wide and confused; it takes in apparently unrelated subjects so far apart that it gives me a pain in my stomach. As a matter of fact it is more like digestion, but it has results.

The worst case of it was the Russian Revolution, which seemed to me to require a complete change of my mind, just, for example, as Einstein's relativity does. Nothing that I used to think could stand in the face of that Russian experience, nothing that Fred thinks in his book is left to me. Liberalism is gone. I could not have talked fast enough to anyone to mention in a flash as I "saw" it, the details of the wreck of my political philosophy in the war and the revolution, AND the threads of the new, and better, conceptions which lay mangled but traceable in the debris. I was alone over here when I was going through that process, not of thought, but of psychological revolution. I mean that I must have appeared to an outsider as my grandfather and my own father appeared sometimes to me when they were brooding. That is what my mother called it and that is what it was. Is. I must tell more about it. But later. As I write about my boyhood I seem to get back into the merely wondering mentality of that age; if I put in comment it is because I have reread what I wrote and seen it with my present mind. I doubt that I should do that. I am not sure,—I am asking you,—whether it were not better to run along like a boy until I actually did look back and see what it all meant, and then interpret.

I am glad, Marie, that you are back upon your job. And such a good job. To have to tell about a modern woman, of today, as a complete history of a woman of the past! Don't get too interested in the controversies about her. Never mind whether she was cruel to her lovers or no. She was a woman, just like you and Peter, and she set out to live her own life, have what she wanted. George Sand, the Woman of the Future,—a good title for you; or, at any rate, a good subject. The only theory I would like to see added to her story,—if you find any facts for it,—is that such a woman ought to be a glorious wife for any man that is up to her level of development. Maybe there is none. I would not be. I can see, I could not love such a woman, but I could, if I could "think" along the line of personal relations as rigorously as I have my own political line. It is a matter of attention and you can, with your George Sand, get and fix the attention upon personal relations of both men and women.

You have my second chapter now. Peter is giving to the typist today the third and the fourth. All of these are sketches; they all have to be rewritten. It seems fierce to me to pass on to new chapters with old ones as bad as these,[1] but it works and I shall stick to it.

Affectionately,
Steffens

Alassio, Jan. 12, 1926

Dear Marie:

. . . The best news about our trio is your second chapter and your improving grip on the essence of your job. The second chapter, which is gone back to you, is a perfect piece of narrative, perfect in development of both story and character, and a model for the following chapters. If you want to see an example by someone else of what you are doing, read Strachey's *Queen Victoria* again. Straining a multitude of facts to get the current of a theme yourself you will appreciate how much he read and how much he rejected to keep his illuminating tale simple and yet complete. I found out what that sort of scholarship meant when I was doing my cities, making a short article out of a bookful of stuff. But I discovered a trick to help me. I would feed up on Cleveland or Philadelphia, then go away home and there, away from the data, away from the temptation to get more and to write all, I let my memory edit the stuff. My memory proved a good editor, better than my conscious judgment. I wrote only what I could not forget, the *unforgettable;* and that told the story every time. I suggest that some time when you are filled full of the stuff for a chapter or two you leave your authorities, come down here and write what you remember. There may be some dates or phrases, some minute points you will have to look up again. But them you can leave blanks for and fill in when you go back to Paris.

"No," you will say, "not now." And I agree, not now. My advice is to go on now till some day when you are distracted by the mass of stuff and then try my method. . . .

---

[1] These were the chapters as they now stand.

To Mrs. A. Winter

Alassio, January 12, 1926

Dear Grandma:

I haven't written to you for some time, not since you wrote to my mama that you might not come here to see me. That surprised me very much; not my papa. He laughed and said: "Ah, ha! Didn't I tell you?" That hurt too. For some reason I don't like to have my papa turn out to be right, especially when he talks about human nature. Your thought of not coming to see me,—that, he said, was the way with human nature.

"You must study man," he went on happily. "You should watch your fellow men carefully and you may even love them, as the Book says. But you must not trust human nature; it will always go back on you, and if you have learned as a child to put faith in it, you will suffer what human nature calls a disillusionment, which is the Main Street slang for getting rid of bunk."

"But," I says, says I, "I am not talking about human nature and Man. I am suffering from a slight by my grandma. Grandma isn't human nature, is she?"

"Yes," he answered cheerfully. "A grandmother has more human nature to the cubic stone than any animal in the world at present. They are a sort of accumulation of precipitated human nature concentrated to the nth degree, and I am glad that you have found out so young the scientific and poetic truth about yours. When a fellow gets his disillusionments young he becomes used to them and so learns to take the unexpectant scientific view of things without bitterness. If your grandma shall have taught you not to trust her or anybody else thus in your second year of life, she will have rendered you a great service."

I asked him whom I could trust, for I have to lean on someone, and he said, "Your parents, Pete, especially your dear father."

Well, it was that that made me write again, that and the pair of creeping pants you sent me. Since I cannot trust my papa; he is all very well to play with; almost as much fun as the kitten they have given me; but I can't put my faith in a thing that he says, so,—I had to hang onto my grandma. And you do understand a feller. That's what the pants show. I have been creeping of late. I can go it fast and far, as far as there is an open door and as fast as is necessary to escape my guards. I go on two hands, one foot and one knee, which my parents and servants think may be a sign of originality. . . .

And I have to show you that Pete can now go dry from seven to ten and from two to six or seven. Which shows that there is some American in me; I am not all English, and, as for the German, that is a secret and must remain so till the next war, when my untrustworthy papa says the English will be helping them (us) to lick the French. He says the English policy is to help each nation to wipe out every other people till there will be only the English left. Yes, and he says you like the English and their policies and their morality, which he says isn't morality at all but the reaction from their conduct in private life and public schools. Do you?

Well, dear Grandma, there is the call to supper. Chow, chow. Pete must leave you, all but his heart. With love to my uncle and aunt,

Your affectionate

Pete

To Marie Howe

Alassio, Jan. 23, 1926

Dear Marie:

. . . I do appreciate your interest and the thought you are putting into my job. Your amendment about going into and finding company in my own mind I accept. I meant that, and I have no fear at all of being egotistical. The boy I am writing of seems to have no connection with me. I could praise him without a qualm. As a matter of fact I am showing what a goose he was, how slow my realistic intelligence was to develop. I was always naïve; I am yet in some things. And I have never been disillusioned,—tragically; not so that it hurt, probably because, as I tell in the next chapters (going with this), I began to have my idealizations crushed early. The racing chapter will tell you what I mean. I am glad you don't disapprove of my mature comments here and there. They just occurred, as you guess, and I don't think myself that one minds that some of them are of today, some of earlier periods, some childish. I find that I write sometimes now as if I were the boy, naturally; I get back to that state of mind actually. Sometimes I am an outsider telling about the boy. What of it!

. . . I am glad you held out against Wells' wish for a fiction story about G. Sand. Novels are becoming more and more autobiographical these days and Lives are becoming fictionized. They will meet soon.

We shall be having Lives written not at all as history; history will remain another, and probably a more scientific thing; but writers will use the facts of a period or of a person as material for a freely imagined biography, and I think that Marie Howe's *George Sand* will be the first one. You know what I mean by freely imagined. Shakespeare did his plays that way. He took what he could get about Caesar, grasped the man and his story, picked the guts out of it and then wrote a play as free from the historian's meticulous caution as a novelist writes an invention. He got the present meaning out of his stuff, as Shaw did out of Joan of Arc and as you are out of George Sand. All I would ask for further is that you go on working, not for precision (though your conscientious care is artistic as well as scholarly), but to discover what Shakespeare got and Shaw may have missed: the eternal meaning of Sand; her meaning as a human as well as a woman. However, I would not hang on hard even for this. You are doing it right, dead right, and well, so that what I would stick for is that you go on as you are going: doing just what your art sense demands, with no respect for old forms, opinions and traditions.

. . . George Sand, as you open her to me, is fighting, not only for what every woman should have, the chance to find and be herself in every way, but for what men also should have. Women are in error, in my judgment, in asking for what men have. In the first place men have not what they want or need and in the second place women have some peculiar requirements, which they can get only when they make the double fight: women's rights for women as such and human rights for women and children AND men. Take economic independence, for example; men have it not. They have jobs, but their jobs are their slavery. A man also has to win his economic independence. Fred got his and I got mine,—under our system,—but we also are gripped by the circumstances of our money and money-getting. We are merely Greek freedmen in Rome. We and you, George Sand and all men and women, have economic independence to achieve for everybody.

To E. A. Filene

Alassio, February 7, 1926

Dear E. A.

Your letter came to me this morning as a shock. I had no idea you were not perfectly well and then comes this information that you have been seriously or at any rate painfully ill. I am going to ask you to arrange somehow so that if you are ever ill again I may be told. There is nothing I could do; I am not thinking now of being of any use; it is simply that I want to know and, let me say baldly, that if there is anybody in the world that has a right to know how you are and not to be ever surprised about you, it is this same me. We are and we always have been much more related than you have realized; we are really friends in these days when friendship is rare and our friendship is built solidly upon understanding; not agreement in ideas and not mutual interest but instinctive comprehension of what each other was and was up to.

However,— Now that you are well, why not come over here to us? People like to come to us; they seem to think we are so happy, all three of us, that we spread it around. You will be surprised at our visiting list. Leon and Mrs. Graves (a Pinchot) drove over from Nice to have lunch with us, and more amazing still Mrs. Harry Payne Whitney came over by train from Bordighera to see us and Jo when he was here; and she, looking over the garden and house, the sea and the woods, turned to Jo and said: "Why haven't we the sense to get something like this?" So I say to you ditto: why don't you have the sense, etc. But I know the answer. People who have developed their wisdom in the service of the public or of others have none for their own uses. That's why writers are fools in their private lives; they can tell the reading public what to do, but they themselves cannot do it. . . .

I may have to go to New York. My *Moses* will be out this year and publishers are after my *Life*. Macmillan cabled for it; I was amazed at that, but everybody seems to be sure my *Life* will go. Those who have read the first nine chapters already done think I should make it a book only of my boyhood; they so like the stories in it. But then I have got on only to my fifteenth year and what follows is better still. Anyway I may have to attend to the serialization and other related business connected with this book.

Your two suggestions are in that direction. The *Survey* could not afford to pay me enough to come back to New York just to write such stories as you want me to do for them. I used to do them on my newspaper, and the readers loved them; they were circulation-builders. And they were just, more just than the law. The true story of a crime tells exactly those human facts which are, under the law, not evidence: the facts that explain how the evil happened to be done. The last one I ever wrote was for Glenn Frank; it was about Sinclair and the Oil scandal, and I tried to show in that case what I learned while muck-raking from all sorts of accused and guilty business men and politi-cians: that circumstances, the conditions under which business has to be done, must bear part of the blame for their crimes. This is not only true and just, but it is a fine, human, dramatic way to teach the public gradually to cease from lynching the villain and look for the cause of evil-doing. It is the lesson I learned so slowly as a journalist but which, when I did finally get it, put a stop to my muckraking.

As to your life, this letter shows that it should be done. What you say so sincerely about your failure is evidence enough for me that you are ripe for the job. Only you must stop having doubts about the com-pleteness of the failure. The whole point is, not that you failed, but that we all fail as you have. Your story has value because it is so com-mon. Your boast can be mine: we know what the successful men do not know, that their successes also are tragic in their disappointment. If I did yours, I would want to go on and do others: Owen D. Young, Wilson, Gary, Rockefeller. The difference between you and your brother, Lincoln, and the other partners, and most other men I know, is that they did not see enough of what they had to do to succeed to know that they have failed.

But this letter is getting too long. Let's wait and meet and talk; and soon. Why not come early to Europe, drop down here in the sunshine and all work out our problems together. And, E. A., one of our prob-lems is to make wise and beautiful the last period of our lives, age, the best of all. I have some ideas on that, some that you need. As you need sunshine and as you need the love I—we can give you. Little Pete alone is worth coming to see; lots of people will tell you that. His only competitor on this earth is the sun; they rise and set together, they shine upon the just and the unjust; I mean Pete will smile upon you as he does upon me, regardless of your lesser merit.

But do give instructions that, if you are ill, I am to be told. See?

Affectionately yours,

Lincoln Steffens

To Hutchins Hapgood

Alassio, February 7, 1926

Dear Hutch:

You are a good friend; I mean that you are a cracker-jack advance agent. I knew before this letter of yours came in that you had been at work. I had a cable from Macmillan and a letter, with a gift of books from Liveright, asking for a chance at my *Life*. This is a great service, Hutch: publishers and editors seem to have the rather common human tendency to prefer what they go after to that which is offered them.

You yourself need have no fears as to the character of my *Life*. It is far enough along for me to see what it is going to be. Though I have done nine chapters and all are about my boyhood it has taken form and shown its own disposition to talk about men and women in their human phases. It is not muckraking, philosophy or even fact knowledge. I think it is an understanding story which anybody can read and like and join in on. Indeed so far, it is a series of short stories, some of which you know: about me and my pony and my colt and my boyhood friends. Marie Howe, who has seen what is done, thinks it could go out as a story of boyhood,—a classic, she calls it, but of course I mean to tell how the fool boy hero of it discovers the world bit by bit; he was looking for the "good" and found nothing but the beautiful. The optimism of it may affront you; it certainly will astonish my old readers.

We here are all busy. Peter, my wife, is writing a novel about a little girl; a good thing, very true and searching and fine. I am writing daily, as you know; and both of us are attending to a garden, a house, and to,—Pete, who in turn is absorbed and absorbing in his business of growth. He is a bully boy, Hutch, healthy, happy, bold.—

On this theme, Pete, I could write pages; and I find I do, even to people who don't care a damn. So I have learned to mention Pete last and then stop off short, just like this. He,—

Give our love to yours, and come when you can. AND thank you for your boosts. You know how to help.

Affectionately,

Lincoln

To Horace Liveright

Alassio, [Feb., 1926]

. . . But I want now to talk about two other subjects. Fremont Older has offered you the story he published part of: Jack Black's *Life*. Take it. It is, as you see, a fascinating narrative and an amazing revelation. How do non-writers manage to set things down so—artfully? Any novelist or tale-teller by profession would be proud to tell a tale so well as Jack has done his story. I find by accident that girls and other people who know nothing of the underworld waited almost panting for the sections of the serial as Older published it. It is a new and a romantic world they see in it and a drill in tolerance and understanding. But there is another aspect of this book that hits me hard, one that the preface or introduction must bring out. This is not the confession of a penitent or a sick burglar. We are learning to understand that some crime is due to abnormal states of being which require, not punishment, but medical treatment. Darrow has rubbed that in in his most celebrated cases, and the world is coming to take a scientific view of such cases and is providing gradually hospitals for the criminal sick.

Jack Black presents another kind of case. He shows that he is not sick or even weak; a man who can cure himself of the dope habit is an example of health and more; Jack Black is an exceptionally strong character. He can, at will, rob houses or not, eat opium or not. He knows and he tells of other such men. What are we to do about this sort? Them we can imprison and punish, surely. I mean that if there are human beings to be treated by our old penal system, Jack and his pals are the ones.

But Older has treated Jack in another way, and won out: he has made Jack an unusually useful citizen. Older has done with this able man what Ben Lindsey has done for twenty-five years now with strong, bad boys. Ben has specialized in strong boys; he dropped the old category of "good" and "bad," adopted his own of "weak" and "strong" and discovered and announced that the strong boys, who did the worst "crimes," are the best boys. And I say that they make the best men. Jack Black illustrates this truth which the world has to learn now as well, and better, than it has learned about the weak, sick and medical cases. The problem is, What to do about the Jack Blacks and the J. P. Morgans, the Dick Crokers, Murphys and, also, the Sinclairs (oil magnates) who now do as much harm as they might do good?

Take Jack Black's book, see that Older or whoever writes the introduction presents cleanly the controversial point that I suggest, and you can draw out comment which will circulate the book and let it do its work, a most useful and exciting service. I think that the Jack Blacks have to be got early, when Ben Lindsey gets the bold boys of Denver, and assigns to them jobs that require all their strength, nerve and abnormal vitality. If I can contribute to the introduction or by comment outside help to arouse an interest in this book, I would be glad to do so, and Older and Jack Black would let me willingly, I am sure. But my first purpose is to have you, whether you take it or leave it, not miss the fact that you have on your desk a new kind of criminal confession, a new sort of author with a new problem. You should know Black as I know him; he is one of the most interesting and impressive men I have ever met. I can sum up my estimate of him by saying what I have said to Jack himself; I want him to have charge of my boy's character education for a year or two in the hope that the little fellow may "catch" from him some of the dignity, honesty, loyalty and self-control of Mr. Jack Black.

Hutch Hapgood would "get" Jack and his book, and would have to help us put it over. And there are others, many more, who, once tipped as to its significance, would boost this burglar up to his best job, the burglary of the house of Respectability of all its moral jewels, cash and clothes.

Sincerely,
Lincoln Steffens

To Marie Howe

Alassio, February 8, 1926

Dear Marie:

You have returned my last chapters, with your comments, and so have caught up with and passed me. I have no more ready even for the typist. It means a respite, but not for long. I am sure to go on with it to the end, though it is going to be hard to keep the balance later when I get into things all men know, have to reveal them as they came to me and show how they disturbed me, changed my picture of the world; and then how I went on writing one way after I began to see more as I do now. I had to see Tom Johnson through, and Frank Heney, and the rest. I had finally to stop writing articles and turn to fiction.

Fred, who has written me a fine long letter, thinks I would better cut the sex paragraphs. Fred is right in this, that I am not an expert on sex; I have little understanding of love to contribute to an oversexed world. But the incident of my childhood, when the neighbor's bad boy showed me things I could not grasp, has a light to offer later. As I grew up I discovered, somehow, that men and big boys disassociated the romance and the animal sensuality of love. There are men who cannot love fully a refined woman (their wife, for example) and so seek out now and then some gross creature who represents to them what sex is to them; a rather dirty, loose thing of vice. I was started off in this direction by that first experience of mine which coupled dirt and disgust, a sort of horror of fascination, with my image or sense of love.

Also I want to bring out that men suffer all their lives from being loved too soon and too easily by their mother, sisters and first sweethearts. They don't have time, they don't have a chance to learn to love. They go on through life getting love and missing the greater joy that women have of giving it. The best rectification I have ever had is Pete, who lets me love him more and more and ever more, and does not return any but the slightest affection. And, as I get at last my chance to court and to give affection, he is losing it,—so far as I am concerned. I hope to demand love from him later, for his sake. I don't want him to miss loving. I would like to make of Pete a perfect lover of women, emotionally, respectfully and (technically) physically. And Peter will help there. I notice that even now, she is as much more like the typical father, who does not indulge his love for his baby, as I am more like the typical mother. I mean that I think that Peter will give Pete a chance to do some of their loving.

At any rate these two lights I have to throw out for the dub male lovers, who really do not know how to love, who satisfy no women therefore, and are so conceited that they are sure that they know all about loving and therefore will not study the subject. However, this might be a separate essay or story. It need not go into this book. No one expects from me any ideas on this subject and these moot paragraphs will not be missed from a book of mine. As a matter of fact I got them clearer from an American woman, who learned them from her French lovers and is now teaching them to rich American men at very high prices. I must tell you about her some day. I really think she has the stuff wherewith to help solve the marriage question for America.

Now for your new George Sand chapters or parts. Your story of the helplessness of Alfred and the sage, intelligent consciousness of George is magnificent to me because I see it as typical of the male and the female. I remember how surprised I used to be when my wife, Josephine, after a dinner with guests, would sit down and relate incidents that I had not seen at my own table. I had been talking or listening, following the spotlight through the conversation, as if all that happened must be what was enacted in the centre of the stage. She had seen back of the lights and, by Jove, she had both what I had and what she (and probably the other women) had also. Well, Alfred and George are just like that. He is being himself,—alone. He and most men would say he was single-minded, honest, rational and,—a lot of other fine things. You show the truth, the universal truth: that she, the woman, was all that he was, and more; she let him play his childlike pranks, she joined in and played them too; she was herself as well as he was, but also she was on to him and herself.

My theory is that the woman's mind is as maternal as her body and her heart. She knows that a poem is a poem (not a reality) as well as she knows that her poet is also a dub or a baby. She will jump off the cliff in passionate imagination, but she knows that if they jump off bodily they will be killed or mangled. The trouble with your example of the common relativity of man and woman is that it is extreme. Alfred is such a child that all the other men who are like him will see, not the resemblance, but the extravagance of his conduct, which they will call exceptional and so miss seeing themselves. Peter thinks you are too keen for your propaganda; I think you are not keen enough. You have shown who is at fault in this story; absolutely. You have settled the controversy between Alfred de Musset and George Sand. You have not yet shown what is the matter between John Smith and Mary Brown. I don't know how to make us men see ourselves in Alfred and our wives and lovers in this Sand woman who saw all around her lover; and liked his weakness and folly so much that he had no chance either as a man or a lover or a poet. Maybe George Sand said something at the time or in her novels to enable you to put it over on us.

Anyway, keep this in mind, as you go on: that women do see and understand more in a situation or a relationship than a man and that, having the greater intelligence, they are at fault for not using it on their men. They have no business to love their idiocies; they have no right to mix up their maternal and their wifely love. I don't know what they should do. But I do think sometimes that wives and mistresses should begin to beat their husbands and lovers. Your job, however, is to make us see ourselves in Alfred and to make women see themselves (and their responsibility) in George Sand.

But enough. Peter is reminding me all the time that I ought to be at work. She should be warned by some wiser woman that a wife should avoid identifying herself with her man's conscience. She says it is all right to write to you, but all other letters are violations of my duty to my publisher. I sometimes think that she, like George Sand and her protagonist, sees all around me and so notes well that some letters are excuses to get out of work. No matter; however, you should tell her to lay off my conscience, for no he-man likes his conscience; it is the intelligent part of him, the effeminate streak that disturbs his— childishness.

Yours affectionately,

Steffens

Dear Marie: Alassio, February 14, 1926

. . . Love is coming of age. There are men and women who do not go blind drunk on love, but can see themselves in the throes of that primitive passion and, in some measure, control themselves. Love will include the intelligence some day, and some other day it will include the affection. The old, wise Chinese do not write poetry about love till it becomes friendship. But that is because, not only the race over there is grown up but the poets also. Poetry is not left to boys and girls; some old men write it. Read Chinese poetry and see for yourself.

I expect to tell in my chapters on my college days how the very clever boys, finding they could get "through" without working, loafed and did not learn. Poets would not study. Oh, they read poetry, played with prosody and did their jingles; all easy. But they took no interest in biology, physics, chemistry. I did not notice that this mattered till here of late when I have been reading and trying to understand the discoveries in relativity and in the construction of the atom, ideas which alter our whole conception of the universe. I cannot get these ideas, I can't see these pictures. The writers themselves, who set out to tell me about them, say that they cannot convey what they mean be- cause they do not themselves SEE the new world. Most of them de- clare that only a mathematician can grasp indirectly the formulas which arise from and imply the truth. But one of them says in so many words that the real reason is that poets won't work in their field, which suffers from the lack of constructive imagination.

Poets won't work in any field. The realm of poetry is science. There is where the beauty is, and romance and adventure and light: in mathematics, history, biology, chemistry and physics, but the De Mus- sets, running around with their hands (and their minds) on their genital organs keep on singing of their loves and their doves just like the children poets of old. And the novelists too. Some of these have dabbled a bit in psychoanalysis but, for the most part, they are all like the gifted versifiers in college. They can get along so well with so little that they have no incentive to work. De Musset was a waste simply because he was content to blow off what he had; he never learned anything, not even of love; his loves were all like this one, I am sure.

So I say skin him alive. . . . I think women have to put science and art into love if not into living too. Men never will.

Alassio, April 3, 1926

Dear Marie:

. . . And don't you think for one minute that I am not eager to have money for little Pete. I am for economic independence for women, why not for my own son? I got mine early and it cost me something; I want Pete to have it from the start at no cost to him. The theory that a boy or man is "made" by the struggle for economic independence is one of the bunks. As a radical I am for a world in which no one is to HAVE to knuckle under and slave for his living; I believe that when men do not live under such a compulsion they will be better and make a better world. As I was rehearsing before my Peter tonight; our intention to leave Pete free of money cares means that we have to educate him to survive it and that can be done by stimulating into a ruling passion, the curiosity which makes him open closet doors now. I expect never to tell Pete anything satisfactorily; I shall answer any questions of his that burn, after they have burned a while, but always with a lead to another question which may keep the fires burning.

Children do not ask questions for information except as fuel or food for their minds. They do not want to know, they want to find out things, and when we in the schools and colleges give them knowledge we do exactly the wrong thing. I would not tell my boy about the stars; I would prefer to ask him about them and when he had read or otherwise got enough to appease his curiosity about the heavens I, on my side, would try to show him how little was the information he had, and go on to indicate what no one knows, what we and the astronomers are asking, and so open his mind to the unsolved problems of astronomy. The unknown in all the sciences is what I want my boy to know; not the known.

I can't see how a boy brought up on that principle could use money in any way except to free himself to explore, whether in the arts, politics or science. Explore and marry or love and have babies and fun all his life. No indeed. I would not be so happy in Pete if I thought he would have to serve the slave-drivers and soul-suppressors and the standardizers. I watched him asleep today; he had been swimming in the sea with Peter and was done up. It was perfect abandonment and trust in us. And I thought: "You are all right, Little Pete, trust me and you will be able and free and intelligent some day to tell the ——s to go to hell. They cannot work you." I don't want any more money for myself and very little more for Peter, but for Pete,—yes.

To Mrs. A. Winter

Alassio, April 3, 1926

Dear Grandma:

I haven't been thinking of you lately. That's why I haven't written. We have had company. . . . And I can tell you that while the crowd was here, while I was so busy I,—like my papa and my mama,—I kept on with my work. I had taken some steps before to learn to walk; while they were here I perfected myself pretty much in walking. It was safe, you see. With everybody sitting around the room, expecting me to entertain them, I could start from anyone and walk or run to any other one. I don't know whether you remember it, but walking is a process of falling. You stand up straight, balance a moment, then you lean forward as if to fall; and then instead of falling and to save yourself from falling, you just rush to someone ready to catch you. It is most thrilling, because of the risk. . . . And I have got on to another trick: I stand up behind my pram and push; it moves and I follow, walking, and the silly grown-ups shout and call it great. But you know and I know that while I push the pram I am really holding on for my life and so the pram keeps me up while I exercise my leg muscles.

I can do other things, some of which a careful grandma would not permit. Even my parents don't like it, but when they are at work and not looking, I can climb all the way up the marble stairs, not only to our bedroom floor, but on another flight up to papa's study. It is wonderful, because, you see, if I once lost my balance I would tumble all the way down stairs and probably break my head. You would not mind this; like me, you don't think brains very important, but it trou-

upper left: ALLEN H. SUGGETT AND PETE, SAN FRANCISCO, 1927.
upper right: LINCOLN STEFFENS AND PETE, CARMEL, 1928. *lower:*
JO DAVIDSON, H. G. WELLS, AND LINCOLN STEFFENS, BECH-
ERON, FRANCE, 1930.

bles my papa, who says if I break my brains, I might have to become an Englishman. . . .

Pete.

To Allen H. Suggett

Alassio, April 4, 1926

Dear Allen:

. . . Day after tomorrow is my birthday; I shall be sixty years of age. I don't feel sixty, today; I may two days hence. Certainly I shall begin some day to feel old and I have a hunch now that I may want to return to California then and live happy ever after; no more foreign business, no more travelling, no more work and worry. I have been quite homesick lately. . . .

I would like to get a house, not too small, with enough ground to make a garden and have plenty of room for Pete to play about in and have his animal friends with him, somewhere within reach of both Dot and you. It might be best to have a beach, though the woods might be as well. I don't know yet which is better for the boy. I would have a cheap auto but I would like to be near some of my friends, for I find that I think less and less of countries now and more and more of friends; California means certain people to me, not only a climate and a beauty. And most of all it means Laura and you. . . .

Max Eastman is here; he came yesterday on his way to Austria; he leaves tomorrow. He knows and is telling me the present inside of the Russian situation. Very interesting.

Affectionately,
Lin.

To Laura Suggett

Alassio, April 6, 1926

Dear Laura:

This is my birthday, a date I don't usually notice, but I am sixty years old this time and that sounds old; or, it used to. But nothing is ever just as one expects it to be and so sixty is not. It only sounds, it does not look sixty. The only difference I notice is an increase in my instinct to go "home" and stay there, and home is California; not a house, not a spot, but a community of people that I love: you, first, and Allen, Dot and hers, Older and Frank Heney and,—so on. You know them all.

Jane has stimulated this feeling. She has been tempting me to up stakes here to return with her and, from some stopping place, set out to find a house and a garden where I can be and be busy and not busy. Some day I shall do that. I think that, if you were more ready to take me in in my complicity,—as a man of family,—I think I would go home this fall. I could use the offer of the *Survey* (and E. A. Filene) to do some work for that magazine to pay my way first to New York and then on westward. With my books coming out I might talk across the continent. How I would love to be approaching the Market Street Ferryhouse on a boat from the Oakland pier. But would you be there as usual, you and Doctor and Older? If I had my wife with me and Little Pete? I could not bear to land without you there.

Another sign of something around sixty is that I am more personal than I used to be. I care more about friends. Old Jac up at Grasse says that friends are all that is worth while to him now, but he is much more than sixty; he must be in his seventies. And he has been a wise man in his day, a fine, working mind. "No more ideas, Stef," he said the last time I saw him. We were talking about my *Life,* and he was pleading only for "stories, your actual experiences; no interpretations." And Max Eastman, who is here, asks the same limitation of the narrative, "just what you saw and the men you knew." There is something in it. We'll see.

You may ask, as I think: what about China? I want to go to China, I mean to go to China. I may go there before I return home and settle down. Indeed I may stick to the road and die on the way home years hence. I don't know. I don't know even what I want. I guess that all I really am wishing is that I might not come home, but only have the feeling that I might if I wanted to.

A foolish birthday letter. But it's from a foolish brother to a —— sister. (You can write in the word that will fill the blank.)

Lin.

To Marie Howe

Alassio, April 21, 1926

Dear Marie:

Pete just walked,—yes, walked into my work room up here on the roof. Of course Peter was not far away, but Pete came in here all alone and as stuck up as I was when you approved my first chapters. Absurd. He had his hair cut yesterday; not going to suffer as I did

for mere curls. He looks dangerously like a man-child now, kindo'
he-man-like, the kind girls would shout with horror and joy to find
under their bed.

But I am not to write about Pete. Too easy, too long, too unnecessary. You know Pete is all right or at any rate half right. I sat down
here to report progress and say goodbye to you and Fred. . . .

You have been good, Marie; kind but effective too. I appreciate it
as Peter does. Something must come out of it, something besides a
book or two or three; something personal and fine all the rest of our
lives. I don't know whether you feel it or not, but you are getting in
this little (but growing) family some return for the love you have
given us; as you have so many takers of love. Lots of people love
Marie Howe; I would like to have you know it and know it warmly.
I mean that I wish you could feel the warmth of our affection for you.

Goodbye, Marie. A pleasant voyage, an easy landing, a quiet summer and long life: old wishes but sincere.

Affectionately,
Lincoln Steffens

To Allen H. Suggett

Alassio, May 13, 1926

Dear Doctor:—

. . . All the world over here is watching the General Strike in England. It is very well managed so far: quiet, orderly and firm. The
Government is rattled. I can't see any results worth while except a bit
of training of Labor to coöperate. But England is the place, if any,
where evolution, as distinguished (unscientifically) from revolution,
may be possible. That is the point of view from which I watch it. I
am pretty sure that nothing but revolution can save France and the
rest. I can't see how Labor can win in England any other way. But
the British radicals are so firm in their belief that they can work it
out without an open class war, that it is worth following just to see if
the ruling classes can give in at all in any essential. No sign of it today,
but we have to wait, so we might as well wait and see.

. . . Brand and Mrs. Whitlock are changed very, very little; both
greyer and more sleek, but he is still tall, slender, graceful and slow of
speech; she round and amiable, a bit shrewd-sighted. He has learned
little or nothing that has changed his mind. The world has gone all
wrong, that's all. I suggested that perhaps we had gone wrong before

the war; not the world, but our thinking, which seemed to me to have been merely "wishing." He looked startled, considered a moment and repeated: "Yes, thinking is mostly wishing." But, after the pause, he went right on "wishing" for liberty and all the old bunk. He is a fine man just the same, and I mean fine. He is writing novels, one just out, another just about finished. He is too comfortable, too quiet, too reconciled to things as they are, to do a good book. . . .

Pete's progressing steadily. He walks and climbs everywhere now. He imitates dogs, cats, trains and is working on bird calls. His sense of smell seems to be keen. He goes up to flowers and, without touching them, bends down to smell them, apparently with pleasure. I like that. I never heeded flowers or knew them; he must have got that from his mother, who loves flowers and writes well about them.

Affectionately,
Len.

To E. A. Filene

Alassio, May 17, 1926

Dear E. A.

. . . I see in this morning's *Herald* that Austria has been giving you a gold cross, which we will put into the appendix.

Also I see in the *Herald* that Jo Davidson has delivered his portrait of Herrick and so goes on his road to success with HIS best things all failures. There is a small torso by him in his studio that is more beautiful, more of a classic work of art, than all his "triumphs" despite all their great earnings. Jo made some $125,000 last year and has bought a château in Touraine where Yvonne is down sick from overwork and wishing to sell her business. What do you mad workers want out of life anyway? You don't get it and you never seem able to say it, not so that I can understand. My philosophy tells me that God does not want any one of us to do the whole job; he prefers us each to do his bit and so be happy and well himself. When will you learn that? When the causes that drive you into the belief that you have purposes slacken their force and you can stop a moment and think.

You should retire, E. A. You could do more useful thinking than you can do deeds from now on, thinking and writing, looking on and seeing and reporting. There is a long, helpful, happy chapter ahead of you if you can cease from overdoing, which is neither wise itself nor productive of wisdom. Reflection, meditation, digestion, is your lay now. Think it over. I shan't urge this view partly because I think you are helpless against the forces which are riding you as you would not ride a horse.

Come and give and get some of the affection you nurse like a baby, too professionally.

Yours as ever,
Lincoln Steffens

To Upton Sinclair

Alassio, May 19, 1926

Dear Upton:

However ghostly I may seem to you, you are not so to me. You are as real as an economic force, and I know some of your explosions, the *Letters to Judd,* for example. Never mind if you have sent it. I know plenty of Judds to pass it on to. Also I know that you are running for Governor on the Socialist ticket, and I wish I could take the stump for you. I don't believe in the Socialists very much; they did not prove to be Socialists when the Russian Revolution came to test them. I think Socialists here and in England, France, Germany and Europe generally are no nearer Socialism than Christians are near Christianity. But the Russians believe in Upton Sinclair and so do I. I think you would make a good liberal governor for my state and that is more than the state wants and all that it would allow you to be. No matter, you cannot but do some good by running in the spirit of your election notices, as you enclose them. And, look out, you might be elected. The other side is apt to give you an unexpected boost by some fool bull they may make.

I enclose a small cheque for the campaign. It is money made in Wall Street, so keep it mum.

Dorrance & Co., the publishers who are putting out my *Moses in Red,* are to send you a copy. It may read, to you, like satire, but it is a serious essay on the laws of revolution and, I think, a bully story. It is dedicated to your friend Judd and Sinclair's friend Babbitt, so I think you may like to push it into circulation.

The *Life* will clear up some of the mystification you once expressed about me, but that comes later, much later.[1]

You are doing great work, Upton, as you know; you have really

[1] Upton Sinclair once remonstrated with Steffens, asking him: "Don't you see what you are showing?" See *Autobiography,* 434.

learned to write; you have a clear, personal style of your very own and you see into everything you look at. No wonder Russia ranks you so high. You should go there some time and you must let me talk to you about it before you start. I am sure I can prepare any man for either Moscow or Venice, and these both require preparation. You would get Moscow all right; I could save you some time and some pain. It is all right, but it is not obvious and some pretty good men have fallen down on it. Bertrand Russell is the most amazing failure to get it, and Mrs. Russell the most amazing success. I would go there with you if they were not so disgusted with me. They blame me for the Bullitt fiasco and for being able to state their case and yet staying out of the Communist Party. After this election, consider a trip to Russia via me.

> Yours affectionately,
> Lincoln Steffens

To Laura Suggett

> Alassio, Sunday,
> [May 30, 1926]

Dear Laura:—

It's Sunday, May 30, and we are all packed, some trunks gone to the station, ready to leave here tomorrow morning on the twenty-four hours' trip to Paris. I wrote G. to meet me for a few minutes again at the Nice station. She won't; not worth while, she says. She had written that she had something important to say, but she wrote it in her note. I am not to mention her (either by name or in disguise) in my *Life*. I promised, but it's too bad. What I really am is shown by that story better than any other. The whole will be hurt by the omission.

I got yesterday Miss Ford's copy of the first ten chapters; which means that you have it, too. I'd like to hear what you think of it. . . . I have said very little about my sisters, because I recall few incidents to show the really great influence you, for example, had upon me; and Lou; and Dot. Perhaps the influence was not explicit, but only general and subtle. Anything you can contribute to this phase, either in the first ten or in the later chapters, will be a service to me and to the book, which I hope you will consider worth while. As you know, I am willing to work,—rewrite again and again, correct, cut,—anything to make a thing good. But in a story of the scope of this, I can't do it alone. So far, as you see, it is just a boy's story of unconscious learning, pretty in a way and pleasant, but not significant. Its meaning comes later, when I saw it looking backwards.

Love.

Len.

To Pete Stanley Steffens

Hotel Richepanse, Paris,
Monday, June 12(?), 1926

Dear Pete:

Your belated letter,—strained through your mother,—was handed to me today when I came downtown to live for a few days. It was like a welcome home. I like to hear from you, but you are right not to make me a duty. It is kinder to let me go hang till you want to talk with me. I can stand almost anything better than being made an obligation.

But you are kind. I had a sweet note from your grandma saying that you were good to her. Peter says you are courteous to strangers even in England and she says something else showing that you still are making her feel that you love her best of all. That all is not only kind, it is wise. . . .

I saw a dandy Irish girl for you today. Ann Bullitt is her name. She is about two years old now, talks a lot in two languages and says jolly things; "My mama is my friend," she said one day, and when someone asked if her papa wasn't also her friend, she answered, "Oh, no; he is God." Her mama repeated that to Freud one day, and he was delighted. "That child is articulate," he said. "I have a theory that many children think that. Yours is the first to actually say it." The moral of this story, Pete, is that the great man was pleased because this little Irish lassie had said something that bore out a theory of his. You will find generally that grown-ups are so constructed or so educated that they will grab any facts that prove their case and won't hear or see others that either do not bear upon what they think or contradict it. But I must explain that I call Ann Bullitt Irish first, because she looks Irish; and second, that she looks like her mother. That was my observation all the while everybody was shouting out how like her father the child looked. You are pretty safe as to looks; you look like a little fellow I call Pete and I hope you always will.

Tell Peter, by the way, that Max Eastman and Eliena were at lunch with me at Louise's house and that a man named Parker and a lawyer named Arthur Hays, who tried with Darrow the Tennessee case and the Negro case, came in afterwards for coffee. A Turk was due, but Max and I didn't wait for him. Peter must call on Bullitt with you when you return to Paris. The house alone is worth seeing; it is old and grand. Bill Bullitt gets back Thursday, the day I was leaving for Karlsbad, so I shall wait over a day to dine that night with him and his friends. His novel [1] has been well reviewed and is selling. . . .

There, Little Pete, I must stop or stay stopped. For I felt so bad in my tummy that I interrupted this letter at the end of the last paragraph and have taken a bath meanwhile. Now it is nearly eight, time for dinner and then, if I don't feel better, I'll go to bed; otherwise I'll call on the O'Briens. Be busy, boy, but don't be good. Good is good for grown-ups and grown-ups are not good, as I shall show you bit by bit, inch by inch.

Your sentimental Pop,
Stef.

To Ella Winter

Jo Davidson's, Paris,
June 12, 1926

Dear Peter,

. . . Jo came down to Guy's [2] office to meet me and we all three went to the Anglo-French Press for lunch. George Slocombe [2] presided; he is vice-president; and I had to make a speech or tell a story. A Doctor Gruening [2] was also there. He has been writing on Mexico and is now at work on the history thereof. He urged me to come to Mexico this winter, if I am in the U. S. A., and said he'd tip Calles to write me. We might do it. Why not?

The other night I dined with Mr. and Mrs. William A. Bird. There was a Mrs. Fremont there, a granddaughter of General John C. Fremont, who conquered California, and as she said, "We gave California to the United States." I asked if there wasn't an army with the General who made the gift.

---

[1] *It's Not Done.*

[2] Guy Hickok of the Brooklyn *Eagle;* George Slocombe, at the time correspondent of the London *Herald;* Ernest Gruening, author of *Mexico and Its Heritage.*

Mason Day, the oil man Jo and I met in Russia, is here. He verified what I guessed and wrote in that article for Kellogg:[1] that Italy did get a big hunk of the Macedonian oil graft, more than Sinclair did. You remember my paragraph? How Mussolini said Italy was for a fair peace with the Turks, but that if they (the Allies) were out for loot, he wanted his share? And how I inferred that he got it? Well, that's true, truer than I had guessed. One can read the newspapers and get the news if one holds the key,—graft.

E. A. said your mother called on him about the coal-strikers and he gave her—advice. I said you and Jane and others gave her money. "I suppose," he said, "that I should have given her some, too."

"No," I answered, "Mrs. Winter is a student of character; not interested in money or in miners."

The rich are the poorest souls in hell, useful only as arguments for socialism or, better still, for the Red Terror. But Filene "got" me even if he and your mother didn't get each other.

I guess Bullitt has been having some more aunts and uncles dying. He is rich, richer than ever, and their apartment is gorgeous, the lower floor of a house in a court with a picture garden in the rear.

Jerry Blum said he was painting. "What?" I asked.

"My wife," he said.

I looked at her lips and said: "I see."

Jerry fell laughing into a chair. "How much will you give me for my next real picture?" he said.

"Ten thousand dollars."

"Gee, that's a lot of money to—not get," he grieved.

Jerry has lost the gland he used to paint with and it's funny to see him wandering around wondering why he can't paint any more. I described him thus and the company all wanted to write it as a story. "A painter who can't paint any more." Jerry said it was done, that story. "Stef's done it just now."

Jo gave me your nice long letter, with the Epstein reproductions, which made a hit with Jo and Yvonne. They were stunned by them; their admiration was almost involuntary, and they looked again and again.

I went to dinner by myself last night, and I was good company. We had a nice talk about the Petes and such things, differing on some points, but amiably; we didn't argue. And so when we got home at

[1] Paul Kellogg, editor of the *Survey-Graphic*.

ten I went to sleep and slept till Pete's waking hour, and then on till eight. . . .

Stef.

To Allen H. Suggett

Paris, June 15, 1926

Dear Dr.:

Your letter is here with your comment on the first ten chapters of the *Life*. Thanks. It's a boost, an explicit, evidently sincere approval, which makes me feel like going on. . . .

Jane is in London with the Petes and she writes clearly about some experiences she is having. She and Peter have been begging under a banner on the street for the wives and children of the coal strikers, and they both have written about the things that were said to them. No money, but only some savage, not very polite comments from the rich; money, praise and some tears from the poor and the workers. Jane sees the class line and the manners of her class off parade. . . .

The Finance Minister is resigning. It is not in the papers, but it will be, and it looks as if the ministry might fall with him. Herriot may come back. None of this matters. There is a financial war on between the Old Banking crowd and a new group. THAT cannot be settled, I think; it has to be fought out to a finish; and it may finish France. The bankers don't seem to care, though some of them are Frenchmen. All the Old Gang are French. There are American bankers in the new group. Some people think that Morgan could decide who wins. He could if he played with the Old Gang, but up to now he is with the new men who are not sure of his adherence. A Mussolini is wanted here. There is none in sight. The newest dictator is the Pole, Pilsudsky, who is a corker of a criminal boss. He talks of "the whip" openly as Mussolini did privately of oil,—castor oil, I mean this time. It's a funny Europe, ridiculous, not pathetic, except that the people will pay. But then that is true everywhere.

I saw Ernest Poole today in a restaurant; and Charles Edward Russell on a street corner. I used all Russell's facts to defend my optimism against his dismal pessimism, and left him laughing for the first time in years. "By G—," he exclaimed, "maybe you are right."

"No, no," I protested, "don't accuse me of that."

Love to Laura.

Len.

To Ella Winter

Jägerhaus, Carlsbad
Sunday, June 20, 1926

Well, Peter,

Here I am, just arrived, unexpected but remembered by sight, and so have a room,—for the present. . . . But I must go back and tell all— On Saturday I did the last of my errands and by early afternoon had nothing to do but wait. Jo was kept at home to receive Douglas Fairbanks and Mary, so I went to the Antheil Concert. And glad I am. This young man is the reddest of the new school who has a standing among all musicians. His things have been too radical for production heretofore, but a great Russian composer and educator had undertaken to produce his symphony, which Damrosch had just bought for New York, and his "Mechanical Ballet." It was a sight as well as a sound. Getting there early, I stood outside and saw, I think, all the queer people in Paris, French and foreign, men and women. Wild hair, flannel shirts, sticks, no hats and big hats for both men and women, and, note well, many intelligent faces. "Everybody," in brief, that is anybody: all the correspondents and their wives, all the painters, poets and, of course, musicians, with Rolls-Royce and Hispano loads, too. I sat alone but when the first number began (Weber's "Freischütz") in came the oldest of those three American girls we knew at St. Cergue, the violinist. I didn't greet her; the music was too, too beautiful, and she didn't see me, as she sat down on the step right beside me; and after the orchestra stopped I held out my hand. Shocked at first, she soon recognized me and asked about Pete, Peter, and I asked about her family: all together in the same place and intending to stay in town this summer. There was another number, and then the Antheil symphony: a beautiful thing. I don't see why the kicks. It's new; it was "discord," true, but beautifully, as one uses rough prose to lead into harmony. And the crowd rose to it. Antheil had a triumph.

In the intermission, Mary and I promenaded a bit, till I left her to join our crowd, the Hickoks, Birds,—all the correspondents, Jerry Blum and wife, Arthur Hays and wife, Ezra Pound and the music gang. Then I had to go,—for the hotel, where Jo met me and took me to the station. Doug had called alone; Mary ill, but there may be a bust in it just the same,—of one or both.

My train travelled via Nancy, Strasbourg, Karlsruhe, and so off the line of the Orient Express via Nürnberg to here. . . .

I had to lie down at this point, and I have slept,—I don't know how long. Not so very. The orchestra, which plays every afternoon here, is still playing, the same lovers are passing and the same clouds. I'll go out and look around us with Pete's needs in mind, but I'll send this off if I can find an envelope and stamp *en bas là*.

Stef.

To Allen H. Suggett

Carlsbad, June 21, 1926

Dear Doctor:—

I left Paris June 19, just broke away, to come here to work. Jane and the Petes are still in London, and I was getting into the life of my old bachelor circle, deeper and deeper: art, music, literary revolt and the money politics of the French. No use; not to me. I decided to cut it all out and run; I did, and here I find everything about as I left it in this funny little *Wald-café u. Restaurant,* high up on a hill above the town, where they take in a few lodgers. Filene found it; I was here in '22 with him; and "they," the boss and head servants, remembered me and made me special rates.

I began the cure today, and shall take it all tomorrow and thereafter. It may amuse you to know the routine. One gets up at 6-6:30 and goes down to the springs which are housed like gods along the little river in the town. There the orchestra is playing good music. You get your own numbered glass or mug and, letting the little girl attendant fill it at the running faucet, you join the crowd of parading drinkers. Two glasses you drink slowly, taking an hour to sip your allowance, then you follow the string of people through the town out to the open-air restaurants in the country. There are a string of these restaurants in town and out, and you may choose one near or far. They serve you the supervised coffee and rolls, with eggs or whatever the doctors tell you. It's a pleasant breakfast.

After it, some of the demons go walking or tennis playing or,—some exercise. I shall climb to the hill to my room here to work. Some of the patients drink the waters an hour before the midday meal, too. I shall stay here till the 4-5 o'clock concert and drinking bout and then take supper downtown, which means a walk home in the dark through the woods,—all on well-marked paths of which there is a choice.

My information about Paris is from bankers; and bankers rule the French Government and press. As one of them put it: "We can't do what must be done; not yet. The expectation that Germany would pay and that the U. S. would let us off is gone, but not the hope that something will turn up to save us from bankruptcy. So no government can live that honestly accepts and deals with the situation as it is. The franc must go still lower before that can be done, so, with checks, the process of indirect bankruptcy must go on; except for—"

"Except for—?"

"Oh, for a Mussolini!"

It can't be summed up briefly better than that, I think. Of course this banker and all Frenchmen would add that there is not in sight and could not be anywhere, a Mussolini in France. But as I explained in my article sent to Paul Kellogg for the *Survey* magazine,[1] Mussolini says: "That is what they said of Italy," and when he answered for Italy and the Italians lay down under his rule, the rest of Europe said: "You can't do that in France, Spain, Germany and England." To which Mussolini says:

"What is done in Russia, Italy, Spain and now Poland, can be done everywhere in the world."

I predict for France a slow fall to a break,—Left; then The Man and a dictatorship, either Right or starting Left, going Right. The only alternative that I see in history is,—the revolution (and I wish that too much to believe in it) or what happened in Austria and Germany.

This place, Carlsbad, is a wound left by the fool, crooked Treaty of Versailles. Here live and hate and wait some 2,000,000 Austrian-Germans under Czech rule, a silly, nationalistic government by a young nation as full of patriotism as they are of a sense of inferiority. They take down all German signs, put up Czech signs, which nobody can read; and remove a German monument to Goethe! The Germans, sure of their superiority, are abiding their time. It makes no difference that they did to the Czechs what the Czechs are now doing to them. They have had and they expect again to have their day. The Czechs have a standing army larger than the imperial Austrian army was; and they have more government officials than all old Austria ever had.

You hear nothing but German here now. It's before "the season," when the English and Americans come,—in late July and August. All the *Kur*-guests now are German and Austrian, with a sprinkle of

[1] "Stop, Look, Listen." (Mussolini the Fascist.) *Survey-Graphic,* March 1, 1927.

other races, mostly Balkan. The styles and colors displayed in the promenade and shops are a sharp contrast with Paris, and it's funny to be where no one notices the franc, where all are excited about the row in the parliament at Prague and the vote on the Princes' properties in Germany. And one soon catches the new interest; at least I do.

Jo Davidson gave me some photos of his Rockefeller. I'll send you one of them soon and I want you to set it up before you and let the pathos of it and the cunning sink into you. It's a work of art. Show it to Older and to your dentist gang, yes, and to everybody. It's the way I'd like to write, without comment.

Love to Laura.

Affectionately,
Len.

To Jane Hollister

Karlsbad, June 21, 1926

Dear Jane:

This is to be a personal letter, to you only. I have been wanting to write it for two weeks, and haven't because Paris was so distracting and I didn't have anything to say, as I haven't now. It isn't a thought or a fact that prompted me to write, only a sentiment; a feeling of affection for you. I love you; not as I love Pete and not as I love Peter, but also not as an uncle loves a niece. That might be formal and superior. I love you as I might, but don't often, love a friend. Anyway it's a warm, equal sentiment of respectful affection most pleasant to me.

We have been together some time now. I have not judged, but I have felt you out and I have a sense of you, I think, a sense of your solidity, but with a molten interior: like the earth, a firm crust around a liquid nucleus which now and then breaks through. I have not missed the tear or two that you have dropped. And I certainly have not failed to admire the dignity and strength of your self-possession. You are a real person. You are going to be such a mistress of your own soul as Jack Black is of his and as Walt Whitman sang of his. No one must ever intrude upon that; least of all your friend Stef, who ranks you higher than anyone else has ever done yet, I think. I, first, have recognized that you are grown-up, a woman. Of course my disposition helped me to that. . . . You may be only emerging (as one of Jo's figures is right now appearing, out of the rough stone in his studio) and I may be a bit previous, but I have met you man to woman from the beginning of the pleasant chapter of our common life and so, as you have felt, we are friends and equals. If there is any difference, due to age, it is that I have the advantage of experience and you have the equal advantage (maybe superior) of a freedom from the prejudices of my experiences and my generation.

But,—this is, I discover, what I wanted to write,—we must not miss, you and I, the uses of a friendship such as ours. We must not be so content with the assumption of mutual understanding that we take for granted what ought to be spoken. I think,—I may be wrong, but I have had sometimes the thought or feeling that you are struggling inside with wishes or perplexities or doubts and problems that might better be brought up into the light and air. Especially if they are vague, they should be revealed and so made definite. I might help you with them; or Peter might. That is for you to judge. As between Peter and myself, the choice is for you to make. Only don't be hesitant about being open with me or both of us. Use us as friends, as real friends, to be trusted like pals.

I am referring, actually, to the signs of emotion I have seen which you never spoke of afterwards. Not many; one or two. Don't suppress. One of the few discoveries of our day, of personal use to us, is that of the danger of over-repression, over self-control; a new sort of tyranny, the mis-rule of one's self. Speak them out, if they ache at all, —if you wish.

And, Jane, if you don't want to, don't you say a word. For I am pleading, not at all for your confidences, only for your confidence. It were enough for me to have you know that, if you want to, you can talk to me,—or to us; and not be treated as a little girl to propaganda. I mean that you can sit down and think out loud with me as Jo Davidson does or Yvonne or Peter.

I wish you would all come back to me, you and the Peters. I haven't said that to Peter; I don't want to make her feel driven or pulled. I can't ask her to come, therefore. But I have no "authority" over you. I can tell you that I am homesick for my family, which includes you, and ask you to lobby a bit for me, suggesting to Peter that, when she has seen and done all she wants to in London, you come, fast, to Karlsbad. It will be a glad day for me when we are all together again here or,—anywhere.

Affectionately, your friend,
Stef.

To Pete Steffens

Carlsbad, June 23, 1926

Dear Pete,

This place will suit you I think. Down three flights of stairs is a restaurant through which you will go to either an open café in front or on a side toward the town to a large graveled playground. There is not much for a little fellow like you to do on this playground. It is the grown-up idea for a place for kids. A bare yard where there is nothing to break and nothing to get hurt on. Safety first is the law for children, but you will have your ball and we will find you a half-developed *Deutsches Mädel* to play with, so that you can learn to think in another language. Sometimes we can go in back of the house to a playground for grown-ups. That has a net and balls 'n' everything to amuse the big children who can't play with nothing like a baby. They have a game called tennis which they work at hard rather than do anything useful. It's thought to be degrading to work; and it is. It is a sure sign that your father was an honest man and never got any graft, if you have to work for your living. I hope to arrange it so that you will not be ashamed of me; I leave you my graft and I'll show you how to get more if you need it. If you work, you will work as a scientist or an artist, for fun, not for money. Money *cannot* be made by labor. But work, real work, for what we call duty or the truth, that is more fun than tennis. Sometimes we will sit, you and I, and look at the human beings that crawl around here, and when we have had our fill of that sight we will walk away a few hundred feet and look at the trees, the beautiful, tall straight trees that have no bellies and no bad tastes. They are dignified and well-dressed. I'd like to have you appreciate trees, appreciate the difference between them and men, and then, some day, believe that, under decent conditions it will be possible for human beings also to have souls. They haven't now; only bellies, pockets and the poor little beginnings of a mind.

Your mother or your Cousin Jane will explain this to you, if I am gone. They will tell it to you honestly and humorously, Pete; they will not propagand with you; with all others maybe; but not with Pete. You are to have the straight of it, my boy; and the straightest of the straight is that we don't know anything; not any of us; not Jane, not Peter, not I. Nobody understands things as they are and the proof of this is that nobody,—not the greatest scientist, not the tenderest poet, not the most sensitive painter; only, for a moment, the kindest lover can see that all that is is beautiful. I can't, I only believe that.

It may be wrong; there may be ugliness, like the sick bellies these miserable *Kurgäste* come here to cure, but I have a funny old faith that, if a little fellow like you is shown everything and allowed to look at everything and not lied to by anybody or anything, he, even Pete, might do better even than Joyce did what *Ulysses* was meant to do; he might see and show that there is exquisite beauty everywhere except in an educated mind.

And an educated mind is nothing but the God-given mind of a child after his parents' and his grandparents' generation have got through molding it. We can't help teaching you; you will ask that of us; but we are prone to teach you what we know, and I am going, now and again, to warn you:

Remember that we really don't know anything. Keep your baby eyes (which are the eyes of genius) on what we don't know. That is your playground, bare and graveled, safe and unbreakable.

Love your mother, but don't you believe and revere her; and, as for your father, laugh at him as he laughs at himself till the tears start.

L. Steff.

To Laura Suggett

Carlsbad, June 25, 1926

Dear Laura:—

I'm alone here, and lonely. Sometimes I like to be alone. . . . Well, about a month ago, I took Peter and Pete to the train and I pushed them away,—to London. It seemed to me then that if the train did not start on time I would bust or scream. And I rested for a while, in Paris, slept by night and relaxed all day. Then there were things to do and people to see. I soon was going it hard. So I cut out suddenly and came here where there is nobody I know,—yet. I am alone, as I wished, and I am getting so that I can hardly stand it. If it went on much longer, I would pick up some acquaintances and become friends with them. . . .

I am thinking about this because I am writing now the chapter about meeting and marrying Josephine when I was engaged to G. I don't name or describe G.; she forbade me to, but I just have to tell the story. It belongs; it shows, not to me; I don't understand; but it must reveal to others what is the matter with me. I want someone with me; I want to be alone. I want to travel; I want to stay home.

I get my relief here at the concerts, hearing the music and watching the crowds. So many concerts, at all the great hotels and garden cafés, at the *Kur*-houses, for breakfast, for afternoon coffee, for dinner. And such crowds. Almost all Germans so far; the season is in July and August, when the English and Americans come; but it's cheaper now, so the Germans are here. I have forgotten how gross they are, with their enormous fat bodies, big bellies on weak legs, double chins, tripled necks and wrinkly, close-cut heads. Their manners are rude and their clothes loud. You would think there was no refinement in them or taste. But see them listening to music.

This afternoon while the best orchestra here was playing Beethoven's Fourth Symphony I was looking at a great, old hunchbacked woman with her sick daughter, both as ugly as can be, but they were taking in the music, "getting" it, I mean, and exchanging glances of appreciation. There's a passage in the early part of the second movement when the orchestra throws the theme upon the air, the first violins catch it, pour it over to the seconds, who let it run like a plaything or a rill over the violas and bass violins to the drum where it falls with a bang, and, there at the bottom, the piccolos pick it up and run away with it like a boy whistling. Well, that hideous old German Frau and her myopic daughter laughed out loud. I could have sent them flowers. It was funny, beautifully playful, mischievous. Nor were they the only ones to show delight in—that, and in other parts. I saw huge merchants, looking like murderers, listening like angels to that music.

There's something in the Germans. There's everything in music. Like Little Pete, it can say everything without any words. . . .

I'll be another week alone, when the London crowd comes (with Pete), another week and E. A. arrives. Meanwhile, in between, come the Graveses [1] (some Paris friends) and the Kreislers (Fritz and wife), who all were here when I was before; they come every year. The Kreislers are good people. "I can't understand modern music," he says, and he looks like Jo Davidson before some of the cubist paintings: humiliated, lost. I can "get" it. I love some of the moderns in all the arts; they are no harder to understand than Russia is; they are not so hard as this funny little new government of the Czechs, over the Germans, who hate to have done to them the absurd and cruel things they used to do to the Czechs. . . .

[1] Leon Graves, of the Guaranty Trust Co., Paris.

To Allen H. Suggett

Carlsbad, July 2, 1926

Dear Doctor:—

Clemenceau, the old devil, said a good thing during the recent cabinet crisis in France, when Poincaré (the most scholarly brother of the famous mathematician and astronomer) and Briand, the one-time Socialist, were sticking up in the news. He said that P. knew everything and understood nothing, whereas B. knew nothing and understood everything. . . .

My writing won't go. I sit down to it every day, but nothing happens but rejected shreds of paper. It's the Josephine chapter. If I could get over that, I'd sail: Reporting, Wall Street, Police Headquarters, Tammany, T. R. and then the muckracking, the war, the revolution and the peace. G. doesn't want me to write her story, however covered up, and it's hard to get around it. It means so much.

Please ask Older to write to Horace Liveright and get from him a letter I wrote him about Jack Black's book. I'm not sure; I can't remember exactly, but I think I said best in that letter some of the things that ought to go into Older's Introduction. I didn't say so, but I think that the problem Jack illustrates is to be resolved only when the social problem is solved. His unrepentant story is really a document, as well as a rare piece of narrative. *But* the paragraphs *inserted,* for circulation considerations, should come out, every one of them. They spoil the story and they misrepresent Jack and his case. They are not true.

I'm glad Fremont does not know, as I get them, the rotten, petty politics of the Hearst organization over here. Journalism is sinking fast. Too bad. But, then, so is our civilization or its culture; and the new order is coming up, slowly. I wouldn't know what to steer Pete into, even if he would let me guide him. Some art or science, I guess. He's too humorous for a revolutionary.

To Matthew Schmidt [1]

Carlsbad, July 20, 1926

. . . Fremont says you might both go to Russia. I can't make out whether he means that deportation would be a condition to your parole or that you desire to go there. . . . In any case I am far from sure that Russia is your solution. Some people loathe Russia now, others love it; and it isn't merely a matter of Red visitors or White.

[1] Sentenced in the McNamara case to life imprisonment in San Quentin. For a brief period in 1926 his parole seemed possible.

Emma Goldman and her friends hated it; Liberals got the shock of their lives, and of course conservatives react against it typically. Yet there are Tories that "see it" and Liberals too, and Reds. I have likened it to heaven and hell, which Russia taught me is one place where everybody goes: to some it is heaven, to others hell. I met individuals among the several thousand radical organized labor men who went early to Russia from Germany and I got from them why they cried out to be brought back to Germany after a few months in Russia. They said they could not stand the dirt, the inefficiency, the loafing on the job and the interminable talk and debate. Bill Haywood suffered from their indifference to him, his services to the cause and his ideas. They pensioned and forgot him. It was awful.

And then Bill himself forgot some things and he missed his chance. He forgot that the leaders in Russia had themselves suffered for the cause, Siberia, prisons, whipping, starvations,—hell. A few years in a clean American prison for the cause does not seem much to them, so it doesn't count. But they did listen to Bill at first. They had him at a meeting to which everybody went to hear his ideas, and especially his report upon the outlook for a revolution in the U. S. A. And Bill spoke, and to encourage them, he painted the U. S. red; he held out hopes for the revolution over in the U. S. A., said Labor was ready for it and,—altogether,—lied. Now they knew better and they are fierce realists. Before Bill had ended his optimistic speech, Lenin got up and went out saying: "Another American salesman."

It killed Bill for Russia; he was the loneliest soul in Asia when I saw him. Only fellows like me from the outside paid any attention to him. He sighed for prison at home; and it was hard; it is hard. It is understandable. They are men who think they have the truth and they have fought and fought hard, against enemies at home and abroad, yes, and against friends in their own crowd for that truth. They are certain that they are right, certain, as sure as people with a religion, a live religion for which the believers still suffer martyrdom. They are righteous, therefore. They kill as they are killed. I admire them tremendously, but I don't like to be with them. All that counts in your record are your mistakes, which they blame as we have learned not to blame; they blame and they punish. All they ask of you is what you are doing "for the cause," and they expect you to furnish, not only the bricks but the straw. They are the unkindest, they are the damnedest set of stinkers I ever met.

But they are heroes too. I am for them to the last drop, I am a patriot for Russia; the Future is there; Russia will win out and it will save the world. That is my belief. But I don't want to live there. It is too much like serving in an army at war with no mercy for the weak and no time for the wounded. Youth can stand it; youth loves it, but for me who am ruined by the easy life of the old culture Russia is impossible. My service to it has to be outside here. It is like the Christian who knew he was going to heaven when he died and knew also that heaven was a state of everlasting bliss but, gosh, he did not want to die.

We can talk this all over when we meet, as we will of course, before you go out. I am not against your going to Russia. But I am not going to let you start off with any illusions. And I mean to see to it too that you are expected there, and, if possible, to have jobs ready for you. I can't do much; I am not credited in there. Lenin never forgave the failure of the Bullitt mission, for which he blamed me, not Bullitt and not Lloyd George. I was the Red, the others mere Whites, and Lenin had no time to be just. And the rest of them cannot understand "how a man can state the whole case of Soviet Russia aright and not be a Communist." They are harder on me than on Emma Goldman, therefore, but I have some friends in there who understand and who surely can present your case, your claims, which will be, of course, for a place in the system to work. All you will need is a chance, a start. They will soon find that they need you.

Bill Shatoff, the Chicago I.W.W., is an illustration of the use they have for an efficient man. He is an Anarchist, not a Communist, but the first time I went in to Petrograd, Bill was Chief of Police. Before I left they made him also civil commissar of the Red army that was defending Petrograd. The next time I went in Bill had been head of the Southern railroads because they were running badly under an inefficient Communist and just when he had arranged to come to Moscow to meet me, he was switched to the presidency of a bank that was being robbed. In between he was tried and ordered shot for some of his anti-communist talk as an Anarchist and was saved only by Lenin, who sent for the judges and said to them: "Shatoff is efficient, isn't he?" They gave a reluctant "Ye-e-es." "You have no one to take his place?" "No-o-o," they answered. "Well, then," said Lenin, "I think I wouldn't shoot Bill till after the Revolution has made good and can spare him." So Bill, whom you will meet if you will go in there, is really on parole. You must hear him laugh and tell you about it. A government of Labor Leaders with here and there a wise guy to save the rest.

Russia isn't what one expects. It is a thousand times worse than most people look for, but it is a thousand times better than it might be. You will like it if you are prepared for the worst, and I can tell you the worst better than any Tory spy, I who am for it, and for you. We can do whatever you decide to do, but let's think it out first and so proceed to our job, both in America and Russia, deliberately, knowingly, realistically. . . .

To Mrs. J. James Hollister

Salzburg, Austria,
August 4, 1926

Dear Dot:

Your two letters about the sex parts of the *Life* reached me in Carlsbad, and I should have answered them at once, to set you right upon the only point in all that you said that I objected to: your apology for your opinion. I asked you to read and to criticise the *Life* chapters, and you have done that; I am sure that I have got exactly your reaction,—yours, not someone else's. No one could ask more, no courtesy could give more. Why then should you worry about it, think at night over what you said and write again the next day to your brother, who might be supposed to know you and so be able to allow for idiosyncrasies or the opposite?

As to the general proposition that I omit all sex, I am in doubt. I don't mind losing some readers or some uses for the book, and I don't feel as you do about such subjects. It will be better for us all when we can talk about all phases of natural life without shock. But you say that I have not succeeded in writing naturally about my little sex experiences; that has to be verified by the impression of others. And my own feeling is that I happen not to know enough about the subject to write about it usefully or clairvoyantly or even beautifully. Perhaps I ought to stick to what I do understand. All that I have against that is that an autobiography should be, if not complete, at least balanced; and my sins, my crimes, the acts which expose the weak or the wicked side of my character, are rather personal than professional. If I tell only the professional tale of my life I shall be more of a hero than, for example, G. knows me to be or my sisters.

We had a hard trip here from Carlsbad, due to the European system of bribery according to which some fellow can come along late and buy the reservation you made weeks before. I have used the system a lot; indeed usually I am on the briber's side, and that is a most comfortable side. Peter has enjoyed the privilege thereof several times, especially when she was carrying Pete. But when we got to Prague and the tables were turned; when some son of a gun had bought out our berths and we stood there, Jane and Peter tired, Pete fretful and I with a cold to guard, Peter saw and said: "So this is the way it feels when one does to us what we have done to them."

We got here, by more bribery, but most uncomfortably; only Pete could sleep all night, and the first day and night we all slept most of the time. We have seats for every single performance both of music and the theatres for all of us. Jane and Peter really learned something from that music master in Carlsbad that makes them enjoy concerts and seek them. I think Jane feels that she knows what music is all about, and it is a pleasure to see her confidence grow. I wish she could get the same feeling about pictures and politics and,—everything.

I have hit upon a fine way into Jane's mind. She is reticent, as you know; as reticent as Jim. She does not talk well about herself. But when I talk about Pete as a problem I can put the case of Jane so vividly and so objectively that Jane can see and discuss it; and often with a shrewd remark about mother (you) which shows that she is applying it to her case and yours. If Jane does not learn her mother's and her father's view of herself and of the parents' problem in general, I shall be astonished.

We had sunshine yesterday, so we all woke up early and got an auto in which we drove out to St. Gilgen, where we called upon Mrs. Sinclair Lewis and her little son, nine years old. Very pleasant, very interesting. The boy is already writing stories, and, she says, pretty well. We shall be making excursions all month, but the first ten days after Saturday will be all music and theatres, morning, afternoon and early evenings. It is something like making a business of culture, which is good for these girls who are so eager for it all and so ready now. For of course we hear criticisms of actors, managers, conductors, composers, and scene-makers, which, however bitter and personal, do open a mind like Jane's to the problems involved in these arts. In short, Dot, I am sure it is all to the good.

Salzburg, August 18, 1926

Dear Dot:

Jane is not here. She and Peter were called for two days ago by a man and his wife to come down to the German border and help investigate for a psychic magazine (of London) [1] some notorious spiritistic phenomena revealed in a simple peasant family.[1] They went day before yesterday, and I was glad to see Jane go because she had disclosed an interest in such things, a curiosity developed by one or two of the White boys.[1] One night in Alassio she and Peter wanted to try table-tipping; we all sat in and sure enough,—the table tipped. Both the girls were profoundly moved till I admitted that I had tilted the table and added that I believed that, when a table moved thus, someone always did it, cheating. This was all right for my purpose, but I noticed that tears started from Jane's eyes. She was really hurt, really wanted to know, so here was a chance for her to see the real thing.

Little Pete is having trouble with his teeth, fever and a stiff neck, so Peter could stay only for the one night. She came back yesterday, saying that there were manifestations, puzzling, mysterious knocks and movements, with a lifting of the medium bodily into the air. "If they are frauds," she said, "they are very hard to explain." But she said that she and Jane were convinced that there was trickery and that Jane wanted to stay and try one more night for an exposure. "Jane seemed to be mad," Peter says, "irritated to think that they should think that they had put it over on us." The next séance is tonight and Jane will be back tomorrow, when she will report to us and write to you.

This family of mediums is the most famous case of today, and others are investigating it. The trickery, assuming that there is fraud, is of no known kind; it has survived all inquiries so far. The point I make is that, if it is not trickery; even if it is genuine, it has no results to show as an addition to our knowledge. But no matter. It is another, interesting, experience for our Jane.

She has probably told you about her theatregoing and the concerts here. With them have gone meetings with the actors and managers, a little glimpse of the inside of the business and the romances (or scandals) of the art world. I don't know what Jane is thinking about

---

[1] *Psyche,* edited then by Warren Vinton. Bees White, of Santa Barbara, a brother of Stewart Edward White. The Schneider family of Braunau, which has been widely publicized, by Baron Schrenck-Notzing of Munich, and others.

it all. We were invited out to Reinhardt's[1] castle after *Turandot* the other night and there were all the theatre world, discussing results and plans, Gest considering with Reinhardt and his staff whether to take it to America. It was a rather gala scene in those great rooms in the old castle of the Emperor's brother.

Jane showed me one of your letters lately; it was a gossipy account of life on and about the ranch; about Aunt Jane and Jack and the visitors AND their characters. When I handed it back I told Jane that it was (as it is) a model letter, just such a personal picture of a section of life as she might try to write you from here. You write well, Dot, when you have not much of importance to say; when you think you are writing nothing. But in this letter I could show Jane how it was done, how to do it.

Love to all.

Len.

To Ella Winter

Salzburg [Aug. 29, 1926], Sunday Afternoon,
Before Pete's Return

Well, Peter,

This has been a busy day after all. I'll call it the Theodore Dreiser day because I was with him, mostly. Pete and I had agreed to make a short trip on some train after the concert; but,—no time for either of us. I was seeing D. and Pete called on Mrs. Crane. But I must begin at the beginning.

I was invited to sup with the Cranes last night; and also by the Nilsons.[2] I preferred the Nilsons. The inevitable Metzler met me at the hotel, took me to the table reserved for the N.'s and he and I ordered and ate before the theatre crowd got back. The Cranes arrived first, so I had a visit with them till the Nilsons came in. They rushed me. Those flowers! She wore some of them. They talked openly of their divorce and their continued friendship; and they were really affectionate. The young husband (to be, I think, this week, not last) came to our table and kissed her hand, passionately. When he bade us good night, she said, "And do you know there are people in

---

[1] Max Reinhardt, German producer, and Morris Gest, theatrical producer of New York. *Schloss Leopoldskron* was Reinhardt's home in Salzburg.

[2] Mrs. Einar Nilson at this time was marrying Count Franz Schaffgotsch.

this town who find it hateful, our divorce and our friendship, all three of us together?"

"It seems right and natural to me," said N. "And I wouldn't care what the stupid say."

I told him our idea of getting a divorce before the hate set in, while we are happy together, and he approved heartily. But she said it was only my way of holding you. To that he said, shaking his head:

"You can't hold a woman."

"Not if we look together for the next husband?" I joked.

"Ah," she said, "when she really begins to seek the next man, she will do it alone; not together then any more." . . .

Home again at 11:40, I asked anxiously about Pete. Mr. Heise said they had watched and listened, but not a peep. I was relieved, but as I went up the stairs I heard a sound I thought I knew,—Pete crying? I hurried up, and there he was sitting up and crying. I felt him; dry, and so held him out. He was mad at me and wouldn't, so I took him out on the veranda and he caved; he heard a train and forgot his rage till we went in. Then he saw I had tricked him and was very indignant; mute, but he wouldn't look at me. I bent over, looked at him till, gradually, he had to smile and, having surrendered, he put his hand on my cheek and said: "Papa." Some triumph!

All night we slept. At 5:40 I heard a "chu-chu" and got up. He was asleep, but his lips were moving: "Chu-chu," so I hauled him out and we both peed. Then we both got back into Pete's bed and slept till 7, when I got a bang in the eye. Up we got, stole into my room, Pete looking for Mama. And there was no Mama. He could hardly believe it; he had to look under the covers and I thought he would cry, but, no, he heard a train again and—

We rang for water, shaved and had a funny kind of a breakfast, just us fellers. It was fun. We ate up everything. When the girl came promptly at 8:20 we were ready for her. We were washed, dressed and separated by 9.

But on the way to the concert I met Dreiser and (probably) the heroine of his next novel, a pretty German girl who loves music. We walked together to the Festspielhaus, met between the acts and after the end I led them to the left to the Festung. He got me talking about Mussolini, so I did all the talking till after my dinner at home alone. Then he told me of his plans: Wien tonight, Budapest tomorrow for a few weeks and then Paris for a month or so. I was to have met them at the café; they didn't come. Metzler sat with me, of course, and a lot of actors and actresses in succession. I forget their names; they hadn't a word to say till Pete drove up in his car. They liked Pete and Pete took to them, but I gave him a card, Mr. Pete Stef., and sent him with Hilda to call on Mrs. Crane.

He was there a long time and when he came back he was loaded with chocolates, grapes and other fruit. Hilda said he was great with the Cranes. He walked in, shook hands and captured the whole lot, the family and their friends, who were fascinated by his geniality and *savoir faire*. They couldn't find enough to give him. I called later, but saw only Richard himself; his wife and the others were lying down. So I chased off to the station to see the Dreisers, who had not come to the café because they got into the castle and couldn't get out till it was time to rush for their train. It was at the *Bahnhof* that he spoke of his plans.

It's now 5:30 and I'm waiting for Pete to come home to report the rest of his day. At the café I struck a bargain with Metzler. I said I'd stay home and take care of Pete tomorrow afternoon, if he would give Hilda a ticket to *Jedermann*. He promised, and he meant it; told her just what to do. She was pleased.

This is the last letter I'll try to get to you. I doubt that you'll get it, but nobody else can read it so it won't matter if it strays. The Cranes leave Tuesday; Mrs. Crane said she'd like to meet you. They live in Virginia, where she was bred. Hope you get back in time to call. I miss you; it's silly, but there you are.

Some love to Jane.

Stef.

To Allen H. Suggett

Salzburg, August 31, 1926

Dear Allen:

Peter and Jane, who have been sight-seeing Vienna, are due back at noon today, and we shall pack up and get out of here. It has been a pleasant month. All music and theatre; everybody talks art as at Carlsbad everybody talked health. Art is better as a subject of conversation. . . .

I find I can handle Pete all by myself. He is railroading these days. I can remember this stage, when I turned everything movable into a train of cars and worked at the transportation problem. Do you? I don't recall that I was as busy at it as Pete. He put in all day yesterday pushing his own baby buggy; didn't ride in it except when, exhausted, he was forced into it to sleep. When he came home to me here he got right down on the floor and him and me we made up trains and ran them all over the two rooms and the hall. People in the house stood by to watch, but Pete never saw anybody and at supper time he had to be fed when he wasn't looking, so as not to interrupt the traffic which was moving on the table; pens and pencils and boxes.

I infer from the way he does all this that the desire to work at something comes first, the motive to gain is later and may be learned from us. He is a mere artist so far, not a business man at all. . . .

Dot has sent to Jane a very interesting book, entitled *Ouroboros,* by Garet Garrett. It is one of the E. P. Dutton's "Today and Tomorrow" series. Don't miss it. Maybe Jane will send it you now that she has read it; I'll see. If it doesn't reach you soon from her, buy it over there. It is a big survey of the Mechanical Extension of Mankind and shows how all the nations are on the same track, missing something by imitating one another, and playing with the fire of war. He is a scientific man, but a good writer too. I know him of old. Jack should read it. It may suggest to him that some other business than the bank, even ranching, may turn out to be the thing in this next fifty years. . . .

Love to Laura and all.

To Laura Suggett

> Manoir de Bêcheron,
> Saché, Indre-et-Loire,
> France, Oct. 4, 1926

Dear Laura:

It seems an age since I have written you; it really must be about ten days, but a lot has happened. Pete has been modeled in clay, cast in plaster and will soon be a finished work of art, to live forever. It is a life-size statuette, standing, hands on tummy, head down, a very baby-like figure. Jo likes it himself so well that he means to show it, and an art dealer made him an offer for six copies for a fountain figure. Pete posed on and off for three weeks; that is to say, he played around Jo's studio every afternoon or morning for that time. He did not sit still for a moment. . . .

We are here for the winter. Yvonne is moving to town to round up her business, Jo is going to America to work. They are turning over their house to us. . . . It is a lonely place. The nearest village, or post office, is Saché, two kilometres away; the nearest market-place is our railroad station, telephone and telegraph centre, Azay-le-Rideau. The nearest city is Tours, twenty kilometres away. We are four hours by auto from Paris, five by railroad, on the way to Biarritz and Spain.

What you say about creative work is right, of course. It is Peter's religion; also it is her habit,—to work creatively. If we loaf around, as one must in travelling, and keep it up too long, she seems to go almost mad. I can idle longer than she can because I can go on working in my head. Mere talk therefore relieves me. But you seem to want to put your ideas into something more substantial than words; you want to do something; and Peter is content at present to write words. Sometimes I think she ought also to do deeds.

Len.

To Mrs. A. Winter

Bêcheron, Saché, France,
October 15, 1926

Dear Grandma:

I haven't written to you for a long time. Too busy. A new house and garden may seem to grown-ups to be about the same as all the old houses and gardens, but to me a new place is a new world, which has to be explored all over again, and thoroughly. My funny parents, they sweep their eyes around the courtyard, for example, and they know it. All they can see is that it has to be cleaned up, planted here and there and generally be made to look cared for. But I,—there is a stairway up the side of the west wing of the house. It did not interest the grown-ups at all. It fascinated me. I think it would have attracted you. Anyhow I had to climb up it to see, first, if I could; second, to find out where it went; and, third, to see if I could get down alone. It led to a closed door, which some day will be open. And I did get down without a tumble. I saw the gardener, his wife and my papa watching if I broke my neck; they were glad when I didn't, so pleased that I did it again and again. . . .

However, we all work in the court or the garden, me and my mama and my pop. Mama plants things, I dig them up; my pop cleans the dirt and leaves into piles, I scatter the piles and generally make work for him. He says that under our system a fellow that gives work is called a benefactor, so I am—a whatever that is.

I have been made permanent, you know, by my Uncle Jo Davidson, the mud man. He has made a monument in infancy out of me and is going to show it all over, he says. Me and Rockefeller or maybe it is more polite to say Mr. Rockefeller and Ella Winter's baby.

And still I can't talk. I want to, I need to; there are things I have to say to my upbringers or they will ruin me; and not in your nice way. I have been often on the point of talking when they changed the language on me, Italian to German, German to French and all the time a mixture of English and 'Merican. I hoped when Miss Charlton came with her steady flow of real English I would get a chance. I was all ready to shoot, while she was with me in Paris and here, but, no, I never got a look-in. She will remind me of a waterfall after I have seen one. Anyhow I got so discouraged that I have decided to wait till I get French from Madeleine. She is my new nurse. I like her; she is quiet, pretty and knows what she wants even if she doesn't know what I want.

But then I like everybody here, the cook, the gardener who is fired by all but me, and his wife, and Pum and the cats and the bunnies and our new auto, which is quite tamed already by my mama, who can learn anything; it still kicks at my papa, but that is because I think he abuses it. A car wants,—like me, to be treated gently but firmly.

This place is nowhere in particular. It is just like somewhere in France, a plain, undistinguished piece of country, French country, and that is what is so nice about it. I like it. It keeps me busy in my head, eyes, hands and feet. I think I might not have written to you for a long while yet, only I hear Aunt Rosa is coming home, and I know that, if I don't remind you, you will be all taken up with her. I feel bound to recall to you that there is still, as always

Your Little
Pete

To Jo Davidson

Bêcheron, Oct. 22, 1926

Dear Jo:

The meadow down toward the river is green and fresh now. There has been rain; not much; not enough really, but enough to water all living things with the hope and the sense of life. One of the pleasures of country life is to understand the wants of the trees, plants and grass, and so to feel their satisfactions. We like sunshine for ourselves, but, here, where the soil can be so dry that one can thirst with it for a drink, a rainy day is a joy, a relief. And so it is a matter of deep contentment to look off across the pasture lands and see them fat with green and red. Red, I say, for the autumn colors are glowing on the brush and the trees. In brief, Jo, Bêcheron is lovely with a new beauty. I wish you could see your home. And feel it. The house is warm, and so comfortable. It is cold outside, you know. Peter just drove her car out of the garage (did it all by herself) to go to Azay and Tours. She was wrapped in her Burberry, and Pete, who goes with her, is dressed in his Arctic white. Adrienne, the cook, gets a lift to Azay, where she gets out to visit her bereaved sister, and the chauffeur teacher gets in. He must, because Peter has no permit yet. Our examination is in Tours next Friday, a week from today. . . .

Happiness is lost often because when it is here, the triumph of a career, one is so busy that it is over before it is realized. Goethe made out that the moment Faust should say: *"O bleibe doch, du bist so schön"* he would go to the devil. I think on the contrary that that is the call to heaven. Don't you keep this glorious period of your life to look back to. Face it now. Grab it, rejoice in it. If you do, you will be happy now and, by the same token, you will recognize the other glad seasons as they come. You will love the autumn as we do at Bêcheron.

From the little you have told about him and his wishes of you, I believe that your Mr. M.[1] has somewhat of this philosophy or instinct. He has triumphed and he seems to know it, and he seems to want, now, to gather the fruit of his victory. He wants all that money can buy for him, and what does he ask for, say, in art? The other rich buy pictures, but having no real sense of painted beauty, they collect the standard masterpieces as a boy collects his stamps. There is a pleasure in that and a service too, but there is none of what I mean. There is no self-expression, no happiness in it; nothing but more victories.

But this unusual man wants his art to celebrate and, yes, appreciate the familiar things and people about him. If I understand his order to you, he wants you to see and to fix forever the beauty of the

[1] E. W. Marland.

figures of his life; not Madonnas, not naked women; these were the things beautiful in the lives of the priests and the men who were the victors of the Middle Ages. And they were right. What does a painter care what he paints? Painting is his business and his happiness; so he painted what the patrons of art wanted done. And they wanted painted the subjects of the Middle Ages. I think that you, an unscrupulous sculptor, I hope, might do damn well artistically and philosophically to enter into the mind and the very heart of men like M., see what they see as beautiful (and I mean look till you do see eye to eye with them) because they, these captains of industry, are the seers of our day. Artists have no quarrel with them, except as they, the artists, are chained back to the subjects of the old art ages and think because the old artists saw beauty in a Christian saint or an Egyptian monster, that they chose the themes, not the captains and Popes and Pharaohs, but the artists themselves. I believe that artists never chose their own subjects, never at least when they were expressing their times, never when they were at their best. Perhaps I can say what I have in mind if I apply it to my art, writing. If I could get the story of a captain of industry, all, as he lived it and as he saw and sees it, the force, the very violence, the fun, the daring and the tragedy of it all, the crimes, if you please, and the beauty of the career of, say, a Rockefeller,—then I say that I might write you THE American novel. And now, if you have got me, we can get you. To wit: If you could so listen to your Mr. M. and listening, get what he sees and as he sees it, you might express the inside of our day as well as you have expressed the outside in your Rockefeller, which is your masterpiece so far, Jo.

But whether you do or do not do this, do learn from him or from me to appreciate this, the moment of your triumph, and the little things and the simple people who are of it. . . .

Funny letter, this. I started it only to tell you what I saw out of the window of Bêcheron when I looked across the meadow after lunch today. See what became of it. . . .

Stef.

To Laura Suggett

Dear Laura: Bêcheron, October 22, 1926

I wish you liked Little Pete. There is nobody I can write to when I want to talk about him, and that is often. He is a small boy, but

upper: "THE GETAWAY," CARMEL, CALIFORNIA (photo by Sybil
Anikeef). *lower:* LINCOLN STEFFENS AND PETE BESIDE JO DAVID-
SON'S STATUE OF PETE IN CARMEL.

he takes up a big part of my being. When I went into the dining room just before lunch today, he was there with the maid, who is also his *bonne,* eating. He looked up, held out his hand to shake and smiled. And having smiled at me, he turned and smiled at Madeleine. He is polite, but likewise he is fair. He is a good deal of a gentleman, in his way.

The other day, when he had been playing long alone, he came running in to his mother as if he needed her. Climbing eagerly up on her lap, he put his arms about her neck and kissed her. Snuggling down into her arms he seemed about to stay there. But I, joking, asked him if he wasn't going to give me a kiss too. He slipped down, came to me and embraced and kissed me. And then he held up his hands to Madeleine who had come in for him, and he kissed her.

She is good with him; all peasant folk are right with children. They don't talk down to them, never use baby talk; they treat a child like a grown-up, on the level, man to man. Our servants in Italy were just so. Like Madeleine they express themselves and exactly what they feel. If Pete is rough with them, they remonstrate with as much indignation or impatience as they feel. No policy about it. They are not thinking of Pete's good, so they sound always sincere. I think Pete understands that. Visitors who adopt a certain grown-up tone with him and by way of noticing him praise something he does or wears, instantly get from him a manner, a pose: he shows off. "That is spoiling," says Madeleine. And she hurries Pete away to play or work with her and the dog and cats, who always treat Pete aright, as he treats them. If he pokes the cat, she scratches him. He takes that as he should, without complaint if he is alone. If any of us is about he "tells on the cat." Sure. But most grown-ups hereabouts don't take Pete's part. Madeleine won't even pick him up when he falls, as he does a lot, of course.

But we all let him have his tumbles; if they are bad and hurt a bit, we laugh. It is for that, I think, that Pete does not cry. He even laughs himself sometimes. He is and he feels on his own. Most of every day he plays all by himself and our reward for that is that he is independent, resourceful and happy. A recent article on experiments with children reported that when they were put into a room full of toys they were helpless, not knowing what to do; and when shown their uses repeated what they had been shown. No invention. Pete will himself find out what a toy or a tool is for, use it for all it is worth, then turn it over and find other unintended uses for it. I say, "Of course." It seems to me any child would do that. Certainly Pete always has been ingenious about amusing himself.

He will soon be talking now. Madeleine talks to him in simple, correct, good French and has caught his attention at last to a language. Others have talked too much, meaninglessly, and he imitates them. He talks in his baby language, talks a streak, as unintelligibly as some of his attendants have talked, saying as little. But lately I observe he talks as if he knew what he was saying. When he comes in from a walk or ride, he will come up and get off what sounds like a sentence, pause, and in another tone, with a different spirit, report something else. But Madeleine says that when he is out for a ride in his pram with her he doesn't talk, he sings. He enjoys the few things he sees hereabouts: cows, horses, chickens, autos, etc. It is such sights that he probably talks about when he comes in. But that he sings or hums to himself is pleasing to me since it fits in with his obvious love of music. No matter what he is doing, when we turn on the radio and get a concert from London or Paris, Pete stops to listen, and if it is dance music he dances, if it is other music he "conducts" as he saw done in Germany.

It's no use. One photo tells more of Pete than ever I can write. I quit. Enclosed is a review of *Moses* in the London *Herald,* the organ of the British Labor Party; it is by Norman Ewer, the foreign editor. It's the only notice I have seen anywhere. I'm trying to write a review of the books of Jack Black, Older and Ben Lindsey all in one, probably for the *Survey*.[1]

Len.

To Allen H. Suggett

Bêcheron, November 1, 1926

Dear Allen:

For the first time in my experience, partners of J. P. Morgan are making propaganda. Two of them in public speeches lately have said France (and, indeed, all Europe) would before the end of 1927 have their money stabilized on a gold basis. Meanwhile the French Government has done nothing observable about either its money or it debts, and the franc is going up, strong, and her bonds, etc., are

---

[1] This was written and published in part in the Paris edition of the New York *Herald*.

improving steadily; all under the lead of New York buying. I think a deal has been made by which Morgan undertakes, for some consideration as yet undisclosed, to restore and stabilize the franc, put up her securities and credit and otherwise adjust her finances. It's the biggest job American capitalists have ever undertaken. I'll bet they do it. I would rather know the terms, the plans and the fact of this combination than any news in the world today. . . .

To Fremont Older

Bêcheron, Dec. 4, 1926

Dear Fremont:

I am willing to help, of course. My offer to travel from here to Los Angeles is assurance enough that I stand ready to go somewhat out of my way to get justice or liberty or whatever J. B. and Schmidtie want. But J. B.'s notes to you do not tell me what they are after. I worked with Darrow once in their case, took his orders, so to speak, but this time I would rather know explicitly that I am doing what the two principals desire, and how they would like to have it done. There is the difficulty, however. I really can't make out whether J. B. wants to get out, he and Schmidtie, or to have a fight with certain labor leaders. He says in one of his notes that he doesn't want his indictments dismissed! I thought that that was what I was to try for at Los Angeles. My hunch is that I can do that. I believe I can persuade the capitalists to do almost anything in this line, but I cannot help much in an inside scrap with the labor machine; though I would like damned well to do that too. I see the labor organizations as the chief opponents of the revolutionary movements in every country in Europe as well as at home. Wall Street isn't in it with the A. F. of L. (in America or abroad) for defence of the capitalist system. Look at the British General Strike! And as for the coal miners, they are left high and dry exactly as J. B. and Schmidtie are. That is the labor situation, but it is hard for an outsider like me to tackle that; give me a Wall Street errand and I can do it with some hope; or Detective Burns; but Labor,—no, let the labor men themselves go up against that stone wall. And if they do, if they want to open up and fight, why of course I can make a statement which will relate how the agreement I made in good faith with Los Angeles was broken, and not only in the case of Schmidtie. It would show also that J. B. and J. J. did believe they were protecting their partners.

But I have nothing but inferences to illustrate the betrayal of all these men by Labor itself. In brief, I think I can be of use in a drive for liberty, but not for justice. I will serve in either, or for that matter, in any plan to my uttermost. Of course. All I am asking is that, not Darrow, but J. B. and Matt themselves decide and tell us what they want done and how; in what spirit, I mean. . . .

To Mrs. A. Winter

Manoir de Bêcheron,
December 6, 1926

My dear Grandma:

My Pop has been reminding me for some time lately that I owe you some expression of gratitude for the gifts you sent me for my birthday. I knew that; I know that it is not sufficient to feel something pleasant in one's heart. I have learned that people want what is felt to be said also or shown. And do you know how I discovered that? I can tell you exactly. My mama has been learning to drive an auto; she does it very well, only when she is at it she becomes so preoccupied that it seems to me that I am forgotten. Of course I know that she can't forget me, but just the same I awfully want to have a sign from her that she is aware that I exist. So I stand it as long as I can and then when I can't stand it any more, I hold out my cheek to her. At first she didn't see it, then she looked puzzled, but she's intellectual with a trained brain; she is so intelligent that she can even understand a child; so she slowly gathers what I mean and desire, and she kisses me. The first time I did it, she nearly drove off the road, but now—so clever is she!—she "gets" me quick and I get my connection. See? . . .

It looks now as if I would be moving to California early next year, and since that means boats and chu-chus, I am for it. Not the end. I am not educated yet to understand that the end is the end of travel, work and play; it still seems to me that the going and doing and being are the things, and that the end is nothing but a full stop which lasts till you get going again. . . . So you must be sure to call on me before we sail. Ah-wah, ah-wah,[1] Gran'ma.

Pete

[1] Au revoir.

Bêcheron, December 10, 1926

My dear Mother-in-law:

Your telegram, offering us the *Herald,* the *Tribune* and the flat, did not exactly reach us; it really touched us, all but Pete. He said: "But, of course. It's me." And maybe it was. Even so we responded to the sentiments expressed. I mean that we understand what you meant. I mean that we felt that the wire was not only an invitation, but a little message of,—oh, well. You know.

Peter took Pete to Azay-le-Rideau today to have a haircut. There was some workman or peasant in the chair when they entered the shop. "Bon jour, M'sieu' Pete," he said, and Mr. Pete responded, as usual, "Ah-wah," which to him is a salute going and coming. And Peter still is wondering who Pete's friend is and where he meets them all. For Pete knows and is known far beyond our utmost circle. But what I set out to say is that Pete got his hair cut and looks better, more masculine, more like his mother. . . .

Pete can argue now. He came up to me one day, all of a sudden, and rattled off the darnedest rigmarole of what sounded just like language, and I understood that he had seen somewhere some grown-ups reasoning together. I came back true to form, with my reasons, so to speak, against his obvious proposition, and so we had it out, both talking simultaneously, neither listening. Peter said that Pete beat me. I smiled first. But Peter, whose education often stands her in good stead, admitted why. "He gets the best of you because you do have to say something, whereas Pete's reason is pure, like Kant's. He doesn't have to think at all." But we often have arguments now just to make Peter feel at home. I don't care if Pete does win. I know that he will grow up, get a college education and then I will be able to beat the stuffin' out of the son of a gun.

I have just re-read this note to see if I have said what I meant to say. And I see that I haven't. What I had in mind to express was the sincere thanks of my family to you and yours for your heartfelt message. I mean that our hearts felt,—yours.

To Allen H. Suggett

Bêcheron, December 14, 1926

Dear Allen:

There was a letter from you in this morning's mail, started by Laura and finished by you. Also one from Older, who says that Jack

Black has been cured by the success of his book of his old burglar-complex. He seems to have had it ground into him that he was a thief and never could be anything else but a thief and ex-convict. Now he has discovered that he is a writer and so comes into a room just like a regular human being. Wonderful, isn't it? Both that a man can be made to think that he is something: a burglar, a banker, a librarian or even a Red, whereas he is really only a human being acting like a burglar or a Red. And wonderful what a little can release him from his complex! . . .

I am sick for home, sick. I wish I could come now, next week. I think that we will be here till February, then go to Paris for a week or two, then London for ditto, and then to the ship.

Len.

To Jo Davidson

Bêcheron, Jan. 7, 1927

Dear Jo:

Peter offers me space in her envelope to you, so here goes. I have nothing to say, everything to hear this time. You have been to California and will have been to Mexico! You simply cannot write into a letter all that I want to hear of those two visits. I know them, of course, but it is just like the time I wanted you to see Peter. I knew her too, but I did want to hear what you would have to say about her. I would rather hear you on Mexico and California than anybody I know. Since you have "got" the West and the Westerners, I am sure you will "get" my two favorite parts of the earth. And you have seen so many of my friends too, or will have: Older, Jack, the Suggetts, and Calles and his crowd. I wish you could do him and Obregón. It would be great if you could get an order for some Mexican busts so that we could go down there together and I could talk life into their faces while you catch it in mud.

The place here goes fine. The garden is almost all remade, along the same lines but renewed and perfected. The house is a bit backward. They are at the lighting plant still, working this morning, for example. It's all right, only unexpectedly slow. There have been leaks, freezes, thaws, etc., but we have repaired what we could not prevent. I have gone far in my *Life*. The *Moses* is making no stir; it's not read, I take it. For even Yvonne, who says she did not want to read it, did finally tackle it and she likes it tremendously. I am amazed at her enthusiasm. I wish somebody would jump on it hard enough to get it read. Can't you stir up some Bishop to go for it and me? . . .

Affectionately,

Stef.

To Mrs. A. Winter

Bêcheron, February 13, 1927

Dear Grandma:

Grown-ups,—except gran'mas, of course,—take a queer view of things. Everybody has been remarking lately that I have grown; the cook says she had noticed it the last week. My mama weighed me and she joined the chorus: "Pete is bigger," she said. Now what I have noticed is, not any change in me; I may be small or big, but I am the centre of the universe, and it is precisely this world about me that has altered. It has become clearer.

You remember that moon I discovered and told you about? Well, there's a sun too. You probably never saw it; it shines so that I turned away my eyes too. But the other day there was a mist; I could look at the sun and I did. I thought it was the moon, and so I said to my papa: "Sechee, moona," but he shook his head, no, and pointed to the old moon off the other way. And so I looked first at one, then quick at the other, and there were two, the moon AND the sun. I hope you are interested like me an' my papa.

Another thing: Maybe you remember how I used to dance when I was smaller, according to my mama. My papa said he was kindo' glad that I liked music. And I do. But that's no reason for getting music and dancing all mixed up. They got to turning on the music can over and over and for a while I liked it because I couldn't seem to get enough of dancing. But here lately I am getting fed up on dancing. After two or three one-steps I want to go back to work or to sit and hear some music. My parents, the servants, everybody, can't understand it; they turn on the can again and again till it hurts. Last night I couldn't bear it any more. When I had had my dances out, they turned on another piece and I ran at them crying, "No, no, no; stop." And they stopped, but they looked dazed. They cannot seem to understand that jazz is not music; it is movement, it is time, it is measure, but music? Music is something else. That is what is becoming clearer to me. That is why,—by the way, I could never understand the radio. As my pop says, it is marriage without love, it is working for money, it is courtesy reduced to obedience, it is affection made into a duty. . . .

With sincere affection,

Your only (so far) grandson,

Pete

To Laura Suggett

Dear Laura: Bêcheron, February 13, 1927

. . . Pete beats me; can't quite make him out sometimes. One of the maids we had for him in Austria taught him to "go stand in the corner" when he had done something wrong. I took the sting out of it by laughing when he was put there, but he recognises it as a punishment. We never tell him to do it; we do not punish at all, but if he spills anything he will himself go into a corner and hide his smiling face. Fine, I get all that. But here the other day he asked us for something, his mother's glasses, I think; anyway something he might break; and it was refused him. He persisted, so did we, and he, quite angry, went and stood in the corner. As a punishment for us? Maybe he is a philosopher who thinks of punishment as an abstraction; it is a shame, not for the server of the sentence, but for the witnesses, for all. Something in that, a lot more than an adult could "get" unless it were some grown-up like Older, who will agree with it. He and Pete would see that the prison term of Mooney is a disgrace, not to Mooney, but to the rest of us. . . .

To Ella Winter

Paris, Sunday night, Feb. 13, 1927

Sweet Peter:

I've seen Georgie. He had a friend with him, one of the New School,[1] the Polish Jew, whose name I forget. We lunched at the Universal Brewery and for three hours (I started to say years) we talked,—slowly; my tone, not theirs,—but I hardly know what was said. I don't have any clear idea of "the universal purpose." It is "Youth" and it is "Life"; but it is not young people. My mind has it: the power to renew itself. And it is not life as it is lived, except by the prophets and the philosophers. It is potential life. What has happened to and by men so far is a result of their fears and weaknesses,

[1] *Esprit,* a philosophical "school" and magazine run by a small group for a short period in France.

their needs and their materialism as well as of the virtuous desires of their higher mental life and being. But it must not be defended, really: it cannot be stated.

"We are mystics," said Georgie.

"Yes, we are mystical," said the Pole.

"Oh, no," I protested, "don't take on a name, don't cover your idea with a word, don't put yourselves in a pigeon-hole."

"You are right," said Georgie.

"We are not mystics," the Pole agreed.

"There is nothing mystical about us," said Georgie.

This was at the end, as we parted and said, "Ah wah." For Pete had come into it; I showed them his prophet's mantle, the Bedouin costume. And you came into it. You,—or my conception of you,— breaks up one of the departments of their thought, the chapter on Woman. Georgie said,—he recalled what I said at his mother's table about our marrying, not for love or money, but for fun, and he said: "No. Ella did not. You may have, but not Ella. She has not such a humor. That is too wise for a woman." I stuck; you did have a sense of humor, or, at any rate, of fun. "No, what she has that you think is humor is the reflection of your mental gaiety." He holds to his first impression of you as an earnest young thing. When I hung on and cited Pete, your jester child, he said Pete got *that* from me.

It was fun, too. They want some more, one more meeting, "say, Tuesday," but I said, "Hold! Enough." So Georgie said he would 'phone his goodbye. I suggested flowers, and so,—he may not even 'phone. Why goodbye? The Pole gave me up when I asked for flowers; he gave me up several times during the afternoon, but Georgie always came to the rescue with the explanation that, well, that I did not always mean flowers. . . .

Is this enough of that? It is for me. . . . I'd like now to meet the leader. He may have something so clear that he can say it. These boys can't; not yet.

To Laura Suggett

Hotel Richepanse, Paris,
March 12, 1927

Dear Laura:

I don't know whether you like a letter in bulletin form, but I had to write one so. News is all right in its way, but I'd rather sit down and write quietly nothing of news to you; that's a comfort, just to lay off and be with Laura and Dr.; like this Saturday morning. With the Petes gone the room is empty and I am alone. Jo Davidson got back yesterday with a lot of lovely old Egyptian fragments of sculpture. And for once I liked to see the stolen treasures in a foreigner's hands, for he understood them. He would hold up a bit of stone with a curved eye and so see the masterful beauty of it that I felt as the original artist must have felt, appreciated and happy. Jo is going to be influenced by the ancient things he has seen in old Egypt. For one thing, they spoil his view of the freak sculptures in Nature's museum. But I mean, really, that he will simplify his own portraits, make them less likenesses and more essential. His "Pete" is more like what he will now do, I think. That is Pete all right, but it should be known as a baby boy. It is so like the others, like all the babies of all the people; just rising erect, straightening from a little monkey into a man-cub. Pete may be one of Jo's best things.

Mrs. Whitney came back with the Davidsons. She has been having a house party or a house boat on the Nile. Jo says it's a beautiful way to live for a while, terribly expensive, but almost worth it. Jo's host and guide was a famous old Armenian dealer [1] who knew everything and everybody. . . .

To Allen H. Suggett

Paris, Sunday, March 13, 1927

Dear Doctor:—

. . . Pete took his mother to London, and she reports as you'll see in her letter, enclosed. He is all right; not nearly such a baby as she thinks and implies in her letter. The other day when I was here alone with him, he said, "Mama n'est pas là." He said it like a Frenchman with hands spread out as at a loss and a sad, sad look on his face. It is too comical. For he is never sad or bereft. I bade him go and say it over again to the Pete in the mirror, and he did. He faced himself and, spreading his arms and putting on the proper French face for a person abandoned, he repeated, "Mama pas là—pas là!" But as he said it and saw himself he saw the absurdity of his affected bereavement and stopped, looked up at me and laughed. Then he did it over for fun, and he laughed like a fat man. After that he would go and mimic himself every now and then. And when his mama came in, he pulled

[1] Kelekian of the Rue de la Paix.

her to the high mirror and did it for her, only he made it papa. I was there, but he said, "Papa n'est pas là," tearfully; and laughed.

He's a great kid, Doctor. Even Jane, who is too young to be taken in by youth, fell for Pete, whose pretensions are so humorous. But then, Pete soon saw (at Alassio) that Jane could not be fooled by the baby bunk that took us in and he cut it out,—for her. I mean that, if he was acting up for us, and Jane expressed her disgust in her face or words: "Ah, cut that, Pete," he would hesitate, look from her to us and back, and, laughing, quit it and eat (or whatever it was) like a regular fellow. I caught on from Jane, so I am in on the ground floor. Only Peter is left out. "Come, Pete," she pleads, "let me put on your shoes." He won't. I come in, give him a look (like Jane's) and say: "No, let him go barefoot and stay in the house." He saves his face by asking me to put on his shoes. Pretending it was not the shoes, but his mother he objected to, he says, "Papa—shoes," and pointing to them, lets me put them on. He cries when he falls down with her; with me he looks ashamed or amused and gets up. He will do this when it hurts too. "Ooo," he says, with his hand on the spot, and I can see it was a real bump.

The maids taught him to go and hit the thing he bumped. I go and pat the thing and make him soothe the table or chair, not Pete. The result is that his behavior is different with different people. I'd like him to be alone with Laura for a week or so, long enough to get her attitude. She would encourage his natural disposition to put things back in their places. Neither of us does that, and I have had Pete insist that, after he has used his pot, I put it back, not near, but just where it was. "Pas là," he says, pointing to the proper spot, "là."

Did I tell you that I wrote to Bertrand Russell for a reservation for Pete at his school, and got it, cordially. Peter is to see Russell and the school with Pete now, in London. We know him, both of us, and his idea is not to teach kids any bunk, not to give them the old physics, mathematics and economics, but from the start teach the new knowledge. "The sun does not rise and set; the earth turns." That's my idea too, I can myself *see* the earth turn from the sun at sunset, but I had to learn to; I had to correct the false vision taught me. I want Pete to see that first, and Russell seems to mean to have teachers teach everything that way: 2×2 is a theory that works pretty well, but not certainly; the shortest distance between two points looks like a straight line, but it's really a curve.

I can't teach Pete to obey; he is too independent and too obstinate, but he is very deeply courteous, he likes to please (like Frenzy), and he will consider me or others and do much for us, if we don't set up our will against his. I do that too, sometimes. When it's an emergency, like getting on or off a train, I compel; I grab Pete and go. But I explain afterwards and make it up. He doesn't understand my excuses, but he does "get" the fact that I am apologizing. He *likes* manners.

Someone taught him to kiss the hand as a greeting,—the French maid, I think,—anyhow he does it with pleasure and with grace. He has lots of little French ways that will soon be lost, I guess; and that does not matter; they are pretty and they develop his instinct for forms that express his courtesy; which is so deep in him that I think it must be natural with all children. Other children, especially some American boys he has met here, amaze and anger him. They are so loud and self-assertive. I like to be there when he is with other children, so that I can break a fight, and suggest taking turns. Pete can get that quick, quicker than the other children, whom also I have to curb to get Pete his turn to jump off a trunk onto the floor.

Some day after we get home, I want you to drive out with Pete alone with you on the front seat. He worships engineers (of locomotives) and chauffeurs. That will be a good start for you, and the rest (of what I want) will follow. You need not wonder at my wish, or feel exceptional. I want Pete to "feel" Jack Black, too, and Laura. I think that children feel and absorb character and that, if Pete can be under the unconscious influence of picked people, his good little character will feed up and grow. Jack Black is a masterpiece of self-control, and that's Pete's need. If he is to be wilful, his will must learn to handle Pete; his will, not mine.

Gee, I guess I was wrong. I didn't only want to be with you; I must have been missing Pete, my masterpiece,—so far unspoiled; rickety, but,—all right.

Love to Laura, Dot, Jim, Jack and to Doctor.

Len.

X

HOME
(1 9 2 7 - 1 9 3 1)

AFTER brief stops in New York City and Chicago Lincoln Steffens and his family went to California. At first he believed his latest attempt to secure pardons for "my dynamiters" was to be successful, but once more he was disappointed. After visiting both the Suggetts and the Hollisters, he began to look about for a place in which to settle. ("How I want a *home!*" he wrote Laura.) Carmel suited him, and he rented a house for the summer. The next autumn he bought the Carmel house that he called The Getaway.

He made a brief lecture trip in the East in the autumn of 1927 and another in the autumn of 1928. He twice visited E. W. Marland in Ponca City. In the summer of 1929, while Ella Winter and Pete were in England, he gave a course of lectures to students in Colorado, and spent some weeks in San Francisco. The next summer, while Ella Winter went to Russia, he and Pete stayed with Jo and Yvonne Davidson in France. On their return to the United States, they took a house for the winter in Croton-on-Hudson, to be near the publishers of the *Autobiography*. In the spring Ella Winter went to Russia again and Lincoln Steffens and Pete went back to Carmel.

When Steffens began the *Autobiography* in 1925, he thought it would be finished in a year or two. He wrote the last chapter at Bêcheron in August, 1930. He always thought of his life as a story, often speaking of its chapters, and it was a story that he had to tell. Moreover, the *Autobiography,* he discovered as he wrote it, summed up all the various books that, since Versailles, he had thought of writing. Naturally, therefore, despite some bad moments, he enjoyed his work. Toward the end, however, it began to seem an unconscionable burden. "Freedom to me," he wrote Ella Winter in the autumn of 1929, "means to have that job done and then, to take on no other 'job.' I'd write, but not long things, not duty things that have to be done." And when it was finished he told her, "I weigh less than I did this morning by a ton." "It is not bad," he said, "I am not satisfied; I could not be; but I am about through. I can do no more. I, too, must live, and I can't while this job is upon me, day and night."

Steffens wrote in the final chapters of the *Autobiography* the conclusions to which three years in America, after a long absence, had brought him. He felt that his own country, which he had been saying was not worth watching, pulsated with a life as new and as extraordinary as the life of revolutionary Russia. The proof that men had solved the problem of production was apparent everywhere. Now the new capitalists, as they were called, were saying that they were ready to solve, scientifically, the problem of distribution. What, he asked, was to stop them? "Really, Jo," he wrote Davidson, "the unconscious experiment this country is making in civilization and culture is equal to that of Soviet Russia. The race is saved, one way or the other, and, I think, both ways."

He was acquainted with some of the new capitalists,—Owen D. Young, E. A. Filene, E. W. Marland,—and he talked with them. He also talked, and largely agreed, with Garet Garrett, one of the most eloquent prophets of a new era. The important struggle, he began to believe, was between management and ownership, not between labor and capital. If the managers, the really scientific men, could be freed from the dictation of profit-seeking bankers, they could distribute the wealth they had learned how to produce. So he became a believer in the new capitalism; but in the newness, not the capitalism. "I asked him," he told Ella Winter in reporting a talk with Garrett, "if he didn't find himself defending Capitalism. He thought—not—not consciously—maybe—he thought—not. I warned him that, if he did, it would darken his vision in spots." Steffens was as ready to abandon the new capitalism, if it proved a failure, as he had been to accept it.

When the *Autobiography* finally appeared, he was surprised by its success, and of course pleased. It was more than twenty years since he had been so wholeheartedly recognized by the American people. With the decline of muckraking, and his loss of faith in reform, had come the decline of his reputation. He had greeted with pleasure the opportunities that came to him with the short-lived enthusiasm for his settlement of the McNamara case, with his success in influencing Mexican policy, with the public reception of his lecture on Russia. But his triumphs had been brief, and he never regained the prestige and power he had had at the height of the muckraking movement. For years he had been in Europe and had come to feel himself hopelessly isolated. ("I thought I didn't have many friends left," he wrote Filene after landing in New York in 1927. "All wrong," he continued, with almost pathetic joy. "We were invited everywhere.") And now, in the spring of 1931, his book, the story of his life, was being called "a sort of classic of our day." The long years of watching had borne fruit at last.

With the book finished, he could enjoy the freedom to which he had long looked forward. Many years before he had said that an essay ought to be written on the art of dying, and now he proposed to practice that art. "Life grows better and better as I live it. Every chapter is an improvement upon its predecessor. I am sure that old age is the best of Life, mismanaged though it usually is. I mean to manage mine and save it, as I used to food, for the last." He preached to Gilman Hall and E. A. Filene "the wisdom of reflection for men of action who have had deep experience of life." There was loss, he said, in dying with one's boots on. "I would like to have a home somewhere to feel that I can, not live there, but die there, my way of dying without haste but without killing anybody else."

The baby and the book had divided his interest for nearly seven years,—and he wrote far more, as this chapter shows, about the baby than he did about the book. Now the book was the public's; the baby —the boy!—was still his. He had often told Mrs. Hollister that he was interested in her children, not merely because they were related to him but also because of the generation they belonged to. Always he turned to those younger than himself with a friendliness that they could not resist, and that friendliness was based equally on what they were and what they represented. His relationship with his son was, in the same curious way, a mixture of the personal and the impersonal. None of the child's sayings was more genuinely welcomed or more widely repeated than his declaration of independence: "Pete's Pete's." Steffens's love for Pete, so deep and so tender, was inseparable from his passionate interest in the future.

To Mrs. A. Winter

Santa Monica, California,
May 9, 1927

Dear Gran'ma:

After I left you the other day I got on a boat, which floated off over the water and picked up my papa. I was surprised that the boat knew where he was and where I was. I guess you, who know everything, told him and the bo-at where to meet. Then I went to sleep sleepy, and when I woke up there was nothing but water outside and mostly sea-sickness inside. I got my insides out the first day, but my mama,—she kept trying to turn inside out all the way. Since I could not help her, I played on the deck, mostly flirting with people, first, those that liked me at first sight, then having dropped them I worked on those that wouldn't look at me or looked as if I were the kind of food that made people sick. This I kept up until I had the whole ship on my side. The only interruptions were when the ship rose up and hit me, as a boat does, you know. My papa, who had to attend me, he said that I fell down, but I want you to believe that the boat fell up. I didn't get sea-sick any more because my papa took me up to the front of the boat and got me to moving up and down with the bow till I had the motion just like when you dance, which was all right till we came to land. Then when the land did not move and my insides did, I fell down some more and I thought and I told everyone that it was the boat again I would get up, point down to the floor and say "bo-at" and everybody would laugh.

New York was glad to see me. It seemed to know my papa, to be curious to see my mama, about whom it had had some doubts. These were soon dissipated, my mama was what these here movie people call a hit. I know this because I could see my papa swell up at her success just as if she were his daughter, as if he had made her instead of only me. He took her everywhere with him to see not only his friends, but editors as well. I was left all alone with Anna,—lucky we took her,— and when I asked him why he wouldn't give my mama any rest, he said she helped him in his business. As for me, I won everybody. I found out that they all like my French language and manners, so I kissed women's hands and said "bon jour, Lady," till I got hugged and kissed so much I had to cut it out. Now I speak English and am acquiring American manners, which are much easier. I keep my French for people I really want to "get," as we Americans say.

Then, when we had conquered all New York, we got a chu-chu which just shot us to Chicago, where I went to live with some dynamiters while my papa and mama went to live with book-shop folk. The dynamiters liked me and when I got sick, they did too. It was like a house in mourning. But the head dynamiter, he laughed at Anna. Once when he asked her something and when she answered in her meek, low voice, he said at her: "Why do you shout so, Anna?" and Anna looked surprised because she had not been shouting. I think it was because he is a Labor Leader and hates to see Labor humble. He wants it to throw dynamite around and of course my Anna does not even threaten to do that.

Well, and then we got on a chu-chu one night, had a room and we stayed on that chu-chu so long, days and nights and days and nights, going over rivers and mountains and plains till I thought that finally my papa had settled down and we weren't going to travel any more. But, no, when we rolled over the last mountains and slid down into the last valley, we came to another city floating on the ocean in the sunshine, called San Francisco, where my mama and I, we conquered my Aunt Lola, who had thought that we were bad for my papa. Don't grown-ups get funny notions? My papa says that you thought also once that he and I were a hindrance to my mama's career, and a disgrace to the family, but I don't believe all that my papa says, especially about my Winter side. Anyhow, no sooner had we got to San Francisco than my papa said to me, we had to come here, "lest they get on to us," he explains; and so here we are in a hotel on a beach where I play around on the sand and sometimes wet my feet up to my pants in the water. I am turning brown as my mama's eyes and as healthy and sound as my papa's ideas. While Anna and I enjoy life, my parents go off seeing the movie people and their play-places, which any child would love. But the grown-ups call it business and are as serious about it as I am about running my yellow taxi on the hotel porch.

In brief, Gran'ma, I shall have lots to tell you when we meet again and more to ask you about adults and their silly ways. I can't now. I have time only to kiss your hand and to throw some to Aunty Rosa and Uncle Rudi.

Your loving grandson,

Pete

To Fremont Older

Santa Monica, May 14, 1927

Dear Fremont:

Your letter came yesterday. Asa Keyes, the District Attorney, is for our proposition. Since he is not a "Chandler man," but a victor over him, I decided to see him first. I called yesterday, made my suggestion,—pardon, commutation,—and he interrupted to ask if they were not eligible for parole. I said they were, but that I hoped for a more clearing and generous act. In any case, however, there were the old indictments to lift. He did not know that, having only the recollection that Matt's were cleaned up. I did not ask him if he would help for a pardon; I avoided anything so explicit, but he was soon considering with me how we might go at it or a commutation, whether the Governor would take such a step, and when I asked him what opposition there might be here in Los Angeles, he thought a moment and said: "Only from the *Times*."

"If I can get Chandler [1]—" I started to ask.

"If you can get Chandler," he broke in, "all will be clear down here."

That was plain enough that he, Keyes, would not oppose us, but I wanted to be sure, so I said: "And those old indictments against J. B.?"

"I will attend to them," he answered.

"Shall we have to have an attorney to make the motion?" I asked.

"Yes," he said, "but I will attend to that when the time comes. You go see Harry Chandler, tell me what he says and then we'll plan the rest."

So I left it and went off to call on Chandler, who was out, of course. He had but just got back from New York and no doubt is busy. I made a request for an appointment any time at his convenience next week. I don't dare hurry him or his secretary.

I am sure I proceeded aright, going first to Keyes and getting him to send me to Chandler. Maybe now Chandler will send me to Keyes. Moreover I can see, by the way my propositon went with Keyes, that I have it in the right form. Indeed, Keyes said that he thought that my success with both Chandler and the Governor depended upon how I put it, and he nodded his head as if he approved the way I put it to him. But he (Keyes) is an unusually quiet, thoughtful man. That appeared when I opened up the subject of bandits and the crime-waves before I stated my business. He could see the strength of the boldest

[1] Harry Chandler, publisher of the Los Angeles *Times*.

bandits and the waste of our way of dealing with them. We talked agreeably about Jack Black as no born criminal, as not sick, but a fellow useful to society, if it would have found him early and given him adventurous work to do. Also he joined with me in wishing for a distinction in treatment of "criminals" and class-fighters, like Schmidtie. He knew all about Matt's prison record, by the way. If this man were governor we could do some things in this line.

You will, of course, regard this report as confidential, telling only the two men concerned and, perhaps, it would be well to convey to them at present only the substance of my bulletin, viz.: that the L. A. District Attorney has no objection to our plan and will lift J. B.'s indictments "when the time comes" to act. But I want you also to show this letter to Andrew Furuseth. We talked over the matter when he called day before yesterday and he deserves to know what happened yesterday. I have not written a word to Darrow yet, but I have no objection to your doing so. I think my feeling is that a letter from here to Clarence Darrow, Chicago, might be opened here. You could write from there with safety, and he'll be relieved to hear of our progress.

From what I hear about Young [1] I think he might help us, somehow, unless he should consult Hiram, whom I fear in all such matters. He is so "just" and so righteous, lawyer-like and hard. Hiram never felt the need of "mercy."

Affectionately,
Lincoln

Santa Monica, May 17, 1927

Dear Fremont:

I have just come from Harry Chandler, and he consents to whatever I can get done. He agreed quickly, easily, without any objection. I spent an hour with him, but it was all about labor history down here since "we" settled the case: he said "we" all through. We talked Mexico, everything; we even discussed whether we could get the Governor under the circumstances, the *Times* having fought him. But he fell in with my idea of a pardon, commutation or parole without a hitch.

I went straight to the District Attorney's office to report as I had promised to do, but he was out for the afternoon, so I left a message which he will understand. I shall call on him tomorrow, but only to

[1] Governor C. C. Young of California.

arrange details. He was all right before, asking only that I get this consent from C. . . .

I can come up to go to Sacramento whenever you feel we are ready. I am not ready myself. I need to know whether both Matt and J. B. are eligible for parole now and how they want me to proceed. My idea is that maybe someone else might better deal with Young, but if I am to carry on through, I propose to ask for a pardon; if that fails, to fall back to commutation and, as a last resort, if all else fails, to stick for the parole, which the Governor could simply let happen,—on the theory that if he said he would not oppose, he might really give instructions to grant the parole.

I feel immensely relieved; as if I had feared a failure down here, and no doubt you will be glad and happy. But don't raise too high the hopes of Matt and J. B. The worst is yet to come. I can't seem to get any sense of what sort of fellow Young is and I keep seeing Hiram in the background.

To Marie Howe

> Hollister Ranch,
> Gaviota, Cal.,
> Sunday, June 6, 1927

Dear Marie:

I omitted it from my *Life,* but I was reminded by your last letter to us of an incident or an experience in my boyhood. There was a little girl, a mean slip of a thing, who used to come around and trouble us fellows by saying:

"I know something that I won't tell you."

Lots of people knew and will remember her. I'll bet Fred ran up against her. She got you all curious and guessing and, then, when you simply had to know what it was that she had found out and would not tell; when you ate dirt and offered to trade her anything you had, she still would not tell. And you had to make yourself believe that it wasn't anything at all or anyhow nothing that you would want to know; and that that was why she could not tell it. Even that never moved her. She would stand around with her secret, look mysterious and shake your gallantry to the point you would have liked to just hit her one.

Well, I have often wondered what became of that mean thing, and now I know. She grew up into a fine woman, perfect, except that she still writes to her vain and most self-satisfied friends, saying that same old mean thing. "Your *Life* is well done with that one exception, which you must know yourself. If you don't I won't tell." You feel like reading the darned thing all over again, and since that is too much you hardly dare to go on writing it "all very well except for that one thing." I can't do it. I am going to beat that pesky, mean grown-up little girl at last. I am going to tell her that I ain't a-going to write another line of my *Life* till she comes through with her secret. See?

And I ain't going to write no more to her either. So there!

                                                              Steffens

To Fola La Follette

                                          Gaviota, California,
                                          [June, 1927]

Dear Fola:

I have just been reading your review of my *Moses,*[1] and I thank you for it. It is a helpful criticism. But I want also to congratulate you upon your understanding of me. I do not mean that it is well to understand me. I mean that it is great to be able to understand anybody or anything as you have "got" me and my book. But then that was always your gift: to understand. And I have no doubt that that gift came from your other gift, the courage and the strength to love. Anyway your review of *Moses* reminds me of the time when I was making a speech, with John Haynes Holmes in the chair. After I had struggled for an hour or more to account for my conduct, he reviewed my speech in a five minute talk and said, really expressed, what I meant.

You are going abroad, you say. I am glad of that; you like it over there as I do. I shall be staying over here for a year or more, but I would like to follow you in your travels. Can you not give me your itinerary? And will you write to me once in a while? It should not be a burden, since you will know that a word or a name will throw me a picture, and we should get closer, Fola, you and I; we are almost old friends now, and old friends become, not only very dear, they become necessities. They are the only people one doesn't have to talk with; they understand all about it by just being together. I hasten to

---

[1] In *La Follette's Weekly.*

add that old friends don't have to be themselves old, not both of them; I can have a lovely time, for example, with Pete without words, and he is younger in years than you are. And then there is Peter. You don't really know her yet, not even as well as she knows you. She has heard about you from Marie and me and you have heard of her only from Marie. But some day you and Peter will like to sit down together and think about some people you both knew pretty well.

Wherever two or three of my old friends are gathered together there I shall be also.

Peter and I have had a great time at Hollywood. We let it be known shamelessly that we believed that the photo-play was a coming art and that we wanted to hear about the serious side of it. When they felt that we were sincere and had no fear of being ridiculous they opened their secret sincerities and we saw something worth while. The cynics laughed; but there were some that dropped the "all-for-money pose." We talked art in Hollywood and we got away with it.

I am working on this quiet, beautiful ranch; writing on my *Life*. Peter is doing articles but soon will resume her novel. Pete is down on the beach at the moment, but all the time he is discovering mountains, cattle, insects and his own legs and stomach. It is good for all of us and not bad for our hosts, my sister and her husband, who live so much alone. We watched a round-up yesterday, a rough and bloody spectacle, but usually we stay within the limits of the house and garden, which are as peaceful as such a multitudinous life can be: alive with birds, bugs and beasts, all busy and all talking at once.

Life grows better and better as I live it. Every chapter is an improvement upon its predecessor. I am sure that old age is the best of Life, mismanaged though it usually is. I mean to manage mine and save it, as I used to food, for the last.

A hail to Mid,[1] whom I can see delving and questioning into Old Europe. A fine, everlasting interest.

But here comes Pete, back from the beach with something to report. I kindo like Pete and his discoveries and his true reports of news. I guess I kindo like more and more people more and more. But I know I like my old friends, like you, Fola.

Affectionately,
Lincoln Steffens

---

[1] George Middleton, the playwright, Fola La Follette's husband.

To Mrs. A. Winter

Gaviota, June 7, 1927

Dear Mother-in-law:

My wife will be indignant at me for writing to you this morning. She wants me to work on my book and she knows that Anna is attending to Pete's correspondence, better, they all say, than I do. But I promised you once that I would always report to you when anything was wrong with your daughter. She is laid up in bed with a sore throat and an insulted coccyx. No, you need not be anxious; it hurts but it is not dangerous.

She was out horseback riding Sunday (June 5) with Janey. They got into an overgrown, washed-out trail and decided to turn back. Peter dismounted, started to turn her safe old horse, when he slipped and Peter sat down on a pointed rock. She discovered that she had a rudimentary tail and that, like all useless, passing organs and people, her ex-tail was sensitive. She was able to remount and to ride slowly home,—so slowly that they were late to dinner; she went to bed and there she is now, being very gentle with herself and the symbol of her long, long pedigree. It is getting slowly better, else we would have a doctor out to examine it. There shall be no neglect even though it takes a doctor all day to make a call here and costs about twenty pounds or guineas.

Otherwise Peter is well and busy, like Pete and me. She has conquered everybody here, as she has everywhere along our long road. Some people congratulate her on getting me (and Pete), but most of them congratulate me on getting her (not counting Pete). In a word, she is a social success and most people don't know how much your labors upon her have been reënforced by my anxious care. They think I just found her just as she is. She is not working on her novel. She feels so full of new facts, experiences and ambition that she is writing for the papers and magazines. She has planned other sketches for the *Manchester Guardian.* . . .

Pete too is growing. He is taller, heavier and much browner. My sister Dot says he is getting handsomer too. I agree with this, he looks more and more like his mother. We all get up early, about six-thirty, and have breakfasted by seven. Then Uncle Jim and Jane ride off over the range on their cattle business to be gone sometimes all day. Jane does a man's work and gets from the estate a man's pay. Pete plays around with Dot, Peter or me, till Anna has done her housework; she takes in our washing and cleans our rooms. Then at 9:30 Anna goes with Pete "down-a-beach." They have a bully long morning in the everlasting sun, sand and water, till the eleven-forty-five train goes by. Dot has changed dinner from twelve to twelve-ten to allow for Pete's greeting the engineer and passengers on that train. After the meal Pete sleeps, and we all miss him; for we sit around talking. But after his nap his fun begins again.

Yesterday was a great day. Pon, the Chinaman, had emptied the swimming tank, scrubbed it and was letting water in afresh. It was Pete's depth. I took him down into it and he waded around making a splash and noises in the sun-warmed water. When he was dried and dressed, Jim and Jane came home and told Pete that they had brought home a horse all for himself. We went up to see it; the children's old Shetland pony, and as soon as they can find his bridle Pete is to ride it, Anna or I leading. But it is, as Pete claims already, "Pete's da-da." Pete is down-a-beach now, but this afternoon the water in the tank will be deep enough for him to begin to learn to swim so that if we sail to China and he falls overboard he can save his own life and swim ashore. . . .

Yours affectionately,
Lincoln Steffens

To Allen H. Suggett

Gaviota, June 15th, 1927

The Governor will let the dynamiters out on parole. I saw him today and he did all that I was asked to request of him but I asked for so much more that I feel defeated and he followed me to the door apologizing.

"Don't think me 'backward,'" he said, "you must remember that you have thought more intensely than I have upon this subject."

I had asked him to pardon Miss Whitney,[1] Mooney, Billings, Matt Schmidt and J. B. and when he exclaimed, I tore on and answered, "Nor is that all. I am asking for a liberal leader, for a man who will do all these things at one blow as a call to men to stop all this hate and be generous and fine." He and Gov. Fuller alone had chances to strike the new note, pardon the class warriors and make the gesture this country is ready for. So I said, and he, struck by the thought,

---

[1] Anita Whitney, under indictment for Criminal Syndicalism, was pardoned by Governor Young on the eve of imprisonment.

backed off. I must get my friends in prison to apply for parole first, then,—when they had made good outside as they had inside,—then we may talk of pardons. By that time we were so intent upon the larger thing that I hardly noticed that I had what my friends and Darrow wanted. We went on into the Whitney case and the new crime laws and when I rose to go, I was disappointed. He rose with me protesting. Why?

"Oh," I said, "I came here for a gesture, a call to liberalism, a leader, and all I got is what my two prisoners are entitled to under the law."

He knew, he answered, and then it was he asked me to remember my advantage over him. He pledged me, if I ever saw another chance, in some other field, for him to give a liberal call, to come and tell him.

To Marie Howe

850 Francisco Street,
San Francisco, Cal.,
June 25, 1927

Dear Marie:

Thanks for this good letter, which is helpful and wise. The only thing I can't understand about it is why you were so reluctant to write it. Criticism does not hurt me; certainly not such friendly advice as this. I shall take it in mind as I write and rewrite and no doubt fix it, with gratitude to you. I may not change it as you suggest. The egotism of my first person was so essential that I think I should not always alter, but increase it, sometimes. I mean that, instead of cutting it out, I might insert a paragraph explaining that I did feel immensely superior to T. R. I had respect for Riis; he knew something about the police; I had awe of Max, Riis' boy; he understood everything. But Roosevelt? He knew nothing and I could not see how he was ever to be taught all that I had to teach him.

What is more, I think he also felt his ignorance and wished he knew as much as Riis and I did. This all amused me as I wrote it. Remembering my conceit, I wrote passages in the exact state of mind of that period; I was the superior, "wise" police reporter again, and my mistake was that I thought readers, like you, would laugh and enjoy it too. What you say shows that there is something to do to the manuscript, but just what remains for to see. You speak of my inferiority complex. Perhaps. But I still feel as to cities and politics when talking with an audience as superior as I did when I was instructing T. R. in the A B C of police corruption. I may be modest about human relations and women and astronomy, but I have no inferiority complex on my own subjects, nor do I affect one. . . .

Neither my life nor yours is going to be a failure. What we may have consciously sought will have eluded us, but what we will have done will be victories, to our surprise.

Peter says I must explicitly write what I so often say of your book: that it is so well written, that it is fresh prose, that it is something new in literature.

Another thing: you seem to dread the proofreading for little things. If you wish me to, I will read your galleys, willingly; and you should ask other friends to read them too. You can call upon your friends as well as let them forever call upon you. Never thought of that, did you!

Steffens

To Fremont Older

Tahoe Tavern,
Lake Tahoe, Calif.,
July 9, 1927

Dear Fremont:

I haven't written because you were away and should not be bothered. But there are incidents to report and action to take. Darrow is putting it back up to you and me to see Hearst, as you will learn from the communications enclosed.

The first of these is a letter from Darrow saying that he really should not come West in the summer heat. Ruby wrote also more urgently to the same effect. I replied to these letters in a wire to the effect that I did not think it necessary for him to come, if he would write to Hearst asking that he see me. One of my reasons was that Darrow shows all the time that his mind goes back to the evidence and wants still to prove that J. B. did not intend to kill the men and burn the plant of the *Times* building. I have not found any interest in that question; we can do what we want to do, if at all, on the assumption of guilt. The matter of J. B.'s innocence would be a diversion, a disturbance. Anyhow Darrow wires me this morning as follows:

"Am sending you a letter to man. Fremont should find someone to see him. If he went along would be good. I feel sure you will convince the man. He really is understanding. He is now in Los Angeles. Sorry I cannot help by wire."

This seems to mean that he suggests that you get someone to arrange with Hearst in Los Angeles now to receive you and me when I get his letter of introduction to Hearst, and that you and I tell H. the story. We shall be leaving here in a few days, going to Carmel first, then to the Hollister Ranch. The elevation is too much for some of us. When you get this, write me your address and I will communicate with you. Meanwhile, if you are near Hearst, you might call on him and explain what Darrow wants; you can arrange for our meeting with Hearst or, better still, you could present the whole business alone. Not that I would not gladly go to Los Angeles or anywhere else to do my part with H. I would like to see "the man."

Meanwhile I enclose also a letter from McClatchy acknowledging receipt of the letter I wrote him for publication.[1] He will print it, as you see, and the Governor is likely to see it. Maybe too the President of the Parole Board and others. C. K.'s letter is more formal than his conversation was; he has had time to think it over and may have gone back to his norm. I can't tell. All I know is that he was warm, even moved when I was talking to him. He wrung my hand when I rose to go and he asked me to "write this; I want it in my paper." . . .

To Laura Suggett

La Playa Hotel,
Carmel-by-the-Sea,
July 31, 1927

Dear Laura:—

Hearst said, when I had finished my very brief statement, he looked up, smiled a puzzled smile, and said:

"You suggest nothing that 'we' wouldn't have done anyhow."

"I know that," I answered. "But Darrow and Older wanted you to have the exact facts, which I best could tell."

He added, "Thanks," and so ended the lesson. He had greeted me pleasantly.

"The last time we met," he said, "was that interview,—long ago."

"Yes," I said. "I've learned a lot since then."

"Come in," he invited, and he led me from the secretary's room

---

[1] See Appendix V, p. 1044.

where there were people, into his own. We sat and I talked fast. I wasn't there more than 10 minutes. The appointment was for 3 o'clock Friday afternoon; he came in at 3:50 and at 4 I was out. I complained to the secretary that his delay in getting me an interview had prevented my making reservation on the night train.

"I'll fix that," he answered. "We have a drag on the ticket office," and he 'phoned for a lower for me and got it within an hour. So I came up Friday night, reaching here by 9, one hour late. Peter was out with Pete, Anna explained, and she went after them. Meanwhile Older happened to 'phone and I reported,—to his great satisfaction. He can help now. He wanted to go, both of us, to see Young and Neumiller,[1] right away, but I resisted that. "Wait a while, I want to do some work." He had got the parole board to postpone the case, so we can move later, any time before July end, and I can do other things the same trip. Time,—thrift.

I saw Ben Hampton,[2] Roy Howard[2] and a lot of Ben Lindsey, who is most interesting. His stories are rich, but the movies don't want them. They are asking and paying him high for what he cannot do.

To Allen H. Suggett

Sand Box, Carmel, August 3, 1927

Dear Dr.:

We moved over Monday at noon. I like the place. We all do. Peter has gone mad on the garden,—or as Pete said when I asked him yesterday where his mamma was: "Mamma gone clazy." But Pete himself is not so sane. He explores the garden over and over again, though it is the garage he likes best. There is an old busted Ford tire that he labors with tirelessly. And, last, there's me; I feel at home here and so settled down to work yesterday. I started my muckraking part and did easily half the first chapter at one sitting. I should finish it this forenoon or, certainly, tomorrow; if I make, as I may, the chapters longer. They are to be offered to Harper's by request for a serial.

I am really happy here. Some big instinct for a home I guess. Maybe it will be satisfied and I may want to travel again. But now I feel like staying here forever.

[1] Chairman of the Parole Board.

[2] Ben Hampton, former muckraker and owner and editor of *Hampton's Magazine*. Roy Howard, part owner and publisher of the Scripps-Howard newspapers.

To Laura Suggett

> Sand Box, Tuesday,
> Aug. 9, 1927

Dear Laura:

. . . Here's a line from Pete that you will like and can use. I asked him if he wasn't my boy. Peter butted in to ask if he wasn't her boy. And Anna claimed him, too. "You are my boy, aren't you?" Pete looked from one to another of us. Then he doubled up his fist, banged the table and said: "No, no, no. Pete's Pete's." And he finished with his fingers stabbing his own chest. Repeating "Pete's Pete's, Pete's Pete's."

Little Jane Hopper [1] came down with her mother half an hour ago to take Pete down on the beach. "Oh," Pete shouted, "Janie!" and he rushed up to her, hand out. "Hello, Janie." When he heard what was fore he said ecstatically: "Pete going down-a-beach with Janie? Oh, Pete'n' Janie goin' down-a-beach." They went off together in their bathing suits, with towels flying like flags. . . .

We dined with Jesse Lynch Williams,[2] last night. Just the family: two nice boys, one very intelligent, a student of birds at the U. of C.

> Carmel, Aug. 18, 1927

Dear Laura:—

Older writes that he has made an appointment for us to meet Neumiller Monday morning. Mrs. Hemingway is to come here and stay with Peter, bringing Bumby to play with Pete. They can keep house together as well as separately, cooking one meal instead of two.

Di Prida, the little Mexican scamp, about whom I have written several stories,[3] called Monday and stayed till late next day. I got in all the writers to listen to his tales. He is just back from China, where in a pinch for money, he acted as assistant executioner at fifty pesos a head, bumping off his share of 174 revolutionaries. Jimmy Hopper and the other authors were fascinated, like Peter, who is also astonished to see how truly I got Gaston in my stories and how correct were the stories. For he repeated them here, the best of them. He is what they

[1] Youngest daughter of James Hopper whom Steffens had brought on to *McClure's* Magazine.

[2] The playwright (author of *Why Marry?*) and short story writer.

[3] "Thirty-threed," *Everybody's,* July, 1916; "Bunk," *Everybody's,* Feb., 1917; "The White Streak," *Everybody's,* Oct., 1919.

call a touch artist, but he refused to borrow from me. "I have sixteen dollars and a half," he said, "and I am to see Doheny in Los Angeles." He will bum his way there from automobile travelers as he did here. Run out of Mexico, he is to find out if he can return now after months in exile. His job is to help a governor graft and his troubles come from grafting on the governor; double-crossing in brief. But he will assist anybody steal. He offered to steal a stolen car for us or to smuggle into us a Mexican book. . . .

To Allen H. Suggett

Sand Box, Sept. 8, 1927

Dear Dr.:

. . . Jane writes that she can't come to see us because she has cost the family so much by accident. She got out of her car to kill a rattlesnake she had run over and, while her back was turned her car set off down into a canyon, turned over on the other side and busted the top and some other costs. Good car, she concludes, because it could still move under its own power.

Col. Wood, Sara and Kay [1] are here, at the Inn. We have seen them afternoons, called with them yesterday on the poet, Jeffers. We go to a picnic with them and the Jefferses today. Pete too.

Friday.—The picnickers came for us at this point yesterday, and I had, to be polite, to cut and run. There were two cars of us, the Jefferses in theirs, the rest in Wood's Cadillac. We ran along the 17-mile Drive to the spot the poet knew, got out in the sun and, led by Pete, made for a small protected beach near by. No wind. Everybody had a good long swim or play in the water and on the beach, till one o'clock, when Pete got hungry and reminded us all of our tummies. We had a nice, slow, quiet talk and lunch at the cars, and spent the afternoon walking or lying around together or in groups. I don't like picnics as a rule, but this one was a success. . . . Everybody was asked by Sara to observe that Pete had not cried once all that hard day. Even when he cut his finger, he only came and showed it to us, saying, "Poor Pete, hurt-a-finger." I used him to make my point: that it is an advantage for a baby to have an older father.

The Woods have their first meal with us at noon today; Anna wished it. And after the lunch, they start off home. They *are* rich people, and it was worth a lot to meet Jeffers, who is the real thing, as his

[1] Daughter of Sara Bard Field.

wife is too. They know what they want, and how to live and get it out of life. I expect to tell you more about it during the winter.

Now I must quit this and go to work.

Affectionately,

Len.

To Laura Suggett

Sand Box, Sunday, Sept. 11, 1927

Dear Laura:

. . . This has been a full week, full of work and play. A chapter done, two articles sent out to editors, one by me; correspondence and telegrams about lectures; and callers. The Woods; Fremont Older Friday morning; Ben Lindsey that evening. Older had no news. Ben was full of stories which he tells so dramatically and with such a sense of their meaning. Putnam heard some of them and his point both for Lindsey and for me is good.

It was that Lindsey drop his children and that I drop the public and that Lindsey work upon the judges, to teach them how to handle crooks, both young and old; and that I concentrate on the great captains of industry and try to meet or tempt them to "lead the people instead of merely plucking them." Of course, this is an old idea, but Putnam made it definite and attractive. I think I'll experiment with it in N. Y.

One never knows who can help one. It's best to listen to all urgent talkers. Of course, Putnam wants to convert me to his beliefs [1] too, but that doesn't matter. He does know something else. I guess that the truth can't be found because it is all broken up in bits and distributed, one tiny piece to each of us.

Addis Place, Carmel,
Friday, Sept. 16, 1927

Dear Lo-la:—

. . . I had to sweep out the garage and while I was at it, Pete came into the dust with his wagon. I asked him to go away. He paid no heed. I asked again, and sharper; he heard and said: "No." I bawled him out, loudly, angrily, and set him and his wagon up the auto drive out of the dust. He stood and looked at me, as if minded to move back in my way, but he didn't. He tried me out, first:

"Papa, now say it nicely."

[1] Christian Science.

Gee. I felt called down, but I said it "nicely"; I was so polite, apologetic, that he forgave me. . . .

It's raining today; began with thunder after 2 A.M., rested after a shower, and has only now set out to rain steadily. The wind is southwest. In the interval, after breakfast, Pete and I went to see our aeroplane. It sleeps about 100 yards from the house. Pete saw it come down yesterday evening. Fascinated, he dragged me down to the field where we watched it circle around, down, and run along the ground like a road-runner right up to where we stood. His whole mind, his whole being was concentrated on that machine as, in silence, we saw the man get out, cover it up, put it to bed and go away. Then Pete came, reluctantly, home. As we came he said:

"Papa, first do-do, then aeroplane?"

And I promised. In the night, when I took him up, he reminded me: "First do-do, then aeroplane?" I said "yes," and at breakfast he asked me again, but I gathered that he expected to "up aeroplane," so I had to change that, to "No, not up, not Pete, not yet. No. We'll go and see the aeroplane go up, Pete and Papa, but we'll not go up till Pete's a big boy." And we did go and see,—we ate up that big aeroplane with our eyes, but we had to be still. "Ssh-h-h," Pete whispered, "aeroplane do-do." It was all covered and no one about. So, after a quarter of an hour of profound contemplation, we tiptoed away.

We all felt something here yesterday, evening and night; we wondered what it was till Anna solved it. "The silence," she exclaimed. No surf. Such a difference! Such a rest! And yet we liked the surf at Sand Box. It must wear the nerves even when it is pleasant.

Carmel, Tuesday, Sept. 20, 1927

Dear Laura:—

I've been abed with tummy trouble else I'd have told you yesterday of an unpleasant adventure Anna had coming home Sunday night from the movies. A man followed her down the Ocean Road. When she turned into the Camino Real, he paused till she got a bit ahead, then ran after her and when she was near La Playa spoke to her: "Are you lost?" She turned sharply, said "No" and hurried on. She felt, she could not hear him pursuing her, and as she was about to turn to look, he struck her from behind on the side of her face and knocked her down. She screamed. He leaped upon her, uttering obscenities, struck her, tried to hold her mouth or to throttle her. She fought. Her arms

LINCOLN STEFFENS, 1931.

(Photo by Edward Weston.)

are strong and she held him off enough to scream again and again. He cursed, tore up her clothes and she was almost unconscious when 'Gene, the porter of La Playa, and the clerk, came up to them. The man was gone. The others helped her up and into the hotel where Mrs. Nutt bathed her face. The Police Chief came instantly; he had heard the screams too. He and the hotel men went out to look for the rapist who had assaulted two other women that same night. But they stopped in to tell us not to expect Anna right away, and, then, in a few minutes they brought her home, all bruised, crying and frightened. When I said, "Too bad; it takes away your sense of security, Anna," she answered: "Yes. I can't stay alone with Pete now when you go East. We must have a dog or,—something."

She feels better now. The Chief brought in a prisoner yesterday forenoon for her to identify. He was a Mexican who got back to his camp late, at midnight; that was the only evidence they had. One of the other women who had been attacked came along, a Mrs. Crane, whom we know. Neither she nor Anna could say the prisoner was the man. I don't believe he is. He liked Pete, watched him, smiling, in the room and then, when the Chief drove off with the whole lot of them, and Pete was calling "goodbye" and waving, the Mexican was the only one that waved back at Pete. He did not look frightened; said he'd been to a party in Monterey and could prove his alibi.

Pete saw his aeroplane fly yesterday. Peter went down to the field and there he was with some other kids gazing their hearts out as the machine rose, flew and came back with its passengers.

Anna stayed in bed yesterday, except for the viewing of the prisoner. She's up on the job today and rather enjoys the interest in her, as shown by the delivery boys and our guests. The town is excited. There are 40 old maids living each by herself in Carmel and they are having some sort of emotions over the news.

The weather is perfect now. No fog. Some clouds, but mostly sunshine with cool breezes. Pete lives in his bathing suit and sometimes only half of that.

Carmel [Sept., 1927]

Dear Laura:—

Peter, Jane, Butler Cox and Mrs. Jeffers drove off this morning to call at The Cats¹ for Margaret. I'm alone here with Pete and Anna.

¹ Home of Colonel C. E. S. Wood and Sara Bard Field at Los Gatos.

My chance to educate Pete, but I struck a snag. He's been telling every-body of late that "Pete's wonderful." I tried to get him at least to in-clude me, and he did. "Yes, Pete and Papa's wonderful," he said, and Anna laughed. So I took the next step. "Anna is not wonderful, and Mama's not wonderful." He reflected a moment, glanced up at Anna and said: "Oh, yes, Anna is wonderful." She grabbed him up and took him off to sit on his pot. When she came back she said that at the height of his straining, Pete gasped, "And Janey's wonderful." When he came back I said, "Who all are wonderful besides Pete?" He put his whole mind on the matter and then, slowly, thoughtfully, he de-clared:

"Pete's wonderful. Papa's wonderful. And Anna and Mama's won-derful. And,—and Lo-la is wonderful, and Al-len." (Pause) "And Charlie is wonderful an-and Julia is wonderful."

"And Janey isn't?"

"Oh, yes, and Janey is wonderful."

"Well, then everybody's wonderful," I exclaimed in disgust.

"No, no, no,—'body isn't wonderful."

"All right," I agreed, "then who isn't wonderful?"

That was too much for him. He reflected, but he couldn't think of anybody to put on his black list. "Pete want to get down," he evaded, and he's now showing Anna the photo album, naming people. . . .

He's getting, not less, but more and more charming; his thoughts or observations are so far ahead of his vocabulary. It's lovely to see him start a narrative and then,—give it up.

Carmel, Oct. 14, 1927

Dear Laura:—

The page proofs of my Christmas story [1] are here requiring prompt correction, so I must be short today, just when there's a lot to report. But Peter says she'll tell you about the lecture, etc., if I'll only go to work. And I will, but, first, I must say a few things.

That the lecture was a success, I felt as I delivered it; I felt full-powered, well, in perfect command of my facts, my words, manner and of the audience, which was a good one, earnest, eager, expectant.

[1] "A Miserable Merry Christmas," *Pictorial Review,* Dec., 1927; Chap. III of the *Autobiography.*

My bad name for Redness only helped to excite their belief that they were to be thrilled; as they wanted, and yet feared, to be. For that Woman's Club is made up not only of swells, it has a lot of teachers in it, and artists or art students, and workers, who are suppressedly discontented with the rich, parents, etc. Every town has some such; one forgets that; and so every audience has some people who want to be expressed and have the "better people" jogged out of their complacency. Well, though I was careful, gentle, almost tender, I did say what I had to say, and so when it was over and the audience came up on the stage, they all thanked me with weak words but expressive hands and eyes, and a few, whimpering congratulations beginning, "I'm a teacher," or something like that, told me why. But, Laura, there's another element to be counted on: the women who are wives. At least a dozen women said: "Oh, I do wish my husband could have heard this." Evidently women are more liberal in my way than their men, and they feel it and would like to have their husbands kicked out of their ruts.

But the conservatives liked it. Dot was the most enthusiastic of my applauders, Jim was gratified and relieved. Jane's eyes sparkled with her satisfaction. The audience did not applaud as I went along; they hardly laughed and then only quickly. No, they leaned forward and wanted me to go on and on, they were too well held to interrupt. Some of them said they were seeing pictures they'll never forget, the mob scenes, the trenches, Mussolini. One woman who knew him personally laughed with delight at my mimicry of his contempt and bluster. "I saw him again as I saw him in my home," she said. "It was a perfect portrait." I did not have or want to stop to tell any anecdotes; I made the whole report a narrative, so I had no need of stories. And Peter, who is so strong for my stories, was well pleased. She liked it too that there was no propaganda; not a word; all reporting.

I'll be called back to Santa Barbara. One head of a girls' school asked me if I'd give a series of lectures; another teacher wants me to talk to her girls "on anything," she said. "It's your attitude I would have them get; not only your facts, your way of seeing,—anything, everything."

Peter may exaggerate my lectures, but she does set me up and make me feel like talking. I think she tends to *make* me graceful and artistic. That is one reason why I want her with me.

Carmel, Monday,
[Env. marked Oct. 17, 1927]

Dear Laura:—

It's funny how one fails to realize or picture what one knows. I knew that Older's ranch is not far from S. F. but I did not really grasp it that when we were there we were within 47 miles of 850. It was a complete surprise to read it on a mile-mark just as we left for home. Peter, too, was struck.

We got to Older's ranch at 12:30. There was quite a crowd at the open-air lunch, but Pete, in his bathing suit, was the first into the new, pretty pool Mrs. Older has built. Peter waded in with Pete, but it was he that opened the waters. And he did it bravely, with laughter and shouts to the ring of spectators. It was warm, but the sun shone only at intervals between clouds, and the photos may not be very good. We were the first to leave, at 3:30 and we didn't get home till 7. We came by San José, Gilroy, San Juan and Salinas, and the S. F. Sunday trippers were in procession going north. Anna had supper ready, and we all went to bed, tired out, at 8. Even Pete was eager for bed. "Pete's tired," he said. "Is Papa tired? Yes. Pete and Papa going do-do right away."

The best of Pete is a certainty. He has a personality, and it's a fine one. It doesn't matter what he does. He is sure to be a fine man. He bowled over Annie Laurie [1] yesterday. She is big, you know, very impressive, in her blond, jolly way, and everybody stood back as if in awe when she emerged late from her auto. Not Pete. He walked up to her, held out his hand and said:

"How are you? Glad to see you."

She shook his hand, but she looked over her head and around at the crowd, asking: "Who is this?" Pete said this was Pete, but she wasn't satisfied. "But whose is it?" She was really impressed by Pete's independence and smiling courtesy. Somebody said Pete was mine. "Yours!" she exclaimed, and I set her right. "No. I'm his; he isn't anybody's." And later, at the pool, when Pete took the centre of the stage, she said that he "thought he was the centre of the world," and I rebuked her: "Bunk! He was born in the centre of our family, which *is* the centre of our world, so he knows,—he doesn't think, he is the centre of the world. Look and see."

She looked, and she said: "It's true. I see. He isn't conceited; he is

---

[1] Also known as Winifred Black; columnist of the Hearst newspapers.

just sure of himself." As he is. She was amazed, but it is true. Pete
is going to keep, I think, what he has, an equality complex, and be
no prig.

Carmel, Oct. 18, '27

Dear Laura:—

. . . We drove, Peter and I, to see a new offering on the real estate
market here: a perfectly lovely old house that belongs to a married
pair of artists [1] we happen to have met at Jo Davidson's studio in Paris.
It's the best lay-out we have seen. The grounds are three lots on the
next street above Scenic Drive and two (vacant) lots from the Main
Street. It faces and commands a fine, wide view of the sea. There's a
very large living room and studio, with a veranda, up, off it to the
front; four bedrooms with lots and lots of closet room. There are store-
rooms besides. There's a room outside and a room under the veranda,
either of which would do for Anna or a study. One has a shower. The
garage is single, but it is easy to double. The garden is big, but
neglected; it could quickly be refreshed. We'd have to build a fence
on one side only; the front and the other side are protected. The whole
thing goes as it stands, furnished, and, though I did not look closely
at the furniture, the interior had charm. Those artists had taste. . . .

Carmel, Thursday,
Oct. 20, 1927

Dear Laura:—

We own a house. Our offer was accepted, and we'll sign the agreement today. . . .

You may not understand how I want a *"home,"* a sense of permanence. Your experience and taste and psychology are so different from
mine! But you must try to understand mine. When I get that house
right and once have moved into it, I shall feel settled in my very
stomach. I was homesick enough before, but since Pete came I have
felt I must settle for my last chapter. I shall even travel more easily.

I would like it if you and Doctor would drive down here some time,
look over the place and be prepared to join in the plans to make the
house right. It's going to be yours and Doctor's in the sense that 850
was always mine. I'd like it to be our family home. We'll make a set

[1] Cornelis and Jessie Arms Botke.

of rooms or a room for the family,—you; set aside something, and then try to get you-all to thinking of it as yours. Dot, too, and her children. And a storage place for our blessed "things."

We were going off on a picnic with the Jefferses at noon. Peter is gone to cut that out. We'll look over the new purchase, get it into our minds so as to think about it in S. F. and on our travels. It will be a good chance for Peter to try her hand at *making* a home. I think that we can get other people to come to live at Carmel. I may even go into the politics of the place, and work from the outside for schools, etc. Carmel should be a children's town, a Pete's Place. But we'll talk this all over when we meet.

Chicago, Monday,
October 29, 1927

Dear Laura:—

A wire from Dot this morning says Pete and Anna arrived on schedule Saturday night. Pete sat quiet in the train, interested, and when he met Dot and A., tried to tell them all about it, and couldn't; "words failed him." And, Dot adds, the next day it rained.

A pretty vivid telegram, which Peter is acknowledging with gratitude. The message shows that Pete got there just in time, before the rain washed out the road.

All goes well here. Darrow and I have fixed up a debate here on November 21st. "Will Democracy Yield to Dictatorship?" I take the affirmative. It's to be in their biggest hall, holding 2,500, and D. thinks we can almost fill it. "I can," he said in his humorous way, "but I have a reputation for sincerity. You, the joker, may keep them away." He says they don't like debates between him and me because "they" suspect us of really agreeing. But he is sounding for a second debate in New York on Prohibition. I for, he against.

I speak here tonight at a very big forum, which has a stunning list of speakers for the winter. My subject here is "The Bankruptcy of Liberalism." On Tuesday we go to Washington, where Darrow, who left here yesterday, will introduce us to some of his psychiatric friends, authorities. This is really for Peter, who has a good start in criminal psychology from her work in London and Cambridge. We all go together to Baltimore, where, at Johns Hopkins, a friend will show us his results, patients and colleagues, then on to New York. My time is filling. There may be a debate in Milwaukee with Victor Berger on November 20, unless he has gone to Washington.

Good weather so far. No stomach trouble. But an awful lot of friends. I think of the house in Carmel as a refuge for safety and quiet. If that fails me, I'll be a goner.

Carmel, Thursday,
[Dec. 1, 1927]

Dear Laura:—

Peter and I arrived at Monterey on time yesterday morning. Pete saw us first, waved and ran to greet us. He had such a lot to tell, and such a lot to ask. He thinks we've been to San Francisco to see Lola and Allen, and he asked about you two. We carried the conversation into the car as we drove home. His growth, in mind and manner, is quite a shock. . . .

You warn us not to invite people too cordially to come here. We don't invite many to come, but those we want, we ask with all our hearts. I wish you were coming this week, but I can wait. We have to go to S. F. soon, both Peter and I, and, Laura, if you want Pete alone for Christmas, you can have him. Anna can take him up, visit her friends and bring him back. I like it that you claim Pete; I'd like him to be the little friend of all of us. But coming back to Christmas, wouldn't it be fine to have the tree and all here in the country, in Pete's own house?—We can talk it over when we meet.

You have no more dread of parents than we have, and we do hope to beat the difficulty, if we can. Peter tries, and she succeeds, in keeping her hands off; I treat him as a regular fellow, and he must feel it. He's been calling me Tef or Papa Tef since I've come back and when he does anything wrong he tells me "Don't look," and we lie together, laughing, saying, "A big boy like Pete wouldn't do a thing like that, would he?" He loves that game. He certainly has no fear of us, and he has a lovely sense of equality. If a thing is wrong for Pete, it is for us too. "Papa, don't say by Jove," he cautioned me this morning. Peter had said it to him, so it goes for me as well. . . .

Carmel, December 24, 1927

Dear Laura:

. . . The house is full of workmen today, as it has been,—lately,—all trying to get things done before Christmas. A rainstorm is brewing, wind is rising, surf high, getting ready for a real winter holiday. Pete is to sing in some Christmas carols, see a Punch and Judy show and a tree, unless the weather stays the festivals. Which won't matter, since he has presents enough hidden right here in the house. Anna got hers last night: a purse bag she awfully wanted, from Pete; some stockings she terribly needed from me; some things I forget from Peter; and the handkerchiefs that delight her from you and Dr. We got your map of California, which even Pete enjoyed, to be hung in my study; Peter wanted to frame it. Shellacked, these maps look like antiques, which makes them still more humorous. But the way Pete put this map down on the floor and pored over it was amusing.

But I must go to work. I want to get this *American* article done so as to start the New Year with the *Life* again.

If you and Dr. have a Merry Christmas, you may credit it in part to us; we are wishing you one.

Affectionately,
Len.

This was not sent off, as you might guess. I got to work and forgot everything. But I did finish my article for the *American*.[1] It goes off in the same post with this.

Pete had a good Christmas. I told him about Santa Claus at bedtime Christmas eve. He was fascinated. "Papa, tell it again." I repeated and repeated and repeated it. Then he told it to Peter. And in the morning, sure enough, there were the things,—the wonderful things Santa Claus had left. Your automobile was the star. The wheelbarrow was good; it got some attention, but the auto was the prize gift. It was like my pony. The other things were a mere disturbance, a distraction. He went back always to the auto,—"Pete's auto."

It was raining so we could not go out. Luckily we had to stay in and at last we found a use for the big studio. It was big enough to ride an auto in, and Pete certainly rode rings around the room. He actually learned to steer. He can't move it with his little legs, but Papa and a big old broom made good enough motive power. I got some indoor exercise too. He can't use it out of doors yet, so today, with the sun shining, he is running his wheelbarrow with the express wagons, etc., of the other kids.

He went to a Christmas party last evening,—6 to 8,—and he could

[1] "Becoming a Father at Sixty," *American*, Aug., 1928.

not sing carols, but he and he alone could dance to them. He didn't want to go to sleep last night, but it was a great day, just the same.

And this morning his papa finished his story of Pete for the *American,* while Peter does the dirty work around the house with her one good eye,—the other is poisoned oak.

Ben Lindsey's lecture agent for the Pacific Coast asks me to debate with the Judge on Companionate Marriage in Seattle, Portland, L. A., S. F., and San Diego. I am consenting.

Carmel, [Jan. 17, 1928]

Dear Laura:—

I am not sure we can blame it on to you and Doctor, but I sat down here in my study this morning and wrote so well and so fast and so intelligently that I had to go over and tell Peter:

"Say, I'm writing like a song this morning."

"So am I," she said, looking up, surprised and happy.

And we talked a moment, long enough to agree that the visit you made (and the lovely way you did it) had set us up and given us a shove off on the Job. And Pete, too.

Peter took him over to his nursery school this morning, early; all dressed nice and warm. He was eager for it. When she got back, she said that Pete walked right into the gang and forgot her. He was not a bit shy. He saw the other children, but he saw mostly what they had: bears, and lions, and elephants, and camels and—

Pointing to the camel, which he knows well, he couldn't think of the name. A little girl told him: "That's a camel." Not to be beaten, he showed and named a bear; and then another bear. "Two bears," he said.

"What's that?" another child challenged, pointing to an elephant.

"Elephant," said Pete.

"My," said the other child, "he says elephant. My brother, who is four, he can't say elephant. He says—"

And she mimicked her brother's pronunciation.

Peter hung around just out of sight a few minutes to see if Pete would want her. He didn't. He was "in it," so she came home.

Do let's see you often.

Len.

My chapter is almost done, the hard one, the one I had lost and had to remake; which is no fun.

To Gilman Hall [1]

Carmel, Jan. 19, 1928

Dear Gim:—

. . . I have long had it in mind to write an article on the wisdom of reflection for men of action who have had deep experience of life. As they live now, they take their experiences as they come, think a little in between, and pass on without ever really summing up what they have learned. This is what is called dying with their boots on. There is a loss in that. I can almost prove it.

When Pete, my baby boy, came to me, I had to stop, look and listen. I wanted to educate him, myself. It would take time and reflection; I must not jump at conclusions for him; I had to be prepared to consider as deeply as I could what I really knew and give him the gist or the light of it. I am doing that, and one result is that he is a charming child. He has no inferiority sense, and yet is not a prig; he is cautious, without any sense of fear; he is not obedient to commands, but very courteously considerate of requests; he is a little gentleman, with exceptional manners, which people like; he has never been humiliated, though he leads his class at school where all but one of the children are older than Pete.

But it is the effect upon me that may interest you. The compulsion upon me to be careful what I teach him and yet to give him the advantage of my experiences, makes me cautious, not only in what I say, but in what I think and write. It is just as if I had to be sure, before I drew conclusions, that I had assembled and digested all that I knew, not a part, but all. I am forced, pleasantly, to refine into wisdom whatever of knowledge I think I possess and make it applicable to the life of a child that is dear to me. In a word, I have to be practical and yet bold. I think the general result is that I am more radical than ever, but gentler and less positive; and never clever.

This has been good for me, and I am rather inclined to infer that anything, a child or an illness, that makes us men of the actual world stop and review life and think to conclusions, however tentative, is good, especially if we report to others what we "know." And so, when I think of you, forced to quit business and driven to sit out in the sun, physically idle and quiet, mentally at leisure but thinking, I cannot but

[1] Editor of *Ainslie's* and *Everybody's* magazine. See *Autobiography,* 442. He had had a stroke which left him paralyzed.

feel that it is a blessing. You are kind, Gim; you always have been devoted to your friends. You will continue to be that. I think that you will be fascinated with the truths you will find in your own rich mind and that we, your friends, will be enriched by your tips on the Truth. Try it. Just think, and tell us what you think. Your life has been most unusual and yet it has been in the current; what about it? What is it all about?

The rest of your life may be the best, as I find my last chapter is my best; and happiest.

To Allen H. Suggett

Carmel, Friday,
[Feb. 10, 1928]

Dear Al-len:—

We came straight, fast and safely home. . . . Pete, at sight of us, ran and literally jumped into our arms, saying almost with tears, "I am so glad to see you." No doubt of his sincerity, and yet Anna said he had been quite content with her alone. Any one of us is sufficient, but he loves us, all three. And you. When we had repeated a few times that we had been to San Francisco to see you and Laura, he exacted a pledge that some day,—not yet, but later, "Pete and Mama and Papa and Anna,—we all go San Francis-a-co see Laura Allen on the chu-chu." And I comforted him further by saying that "Not yet, —but later,—soon," you would be coming here to see him. "To see Pete?" he asked. "To see Pete," I promised. So there's an obligation.

It was pleasant to get "home." The house looks neat and individual; not a type. And the garden is fine now. The grass is high enough to mow. It is not equal; there are spots; the grass has to spread even, but the great space of open grass is refreshing. Many flowers are out; the buds are showing, the vines beginning to show life and ambition. Pete's "yard" alone is informal and not kept; he uses his space, leaving his tools about. But we propose to let him have his place "all by 'self," to use, abuse and "own." Peter has set out shrubs and trees to curtain it off some day and leave him his own, whole world, from which he can raid into ours; as he does. He uses the road and the walks more than he does his own space. A happy child. And so affectionate. Until he went to sleep last night, he kept stopping his play to come to Peter or me to say: "I'm so glad to see you, Papa" or Mama. "So glad!" And his arms and legs would circle and squeeze us.

It's 10:30 A.M., so I'll quit this and go to work. Love from all to—all.

Len.

To Fred W. Kiesel[1]

Carmel, February 25, 1928

Dear Fred:

This is to be handed you by John James Hollister, better known in Harvard and high financial circles as Jack Hollister. He is going to Sacramento to attend the meeting of the Sacramento Brewery Co. and to meet you and Gerber. He not only represents, he personifies the Steffens, Hollister and the Suggett families not only in money matters but in good looks, kindly disposition and a humorous view of life. Please pretend to like him, and let him see the fair outside of the banking business; when he is older and stronger we can take him between us behind the scenes and make a banker of him, as he means to be, on his road to financial power and preëminence. And don't forget that Jack is Dad's grandson.

Yours cordially,
Lincoln Steffens

To W. E. Gerber[2]

Carmel, February 25, 1928

Dear Gerber:

Do you remember how Dad used to haul down to the bank in a wagon a baby boy who looked up at you and said never a word? Dad's first grandchild? Well, this is he. You know something of his past, but of his future you have no idea. I can tell it you.

He is going to be one of the leading financiers of the Pacific Coast, if the Coast grows fast and big enough. He has been a bit deformed by Harvard, but we, his relatives, Wall Street in San Francisco, and a wife he is about to take, are reforming him back into shape. He is a bond broker at the moment, learning the game which you know so well. We have given him our proxies to attend the meeting of the Brewery Company in order that, by watching you, he may learn how to behave at the funeral of a great business enterprise. We have given

[1] President of the California National Bank, Sacramento, California.
[2] Steffens addressed this: "President Emeritus of The Bank."

him a letter to Fred Kiesel so that he may be in at the height of a great financial career and be shown over the bank building and see high finance expressed adequately in the art of architecture. I rather expect my nephew and Dad's grandson to be, first, a director, then president or something of the California National and (or) other banks, and finally like you and old J. P. Morgan, the retiring but secretly directing boss of Business. See? I don't want you to judge Jack Hollister by appearances, but by what I tell you of his future.

Yours affectionately,
Lincoln Steffens

To Laura Suggett

Carmel, Friday A.M.,
Feb. 27, 1928

Dear Laura:—

Your letter of Tuesday came only last evening, to remind me that I had not written since our week-end,—about the rest we've had. But all our visits are happy; and they all leave me so. It seems to me that life is just bully. What I say in the opening paragraph of my *Life* is coming true and truer: each chapter of my story is better than the previous chapters; and the last is the best. . . .

We had a very successful dinner last night for Mr. and Mrs. Breinig (Pete's teacher) and Rhys and Mrs. Williams. Anna's little dinner was simple, but perfect; and Peter managed the conversation so that it was a conversation. She couldn't do it a year ago. Last night she broke up side conversations, kept everybody in the circle on the subject before the house. Mr. Dickinson [1] and Laidlaw Williams [2] came in for coffee, and everybody talked. Rhys Williams led on Russia, I steered, but Peter did the managing. It made a pleasant evening, which everybody enjoyed; they stayed till after 12 and we didn't get to bed till after one.

Peter told you how Pete has learned to respect our refusal to play with him when "we have to work." I can prove it. Peter asked him to do something the other day, an errand or to help in the garden, and he declined: "No, Mamma, Pete has to work," he said, and he went on working.

Mrs. Breinig said last night that I generalized too much from Pete,

---

[1] Henry F. Dickinson, retired lawyer from Chicago, living in Carmel.
[2] Son of Jesse Lynch Williams.

that, for example, all children are not as courteous as Pete; that his courtesy, which they notice at the school, is unusual. She said that only yesterday, when the children went off to do something "all by selves," after they had started, Pete came back and assured Mrs. B. and the other teacher that "We'll be careful." And Peter tells how, when some other children noticed with shocks and pity that one little boy had no shoes on, Pete lifted the two bare feet and pointed out that "But he has two feets," so he was as good as anybody. . . .

Her impatience with him works just as well as my good nature, sometimes I think it's better. He treats me like an equal; I'm easy. But he has to work to win Peter and keep her "nice at Pete." I guess the only rule for grown-ups is to have no pose or policy, but to freely treat a child according to their own (the adults') nature. You remember how Lou could stick needles into Frenzy, kick him about and generally abuse him, while Doctor had to be always nice. Well, this is good, for it shows that Pete has learned already seven or eight different ways of dealing with that many different people. . . .

Len.

Carmel, Tuesday,
Feb. 29, 1928

Dear Laura:—

. . . Did I tell you that Peter and I are to debate "Will Democracy Yield to Dictatorship?" before the local Forum next Thursday evening? She has never been satisfied with the negative presentations, neither Kaltenborn's, Darrow's, nor Newman's.[1] She always, afterwards, brought up points which they might have made and she did indeed grip the issues better than any of them. But her chief complaint has been that my opponents did not make a good enough case to force me to state my thesis completely. Anyhow, when the Forum came to ask us both to speak, we proposed both to speak, but together. The manager was delighted, the date was fixed for this week and Peter is preparing rather carefully.

Her real purpose is, as I can see, to make me make a good case; to bring out the philosophy (which she agrees with) and I think she will "win." Her main argument or point is one I'll have to agree to: that, since Democracy yields to Dictatorship only for the emergency (of revolution) and seizes power for the purpose of laying down

_____
[1] Rabbi Louis I. Newman debated this subject with Steffens in San Francisco.

conditions of economic democracy, then and therefore, Dictatorship will eventually yield to Democracy. As Lenin said and planned. Winning or losing, however, you can see that by this plan the whole philosophy and the whole program will be stated. I think it will be fun and good propaganda; if it turns out well, she and I can do it elsewhere. I wish you could hear it, but it should be better some other time when she will have done it a few times.

The editor of the *Peninsula Herald* asked me yesterday to address the Rotary Club of Monterey at noon the same day, Thursday. He is a fine young fellow; a reporter who married the daughter of Congressman Hayes of San José and so got this paper. He likes us, we like him and I am glad to serve him in an emergency. He said I could hit the Rotarians as hard as I liked; he did, he added. I didn't answer that, but of course I'm not going to kick that dead dog.

Carmel, March 2, 1928

Dear Laura:—

I spoke for Griffin, the young, free editor of the *Peninsula Herald* at the Rotary Club at Del Monte yesterday noon. One of my very best. I could see that they were struck into thought or insight. As Griffin said: "God! They even stopped smoking." My theme,—it was a short 35-minute talk,—was the understanding of foreign countries. I gave the keys France, Germany, Russia and Italy, and was asked to and added England. Someone had exclaimed (when he heard I was to speak), "What, that radical!?" So, as I gave sympathetically Russia and its opposite Italy, I remarked that when I gave Russia alone I was called a Bolshevik and when I gave Italy alone, I was a Fascist. At the end, after the questions showed that they had "got" me, for my close, I said,

"Now, gentlemen, I am become your neighbor. I want you to know me as a reporter and, if I should go, for example, to China and report with understanding the struggle of the Chinese, don't,—please don't call me a Chinaman."

In the evening we got a young girl, who cares for children, to come in to stay with Pete, and we all three,—Peter, Anna, I,—went to the theatre for the debate. It was pretty well filled, "mostly with old women," Peter said. A caustic, self-possessed old lady presided, well. I led and made my argument direct, with no jokes or frills, "too earnest," Peter said. Peter answered, as she had to of course, with points, arguments. She told some anecdotes, but she had no story as I had; no one narrative. She was good, made more and more searching points than any other opponent, but she had to use her notes and did not make a speech. What interested me was that, agreeing basically with me, she said so and, even for the purposes of debate, was too honest to say any insincere things. . . . There was a standing vote, and that Peter won, plainly. The majority was for her or for her side of the question.

Anna adored it. I saw her as I spoke; she sat on the edge of her chair, her eyes wide, her face aglow, as if she were seeing a light. She ran back to Pete the moment we closed, before the vote, but she said this morning that it was "lovely" and it seems to me her attentions are even more friendly than before. . . .

Carmel, Sunday,
March 26, 1928

Dear Laura:—

. . . Albert Rhys Williams, who has been 7 years in Russia, and with the peasants, turned up here Saturday A.M. and said he wanted a place to work,—to write. Peter took him to an agent, who showed him three small houses; he chose one and yesterday he moved in and sat down to his job: a book on Russia. Meanwhile he stayed with us all Saturday and half of Sunday, and poured out his news, which is all good news and authentic. Things have progressed so far that I don't have to admit any more some of the faults found with the new country. The dictatorship is relaxing; it is hardly felt at all by the peasants, who have universal suffrage for all voters, men and women, over 18; and living conditions are good, better than over here, because while no workers there earn so much as some over here, no one gets so little. There is no unemployment, no bread line. In a word, they are rising and, as prosperity comes, they all are sharing it. It's a people that is coming up.

He brought some examples of craftsmanship, and we're to have all the local artists in some day soon to see his samples of art work and hear him on the peasant sense of beauty and skill.

One of the things Jane got from me which she mentions as helpful was my assurance that this place,—our house, is hers. "Think of it," I said, "as a hole into which you can retreat and hide any time you want to run away and have time to breathe and think and feel safe." That she prizes. She understands, too. She may never come; that's not the point. What she likes is the thought that it will be always there and that she can dart into it like a squirrel whenever the hounds get too close. One hole is enough, but you can give her another if you wish. Only, it must be a retreat, possibly, from her own family, you understand, and from all plans to help her. Pete expresses it exactly. Every once in a while he comes climbing up into my lap, saying, "Papa, let's rest a while."

Other criminals have it. That was the origin of monasteries and nunneries for saints, and, as you know well, a burglar always wants to have a getaway. He never robs a house till he has seen and marked out a getaway.

"The Getaway" would be a good name for this pretty, little, snug place of ours.

Carmel, April 2, 1928

Dear Laura:—

. . . Older drove down yesterday alone. He got here by 10:30 and stayed till one o'clock talking over our friends in San Quentin and other business. We all called with him on Albert Rhys Williams, who reported more of his good news on Soviet Russia. Older drove off well satisfied with his visit, promising to come again, often. He and Pete are forming a warm friendship, though Pete could not recall Older's name. It amused Older to see him try and try, puzzled and embarrassed, and then, when prompted, laugh the name and jump into Older's arms. It seemed to move Older, for, obviously, Pete knew the name.

It came out this morning again, how important to a child is the saving of face. The big gate was open, Pete ran his auto out into the road and Peter had to fetch him back. When she closed and latched the gate, Pete said:

"Mama, why do you lock the gate?"

"To keep Pete in," she said.

"No, no," he protested. "It's to keep the flies out," and when she accepted the amendment, he was satisfied. Keeping the flies out is an excuse I invented at the Addis Place for closing the gate; he remembers it. It's bunk; he knows that, but bunk is better than spoiling one's face, as Pete and the Chinese and Papa all know well. . . .

Carmel, April 12, 1928

Dear Laura:—

It's Jo Davidson's fault; his and my tummy's. He was so full of news that I got all worked up the first two days and went to bed the third and part of the fourth. Now I'm used to him and it; and feel better, so much better that I think I'll go with him to Ponca City. My secret purpose is to see if I can't get his help and approval to go East and butt into the Sinclair case: write it or attempt a settlement, —on my ground. Of course I can't, but, if they'll let me and tell me the facts, the failure won't hurt any more than the McNamara case did.

I got your nice letter this A.M. and I'm sorry I did not write oftener. It seems an age since I confessed to you. But Jo does fill the house and the garden and one's life. He is rich. He stimulates even Pete.

"Pete thinks Pagliacci should be fast," I heard him say to Jo, who disagreed and won. Pete set it for half speed and his funny little expressive face showed that he did think it was better so. But what a subject for debate between him and Jo. Pete sets other music for half speed now, all but dance pieces. He may be imitating Jo, he may really have felt and liked the difference. I don't know. All I can see is that he is growing and, as Jo says, not losing his early charm. The other day we were out calling on the Jefferses. Pete was outside playing with the Jeffers boys (11 years old) when he ran into the living-room,—jumped into the middle of the group and shouted:

"Gosh! the Willums! The Willums are coming."

And Jesse and Mrs. Williams came in, laughing.

The next day, when the Williamses had us all to a dinner out in the country, I gave as a toast: "Gosh! The Willums." And they loved it. . . .

The California Limited,
Leaving Albuquerque,
Friday, Apr. 20, '28

Dear Laura:—

My report of the talks with Marland will be interesting, especially to Doctor. The last night at his house, E. W. Marland laid open the whole inside story of the S. case and the presidential election of Harding, which was a "deal."

As I have just said in a letter to Dot, it is amazing to me how easy it is to get the facts. I knew it as a muckraker, but I'd forgotten that all you have to do is to ask the insiders who know; they will tell you as soon as you win their confidence.

Jo and I have made this man a friend for life, and it was done by simply not laying down to him as his staff does. These bosses prefer and promote yes-men, but when they strike independent people who contradict them, they come to life and like it. And we almost quarrelled with this oil man; we licked him to a stand-still on art and his patronage of artists, changing his ideas and plans, and so got him to really consult us on oil(!) and to trust us with his knowledge on politics. It was a rich experience for us and he said,—for him.

To E. W. Marland

Carmel, April 23, 1928

Dear Mr. Marland:

Bread-and-butter letters are not bunk, not an empty form, as I used to think. After a visit such as we had with you, there are things which one wishes he had said, conversations that should be continued, a relationship established which should not be cut short. Jo and I felt and said something like this on the train to Newton, and I meant to write to you a few of the thinkings you inspired. I have waited too long: I have too much to write. All I can do is to thank you for the hospitality of your house and of your mind, yes, and of your "gang." I am all stirred up; it's as if I had travelled in a new country.

The shortest way to sum it up is, perhaps, to say that, if you had a bunch of novelists there and talked to them and made them show what they thought they knew as you did with us, you would advance and change the very stuff of American fiction. Your mind is on art: painting and sculpture, and you are going to influence them more than you seem to realize. But I think in terms of my art, writing and seeing and thinking, and I see, as I reflect upon what we said to one another, that fiction does not touch upon the matter we discussed, which is of the very stuff of American life.

Love stories occur in this country, but they are not "the" stories of America. The real tales of this amazing country are such stories as you told about the election of a president, of the governor who is guided by the astrologer and the palmist, of the bandits who became mayor and chief of police and afterwards heads of the company Jo has stock in. Grand dukes, princes, even bankers occur in our novels, but *you* have never been written and your "still-faced boys" [1] are unknown to literature. There are romances of diamonds and gold, none of oil and not a single good one about business. I think the reason is that our writers do not meet and really know you and your sort, not on the job; artists and writers meet the sons of captains of industry and sometimes the captains themselves, but only socially,—in "society," where the business on hand is drinking or flirting. It is absurd, and the results are ridiculous. One of them is that you don't, you can't, read fiction. The leaders of our life don't read our literature.

If you and your beautiful new house alter that, you will render a greater service than you intend, and, if I have anything to sell you, it is the sense of that and the gratification of knowing it. But I said that to you when I reminded you that your sculptured record of characters and costumes will be also a gallery of modern art. Jo's salesmanship is bent on getting you to enjoy the art as well as the record. But really, Mr. Marland, I am not out to sell you anything; on the contrary I am not exactly buying, I am grafting upon your knowledge, your experience, your wisdom of which you give so generously.

I hope you will not forget, when you come to Del Monte, to let me know, so that I can call or, better still, that you will come over here to The Getaway to call upon Pete. He, at least, is your equal: fearless, unhumiliated, wilful and very courteous.

Please remember me to George Marland and to—all the other happy men about you, happier than they know. And thank you, and thank them.

Yours sincerely,
Lincoln Steffens

To Laura Suggett

Carmel, Sunday,
May 14, 1928

Dear Laura:—

The sun came out yesterday, and so did Pete. Very much. About noon he disappeared even from the garden. *And* the gates were closed and fastened. Peter ran out into the road and there was Pete coming back from,—somewhere, all a-sweat but happy. "Jo isn't in his house and Johnny isn't in his house," he said. He had been calling on friends who were "out."

---

[1] Term used by E. W. Marland for bankers.

"How did you get out, Pete?" we asked.

"Over the gate. Pete climbed it."

"Which gate?"

"The Pete gate," he said, meaning the smaller one, near the garage. We must do some wiring. But he'll soon be free, able to climb anything, and we'll be having our runaway scares. . . .

Jesse Lynch Williams called last night when Mrs. Edson [1] was here and we got into what Peter calls my "philosophy." I objected that the things I was saying were the result, the application, of a philosophy, not the philosophy, which, I said, I had never stated even to myself and couldn't state now. "I can," she said, and, challenged, she did. I was amazed. She reeled it off in good order, beginning with "principals and heelers" and going through with an understanding that interested me and, really, illuminated and suggested the writing of the whole thing as she put it. I don't like to make her too conscious, but I have to think now that she has got it all and made it her own. I sometimes have thought that her mind was too quick to be solid and profound, but by Jove she has, in some quiet way, somehow taken it all in. Of course her own experience in the Labor movement and the war and peace times has made what I know (or think) real to her.

Peter is going to be able to carry on my ideas—after I am gone; they will be hers then. She won't have to quote me at all. I believe she could finish my *Life* if I left it incomplete; not telling the narrative, of course, but giving the outline of my mental development.

She is fine, too, about my teachings to Pete. My use of lessons in disobedience to develop will power has inconvenienced us and she has protested. Appeals to his understanding and coöperation work, but too slowly. And I have, as a matter of fact, received obedience now and then. But, with all her protests, in spite of her fear that I may be wrong and do harm, she has not asked me to stop or change my course. It interests her too much; she sees the point, and puts up with the consequences, however disturbing they are in Pete's actual conduct. I think, therefore, that I'll win through; that Pete will respond to requests and resent commands, as I wish he would. Meanwhile Peter goes her way with him, which is different from mine. And so does Anna. . . .

Love to all, from
Len. & Co.

[1] Mrs. Katherine Edson, active in women's organizations.

To Allen H. Suggett

Carmel, May 14, 1928

Dear Doctor:—

Pete is back in school. The weather is cold and wet again; a little rain last night. But Pete is so well again that it's all right. He is growing visibly, especially in his funny little mind, which sees more and more and expresses it. . . .

Len.

May 15.—I didn't post this letter, so—

Pete fell off the bed yesterday while playing, as we had warned him he might. He hurt his toe, a little, and cried. We paid no attention for a while, then I asked what he was crying for; he wasn't really hurt, as I knew, for I examined his toe and went on shaving. He explained it all.

"Pete's crying because he hasn't got any friend."

Lovely. He knew it was his fault, that we knew it and that therefore, he was without any sympathetic ally. He was all alone in a hard, just world.

When Peter went to fetch him from school, one of the teachers who had been working with Pete and evidently thought she could show that, for the moment, she was nearer than his mother, said:

"Whose boy are you, Pete?"

He looked up, thought a moment and then gave his old answer,—in one word.

"Pete's," he said.

He has learned the word friend. We were dining out with the Carlos Hittells [1] and I was remonstrating with Peter for something. Pete must have felt the situation. Very sweetly, very sympathetically, he said to his mother.

"Mama, Pete is a friend to you."

Even if I wasn't; she was not to be abandoned and alone.

Yesterday Pete and a pal of his own age were looking at an old cat with kittens. Pete put his hand on the mother cat and said to his chum:

"That's the papa cat," and the other little boy answered: "No, that's the mother cat."

Both were right, according to their upbringing.

[1] Now living at Pacific Grove, a few miles from Carmel.

To Mrs. A. Winter

Carmel, September 13, 1928

Dear Pete's Grandma:

Pete is in our bedroom above me here, shouting and laughing, with his fractured leg in a plaster cast. You will see all about it in the *Carmelite* and, as Peter says, must hear about it from us. Well, he walked uptown with me last Tuesday to see his mother, who was getting out the paper all by herself. I talked to the printer about Peter and her triumph and Pete climbed on the mud guard of Peter's car, stood there a moment, and the next I knew he was down out of sight, crying. I ran to him, felt his leg which he said was "almost broke," found nothing and, as Peter came out, we tried to comfort him. But we couldn't. Peter drove him to the doctor, who said also that it was probably only a bad bruise, till seeing that Pete continued to whimper said, "No, Pete doesn't cry for nothing." He took an X-ray and it showed a crack up the middle of his leg-bone, not near either knee or ankle joints, not complicated at all. He put on the plaster and we got Pete home and in bed. He suffered a lot all that night, at intervals, every time he moved.

The next day he was better and, as people came in to see him and he showed them his leg and heard their exclamations, he remembered his superiority complex and became so proud of his distinction that he proposed to me, on the quiet, that we might break his other leg or an arm. You can't down Pete Steffens. I still hear him raising hell up-stairs, shouting, laughing, throwing things around. He wants to get up and when we said no, he got mad, but I turned around and said yes. He tried to move his leg and quit. He knows now that he doesn't want to get up. He takes it out in noise. And there is something to take out. He is so well, pink-cheeked, red lips; vigor like his mother's.

I think that he tried to step down from the mud guard to the hub, got his foot between two spokes of the wheel, fell and wrenched his leg. It is a fracture, a "green stick break," not a break. No displacement. And Dr. Kocher, who likes Pete and us, will see that it heals right. You need not worry. Pete is all right. He has no mother, but there is his father and Anna and the neighbors to take care of him like a lot of grandmothers.

Pete's mother is having a great triumph. She entered into the making of the *Carmelite* as she goes into everything, with all her being.

Peter got the composing room, the editors, the advertisers, the writers, all working for her, heartily, happily, laughing. One printer, a hard-boiled union man, kicked to me, thus: "Say," he said, "you know how Ella Winter runs,—she never walks anywhere,—always a dog trot. Fine for her. But, God damn it, it's catching, and every once in a while I find myself trotting around like her, on a run. And, say, I draw the line at running. It's against the union rules and what t'hell. Why should I run?"

There she goes now downtown to attend to something. She had spent a minute with Pete; a minute. Poor little orphan! We took him to a formal tea the other day at a swell house and he was crawling around playing bear all by himself on the floor. A woman talking to me felt him go by; she looked down and said, "What's that?" I said it was a poor little kid that had no mother, only a papa. "Whose child is it?" she asked, touched. "Mine," I said. "Yours! And where is its mother?" "Oh," I said, "his mother is the editor of the *Carmelite*." She gave me a funny look, walked off and I saw her pointing me and Pete out to a bunch of swells, who glanced over and laughed. They understood.

And, as for Pete, you need not worry about him. He has a papa, he has the town with him, and his grandma. And he has Pete, who is the only kid in Carmel that has a fractured leg in a plaster cast that peo-ple flock to see. He is learning to move it by myself. He called me up at two o'clock this morning, I thought to help him turn over, but, no, when I put on the light and came to him, he said, "No, Daddy, you watch and see. I can do it all by myself." And he did, and I was free to go back to sleep beside my exhausted editor of the *Carmelite,* the coming organ of public opinion of this Peninsula of Monterey. As I lay down Pete called over: "Papa, I will count and you and I will go first to sleep together." And I counted, "One, two, three, go."

Love to all.

Affectionately,
Pete's Papa

To Ella Winter

The Players,
New York, Nov. 16, 1928

Dear Peter:—

. . . I have so much to do, so many people to see, and all I've done so far is to see and have a long, good,—a really amazing talk with

Hemingway (talk about artists!) and Isaac McBride. I'm waiting now for Charlie Wood, the writer. I see Frank Polk this afternoon. And there's the Roes, the Howes, the editors,—you know the list. I can't do it all. I may have to come back here from Boston.

Interrupted here by Wood, I took him in to lunch to persuade him to consider doing E. A.'s "Life." As we sat down in came Glenn Frank, who joined us and helped work for E. A. E. A. said he'd pay me $5,000 if I and Frank would edit Wood's work. Frank asked me why I had never come to see him and I answered only with a look and "You're a busy man." He showed not the slightest sign of guilt. He told me some good stories about his experimental school, and we are to meet tomorrow if I have time. Wood consented to see E. A. and talk over the Life with him.

I went down to see Frank Polk about the Book League he is a "judge" for and we had a jolly talk. He told me all the troubles he had on my account (because of a letter he gave me to the embassies) and enjoyed them, the troubles. But I had never imagined they were so many.

It's warm and misty today; has been for several days here and in Boston. I had to talk but I called up the Roes and went to dinner at their house. Then, thriftily, I hinted that there was a great Russian revolutionary movie in a celebrated little new theatre. They caught on and we went. I'll tell you of that later.

I can only outline diary-like now. For instance, last night after dinner at the Crandons'[1] they gave me a regular, very successful, very very interesting séance. "Walter" came out whistling and I had a talk with him, and the others too, but it was my night and I asked him some questions which he answered well. He made one odd mistake. He referred to me as "a physicist," and I say odd because Crandon and Margery both know perfectly well what I am and that I am not that. He said he might come out and visit me in Carmel. He wouldn't promise; he would consider it and let me know through Crandon. But Crandon says Walter can't appear unless there's a medium, so he suggests that we put it off till he and Margery come out there (as they plan) for a séance with Stewart Edward White. Jane must be there.

[1] Dr. L. R. G. Crandon, physician of Boston, Mass. Mrs. Crandon is the medium, "Margery." "Walter" was supposedly "Margery's" brother.

I have no conclusions to offer about this, don't even feel pressed to explain.

. . . There were a lot of old friends at Ford Hall to greet and hear me. Some of them stood in line at 6 P.M. and by 7:30, when we got there, the place was packed; the platform full and many standing. It was a very friendly, very quick audience. You were referred to, and Pete, and when the chairman explained about Pete's broken leg as the reason for your absence, the audience actually started, groaned or exclaimed sympathetically, so that the chairman had to add that it was getting well. Then the crowd actually sighed. Thus started, I spoke as well as I ever have in my life, and it was a triumph; really. E. A., Clint,—everybody said so, but best of all were the questions and answers. Good questions, and short answers, sometimes a word, once only a gesture which brought down the house. Coleman, the chairman, laughed so hard once that he almost lost his control. And there was one hour of the questions and answers. I must have been in fine fettle, after my other talks, the one Saturday night in New York, the other at noon in Boston Sunday and practically the whole small audience of the Ethical Society came to Ford Hall.

To Charles Erskine Scott Wood

The Getaway, Carmel,
February 13, 1929

Dear Erskine:

When we drove home from The Cats Monday, I felt that I had been in a place of beauty, and I wondered why we didn't go oftener to you. The drive there is beautiful, the house, the hosts, the guests, the spirit of it all,—the whole and every part are beautiful. Los Gatos is a work of art. A play of art. For one feels that the design is unconscious, as if it were a garden where beauty grew and became aware after the blooming. And to me, to a guest, it has the extraordinary effect of taking one in and making you also beautiful, as music and poetry do. You have a rare triumph in your continuous creation of The Cats, for it expresses you and Sara more completely than anything you two have ever written.

I would like to feel often as I feel at The Cats. No, I mean more than that; I would like oftener to be as I am there. So far as I could make out, I don't go because I have a sense that you and Sara are troubled by the many visitors; that you think that your writings are more important than The Cats. I don't think they are, but I have to respect your foolishness as I do your wisdom and your good health; and I have to remember that maybe this is only an excuse for my own inertia. I shall continue to stay home too much, but I do want to say that we all have a right to go as often as we will to a temple as beautiful as you two have made and that, as poets and priests, you are bound to realize yourselves that you and this creation of yours are greater than everything else that you have ever done.

I may be wrong about this, but I am truly telling you the feeling I have after a visit to you. And just this once, let me add that as between the house and yourselves, Erskine, and you, Sara,—you are the more perfect. You are, both of you, each one of you, beautiful works of art. One must not say a thing like this twice or to the face of the hearer, and I will not repeat it; and you won't answer it. Please. It is enough that I have got it out of my system, the thought that we humans can achieve beauty in ourselves, and that we are our own works of art. That is what you have proven, and that is what you illustrate.

Yours affectionately,
Lincoln Steffens

To Jo Davidson

The Getaway,
February 18, 1929

Dear Jo:

You-all have a nerve to ask a man of my rank to travel all the way to Ponca City just to see you-all, but we'll do it. We have talked and kicked it over till today we decided to wire E. W.[1] that we'd go, and we will, all two and a half of us; Pete too; but I shall have to work mornings on my *Life* and Pete will have to have someone to play with, someone that can keep him out of the lake. This unless something unforeseen happens. But the point is that we are to see you and Yvonne and E. W. and his'n. It's funny how glad I am that this is so. I must have bad taste in people.

Really, Jo, the unconscious experiment this country is making in civilization and culture is equal to that of Soviet Russia. The race is saved, one way or the other and, I think, both ways. And E. W. is right in one small particular: artists, whether the painters or the writers, don't see it; and they must. The artists are the real tories, not

[1] E. W. Marland.

the capitalists. Big business in America is producing what the Socialists held up as their goal; food, shelter and clothing for all. You will see it during the Hoover administration, which proposes to deal with the problem of unemployment, profitably; the employed have been taken care of, as consumers, as the market, which, therefore, booms. I remember that you saw some of this on your last trip, but you didn't see the cause, only the effects then. We can trace the causes and perhaps the future when we meet, with E. W. furnishing the raw material for thought. It is a great country, this; as great as Rome. What it needs is a bit of Greece, and the artist won't give us that.

Stef.

To Jo and Yvonne Davidson

The Getaway,
Carmel, March 22, 1929

Dear Jo and Yvonne:

We ran out of the dust of the prairies into rain and snow in the mountains, then down into the heat of Los Angeles and the oranges. The cool fog of Monterey Bay, which welcomed us home, was refreshing even to what they call in Carmel, our souls; we were glad to get back. We were better people here, less cross, brighter, kinder to one another. But Pete did the expressive thing. Put to bed for his nap at three, he slept till nine and then returned to sink into the night again, very, very busy.

. . . We had a good time, Jo. You too. It makes, as I warned Peter beforehand that it might prove, a fine chapter in our lives, one to remember. We could have had a lovely visit anywhere, we five or six, but in the setting of Ponca City, with its characters and its background, it was like meeting in a novel or a picture. At any rate I felt it so. But I see Marland and the girl, the house, the town and the people as stuff for fiction and I regret that I can't write stories any more. (I found the manuscript of a short story returned when I got home.) Yvonne might write it. She saw it best, and she writes, you know. She will put it into her diary; I would like to see that diary. But I wish she would make a round, perfect thing of Ponca City. Think of the scenes in it: that afternoon tea in the studio when the busts were all done, the one showing, the Negro's covered and everybody presenting themselves happily for the moment,—you, proud and triumphant; P——, the model, utterly out of place; Pete inspired by

P——, Jr., the gunman; and Peter and I; and Marland and his bride. What Proust would have done with all that! No French writer ever had such a jumble of raw stuff to play with.

I felt the relief of Yvonne's betterment. I had pictured her as more ill than she was, so that her health and the freedom of her mind were a delightful surprise for me as well as a satisfaction. She has what Peter calls the wisdom of the French now, and all handy for whoever can use it. And you on a peak of your power; well, robust, with your undoubted genius at your fingertips, at your thumbtips. You can do anything you please now with your medium, anything whatsoever that is sayable in bronze or stone. A great artist, and a superb person. I am not going to talk this way very often, but I do believe that it would be good for you, for all men, if they would pause once in a lifetime to realize and confess to themselves that, now, they are full-powered, gifted, a flower of the race in full bloom. I shall never forget you as I saw you in Ponca City; and I think I can add, as Yvonne saw you. For she "gets" you, Jo. I saw pride of you in her one day.

Yes. Ponca City was worth it.

I'll go to work now. Maybe I can finish my book in July. If I do we shall be free to go,—wherever we want to, China, France,—we'll see.

Love to Yvonne, to the boys, to you, Jo.

Affectionately,
Stef.

To Marie Howe

The Getaway,
May 4, 1929

Dear Marie:

The clippings did what you thought they might, but I'm not going to comment on them. Peter won't let me. I am held to the *Life* hard these days; no rest, no play, no letters, and she is winning; I am doing "Ohio and Tom Johnson." Pretty far along, you see. The cities are done, some states; I'm half through the muckracking. The revolutions come next and the war and the peace. I must be half through my *Life*, but it's fierce; how long I did live.

That little clipping you sent Fred about me being fashionable was done by our enemy, the editor of the *Carmelite*, "my admirer," Peter calls her.

You know, don't you, that Peter, Pete and Anna are to leave me alone this summer? They are all going "home"; this house is to be let. Anna goes in a tourist group of Welsh folk. Pete takes his mother all by 'self. They will be trying to see you in late June; I hear them talking about it. Sometimes I wonder why Peter goes to Europe if it's only Marie she wants to see.

It's still cold here, but sunny. The garden is abloom and the walks neat. The best bourgeois garden in town. Pete is happy. He's in the lying stage, tells whoppers the way I did when a child. Stealing comes next. I have an article in the current *North American,* which Elsie McCormick might like to shoot. All but the title is mine; the editors did not like mine, "There's No Mystery About Children." [1] I wish I could write only for fun, like that.

And I wish you'd write oftener to me or us.

Affectionately,
L. S.

It's sentimentality that makes people laugh at a young father; they laugh lest they cry. I think an old father is much funnier, if it's his first child. He's as ridiculous as a young mother, and it's all right to laugh at an old father. He doesn't care a damn. He's having his maternal joy and pride and illusions, and he knows it, but he knows it's worth it, as women do. He pays the price gladly.

Stef.

To Mrs. A. Winter

Carmel, June 12, 1929

Dear Grandma:

Now that it has been decided that Pete is to take his mother to Europe this summer on the S.S. "Minnesota," sailing July 13, I feel called upon to caution you not to spoil them and their vacation. You should rather suppress your grandmotherly instincts than ruin the good work I have been doing with and for them.

Pete, remember, is being brought up as an American internationalist, not as an English imperialist. His spirit is not and must not be broken. He does not know that there is anyone in the world superior to him in authority, power or age, and I don't want him to discover that yet.

[1] Published as "I'm Teaching My Boy to Defy Me."

An English nurse, such as you proposed, might try to put him in his place. She would encounter resistance and, in fighting for her life, might touch Pete; or she might apply discipline and take the joy out of his visit to his grandma. I am afraid for Pete, for the nurse and for his grandma. If you will be patient you will discover that Pete is something of a little gentleman, who goes abroad partly to ride on trains and boats, but mostly to see if his grandma is as wonderful as Anna and his father are. You will have a pretty high standard to live up to for two or three months; and I can very well understand that, as you see him studying and sizing you up, you may like to have help, someone to relieve you for a few hours a day to drop your pose and be natural; at rest. But don't you do it. Take a chance; Pete is not infallible as a judge. In brief, don't try to form or reform Pete, let him do that to you.

Now, as to Peter: She came to me, you remember, to be free, to escape the domination of love at home, and, of course, as you no doubt expected with a smile, she fell out of the frying pan into the fire. She finds herself dominated by our love as much as she was by yours. I sympathise with her. She ought to get a divorce from me, but when she goes home for the summer she ought to have a taste of that freedom which alone can send her back to me glad to be cared for, planned for, protected—dominated once again. I would suggest that you let her come to London, thinking that there are no plans into which she must fit. You may make a program; you will, you must; but do let it be tentative with you and unconscious with her. She thinks of arriving home in London to see you and the rest, not dutifully but for sheer joy; then, she expects to be invited here, there, anywhere, to Germany, to France, out into the country in England, and to accept as the moment prompts her. If she finds that her time is all claimed out she will be very unhappy, and she won't enjoy visits that she otherwise might love to make. You may feel disappointed that she is so interested, for example, in the Labor Government; she may be running off all day and night after information and be seeming to forget you and Pete. She does that here sometimes and I sit at home like the mother in the woman's place; I take it all right; she always does come home to me finally. I urge you to be prepared for that and not to take it amiss. She is still young, very young; and thank the Lord, very interested in the world. She and Pete are more like sister and brother than mother and child; which is good for Pete, for her, and, I think, for us grandparents.

It is in this spirit that we are experimenting with divorce. It was our original plan, you remember. To obviate the difference in our ages we agreed to live together married for five or so years, then, before there was any hatred and before Peter was so old that she would have no chance to remarry, we would get a divorce which would free Peter to go, if she should ever wish to go away; equally free, however, whether married or single, to come back to me and my home as she can always return to yours. Or she may never leave me, if she can stand me through the years. We meant to do this secretly and her attorney advised her we could. But when she filed her "complaint" the other day, some reporter got hold of it and it was published. The papers have spread it all over the country and possibly it may have gone to England and Paris. Too bad. We planned to tell you when Peter got home; and first. We are tempted right now to call it all off, for the present, and do it later, somewhere else, privately. Luckily there is no inner urge to force us through with it. On the other hand, since the damage of publicity has been done, we think we might as well get it all over right now; next week, before Peter sails. We'll decide soon.

Peter says that, with your ideas of the family and divorce, you will be shocked. I am sorry, but we have shocked you before and our queer way did not turn out so shocking. And, let me ask you, how would you solve the problem of our difference in age, with the consequent difference in our interests? I have seen what Peter wants to see, the world. I can sit here watching Pete and understand what is going on outside Carmel. Pete and Peter can't. And I can't, and I should not, tell them what it all is and what it all means. I have shown Peter lots of men and women, great and small, and some events, big and little, but I can show Pete bugs in the garden and the rollers on the beach. Yes, and I can encourage Pete to build castles in the sand and Peter to write a novel. But I cannot give them what they may only *think* they want: their own comprehension of life; that they will have to get for themselves.

While Peter is away, Jane and I are going to sound around for a good job for Rudi, something in his line but with American prospects. He says he would consider an offer; he liked it here; he liked the taste of this country; and we liked him. It may be that we can all get

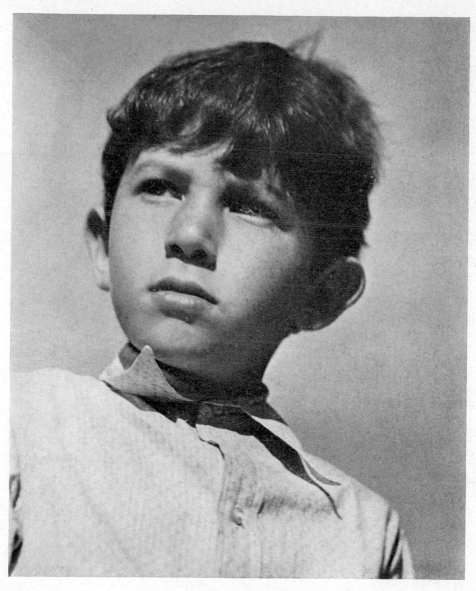

PETE STANLEY STEFFENS, 1931.

(Photo by Edward Weston.)

together over here and,—live happy ever after. I think you might like to be in a great family of which Pete is the head, so be lenient, diplomatic, tactful with him and his mother this summer. Win them if you can.

Yours affectionately,
Lincoln Steffens

Try to encourage a divorce without a separation.

To Ella Winter

La Playa Hotel,
Carmel, June 28, 1929

Dear Peter:

Your love letter came in a few minutes ago, and I found myself thinking of old days; even of the moonlight on the Seine. So far back and deep down did it reach. But it reached forward too. I thought,— I said almost aloud: "And I'll be getting love letters like this!"

It's worth the separation, that is; just the love letters. And, as you say, it's worth it all to feel the spring of love and find out how much we adore each other. Yes, it is all to the good; all,—except your depression. And, as to that, I have my little vengeful laugh. You thought I was absurd to feel marriage so much; I think you absurd to feel divorce so much. But you mustn't go on this way. We'll not be ever different, if you don't want it changed. The matter is all in our hands again; out of the law; free of courts and other people. We can do it as we wish. And apparently, when the test comes, we wish the same thing. We want each other and our lovely relationship. All right. Then we shall have that.

You go rejoicing on your way. See all your old friends and places. See yourself through. Be honest with yourself. Do what you will or must, tell me and we can deal with anything freely and finely. Don't be depressed. Don't be afraid. Behave as you are, be sure of yourself and me and make the world take you as you want it to: remembering always that others will take you as you give yourself, with no more doubt than you yourself feel. Don't hurry, don't worry. I'm here and waiting, but without hurry and without worry now. . . .

Love,
Stef.

Carmel, June 28, 1929

Peter dear:

Pete's asleep and I'm going too. But first:

I dined with Garet Garrett[1] tonight and I told him of your love letter; not the terms of it, but just that it was a love letter. Garrett rubbed his face, thought a moment, looked puzzled at me and said,— at last,—

"Well, by God, only Freud himself can get the guts of this damn Steffens affair."

I laughed, and Miss D. laughed; he was so dumfounded; as if his theories had busted and blown up.

Mrs. Turner[2] called to see you. I walked out with her, and said a few words about us. She got it at once and was so glad that it showed in her face. "I'd like,—I'd be tempted to write that into a story." She invited me to make John drive me out to their house. They really like "us" and Pete. I say Pete, because her only inquiry about our news was as to Pete. "He'll always have you both?" she asked. "I don't believe in letting children hold people together, but Pete,—is different." The little I said was vague, but enough to make her look happy. . . .

Good-night.

Stef.

Carmel, July 1, 1929

Dearer Peter:

Dearer than ever I mean.

Garrett did not go away this morning, not until noon, and then, as he was starting, he saw me and Pete returning from Weston's[3] studio. Garrett stopped, mused, asked if he could lunch with me before starting and, when I agreed, drove and got Miss D. As we sat down at table, he mused again and finally said, as if to Miss D.:

"Do you know,—God damn it,—I hate to have about anybody or anything the god damn sentimental feeling I have for that man" (nodding at me). We laughed; he looked and sounded sincere, but he abruptly changed the subject. . . .

In the mail was a letter from Mabel Dodge, asking me to go to

[1] Garet Garrett, journalist and magazine writer, had just spent a month in Carmel and struck up a warm friendship with Steffens.

[2] Mrs. John Kenneth Turner (Adriana Spadoni), the novelist.

[3] Edward Weston, the photographer, at that time living in Carmel.

Taos, even before she gets there Aug. 1. She says Hutch and Neith are there all July. I may.

Pete caught me out this afternoon. He drew me to the bathroom and showed me I had left the light on. "That is a waste," he said, shaking his finger at me. I was guilty, I confessed, but I was so ashamed that he took my hand and said, what I have said at times to him: "But never mind, Daddy. I like you even when you are bad like that; you are a nice Daddy all the time and naughty only sometimes." We've had hot days for a week. The fog was welcome today. . . .

Stet.

Sir Francis Drake Hotel,
San Francisco, July 6, 1929

Dear, dear Peter:

I am writing this just before supper, to send it by air mail. It is probably the last letter you'll get from me before sailing. We,—Pete, Anna, Mark, I,—we start tomorrow, Sunday morning. I can write on the train as you did, but I can post letters only at air mail stations; anywhere else would be useless. And I might give Pete a note to you, but, I'm going to say goodbye. . . . I love you, Peter, you and your ways. I admire, I respect, I believe in you. I want you to come back to me. I hope you will love me long, but I want you to be free too, to love me or not, to say so or not. For, whatever happens, we are friends, rare friends. The Chinese know one thing. They know that friendship is better than love. . . .

Later.—Well, it's been all evening. Allen didn't come; Miss D., Garrett and I warmed right down to cases. It's too much to report. Personally G. feels, he says, that we are about "the most intimate friends" he has; that was his phrase. He would like to come West and live and, if he does, it will be to Carmel. . . . He sees the evil of the inheritors of riches; he'd abolish inheritance. Speculation and the stock exchange are "obsolete," can't last long; not needed now. The profit motive, the money motive,—not essential,—not primary. Sees the possibility of what I saw in Russia: vanity in place of money. I gave him some idea of what I'd got from him. He said, "Hell, it's been a balanced exchange." He has quit psychoanalyzing us; takes us at our face value and accepts our reasons for our deed.

Now I'll post this. . . . Good-night, Peter.

Wellington Hotel,
Denver, Col.,
July 10, 1929

Dear Peter:

This is to meet and greet you in London, at "home," your home, you and Pete and his grandma. It will be a joy to your mother, but also it will be a tragedy. She can never understand it all. She will want to change it to fit her ideas. She may make it hard for you; certainly when she expresses her own doubts and fears, you will want to fight. Don't. Explain as best as you can, but don't argue. Leave it at that. . . .

One of your envelopes contained Gilbert Seldes' *Back from Utopia.* I saw another of the series on the train and I could not read it. He can't write and I think he can't think. Garrett said something about him and other ex-radicals that suggested to me that Lorimer and Co. (*Sat. Eve. Post* & Wall St.) are counting on and encouraging what they think are ex-Reds, to confess. They might take a "confession" from me. G. said they would take an article on my present views. But I told him that I could afford to write what I think now for a liberal or radical paper, but not for the *Sat. Eve. Post.* Seldes, however, never was a Red; he was only the son of a liberal, really a Liberal. . . .

I find my mind picturing you on your rounds of relatives, old friends, parliamentarians; in London, Paris,—with Jo and Yvonne, Guy and Mary, Billy and Sally, everybody. You'll have fun. Try to find Jaccacci, possibly at the Crillon. Give my love to each of them. Makes me kind of homesick. I *could* spend a winter in Paris, yes, and in Rome. The key to my life is the *Life.* I must jam it through. I wish I could do it this summer and fall. Then,—the whole world will be open to,—us. We'll have some fun, Peter, you and I and Pete. My error is not in failing to know what you want, but in thinking too much that you can wait for me to finish. We'll change all that.

But do realize that you are free of me and my inhibitions; you are bound only by your love for me; not by mine for you. This last is thrown overboard. I wish I could make you feel how free you are, really and truly free. That's one of the advantages of my narrow view of marriage and divorce. I feel you to be freed, and I can't see why you don't feel free. You can go anywhere, do anything, love anybody, —including me. And I'll always love you. We'll always be friends whether we're lovers or not.

Denver, July 12, 1929

. . . As to the Labor Government, ask if they are going to be content to prove themselves safe again; or if they propose to strike out and lead. They can't do much, with the Liberals holding them back, but they can do something. Anyway the world hopes they'll so act as to distinguish themselves from the Liberals or even the liberals. Will they?

Show them how, over here, there's a rift that may become a split between the management in industry and the ownership, which is a bit bigger but along the same line as labor and capital. And it's the old, dead, parasitic owners that are holding back industry in England; vetoing new machinery, new methods, new men. We have it in old industries, like coal and cotton; it's only our new businesses that are going ahead to adventure. So it's not American or English. The crisis, the coming conflict, is between the old and the new, the contented owners and the young administrative managers, organizers, inventors and workers, everywhere, and the British Labor Party could find and open it by favoring and winning the managers of industry and balking the owners clearly. The British Labor Party could lead American politics and French as well as British,—that way. See if they see or can see this.

Are they going to take care that work given the unemployed is productive and not merely a dole or any old work?

Are they clear about dealing with the causes (economic) of war, rather than with treaties and pacts and disarmaments?

Are they scientific at all, or only moral, sentimental, liberal?

Are any of them conscious of the corruption of social entertainments, dining with the King, etc., and titles, etc.?

Other questions will develop out of these and out of and during conversations. . . .

The Alexandria Hotel,
Los Angeles, July 22, 1929

Dear Peter:

. . . And what a lot I have to say. I found that out in this lecture course. Six lectures, and I didn't get it all out. The reason of course is that I have an angle on things which enables me to say everything or anything over again and just a little bit changed. It's not new; it's the old things all seen afresh from a new point of view. My ever-increasing crowd in Greeley, which grew from a few hundred students and professors to many, with an addition of business men, seemed to sense this. They were puzzled, but they followed and asked for more: it was as if they were asking, "Well, and how should this look now?" I was at my best: easy, quick, humorous; serious, too, but prompt with a jest. I got really witty at times. I answered nothing directly; always with an anecdote or a story. "You make us think," they said.

But I noticed also that my disciples became more and more personal. They hung on and hung around; and as one woman said: "It's you, not only your ideas, but you." And I quoted the woman who, when I reproached her for not asking her question in the open meeting, said, half bewildered, "Oh, well, I guess it's because I just wanted to talk with you." And the men, too; even the professors. Garrett seemed to be like that. When they sat down to question him, on Costigan's [1] Saturday Night, and offered him and me chairs at opposite sides of the room, he whispered to me: "Don't go over there. Stay here by me and back me up; and answer for me."

I'm a bit bewildered myself. I wonder if speaking and not writing isn't my game. But, then, why am I not called back more often to the places where I made a hit? Salt Lake City, for example. Unless it is that my hearers go out and try to quote me and make me sound all wrong or queer. I can't get that. There's something wrong and there's something right. Which is which?

The lecture man called and we had an understanding which Frank Heney contributed to; he came in while we were talking. Then Frank said Bob La Follette and Fola were at Santa Monica and asked me out to his house for lunch, promising to take me to the Miramar afterwards. I went.

After dinner Dr. Gerson took me to the Bowl for a concert, a lovely symphony concert in the greatest setting I ever saw.

Stef.

Gaviota, Cal.,
July 31, 1929

Dot drove to Gaviota yesterday afternoon because she learned by phone that there were a lot of letters for us. There were, but none of it was interesting or personal, and Dot was so disappointed that she said what was on her mind. "You were right," she said, "nothing from

[1] Senator Edward P. Costigan of Colorado.

Peter." And I realized by my feeling that I had hoped for the first letter. I had argued against it, calculating the time, and been hoping for one all the time. I can't get one till the end of this week and yet Dot is going in really to look for "something from England." The worst of it is every time she is disappointed or whenever I show by my eagerness that I love you, she breaks out in a rage at my folly in the matter of a divorce.

Dot and Jim are good hosts, cheerful, easy. They talk a lot about Pete; thinking of his future. "The ranch is no good for Pete now," Dot said yesterday; "he is too young to avoid rattlesnakes and pests and cattle, but some day, later, when he can come here and have the run of the whole place and ride and rope and brand, the ranch will be a godsend to him." And to his cousins, I add. He will be the oldest of the whole tribe of children: Joe's, Jack's and, of course, Jane's and Clint's. He can come here for vacation and lead the bunch into and out of mischief. I have not thought of that before but, of course, I can foresee him coming here to work with cattle, and to play, even into his college days. . . .

I am listening to the "farm relief" talk of Jim and Dot, both well up on the farm problem, and I can see that that, the conflict of interest between farmers and others, is just as acute here, as is the clash between peasants and labor in Russia, Germany, France and the Balkans. But I can't get the nub of it yet. Hoover may force it to a crisis, but I think not.

Gaviota, Cal.,
Aug. 2, 1929

Dear Peter:

Bob and Fola came yesterday. Jim was in Santa Barbara on law business, so we three sat on the veranda and talked politics, which, as usual in the U. S., is really economics, business. Bob sees as I do, the situation even down to the split between management and the banks, but he does not see through it; as I do not either. He is right in his feelings, however, as right as any of us, and much more radical than his father was. As Dot says, young Bob goes farther toward the farmers' view than Bob, Sr., did. His one complaint is that in the old crowd, both in the Senate and out among the reds and liberals, there is nothing but cynicism, disillusionment and,—"What's the use?" There's no good advice for him, Bob. He can't say, "What's the use?"

And he can't go into a fight like some Senators, saying, "We'll be beaten." He is depressed as well as sick.

What shocks me is that I, who used to be able to see through a problem of economics into politics, I can't do it now. We talked till Jim came home at supper and then at table and into the evening up to eleven P.M., impressed with it all, and I had no counsel to offer. What sort of a guide is it to a U. S. Senator to see that management and ownership is splitting as labor-capital used to? What is the U. S. Senate to do about foreign affairs, strikes and legislation on the tariff? The tendency is to fall back upon old principles.

We are not up to our times. I am passed by at last. So it seems. I must read and know and think more. What does it mean that Ford should say on his birthday that business is going to have to be run without profit? He showed that he meant that, even if there were profits, they'd have to go back into the business, but what he said was that the best, the most ardent managers (like him) were setting the pace, to manufacture for sale, regardless of profit, and that the lesser, more money-making competitors would have to be content like the leaders, in the job, in the businesses, in the management (like artists) and to hell with the profits.

Let some of your English economists chew on this.

Anyway there is something new under the sun.

I had an embarrassing surprise yesterday. I received a diploma, and a medal: a decoration from the Lithuanian Government. If it were from France, Germany, Italy, I'd send it back with a polite apology, but Lithuania,—no use rebuking that small backward nation, which is only trying to thank me for a service I failed to render it years ago, when they asked me to help make an approach for peace to Russia. At least that is the only "meritorious act" I can recall as within their knowledge.

Stef.

Gaviota, Cal.,
Aug. 6, 1929

Well, Peter dear:

My oil well came in yesterday; Dot's didn't. Mine is a gusher, what they call a "major flow." There were four envelopes: the long, bully boat letter,—21 pages long; your first letter from home; the over-looked diary pages that belonged in the steamer story; the clippings and the photos. I was dee-lighted, and read you all the way from

Gaviota into Santa Barbara. The letters, which I read aloud to Dot, were fascinating to me, so complete, so vivid and so sweet, and Dot called them "great." You are her best letter-writer. And we both felt and commented upon the girl-writer who came through so alive and so "noble," as Dot repeats. I'll bet you didn't see how distinctly you sketched yourself, and what a straight character you displayed,— straight in the honest crook sense.

But I'll not answer all that you say, not today. I'll be answering these letters, at least till the next ones come. I went to work today, so I'll write only enough to let you know that I feel connected up with you and Pete, knowing that I'll get news from you in each steamship that brings mail. Don't make letter-writing a burden; just enough each time to keep up our touch and make our diary complete.

I read Mary Vorse's[1] story last night; Dot hasn't yet; but it will hit her hard. It did me. Youth has gone over the top all right. Sure. Made me feel as *All Quiet on the Western Front* did. But I read most eagerly, and with feeling, the first letter from ashore. And first: do get some of your parliamentary friends to get my name off that stupid black list.[2] A folly or a crookedness to begin with, it is an example of English inefficiency and stupidity now. It's like that soldier the Prince of Wales saw on guard in Rotten Row and asked about, only to learn that some one of his royal ancestors had once had a mistress across the street. No one had ever changed the order. They leave the past sticking up half buried all over England.

Tell your friends in power that I am not likely to come over and tell the truth about Lloyd George, and that it is absurd to leave my name there forever, to stop my wife, my child, perhaps my grand- and great-grandchildren at the front door of the Empire to interrogate them: why their editor-ancestor was once suspected by old England of having reported on the Russian Revolution. If you don't get it fixed, I'm going to write an article about it or a chapter in my book,—to make the English look like the asses so many of them are.

Pete's landing first was a picture; and grandma. Not enough of that. I want to hear what grandma says about Pete. . . . And Peter, you'll always have me, who wants you, and will be there always for you. A real backing as long as I live; and after. . . .

Stef.

[1] "Tourist Third," *Harper's Magazine,* March, 1929.
[2] Ella Winter and Pete were held up and questioned on arrival in England, and informed that Lincoln Steffens was still on the British blacklist.

Gaviota, Cal.,
Aug. 12, 1929

Dear Peter:

. . . Your letter, partly typewritten, is a corker, interesting, clear, and, as usual, complete. I like the personal, about Pete and Rosa and his grandma. Always give me some of that. The talk with Wedgwood is fine. I could almost see it and it sounded so right; and so English and so,—hopeless. Wedgwood's economics are old, but he has some. And the "passing a law to keep the Africans from owning land in Africa" is world news. We used to think it was American, our California legislation to forbid the Japs from owning land in America, but I see now that we should have forbidden the Japs to own land in Japan.

England is the seat of an empire; it is not a normal country and I see no way out for her. But we don't see very far.

And that is the point about all of this. We are not thinking, we are working out our problem, and when Marion [1] cannot see the end, or rather when she does see the end, she is thinking; and she is thinking out of our own concepts. But Ford sees to an end; he is no thinker; he has only flashes. It seems to me that we are seeing a clash with and the end of ownership,—by another road than that of the Soviets. Ask Marion which she thinks is the deeper-boring issue,—Capital vs. Labor, or Ownership vs. Management. This is the idea that Garet Garrett took away East with him from us. He'll be trying it out on some of his managers and we'll be hearing from them through him. The ideas in people's minds count, though they are not, as you carelessly say, as strong factors as economic forces.

Of course England is not dead. It seems to me to be dying, but who am I? The thing for you to get is what they are thinking and doing; and I think you might get some such news there as G. G. got here, but listening, not only to the intellectuals, but more especially to the hip-thinkers. Why not call on that editor of some weekly who is an economist—what's his name—Keynes? Talk to him about G. Garrett, etc., and then listen to him on English ways out on the sick industries, mass production and on what English industrialists are really, unconsciously doing.

I am not so sure we can't have mass production in agriculture. Jim read from *Wallace's Farmer,* his agricultural weekly, that owners who

[1] Dr. Marion Phillips, chief woman officer of the English Labor Party.

lease land in tracts to different farmers are learning to put an expert over all the renters with power (under the lease) to supervise, and that works out. They have tried to farm on a grand scale with hired labor; that will not do; and renters are careless. But Jim himself is now learning in terms which permit him to manage, and he sees there's a way out into mass production. The other way, which Hoover is furthering, is cooperative farming under business management.

Jim came down from a ride last night, late for supper, and said, "Well, it's done. I have made something that will be there as long as the hill." It's a part of his water-work system. That is art. As you see. I really think you see America right. Anyhow, if you could say it all as you see it, it would be art; and about art; by an artist. I hope Pete learns to see it as you do, as coming, as growing, as sure to do and be something.

I am well into the fourth chapter about Ben Lindsey and Denver; and W. S. U'Ren. It's going fast. I am over the top. And Dot, who has been reading the MS. Older left here, likes it all. Very much.

Why not tell Pete that what he sees with his eyes shut are dreams? And show him the difference between day-dreams and dreams. . . .

To Pete Steffens

Gaviota, Cal.,
Aug. 14, 1929

Dear Pete:

I haven't written to you for a long time, a quiet, busy time for me, on the ranch. You know, Uncle Jim's ranch, Aunt Dot's ranch, Jane's. You were there once or twice but there is no one else here now, only the Senator [1] and Aunt Dot and I, except of course some thousands of cattle, hundreds of pigs and sheep, and millions and billions and billions of birds and bugs, and a few deer. Oh, yes, and a Chinaman, named Gin Chow. I'll tell you a story about Gin Chow. It rained here this morning. It never rains here in summer. The first rain is due not till the middle of November, and there has been no exception to the rainlessness of the summer. But Gin Chow, who works in the vegetable garden, looked up one day two weeks ago and said to Aunt Dot: "It's going to rain the middle of this month"; he said the fifteenth.

[1] Pete's name for his Uncle James Hollister, a member of the California Senate.

Dot laughed at him and came home and laughing, told what old Gin Chow said. And we said: "We'll see."

And yesterday it clouded up. The newspapers reported what they called a freak storm in the southwest of California. Imperial Valley, which is below the level of the sea and has but half an inch of rainfall in a year and always in the winter, had a slight precipitation, and the desert had a few drops. So when we saw the clouds, we thought of Gin Chow's prediction and Uncle Jim said: "Well, we're going to see." And this morning when the gong rang at 6:00 A.M., there was a patter on the roof and Aunt Dot called out of her window to me:

"It's raining. Hear it?"

"Gin Chow knew," I answered. . . .

I have a letter from grandma, who says you are nice and that she likes you. That's right, Pete. Make her like you. It is easy. All you have to do is to be a nice boy and like her; and say so. You know. "Ladies like it." Don't forget to kiss the hand, Pete; and be quiet at table and eat.

Have you told grandma any stories? Do tell her all about Charlie Lindbergh, and how quick he was; and ready; always ready to go. She will like that story. And there are other stories, you know. The millions and billions and billions of cats; [1] and,—all of them.

I must stop writing now. Aunt Dot is driving to Santa Barbara and she can post this. Maybe she will bring me back a letter from Mama.

So goodbye, Pete. I am so glad you have cut out your baby tricks and become a traveled big boy of the world. Give grandma a kiss for me, and Rosa, and give Mama two. . . .

Affectionately,
Daddy

To Ella Winter

Gaviota, Cal.,
Aug. 14, 1929

Dear Peter:

Older phoned from Gaviota yesterday A.M. but he could not drive in to see us. Had a summons from Hearst and had to hurry on to San Simeon to see him about Mooney. There was some sort of row on in Los Angeles about the report of that Mooney meeting. I saw in

---

[1] Wanda Gág's *Millions of Cats*.

the *Examiner* the next day a report of half of Judge Griffith's speech,
—the part showing what had been proved against Mooney and to
whom; this was obviously to have been the basis of the Judge's showing, that all those witnesses and *all* the testimony was perjured; but
the paper omitted this part that proved Mooney innocent. I infer that
Older roared to Hearst and was called to explain; anyway the rest
of the Judge's speech was printed yesterday, the whole of it. . . .

Do you remember my explanation of the trouble with foreign correspondents: that they soon lose interest in the American questions
they take abroad and become absorbed in the French questions in
France and the English questions about England? And my story of
the Bullitt mission: how we wrote down our questions before we
entered Russia and read them after we had been a while in Moscow?
Well, you are like that. Our questions are fading and you are consciously becoming interested in the imperial, colonial and local problems; and it is all right too. It is *you*, to enter into the problems with
the people you are with; it's a virtue in you.

The last letter leaves two stories to be continued in your next: one
of them is tea with Stella Benson.[1] The other is the call from the
Grant Richards man for your MS.![2]

In town Dot invited Joe Wheelwright to luncheon at the Paseo and
I had a chance to talk with Janey's choice. . . . He was a bit repressed
at first; Dot said he was in awe of me. But I boosted him out of that.
I asked him if he wasn't the hero of a love story I had been hearing
lately and he blushed and then laughed. . . . We drew him out on
his subject, the education of rich men's boys, and then stuck him on
some of his phrases. And I talked a little on Pete's education,
and he got so interested that he asked leave to come out here for
more. . . .

To Pete Steffens

Gaviota, Cal.,
Aug. 17, 1929

Hello Pete:

I've got something to tell you, something I promised in a letter to
our mama to tell: how I was stung the other day by half a bee.

[1] English novelist, author of *The Poor Man, I Pose*, etc., which Steffens admired.
[2] English publisher. The MS. is Ella Winter's unpublished novel *Wait Till
You're Married*.

You know about bee stings, you 'bember [1] when you were swimming in Mrs. Older's pool something seemed to bite you on the under part (where it is soft) of your left arm; I looked and I saw a bee, and I pulled him off and his stinger. Well, that was a bee-sting, and it certainly does sting. But half a bee? How can half a bee sting? I'll tell you. I was mowing the lawn here and, when my grass basket on the machine was full, I put my hand under the cut grass to pick it up and stuff it into a bag. I felt a sharp pain in my little finger.

I yanked it away quick, very quick, and there I saw sticking in the flesh half a bee. The head and half the body had been cut off probably by the machine, and I guess it was dead, that upper half. The half on me was so full of life that I think that the soul of a bee is in the lower half, at the very end. For it had stuck its stinger deep, deep in me; the rest of the lower body dropped off, and still the stinger stuck. It stuck till I moved it off with the blade of my knife. This I did thus so as not to pinch the stinger. If you pinch the stinger you press the poison from it into the wound. I didn't want to do that. I had enough. The poison that that deadly mad bee shot into me made my finger swell and ache and in the night time my hand also swelled and ached and it is swollen and painful even now as I write, two or three days after this all happened.

All I got out of it was this story to tell Pete, so that some day, if he is stung by half a dead bee, he will think of his daddy and,— smile. . . .

Dad

To Ella Winter

Rancho Bulito,[2]
Aug. 20, 1929

Well, Peter, it's done. I feel as if I'd be having writer's cramp before long, but Chapter 14, Part IV, is finished and filed on the pile. It was all about leaving *McClure's* and making the *American Magazine,* with anecdotes of Peter (Dooley) Dunne and the story of my first

---

[1] Pete's word for remember.

[2] Mrs. Hollister writes: "When we first returned to the ranch to live twenty-eight years ago we thought the old name of the cañon was *Las Bolitas* for the thousands of little oak balls that fell from the oaks; but later on we changed it back to what it really was, *El Bulito,* which means a little drinking horn or gourd, we think named so because of the shape of the cañon. It is named so in all the old maps."

article, on Hearst. I'm surely going to have that feeling you wished for me: the feeling that it is all done, that interminable *Life,* that big, too big book. And, I think, before you get home!

What you say about the life left in England reminds me of a rejoinder I made in Cincinnati when I was challenged for saying the city was dead. Someone pointed to the life in the streets and the business. I said, "Yes, but the people you see going it so fast are eating up their own city and its people and its wealth. It is full of life, true, but so is any carcass, the intense life of maggots."

England is not that far gone, but years and years ago the English gave up agriculture; it was unprofitable; they went in for manufacture and trade. And to get markets they conquered colonies and created an empire, which bought from the old country. The colonies traded raw materials for the manufactured articles of England, till, of late, those colonies have begun to manufacture stuff of their own out of their raw materials. The U. S., Canada, Australia, even India, are competing with England, and they all are self-sustaining; they have agriculture. England cut out agriculture; is not self-sufficient, and now is losing the business it must have to live. And, meanwhile, the old industrialists, the old statesmen, the old culture, the old factories are all obsolete, and the English don't know it. They are industrial-minded, or often merely industrially habituated; they don't think of either the new machinery or the new problems. And the new party won't even recognize Russia and is fighting against the Young Plan, —to get their share of the graft. Well, they need it. It's funny to see the Labor Party going after it for them, but they sense the need of their "just share of reparations." I suppose it's no use talking to them about it, but when Marion says that it's no use raising wages (for labor and profits for farmers) in England, she states a fact, but she misses a Socialist, a practical, scientific truth. She is thinking like a Tory; and she is thinking about,—a corpse, or a dying thing.

Did you take Pete to the Wolfs'? I'd like them to see and know him; and I'd like him to remember them and their habitation in that deep court,[1] so English. It's an interesting trip for him; underground and bus, isn't it? And, if Pete could always carry in his memory a picture of that fine, wise, honest man and that affectionate, competent,

---

[1] Lucien Wolf lived in Gray's Inn off Holborn, one of the old courts in the heart of London.

kind Margaret, it would be good for him forever. I do, you know. They keep me sometimes from saying smart things; they belong to my collection of Christians, of whom there are so few in the world; and so few of those few church Christians and so many—Jews. Yes, make a point of a meeting of Pete and Lucien and Margaret Wolf.

Stef.

To Sara Bard Field

Rancho Bulito,
September 1, 1929

Dear Sara:—

This is the day,[1] Kay's day and her Jim's, and yours. And nobody's else. Our Jane put off her wedding; just can't, not yet. So it is Kay's day, and I know what I am missing. Your few words of the plan only fill out the realization I had that it would be all beautiful. And, as Barry's amoralist shows: that is what you are and what you blossom: beauty. This wedding is a flower, as Kay is herself, of you.

I wonder if you and Erskine know and get the earned joy of your loveliness. The most perfect people creating by living it the most perfect life that is possible on this earth. I wish you could acknowledge that. It's too bad that people can learn to confess their sins and are afraid to face their virtues and their triumphs. I would be willing to use force to compel you two, you and Erskine, to close this wedding with the happy acknowledgment to yourselves, to each other, that you have succeeded in life. You have not only made poetry, you are poems, one poem.

You see, don't you, that I am thinking of you rather than of Kay and Jim; for the moment. They and their union are, to me, but buds breaking forth upon the bush, the beautiful bush, which apparently is to carry on and on. Kay and Jim and their marriage will reproduce other flowers like themselves and other loves like theirs and yours.

I feel, I almost see, as you can see, the loveliness of the work of art that is to be on the hill of The Cats this day. I could sing my joy in it.

Love to you all.

Affectionately,
Lincoln Steffens

[1] Wedding day of Sara Bard Field's daughter Kay to James R. Caldwell.

To Pete Steffens

Rancho Bulito,
Sept. 9, 1929

Dear Pete:—

We had an earthquake last night as we were going to bed around 9 o'clock. You bember, Gin Chow predicted one a few weeks ago; he said it was due and might occur about Sept. 13. It came too soon for him, therefore, and it was not a big one. It began as a slight trembling, stopped, started again, and got sharper and heavier before it ceased, say, 20 seconds all told. But maybe there will be another, others, for the old Chinaman's records show that it is an earthquake cycle; as it is also a time for a very wet winter. You may have to wear your rubber boots a lot. And I may have to rake back the wash of the road in our garden.

Clint, by the way, said he liked you, he liked the way you did not cry when you were hurt and he would like to be your friend later when you go to school and college. Clint is very strong. He can swim fast, shoot straight and stand on his head. He was just graduated from Harvard and is about to begin an eight-year course in medicine. . . .

Your daddy,
Lincoln Steffens

To Mrs. A. Winter

San Francisco,
Sept. 14, 1929

Dear Mrs. Winter:—

. . . Peter does hold what she learns. She was evidently able to apply in Europe the scientific culture that is coming everywhere. She does not reason as she did when I first met her. She looks to see. She forms theories, avoids convictions and conclusions, observes drifts or currents of conduct as experiments and can await the results. Our intellectuals can't do that. They still reason, and they reason from the false premises of old, exploded ideals, like right and wrong, liberty, democracy, justice. It must interest you to see or to hear that only the scientists, the business men and the Bolsheviki have gone over into the culture of experimentation.

I am wondering whether Peter could put it over on Bernard Shaw, who is the last of the old school of literature and ethics, just as your Bertrand Russell says Einstein is the last of the old school of science;

not the first of the new form and phase of thinking. I myself can think in the new way, but I cannot act it. That's why most of what I say and write is funny, humorous and satirical. The new writers will not be contrasting the old and the new; they will be soberly over in the new, seeing things and saying them as matters of course. I know no one that does that yet. Maybe Peter will do it. If not Peter, then Pete.

And, speaking of Pete, what do you think of him? I don't mean how do you love him. What do you think he can do or be best? Parents (and grandparents) and teachers have been licked to the point where they say and believe that they cannot foresee what children are gifted for. I think this is wrong. I know it is hard, but somebody must learn to educate a child individually to his own province and the child can't do it. The parents and teachers must. We must study a child, we must look and see what he shows the most abiding interest in and does longest and best, and form theories as to his gifts; and then try them out in school and in play. Pete, as you see him now, is, in part at least, a result of our encouragement of what we saw in him: a child born with a sense of courtesy and great self-confidence.

He has shown so far no sign of manual dexterity; no mechanical gifts except gracefulness. But he has intelligence, and that intelligence is made up of imagination, some humor, a tendency to whimsicality, and a gift for words: as I see him. What more (or less) do you see? And how and to what tentative end would you educate him? I would go in for mathematics, beginning with mental arithmetic, to get his imagination to work; and stories, and some acting and dancing. The last to develop his grace. . . .

> Mark Hopkins Hotel,
> San Francisco, Sept. 17, 1929

Dear Mother-in-law:

Please send word to the boat for Peter—if she has started for the United States—that Dr. Suggett and I received yesterday a telegram couched in these terms:

"Freedom regained no longer rebellious married secretly today love." It was signed "Janey."

I would like to see the Santa Barbara papers on September 20, when the wedding was announced to occur. And I would like to see Dot's face; and Jim's. This generation is the open season for parents. . . .

San Francisco,
Sept. 17, 1929

Dear Grandma:

Older told me yesterday that Hearst had thanked him for the tip about Peter's interview with Shaw and had cabled his London man to see her. He asked Older to cable Peter and Older read me his cable. I am astonished that Peter did not herself realize the value of her talk; that she did not know what papers would pay for it. And her title: "Shaw as a Political Philosopher"! I suggested a better one, more Shavian: "Bernard Shaw's Interview with Me." On the other hand, the *news* of it is, if I understand what it was about, that Shaw is talking on America. "Showing Shaw America" or "Shaw Sees America." Peter should be good on titles by this time.

I may make Europe another visit, long or short, but I don't want to settle and live there. Russia, China or these United States for me. And I don't want Pete to be brought up in such a hardened, hopeless, class-lined society; with no chances for youth or for adventure; and no education. Nothing but culture. The way Peter says he is spreading his a, shows that he is sensitive like her to his surroundings. He would become in England a regular Englishman, the very type, standardized and full of the knowledge which is dead. No, Pete should see enough of his grandmother-country to like it, but with a smile; not to be of it and smug about it. I would have him see America also objectively; all countries should be foreign to him. But of them all, England should be the last one where he should go native. . . .

To Ella Winter

San Francisco,
Sept. 21, 1929

Dear Peter:—

. . . That Science publication brought yesterday an article by a Johns Hopkins psychologist on a theory that there can be "no progress without crime." The state should make laws and enforce them; that's the only way to get any stability, by establishing conventions. But, for progress, there must always be lawbreakers, who show what laws are wrong and force changes. Perfect obedience, he says, causes death (to thought and growth) in individuals and in states, and he gives examples. We are going ahead in the U. S. because we are breaking laws and conventions; other peoples have stopped because they are law-abiding. England, par exemple, where I couldn't get a cigarette at 9:01 P.M. For the past, I'd like to study China, where it is really old; for the future, America and Russia.

The chapter I finished is the one, after San Francisco, about Los Angeles and the apple speech. It makes a good summary for the ending of the Fourth Part, which will be done this week. Then Europe, Mexico, the war, Russia, peace and the New America. That will be all,—about 8 more chapters.

Your visit with Pete to the Wolfs was a gratification to me, as I got it in your account and Margaret's. I like them to like Pete, too, as well as you and me. I hope you see them again in Paris; and that Pete goes to Gray's Inn to say his goodbye. And Pete and the autumn leaves, and you! Lovely.

But the gem of your collection is the part about Stella Benson and your note to her, which you should have sent her. Why did you not? Why only to me; if you did? Your report of your interview with her is an article, or, it would be with a few amplifications. It shows her as honest and self-trusting, to the degree of genius, but not wise; too impatient of others. So many gifted people are like that, not all; Jeffers is not. He has serenity, and a broad vision. The error comes from judging, which Stella Benson indulges; Jeffers does not. . . .

Stef.

San Francisco, Sept. 26, 1929

Dear Peter:—

Doctor read to me just now your radiogram saying you sail "Majestic" Oct. 16. I am *so* glad. You have given up "till Xmas." Dear Peter. You shall have another trip to Europe soon for that. My, it's exciting to be foreseeing your homecoming. . . .

You say Pete is at school, a Kindergarten. That is very wise. No matter how short the time, it will leave an impression on him. Jack and Clint Hollister urge that we get Pete ready for college early. They were late, you know, so they are speaking out of experience. We'll have to think about that and plan a bit lest Pete feel the way Jack and Clint do, that their parents might have been more on the job. With my book done, I may be able to do some actual teaching and see, for instance, that he gets from the start an insight into mathematics; see numbers with his quick imagination and not merely on paper, the way you and I did. . . .

I can make him eager and quick to learn geography, and history, by getting him curious about how things lie and how they came to be. That's the parents' part: curiosity. Let the schools satisfy it, and try to kill it. We'll open more holes in his head than they can ever fill up. And so with college. We can make him want to know about metaphysics as well as other boys will make him want to know about football and rowing. Yes, I am glad he is at the Kindergarten; as I am glad that he loves his grandma and feels her.

Affectionately,
Stef.

San Francisco, Sept. 27, 1929

Dear Peter:—

Those two letters from Rue Cambon were not from Guy and Mary. They were from you! I wasn't so very disappointed. . . .

In my cable I apologized for my irritable letters. In these letters you explain yours.

In my last letter I tell you that I have been learning something. In one of yours yesterday you say you "have been learning some deep truths." One of yours is about "marriage."

You say "There must be a point where one thinks as one really feels." I'll match that with this, that I have been learning: "We think one way, then another; what we do is right (for us), what we think is wrong," so you've heard me say, not surely. My new idea, which brings this to an intelligent fusion is: We think out of our pose, we act out of ourselves. That may be what bothered Stella Benson. Your remark shows that you are feeling your way to a union; and, not merely by a process of self-justification.

The artist, the writer, may be the one that achieves this complete identification of himself, of his feeling, his thinking, his doing, a union of his pose with his being. One's pose must be related somehow to one's self. The choice of the character to choose to appear as, must indicate at least my taste. But, what I have always liked about an honest crook is, perhaps, that he has become aware of his pose, sees through it and lets down when he meets an equal,—crook, who also is "onto" himself. There is something for a novelist to write herself clear on in all this.

But,—enough. You were going, in your last, to be busy shopping in Paris, visiting Bêcheron, revisiting Paris and you might not write much. I'll expect no more letters for two or three days. I may not have time to get an answer to you to those letters; this may well be the last direct reply you'll get. And it doesn't matter. We are running parallel again, thinking in, at least, the same circles; we are married once more. The trip is turning out other than I expected. I thought it might lead to a separation, and I was making myself ready to stand it; I am so glad that I was wrong that I did a strange thing yesterday. I wrote to Sara and Erskine a short letter which I hope won't mystify them. I let out my joy to them, as one might have gone to them with a great sorrow,—for sympathy, for a chance to express myself. I think that they will understand that. Otherwise they will wonder. I shall be interested to see if they "get" it; that I was so happy that I could not contain myself, and there was no one else to speak to in the emergency.

Now, I'll go to work. It is late; nearly 9 A.M. But nothing matters. My girl is coming back. My boy, too. But it's funny how much more I yearn for you than for Pete.

Stef.

To Mrs. A. Winter

San Francisco, September 28, 1929

Dear Peter's Mother:

Lest she and Pete be gone, I shall write to you. . . .

The only news, but the inspiration of my gaiety, if you please, is that I ended a moment ago the chapter I reported half done. It is about Wall Street, the control of credit, American sovereignty and *Everybody's Magazine* when I was on the editorial board. I am working in a new mood, less serious, more humorous, telling big things merrily. Pete's fault, I think. I have got to imagining him reading some day his daddy's life, so I am telling him the things I do want him to know in the spirit in which I would have him take life. No reverence, some fear but not much respect for law and the powers and the conventions; how easy it is to play and win at the game.

So I am showing Pete what I learned as I learned it and showing him that he can go forth and learn whatever he wants to know, so long as he will look at the facts and not listen to men or read their books too credulously. I am glad to gather that you have been working along the same line with him instead of along the line of your education of his mother. Or am I wrong? . . .

Peter still suffers from sincerity. She is very much in earnest, but she is better than she was when you delivered her to me; don't you think? She says you like her now, that you are tolerant of her ideas and conduct. Unless this is despair, it is approval of what used to worry you. Of course she has been held back by her marriage to me, but the divorce will lighten that handicap and, if it does not release her, there is a separation to try. I don't know how you feel about our program; you don't say a word, and somehow I don't feel that in this case silence is what it is cracked up to be. You may talk to me, you know. I listen; and we keep learning, Pete and I.

To E. A. Filene

San Francisco, October 10, 1929

Dear E. A.

Your nice, quiet letter, announcing your arrival home, got here yesterday and gave me a warm feeling about you. You are all right. You are facing your problem, and I would like to have a voice in the solution of it. I have no advice for you; I know only what I would do in your case, but that might not be the thing for you to do. What I'd like is to talk to you slowly enough and long enough to get you to know what you would like best to do. . . .

Isn't it strange that men who know these days have so little sense of the need of reducing what they know to wisdom? It is, I think, because knowledge now-a-days is attainable only for men of action, and men of action have not the habit of reflection; they only reason or act. I would have you, for example, enter upon no new undertakings, but just idle and think. You probably could not stand it. An habitual propagandist, you will have no doubt to spend all the rest of your life continuing to persuade men to do what they are doing and can't avoid doing, instead of watching them work in spite of themselves and their old ideas along your way. Mass production is here; it will move on like a glacier; no one can hasten or stop it. The only question is what does it mean as to other things? What does it mean as to the education of Pete, the relations of men and women? What ethics will it call for, what philosophy of life? What kind of politics? Won't there have to be bribery and lobbyists to help force the laws of man to conform to the laws of economics? Who is to think upon and write and talk about such things in the new era? Well, not E. A. Maybe Garet Garrett. Maybe both of you will leave it for Pete to do; or Peter.

But, E. A., if you do get sick of the fighting in Boston and the propaganda in New York and Washington and Vienna, remember that there is a quiet spot in Carmel, California, where you can always be loved and insulted, laughed at and admired.

Yours affectionately,
Lincoln Steffens

To Upton Sinclair

Dear Upton Sinclair: San Francisco, October 13, 1929

I have started to write the Boston chapter of my *Life,* and I want to know what you got out of the book I wrote about Boston, Mass., New England. You had it; did you read it? If so, what did you make out of it? Do you see why no publisher would take it? What I thought I was doing was to muckrake the ideals of America that came down to us from Old England through New England and which I had found "not working" everywhere in the West, Middle West and the East. What my committee expected was an exposure of the political conditions, which I simply could not go into; it was such an old story. No one expected and no one cared for an exposure of our American virtue as a source of evil. Maybe you didn't either. You and Bernard Shaw both possess and practise those virtues and you attribute the evils of society to economics, only. I notice that the Russians are very particular to inculcate the new ideals and virtues of Communism; they act as if they thought ideas counted. As I do. At the time I wrote the Boston book I felt only that ideas did harm; that there were two causes of evil, one economic, one moral or ideal, and I was trying to "show up," not only the bad influence of the non-practise of our American ideals but of those ideals as ideals. I can see that my book could have been of little use to you in your book, but I would like to hear from you what you thought of what I wrote aside from your purpose at the time. Have you time to tell me? I want your answer as a guide to what I am writing now, right now.

To Ella Winter

San Francisco,
Oct. 17, 1929

Dear Peter:—

. . . Would you like to know what I think is the wisest, most penetrating and imaginative thing you have said (or written to me) all this summer? It was an exclamation in a letter of amused exasperation at me; something like this: "You do let the funniest things keep you from action!" It wasn't well expressed. You should learn from Stella Benson to wait and look and study a scene or an idea till it takes on words. But this insight into me was a lightning flash. I have watched it and seen it at last; it's been there all my life. An imaginary chalk line can keep me from doing something all ready to do.

I thought this last night when I was trying to balance up the pros and cons to a conclusion: whether you are a writer, of fiction, say. I did not decide, but I did recall observations of yours that show that you can see, and into people, too. It seemed to me that you lacked only the instinct for words, and I wasn't even sure of that. Your inadequate, your "uninspired" phrasings, may be due to your excessive quickness, to your impatience. Maybe you could learn or be taught to love the pat word. In your interview with Shaw you quote me as asking the Oil King, Marland, whether, when business goes a bit bad, they will cut wages or *profits*. Correct enough, but to make the point and the picture, you should have said what I said: "dividends." Not profits. When profits go down, I meant, will they cut the wages to labor or the distribution to the unproductive shareholders. You got the idea, but not quite the point. Stella Benson, Hem,[1] the best of them, all think it through to precision in words; just as sculptors or painters model up to an edge, to perfection. Why not try, in conversation at first, to wait a few seconds more, and hit the nail squarely on the head?

Stef.

To E. A. Filene

San Francisco,
October 17, 1929

Dear E. A.

I have, and I have read Wood's[2] first chapter; and I am relieved. He will do the Life. This chapter is written, as writers say. It is well done. It is easy to read and whoever starts it will carry on. It is interesting; it is alive. It is important, too.

I am sorry, though, that Wood does not quite see that you are a failure, and you must make him see it. It may mix things up to say it, but the point of the whole story, the use of it, your success, is that

---

[1] Ernest Hemingway.
[2] Charles Wood started, but did not finish, a Life of E. A. Filene.

you are and that you see that you are a failure. Everybody fails, in some sense, but not everybody "gets" his own failure. As you do. I would ask that Wood let you tell him again, and that he open his mind to believe, that you have made a failure and that you know it. How else can you and he relate the story ahead of you in such a way as to account for your failure and so show others what to avoid?

But first, let's grasp the failure, the failures. You, a boss, set out to get your employees to take over your business and so achieve democracy in one spot in industry. They did not rise to the chance in a business, just as they have not risen to the opportunity the ballot and our democratic charters gave them to "take over" political power. Why not? Just to stimulate Wood to reflection, I will suggest that the cause of this failure may mean that democracy as a theory of action is the bunk and that one of your mistakes was in your theory of democracy. Maybe your life shows, among other things, that Mussolini is right when he says that the people don't want to govern themselves, that they want George to do it. But in analyzing the events to get at this conclusion you must tell him how you gave power also to your partners, and how they, typically, I think, used their power, as the employees used theirs, to get lesser things: high wages, bigger dividends, prestige and finally all power. They took over the business, and not in the interest of the business, but in the interest of their careers. Wood will find rich digging in the story of that failure. He will learn from it something so scientific that he will be able to predict what is likely to happen in General Motors, etc., as well as in a new Western state. There is a Truth hidden in that stuff which Wood has his hands on.

Second: you set out to reduce the percentage cost of distribution. It has increased. Ford succeeded in cutting the factory price of autos and he showed that the cost of distribution could be reduced and he did not solve that so well as he did his own problem. Evidently it is the harder, as it is also the more important problem. Why is it so hard? That question might be answered and the problem might be stated so clearly out of an analysis of your failure (and everybody else's; even Ford's) that this book might lead to its solution; which would be success. I think that, in dealing with this thread of your story, Wood or you or somebody should consult with Ford, Garet Garrett, the General Motors people, and any other men you know that have ideas or experience along this line, but principally you should tell and retell the story till Wood and you see what your mistakes may have been.

You made other failures. You got little or no credit from your creation of the City Club, from the League of Nations, from the reorganization of the Chambers of Commerce. You may not care, but I do and Wood will, for you thereby lost control and a good influence over these tools or weapons; and the failure was due to a mistake, to a defect in your character or in your thinking. I am not going now, in a letter, into all of this; there is too much of it. All I want to say now is that you have not yet put yourself over on Wood or he has not opened his ears, eyes and mind enough yet, he has not got you; neither your sincerity nor your weaknesses. If he can see just why, he will have another element in his story, for your failure with him is probably the same as your failure with your employees, your partners, your friends and associates. Let Wood ask Brandeis, for example, why he misses you; as he does.

I would beg Wood to see and verily believe that this story is worth the doing, precisely because we have at last a successful business man who sees vividly and even tragically the failure of what we all call success. It will show the failure of success. And, if you can but put yourself over on Wood, you can achieve your ambition; you can make your Life the real success that your life is not. In a word here is your chance to succeed. If I were you I would do nothing else till this Work is done.

I can't work closely with you and Wood now. My *Life* is important too; it is just as much and as meaningly a failure. I must get that done. When it is done, I will labor some with you, as you suggest. Meanwhile, we will do what we can by correspondence and,—why can't you two blokes come out here for a month or two? Mountains and prophets have compromised before. And got together.

Affectionately,
Lincoln Steffens

To Mrs. A. Winter

San Francisco,
October 24, 1929

Dear Grandma:

There was a nice little letter from you yesterday and I should wait till tomorrow to reply to it. Pete arrives then and I know that you would like to hear how he is and what he says about his grandma and Merry England. He is coming with Anna. But we shall be going right on to Carmel, where we'll be opening the house, and then I have to go south to meet Peter at Los Angeles; probably with Jane in her car. I'll have no time to write letters, for a fortnight. . . .

It's strange how those old countries fascinate Peter. You don't find it so. I note that you object to my theory that England is dead and you offer as evidence against me that there is a lot of interest and life in the troubles of the people around you. Of course. Dead things are full of life, but there is no growth in them, no progress, no adventure. The trouble with Peter—her virtue, her weakness—is that she is sensitive to the influences about her; she likes where she is. When she is here she may like it here. But, as you say, she will decide for herself.

But what's the use of writing letters with Pete impending. Just think, I shall see him tomorrow coming striding off *his* ferry boat, a well-dressed, independent little gentleman, with his secretary close behind him, saying, "Hello, Daddy." I shall at least shake his hand and then, in the car, hear all about Grandma, trains, boats, the Labor Government of England and how he can read, write and do arithmetic; for I am sure you taught him a lot of things besides Labor politics. I'll have to take care of him for a day or two, while Anna is busy with the house; she can't be bothered with him then; and then I'll go to Santa Barbara by train, get into Jane's car and drive down to fetch Peter, the renegade, and poison her against Europe and her friends and relatives in the old country.

Meanwhile, by way of news, I finished the third part of my book the very day Pete landed in New York. I'll have the whole book done by Christmas and then we'll go somewhere. . . .

Affectionately,
Stef.

La Playa Hotel,
Carmel, Oct. 27, 1929

Dear Grandma:—

Pete's here, all well and happy. He wired me to meet him at Oakland Pier so I crossed the ferry and saw him, not as I had anticipated, marching off the boat, but beside his train with Anna, who spied me first. She told Pete to look and he turned, gave an hysterical cry and leaped into my arms. "My daddy, my daddy, my daddy," and then, right away, "I've got a truck, see, a big one, heavy," and held it up for me to see.

Anna's man, Leslie, appeared and there was a quick bit of planning. Anna wanted to drive over with him, so I took Pete and the baggage onto one boat, while Anna and hers drove onto the other. Pete and I had to hurry. When we were safe aboard, the deck hand raised the apron bridge and closed the gate. Pete had to stand by to see that done and I had to hold my questions. And then, when it had started it looked as if the pier were moving. At last Pete could answer questions.

"Where have you been all the time, Pete?"

"At Grandma's."

"Is she nice?"

"Yes."

"Tell me about her. What does she look like?"

A silly question, which flabbergasted him.

"Her face is green," he said, and I was properly rebuked.

"But where does Grandma live?"

"London."

"So you were in London, at Grandma's."

"That's London. Grandma's is London."

He wanted to show me his truck, so I watched him run it up and down the deck and meanwhile looked him over. He had on his new grey overcoat that looks so grown-up, and a big black hat with wide brim that looks so foreign. But he was well, no sign of fatigue, and he was heavier, but still such a little Pete. And he spoke with an accent, English, clear and precise, with his mouth closed in. After a while I asked him whom else he saw in London.

"A boy," he said, "a little boy, bigger than I am, but a little boy."

He choo-chooed his truck a bit, then told me about passing through tunnels, lots of tunnels that are snow-sheds. That was that day, as I knew, coming over the Sierras. "But there was no snow," he said. "We did not see a bit of snow. There was an engine, a great big one." Pause.

"Have a nice time on the boat?"

"Yes. The boat was the 'Majestic.'"

"Glad to get home?"

"But this is not home."

He played with his truck and I let him, till we landed in San Francisco. Then he forgot his toy. He liked the city.

"Uh-h. Let's stay here every day."

We had to find Allen. Pete did. He recognized the car, climbed in and kissed Allen, while I went to fetch the baggage and search for Anna and Leslie. They soon came, driving off the auto-boat. We sorted the bags, I took Pete's and Leslie Anna's. She did not want to go straight to Carmel the next morning; preferred to stay up with Leslie till he drove down,—today, Sunday. So I arranged with her to meet me at the house Monday (tomorrow) morning, to open it up.

Pete and I and Allen drove up to Jack Hollister's flat, where I was for going right to bed. But Pete wanted to play with his truck, so I undressed us both while he was loading and unloading,—Canadian pennies. When we did get to bed, Jack came in, had a short visit and then we all quit and,—slept. It was 9 P.M. We slept, all of us, till 7:30, then up, a bath, and downtown in Jack's car to breakfast at the St. Francis, where Pete's chief interest was in the whirling weather door. "London has one," he said, by the way. At breakfast Jack tried to pump Pete on London. No use. He did find out that Pete had ridden an elephant, but London and even the *"Majestic"* had been wiped out by the journey home, and the boat by the train. Pete lives in the present.

Allen looked over his teeth, carefully. We inspected Jack's factory, had lunch and went to the train which left at 3 P.M. Pete played with his truck and pennies up and down the aisle most of the way. He remembered the stations, San José and Monterey; he was delighted to get on *his* bus (the bus he goes to school in) and asked for the driver, "Big Pete." "He's big Pete; I'm little Pete," he said. The bus took us to La Playa, where we had dinner, interrupted by Pete's discovering that a little girl friend of his was still in the hotel. He flirted with her, but also he ate a good dinner. Then to bed.

(Pete just came awake and asked me what I was writing. "A letter to Grandma. What shall I say for you, Pete?" "Tell her I came on two ferry-boats, two big ferry-boats."

"Any love for her?"

"No. I want to keep my love for Mama. Will you write to her? Then tell her my love; it's for her, my love.")

Sunday morning, after breakfast, I let Pete go to the beach with his girl friend and a big boy. When I went down an hour later, they were having so much fun that I stayed till noon. After lunch a nap, then down to Pete's house. Pete rejoiced, looked all over. "That's where I climb." "That's where my mama writes, and that's your room, Papa." "And that's Anna's room. Oh, look, it's open." Her room was the only one that was open; the house is still closed and I can't get the key on Sunday. No matter. The garden was enough. It has grown so much that Pete noticed it. "Daddy, they have planted more trees and yes, more flowers. Won't Mama be glad?" Of course, there have been no more plantings, only the old things have grown or spread and the place is so fat that we'll have to clear out a lot.

Monday, Oct. 28.—Pete looked past me at breakfast and his face lighted up. "Anna! It's Anna," and there she was. We finished up breakfast and agreed all to go to The Getaway, Anna via the real estate office to fetch the key. She opened the house and said: "It's clean. There's no cleaning to do," and she was pleased. We opened all the windows to let the sun and air in, and then Pete and I did some work in the garden, ran an errand uptown (to have the electric light on) while Anna prepared the house for us for tomorrow morning.

I am glad to be home. Pete and Anna have gone this afternoon to Monterey to see about Anna's baggage and ticket, I came down here after lunch to do this bit of writing, at my old desk. No doubt Peter is on the way home, but I've had no wire saying when to meet her. One will come tonight, I hope.

Affectionately,
Stef.

Tuesday.—We are moved over into our house. Pete, pulling off cobwebs from the eaves, knocked over a flower pot. "What a to-do!" he exclaimed. Old English. Where did he get it?

To Upton Sinclair

Carmel, December 5, 1929

Dear Upton:

Get ye behind me. Here I am trying to concentrate upon and get done the story of my Life, with a publisher naming dates, and you come along with an offer to let me read your new novel! No. I must not accept. I must stick to my job, which would be easy if I had got where you have got: where whatever I wrote was just so good, no better, no worse, ever. Do you realize that achievement of yours, that you have found your style? And your stuff? And yourself? Lucky devil! Unlucky me!

No. I won't read your novel till my thing is done. I know just how good your novel is, anyhow. Firmly I am, but

Affectionately yours,
Lincoln Steffens

To Mrs. Gilbert Roe

Carmel, December 24, 1929

Dear Netha:

Peter handed me, open, the sudden message you so thoughtfully sent us out of your sorrow; she had read it, and, as I was taking the shock of it alone, I thought, I noticed that she was feeling it as I was. And she said: "He was so kind, so wise to me, and such a friend—" Then I realized that time had nothing to do with the friendship of our friend. We had no great advantage over his later, younger friends, like Peter.

Gil had love to give, and understanding, and Peter got the full force of it in a few minutes as you and I have had it for years. And she knew that and had given it back. My grief (there is always a remorse) is that I can't remember ever having expressed to Gil my love for him; it's as if I had taken his and never thought that he might have liked to know about mine, which wells up warm and big now that it is too late for him. Not for you, however.

If there is anything I can do,—if there is ever anything we can do together, you and we, let's do it. He would like that. We would like it. If there is anything I can do for the children— I hope that, since it happened around Christmas, they were there, so that he could see that he was going right on in them.

Our children are our immortality.

I can't say the rest, but I don't have to; you know it all. You know, as I trust Gil did, that we love you.

Affectionately,
Lincoln Steffens

The Getaway,
Carmel, January 7, 1930

Dear Mrs. Roe:

Jack writes me that you did not get my letter as soon as you expected and I have explained to him that the telegram, which came promptly, hit me in such a way that I could not reply right away. I

ELLA WINTER, 1933.

(Photo by Sonia Noskowiak.)

fear that I gave way to my grief, which I would not have added to yours just then. You had enough of your own and, besides, mine was lonely; that is why I was so struck when I saw that Peter felt the loss as hers. I am sorry I disappointed you.

I see that Young Bob is going right on doing in the Senate what his friend and his father would have had him do. There is immortality. And I felt that in Jack's letter: strength, courage, independence, even a bit of defiance of custom, which, I remember, Gil thought worse than the law. "I can see," he said once, "how we may get by the law, but how we are ever going to overcome custom I cannot see." Jack was speaking of the funeral, but he was showing how we can beat custom,—by defying it.

I have been recalling a lot of things Gil said and did in his so quiet, wise way. I have been thinking a lot about him, and you.

What are your plans? Why don't you come out here to be in the sunshine? Have you much to do? I don't want to ask you to write us; I would not add to your burdens, but we both would like to know how you are and what you see before you. I am, we both are yours, you know,

Yours very affectionately,
Lincoln Steffens

To Frederic C. Howe

The Getaway, February 12, 1930

Dear Fred:

. . . I can't go to Europe with you this year, and, besides, I don't want to "see Europe" any more. That's checked, that continent. I might like to go to some spot where it is reminiscent, pretty and cheap to live, but to learn I would rather travel in Russia or China. Send me your tour leaflet, however; I may get you someone else. And tell me what tours are preparing for Russia.

You mourn your losses in Wall Street and speak ill of tips. But I think I can see from here a renewed bull movement and, if you have got your banks to carry you, as you say, you may recover losses and have another chance to take paper profits. I want to see your book on Banking. I am no Anarchist apparently; I do not understand money. I only suspect it. How are you able to see both money and the land? You must be bi-sexual or something.

I wish you would come out here some day and see how well everything is going with me, with us: Pete, Peter, Anna (our most important maid) and me, I am getting toward the end of my *Life*. Two volumes, Fred. I wish you'd help me cut it. And I have left out about one volume in the writing.

Do you know Garet Garrett? He was out here last year; I listened to him. He has some facts that make a picture of America. George Hughes was here a fortnight ago. Remember? Atchison, Kansas, single taxer, a queer duck. Sinclair Lewis is here now; he wants to do a Labor novel.

Have you any ideas on town planning a village? Or references? We are having some fun with the future of Carmel in our paper, a weekly.[1]

Why go to Europe when you might come here; and Marie, too. What of the summer school? A good letter, yours, but it suggests more questions than it answers. Write again or come.

Love to Marie.

Yours affectionately,
Lincoln Steffens

To Committee of Admissions, The Players

The Getaway, 22 April [1930]

Gentlemen:

I have known Ernest Hemingway since the Armistice when he came to Paris from the front in Italy to report as a correspondent for some newspaper in Canada. He was fascinated then with cabelese, as a language, and working secretly on his short stories. He was subjecting himself to the conflicting influence of Gertrude Stein, Ezra Pound, James Joyce, but laughing, shadow-boxing, skiing and bull-fighting through them all to his own. A gay kid, he was a charming companion. Big and strong and handsome, he was physically alive, mentally forever at play. His labors were unknown to us. I never heard of them till intimacy grew; then came the discovery that he was profoundly in earnest, beautifully honest, industrious, sure.

"You can write," he said to me. "It's hell, but anybody can do it. I haven't yet. I will though, you'll see. And you can. Anybody can."

That's his propaganda, apparently. I heard him give it to Dos Passos, to my wife, to Guy Hickok.

The happy boy was an artist, I found, and I think The Players will be delighted to find that the novelist is just a happy boy, a born Player.

[1] *The Carmelite.*

It is a pleasure to know tnat one may see him at the house. May others of that set or ilk follow.

With sincere respect,
Lincoln Steffens

To Alfred Harcourt

The Getaway, April 24, 1930

Dear Mr. Harcourt:

Your wired inquiry about a title has just come, and I am telegraphing as follows: "Title undecided. Letter follows with suggestions. Meanwhile use My Life."

I have not been thinking of a title, so absorbed am I in the last chapter which I am doing now. But I find that I still prefer the original "My Life of Unlearning." All the time I was muckraking the opposition asked why I didn't take things as I found them. Well, I have at last, as you will see; so it occurs to me to make the title "Taking Things as I Found Them" or, shorter, "Taking Things as They Are" or "The World as I Found It." "Seeing It Through," "What's What in America," "Back of the Fronts," say something pertinent, but the last suggests a war book. I shall reflect further and report anything worth while.

Ella Winter has gone to Santa Barbara for a few days, but I think she wrote you that I have a man, Spud Johnson, the editor of *The Laughing Horse,* at work on the manuscript, editing it for repetitions, errors, unclearnesses, etc. As he turns in copy Peter (Mrs. Steffens) reads it for the same, and, when I get through writing, I shall finally edit the whole thing. I am well into what I think is the last chapter, a survey of the United States in the light of Europe. It will be done in a week, I verily believe. The editing should go fast and, I hope, it will cut a good deal. Have you considered illustrating the story? Do you think I shall have to go to New York to read proofs or for any purpose? I ask this to help me plan my summer. We have let the house here for June and July, but I would rather not go East unless you will need me.

If you are to consider titles with me, you should know that my last and summary chapter finds that this country is going its own way too strong to stop or turn, and that way is the very process of corruption which we reformers and liberals opposed. Bribery looks now to me to be necessary, if not right: an act of God. Mass production is here, mass distribution is coming. Trusts, combinations, mergers, are steps toward the organization of all industry, all business into one unit, which will eventually be the sole government. We shall have no political government. And probably no stockholders. No middle class. Criticism, muckraking, hereafter should be on this basis, taking things as they are, trying to foresee the ends in sight and choosing the end we prefer, by dealing with the causes of what we call evil and good, always pretty sure that we can control our environment, if we want to. We can be free, or democratic, or safe, but not by wishing; only by economic arrangement of the circumstances of life. We can be good people, or happy, or brave, or wise, but it is no use introspecting for this purpose; it is only by seeing what moulds us into what we are and making conditions that will mould us into what we would like to be. Aside from this management of conditions or because of it, we have to get rid of our old moral culture and learn the new culture, already here in science and in big business: what I call our experimental culture. No more thinking, nothing but theorizing and experimenting; no more positive knowledge, but only working, tentative hypotheses. American business is nearer right than American ideals.

Yours sincerely,
Lincoln Steffens

To Ella Winter

Bêcheron, July 6, 1930

Dear Peter:—

We are back from the Château de Candé, but Pete is gone with Jean and his pal to Azay-le-Rideau and Jo is talking to the great art dealer of Paris and Berlin about an exhibition of Jo's works in Berlin. I am free.

The Bedaux place is a castle, an old château up in the woods on a hill, a picture. The grounds are a country, a beautiful country through which on moss-banked, shady roads, you mount to the castle, all restored and equipped, inside and out. We were received in front, taken in, down to a regular barroom in what may have been the prison; then up to the grand dining-room. The other guests were all titled French (and one Swiss). The dinner was swell, and Bedaux[1] was not different, as Yvonne predicted; not formal and busy, but devoted, humorous, Satanic as with us. But Yvonne explained that this was so

[1] Charles E. Bedaux, the efficiency engineer.

because he addressed himself always to Jo and me, even when he talked (over their heads) to the other guests. They were really disappointed that you did not come, but they were interested in your trip to Russia. They talked also about Pete, who seems to have made an impression upon the Bedaux, who scent something unusual in all of us. When we left they proposed a picnic soon, and I told Bedaux we must meet again. "You know something I don't know," I said, "and I think something you don't think."

"Yes," he answered, "you think something I cannot think."

I had accused him of mistaking God for Satan or vice versa and he seemed quite jarred. He does. He thinks of Satan as goodness, unrecognized goodness, whose apparent evil deeds are for our good, disciplinary.

It was some fun.

French is getting on Pete's nerves. It annoys him when people speak it; he will not look at or answer anyone that speaks it to him; and when I use it, he appeals to me. "No, no, Daddy, not you; don't you talk that." He says he will never learn it. He picks up words and phrases, but it seems to him hopeless, that he'll never be able to "talk that."

They say, the dubs, that children acquire tongues easily, quickly, but I can see that it only seems so to heedless adults who do not see the process. To the child it is slow, hard, and there is some suffering in it. Pete feels for the first time in his life, not "in it"; a sense of inferiority. . . .

Bêcheron, July 13, 1930

Dear Peter:—

Pete came up, whimpering, from lunch. He felt bad in his chest, he said, and his bones. I touched him. A fever. Jo followed; he had noticed that Pete was not right, and he made Pete go to bed. . . . I just looked in on him. He whimpered at the sound of my footstep. He is quiet, but not asleep.

"I'm not going to die," he said when he was undressing. "And if I do I'll go to heaven."

"Where did you get that 'heaven'? That's the bunk," I said.

"Well, then, I'll go to the bunk."

Who has been telling him about heaven?

10 P.M.—Pete slept 2½ hours this afternoon, woke and asked Jo to

read to him. I got up, took a bath and dressed for supper. Pete wanted his soup, but barely finished it and that's all we offered; it was more than he wanted. It hurt his throat to swallow, he said. He lay quiet till I came up from supper, slept a bit, on and off, till just now I took his temperature,—37.5, which Yvonne said was a temperature but not alarming. Jo also reassured me. They have a good doctor, who will understand; knows kids. He will be called in the morning. It's curing me all right; my bronchial symptoms have disappeared. I'd rather have bronchitis and die than have Pete sick like this. He's so sweet about it. He muttered "Mama" but when I asked him what he meant he said he meant "Mama and Papa," and he smiled contentedly.

Bêcheron, July 18, 1930

Dear Peter:—

. . . Yours of July 15 arrived this A.M. and I read parts of it to Jo at breakfast. "A beautiful letter," he said. "She does write well in that form. I should think she could do a novel."

You liked Williams' book and thought you'd want to stay longer than planned. Well, we had agreed on that. You had an idea for an investigation, which might be good. You doubted their statistics. So did Lenin. "Don't bank on our statistics," he warned. "They are unreliable." They may be better now. But your proposed inquiry doesn't sound statistical; certainly the one as to kids' delinquencies is not.

My hunch is and has been that you would get more and better stuff out of a first, short, general survey, a sort of general seeing and hearing what happens to come up. This, for the conception, the new view of things. Come back with this and the answers offered to a few standing questions, like: is ambition, pride and vanity, enough alone to make men work well? Is profit, wealth, which is our so-called practical, essential incentive, unnecessary? How far does the esthetic impulse: to do things well, carry men? How many such artists are there in a hundred? There are other questions, of course; you know them. The answers to such as they are would be more popular to write about and more suited to your own intellectual needs. How are they getting along with their plans to develop the new democracy in the self-government of shops? Is it true, as I have heard, that the workers, having lost their fear of government and profiteering bosses, want their communist foremen to do the governing? Let George do it? That bears on and points your fear question. It's a waste to concentrate on one fear; ask about the others: punishment, property, losses, poverty. I think that this, with all that you happen to see, hear and experience in a short visit, will be good enough for thought and writing. But this is only my view (and my experience). Rhys W. went after quite other things, and he lost by it something that I got: the essence of it. But you decide.

Bêcheron, July 24, 1930

Dear Peter:—

. . . The word "corruption" was big and understood in the vocabulary of my day. It meant diseased, politically, and was so taken. It was not so used in England. The English have always kicked at it. It does imply a moral judgment. The muckrakers were full of moral judgment, as our time was, as we all were. It belongs in my *Life,* till after Russia. And it did presuppose an ideal state of affairs; an ideal described in American charters and constitutions. And my reporting was to show that this ideal and these described governments were corrupted, not by bribery alone, to change them to represent what other governments represented, a government by a class, to destroy the health of our state and to split the minds of people so that they said and believed one way and did another, unaware, to their psychological distress. It may rank, this word, with scientific slang, only it is better understood by my readers. If I could carry on my *Life* to my own conclusion, I would show that it was the ideal that should die, not men's conduct; the ideal state, not the business that sickened, weakened, corrupted it.

Do you see what I mean? The turn comes with the statement that "Bribery is an act of God." Modern psychology might explain all this, but I rather think that this explains modern psychology, which is all full of the idea in conflict with conduct. The modern psychologists traced all to sex, etc. My book might show that the conflict is universal; it is in politics, business, literature and the language of the psychologists.

My hypothesis is that organized society is passing out of the agricultural into the industrial stage, and that most of our conflicts, sicknesses, corruption, is due to the misfit of our ideas and ideals with what we were brought up to think, and to the blind struggle of the industrialist to make a fit; to make a state and its laws, for example, suitable to and represent what has and still is happening. But I don't want to write this into the chapters where I did not see this.

Bêcheron, August 1, 1930

Well, Peter, I have been through the *Life,* once, slow, hard; all but the last, untyped chapter; which I must look for and "do." I'll go through the whole thing again, now, to see how it all fits. For I have made some cuts and written a lot of inserts. I have not cut so much as you indicated; I need repetitions; they are unavoidable in a long work. An idea or a fact stated in one connection, bears upon or is made evident again, sometimes clearer, in another connection. I have been light and short and reluctant with inserts; the whole is too long already. But, on the whole, I am coming to the conclusion that this *Life* is me and my story as I see it and want it seen. And *it is not bad.* I am not satisfied; I could not be, but I am about through. I can do no more. I, too, must live, and I can't while this job is upon me, day and night. I shall run through it this time, run, not crawl, and part by part, I shall ship it to Miss Ford to recopy the worst pages and so send a neat, presentable, finished MS. to Harcourt. So there. If I am not quite up to my own facts, experience and conclusions; if I don't write it all in my own light, let the psychologists do what they will with it,—when there are some psychologists. See?

I have found my last chapter, the end,—one page missing, which is O.K. I have to rewrite some of it, but in the main it is as I want it to be. I have thought of a fine, humorous last paragraph. I'll have it off to Miss Ford in a day or two. In a word, I think now that I'll be done, all done in time, and have it delivered by September, as promised,—all but the illustrations.

Now I am ready to take an interest in your plans. I have asked for, I expect soon, your several dates. I weigh less than I did this morning by a ton. But,—the tub is full, and Pete's not here. I'll go and whistle.

Stef.

To Anna McCarthy [1]

Bêcheron, August 6, 1930

Dear Anna:

I have been working. That's why I have not written. But I have heard your good news and I have been glad. I want to be home when the little one comes so as to be sure that you treat it right from the

---

[1] Anna, the Steffens's Welsh housekeeper, whom they had brought to the U. S. A. with them, had married Leslie McCarthy, Carmel electrician, in March.

beginning and have everything it can possibly want. It is to be our baby, you know, as Pete was and is. I suppose you prefer a boy, but I want a girl; and why not. We have a boy.

I have stayed right here at Jo Davidson's country place and I have kept Pete. Peter went off quick to Munich to study in a German clinic. A month she has been there, but now she is gone to Berlin to start for Russia for two weeks or more. She wants to stay longer there, but I think she won't. My book will go, all finished, to New York in September and we'll probably have to follow it there in October-November. So we may get to Carmel by February.

You and Leslie must do the best you can alone, without me. And you will do pretty well, of course. If I am late and I find that you have made any mistakes, I'll correct them when I get there.

The only great news I have for you here is that Pete eats. Eats? He gobbles; nobody has to ask him to. He gets hungry and begs,—I have seen him cry for *more carrots*. And I think it's because he is growing. He does not speak French yet, but I'm sure he'll have it before he has Welsh or Irish.

Best greetings to Leslie.

Yours affectionately,
Lincoln Steffens

Pete says "my love to Anna and my love to Leslie."

To Ella Winter

Bêcheron, August 8th, 1930

Dear Peter:

You'll get this in Russia where foreign news sounds so foreign; and everything is foreign, especially domestic news. However, here goes:

Pete's governess is here. She came just before supper and Pete is examining her. Can't make up his mind. "Do you speak English?" he asked her, and, fortunately, she said, *"Non. Il faut toujours parler français avec moi."* I say fortunately because while she is a French governess who "speaks English and German" her English might inspire contempt in Pete. She is to teach Pete to read and write English, and to speak French. And work. I bade her put him at reading and keep him at it a little longer than he wishes, each time, increasing the time with each lesson. He must learn to stick to a job.

Wells comes day after tomorrow with his girl, who, they say, is a character.

Pete was ploughing today with a man and horse. He is interested in the various kinds of farm work going on around us. Also he is having a phase of climbing, which is not so amusing to me. I let him, but he does take risks. He and Marie Louise [1] were playing ball on a wall today. It gave even Jo a thrill.

You saw the Mooney case news. New trials begun, with fresh charges added: Mooney and Billings in a conspiracy with (Emma Goldman's) Berkman as chief to blow up the parade. Since they can't prove he did it, they will prove he intended to.

It's late. I'll go to bed, feeling you will be impatient of all this and thinking to yourself: "So this is Bolshevik Russia; where are all the concessions?" I shall be interested to hear first impressions, but, then, I'll be glad to hear what you got in Berlin, too. No letters from there, yet; none for two days.

I am writing a lot now into the last chapter, making it very long, but I can't help it. I'll make the preface short.

By the way, this governess served, she said, Scott Fitzgerald's little girl. But I am not sure she has the name right. She called it Scott to me and Fitzgerald to Yvonne, and it was Yvonne who put the two names together; she asked me if I knew of a writer called Scott Fitzgerald.

Good night, Peter; my greetings to Russia, and to my few friends there.

Bêcheron, August 10, 1930

Dear Peter:—

Wells is here with Her. . . . He remembers you. "I know her very well," he said. "Better than I know you. For instance, she wrote me about you, and who and what you were when she was first with you, and I never knew till I got her word for it, how great a man you were. She told me."

I asked him why he didn't go into Russia again.

"No," he said, "I have come to the conclusion I am not a good observer. I get my field facts from others who can see better than I do." And that's why he doesn't go to China, I notice. He expects nothing big from India. Russia must make some success, "else we'll never have another chance to offer a planned organization of society." He bemoans the Communist malice. He has heard that Russia is strewn with

[1] Niece of Yvonne Davidson.

tractors and other machinery that is going to rust unoiled, unused, unrepaired. He hoped I'd be able to deny it. All I said: "Whoever told you that saw some such machinery. Everything you hear from Russia is true, but never the truth." He accepted that, absolutely. "Of course."

I told him a few of the high spots of America, "the high-wage market," Ford's declaration that business would be run without profit; which (profit) would go back into the business. "I am writing a book on that," he said. "We are failing,—a crisis is coming,—because we don't know how to distribute people economically, well."

Jo is touching up his bust; in wax, and it's awfully good.

"He's taking the sorrow out of it," Wells said. Jo is getting all the humor into that little head and face. Wells is going to New York in October,—next year. He is interested and agrees with everything I say. He is fine on the use of tradition. "We are, we must break up the old ones, most of them. Fine as some of them are, the liberal, for example. But we must have a new tradition."

"As Russia has," I suggested.

"As Russia is creating," he answered.

I asked him what question he would ask if he were there; you would get the answer, I said. He said: "We hear that some men are arrested, held and then asked if they don't want to work out their time without salary. They do. See if there is any or much of that sort of forced, penal labor. Especially among experts: chemists, scientists and professional managers." Doesn't sound very general to me. Probably one or two cases that have been multiplied by reports.

He is for a standardized, but very advanced education for the whole world, so that all people and peoples shall have some economic, geographic, historical knowledge in common.

He spoke very well of Darrow, with some imagination. . . . I read them two of Dorothy Parker's stories.[1] He enjoyed them. I said there's as much in one story of hers as in a whole Wells novel. "More," he answered.

Bêcheron, Monday [August, 1930]

Dear Peter:—

Two days of sunshine and it's bad weather again. "English weather," Wells calls it. And, by the way, he got to talking again about D. Par-

[1] *Laments for the Living.*

ker's stories, the knowledge in them, the understanding, the force. Like Hem she makes the inarticulate express themselves and she tells tragedies in the casual, comedy vein. Fierce, some of them. As W. says: "She knows the women who have sex relations with all their friends and so have no friends among men. They go to other women." And he pointed out the dedication of D. Parker's stories. And she has the drinking women, too; their dull tragedies when they can't get any more kick out of drink.

But what you will get, after Russia, is the irrelevance of all this stuff. The stories of a decaying culture won't touch you as they might once have done. There's another life for you, a young, vigorous, hopeful life that asks for no artificial "kicks." I'd like to hear you when you come out on the servant problems that trouble Yvonne; and the boys' problems; and the taxes that bother W. He fears going to the U. S. lest he be met with an enacted surtax. He tells of a man who keeps a mistress and then goes and lives on her because in France a kept woman is not taxed. The French politicians who keep women have fixed it so that they thus can escape their dues. Her house or flat, her furniture, her income,—all free, and all that live with or on her get off. Think of this in Russia and smile; as you would if you read D. Parker in Russia.

Good-night. Regards to all my friends.

S.

Bêcheron, Aug. 16, 1930

Dear Peter:

Your first from Moscow, dated Aug. 12, at 7 A.M., arrived in this morning's mail, four days. And such a letter! I read it to Wells and Jo, who saw that you got it. "It's true." That was what I told Max and the others like him in America when I came back; and that's just what they can't believe, any of them that have not been there. "It is true." The Russians have made the great turning, and when you write as you do I know that you have made the turning. You will see everything better now. You will be yourself different. But what you say about Americans in Russia is typical of all who don't get it. Wells, who sees the need of a planned example among nations; whose mind wants Russia to succeed,—he can't believe it. Jo grinned at your letter, happy. Wells stared, nodded, yes, but,—but what about this? What about that? He can't. His mind will not change. Jo's can. Yours has. There are lots of things you will never say or see again. But go on gobbling. Get it all. For, if you get enough, you will be able to judge even Russia; as only a philosophic communist statesman can.

Do you know what line from your letter hit Wells the hardest? It was Jeffers's "few of you have energy to hear." That he knew. The rest he has to believe.

He is still here, Wells; she left today, but Wells can't go till Monday or Tuesday. His car is in need of parts that have to come from Paris. But also he likes it here. As Yvonne complains, her guests certainly do stay. I guess she means me, but I can't go till you come and take me away. I'm getting like that Dutch writer [1] who could not cross the street alone. But let me get back.

Ask your American sceptics to try to use a psychological fact: that their brains are laid out in compartments. Let them have a Russian compartment, put all the Russian facts and philosophy into it and not either distrust or judge with the old parts. Take Russia in without asking if it's right and what does it mean. It's the thought of having to do something about an idea that prevents practical minds from accepting one. What would they do if they went to Mars? Would they look or would they judge,—and close their eyes? Tell them my story about Emma Goldman going to a Socialist heaven and finding it hell. Concentrate on Barkley,[2] who seems most worth while. He can prob ably see that there are two ways of doing things, the Russian and ours, and do tempt him to see that our anti-trust policies are reactionary. I am glad you found him. I'd like to meet him. And Wheeler?[2] How is he? Just a good liberal? You must see Bobby La F. when you get back.

Wells is very reactionary in some ways, or he is very wise. I don't know which. He may sound to me as I sound to my old liberal friends. He goes far with me, but he is writing about and urging traditions, now, but to be hard and fast; discipline; liberty. I can't put these together, but I can't make him consent to the idea of time, relativity. Like Shaw, he has no sense of or respect for beauty. It has been a very interesting visit, his, though I am troubled by his growing age and his wandering attention. He is fascinated by Dorothy Parker; we

[1] Hendrik Willem van Loon.
[2] Alben W. Barkley, who was on that tour (conducted by Sherwood Eddy) with Senator Burton K. Wheeler and the late Senator Bronson W. Cutting.

all are reading that one book. "She is an extraordinarily intelligent woman; has a great gift," says Wells. . . .

Go on, dear, get it all; all but the details. Get it as a whole. Let it lift and clear your mind. It is better to be a revolution than to see one, and Russia can put you forward centuries in civilization. It can jerk you up to where it has got, and then show you the future. And Pete will profit by it, and I will. Russia is just what Dorothy Parker, Hem, Dos Passos and all the Youth school of writers lack and need. They seek it in drink and get it in cynicism. You can take it, as it is, in the living form of a people on the job, in a religion. Faith, hope, liberty, a living,—Russia doesn't need to drink.

Sunday.—I missed the postman this A.M. He brought your second letter, as good as the first. I read it as before to Wells and Jo. Silence on Wells' part. He can't. He is really old.

Love, Peter.

Stef.

Wells thinks we, he and I, will live to see the collapse of our economic system in Europe.

Bêcheron [August, 1930]

Dear Peter:—

It occurred to me this evening while I was playing billiards with Jean that it might be better for you this first time not to stay long in Russia. One of the most thrilling experiences that anyone can have is a first impression of that new world. I have talked some about the troubles of correspondents anywhere abroad. They are corking reporters when they first arrive in any foreign country partly because they are full of questions from the outside, which are leads to a first, fresh impression; and partly because they can see so sharply while conscious of the contrast of what they expected and what they see. But there's another difficulty for them and for you. After a while we get over, we forget the first impression. To you, who are so well prepared with the philosophy and the point of view, this first impression will be your most valuable acquisition, whether you write it or only keep it for yourself. I am afraid that, if you stay after the party leaves, you will get too interested in some of the special inquiries you want to make. In getting the complete answers to them, you will dull something much better,—greater, nobler, more astonishing. A big, superficial survey is what I advise you to take now. Get the other or others some other time. You will be going as often to Russia as Pete is going to Europe and America.

But, remember, this is only my impersonal advice. You decide. I am for whatever you want to do.

Have you in mind the questions I wanted you to ask. (1) Are they finding out that men can work, hard and well, without the incentive of profits or high pay? (2) What are the evidences of this, if it's so; and, if it is not so, what experiences illustrate it? (3) Is it true that the workers in shops will not take an interest in self-government? (4) Have they lost fear; fear of the boss, fear of the government; and, generally, fear? Bill Shatoff would be wise on these questions; he was always an Anarchist, not a Socialist; an extreme liberal, therefore, but he could learn and change his mind. Ask him, too, if there is any improvement in the skill, inventiveness, discipline of the workers. Don't fuss with such subjects as Trotzky and his fate and Stalin and his policies. Russia is not like that. Get at the policies and ideas of the government, of the Communist Party.

Don't bother with the "wild boys"; there's not even news in that. How they handled them is part of the question as to how they handle crime. What experiences are they having with concessionaires and expert employees: managers and others hired for their uses? And do get if you can what they admire in the U. S. and, if you like, other countries. See if they can see what we see in the U. S.; mass production and high wages; the unimportance of the rich as consumers and, therefore, the waste in dividends from stocks and interest on bonds; the rising conflict between management and ownership, instead of labor and capital. You will see theatres, concerts, operas, of course. Their galleries are rich in old masters; are there any modern pictures and sculpture to see? And, for fun, note the reactions of the party in the language it is expressed in. Do all this and get quick answers to your specialist questions; that will be enough for one dose, I assure you. You will take a year to digest it and the sights you see on the streets, trains, stations and theatres.

To Anna McCarthy

Our dear Anna: Bêcheron, August 20, 1930

Peter is in Russia, and happy there. "It's true!" she exclaims. "They have got it." But she won't get your letters for a fortnight when she comes out and back here to me and Pete. . . .

I can't yet answer definitely about our plans or the house. It is being offered for the fall and winter months, but it is unlikely to be taken. And I am glad of this. I want to go home and live in it myself. I am really finishing the editing of my book. Half of it has been delivered; the rest must and will go to the publisher in September. We'll stay on here till October when I have to go back, probably with Peter, to see the book through the press. After that,—we don't know. I'll be for Carmel, Peter may be for Europe (Germany or Switzerland), where there are good up-to-date schools for Pete. . . .

Talk to your baby, Anna. Never mind talking to Leslie, if he does not want to. But your baby,—let him live in your thoughts, think of and talk and listen to the little fellow, so that he will come out smiling at and loving you. He is alive now, you know. He is a part of you, shares your blood, your food, your thoughts and feelings. I used to talk to Pete before he was born, more than Peter did,—and I think we got then to be the friends we are now. And you, so much closer to him, you can give him your intelligence, your love, your humour. Don't be modest, Anna. Be proud and not only of the baby, but of his mother. I taught you to see some of your worth, but not all. You are so much finer and wiser than you think. Tell that to the baby, tell him or her that he is going to have a clever, kind, wise mother, proud and smiling. He and Pete can beat the world if you will only believe it. You must,—you must have faith to give him, faith in himself.

Goodbye, dear Anna. There will always be one man that values you.

Yours affectionately,

Lincoln Steffens

To Mrs. A. Winter

Bêcheron, Wednesday,
August 28, 1930

Dear Mother-in-law:

Peter is not writing me any particulars of Russia. She left Moscow to go to Leningrad with her party, but was to return for two weeks more of Moscow and the country. She "thinks" she may come out in the "last half of September." I'll have to be in New York in October for proofreading and she was to attend to illustrations.

We have had here for a visit George Slocombe, the foreign correspondent of the *Daily Herald,* who is just back from Gandhi and India. He thinks Something is to happen over there to the British

Empire,—soon; within four years. He was fine on Gandhi, with whom he had two long interviews, partly for publication, partly for private conversation. He says Gandhi understands the English better than the English do. That's easy. Any foreigner can see the English better than the English can see themselves. Even I can see and say that much. And Gandhi has lived in England; he was a barrister of the Inner Temple once; he has been up against them always.

Peter says Russia is and makes a revolution. She is all upset. All values are altered. "The land of impossibilities," she calls it. It sounds as if she regarded it as greater than psychiatry. She would like to be a correspondent there.

Affectionately your
Lincoln Steffens

To E. A. Filene

Hotel Schuyler, New York,
November 11, 1930

Dear E. A.

This is only a warning that we are here for a couple of weeks; and that I want to see you. Pete has gone off to boarding school,[1] so that he does not care anything about you. But I, and Peter,—if you come to New York, call us up.

And please come prepared to help me with pictures to illustrate my book. I want good photos of you at the time I was muckraking Boston, and Brandeis and Martin Lomasny (Martin will get you something of him if you tell him what I want) and anything that bears upon Boston, 1915.

But principally I want you to bring your blooming self and all your troubles. I love the troubles of other people, you know. Pete says of troubles that they are for tomorrow, only never for today or for day-after-tomorrow. How is that for wisdom! Another thing he says is that "Daddy is always wrong, Mama is always right, and as for Pete, Pete is half wrong and half right." And the way he says it seems to indicate that he thinks that to be wrong is somehow better than to be right. Anyway he laughs when he says it. I am sorry you can't see Pete, but I can reflect some of the light he throws upon life, the light and the laughter.

Yours,
Stef.

[1] Hessian Hills School at Croton, New York.

To Yvonne Davidson

Croton-on-Hudson, N. Y.,
December Something Like 18th, '30

Dear Yvonne:

The day is done and Darkness falls on the wings of night, but Pete is having his early supper and there's a letter from you, a regular love letter. Dosch-Fleurot[1] had been to dinner and started you off thinking of us and the result is such a letter as one gets seldom from you, a letter in which you really give yourself away, expose your heart and,—and make me feel homesick for Bêcheron, and Jo, and even Jean, the intelligent. (If that boy had a bit more intelligence he would know that he had the stuff and would train his mind for the purpose of using it. But he isn't so intelligent as that; still inferior to me and Jo.)

But I must go to work and make my report. My part on the book is done, the galley proofs read and corrected. Peter is reading them now and assembling the illustrations. Jo's contributions are here. Thanks, Jo. I think all will be well. We have no title for the book. Peter proposed and lobbied for *Reporting Myself,* but Harcourt and I and others preferred no title, just *The Autobiography of Lincoln Steffens*. It gives a nice false impression of dignity and self-sufficiency. Peter makes a wry face, but her face soon cheers up.

She did not take that Berlin job. The U.P. here decided that they did not want a woman in that place. She was lucky, I think. She still intends a career. She is content to make it here, however, and I am waiting around New York for her to get it done. How long does it take to make a career? I think that three or four months should do, but I'm not sure. It might take a year, which is a long time to sit around in the cold just to wait for a wife.

Well, we are up here in a tiny bungalow to be near Pete, who was boarding in a school. He left us in New York without regret and gave out here not a sign of missing us. The teachers said that he fell in with the gang and its ways more easily and quickly than any child they ever had. It was not for Pete, then, that we quit New York and came here. It was for us, his parents. We missed him. And it is a joy to be at hand, to send him off at nine in the morning to walk half a mile to school and to have him rush home at four in the afternoon.

[1] Arno Dosch-Fleurot, foreign correspondent for the New York *World* and later for International News Service.

Business is bad, but it isn't as bad as Wall Street and these blooming business leaders think. There may be some failures impending, like that of the Bank of the United States. On general principles orders put in at any break during the next three months would, I think, be swell for profits.

You sound well and happy, Yvonne, and what you say about your health and what you imply as to your philosophy account for the tone of your almost cocky letter, which made me laugh with pleasure. As for Pete, he's at school, but I asked him yesterday if he remembered Jo. He said:

"Yes, he is the boss of the studio."

"Of Bêcheron you mean."

"No, Yvonne is the boss of Bêcheron. Jo never put you out of Bêcheron, and he did out of the studio. If he wanted to, he could make you stay out of the studio." This with awe, reminiscently.

He recalled too that he was the boss of the garage, of the dogs also, but evidently he appreciated more the idea that he was Bill, the garage man. Jean is the boss only of the motorcycle in Pete's memory. And I like that. I just love anything that puts Jean in his place. But I must get my hands on Jacques, who lives all inside himself and rarely comes out.

Peter had a summons from Bedaux the other day to come to dinner and go to the Opera with a party and without me. And when she went he asked her to talk Russia and the Revolution with the president of his company. She did yesterday, and had a lot to correct, but a lot; and did that too. The president was going to make an address on Russia and Bedaux evidently was a bit worried. B. wants to be invited to Russia some day. Peter talks better than ever on that subject, but she hasn't sold any of her articles yet.

I must quit this. I started last evening, resumed this morning and now it is high time to stop playing and go to work. Goodbye, Yvonne, and Jo, and Jean, and—everybody. I would like some details, you know, about gardeners, butlers, cooks, etc. I think I should be treated as a minority stockholder in an honest company.

Affectionately,
Stef.

Tell Jo we, and especially Peter, have been seeing and listening to and being thrilled by Jerry Blum. And, yes, you should know that the *American Magazine* was invited by Hoover to have an interview with him. They chose me to do it, and the President would not accept me. Our philosophies differed too much, he said.

To Ella Winter and Pete Steffens

12 Otis Place,
Boston,
Christmas Day, Dec. 25, 1930

Dear Peter'n'pete:—

Just the same it seems somehow wrong for me to be here and not there at this time. Christmas is terrible in Boston: business is so good and the lighting is so unusual: the carols— And yet it gets you and I wish I had done something about and with my little family. All I can do now is to hope that you gave Pete his sled. . . .

I had a nice, long luncheon talk with E. A.'s partners; no result, but very entertaining. I called it a hate lunch and so kept out some hate. Made conscious, they had to laugh. I urged them, and I wrote Bob Minor to see *Overture*,[1] others, too.

E. A. and I called on Martin Lomasny; he was out, but he 'phoned later, and I never have heard and felt such grateful warmth as he blurted in his offer: to "come anywheres to see you, anywheres any time; I think by God that we get each other, you and me." I'll see him after today.

Last night Nolan, the greatest of the city planners (professional), came in and he gave me not only stuff for my little article on cities, but ideas, views and even vistas. He was really wonderful. But they don't any of them know what to do about our congested cities and the traffic. The only solutions require bitterness, rebuilding and some disregard of private properties. . . .

To Jo Davidson

Croton-on-Hudson, N. Y.
January 5, 1931

Dear Jo:

We cabled you night-before-last to the effect that the tailpiece of Little Pete had arrived and that we were grateful to you, not only for that but for all you have done so promptly for the book; and for a continuous stream of kindnesses, thoughtfulnesses. An editor sounded

[1] Play by William Bolitho.

me the other day upon writing a sketch of you in your sittings and he asked what I would call it. I said the best title would be: "Jo Davidson, the Rich Man," adding that you were the only rich man I had ever met and that even your wife called you that, saying that you were magnificent even when you were a bum. Well, Peter says it now, and she is thinking only of your magnificence with our book. We are thinking of putting on the title page the line "Illustrated by Jo Davidson." . . .

Pete has just come home from school. "Who you writing to?" he asks. I say "Jo Davidson" and ask him who is Jo Davidson. "Jo Davidson is my friend" is his sufficient answer. But he dictated to Peter the other day a letter to you. I heard him and not a word was prompted. I'll let Peter write that. She is in New York today on your book and mine. It is astonishing how much there is to do after a book is all written and I am glad I have Peter to do it. She nearly broke her hip four days ago: thought she could sled like Pete and his pals. As Pete said she did not steer right, so she ran into a tree. But she is recovering from the painful, very painful bruise to the edge of her hip.

Give my love to Yvonne, my respects to Jean (tentatively) and keep a warm smile for yourself.

> Yours (literally),
> Stef.

To Charles Erskine Scott Wood

> Croton-on-Hudson,
> February 3, 1931

Dear Erskine:

I am not writing today to thank you for your corking blurb for my book. I do thank you. Also I appreciate the imagination which went into the form of it, the thought of what would work. You are a very practical poet but I am not writing to say that; nor just to send my love to Sara, though that goes too. No, I have a better reason than any of these, better for me.

I am writing to you because I have at last read the very last of my proofs, galley and page. The darn book is done and out of my hands and off my blooming mind. I rejoice and I wanted someone to rejoice with me, somebody that understands what it is to be through with a job and free,—free to do anything else. And I know none like you two workers and rejoicers and libertarians and,—and lovers.

But I am going to add a few lines. We are still here in this cold, cold land of unthinking business, still at our several occupations. I have still some politics to do for reviews of my book, and my appeal to my writing friends to review my *Life* without reading it, to get them to tell what my story should be; not to wait and see how I have fallen down. Some job that. My friends are in the habit of receiving all suggestions of mine with a grin as if I were not a serious person. Peter is making her career, which bids fair to go on for several months more. Pete is starting his career with never a thought. He is in a good school, a school where he is being educated unconsciously and happily. At any rate he likes to go to school, even though it is all burned down, the buildings, I mean, and he comes home able to tell me only that he has learned to skate and sled. All is well, therefore, with us here, but just the same I think I shall soon be heading West. I have to go to see if Rolph [1] and Fleishhacker [2] will not let my dynamiters go. I want to go to see some friends of mine who make my heart smile. I hope, when I do go, to read the finished manuscript of Sara's (and my) poem on Barabbas.

And here, the other day, Garet Garrett challenged me to drive west to San Francisco via Texas with him, say, in March. Otherwise he threatens to go all by himself to Florida. Florida! Did you know that there are people out this way who think of Florida somewhat as we think of California? It's a sort of alternative; a something just as good.

The most unexpected phenomenon hereabouts is the detestation of Hoover,—it is so violent and universal that I begin to have some sympathy for him, and the denunciation of him in Wall Street convinces me that there is something good in him, and I look and inquire, but no, nothing. And yet there is Wall Street talking my way! Now whom do you suspect? I have never been caught in that position before.

I've been looking all the time as publicly as I could for that big business man that is going to think. You heard the rumor: that if this depression keeps up much longer somebody in business will begin to think. It sometimes sounds like a mere empty threat, but gosh! it might happen and I'd like to get a scoop on that thought or the

---

[1] Governor J. J. Rolph.
[2] Herbert Fleishhacker, banker and shipowner, of California.

thinker. A world beat! If you see or write to any business men I suggest that you ask them if they are the One, and if you catch him, wire me. I'll sell the story and go you fifty-fifty. Be sure to get a photograph of the thinker and, yes, don't forget to get the thought.

If you write us a polite acknowledgment of this please report on the health of both of you. And Older's. Laura is better, but she is not well. Her library system is established in Soviet Russia!

Well, Erskine and Sara, I will stop this nonsense if you two will give each other my love also.

To Anna McCarthy

Croton-on-Hudson,
March 20, 1931

Dear Anna:

I have not written to you how I rejoiced with you and Leslie over the little girl and the stout and courageous way you have borne her and your crisis. I feel as if we had now a girl in the family, and I always did want one. Pete and I both regret that we are not there to enjoy the little one. We may be some day.

But also I want to tell you that Leslie's letter, announcing the birth, was as humorous and complete as you could have written it. And tell him that that is high praise because I discovered first, I think, that you have both wit and humour.

All goes well here with us. The book is printed and will be published April 9. After that I may be going West.

Give the baby a kiss for me, give Leslie a warm greeting and take yourself my love.

Your friend,
Lincoln Steffens

To Netta Cooper

Croton-on-Hudson,
March 22, 1931

Dear Netta—

Here's a letter from you—which has just arrived this minute— and mostly about my book. It's a letter I would have been glad to show Theron.[1] He would see in it that he was being understood. It was a nice letter, and I'm so glad.

[1] Theron P. Cooper had died recently. Theron and Netta Cooper ran first the Walden Bookshop, then the Concord Bookshop, in Chicago.

Mr. Flynn's blurb is bully. I'll show it to Harcourt, Brace and Co., who, all of them, are concentrating on my *Autobiography*. They have set aside an unusual sum to advertise and push the book. Some New York orders are coming in. It looks as if, despite the size and the price, the thing might be sold, even in these times. Your order gave them all a cheer, especially when it came so early (you are a friend).

Of course you may throw a party for me (and the book) if you wish. If it is a talk fest, I'll promise to say some interesting things about the book and its contents. If not, I'll gossip just the same. I rather shrink from the radio broadcast, but all right if you wish.

But what I'll want in Chicago is time for a long quiet talk with you. I don't yet know when I'll be going, probably soon after the middle of April.

Yours, Netta,
Stef.

To Rose Isaak

Croton, New York,
April 27, 1931

Dear Rose Isaak:

Thanks for your letter, for the good word about the book and for the rebuke that I had not sent it to the boys.[1] There is a first edition copy for them, of course, but I did not know that I could get it to them directly by mail. I am going West this month and I meant to take it over to them and so make sure of its delivery. Assuming from your letter that it is all right to use the post, I'll do as you suggest tomorrow when I am in town.

I'll be seeing the Johannsens in Chicago on my way out and I'll tell them that you are as ever on the watch. Thank you again.

To Margaret Johannsen [2]

Croton, April 29, '31

Dear Margaret:

All but the exact trains is decided. Peter stays here, to go later to Russia on a book job my publisher is financing. Pete and I leave here May 6-7 for Chicago where I am to be the guest of Hayden B. Harris,

---

[1] J. B. McNamara and Matthew Schmidt. Later the *Autobiography* was taken away from J. B. McNamara by the San Quentin authorities.
[2] Wife of Anton ("Jo") Johannsen, the labor leader.

who will meet us at the station and take Pete out to you for two days of your influence. I go to work. And on the 9th or 10th Pete and I go West on the U.P.-S.P. to San Francisco, later to Carmel for the summer. This is all only a general warning; we'll be exact by wire later.

I wish you and Jo could be here to get the full force of the reception of my book and,—don't laugh, Jo,—and me. If I believed all that they say about me I'd be so swelled up that I'd never speak to Jo again; only to you, Margaret. And E. A. Filene gave a dinner at the Ritz for me and the characters in my book, as you know, night before last. 85 present; the damnedest mixed company you ever saw: From Barney Baruch and Anne Morgan to Mark Fagan, all the columnists, critics and reporters. It was really a great occasion. And what do you think they demanded of me? Another, a third volume.

But don't you worry. I remain, as ever, unconvinced and humorous, in brief—

Yours affectionately,
Lincoln Steffens

To Mrs. A. Winter

Croton, April 30, 1931

My dear Mother-in-law:

My typewriter is out of order; I should not write with a pen, but we are going away from here tomorrow. Pete stays a few days more at school, then joins us in New York, where I have a lot of things to do. Then, on May 5, I go with Pete to Chicago to do a couple of errands and make a speech. Then, fast, west to San Francisco,—Carmel, —Los Angeles,—Santa Barbara for the summer. Peter stays in New York a bit longer to decide, but my publishers offer to finance her on a trip to Russia to make a book she has outlined and I think that she will do that.

I am glad that you like my book. I like your obviously sincere pleasure in it, even though everybody here also seems to like it. I have never seen the critics so unanimous; they all came out together with what looked like a shout of acclamation, and since then they have boosted it quietly almost every day. The first edition sold right out: a $7.50 book in two volumes about me and by me in these hard times gone into the second printing in 10 days! I do not understand it. Filene gave a swell dinner night before last at the Ritz and 85 people came: business men, politicians, writers,—all sorts, and you should have heard the speeches. You would no longer have wondered that your daughter married me and that your grandson, Pete, is so nice. Yes, and by the way, some speakers referred to Pete. One poet said that he was our real triumph: a courteous kid!

It has been fun. I think Peter has sent you some of the clippings. She can't send them all. Too, too many. I really think we have registered a success. The publisher says the book will go on selling for a generation; as a sort of classic of our day.

Love to all. Goodbye.

Stef.

XI

▀▀

CONCLUSIONS
(1931-1936)

IN TALKING about the art of dying, Steffens said that men of action ought, as they grew older, to try to formulate and communicate what they had learned. That was what he had done in the *Autobiography*. However, as he wrote in the foreword to *Lincoln Steffens Speaking*, "When I finished my *Life* I did not die as I might gracefully have done. I lived on and, of course, learned and unlearned as always." He still had something to say,—more, he came to believe, than he had ever had before,—and he said it.

Successively in three local papers, *The Carmelite, Controversy,* and *Pacific Weekly,* he conducted a column of brief paragraphs. He had been asked to write for the Hearst papers, and there had been other offers, but he refused. He preferred to say exactly what he thought, even though he spoke to a small audience.

From 1931 to 1933 he lectured as well as wrote. ("I have learned at last to speak and I love to do it," he wrote in 1932, after twenty-five years as a lecturer.) He spoke at many meetings, small and large, in California, and he made three trips to the East.

Returning from the last of these, in December, 1933, he was taken ill in Chicago. The illness, diagnosed as a heart attack or thrombosis, kept him at home and much of the time in bed. Lecturing had to be abandoned, but he continued to write his column, and he talked with the visitors that came every day to The Getaway. Ella Winter, who had been to Soviet Russia again in 1931 and had been doing much traveling and lecturing, abandoned all activities that took her for any length of time from Carmel. Through her and through friends, Steffens kept closely in touch with the labor movement and especially with strikes in California. He not only watched the little fruit-pickers' strikes, the cotton strike in the San Joaquin Valley, the marine strike and the San Francisco general strike; he gave what aid he could.

At the same time he planned two major pieces of work. His old friend, E. A. Filene, had long desired Steffens to write his biography, and Steffens, seeing a revealing story of success and failure under the capitalist system, was not unwilling. But he did not wish to undertake sustained work of that kind, and he proposed that Filene secure someone to write the book, with Steffens to suggest the approach and guide the execution. Robert Cantwell was selected for the job, and, though the biography was not finished to Filene's satisfaction, Steffens enjoyed the association with the young novelist, whom he admired.

The second task that Steffens contemplated was the writing of a postscript to the *Autobiography,* to tell what he had discovered since the completion of the book. Often discussed, this postscript was never seriously undertaken. In the foreword to *Lincoln Steffens Speaking,* written the day before he died, he said, "I think now that I can really end my autobiography, but later, not just now."

He could "really end" his story because he had, he believed, found his way to a solution of the problems that had "fretted all his life." He wanted to tell how this had happened, and he knew that the readers of the *Autobiography* wanted to hear, for many of them had told him so, in letters, in questions after his lectures, and in visits to his home.

The process is suggested in his letters. In the last chapter of the *Autobiography* he wrote, "The United States is making an experiment second in hopefulness only to Russia, a revelation of evolution as against revolution." In 1929 and the years following he thought he saw the failure of that experiment. In 1935 he wrote,—typically to a student,—"I had come to regard the New Capitalism as an experiment till in 1929, the whole thing went over the top and slid down to an utter collapse. That was clear to all. I went to New York to hear the semi-scientific captains of industry say in words and facial expressions that they did not know what had happened or what was to be done about it. They did not understand their own experiment. Then,—not till then,—did I give up,—and turned to see what else there was."

His attitude toward the Russian revolution had never wavered since his first glimpse of "the future." He had only asked himself if there might not be other ways. Now he was convinced that "nobody in the world *proposes* anything basic and real except the Communists," and that "Communism has to come." The reformer, who had turned to the study of revolutions, now became a believer in revolution as the only way to make "all reforms" possible.

As always, he said what he believed, and he said it so that people listened, if not with agreement, then with understanding and respect. He talked particularly to the young, and he was glad that they came to him for his vision of a new society. "Now civilization may begin," he told them, and he taught them to think wisely of the future America as well as to deal intelligently with the problems of the moment.

"My concern," he wrote an old friend, "is no longer personal and passionate; it is passionate, but for the children. I care what sort of world Pete's generation will have to live and fit in." Even at the time when the depression was most directly affecting him, he welcomed it because the collapse of the old order must precede the building of the new: "I rejoice because I can see that Pete is going to come up in a new and I believe a better world."

The last five years were busy,—and happy. "You are learning about life," he wrote in his last letter to Pete. So was Lincoln Steffens, to the end.

To Charles Erskine Scott Wood

Carmel, June 11, 1931

Dear Erskine:

I've been half sick, all dead-and-alive, since I came down here. The winter of honest work and devotion to others must have worn me out. One solid month of loving care of myself has revived me; I think I shall live. I'm going south tomorrow to see; to see Dot and her family, and the Friday Morning Club of L. A.

I read your book about Liberty [1] and I think I chuckled over it as much as you did in writing it. Sometimes I stopped reading, laid the book down, in order more purely to watch and listen to your internal laughter. You have said it; said it all, I think. I prophesy that this book will turn out to have been the last cry for freedom. It's all true; it shines with truth; and man will always desire liberty, but not because it's the truth that will make him free. He isn't after the truth.

[1] *Too Much Government,* by C. E. S. Wood, Vanguard Press, 1931.

I'm going to inspire my poet, Sara, some day to make an image of Truth,—a bedraggled, fallen woman who solicits men on the street, running after them as they once ran after her, and with one eye out for the cop, inviting them to take her and weeping deeply when they won't. The poor thing. You treat her like a lady. Well, you're a poet too, and you have done her beautifully in your expressive prose. You can write, Erskine; you do write. You express yourself, and you express me; you express our generation. But we're a funny lot of dreamers, as I'm finding out. Have you seen Mike Gold's roast of me and my book in the *New Masses?*[1] He says I'm tolerant. That's his charge. And he is expressing his generation. I must write him to attend to you.

I'll be writing or calling on you when I get back. Meanwhile,—love to you, Sara, Kay and hers.

Lincoln Steffens

To Alfred Harcourt

Carmel, July 3, 1931

Dear Harcourt:

As you see at a glance my typewriter is in commission, so you need not fear to write to me; you will be able to read my answer always.

Henry S. Canby writes asking me to do a first-page review of Harpers' *Leonard Wood,* out in the late summer. I begged off. I never did a review and it makes me anxious to think of writing one now. He thinks I know a lot about Wood and his story, but I don't.

In his letter Mr. Canby says he had looked for me in New York that he might speak "not merely of my own pleasure in your book but also my whole family all the way from son to grandmother. Nock[2] in the review he wrote for me did not express himself too strongly." He closes saying: "Harcourt tells me that your book is going splendidly, —apparently the only one to break through this spring."

Peter cabled from Moscow a week ago, but her last letter was dated from the train between Berlin and Moscow. Her cable said she felt at home in Moscow.

You are not selling so many sets as you expected, are you? I don't care myself. My feeling is that the book is digging in. People are reading it, and they feel it; they talk about it. There is something they

---

[1] "Mr. Steffens Liked Everybody," by Michael Gold, *New Masses,* June, 1931.
[2] Albert J. Nock, editor of *The Freeman* and author of historical and political books.

do not know in it, something they are made to believe, and they talk and talk. I sense that all around me. I hear about it. But I do have one hunch about it. A question often privately discussed here (a typical community) is whether I am sincere. My interpretation of this doubt is that readers, taking my story very seriously, even solemnly, get a sense of my humour, but since they do not know that I am often a humourist, have never heard me spoken of as a jester, simply take it out with a guess that I write with my tongue in my cheek and don't mean what I say. If we could get someone to write of me as a humourist, I think we should meet the case exactly. You may recall that I early suggested this point. The need of it grows on me. Some humourist, like Don Marquis, would do it best, but you know the list and you know how. For you have proved yourself a strategist in the publishing game.

Another thing: Owen D. Young asked for my book to take West with him on a trip two months ago, saying he would have time to dictate a review of it to his stenographer who was to travel with him. He probably found the book too long to read all through on that trip, which was broken by the illness of his mother. I saw in the papers that he hurried home and stayed beside his mother for two or three weeks. I'll bet he has never read the book. But I don't see why you should not write and ask him if he would not like to say something about my book; that it would be a big boost for me; or, if he has not had time to read it all, to run through the two last parts about the direction progress is taking in America and comment on that. This would come better from you than from me, but I'll do it later, if you don't care to do it now.

By the way, I have no set of my biography. My fault, but I would better have one on hand. You sent me a first volume some time ago; I wondered why. Please let me have now a second volume or set of the last edition, with corrections. No hurry; my house-keeper has a set that I use in emergencies.

Yours warmly,
Lincoln Steffens

To Mrs. A. Winter

Dear Grandma: Carmel, July 25, 1931

Pete is doing very well, thank you. I often think of you all alone there in London with no one to love and to love you but Rudi and

Rosa; no Pete, no Peter, no Petest. It makes us sad. It must be awful. But we go on enjoying life. Pete just now is not home much. He gets up early, around seven o'clock, and pays a visit to his best girl whom he calls "Precious Margaret," a young lady about sixteen years old whom all the young people adore. She favors Pete. When I get up I whistle and Pete tears home for his breakfast. He is brown and barefoot; unwashed, uncombed, and dressed in a suit of overalls; and preoccupied. After breakfast he runs back to Margaret till lunch time or till he is sent home by Margaret. Sometimes he goes swimming with Margaret; and how that boy can swim and dive; he is accepted as an equal in the water by much older kids. Sometimes he drives off with Margaret to Monterey,—Pete up in the high rear seat.

A few days ago he drove over with her to the rodeo at Salinas. A rodeo is a gathering of cowboys and girls to ride bucking horses, steers, anything that will fight. He loves that, and he comes home to swagger about town with his "gun" at his hip. He always carries a pistol these days. I have persuaded him not to shoot people, but only the rear tires of their cars. Our neighbors are astonished and disappointed that I let my boy be a rustler and a bandit, but I answer that this is the age for a human to be warlike, conceited and a blusterer. Anyway Pete is the tough of the town, the pal of all the cowboys, crooks and cops of Carmel, the gallant of all the girls. One of the girls, a beautiful, clever high-school student, I have employed to teach him reading, with instructions to persuade him, without discipline, not only to read but to stick to a job; first, for ten minutes, then twenty, then— The other day she said proudly, "We worked for 45 minutes without a break." I complimented Pete on that, saying that Hester was a good teacher. He rebelled at once. "Hester isn't my teacher," he said. "She teaches me, but she is only my Hester."

He keeps up the social end carefully. One woman told me at a concert that Pete had called on her the day before. Since she lives about five miles from us, I wondered how he got there. "Oh," she said, "he came with the grocery boy on the delivery car, so he stayed only a moment. But he was very complete and formal. He asked me how I was, how the baby was and kissed my hand when he bade me goodbye." Mrs. Dickinson, another remote neighbor, said he had called her on the phone to ask if she and her husband were to be at home; he would like to call. "I was going out, I said I was sorry, but he assured me it was O.K. He only wished to inquire how we all

upper: ROBINSON AND UNA JEFFERS AT TOR HOUSE, CARMEL.
lower left: JO DAVIDSON MAKING JEFFERS'S BUST ON "THE GET-
AWAY" BALCONY, 1930. *lower right:* GARTH AND DONNAN JEF-
FERS AND PETE STEFFENS AT TOR HOUSE, CARMEL.

were. And another day," she continued, "we met him trudging along the road. He said he was going out on the Point to call on the Schoeningers. He was willing to go with us and he did; we went down on the beach for a picnic."

I tell you all this so that you may know that your grandson is living his own life, free of the interference of his parents; so that you may see him walking erect and proud, barefoot and dusty but cocky along the roads to make formal, welcome calls on his lady friends far and near.

Interrupted at this point, I took the sheet out to post; as I will. But you must know that Ella Winter is "covering" for Hearst's Sunday papers the visit to Moscow of B. Shaw and Lady Astor. She cabled this to me a week ago. "Seeing Russia with Shaw" should be some fun.

My lecture dates, which take me East in October and back via Texas in December, are increasing rapidly; I'll have all I can do. The book has done it and the lectures will help the book; which sells right along and gets such bursts of praise that I am almost persuaded myself that it is a good story that really does something to its readers.

Jane's baby was due in Peking last week, but I have not heard yet the word that will come by cable through Jane's mother at Santa Barbara. . . .

Stef.

I'd like to hear how the gold crisis affects you and how you feel about it; also any comments by economists and financiers. Not that they will understand it. The U. S. took it pretty well. A slump in prices under heavy, frightened sales was soon offset by support but mostly by arbitrary orders against short-selling, which forced our bears to cover. I expect a resumption of the slow slide down, but I am not sure enough to bet on it. You will have the advantage of inflation for a while; your money goes down, commodities up, but England, as a whole, will be exporting, not importing, and that may revive business some. In the long run, however, the capitalist system cannot, I think, recover except, once more, in this country. How the world does need, and lack, economic wisdom. But, if it had that, we, —you and I,—would be wiped out as loafers and set to work as producers. Which may happen anyhow. I'm having fun telling Pete all about it; about the dumb grown-ups and how his generation will have the chance of centuries to see straight and do straight. An empty throne in every country and every business.

He came into the house last night; I had a caller, and Pete had seen the car. Before he saw my guest,—a hotel manager,—he called out from the door:

"Have you someone here, Daddy?"

"Yes," I said, "come and see who it is."

He came in and saw. "Hello, Dave," he greeted, calling the man by the name I use. "How are all the family?" Then he climbed on my lap like a little child. "I'm tired, Daddy, please help me to undress."

I kind o' like Pete. And Dave said he did. But Dave thought that Pete's generation would set aside our generation a bit too ruthlessly.

Stef.

To Yvonne Davidson

Carmel, July 25, 1931

Dear Yvonne:

You gotta stop that. Making me a duty! The whole tone of your otherwise affectionate letter was to the effect that because you had not written to me for seventeen years I had been lying heavy upon your conscience. That's awful. If it had gone on much longer you would have begun to hate me. I don't want that. Never again. You don't have to write to me. Really. I can and I do often call up the image of my Yvonne and you can tell that I "get" you: I smile, feel warm and nod wisely. I always know you are all right. You never cause me any worry; not like Jean and Jacques and Jo. They ought to write or, better still, cable, but not Yvonne.

And, as to my book, you don't have to tell me that is great. I have it from all sides that it is a "masterpiece," written by a "wizard"; a "classic" done with a "smile." It isn't selling so darned many, about 5,000 sets so far, but Harcourt thinks that is because of the price and he is thinking of making for Christmas a one-volume edition for about half the present price. Don't mention this; it isn't decided. And it is too bad because the publishers had made a perfect book of it, fine paper, good type and a sound make-up. A cheaper edition will have to be,—cheaper, somehow. But the point is that the long book that I got so tired of writing and expected so little of has won the applause of all sorts of people, the literary critics, the newspaper reviewers, the newspaper men generally and has made lots of readers "love" it and recommend it so that it goes right on selling and,—winning. I do wish that, while I was working on it, I had had some prescience of what was ahead. I could have enjoyed it more and done it so much better.

One day about two weeks ago I went with Pete to the swimming pool at Pebble Beach. The swimming teacher there saw him play boldly about in the deep water and offered to teach him in six lessons. I agreed and went south to lecture. When I returned for Pete's fourth lesson, I saw the teacher pick him up, walk out on the high spring board and throw him in. It shocked my maternal heart till I saw my baby tread water, come up and swim smiling ashore. My paternal mind was delighted, but the teacher bade me, "Wait two days more." On the second day there was a show on at Del Monte of young swimmers; races, etc. In the midst of these events I saw Pete in all his clothes suddenly appear out on the high spring board. The man with the megaphone yelled at him to get away from there. "What you doing anyway?" Pete answered: "I'm going swimming." "But you can't go swimming with your clothes on. You get away from there." Pete got up, turned and lost his balance. He fell in aflop and the crowd gasped; he did look so tiny. He went under, stayed a long while, then out came one shoe, then the other, then his jacket and finally his pants. And he swam on his back, floated, did two other strokes and came out amid cheers. He was in his bathing suit. He walked out on the spring board, made a corking dive and struck out like a professional for the ladder. The youngest kid at the show, the teacher's pride. He had learned it all in deep water, never had a bottom he could touch, but the teacher said he could learn like that because he had never known fear.

It's vacation time, of course, but I am having picked young students whom he does not know as teachers teach him reading, writing, biology,—whatever these young people are good at. For I realize that so long as he learns it does not matter what he learns, at this stage. They are teaching him to work or, rather, to stick to fascinating play with good subjects. He is busy, happy, brown and strong. I am idle, content, well, with a big lecture trip ahead with dates east to New York in October and back via Texas in December.

Jo is in London? I get bits of news or comment of his show, a success, like my book, *d'estime*. Not much money? So I guess. But all the world, except Russia, is in the same boat. . . . The U. S. is blaming France now, but the French are the only rational people outside of Russia. They suffer from us because they can't help seeing the facts and acting on the premises of our culture. Logic may lead them into trouble some day, but they will be leading the world when it does. We don't know it, any of us, but we shall follow France, even Italy; and England. The next war will be between Russia and the rest of us, between Communism and Capitalism. The Germans (unless we can save their banks) will be with Russia and Communism. And whatever the end of the war,—in the long run,—Communism will win. For it looks as if we cannot make our system work.

Your boys ought to get a sense of this. It will play a large part in their lives, this struggle. It makes what is happening to them now unimportant. . . .

I love you, Yvonne; I love Jo; and I do love boys.

Stef.

To Alfred Harcourt

Carmel, Aug. 11, '31

Dear Harcourt:

. . . I am getting a curious demand to do articles, a book and to speak on the education of kids for the transition period from one kind of life to the new life ahead. Canby (*Saturday Review*), *The Nation,* my neighbors, ask for writing; professors, teachers, parents, want lectures. The headmistresses of New York private schools ask for a lecture in October; and I've consented. But, for you, a publisher, it must be significant of a real demand, that these calls to me come all at once and yet are quite separate. The feeling is that, as we are passing from one culture or way of life to another, our education of children must prepare for either or both.

I would like to write along this line, but I'll be slow and I'll bet that such an acute demand will soon have produced a book to meet it. So be on the look-out. Or, better still, why not advertise for such a book? And watch the comment and the response. I have to write now to Canby, who keeps after me for something, almost anything.

Peter writes that she would like to stay on in Moscow next winter. I am advising her to do so, get a job and write her book.

I'll send separate another thing that you may not have seen: *The Classmate,* a paper for young people, Cincinnati. That's the lead,—young people,—for the *Autobiography.* I took it for my short article for *Wings,* the Literary Guild magazine.

Yours,
Steffens

To Ella Winter

Carmel, Sept. 2, 1931

Dear Peter:

. . . I went with Pete, taking Hester (in her car), the first day and I was rather shocked and pleased (and flattered) that he had none of the emotions I suffered on my first day at school. No fear, none of my dread of the big fellows, no worry about the lessons. He braced in, head up, shoulders back, and I was amused to watch him go about sizing up the other boys and girls, very deliberately, and the grounds and the apparatus. It was all satisfactory, I gathered from his face. He said not a word; he had no attention for us. And when the teacher called the kids in, Pete shot for the door and disappeared. I had had a talk with Mrs. Trowbridge and I went back at 2:30 for another. She was keen on Pete. When she had all the children settled in the morning, she says she asked who would begin the reading and Pete spoke right up. "I will," he said, and he was off. She thought it odd that, with all this readiness and leadership, he seemed to be quite unconscious of it. It pleased me and made me feel that I had succeeded in that one thing, though it was born in him, you remember: "Pete's Pete's." . . .

Friday we went to San Francisco and, in the early afternoon, Dr. Scott pulled one of his front teeth and took an impression. The little tooth had quite a root, but it came out on a jerk and it did not hurt much till Pete saw the blood. Then he cried a little. I urged him to be a sport and have the other out. "No," he said, "I was a sport for one. Two is too much sport. And I don't want to be too much of a sport all at once."

Garet Garrett writes he is coming here when he finishes his article on Germany, which is ruling the world, he says, by threatening to collapse if not helped. And he adds: "Meanwhile look but disbelieve it, —there is a run on the Bank of England." . . .

Carmel, Sept. 17, 1931

Dear Peter:

Pete says he doesn't understand why most of the kids hate school so much. He doesn't. He likes it, he says. He can beat 'em all. At first Adelaide (whoever she is) could write it on the board eight times to his once. Now he can write it (whatever it is) ten times to anybody else's once.

"And I can write up to one hundred in three minutes."

The new, one-volume edition is not yet out, but it must be announced; I get congratulatory letters, and the book-shop tells me they have placed large orders for the cheaper book. I got last night a nice characteristic letter from Gertrude Stein. It's short; I'll quote verbatim:

> My dear Steffens,
>   Just read your book and like it a lot, I liked the crime waves and I liked Roosevelt and I liked me, and I may say I liked it all, I liked it in itself and I liked it because it brought back my early days, best to you always,
>
> Gertrude Stein

Just like that; I sent it to Harcourt.

The stock market has sunk to the lowest yet, and the sense of depression is deeper, wider spread. California will get it next. The Wall Street drop yesterday,—to the lowest,—was attributed to foreign selling from London, Amsterdam and Paris; all scared by the suppressed English news: the run on the Bank of England, miners parading the streets of London with their picks on their shoulders and a hand out for aid,—and propaganda; food shops guarded. The revolt of the sailors, causing the return of the Fleet; you know, that had to be published. The S. F. *Chronicle* reported a London banker as saying that England would have Communism within a year.

And today we learn that fighting between the Japanese and the Chinese which resulted in the taking of Mukden by the Japs may be the beginning of a Jap-Chink war. Gerard Swope, president of General Electric, comes out with a plan,—the plan Owen D. Young talked to me about last winter, for centralised control of industries in institutes bound to provide for employees. Things are happening, everybody listening and the world aware of Russia, acutely.

I'll be glad to go East to hear more. . . .

Stef.

To Jo Davidson

Carmel, September 19, 1931

Dear Jo:

A letter from you; the news of fighting that may mean war between Japan and China; the stock market slumped (yesterday and probably today) to the lowest yet,—on selling by London, Paris, Amsterdam because of what is impending in England; private information that there was a run on the Bank of England (not reported in the press), that miners shouldering their picks parade London, shops guarded and the British fleet returned to port because the sailors who are the modern starters of revolution, struck at the cut in their pay,—all this and more comes together here in this sunny, cool, comfortable place. There must be some interest and some dumbness in the outside world, something wrong in our social-economic arrangements and no leaders to point the way out. I feel like a front-seater at a great play, trying to determine whether it is a tragedy or a comedy. All I can do about it all is to answer your warm, depressed letter. . . .

Nothing much or new from Peter; not since she started down the Volga. A post card here, there, but still getting stuff, good stuff, which, however, she can't quite master and digest. She too lacks confidence in herself. Where did you get your superiority, whence my conceit? I'll bet Peter has to come to me to find out what she has and what to think of it all! Well, I may laugh and turn her over to Pete.

You ask me, you tempt me to come to Bêcheron for this winter. That would be great. Really. It would feel so safe, so snug and so beautiful too, to dig in there, combine our strength and look out upon the suffering world. But I can't do it, Jo. I must not think of it. Pete has made his beginning at this good school, he has a good teacher who adores him and he is thriving in health and assurance. I would not for the world break up such a good thing. I can see us all around Yvonne, like the queen she is, wise and serene, you at work, I at play, and the house, garden and the country perfectly lovely; a guest now and then; a little trouble with the boys here and there,—just enough to remind us that we are a part of the world. It would be heavenly, but I shall have to take my month or two in the East and then come back here where also it will be sunny and beautiful. My little old income is cut in half, but the book will come along to make up for losses. I shall be secure and Pete will be busy and happy. You wouldn't think, would you, of reversing your proposition, you and

Yvonne, and coming here to my place in the sun? No. You have Jean as I have Pete. Well, then, just remember that you can come here if you want to. I say that because I find it pleasant to say to myself that there's a wing of Bêcheron for me, if I like and can. . . .

Thanks for the clippings, so interesting. But I am not surprised that they led nowhere. Nor are you. You must know the preoccupation of the English and see how far they are from art, from sculpture. I get a big kick from the Gandhi proposition. . . . I feel that you would make a beautiful thing of Gandhi, the spirit, with humour.

I must break off and go to lunch. I'm called. I hate to leave you; I have so much love for you, Jo, and for Yvonne. It is a joy to be thinking of you as I have been all this summery morning. But I promised Pete,—so goodbye,—Bêcheron.

Affectionately,
Stef.

To Mrs. A. Winter

Carmel, September 21, 1931

Dear Grandma:

This is the day when we learned here that Great Britain had had to suspend gold payments, close the stock exchange and become a dictatorship. To celebrate and take advantage of the probable fall of our stock prices today, I ordered a purchase. I haven't heard what I got. Whatever the prices, I may have to hold for a long time, but this country will "come back," even if England does not. Capitalism, which you and I are against, is falling, but not everywhere at once.

Pete went swimming yesterday. When he got back I asked him if he had yet made the high dive,—about fifteen feet. The last time I saw him, he dived off a chair on a table up on the side of the pool, about ten feet. "No," he said, "my teacher wouldn't let me do the high dive, but I did learn to do a back dive." He is the youngest child that swims in that pool; he has a great teacher, a woman, who swears by Pete. "He is so intelligent," she says, "and knows no fear." . . .

I have a photograph of Anna's baby, Betty Ann. It is a wonderful photograph by Edward Weston, the best man in America, I think. It is for Peter, but I am afraid to send it to Russia lest she come out and the picture be lost. You are nearer; you will know sooner than I what her plans are. I may enclose it in this letter for you to see, to show to Anna's old friends and then give or mail it to Peter. She is a beautiful baby, Betty Ann, a pleasure to have in the house here. Pete is devoted and nice to her. And, as for Anna, she is the happiest woman in the world.

My book is still going strong. You know, of course, that the Literary Guild broke its rule against books already out and selling, to take mine for its October Book. They persuaded the publisher, with my cheerful consent, to republish in one volume at a reduced price, $3.75. The Guild bought 20,000 outright to distribute to its members and, since that victory will start sales again, Harcourt is printing forty thousand in one run of the presses, 20,000 for the general market. There will be more reviews, more helpful talk and probably a lot more lectures. Pretty good for hard times. My private income has been cut in half, but Anna, whose husband is out of work, is very careful and we live our happy lives and enjoy the world spectacle just as I used to. I rejoice because I can see that Pete is going to come up in a new and I believe a better world.

Affectionately,
S.

To Sara Bard Field

Carmel, September 21, 1931

Dear Sara:—

I can understand your feelings about Kay. Jane Hollister went through a similar strain of prolonged distress in China. She came through and of course Kay will with her baby; they are women. Men could hardly survive. But a man as well as a woman can look on and wonder and feel even as you do.

The world looks dark today. My morning paper reports Great Britain suspending gold payments, closing stock exchanges and declaring a dictatorship; Germany closing speculation, and the renomination of Hoover in doubt. I bought some stock or ordered it bought in the smash I anticipate today. But it may just be that we shall see the beginning of Revolution in our Western world.

I called on Robin Jeffers day before yesterday and asked him about Lehman's [1] essay on his poetry in the *Saturday Review*. He had read "most of it," thought it—very intelligent. Didn't he think that Lehman was trying to put over his philosophy on him?

[1] Professor Benjamin C. Lehman, of the University of California at Berkeley.

"Um, yes," said Robin, "but everybody tries to do that."

"Everybody?" I asked, struck by the probability.

"Everybody but you," he smiled.

And what had struck me was that I had often tried to make propaganda with poets; you, for example. Robin is about the only one I let go. I wonder why. Anyhow he had noticed my neglect or tolerance of him. . . .

Capitalism is breaking down. One can see it from anywhere. And it's enough for me that our children are to grow up in a new and, I am sure, a better world: not yet free, but not hungry and not fearful. There is something to sing, Sara; not only the bears should do the rejoicing. The new world and Kay's baby will be twins. I'd like to put that idea over on all you poets, Robin too.

Not much chance of my getting up to The Cats. I have a lot of scattered speaking engagements that break up my time. And what's the difference, I am with you two always; really; I feel you and your beauty, and it does me good.

Affectionately,
Lincoln Steffens

To Ella Winter

Carmel, Sept. 27, 1931

Dear Peter:

I see that Walter Lippmann is back from his travels with Tom Lamont and is to have a column in the *Herald Tribune*. It will express Wall Street, I predict. And Wall Street needs a voice; and a mind. You can have no idea over there of the poverty of our best minds and the distress of Capitalism. You hear people say and you see them write all the time that "if Capitalism can survive." Today's paper says Lloyd George is to be the leader of the Labor and Liberal parties, united against Ramsay and the Tories.

A great world in which everything is clear to me. Communism has got to come, apparently, if not now,—in this depression,—then on the next. The causers,—the possessors of the causes of evil,—rule and will not let the cures be applied. I am not surprised that you are so near Communist. I think you only need a revisit to this world outside, to become all Communist. My surprise is that you have not done so already. . . .

To Mrs. Edna Lockwood[1]

> The Getaway,
> Columbus Day,
> Oct. 12, 1931

Dear Mrs. Lockwood:

Thinking it was a holiday and no school I kept Pete home today. I'm sorry. And Pete cried when he learned of the error!

How am I to account for that? I never mourned when I missed a day at school. Did you? And I never scolded my daddy when he gave me a day,—for any reason.

I begin to think that the critics are right; our school ought to be looked into.

Meanwhile I apologise for causing my son to play hooky.

> Yours sincerely,
> Lincoln Steffens

To Mrs. J. James Hollister

> Hotel Brevoort,
> Fifth Avenue, New York,
> November 1, 1931

Dear Dot:

There seems to be a concerted effort on to change the psychology and start a recovery. There's some good news which is presented forcefully, with a solid front, and the leaders, both political and financial, are boosting everywhere. It is very impressive and must have some effect. But I have not seen yet any of the authorities that I can count on, so I cannot advise you or myself.

I go to New Haven today (Sunday) to speak tonight and again tomorrow, which means that I can't get down to business here till Tuesday or Wednesday. I have so many errands to do. But I can say that all goes well with me. My lectures go home with obvious effect and my book, which helps to get me a hearing, is selling better than ever. The publishers promise me a continuous sale; and the personnel, from the president down to the telephone girls, are "crazy about it." "The most worthwhile book" he ever put out, they say, some of them, and I had to autograph the books of all of them, the copies they had bought and read or were reading. I guess I have really done a good book.

[1] Teacher in Sunset School, Carmel.

But, Dot, I can't tell you what you and I personally want to know: how business is.

Peter cables she'll arrive on the "Bremen," Nov. 16. I'll be here a week after that. . . .

Len.

To Theodore Dreiser [1] (*Telegram*)

New York, November 6, 1931

You won't forget that nothing peculiar to Kentucky is happening down there. I think it would be helpful to let the people you are inquiring about know that we know that the very same things always occur in all similar emergencies everywhere.

Lincoln Steffens

To Mrs. J. James Hollister

Hotel Kimball,
Springfield, Mass.,
Sunday, Nov. 8, 1931

Dear Dot,

J. George Frederick [2] says the turn has happened; in September. He thinks the revival will be long, slow, painful. I don't. It may be slow, long, but there is reason to think that we shall have the worst (best) boom ever. There is lots of money idle and waiting; there are speculators waiting and eager. If only the people who ask me if it's time to get in again buy, there will be a burst. And even the captains of industry who anxiously hope to curb the next rise are afraid they can't. J. George Frederick is thinking of the adjustments and all the difficulties preliminary to good business in general. And he may be right.

My humble lecture tour is developing into a triumph. Everybody seems to have read (*and bought*) my book and they most of them have an emotional sense of it. You would be pleased to hear how they like Dad. One man yesterday, a high and technical official of Rochester, spoke of Dad with a tear in his eye; said he wished he had had such a wise father. "When I drank," he said, "my father,—

---

[1] Dreiser went, as Chairman of the National Committee for Defence of Political Prisoners, to report on the terror in the coal area of Harlan, Kentucky.

[2] Author and business prognosticator, editor of business magazines, and founder of the *Business Bourse International*.

well, he wasn't like yours." My meetings are packed by people standing up and they all take what I say,—which is not what they think, —with an obvious willingness to accept,—even that "we reformers are licked; the corruptionists have won, and maybe that is best. Maybe bribery and corruption is a natural force, an act of God." They listen to this, and their questions show that they consider it. It's the times, too, that help, but I and my book are taken as authority. I have had to stress it that I am only wondering, thinking and not at all sure.

The Literary Guild has sold 37,500 of my one-volume book, got back only 2,500, and they say that is a good record. And they predict from the satisfaction of their readers "who kept the book" that those that returned will soon be reordering. Harcourt is selling, too. He got an order for a thousand from one shop while I was with him one day last week. I see it is on some lists as best seller, but I cannot but note in the attitude of my literary and professional acquaintances that I am a success, as some of them say, a second time. I am almost convinced myself. But Harcourt sticks to his idea that he can make a classic of the book, that will go on selling forever. "I think," he said, "that you are going to have in it a property that will pay Pete some day a regular income, not always big, but sure and steady. He laughed, but he meant also that he would have a standard work in perpetuity. It's been made "required reading" in some courses in several colleges: in English, and journalism, in government classes, and in history.

Affectionately,
Len.

To Pete Steffens

Plaza Hotel,
San Antonio, Texas,
Dec. 9, 1931

Dear Pete,

I flew yesterday in one of those big passenger planes from Louisville to Memphis and I meant to fly farther to near here, but the rain and fog stopped all flights that day, so I came on by train. I'll tell you about it.

The plane I was to take was coming from Cincinnati, so I took a taxi and went to the airport in Louisville to meet it. There were some clouds out there but the weather man said we could fly, and when the big plane came swooping in and the other passengers got out, we were told to "all aboard." I ducked low to get in and took a seat on the right side, buckled the strap around me and settled down comfortably. My bag had been checked like on a train. I had a window to myself and there were eight other passengers. The pilots were two young men, about 20-24, who looked strong, confident, very competent. Both went up to their station, which is closed off, apart; they had the motors going already. With one glance around at us, one of them started us across the field; he paused, started the motors flying so fast you could not see them and we raced around the field, took off,—we were flying. The ground sank away as we lifted and turned to take our direction, and what surprised me was they did not seem to go fast. You could see by the way we passed trains and autos that we were going at great speed, but it did not seem fast. That is because, up there, you can see so far ahead objects, like hills, rivers and towns, that you seem to approach them slowly. We sailed along making a great, regular noise (the motors) but we moved evenly, steadily, and swung around heights very smoothly, bending way over. We were going fast, to Memphis, I thought. There was nothing to do for a long while. Some passengers read papers. I watched the country,— all marked up in farms,—blow by under us for perhaps two hours.

Then the motors slowed and we began to swoop down around in a circle. I saw a big town nearby and somebody said it was Nashville, Tenn., but I was surprised; and I was glad, too, when we came down on the landing field of an airport, a muddy field which we tore up badly. And I learned that it was a regular stop-off station. I darted into the rest-room, got a sandwich and a Coca-Cola while some passengers got out and others were buying tickets. We did not stop long. Climbing in again, we raced through the mud, paused, set the motors going full power and so again up, but not so high this time. It was raining, the clouds hung low,—what they called a low ceiling,—and the pilot to see and keep his course had to stay near the ground.

Then we came to high hills,—almost mountains, and we ran into big pieces of fog. That drove the pilot down lower, and from then on we always followed a river or a railroad that was going our way. Cars and horses, pigs and sheep were frightened by us,—so close,— and ran and kicked up, while farmers looked up at us and automobiles halted to watch us as we zoomed along. For now we seemed to be going fast, very fast. The boy pilots took turns and sometimes they were both out there together. A passenger I met afterwards, one who had flown a lot, told me he was scared; and that the pilots were, of the fog. Anyway, it was 1 hour 50 minutes, this time, when we settled again to Memphis; as I was going out, I asked the pilot how long before we would go on. He shook his head and said: "Not today; we'll cancel this afternoon's flight." And they did. My ticket was to Dallas, Texas, where we were to arrive at 5:30 P.M. The agent bought me a railroad ticket and berth on the Pacific Missouri Railroad to here instead of to Dallas. And to make up, the agent took us to a hotel, gave us luncheon and a room to wait in till 7:15 that (yesterday) evening. I had a bath, a nap and came on last night this long, long journey down to San Antonio, which is in Texas near the Mexican border.

It is sunny here. I have to stay here and try to get over my bronchitis in time to speak here on Monday (today is Wednesday); to Houston on Tuesday; and then next Wednesday, I have to fly again from Houston to Amarillo so as to speak at Canon, Texas, at a college. But flying is good here; it is almost always clear, and usually sunny. After that, Pete, I'll be going home, stopping only for a day at Los Angeles. I can't name my date yet; I'll wire that to Anna later, but I think it will be about December 21 or 22: Carmel, and I'll be so glad.

Love to all: Betty Ann, Leslie, Pete, your teacher and the whole town.

Dad

To Ella Winter

Carmel, December 27, 1931

Two young men, one a chum of Jacques Davidson, the other also a Wisconsin University graduate who has studied law and is now doing psychiatry, called at Jo's behest yesterday, the law psychiatrist with his wife, who was a reporter on the Minneapolis *Journal*. They are the most interesting Youth I have met so far in the U. S. Both,— all natural reds; not organized, not partisan, but instinctively for Reality. The first boy was in a research organization that put him into the business of planning settlements for Indians on the reservations in the Northwest. They are, you know, hungry minds, and after a couple of hours with them I bade them stay over so that we could go on today. I expect this morning to have the time of my life. They see that everything is wrong, especially the ideals and attitude and efforts of Meiklejohn [1] and Glenn Frank. Big, handsome, young and strong, we are hoping to get some sort of a line on what is right under our circumstances, and every word I utter seems to throw a light. That corruption may indicate a direction, a natural road; that the crooks may be the men to use; that revolution may be necessary; that there shall be no punishment,—anything like that opens up vistas for them. I told the doctor-lawyer about you, and he wants, he needs, to see you.

I did not know there were such young people.

Carmel, December 31, 1931

Dear Peter:

. . . Max does not really understand the Russian Revolution,—the politics of it,—and the Trotzky and Stalin incident showed that.[2] He is a Menshevik like Trotzky. But we are all capitalists; there are no Communists yet. Max falls down in one place, I in another, you on your spot. I'll bet Max,—nay, even Stalin,—will be making more errors. Some day some real Communist, developed out of Communism, will write a history putting us all in our places. And he may never understand that it was impossible for us to just be what he himself will have been made. . . .

Love, Peter.

Stef.

Carmel, Jan. 5, 1932

Dear Peter:

A fine letter from Brand Whitlock; he likes my book, he writes at length about it, closing thus:

"The nicest thing about your book is that you got your own personality into it. You don't say an unkind word about anybody!"

I am sending off today my "Satan's Version of the Fall of Man" [3] to Canby of the *Saturday Review*. He said he'd like to have it.

[1] Alexander Meiklejohn, then head of the Experimental College at Wisconsin.
[2] On her return from Soviet Russia Max Eastman told Ella Winter that though he disapproved of Stalin he felt he was doing the job.
[3] Published in *Scribner's Magazine*, Jan., 1934.

Mrs. Jeffers called right after breakfast to ask me to let Gloria Stuart [1] have for review her copy of Robin's last book, the Irish poems. She had lent it to me. She said Mabel Luhan had had a failure. She had set out to make Robin come back to New Mexico and he would not, and she acknowledged herself beaten. I said I'd have to report that to you. She says they did awfully like the record [2] of James Joyce's reading and ask leave to bring here others to hear it.

Pete set out like a little major for school this morning, as happy and proud as a boy can be. He is promoted to the First or Upper First, and has a new teacher whom I must see. All he ever speaks of is his arithmetic. He likes that and practices it mentally with me. Whenever I show him a general principle, like the fact that five tens, five thousands, five millions, are just the same as five fingers, or five bicycles, he looks intelligent, thoughtful, and delighted as if he "saw" something. And after a while he makes a comment or makes an example which shows that he "gets" it.

Maybe he will learn to see through mathematics. I didn't and I want him to.

To Mrs. Gilbert E. Roe

Carmel, January 10, 1932

Dear Mrs. Roe:—

I got home here about 10 days ago sick (abed) and tired—of lecturing. It was a terrible long, hard campaign of travel; I shall never do *that* again. But the worst of it was that I did not do what I went East for; I did not see my friends or, if I did, I did not see enough of them. Till the end. On my way back I did not want to see,—I did not want to have any more friends. I was done up.

A week in bed has done something for me. I am recovering. I was glad today to get your little note. I'd like to see you. But,—this is how bad it was,—I did not answer a letter from Gardner Hale [3] and the news of his tragic death hit me a double blow.

It is mystifying to think that that beautiful man is gone, all gone.

[1] Gloria Stuart, the film actress, was at this time working on *The Carmelite*.
[2] Phonograph record of "Anna Livia Plurabelle" from *Work in Progress*.
[3] Painter killed in an automobile accident motoring up the Pacific Coast to visit Steffens.

Yes, Walsh and I got together on a plan, but it has not worked out so far. I'm to have a private try,—soon; see the Governor with the boss for a talk on politics, Walsh's plea for Justice and the Right being no use.

But, anyhow, Pete is happy, and healthy, and a darling. He has a bicycle, and has learned in a week to ride it. He leads his class at school. He leads his own life at home.

Peter is back from Russia, in New York, where she is writing her head off. But she is coming home soon by air and will probably go to work on her book.

You are all right, I feel, so we'll have a good year, we will; however Hoover and the world may suffer.

Affectionately,
Lincoln Steffens

To Netta Cooper

Carmel, Feb. 14, 1932

Dear Netta—

Peter is working on her Russian book with a stenographer, and when she talks it is better than when she writes. As I told her yesterday. Maybe she is not a writer. Maybe, like Darrow, she's a talker. Anyhow, she's so concentrated that she doesn't write letters, or make calls, or go to the show. We are making an exception this week to go to Col. Wood's and Sara Field's for the poet's 80th birthday. And while we are there, to call on the Olders and their dogs. Pete, too. He's pretty busy keeping ahead of his class at school, riding a bicycle, and practising football. But he comes home when it's too dark to work at his self-development, and we see him at breakfast, too.

As for me, I am answering the fans who have discovered and read my now famous book, which seems to have begun to sell around Christmas time. It had sold about 65,000 up to that date. I don't know what the score is now. But as a book fancier, you ought to know that the first edition is selling at from $11.00 to $25.00. And Netta, dear, that is only for the book of my past. Think of the book of my future when I come to write that.

I'm getting two medals I hear, very soon: One from a bunch of newspaper men, who don't give gold medals very often or very lightly. But I'll have to write a letter of humility and deep appreciation. . . .

To Frederic C. Howe

The Getaway, Feb. 27, 1932

Dear Freddie:

It certainly pays to write to you, especially a letter of apology; you not only forgive a fellow, you pour out a lot of golden news,— or light, at least.

You are ripe to write an essay or an article on banks, out of your book. Now is the time. People are questioning the banks, suspiciously; the beginning has been made in Congress by Hiram Johnson, who doesn't know much. What do banks do? And what should they do? As to the break-up of the System, you are too hopeful, I think. Wells says England is finished, but not the U. S. A. And not all Europe. Our overhead is terrific, our debt immense, but I have a hunch that there's one more big boom ahead for us. On my trip East and West so many people asked if it was time yet to buy stocks again. And hereabouts a lot of them are ready for "one more turn."

Won't the railroads sell out to the Government, first, and go bankrupt second?

Is there anything that one can put money into to save it? What do you hold? What could I get for Pete? Or, shall I let him go with his mother to Russia to grow up in the Future?

You see, you might write an article for me and thousands would read it. Anyhow I wish you'd do me another letter before you go to Geneva.

And Marie, what is she doing with herself? What interests her?

My amazing book keeps going,—like a novel. Young people are reading it, the generation that never read our muckrakings. 65,000 sold before the Christmas sales, 1,500 since, but I haven't heard from Christmas. Your *Gold* would go like that. Don't wait to make it too solid. Put out one book now and follow with another, if you will. Remember that what you have is all news.

Give my love to Marie. Tell her Peter is getting on fast with her book.[1] Pete is as happy as sunshine and just as independent of surface rains and clouds on earth. It has been cold, but sunny here. Lots of rain, lots, but it came and went. And now it's like summer; hot yesterday. You might come out here instead of going to Geneva.

Affectionately,

Lincoln Stef.

[1] *Red Virtue: Human Relationships in the New Russia,* published 1933.

To Alfred Harcourt

The Getaway, March 10, 1932

Dear Harcourt:

Thanks for the letter with the news of January sales, the guess at my share of the earnings and the offer to pay some in advance. This will not be necessary. I think that stocks have gone to the bottom for the last time and so, some day when they are low again, I may buy a few shares, but not in a hurry, not many and not on a margin; and I have a good credit at my bank.

My mail continues to bear daily witness that the books which you sell are being read and with a satisfaction that still astonishes me. I feel too a personal note of warmth, even gratitude; my old stuff was new to many readers and my picture of it connects up with what people knew, to complete their picture or make one of their many snap-shots. I have done much better than I knew; as you, wise editor, knew all along. Even Peter advised cutting the muckraking chapters, and the old muckrakers all backed her up. Do you realize that you are the only one that said: "Let her run"?

If I could get a start on that book for children about the world as it is, that would go too; and not only among the kids. I have been practising on school children and college students lately, always with success. Yesterday I made an experiment beyond anything I have tried before. At a high school in Watsonville, thirty miles from here, I cut out all entertainment and gave them what I called straight goods; I told no stories, not an anecdote; for an hour I described things as they are, politics, business, education, science and art without relief. As at Stanford, I saw those kids come up to the edge of their seats, open their funny mouths and their eager eyes and eat it all up. And when it was over the applause lasted two or three minutes, —from kids! from those hard-boiled, sneering children who hate to be lectured to. They asked me to come back soon, and one of them, with the approval of a large group, said that that was the first time they had ever got it straight. You are right about that book too, dead right, and, if I don't do it, somebody else must. And I may not. Whenever I sit down to a job at my desk I get sick at my stomach and I notice, as poor Peter does, that I am falling into the brooding silences my father ended his days in, and his father. I shan't give up yet, but do you keep the project in mind, think who could do it and maybe I could help.

The teachers and parents will back up such a book. Yesterday, in the question period, a boy rose to ask me why the teachers did not tell it to them that way, and when I answered that the parents and the machine would not let teachers teach the truth, the teachers clapped and nodded approval, one man with joy in his astonished, interested face. And then, at noon, when I confessed all this to a luncheon party of business men and women, they behaved like the kids and teachers. People are all right, I repeat; some*thing* is wrong, and the job of the editor is to make the writers understand that they must excite the dull imagination of the readers.

I have been reading Dos Passos. He does it. I think that every young writer should read *1919* and read it too with his eye sticking to the fact that this young writer is one of the three or four kids in literature who are breaking away from the old schools and seeking, and in this case finding, a new way to get nearer to the art of showing things as they are, beautifully. I wish I were an editor over some of them. For I am sure that they would soon be understood and taken by the readers. You could make a new magazine with them. I wish you could get them all under your free leadership. You would if they knew you as we know you. Make Dos Passos introduce Hemingway, but then Dos Passos knows them all. Have a talk with him about making a gang.

Yours sincerely,
Lincoln Steffens

To E. A. Filene

The Getaway, April 5, 1932

Dear E. A.

I'll see you if I go East, of course. But even then I don't want to go on to Europe; not even with you. Spain is interesting and Russia is full of meaning; all Europe is worth while. But the U. S. A. is best now for all of us, especially for me, if not for you.

I am addressing myself preferably to Youth, which has a mind open enough and eager enough to take and use what we have to offer. It is fun to show them that we old folks are up against the fierce problem of distributing a permanent abundance to a mob that has too little. And to tell them that the trouble is that we have fixed ideas in our old dub heads that prevent us from seeing some way out which must be obvious to fresh minds, unless they have already begun, as most of the youth have, to learn from us our axioms. For of course it is axioms that are wrong in business as in science.

Think of the idiocy of taxing back from you what you never should have taken at all. And swelling you up with the notion that you are self-sacrificing.

Peter is working on her book on Russia, getting along fast. Pete would hardly know you. He is so busy in school and in mere living that he is always, like a business man, in conference. I suffer from bronchitis and from my fan mail, which is really formidable. It is youth again that is reading my book: and buying it too. Harcourt says he sells from 350 to 500 a month right along. How do you account for it? My theory is that it is the narrative; that they prefer a story to an exposition like yours, and so I infer that the book for you to make is an autobiography telling how one by one you discovered what you know. I know I could write it for you, if I would or could: too reluctant to work hard now; but you made a mistake in stopping the one you had going. I'll bet I could make a worse character of you than Charlie Wood did and still make both you and the public like you. And if I could somebody else can.

Goodbye for today, E. A. You are the opposite to the world and most of its inhabitants: you are hopeless in principle but in fact all right, a bully subject but a tough object, as I prove by the way I put up with you. . . .

Affectionately,
Stef.

To Elizabeth Nixon Winstanley

Carmel, April 6, 1932

My dear Mrs. Winstanley:—

You have no conception of the gratification that there is for me in your letter and in your poem to your father. I thank you for them. But you need not wonder that I remember so vividly and so perfectly Evelyn Nixon,[1] as I relate he did great things to and for me, he woke me up and set me right and I quote him again and again in conversation and in speeches.

He was a great, wise, very learned man and a teacher in the finest sense.

---

[1] A teacher at the University of California in the eighties who helped prepare Steffens for his entrance examinations. See *Autobiography,* 112 ff.

I wish that he could know how thankful I am and know my appreciation of him grows as I grow ever yet.

It is the next best thing, however, I know, that his daughter knows. It was very kind of you to say so in that letter, and in such a graceful way. I guess you are his daughter as I am his disciple.

Yours sincerely,
Lincoln Steffens

To Mrs. C. J. Reed

Carmel, May 25th, 1932

Dear Mrs. Reed,

Of course I remember and very well, very pleasantly, too. And I should have answered your letter before. But I sent your remonstrance to the club here, to be read at a meeting, and I think they passed it on to another group in San Francisco. Meanwhile I have been in and out of town lecturing, etc. I am sorry to have seemed negligent.

I can't advise you as to what you can do to keep the John Reed Clubs from using Jack's name. I'm not an attorney. But Francis J. Heney is. He is on the Bench of the Superior Court of Los Angeles now, but he is your friend and neighbour. He lives in Santa Monica. He will tell you what you want to know.

I can't do a thing. The last time I saw Jack, he blew me up hard, eloquently, rather bitterly for not myself doing what he had done: come out straight for the Communist Party and the World Revolution. One of the critics of my *Autobiography* was present at that scolding I got and said he looked in my book for my report of it. And he said in his review that I did not mention it, implying that I was ashamed of my part. But the point here is that Jack did go completely over; he ceased to be the free soul that you (and I) remember. He lived the life of a party Communist at the end.

I have told elsewhere how Jack's father besought me when the beautiful boy came to New York from Harvard to keep him free and unconvinced. I have told too how he often frightened me and I thought I had lost out and he was gone to some cause; but he came back, went off again; and how he finally went and stayed and died for his convictions. He became a hero in Russia; he will be for ages a Soviet Russian hero. And, Mrs. Reed, I'm afraid that you are wrong about his not standing for the use of his name by the clubs. My impression is that Jack would approve of that, or if he objected, he would have complained only that the John Reed Clubs do not go far enough. He might say to them what he said to me that night on a street corner in New York: "Go on—the limit."

I know that there is not much comfort in this letter for you. Maybe the sense of that is what unconsciously kept me from writing before. But you have turned to me in your trouble and I can only answer your good letter honestly.

If I get a chance I may call you up and ask permission to see you. I hesitate. I can hardly say more or better than I have written here.

Yours very sincerely,
Lincoln Steffens

To Owen D. Young

The Getaway,
June 1, 1932

Dear Mr. Young:

Is there any service I can render that would justify my appointment to a place near enough to your "economic council" to follow what you do or try to do? The task is the most interesting in the world. It will take all our culture, all our knowledge, theoretical and practical, to find the way you seek; and the answer may decide whether we proceed by a revolutionary or an evolutionary course to our end. You showed your evaluation of it when you preferred it to the presidency. To me it is a chance to bring to a climax all that I have learned and wanted to learn in my life; it might make a third volume of my life.

The part I would like to have is to see and persuade business men to join a program for united action, a diplomatic function. I have had experience and success there. Such men are understandable to me and they have understood me to the point where, as in the dynamiting case, seventeen of them agreed upon "the impossible." You are making an experiment and I have achieved the experimental attitude in working and even in reporting the application of the method. I might seek a chance to do this job as a reporter, but reporting is too swift in this case, and I cannot afford just now to work without pay; I can live here quietly, but to travel and go it or stay in hotels is too much for me. Therefore I ask whether you can find a use for me, an excuse to let me see this great, historical spectacle close up.

I am always glad to see that you are well and, I think, wise. The bow to the presidency and the way you made others bow to your bow, was a delight to me.

Yours sincerely,
Lincoln Steffens

To Jo Davidson

The Getaway, June 3, 1932

Dear Jo *et cie.:*

This is only to show you that I have had my typewriter put in order and can write now to anyone I please, you first. There is a letter from you to answer, I think; I didn't acknowledge yours to and about Will Rogers, did I? But never mind; I do thank you but I don't need any excuse to address you and yours and tell you that I have at last got the machine going. . . .

We here are all well. Pete will soon have a vacation to rest from his labors in school. Peter is toward the end of her book and meanwhile doing all sorts of jobs, the most interesting of which is the organization of a John Reed Club to study Communism. They have nine members, with many sympathisers who would like but dare not join. I gave them a talk on "Why Communists Have to Be Blankety Blanks," which met a thought in the minds of some 120 auditors and gave me some fun. I am wasting and enjoying the lost time, making a lecture now and then for money and amusement. . . .

My book still sells. I did not get the Pulitzer Prize, as so many critics predicted, but I do get next week a silver medal from the Commonwealth Club of San Francisco and I did get a gold medal from the N. Y. Evening Post Association. I saw in a S. F. paper that the book is a best-seller again and I hear that that was proclaimed over the radio last Sunday. All of which helps. And, like everybody else, I need help. This depression gets worse and worse over here. The bankers have been boosting stocks for two days now, or bonds, but that only gives us a rally. The tendency and the psychology is bearish. Stocks are down almost to their real value. It is very bad. My neighbors complain of a cut to one-third of their incomes, and they are nice people who don't do a thing. My loss is about that. It looks as if we might not have to have a bolshevik revolution at all. We are getting there by the swift process of evolution which is not so slow and gradual as the optimists predicted. It is, as a matter of fact, very, very funny.

Your bust of Jeffers has come and it has conquered. All the family like it; they are a bit emotional about it; and their visitors are caught by the bust or by the atmosphere of approval. But of course, you and I know that Mabel Dodge is to be credited with some of your success. She is not here now to steer people's judgment with her reason for not liking the bust. You remember her reason? You made the damn thing in our house, not in hers. A better reason than most people's for an attitude on a work of art.

Well, Jo, I have proved what I set out to demonstrate. You must be convinced that my typewriter works and, since that is about all I have to say,—except that I still love the Davidsons, worthy or unworthy,—I'll quit.

Yours affectionately,
Stef.

To Ella Winter

The Ranch, Monday,
June 29, 1932

Dear Peter:—

It was a hot, baked ride but fast. We got here at 3:30. And your boy Pete was in the pool by 3:34 and swimming. Everybody was astonished at the way Pete could swim and dive. Even Clint approved. Those two are off on some ranch job together now. They left this morning right after breakfast (7 A.M.) and Pete 'phoned from Gaviota that he was working. There's a creek to dam, fences to look to and repair. For Jim has to have cattle rounded up tomorrow and next day for a sale. Some girls have been 'phoned to report at the rendezvous tomorrow morning. Clint is a little ashamed that Pete can't ride a horse yet; and Pete hangs his head till Clint declares that he (Clint) is bound that Pete shall learn not only a horse, but to look and see and name every bird that sings, every beast that moves. Pete seems to agree that it's a shame not to notice and know things on a ranch and everywhere else. And so, Pete is kind to but he has discovered that he has no need for a daddy. He looks as if he thought that every man should be and every kid should want to be strong, quick, able to do anything going like Clint Hollister. He even went back on Dan, the Chinese boy, who was great last night. They took to each other and Pete entered into a contract to help Dan pick oranges, vegetables and,—all that. But Clint was in town last night; drove a girl home. This morning he took command and Pete looked at Dan the way Clint did, and,—oranges, huh?—he went off with Clint to prepare for the roundup.

His new suit,—the overalls,—is rejected. It's too big, and he put on his corduroys. And I don't think it was only because Clint also wears corduroys.

Stef.

The Ranch, Tuesday,
June 30, '32

Dear Peter:—

It's a lost day for Pete, almost. He can't ride a horse, so Clint went off to the roundup after breakfast without Pete. And there are girls, too. They came out from S. Barbara to meet the cowboys at Allegria. All day they'll be driving in. Maybe Pete can drive down tomorrow when Jim goes to boss the buyer's choice of bull calves he wants. But we are not sure.

Pete played around the pool till, when I went out, he had lost the rake in the water and wanted to dive in to get it. We held him out for a while but after ten-thirty we let him go and he had half an hour's swim. He can swim well. We must let him go on learning strokes and dives. He spent half an hour in the orange grove; ate 11, he said. And now he wishes it were afternoon so that he can go swimming again.

Thursday.—Pete, the diplomat, played politics last night and this morning to get to go with Uncle Jim to the roundup. Jim drives. Bud, the cowboy, and Clint, rode away early on their horses to go, the one over the hills, Clint along the beach to meet the cattle. Jim was finally brought to see what Pete wanted to do and asked him to join him. He had to make some promises: to persuade Dan, the Chinese boy, to put him up a lunch; to look out for rattlesnakes and to keep clear of the horses and the cattle. Pete gave his word, everybody was satisfied and now I can hear Pete's voice piping up out of the hubbub at the garage across the creek. . . . Allen and I are to be here alone all day, a foggy day, by the way, which is good for Pete's head, though he wears an old hat because Clint and the cowboys all wear old hats. . . .

Stef.

To Martin Flavin

Carmel, July 23, 1932

It is beautiful, Flavin. It's poetry. And it's a play.[1] I was swept along by it, moved in my emotions and still more in my imagination. It's a great thing. I hope the theater people can see it as I do, up there on the stage, alive, a going concern, true, even "practical." You've even got the generations pictured in it, the good old founder, the newer managers who are understandable to him, and the newest controllers who are not understandable. And the types; the worker for wages, the worker for the work, the inventors, the financiers, the two kinds of directors and the mob. The end is too good, too hopeful; I can't see so far. Or, I'm afraid of my wishing.

I did not know you were so seeing, Flavin, and so knowing. You had fooled me some with your funny hard-boiled poise of matter-of-factness. No more of that now. And you may go to Russia with my permission. You'll see the future there through their dirty, clumsy, infantile present, and you can say it, when you do. You can say it.

I wonder why I feel so grateful to you. But we can talk about that.

Lincoln Steffens

To Mrs. A. Winter

Carmel, Aug. 10, 1932

Dear Gran'ma:

Peter let me read your last letter,—the one about what a handsome, living woman she is and also about your going to the country. I thought I'd make sure that you got an answer.

First Pete. He exclaimed bitterly in the bath the other day that his best friend was his grandma. I had been making him do something, and I asked him why he thought just then of you and your superiority. His answer was rather remote. "Oh," he said, "my grandma is the only one that lets me do anything I want and never makes me do what I don't want to." So it's only by contrast that you loom so high in his estimation. But I notice every once in a while that his memory of you is pleasant to him. I told you that you had spoiled him; as you did his mother.

Carmel is a very busy place in the season, and this is the season. Clubs, concerts, musical politics,—and tourists,—Carmel in the summertime is the busiest hive in the world. But the busiest bee is Ella

[1] *Amaco*, by Martin Flavin.

Winter. She runs herself to exhaustion, but she runs everybody else,—that will let her,—too. Her book is her main job, and it's coming on to an end, a good book, too. But that's only the start of her damned energy. She is the founder and boss of the John Reed Club, which is a near-Communist organization for near-writers and near-artists. It gives lectures. I gave the first one on "Why Communists Have to Be Blankety-Blanks." The last was by a Communist on "Why You Are Not Communists." But the Reed Clubbers do everything, from despising their neighbors to making money on cheap entertainments. And Ella Winter is the bane of the town's existence.

I'm writing a little, articles, fables and a column for the *Carmelite,* our weekly. In general I am campaigning for Hoover on the theory that he and his backers will bring on the revolution. And I am pointing out now that the next boom is on; we have turned the corner and are rising out of our depression into the last great boom of the United States of N. America. . . .

A smile all around.

Pete's Papa

That's what Anna's pretty baby girl calls me,—Pete's Papa.

To Beverley M. Bowie[1]

The Getaway, August 29, 1932

Dear Mr. Bowie:

In the very same mail with your letter this morning came another from the editor of the *Cosmopolitan Magazine,* asking me much the same question and offering me space for the answer.[2] And he doesn't cast slurs upon my handwriting either. I think I shall do it for the editor and let him publish it to you. What would you do? And you say, what is true too, that it is all in my book, which is a long book and should not call for a third volume, even from an admirer of it.

But one word to your inquiry: in our society, where money plays such a large part, men brought up to our ideals of wealth and success are under a constant pressure and temptation to take offers and submit; most men will go along. In Russia, where nobody has or can get and spend money, the same men do not surrender. "Lead us out of

---

[1] Harvard student, son of the Rev. Walter Russell Bowie.

[2] Appeared as part of a symposium "But Will It Be the Same One Hundred Years from Now" with H. G. Wells, Julian S. Huxley, Stuart Chase, Bertrand Russell, Amelia Earhart and others, *Cosmopolitan Magazine,* Feb., 1933.

temptation" is an old wise prayer never answered till now, in Asia. Cut out the apple,[1] as the Russians have, and you will see how different everything appears and becomes. I know a young theological student who in Russia saw that there was the place to preach and to practise Christianity or other impossible ideals. They all are possible there or will be later when Communism is established. You might recall in this connection that Jesus must have seen that his teachings required Communism, for in the Acts his followers are practising it. But—

I refuse to be tempted into that third volume. I'm going to quit writing to you just because I like you so darned much.

Yours just the same,
Lincoln Steffens

P.S.: I wrote something you might like to read about the new muckraking, Seabury, etc., in the *Survey*[2] a year or so ago. I forget the date, but the editor will tell you that and send you the number.

My compliments, if you please, to your father, who also might care to see that article.

To Upton Sinclair

Carmel, September 25, 1932

Dear Upton:

You have seen the warning in this week's *New Republic* that next week Edmund Wilson is going to muckrake us? Well, I propose that you and I stick together and fight him back, for our very lives, and I'll tell you how we'll do it. You, a pacifist, are probably weak on strategy; an honest man and a prohibitionist, you may be no good in this sort of an emergency.

I'm assuming of course that Wilson, an acute critic, will get us right and give us justice. The fact that he lumps us is a bad sign; it really looks to me as if he had seen through us. I am scared. I hate justice, especially for myself. I have asked for it, but my prayers were altruistic. I prayed for others, not for me. No judge who has rendered justice would like it for himself. So I am frightened and I beg you to take my advice and line up with me for a united defense, thus:

I suggest, when we recover our breath from Wilson's attack, that you, Upton, walk right up to him somewhere and sock him one be-

---

[1] See *Autobiography*, Chapter XXX, "Los Angeles and the Apple."
[2] "As Steffens Sees It," *Survey*, Oct. 1, 1931.

tween his too seeing eyes. I, meanwhile, will have sneaked around behind him where I'll bark at him and bite him on the legs or the back somewhere. That will distract his attention so that he can't return your frontal attack; he will look around down toward me. In that supreme moment do you hit him with all your might just enough below the belt to knock him out but not enough to get caught making a foul blow. Then I will jump on his prostrate form and yelp with joy and victory, while they are taking you away to the hospital or to jail on a charge of assault with intent to kill.

Please write or wire your agreement to this plan so that I can sleep and rest and be ready. I feel about worry as I do about justice.

Yours hastily,
Lincoln Steffens

To Alfred Harcourt

The Getaway,
September 26th, 1932

Dear Harcourt:

Your letter of September 16th arrived during a brief absence of mine from home and Ella Winter opened and read it. So part of your purpose was accomplished. All I had to do was to back you up and say that you had the call on her.

Poor girl, she has been working hard, writing and rewriting, and the work was necessary. So was the time. The book has been not only improved, it has been made that way. And it seems to me to be a good book. I have not read all the revised chapters but I still think it's all right. It will go to you now within a couple of weeks. Chase phones from San Francisco that he will be here Saturday so that he can read as much as he likes of it.

What you say about the sales and my share of the profits of my book is very gratifying, of course. I don't need the money now; I wanted only to know what I could count upon having during the year. You keep it till it is due me. I have told Ella Winter and I want her to think that she has got to meet her obligations all by herself. Perhaps I would better say to you in part, now, what I was going to offer as an introduction, comment or blurb on *Red Virtue*.

She went to Russia to see there all the solutions or experiments with the problems she had come across in England, America and in Europe generally: for Russian answers to American questions, really. Living with me and seeing my book in the writing she became as keen as I was on what we were up against in detail. As a student and lecturer at the London School of Economics she knew well the English questions, the British problems both at home and in the Colonies. She had been specializing for several years in psychiatry. She had been associating with the younger school of English and American writers of fiction. All this was her unique and very fertilizing preparation for a trip to Russia: to get, as I say, solutions or leads to solutions of our western problems.

Over there she found what you and I knew she would find: that everything had been changed a little, some more, some less, but everything was different. Love was different, marriage was different, politics was very different; and business, and ethics, and customs, and fashions. Art and literature were taking a new road; there was an upsurge of science, especially in research. That's a long enough list for now. What does it mean?

I once heard Gilbert E. Roe, a distinguished New York attorney who had once been a partner of Robt. M. La Follette, Sr., say that he could see how we might change our laws, charters and constitutions; we could change our economics. "But," he exclaimed, "how we are ever going to change our social customs, I cannot see." Other prophetic thinkers have thought through to the same stone wall. Peter's book would have enlightened Roe; it will make all our wonderers see that customs can and will be changed. I think it will fascinate you, yourself, to see how such deeply embedded habits as those of love-making and of the family soften under a new economic system and begin again to flow. You will see the Russians falling back on still deeper instincts to think aloud, and rather patiently, about what will happen to institutions founded by the cave-men.

I can't dictate off this way just what I mean, but I must have said enough for you to see what the feature is of this book. With a little pointing up to attract and steer the critics we can give this book a send-off something like the start you gave mine.

The *Cosmopolitan Magazine* has asked me if I would muckrake Europe. They got the suggestion out of the *Autobiography*, where I said I didn't want to do it but that somebody like Spewack should. They had asked Spewack and were negotiating with him when they wrote to me to ask if I wouldn't consider doing it. I have answered

upper: J. JAMES HOLLISTER AND PETE AT THE RANCH. *center:* THE
HOLLISTER FAMILY. *top row:* MR. AND MRS. J. JAMES HOLLISTER
AND JOE. *bottom step:* JACK AND CLINTON HOLLISTER. *behind
Clinton:* JANE B. HOLLISTER. *lower:* PICNIC AT CARMEL HIGH-
LANDS: *left to right:* TONY LUHAN, HAZEL WATROUS, LINCOLN
STEFFENS, ELLA YOUNG, A FRIEND, DOROTHY THOMPSON, JOHN
O'SHEA, SINCLAIR LEWIS, MABEL DODGE LUHAN, RICHARD
BUHLIG. ELLA WINTER.

that I would come to New York to consult with them about it, if they wished; I still didn't want to do it myself, but I might care who the men were that were sent and I might even edit or direct the job. No answer to that yet. I'm doing an occasional lecture out here and procrastinating about four or five lecture calls to Chicago and East. In a word, I may be seeing you this fall, as I should like.

Yours sincerely,
Lincoln Steffens

To Upton Sinclair

Carmel, September 27, '32

Dear Upton:

I've seen it too.

The *New Republic* came in the same post with your reassuring note and verified the good news: that Wilson didn't get and give us away.[1] I'm so relieved. I've always been afraid some son-of-a-gun would come along and see and see through and expose me as a comedian. And when Wilson said he was going to lump you, the tragedian, with me, I was sure he had me nailed. I wasn't afraid for you. My letter to you was all pretense. I knew that you never laughed at yourself. No. I was scared for me; lest this, the greatest critic of our latter days, had seen my shoulders shake in prayer and guessed that the little private sounds I make on my knees were not sobs, and that the object of my deep concern was not really you, Upton, but,—oh, well—

Yours merrily,
L. Stef.

To Mrs. J. James Hollister

Carmel, Wednesday,
[November, 1932]

Dear Dot:—

The sun shines, the forests burn, wheat's on the bottom; U. S. Steel declares an unearned dividend on preferred; Pete and Anna are down and out with 'flu; Peter's book is all shipped to Harcourt who likes the part he had read: and Allen is so silent that I guess he has found a friend. Peter has a call to lecture at Vancouver on her way East, but

---

[1] "Lincoln Steffens and Upton Sinclair," by Edmund Wilson, *New Republic*, Sept. 28, 1932.

her ticket reads via airplane from Los Angeles. I don't know just what she'll do; except, of course, that she'll have to go to New York somehow within a week.

I've just turned down a publisher's suggestion to write a life of all the La Follettes. I have accepted another to prophesy in a symposium with Wells and others for the *Cosmopolitan* on "What Government will be 50-75 years hence." Five hundred words at one dollar a word. That would be high pay in England,—in pounds.

I put in an order to buy a few stocks this morning after the lift on the Steel dividend; my offer is below the market on the assumption that prices will decline during the day and that the turn is here, and that ultimately. Meanwhile I'll get more if the market goes on down. I'm a bear on our civilization, but a bull on the market. One more boom?

Tell Jim to tell Dot to write me once in a long while.

Affectionately,
Len.

To Harlow Gale

Carmel, November 12, 1932

Dear Harlow:—

No. I'm not sick, but I have not been well and oh, so busy. I should have acknowledged getting your manuscript long ago, but I wanted to read it all. I've read only the first few pages. I'll be sending it you soon.

Do I understand that you thought that Johann and I had some sort of sex relationship! We didn't have, you know. It never occurred to me that our affection might look like that to anyone.

I think that you'd better change names of persons and places enough to make all identification impossible. It's a freer way to write, too. Fiction is the best form for the truth, as I know well. I let go in fiction; I repress in fact stories; and it's with the imagination that we really see.

But it is good to hear from you, and get again the feel of you. So unchanged, too. You are a wonder, Harlow, and such a dear. I'll soon be writing again.

Affectionately,
Lincoln Steffens

To Ella Winter

The Clift,
San Francisco,
Nov. 15, 1932

Dear Peter:—

Saw Rolph in Sacramento this morning. Meaning to take the 9 A.M. plane, I got talking to a reporter and missed it. So, having an hour and a half to put in before the 11 plane, I went over to the Capitol and asked to see the Governor. "Sit down." A U.P. reporter spied me and came up; he had read my book. What did I want? I told him. I said: "And has Rolph any humor?" Yes, and he'd show me. He darted into the Governor's office, came right out and ushered me in. Rolph received me amazingly, had often wanted to see me. I said: "And I you. I've been inquiring about you: whether you have any sense of humor. This U.P. man says you have. But I'm going to put a test and find out." He laughed: "Go ahead!" he said. So I put my proposition to choose a moment when the Reds were hauling hardest on their end of the rope and, then, he, Rolph, let go his end. "And why, it,—"

He looked interested, stood up, and was going to say something to put it off, so I said: "No. Don't answer now. Just let it sink in till it gets down to your sense of fun, then— I'm not trying to get Mooney and the rest out of prison. They are too useful and happy there. I'm only trying to find out if you can see the humor of,—politics."

And, a few words of "come again" and "honored," "thanks for your call,"—I was getting out. All in about 8 minutes. . . .

That short speech of mine at the Mooney rally made a hit; on the radio, too.[1] It was the only one heard, so it sticks up like the best. It was heard here by at least a dozen people. I wonder why they listened in at such a meeting. Common people, too.

The Alexandria,
Los Angeles,
Nov. 18, 1932

Dear Peter:—

Just got in from a straight 2 hours flight from Alameda. Too long a stretch. It was clear, smooth, but utterly monotonous; it seemed slow so high up. So I'll go back by the other line which halts twice on the

[1] Mooney mass meeting, San Francisco, early November, 1932.

way. But anyway it makes creeping along the ground on a railroad train idiotic. What I'd like to know from you is whether it is tolerable for a long trip like L. A. to New York. The stretches must be very long. Can one smoke? We couldn't smoke for those two hours.

Grokowsky[1] called up just now. Says the house is sold out and he hopes I'll come out for Communism. The title is: "Can Capitalism Be Saved?" Smith taking the affirmative. I need only say no, but I think I'll try to prove that Communism is inevitable; not desirable, perhaps, but coming sure. I lunch with Smith and Grokowsky today, soon, and I think I'll tell them I shall challenge their whole order of logical thinking and stand for the historical, experimental method of "seeing." I'd like to test that against an able, scholarly debater like Smith. G. says the crowd are hoping I'll go clear through for them, and in that way, I can, to my satisfaction.

No mail here from Anna, so no letter from you. I'm still wondering if you beat that storm to New York. And there's so much else to hear from you. But, then, I'm interesting too now for a few days, ain't I? So I'll send this and carry on my serial for you.

Stef.

To Beverley M. Bowie

Los Angeles, Nov. 19, 1932

Dear Bev. Bowie:—

. . . I am not a Communist. I merely think that the next order of society will be socialist and that the Communists will bring it in and lead it. The Socialists are waiting for a majority; the Communists know that they can proceed (as the capitalists do) with a minority just as soon as capitalism busts. Intellectually they are ahead of the Socialists in this, that they know that there is a job to do and that it has to be done. The Socialists *intend* only to do the best they can: which is not enough, as they have shown wherever they have had any power. Laski is a good example; I know him personally. He wants too much besides Socialism. The Communists want Socialism. That got, they can get the rest.

As to violence in the transition, that depends upon the opposition. The old order will probably fight; it's a fighting order, so the Communists must be prepared to fight.

---

[1] David Grokowsky, manager that year of the Liberal Forum in Los Angeles.

Now, that's enough from me to you. You can answer what I say, but don't. Try to see it. If I had a conversation with you it would not be about Socialism; it would be about thinking or seeing. I cannot write it all out because my writing is illegible. And you are coming along all right, just keep moving.

Yours sincerely,
Lincoln Steffens

I am to have a debate here Monday evening with a very able thinker and a witty talker, Paul Jordan-Smith, on your subject: "Can Capitalism Be Saved?" I have the negative but I shall move over into a positive position by predicting that Communism is coming in Russia only first. We should study history, not logic, as Bertrand Russell says. We are way beyond logic and,—history too.

To Ella Winter

Los Angeles, [Nov. 19, 1932]

Dear Peter:—

I have been recommending you for lectures down here and you'll get some when you come back. They need you; exactly your angle. Practice out there all you can.

I turned in "The Reluctant Briber" to Howard Smith, the story editor who makes fiction into pictures. He said he knew nothing, except that his boss wanted my story. I've hesitated to see Hovey. Lunched with a Mr. Cooper and an actor Cagney, who likes my book, an earnest fellow who wants to act. He's Warner Brothers' best-paid actor, but is eager to do better and better.

A confused young scientist, a botanist, who is a teacher or professor at the university, called today and begged me to meet with his crowd of young university instructors to help them understand what is happening. I've agreed to spend tomorrow evening with nine of them. It's secret, of course. They are a bit frightened.

There are many, very many people down here who are scared at what has happened. Monday night is sold out; and that means between 2,500 and 3,000. And they don't want any fun either. I've been cautioned to be very serious, clear and straight. My opponent,[1] who has been with his wife, at our house, is an old Socialist who quit because he is really only a gentleman and a scholar. But, gosh, he has

---

[1] Stitt Wilson, Mayor of Berkeley.

a beautiful, big, bass voice and he can talk, they say: a real orator. He gave me a line on his argument, and it's easy for me, unless his personality goes over in this voice. We use microphones; I notice that his voice is best over the 'phone. A real debate, I guess, no snap this time. He's an old friend of Darrow, same ideas and tendencies. Hates machinery, violence and all that.

Los Angeles,
[Nov. 20, 1932]

Dear Peter:—

Your train letter has just come in with a big batch of mail from Anna.

What you say about our intellectual bond rang a response in me. I am changing, catching up emotionally with my mind and I think we'll enjoy ourselves again, or, I'd better say I shall. For you have been pretty even all along.

I went out for my evening with all those (10 or a dozen) young professors who wanted an evening with me. All sorts, they are young, going left fast, many of them Socialists or near it, and ate up my preference for Communism. Strange how they accept me as an authority; didn't want to talk, only to listen. Well, I did some good work. They came along willingly as far as they could go,—6:30 to 9. Even the economists were good. One of them said, "I tell my students that all their lives they will have to be hearing and talking or doing something about Socialism and that, therefore, they must understand it."

The talk at the church made a hit, but I didn't enjoy it; seemed footless. And the processions that poured up to shake hands made me feel like poor Hoover. I made punishment of crime look silly, and they seemed to get it.

Now to bed.

Stef.

Pete is giving a birthday party to a group of his pals, very carefully chosen. I saw and heard him weighing his list and I can tell you that Roosevelt will give no more serious thought to his cabinet selections than your Pete has put into his job. And I get letters asking whether Pete really exists! [1]

---

[1] Charles Roberts Aldrich, the psychologist, had written an article called "Is Pete Steffens Only a Myth?" in the Carmel *Pine Cone,* October 14, 1932.

California Hotel,
San Bernardino,
[Nov. 23, 1932]

Dear Peter:—

Everybody said and there were many signs from the big, very big audience last night that the debate was a thriller; and that, if there was any winner, I was he. But I went too far left to have carried any audience; except, of course, the Communists in the top gallery. All I mean is that I showed that my opponent's "wishing" that the capitalists might by reason save capitalism was unprecedented in history, and in fact unlikely.

But the evidence of my success that will convince you came in the person of a young Russian researcher sent here from Moscow to study our movies. He came all aglow into my dressing-room and asked where I lived and when I'd be home. He has to come to see me. "I want to get more of the differences between us and you Americans, in our thinking." I had shown in passing how the Soviet Russians really "got" evolution into their bones; how Russia, with all the "interests" cleared away, could easily accept any new idea and do any new, good thing, impossible here; how they did not do their best, but tried to do the job. He said that my talk was the first time he ever got the key he lacked to understand us. "Your attempt to explain us to Americans explains America to me. I want that, and more. We'll talk about the differences between us, all of them. All of them. I have to take them back with me."

You see? He had never lived under capitalism. Some of our troubles, mental, political, economic, were beyond his comprehension till I, in some detail, explained why the capitalists in power still could not *do* the things they see to be necessary. A revelation to him, his joy illustrates what I have said so often, that pretty soon the Communist order will not be able to "get" just what it was that blocked us; just what the picture is that's back of their phrase. "But the capitalists cannot give up what they've got." I told that fine Russian youth (about 26) to come and stay at the house. I'll make him understand capitalism. And what fun to try! What I'll get of the formed Communist mind that knows no other way! [1]

[1] Steffens often used the illustration of this Communist Russian boy. But he never turned up again.

Carmel, Dec. 3, 1932

. . . My Sunday night talk at the Schoeningers' was a most unexpected success. It was packed, upstairs and down. They had places for 82 and over a hundred came; and all sorts. Lots of young people, but grown-ups, too, and good people. And I had no speech planned. There was a subject, but I paid no attention to it. I just talked to the faces in the audience; I seemed to sense what they were expressing. One woman, I remember, who talked, and talked, finally turned and whispered indignantly to her husband. I thought I knew what she said to him and I answered that. And the look of astonishment on her face was a sight to see! A few (kind) words more, rubbing it in, and that face melted.

Indeed, the most frequent comment afterwards that night and today, —not to me, but to one another,—the exclamation of that crowd was that I was "sincere." And I went the distance too. "You, my neighbors, you don't have to be Communists; but you do have to know what it is and what it means. You can't live on here with me and go on asking your dumb questions. The Communists have got it; they'll save the world, and the only way to beat them is to beat 'em to it and do, your way, what they're doing theirs. And the doubt is that you can; that you can give up your blooming dividends, interest, rent and all you've got for a common prosperity."

My, but it was fun. I have learned at last to speak and I love to do it.

Carmel, Dec. 6, 1932

Dear Peter:—

No. You can prepare the swells to see Fascism as a betrayal. They'll have to go along with it but they will then remember and so know why we do not take it but go right on. Undermining Fascism is a real job. I do it every time now; never miss.

I got a book from Liveright,—*Farewell to Reform*, by John Chamberlain,—all about me and the rest of the Progressives, reformers and muckrakers. Read it. You have no idea how significant I am or was.

Pete just came in, selling the *Country Gentleman, Sat. Eve. Post*, etc. He had a canvas bag on his shoulder and looked just like Stanley Wood's kid used to. Said "a man" gave him the job, with the offer of a prize or prizes,—free.

Like that? You say you like to hear anything about Pete.

Mrs. Isaak told me that Miss Eddy handled a White Russian questioner beautifully the other night. The White, a girl, rose and said, "But they (the Reds) murdered my brother!" Miss Eddy walked down off the platform to the girl, put her hand on her arm and said: "No, not murdered. There was a war, a real war, and your brother was killed in that war. But he was not murdered." And the girl gave up and followed Miss Eddy to get more, and more; and the audience got more and more. Very good, very real and,—fine instinct.

An old unemployed just called. "What are *you* doing about it?" I asked. "Well, I used to do more than I do now. Used to be an I.W.W."

"And now?"

"Oh, now, I'm for all of us, all, to get into the Communist Party." I gave him something, then; and not till then.

There,—must go.

Stef.

P.S.: My bed was full of marbles when I went to bed last night, so I know that my father has come to life in Pete.

Carmel, Dec. 14, 1932

Dear Peter.—

The following telegram is here:

"Manchester Boddy editor and publisher of the *Illustrated Daily News* who is taking the town by storm with series of articles on Technocracy is willing to debate you under our auspices subject to be worded as to whether Technocracy can function in United States or solve our problems exact wording to be decided upon by affirmative. You negative. January 9th. Anxious to have you accept. Will write you in detail. Wire acceptance collect.

"David N. Grokowsky."

I want to accept and I think I'll wire: "Yes, if you will have a substitute for me in case my throat keeps me home."

That essay on Robin by the young American doctor [1] in France says in the preface "but the best source on Jeffers the man is the special edition (or number) of the *Carmelite,* etc." [1] That's one thing you did, a deed done well. Probably last forever. . . .

---

[1] Lawrence Clark Powell. The issue of *The Carmelite* on Jeffers, edited by Ella Winter, appeared Dec. 12, 1928.

Nice lively lunch, talking about the doctorate on Robin, who won't read it; about the rumor running around town that I'm sincere; ghosts, etc. Robin is toward the end of a long narrative poem promised Feb. 1. He made a personal point with me to come out more often.

I suggested to Miss Watrous today that they get the Englishman I debate with in L. A. to repeat with me up here, or, I said, "I'll report the debate in a talk here, all alone, giving both sides, his and mine."

"But that isn't what the people here want," she said.

"I know," I said, "you-all want to see me beaten by somone in public."

"Ye-e-s," she said. "What we'd like is someone who can present our ideas in such a way that you can't answer them."

"Impossible," I said. "No one is clever enough to take the dumb things you Carmelites think and make an intelligent address with them."

"Except you; you could."

And I guess that's what they think of me.

Pete's a business man today again. I wish you could see your red son selling *Sat. Eve. Posts*. He has decided to peddle nothing else. "You make more on the ten cent papers, but you can't sell them. People say, 'Bring me the *Eve. Post* next time,' so I think I'll take only the *Posts*." I bought one. He has sold several; has a lot of small change in his pocket. But now, it's football; I can hear them.

Carmel, Dec. 16, 1932

Dear Peter:—

Your article in the *New Republic*[1] reads very well. You seem to be just telling it. Just the same I begin to want someone to come right out and say what I'm going to say Jan. 6, that "Russia Has Got It." A partisan book, full of free rejoicing, is what I want. To hell with the open minds. Especially in your case, it's a pose and hampers your style, clogs your genius. Is it the same pose in Joe Freeman that takes the joy out of his faithful book?[2] I don't want aggressiveness, you understand; only gladness. What you think of Russia is good news.

[1] "What the Soviet Child Reads," Dec. 14, 1932.
[2] *The Soviet Worker*.

Pete's having a deuce of a time deciding whom to send some Christmas cards to: you or me. Addressed by him "to Daddy" he changes it to "to Mama," and then back. He reasons out loud enough for me to gather that your sole fault is that you are so far away. He can't hope to see how "so prised" you are. I don't know yet what he'll finally do, but if you win you will have to find some way to let him "get" your joy, else I'll get all the presents.

He plays in a "Nativity thing" tonight. He only kneels and walks and stands;—"no words, Daddy." But I'm not going. I have to see "I'm a Fugitive from a Chain Gang" and Pete, who has seen it (in Monterey), says "it is better than his play, oh, much better. There's shooting in it. Not much, a couple of shots, but,—yes, you better go to the movie." . . .

Carmel, Dec. 17, 1932

Dear Peter:—

I "had to" go to Mrs. Blackman's [1] last night for supper and,—you know. A surprise. Mary Bulkley [1] read the December *Outlook* article on Technocracy to the whole gang and she can read. She made every sentence land. I got it like new from her. And I saw the others get it. I *heard* afterwards in the discussion that they got it. Miss Bulkley and I wouldn't let them sneak out either; they had to face it. And it made them contemplate Communism. Even Mrs. Blackman couldn't get off the ground. When she flapped her wings for flight, I heaved a rock at her and she came right down. . . .

M. came in and got fresh orders from the party. She looked driven. With her was the leader for the district, a good sensible fellow who was glad to laugh a little and said he would come in here when tired and get my slant.

All Pete's girls are home for vacation: Margaret, Hester and,—all the college girls. He was in the Nativity play; I was so far back I couldn't pick him out of the kneeling, chanting boy chorus. But it was all horrible. Propaganda to beat the band. But it didn't touch Pete any more than the *Eve. Post* does. And don't you worry about that. He's immune himself. It's only your pride that's hurt. I'll tell him about the *Eve. Post,* but I'll not forbid him to peddle it. I'll let him offer it as a mess of lies, but he may sell it and make his own money. He

---

[1] Mrs. George Blackman of St. Louis. Mary Bulkley, author of "Sonnets at Seventy," both Carmel neighbors.

wouldn't let me pay for his movie Saturday. "No, I'll pay it out of my own money." . . .

Carmel, Dec. 22, 1932

Dear Peter:—

The Central Railroad of Georgia went bankrupt the other day, the first of the railroads. More will follow; all should go. I have $10,000 in the C. R. of G. And I'm glad, not sorry. I'm a bear all right.

A young student Communist came from L. A. last night to see me. He's all the way. But he's scared at Technocracy and I guess the Communists generally are in So. California. Why? My debate at the L. A. Forum is Jan. 9, with Manchester Boddy, editor and publisher of the L. A. *Illustrated News* and the badly worded subject is "Should Technocracy Present a Plan for Economic Recovery?" I, yes. I've suggested a change: "Technocracy *Is* a Basis for a Plan." My idea is to show that it can be applied only after Communism,—in Russia, for example.

But it's going like wildfire in California and, apparently, everywhere. Tell me what the Communists are saying about it. I regard it as great, good Communist news. . . .

I got a wire night before last from San Diego to go there today to address a Mooney meeting tonight and saying the movement would be disrupted if I didn't. Two days' notice! I wired that I was sorry to disrupt the world movement for Mooney, but I could not get there. Damn fools!

M. got too late orders to do the impossible yesterday. She looks worried, driven. It takes a Bolshevik to be a Bolshevik. No Menshevik could stand it.

Carmel, Dec. 23, 1932

Dear Peter:—

In five minutes Anna had the special *Carmelite* on Jeffers laid out to go to your Princeton collector. Picking it up, I ran through it and I got really interested. It's a valuable, good thing. But what hit me with the most astonishment was that the editorial I have in it shows that I saw in 1928 that the crash was coming and all this stuff about mass production, mass consumers. It could be printed today. And your part is very creditable, yes, and you get credit, too. I am proud to have this go out anywhere to anybody.

Will Durant's articles [1] remind me of that old Russian fable about "The Critic." Remember? The shepherd who saw his friend, the pig, disappear into the castle yard, waited till he came out and then asked him if he saw the wonderful pictures, rugs, plate and all the other grand things said to be in there.

"No," said the pig. "I didn't see any such stuff. All I saw was some garbage, and not enough of that."

You might use that on Durant. In a debate it would be lovely.

I'm glad you met and enjoyed Dr. Williams,[2] the psychologist who liked Russia. . . .

And, by the way, I gave my barber my book; he lent it to a relation at the Naval Station at Goat Island in S. F. Harbor. Can't get it back. "All the officers are reading it and passing it around till it's a wreck."

I didn't expect to "get" Rolph with my test of his sense of humor. He isn't governor himself. In the Mooney matter the governor is Matt Sullivan.[3]

College of the Pacific asks me to address a conference at Pacific Grove next week of college men from California, Nevada, Arizona and New Mexico on Russian Communism and then lead a discussion. I'll do that all right. But the point is they want me to; and on that theme. The world *do* move. . . .

Carmel, Christmas Eve [1932]

Dear Peter:—

It *is* Christmas Eve. The tree is up and was lighted for supper. There were presents on it, but no fair touching, so Pete went to bed. Anna came up later with more presents that had been kept hidden in her room, addressed them, placed them and just as she and Leslie went off to bed, there was singing at the gate: a chorus chanting carols. Must have wakened Pete, for he came out of his bedroom, squinting and,—he saw the increased pile of gifts. But "no fair touching," and, slowly, he went back to bed. Now all is still in the house. . . .

I know why the Communists shy at the Technocrats. They can't

---

[1] In the *Saturday Evening Post;* published as *The Tragedy of Russia.*
[2] Frankwood E. Williams, author of *Russia, Youth and the Present Day World.*
[3] State Supreme Court Justice Matthew I. Sullivan.

say it, but I've got it "all by self." It isn't because Scott [1] is a paranoiac and has no degree, etc. It's because like the Socialists and the Fascists, they see something utterly wrong in Capitalism, but they haven't gone completely over. They'll propose the best they dare and do the best they can, but they don't expect, they don't intend to do the job. But look out: the Fascists want the Technocrats and the handling of Technocracy as the Hitlerites and the Fascists prefer to handle Socialism themselves. That's like the Churches handling Christianity. I tell you the idea of doing the job is the Communist virtue and that's what all the world fears, the whole compromising world. But I notice that some of the critics of Technocracy see and say it is Communism, and that's right. Technocracy is a scientific, unphilosophic criticism of mass machine industry and Capitalist finance which leads right up to Communism, which, alone, can deal with the emergency described and distribute mass production and mass leisure. I'm going to deal with it all in L. A., with the Communists there and with them in mind. I want them to grab and claim it. And, as in New York, they must learn to receive and select and drill the non-Labor recruits, but especially the unconscious technocrats, the educated, trained, expert technologists whom I have met, you remember.

Talk with Bob Minor about this. Remind him of what the railroad men, the controllers on the job there and in the telegraph, telephone, light and power services did at the turnover. They must stay on the job here too some day and, if cultivated now, will go all the way, some of them. Well, in this country they are more important and more numerous than in Russia. Dangerous, but essential to start with. . . .

Robin wasn't well, a cold, and so had given up or, anyhow, got out of flying to Mabel.[2] Una said the boys were disappointed; I could see she was. . . . She asked me why E. and S. disliked Mabel.

"Well," I said, "Mabel is all right to anyone she is winning, but to others she has won or doesn't want to win, she's not so nice, not nearly so nice. I've been both. Long ago when I was a key to Jack Reed, she was charming to me; now she is—herself. She hasn't picked on Erskine and Sara as good stuff for her, personally or professionally, so she does not shine to them. And when she isn't shining, she's a wet, cold, cloudy day." Una sat still and took it all in, thinking. . . .

Stef.

[1] Howard Scott, who put forward the technocratic theory.
[2] Mabel Dodge Luhan had invited the Jefferses to Taos.

Carmel, Sunday,
Jan. 22, 1933

Dear Peter:—

. . . One question that has to be answered about Russia is, "What will become of the spiritual in man if they start out with nothing but materialism?" I spit when they ask me that, or get mad. The implications enrage me. Why is it that the less intelligence people have the more spiritual they are? They seem to fill all the vacant, ignorant spaces in their heads with soul. Which explains how it is that the less knowledge they have, the more religion. But the only way my instinct has to meet them is with a good kick in the rump. One should have a sentence, one phrase that will get under their skin and make *them* mad. They are on the school board, too; and there they are for "reading, writing and 'rithmetic-materialists,"—only. And they wonder why we must have a red terror! . . .

Mabel and I have both got started inciting Una to begin her memoirs. Una recoils but I can see that she is tempted. Other poets' wives have done it so she would like to be regular. I asked her about her memory. She said it was good.

"Do you recall the date when you met me?"

"Oh, yes," she laughed. "And I know how important to us that was."

"All right," I said, "then you are all ready to write the life of Robin Jeffers."

She's awfully happy, these days. . . .

That marriage is the most perfect we know, and the best love story. We mustn't forget it when we think about marriage, love and the home under Capitalism. It checks many generalizations and some cynicisms. This comes out in Mabel's account,[1] but she doesn't say it; only shows it. But she made me think it. And I think very important to the whole picture that tears appeared in his eyes as Robin read Mabel's story. I'd like to give him a gossip of the hills that he could string his own romance on and so do it himself. A lonely drunk who ran off with a wife, who taught her to drink with him and who was taught by her not to drink too much. Mabel tells about the last time he "fell." Una woke up to find Robin gone. When he came back in the morning, she learned from him that he had walked all the way to Monterey, bought and drunk a bottle of whisky, and walked back.

[1] An unpublished story about the Jeffers family by Mabel Dodge Luhan.

Her behavior cured him; never again. Mabel says he cannot stand it to see Una suffer; as he can't see an animal or a bird suffer.

It's all very "instering," as Pete says, and Anna now, and pretty soon Betty Ann.

Seems to me I can see these two kids grow, especially Pete. He went canoeing with Kay in the river this A.M. He promised me that, if he got his feet or any part of his clothes wet, he'd come straight home. And he did. He came home long before Kay. "I stepped on the water, Daddy. You can see. So I came straight home. Isn't that keeping my word?" He glowed when I appreciated it, he glowed and changed all his clothes. "A square guy, no kid," I called him.

To Upton Sinclair

Carmel, January 22, 1933

Dear Upton:

You are a dear. Always looking for yourself in other men; and seeing what you look for. Here you are finding a prophet, a leader and a showman in William Fox. Well, he and I know that it's you who are the showman, leader and prophet. You, Upton, not Fox. He can't see the drama you see. He can't seize the opportunity you reach for. You have just written the man's life story and you show now that you've got him too great. You've got him as great as you are.

Some big man in Fox's class and rank will do what you want, the Napoleon you have created to go ahead and do, but it won't be Fox. Write him and tell him I said so. And he won't publish the story you have done of him.[1] And the story won't be true unless he does release it.

But I do love you and your size and your faith and,—and all that; as I love all your fiction.

To Ella Winter

The Getaway, Sunday,
Jan. 29, 1933

Dear Peter:—

Your good letter,—very, very interesting,—from Minneapolis was here when I got home last night. You were tired, but inspired and learning. . . .

[1] On Feb. 12 Steffens wrote Ella Winter: "Upton Sinclair writes that he is publishing himself the Fox book. No publisher would take the risk without some assurance from Fox, and Fox . . ."

My appearance in S. F. was a success, too. The meeting could not begin on time; the lines pouring in were so long. And then, when we started at 8:45, the Scottish Rite Hall was packed and, as in L. A., another crowd was turned away. Wm. C. Wood, Pres. of the Commonwealth Club, who was chairman, opened wittily but briefly, introducing Chester Rowell,[1] who was to tell what Technocracy is. He, like Wood,—all the speakers wondered at the size and interest of the audience, but Rowell told more of what Technocracy is not. He was too light, too contemptuous. Prof. Ira Cross [2] was better in that respect, but still inadequate; and very reactionary. (How he thinks he and I have so much in common, I can't imagine. Evidently the book got him.) John D. Barry claimed Technocracy for Socialism and was very outspoken about Socialism as the cure. And he rejoiced in the fear, curiosity, or whatever it was that made people think.

I came last, and stood for Communism as the cure, the only cure. But I, too, began with the audience, telling a story about the hansom cab horse who sat down, open mouth, at his sight of the first auto truck on Fifth Avenue. The whole hall laughed and laughed; I guess I made a picture. When the laughter ceased, I said the horse was scared; he shied; and ever after I have had my picture of him as a personification of the American people, who also shy at everything new. "So now," I said, "I'm going to do with you what we used to do with a horse that shied: walk you up and down before the terrifying new object." I gave and backed up the graphs, curves, findings of the Technocrats, said that ever since Marx we all knew what the scientists had reduced to figures and said that the time had come when, Capitalism failing, we must act. And like the Technocrats who examined the economic ground, we must look around for the tool, the weapon, the organization to lead us in action. I seemed to find and describe without naming it the Bolshevik, Communist Party. And that was funny. As I proceeded with my description of the organization that was set on *one* purpose, to wipe out the foundation of war, graft, tyranny,—everything,—the audience, foreseeing my destination, sat up, shook their heads, nudged one another and looked alarmed. I halted in the middle of a sentence and in the silence said:

"Yes, I am talking Communism, Bolshevik Communism."

[1] Editor and chief columnist of the San Francisco *Chronicle*.
[2] Professor of Economics at Berkeley.

The hall gasped. Individuals gasped. Allen and others in the audience said it was an audible shock. I went on driving it home that the Communist Party was the only organization that wanted to do the job. The Communists in the back of the hall were cheering, shutting up and cheering again, but the audience generally were backed down in their seats till they looked just like that cab horse, and, seeing it, I halted, walked off a few steps and said:

"Remember my cab horse?" And I dropped my jaw, stuck my two hands up for ears, flapping ears, till they saw the resemblance and my meaning. Then I said, "Fellow Americans, I greet you. Good night."

The house broke into a roar of laughter. It was evidently put. As I sat down they cheered and applauded till Wood signalled me to go and take a bow.

One can't plan a thing like that; and you can't count on it. It just happened to work. Laughing and hit, that crowd stood while Wood closed, saying with a laugh:

"Well, whether we found out what Technocracy is, we did have a good time."

The Communists, satisfied and relieved or expressed, stood apart to watch me put on my coat. The *Western Worker* wanted the text of it. Old radical friends came up to say it was my "best ever." Allen was proud. But all were laughing. They said nobody would ever forget my picture of the horse and its meaning to Americans. "And nobody in that audience will ever be afraid again to look at Communism." A restaurant man took a crowd of us to his place and gave us food and drink. That Standard Oil man was there with us; he's got something out of it. He's a conscious corporation manager who sees the owner now. He sees the use of his engineer's culture and methods in politics, education. When he bade me good-night at the Clift, he gripped my hand and said: "You're all right, all right." He and his wife and children are coming down some week-end soon.

You can talk to engineers, scientists, Technocrats! They have to get it. They can't tell us much, but, with their background, we can tell them. And this the Communists should know. They should not resist, but go after the T's and carry them farther, to action.

When are you coming home? Don't surprise us too much. Give us warning.

Stef.

You might come home to protect me from the Communists who pester me for appearances, all fundamentally important. They act as if they were glad that I'm not a Communist.

Carmel, Feb. 7, 1933

Dear Peter:—

A letter from J. B. enclosed one from a friend saying old Mrs. Mc-Namara is dead. J. B. didn't mention it, just sent the letter. I have written him recalling my meeting with her and her youngest in Cincinnati, when she said of Labor, "They can have my third boy, too, if he is needed." And I promised to go over pretty soon. I'd have gone last time I was in S. F. but Older couldn't. I like to go with him.

Calls all the time from the Communists, all sorts,—and from S. F. and New York. I have to ignore most of them. They bombard one and they never get enough.

R. was in today. Had seen some people from Sacramento, one stockholder in the bank who said it was pretty bad. They would pay depositors about 30 cents on the dollar. Which means the stockholders will have to pay back all the law calls for. I may be assessed for $25,000, twice the par of the stock. It gets on my nerves a little, more and more, in spite of the way I take it. I understand now better how my neighbors feel, with their similar losses, the Dickinsons, Jefferses, Luhans, Blackmans,—nobody talks much about it, but you feel it in the air, not so much as in S. F. and probably not anything like New York.

And yet that professor of banking, who was here, said No, when I asked him whether, if we passed all the *proposed* banking reform laws, we'd have banks as good as, say, Canada. I tell you nobody in the world *proposes* anything basic and real, except the Communists.

Stef.

The Getaway, Feb. 12, 1933

Dear Peter:—

Pete and I drove to the Older's this morning. We got there by 11:30, had a nice visit; lunch and drove home. There was a Princess there, a very nice, refined person, and she laid herself out to win Pete. He was seated next her at table, and he was polite enough, so far as I noticed. But on the way home, when I asked him how he liked the

Princess, he said he didn't at all and he broke out into a bit of perfect mimicry. He preferred Tony. He knows now what a princess is. And when he inquired if kings governed all countries, he listened attentively while I told him all about kings. The Princess helped a lot.

Dot writes frequently now, assuming that I am interested in our busted bank, and she encloses clippings and letters from her old Sacramento friends. There is no definite information in any of it, but it does look bad. But it doesn't worry me in the least. It's just one profit gone where they all ought to go and to hell with the cost,—to me. What do we care for losses,—we all have plenty of them. . . .

The Clift, San Francisco,
Feb. 16, 1933

Dear Peter:—

I'm in between dates, a call at San Quentin this morning and now, pretty soon, Allen will drive us to Napa to speak tonight.

Older wouldn't go over this A.M. because Holohan [1] wouldn't let us see Mooney. (His article about his prison life in the *Spectator* has closed him in again. And he didn't write that, couldn't, not his style or attitude.) So Allen and I went and saw J. B. and Matt. Both very well, very. And both *so* pleased with me; and you. (We're over so far left and going straight.) They told again about hearing my Mooney talk over the radio. J. B. must have been convinced that time (I forget) when I said I was about dead. For when I spoke that day, referred to "the hard-boiled Bolshevik minority that carried the revolution over" the edge; of "doing, not our best, but the job" and "then,— vote for Foster,"—J. B. exclaimed, "Why, the s. of a b. is not dead; he's come to life!" He and Matt wanted to send in "the free man," the head of the "Department of Education" who conducts schools, colleges, etc., and had debates and lectures. He and his wife have been carried away by my book. Well, he came, they left and he wants me to lecture to the prisoners (and J. B. does, too). Barry [2] does often. I said I would.

I called also for a boy named Balfour, a young musician in for forgery, who, J. B. says "got born" by the book, "the first time he ever saw anything." He is a worshipper, almost. Wants nothing but "litera-

[1] Warden James J. Holohan of San Quentin.
[2] John D. Barry.

ture." He spends all his time on music, playing in their band, and is making himself a master.

It was a sunny day, the best kind, a bright day after a rainy night. The bay, the hills,—everything alive and quiet and good.

You ought to write to J. B. He adores, he counts on you and wants nothing but what you give, a touch with the Movement. He knows all that you do, pretty near. J. J. wrote that he'd had a talk with you. "Ella," he calls you. And he always speaks fondly of "Pete."

I said to him that Pete always wants to come to see him. He loves that.

"You've got the boy all wrong on you, Jim," I said.

"How so?" he demanded, concerned.

"Oh, he thinks you're all right." He gripped my hand, so relieved. I must take Pete over next time.

Later I saw J. B. on patrol up in one of the cell houses and he called down some deprecatory remark. (We were "inside," just leaving the Education Department.) I called back, "Ah, don't be so damned snooty," and he got it, and laughed. They are very, very well. A pleasant visit.

To Mrs. A. Winter

The Getaway,
February 18, 1933

Dear Grandma:—

. . . Peter is still East, in New York. She has been out on a lecture tour as far west as Minneapolis and everywhere in between; and she has been making a real triumph of it. She talks on Russia, of course; the same stuff that's in her book; which is a good sign. The book will be out on March 16. I like it and I think it will go. But, like me, she talks better than she writes. She will come West soon on a talk tour. Her life sounds full, active, interesting.

Pete and I are hoping she will be home here a lot this summer, though this small community is not big enough for her. It wouldn't be for me if I were active. But I'm just sitting here in the sun, taking my (financial) losses and watching Pete grow and my book go. For that book still sells, you know. Nearly 100,000 now, and my mail is full of gratified letters. It's lucky it came along to earn some money just for the depression. . . .

Stef.

Our depression, I am happy to say, goes on deeper, heavier and shows no sign of a let-up. I do hope "It" comes. I'd rather have it now while Pete's a child so that he can go out into a decent world. Not this, not this!

Anna's baby is two years old and prettier than ever. Leslie, the father, an electrician out of a job, lives here. It's a very happy household.

To Ella Winter

Carmel, March 5, 1933

Dear Peter:—

Tony drove us, a long 18 miles—one hour—up to the top of the mountains. Hamilton Jeffers, like Robin, is taciturn; he retreated out of his house, and Una and Mabel spread our picnic supper on his floor, on a blanket. As soon as it was dark he came for us and took us to the big telescope which he fixed on the moon. Very disappointing. Showed high and plain one small region, a group of craters, and that's all. The 12-inch next made Mars look half as big as the moon, as we see it ordinarily, just a big star. I was disappointed because there appeared to be no taxpayers on either heavenly body.

My three talks [1] went over all right. The Press was a conversation, half an hour by me to start, than 1½ hours questions and answers, mostly, sitting down. The local and campus newspapermen, all the journalism faculty and other professors, the journalism classes and some literature (English). Everybody seemed pleased as I led them to see the changes coming in conditions, thought and press; from liberalism and why to the service of conscious propaganda either in a red fight or a Communist State,—to change human nature.

A big crowd at night, a couple of hundred expected, 700 there; students, profs., townspeople.

There were many questions, at least an hour.

The next morning with all and only Socialists I set out to describe Mensheviks and Bolsheviks on the theory that as I talked they, the students, would find themselves, be able to say to themselves: "I am a B." or "I am a M." And it worked out well. One Bolshevik, the rest Mensheviks. They asked why I couldn't talk of high-brows (intellectuals) and men of action, science, etc., so as to let men sort themselves. And maybe that could be done.

Stef.

[1] At Leland Stanford University.

Carmel, March 11, 1933

Dear Peter:—

No, I don't care to go to Einstein for an interview on Hitler; I might get one from that very simple old man. And, then, he'd never dare go back home. Another reason is that I'm not interested in what he'd say. He doesn't "get" politics, etc., at all. I know. The *New Masses* doesn't care about any of this, but I do.

Do you mean to say that the *N. M.* would like me to do a column; as a columnist? But, no, it would be no fun to have one in the *N. M.* Their readers are too intelligent. I love best to talk to my own class. They will all be gone some day, soon, and I shall so miss them.

Mrs. Geo. Boke[1] called today to settle it: am I running or no? She's a real person. How she does hate good people, reformers, talkers and writers. "Why doesn't somebody do something?" She said I was only confusing minds already confused. She said that if I'd really run I might be elected. And if I'd say I'd really tackle the school job[2] she'd be for me. She's for Pete, she said, Pete and the other kids, and no fooling. "I like fooling," she bursts, "I love extravaganza, but not about kids and schools."

I think that what's the matter with me is that I'm elated over the world news and my happiness comes out so often that it jars upon the already confused and depressed bears. I should think the *New Masses* would be printing all Christmas numbers, full of joy, victories and the good news. Why bother about Hitler when we have Roosevelt forming our dictatorship? The Germans made a fuss; not the Americans. I tell you we would rejoice and prosper in a Communist State. If only we knew it. And why can't we be told? Why must we always back into heaven only to get out of hell?

I'm getting the most emotional, suppressed gratitude from my hearers at Berkeley and Stanford. And I'm telling 'em, too.

Now I'll go at my pestiferous mail. A stenographer and I cut it down some yesterday, but I hate to dictate and paid her off to get rid of that form of work.

[1] A Carmel resident and wife of Prof. George Boke of the Law Department of Stanford University.

[2] Steffens was talking of campaigning for the trusteeship of the Sunset School: "My platform is to run the school for the kids; not the taxpayers. And my slogan is to take the fear out of the eyes of the teachers, the fear of the taxpayers who want to cut salaries and save. I propose to double teachers' wages and, then, see that the teachers are worth it."

To the Editor of the New York World-Telegram [1]

Carmel, March 30, 1933

Sir:

People who are incensed at the mishandling of Jews and Reds in Fascist Germany should remember that moral violence is of the very essence of Fascism. Fascism is not only counter-revolutionary; it is counter-historical, too. It takes all one's force to go against the stream, as Hitler goes and Mussolini went. Hitler has to seize upon every prejudice, every passion in sight to counter the natural, the economic currents that make for the ending of the capitalist system and the beginning of Communism. He may be sincere in his hatred of Jews; the Germans he needs with him are. Anti-Semitism existed as a force for him to use and he had to use it. A must it was. His sincerity only caused the gross excesses that arouse the world outside. The world should learn, however, that Fascism, threatened everywhere, will and must always behave this way. Communism had anti-Semitism in Russia; it is very strong, very widespread. And that they did not avail of it was, not because they are gentler than the Hitler Germans, but because they did not need it. On the contrary, they needed the Jews. They needed all peoples who could fall in with, help and function under the humanly understandable system called Communism.

It's too bad to miss in indignation, however just, the lesson Germany today is teaching: that Fascism will be fierce on Jews, Germans, Americans,—all economically civilized people. And that they will fit in with and be happily at home under Communism. It is not an outrage, it is a revelation that Fascist Germany is offering us.

To Ella Winter

Hotel Leopold,
Bellingham, Wash.,
April 2, 1933

Dear Peter:—

I haven't responded to the telegram asking from me a statement to be read at the big mass meeting, April 5. I can't. Every time I try it I say what I think. And that's no good for a crowd, a mob protest.

[1] The Committee for the Victims of Fascist Oppression in Germany, of which Ella Winter was at this time secretary, had asked Lincoln Steffens for a statement for the press.

It's not Hitler, it's Fascism that has to be met. The Jews are intelligent enough to see that Fascism is a movement of defense against economic forces that make for Communism. The Fascists haven't got history with them, they must depend on existing psychological forces of prejudice and passion. Hitler has two such that he can use,—anti-Semitism and anti-Red. Well, he cultivates, voices and puts in action both, and they form a wave he can ride on. Mounted upon them, loosing them recklessly, he can do other things that otherwise he could not do. We'll find in this country that something like it will be done. The passion here is against financiers; not Jews. But there is some anti-Semitism and, as Ford illustrated, a demagogue can mistake the hate of bankers for the hate of Jews.

The big thing to bring out is that the Jews have to see, like the rest of us, that the choice is between Fascism and Communism, between Russia and Germany.

But all this is not direct and obvious enough to proclaim to a mass meeting. They want to pit hate against hate. I can't help at that.

I'm having a quiet, restful, lone Sunday here. Bellingham is a mill town on a small plain on Puget Sound; it looks terribly depressed. The mills seem to have been in part demolished, or in disrepair. The people are working men and women; even the young boys and girls are big-limbed and powerful,—a pioneer community. At the Normal School where I speak, salaries and teachers have been cut; it was in the paper yesterday. I have no idea how they are taking it, whether they are meek or indignant, whether they are thinking, or merely feeling. I may enclose a "column" from the Vancouver *Sun* contrasting my little meeting there and the big Oxford Group meetings,—3,000-5,000 people, who are feeling and seeking comfort in the escape from facts and thought. They don't want me, but maybe these teachers and students do. We'll see tomorrow. I may get a line on them tonight when I see some representatives of the School to report and inquire. They've got me down for an address and I shall ask for a question period, of course.

You must know that you made a very deep impression on the many people who saw and heard you in Vancouver. Everybody I met spoke of you and in a way that made me sure it wasn't just politeness. They were explicit. Your looks, your energy, your clearness, readiness, grasp. And your clothes, too. I hope you don't neglect dress, don't affect the Red carelessness. Be and dress yourself. Communism will free taste and beauty some day; why not now? You, in a quiet way, can make the example that will set the pace for beauty, which is one form of that individuality which Communism will release, not suppress. Somebody has to see clear through the Communist era to art, literature, pleasure, as Lenin did to political anarchism. One can't preach it now, but you can *do* it. The idea that beauty, cleanliness, taste and play are bourgeois is absurd; understandable, but not sound. All the good things of life belong to—us. I think we should claim them, take them. Like technocracy—that was ours, as I put over to a start in Los Angeles. There was a gasp, then the Reds yelled with sudden surprised perception. It's the technocrats we were against,— as rulers. The machines and the men that run them under us,—they are ours.

A classless society of workers, well-to-do, and gifted with leisure, will be the best-dressed people in history. I can imagine the handy, open, easy, graceful clothes they will wear. Can't you? Talk to Filene about this; he has done some thinking about it. Says the mass can hire the best designers away from the idle rich, now. He did that once.

Some day I'm going to talk about art and literature in the New World. Along this same line, too.

But,—I recall,—you may not have an idle, empty Sunday to read this as I have had to write it. I'll shut up, adding only a repetition of my advice to you: not to feel pulled West when you want to stay East.

Stef.

Carmel, April 19, 1933

Dear Peter:—

. . . Your book is a beauty. Harcourt's part is well done, the book-making, I mean. Somebody put something into that that counts. Yes, and as I read into it I got a live, fresh impression of you and the new way of living. It's a volume, I think, that will be taken by anyone who opens and flutters the leaves, a dip or two and you want more. So much one wants to know is there. I hope it sells, but I pray that it may be read.

But you must not become so nervous, emotional, excited, about the breach between the truth about what Russia is and the picture people keep in their heads. Your letters, I am referring to now. Read your own book and you'll understand that people can't be expected to "get" all that. It's too much, too new. And your unrealistic feelings about it will make you sick and useless if you don't look out. I do wish you'd come home and stay a while. The world is moving fast, faster than I ever expected it to, and you should sense that and let it re-assure you. It's no use saying this to you. All that will help at all is to come here and rest.

Phil and Bob La Follette cannot,—I mean *cannot,*—understand Russia. I "got" that that last interview I had with Mrs. La Follette and young Bob. Our ways had parted. The Progressives want progress.

Yes. Women are one of the minorities that Russia has really freed, and American women should be persuaded or charmed to imagine what it means to women to be freed. "Economic independence" is a phrase to be filled out for them. And you can do it.

Mabel Luhan delivered here yesterday those hand-made cowboy boots for Pete, beauties, but they are too small. Pete tugged in despera-tion to get them on and so keep them, but no use. He couldn't get them on. So Mabel called this morning to take and return them.

Did you ask Felix Frankfurter if President R. is going to recognize Russia? He'll blow up pretty soon, Roosevelt will; I hope he gets that gesture made before the end. They want it so, the Russians.

Sir John Simon, acting in self-defence in office, illustrates what I mean by the English being more corrupt than we are; the English take *that*. We'd laugh and kick. . . .

There's one petty, personal relief in our "off gold." Ever since I spoke at Berkeley two or three years ago, predicting we'd follow England off gold, some guy has been asking me 2 or 3 times a year, "when?" Now he'll shut up.

Stef.

To Mrs. Gilbert E. Roe

The Getaway, April 30, '33

Dear Mrs. Roe:—

. . . Your first letter seemed more like a call to me than a letter, as if you had had a throwback to old times. I'd have liked to go to see you. I'd like to go right now. We have so much in common, you and I: people and experiences and ideas. I feel like writing a letter to call you. Nobody around here remembers any of the things I remember; other things but not ours. And the world is swinging so far off our old course. Do you remember, for example, liberty? Gone, all gone. Everybody's against it. I practise it once in a while, make a free speech, and it's always so astonishing, both to audience and to me. As if the young people there turned to one another to ask: "Liberty! What's that?" And usually I, too, talk for Communism. For the Communists don't practise or grant, but they are laying a foundation for, liberty as well as for food, shelter and clothing. How I would like to sit down and talk it all over with Gil! He'd understand, I know. He'd see the difference between Stalin and Hitler, between Stalin and Mussolini. But, then, you would, too.

Mrs. Fairbanks' enthusiastic letter recalls the day when it was Mexico I knew and cared about. Now it's Russia. I still see Mexicans, the old revolutionists who are in office and in power, and, as they talk, now, I ponder impolitely the story of the men who started out fighting and ending by winning,—what? The fight's the thing. Victories are ashes. My Mexican winners stop, shocked, when I say to them: "But the Americans, the U. S. are friendly with you now, and satisfied, as you are. What does that mean? What's wrong in Mexico?" They look guilty.

But, never mind, there is Russia where the Bolsheviki did not take to themselves the properties they confiscated; they abolished all private titles. So they are not victors as the Mexicans are.

My concern is no longer personal and passionate; it is passionate, but for the children. I care what sort of world Pete's generation will have to live and fit in. Can't do anything about it. All I do is watch it moving in my daily paper and then look down at Pete at play on the floor. My life is very quiet, sitting in the sun or fog, like a bum in the gallery at a theatre, but with a good play going on way down below on the stage, a play that I think I can understand. You,—in that phrase about the attic at the farm,—you seem to be seeing a play too. How I would like to see you seeing it. Whatever you conclude as to writing letters, you certainly used the last two to me, for an effective purpose. You recalled our love for each other; yes, love.

To Ella Winter

Carmel, May, 1933

Dear Peter,

B. C. called yesterday P.M. He is a tall, handsome young Wall Street man who says he belongs to a group of such fellows who are going left by repulsion from what they see and hear of High Finance—in their business. He heard me at Greene's. He goes along as far as I do, except that he can't,—and they can't,—stand the Communists. What should they do? I suggested that he and his bunch go on and take Communism; get it, study it, understand it in the originals, and then *follow* the Party. Why not be glad there was a front rank of shock troops to go out and do what they would not do: make hopeless attacks, get their heads busted and lead while the leading was so dull, hard and unromantic—from their point of view? Then, when the time came, they could move up front, too. He liked that and said he would take it to New York.

But I found myself dealing with a Party problem. Evidently there are many, very many Americans, petit bourgeois Lefts, who have looked at and shied off from the Party. They can be got, they must be got, and I, we are really, but unconsciously, finding ways to "get" them.

I told B. C. my question and answer:

"But, Mr. S., aren't the Communists—er—all—aren't they rather—?"

"Yes, they are. They always remind me of that little bunch of publicans, sinners, fishermen who followed Jesus around. I don't know just why, but big, fundamental, revolutionary ideas always come from the unrespectable bottom of society; never from respectable people."

I had a nice quiet talk with Allen Griffin today on a drive to his place and back, about an hour. I urged him to know, to be conscious that he was a Fascist; that Roosevelt was no Hitler, but that we'd get one from such thinking as his, Griffin's. It hurt, but he didn't resist much. It was a shock, but he was most disturbed, I gathered, at being caught unaware of the drift of his innocent course. I advised him, first, to know where he was going; and, second, to get clear on and make clear the choice we had,—to limit production (Fascist) or to accept and distribute a-plenty (Communist). He drove away very thoughtful.

I find it best to argue, not for Communism, but for awareness. "Don't be an unconscious dub." Nobody wants to be that, and the alternative vista of dividing an abundance stalls everybody.

. . . A pro-Russia, pro-Communism book is the one that's needed now. I'd like to write it myself. Wish I had up-to-date stuff. I'd make a thriller, not an objective line in it, just a proclamation that Russia had found the way for America. *And* people want it, the book I mean.

They won't, they can't, take Communism, but lots of them are willing to see it. Maybe this is the primer you have in mind. If so, we can do it together. . . .

Stef.

To Mabel Dodge Luhan

The Getaway,
May 15, 1933

Dear Mabel:

Yes, the boots fitted his foots, and not only that, they fitted his budding soul. (Vanity is the size of a male's soul, isn't it?) I think his only fault found with these beautiful gifts is that he can't wear them to bed. And even that's more our fault than the bootmaker's. For Pete would certainly sleep in them if we'd allow him to.

Thanks, Mabel.

Affectionately,
Stef.

To Allen Griffin

Carmel, June 18th, 1933

Dear Sir:

If you and President Roosevelt can frame or force the canners to act together in their own common interest, you and he and they will prove that capitalism can be made to work and that Communism is not inevitable. It's as big as that, this one more attempt to get the canners to govern themselves. History is against the experiment. The oil men, the sugar men,—all the big industrialists, have failed at it again and again. The oil men recently, in despair of themselves, asked the Federal Government to appoint an oil dictator, and the President, on to the business men, threatens to be or name a dictator for sardines. Two European countries, Italy and Germany, have set up dictators to force business men to conduct their big businesses in their own common, capitalist interest. And the other countries are going that same Fascist way. Ours, too. That's what President Roosevelt's threat to deal executively with the ruggedest ten percent of the competing individualists forecasts,—a Fascist dictatorship.

You show the *Herald's* good news sense when you pray for and report the negotiations of our canners. You are watching a local example of a world series of current history. But I think you should show your readers (and never yourself forget) that the economic set-up is typically against success. There is a standing pride that every American covets and that few of us can ignore, there is a profit and possibly riches, honor and "success" for the ten percent of the canners who can tie up the ninety percent in a perfectly reasonable gentle-men's agreement, and then, themselves, sneak through and bust it. We talk of the incentive of profit; it's our most precious working force. Well, that's what makes a canners' agreement and, indeed, capitalism impossible.

Yours pinkly,
Lincoln Steffens

To Whittaker Chambers

Carmel, June 18, 1933

My dear Whittaker Chambers:

My hat came off while I was reading today a story of yours.[1] How you can write! And your stuff—

Whenever I hear people talking about "proletarian art and litera-ture," I'm going to ask them to shut their minds and look at you. I hope you are very young, though I don't see how you can be. I hope, too, that you are daring, that you have no respect for the writers of my generation and that you know as well as I do that you can do it.

Now, I'll put on my hat again.

Yours sincerely,
Lincoln Steffens

To Franklin D. Roosevelt

The Getaway, Carmel,
July 15th, 1933

Dear Mr. President,

As the only confessed politician left in the world I ache to whisper to you the suggestion that a declaration of amnesty to all so-called political prisoners right now would clear like lightning the gathering clouds of labor conflict everywhere.

Wages are low. Little strikes are calling for raises. Every fruit and vegetable is having one. And they are needed,—by the bosses too,—

---

[1] "Our Comrade Munn," *New Masses,* Oct., 1931, or "Death of the Com-munists," *New Masses,* Dec., 1931.

because there is no other known way to raise the level of wages evenly on the mean, as well as the willing, employers.

But your rugged ten percent "get" the sheriffs, cops, courts against the berry and lettuce and pea pickers, and so win. And the present point is that they are winning by jailing the agitators for the period of the crop-picking. See?

Well, now, if you, Sir, would say by an act what I'm sure you mean, the gesture would be understood. Employers, and sheriffs, juries and judges would stop to think: "Oh, so that's what he means." That would halt the process of railroading the leading little workers to jail.

And the occasion is here: the Convention of State Governors here this month. With a bit of diplomacy you, Miss Perkins, I,—we politicians might persuade the governors assembled to join in the declaration of the New Deal for Labor, letting old prisoners of your day and mine go free and so discouraging too many arrests during the period of change just ahead of us.

Governor Rolph might rejoice in the excuse to get rid of Tom Mooney without passing upon the laws and justice of California. My old dynamiters, Matt Schmidt and J. B. McNamara, who have served twenty and twenty-three years, might go home to tell their stories. It would save faces in such cases as Scottsboro. It would take some fast work to complete the lists and lay them ready before the governors. But with you leading and taking the blame, if any, a general amnesty would put over the message. I seem to hear you calling all the time,—to lay off the fighting and fix things up some other, better way.

Anyhow, I offer my suggestion with the compliments of an old, unreformed politician to the man I think of as a poet in action.

Yours very respectfully,

Lincoln Steffens

To Robert G. Sproul [1]

Carmel, Sept. 29, 1933

Dear Mr. President,

I have been asked to speak at a meeting of the Social Problems Club called to protest certain acts of the University students and of city and

[1] President of the University of California. The Social Problems Club, composed largely of left-wing students, had been forbidden to meet on the campus.

upper: SARA BARD FIELD AND CHARLES ERSKINE SCOTT WOOD
(photo by Ansel Adams). *center:* "THE CATS," LOS GATOS, CALI-
FORNIA, HOME OF SARA BARD FIELD AND CHARLES ERSKINE
SCOTT WOOD. *lower:* FREMONT AND CORA OLDER AT THE
OLDER RANCH, CUPERTINO, CALIFORNIA.

county officials against the conduct of the Club, and I have consented, of course. But I would like also to make clear to you my attitude in this matter.

All my life I have urged students everywhere to think and discuss among themselves the social (and other, scientific) problems enough to develop an intelligent curiosity that might fit them to want what the faculties teach. One of the suggestions offered was to form Social Problems Clubs. Walter Lippmann and I started one years ago, at Harvard, and it did exactly what we hoped. And the Social Problems Club at Berkeley has begun to produce there a small but eager minority of students who are interested as much in the intellectual life as the main student body is in, say, sports.

I should like to encourage this nucleus of students to go on and learn to think some things that the majority of us do not think. But I should like, as an old student, to feel that in doing this I am working not against, but in sympathy with the policy of the University.

Why cannot this small but growing number of serious students have room right on the campus to look, now, at the problems they will have to deal with later in life?

I wish there had been a Social Problems Club at Berkeley in my day. It might have saved me years of fumbling. It would have provided something that was missing there when I was a young student.

Yours very respectfully,
Lincoln Steffens

To E. A. Filene

The Getaway,
October 14, 1933

Dear E. A.

Just home from Los Angeles. I can report that I rose to the occasion of the debate to the satisfaction of the crowd. Phil La Follette was fine: young, handsome, able, he showed that he had been thinking and exploring off his own bat and coming to his own conclusions. He was hindered only by the thought that, as an ex-governor and a future—something—he must not go far beyond his following. I, with no following to watch,—I had a great advantage. He said I abused it, some. "Stef can laugh at me and I can't make fun of him," he explained during the debate.

My handicap was that I would not play too freely with the son of my old friend, Bob La Follette.

A promising boy, Phil, all alive and eager, but the crowd was obviously looking for a leader in him, and he wanted to follow,—as they did. Why won't somebody go ahead and lead!

It did me good, physically, to have that debate, washed me up mentally and bodily. I can rise to emergencies still. In the meantime I took Pete to a Warner Bros. lot and let him see a movie scene in the making. As luck would have it, the scene was a monkey show, a lot of all sorts of monkeys playing hob with an abandoned dinner table. Pete enjoyed it.

Now, today, is Saturday, and I have Sunday for rest. On Monday I go to San Francisco to debate with Norman Thomas, the Socialist, that night. And the next afternoon I lecture at the University of Berkeley. Tuesday I fly to Sacramento to see the governor. Then home here. By that time I should be able to write definitely,—more or less,—to you.

Affectionately,

Lincoln Steffens

To Ella Winter

The Getaway,
Oct. 19, 1933

Dear Peter:—

Joe [1] and I set out to drive yesterday but at the Ferry we suddenly decided to fly. We went to the airport, got tickets to Sacramento and back, and soon were off to—the Capital. The Governor,—everybody was expecting us, because (for some reason I can't guess) Rolph had announced that I was coming to see him. Joe was amused; the reporters gathered about me and wanted to know what I wanted to see the Governor about. To stall them, I said I was making an investigation to determine whether Rolph had any sense of humor and we had a funny interview along that line till Rolph came out and called me in. He was most cordial; said so out loud as if he wanted the reporters, all delegations,—everybody to hear. Well, they all heard. Then we went into his private office alone. He asked me questions about the house, the Governor's mansion; [2] questions he said people were always asking him. But, no, they were mostly to determine

---

[1] His nephew, Joe Hollister.
[2] Joseph Steffens sold his house to the state; see *Autobiography*, 128.

whether and how long I had lived there. Funny! I was impatient of
this line of inquiry, didn't know much and hauled him back to the
strikes.

"Bad, you know," I said.

Yes, he knew.

I sketched it all as you know it, told him about the committees and,
finally, drew out the report (of last night). He read it. It's well
written, as I observed, and sure enough he read it again and very,
very attentively. I elaborated and rubbed it in. I said you and the
committees, and delegates from colleges, S. F., L. A. were gathering
down the valley to inspect. And I told him the difference between
going to see and just hearing about things.

"You ought to go and see; you, Governor."

"I can't," he said, pointing to his foot.

"Well, then, send for Chambers [1] and let him tell you. And hear
me." And I lifted up his failures, and the absurdities. I met his points:
failing to find or indict murderers "of our class" and indicting at
the same time "17 strikers." [1] He wiggled, uncomfortable. Then I advised the general amnesty, and a statesmanlike call on the finance
people to yield to the ranchers, so that the ranchers could yield to
the pickers.

He said: "You know you always tempt me. You make a fellow
think, but you ask things hard to do."

"Yes, hard for a man to do who has to consult. Not hard for a
Governor to do who acts off his own bat."

He called for a stenographer and had her mark an envelope with
my name, put the report in it and noted the names "Mooney, Billings,
Matt Schmidt, J. B. and Chambers."

I referred to the breach of contract with me in the McNamara case,
and said,

"Harry Chandler will verify this."

Then came a revelation that gratified me. The Governor said:

"Yes, Chandler did see me somewhere and he backed up all you
said."

Wasn't that white of Chandler?

But I must stop this now. I can only tell it. But the point is that, for

[1] Pat Chambers, one of the leaders of the cotton strike, who was jailed in
Tulare on a charge of criminal syndicalism. Three strikers had been killed by
rancher-vigilantes.

some reason, Rolph *is* really tempted to do something and, if an emergency arises, I think I can go up and get an act.

Joe and I, returning to the airport, got your car and drove home here in time for supper. Then Joe drove back to S. F. with your mail up-to-date. Let him tell you all he can, too.

Stef.

12 Otis Place,
Boston, November, 1933

Dear Peter:

Roger Babson and Coleman of the Forum came to dinner. Babson thinks that we'll change the price system and wind up with some sort of technocracy ultimately; Fascism and technocracy.

Babson said he saw Edison just before the old man died and his parting remark to Babson was: "And, remember, Babson, we don't know nothing about nothing."

Coleman said that the Communists are raising such hell about the Nazi meeting tomorrow that the owners of the building are demanding insurance for the one night and the rate is high too, $90. He showed me a leaflet by the John Reed Club. And there are others, too; handbills, postcards, threats. The Forum has had 2,000 letters of protest.

Niles, the head of the Forum, is amazed that while this protesting and anger and threats of mass pressure against him is going on, the same Communists came to him as a committee to ask him to pay the fine of a good Communist leader so that he can get out of jail in time to lead the mob. The Harvard men asked me to rationalize that on Monday, and I will use it, of course, to stress the difference between Liberalism and Communism.

Norman Thomas has a large liberal following around here. Of course. He is a liberal. And no liberal, no one at all that has any name has ever come out for Communism as I propose to do tomorrow. That must be done in New York too. Someone other than a party Communist has to appear to lead what I call the second line; some hundred percent American; as, I guess, Strachey does for the English.

I keep meeting my readers, mostly Youth, and I can see that they have wept over the pony[1] and are all broken up when I josh or make what they call cynical remarks. . . .

[1] See "A Miserable Merry Christmas," *Autobiography*, 17.

To William C. Bullitt[1]

Boston, November 25, 1933

Dear Bullitt:

I heard once (from Jack Black, the burglar) of a man who beat your record. He was after a guy who was in prison, so he had himself sent to the same prison, only to discover that his enemy wasn't there; he was in another prison. Your superior quietly served out his term, had himself convicted of another crime, and sent up to the right prison. There he learned that the man he was after had been transferred. Enough? No, sir! He finished that term and had himself carefully sent to the third prison where he found his man. And he killed,—he stabbed him.

However, I do congratulate and admire you, the second most persistent son-of-a-gun in my history. The third is probably Litvinov.

A good journey to you both.

Sincerely,
Lincoln Steffens

To Pete Steffens

Boston, Nov. 26, '33

Dear Pete:

You have had your ninth birthday. Turned the critical age of nine. Do you feel the difference? You must. There are a lot of your kid tastes that you should pass. No more stealing, no more lying; better table and other manners. For you have to clear the deck for ten. You will of course. I am not a bit worried.

My trip has been a surprise. No snow, no cold. Just a balmy East. But we'll soon get the weather of an Eastern winter, we are nearly through November, and December is the worst of winter.

I went to the Harvard-Yale football game yesterday. Harvard won by 19-6, and rejoiced because for two or three years Yale has always won. It was team-work that did it, team-work, discipline and skill. One big play was a long straight pass; one man passed to a second man who ran up to where it was prearranged that the ball was to go. Perfect. Another fine play is described in the papers as a nine-yard run, but I saw it and the point I noted was that the Harvard team,— the whole team, opened the clear way for their runner and blocked

[1] On the latter's appointment as the first American Ambassador to Soviet Russia.

the Yale players so that all their runner had to do was to run. See? It was the team, not the runner, that did it.

The papers, the crowds, like and praise the individual players, but football is great because it is the teams, not the individuals, who play it when it is well played. Each individual player has to be good, skillful, perfect, but perfect only as the part in a perfect machine, which is the ideal.

Give my love to Mama, Anna, Betty Ann, Leslie and keep a teeny weeny bit for a guy named Pete. And, oh, yes, if your friend Cagney is still there give him a hug for Pete's daddy.

Affectionately,
Stef.

To Ella Winter

Boston, Nov. 27, 1933

Dear Peter:

We all went last night to the Nazi meeting at Ford Hall which this morning's papers report as a riot or a street battle outside and a disorderly scene inside. Very disappointing! Very quiet! It's one of those events that must be seen, not imagined; the opposite of your strike experiences: less, not more. Our approach was through quiet lines of cops, holding back silent crowds. We got in through a side door to find the big hall packed up to the roof. An appeal for tolerance and free speech; then music; then the speaker, a soft-faced, smiling German professor, Schoenemann.[1] He made a slow, dull, utterly uninspired address, explaining as revolutionary all the atrocities, denying most of them, justifying the temporary mistreatment of "bad" Jews, extolling the "good" Jews. There were a few interruptions, and Coleman became indignant. The talk was really absurd or ignorant. The questions were sharp, definite, and,—evaded. There was some feeling created. There were Jews in the audience (E. A. for one) who had witnessed happenings in Germany, and they asked with suppressed emotion their penetrating questions.

Coleman and other Ford Hall directors came to Filene's afterwards and I asked Coleman if he was not aware that the time would soon come when free speech would be over and people would vent their feelings with force. He said, "Yes, but not yet."

[1] Professor Friedrich Schoenemann spoke at the Ford Hall forum on "Why I Believe in the Hitler Government."

This Liberty business is only for us now because we have not yet decided upon a course of action and so are "open-minded." When we go Nazi or Communist, we'll fight with intolerance. "Yes, but not yet."

I said and I think that his audience behaved unusually well. In a hot spot last night when the Communists and Jews were so mad at the speaker I happened to say that he was so dumb that I believed he was appointed, paid and sent over by Moscow to do the Hitlerites damage. Dennett of Harvard said he'd heard dozens quote the remark and get it and laugh. Roger Baldwin, for example, who was here but went right back to New York.

The thing I can do and that you should learn to do, is serenely to see, and say, and remind our crowd of the straight, "the correct," line. The Communists and Jews, instead of being so indignant at Schuman's evasions and weakness, should have rejoiced that the regular Nazi propagandist was,—what he is. And last night, when Coleman was so angry at the disorder and violations of free speech, was the time to remind them that better, more intolerant times are coming. It quieted Coleman so much to look ahead that he laughed and took my advice at parting. He was going to apologize for his meeting; at my tip he said he would brag about it.

I see Governor Rolph approves the San José lynching of the kidnappers.

Boston, Nov. 28, 1933

Dear Peter:

. . . I have made better speeches, but I've never had a greater success than at Harvard last night. The Liberal and Inquiry Club boys were surprised and hilarious. The big new hall was filled to the brim. "Never saw that before," said Dennison,[1] "and we could never have got them out." Professor Holcombe, who "requires my book," introduced me, saying he had already done so to hundreds of students. He told the story of my proposition to President Eliot and then he warned the students that I was the best, most dangerous high-power salesman in America. And to look out or they'd get some new ideas.

I urged the wide-open mind for half my time, then, suddenly

---

[1] Henry S. Dennison, president of the Dennison Manufacturing Company and member of many governmental-industrial bodies including the National Labor Board in 1934.

turned, and bade them close their minds, to act when the time came. And "the time" is upon us. I got them laughing at "grown-ups," told stories, made jokes (I was in fine fettle), but they were all serious, too, on the edge of their chairs. Holcombe said he never saw such a combination in a speech, of play and serious thinking. The Communists were satisfied down to the ground, for I came out straight for Communism, preferably Bolshevism. Warned them to know which they were. "Don't be like my governor, Rolph; don't be a Hitlerite and don't know it." I answered good questions for half an hour, quick, eager questions. Then Holcombe intervened for a pause to let the fellows go who had lectures or study hours, and they went on for three-quarters of an hour more. The cheering (actually) lasted for a minute at both halts. There is no doubt that I accomplished something, cleaned the whole atmosphere. Holcombe, closing for me, said to the students: "I warned you against this man, so you can't blame me. But there is one item I got myself. You might learn from Steffens that the way to put over what he did, is to be patient, graceful, tactful,—entertaining." . . .

New York,
Thanksgiving Day,
[November, 1933]

Dear Peter—

Awful; two days I've been here; seen lots of people but there are *so* many more to see, so much more to do. Seen: John Strachey, Kyle Crichton, W. E. (Bunk) Woodward, Max Lerner, the *Masses* editors, etc. But I missed Bullitt (and he 'phoned me, too) and, well, you know my list of people to see. I'm in despair about doing it all. Strachey is a big, black Englishman. He said people called him a Jew, and I declared he was. He denied it and I offered proof: "Your intelligence; there must have been a scandal in your damned family somewhere." He came to lunch with Kyle Crichton. I told him the Boston Forum wanted me to preside Sunday night. He wasn't afraid of me. I said I'd explain how he got by with his open Communism; I'd say it went because of his English accent, not because of his intelligence. And that was his theory too. I cited you. He knew you, had read your book; he had conned your book and told anecdotes out of it, which he loved. It's a secret that he may go West to California early next year. He and I (and Kyle Crichton too) got along like pals. He knew about and rejoiced in my campaign for Hoover, liked my (Fascist) view of Rolph; agreed with me that I might campaign for all the things we hate; Fascism, Hitler, New Capitalism,—he young and satiric, I Satanic. We have no one like Strachey in the movement over here and he has found no response like mine.

Harcourt wants a third volume on my Life. Feels the demand and sees in my talk that I've gone far beyond where the book ended. I said I'd think of it; but that I believed you'd have to do it, if it were ever done.

New York,
Thanksgiving Night,
[Nov., 1933]

Dear Peter:

Whittaker Chambers called up this morning; said he heard I would like to see him and offered to call. I suggested lunch here with me. He had been cheered by a copy he got of my letter to him. Really appreciated it because nobody had ever before given him a hand. "Not the other left writers, not the other men on the *Masses?*" I asked. He: "Never a word. We don't do that for one another." I said that that was a Red fault; there must be "warm spots." He agreed; he himself tries now to be one warm spot. But it was not the spirit of the Party. I said I got that at the *Masses* yesterday; they listened, but were unresponsive, and I thought, got or took nothing. "There you are wrong," he said. "They told me that they had had a very impressive, suggestive talk from you and that's why I am here; because they were so impressed, especially North."

The Jewish political editor of the *Frankfurter Zeitung* called on E. A.; recognized me, and said he had met me years ago when he was Washington correspondent. He could, but he didn't say much. E. A. quoted a letter from a German Jew who wrote at length how all was well in Germany and wound up, "As Elisa would confirm if she were not dead." And that was the point, the news that Elisa was dead. He didn't say how.

I had complained to Strachey that the third party movement was an old instinctive evasion always resorted to by Americans. He jumped at my remarks and said he had just written for the *Mercury* an article on that subject; he would send it me. He did. It is here in proof sheets. Awfully pat and timely. An English-American parallel. Good-night.

Dear Peter: New York, Dec. 1, 1933

A frightened letter from you, alarmed at the lynchings and the threats to workers, Communists, etc., and Pete. Take it easy. You are seeing a growing revolutionary spirit that is, so far, going wrong or right or Fascist. It will not soon come to a head. And, eventually, it will develop on our side and frighten the other people.

Now as to free speech for Nazis. If they have speakers like the one at Ford Hall, I say the more they appear the better. And, anyhow, logically, Hays is right. So long as we appeal to the law, Constitution and bunk, as we do, the other side will and indeed has a right to. But we know it's the bunk. We know there is no guarantee of free speech and we talk it because that is all the enemy responds to, ex-cept, of course—. Your real reason is that you are using the enemy's weapon in the class struggle. You are against the Nazis because they are against Communism. You can't say that, but it is the fact. All you can say is illogical, however true. You *know* that their propaganda is deliberate lies. They only *think* that our propaganda for Russia is false.

As you know, I've long condemned logic, liberty, and all the Capitalist abstractions, in public and in private. We have other premises. We want first to lay a basis upon which liberty can exist. We want, first, to establish the premises from which we may some day reason.

Telephone: Taub. . . . He probably has Scottsboro news and wants a statement. Yes, he had a verdict; all to die in the chair. I made a short statement: "Too, too bad. Not unexpected. Natural. Part of the general violence all over the country, down South, out West, everywhere. Fascism, you know." He wants a press conference tomor-row morning. Good-night, Peter.

                                                     Stef.

To E. A. Filene
                                    New York, Sunday, Dec. 2, 1933
Dear E. A.

I'm all up in the air again. But for a good reason. I've found an-other man who can do our job, I think. He is Robert Cantwell, a young novelist, who is on the *New Republic*. He has just finished his second novel; his first, two-three years ago, I have,—*Laugh and Lie Down*. And he sees your life as a story, sees it, I mean, with imagination. I have a strong hunch for him.

I sent him off yesterday to think it over. I wanted to reflect myself and I must see others,—publishers, editors, writers,—who know him. There's no hurry, of course. Perhaps I'd better invite him to Boston to see and be seen by you.

He's an attractive boy, blond and clean and winning. He has a wife and a young baby. He comes out of the West; from the state of Washington. When I showed my list to Malcolm Cowley, he said: "Not, not Cantwell. We want him here and he's doing his proper work, fiction."

A day or two more and I'll return to Otis Place.

Stef.

To Ella Winter

Hotel Sherman,
Chicago,
Dec. 11, 1933

Dear Peter:—

Young Robert Cantwell travelled with me on the Century from Boston to Springfield and, when he left the train, he said with confidence and some enthusiasm: "I'll do your book." And I think he will and I told Filene so today when I wrote.

My Rotary address today was a whirl of a success. 800 present; with some of my (our) friends there: Darrow, Fay Lewis, his niece and her husband, the Johannsens. Darrow said it was the best he ever heard from me. Margaret was delighted. But they all liked it. And it took the Rotarians by storm. I had the microphone removed and everybody heard me. Darrow said: "I thought you always dropped your voice as I do; you didn't today." I wasn't very radical, left that for tomorrow, when I meet the picked Rotarians and business men for a conversation. Darrow, Lewis, Jim McGill and a few of my friends will be there to help.

What I seem to have done here (besides earn $200) is to make the Rotarians feel that radicals have something to say and can get you to hear it, face it, without being an offence. "Now," said Fay Lewis, "they will hear others." And I heard the committee asking Darrow, who had never spoken to this crowd. Also I sold (and signed) about 30 books. . . .

Something has happened,—is happening to my left leg. It weakens and gives me a terrifying tendency to go left. I have to hold on to somebody. I'm hoping it will pass, but I've had it two days and it gets worse, not better. . . .

Sam Blythe was here today on his way home. He has been reporting Washington for 3 months on the *Sat. Eve. Post.* He says Frankfurter and Brandeis are the real power behind Roosevelt: pick the brain trust and the policies. Brandeis! No wonder. And Frankfurter! Not very radical. But it will be well for you to know it. You can write to Felix, some time. Might get an angle from which to move for Mooney. We'll see.

There. Good-night.

Stef.

To Marie Howe

The Getaway,
January 17, 1934

Dear Marie:—

You are the best of letter-writers. Ever hear that before? Well, I don't care if you have. You give,—I guess you can't help giving,—a perfect portrait of yourself and the background of your life and the world. I ought to answer in kind, but I can't now. I am forbidden to by the doctor and I don't feel myself to be able to.

I'm allowed "up" for a couple of hours a day. That's progress for me as one more boom would be for the U. S. But it doesn't mean much in either of our cases. My orders are, when up, to go out in the air and sunshine, but no change of air will do my job. Or Fred's.

But I must not go on with this. I'm tired. I've been up too long, I guess. I'll just post this and try again. I kindo' hope this will bring another letter from you.

Affectionately,
Steffens

To Governor James J. Rolph

Carmel, Feb. 2, 1934

Dear Governor:

Pursuant of my unpromising experimental probing for humor in high places, I am going to ask you to contribute personally a dollar

or so toward a fund to buy a typewriter for Caroline Decker,[1] the tiny
little labor agitator who is doing what no big A. F. of L. leader
has ever dared undertake; to organize the migratory workers of the
lovely orchards and vegetable ranches of California. You remember
her! She is the so-called amazon who led the workers in their well-
led strikes for a living wage in the valleys last year. She has to carry
on the struggle this year, and next year, and the next. She thinks she
can make consumers, citizens, and human beings out of these peon
producers. An audacious experiment, as dubious as mine, and therefore worth boosting. But she hasn't even a typewriter to make clear
to us and to the workers, the strategic plans she draws.

Let's help her to a machine. I will if you will. You might induce
some of the impartial police, personally, to join us; Chief Cato, for
example. I may ask some picked ranchers to come in on it and your
Mr. Secretary Smith could invite the highbrow newspapermen he
sees daily. They might have a sense of humor.

If the fund should exceed the price of one cheap typewriter I'll keep
the difference for the purchase of another if the first one should be
wrecked in some righteous raid.

Yours solemnly,
Lincoln Steffens
Chairman, Secretary and Treasurer
Caroline Decker Typewriter Fund.

To Louis Oneal[2]

The Getaway,
Feb. 9, 1934

Dear Mr. Oneal:

It's all right, of course. I realized when I wrote to you that it would
take a sense of humor to do what I asked. And humor is always inconsistent. But doggonit, I thought you had it; inconsistent humor,
I mean. And I still think you have it. That ten dollar incident with
the young man who called you a menace is evidence on my side. I'll
suggest another bit of evidence.

I suggest that you ask each of your clients on the wrong side of
the class war to pony up a dollar for the typewriter on the right,—

[1] Secretary of the Cannery and Agricultural Workers Industrial Union and
at that time leading fruit pickers' strikes in California.
[2] Political boss of San José. After first refusing, Oneal sent $10.

I mean the left side. I'll tell you a story to illustrate the psychology of the conspiracy I'm trying to draw you into.

Mark Hanna was once paying out money to his workers on election day. As the file was passing through his office, one of. his lieutenants rushed in and whispered to him: "Look out, Mark. There are some workers on the other side in this line." Hanna hesitated, reflected a moment, then decided and smiled: "Oh, well," he said, "let 'em come. If they take my money, they can't fight me quite so—blank-blank hard."

See? Mark Hanna had what we have, you and I; he had humor, not consistency.

If your ranchers help buy that typewriter, they'll hate to see it smashed; they'll hate to think that we are just consistent enough, you and I, to ask them next year to replace the wantonly destroyed machine gun.

And, Mr. Oneal, you understand, don't you, that my gay persistence is due to pride in my judgment of character. I can give up the dollar, but not my hope, not my faith in your humor. We are so few, we humorists; we must hang together. Can't you see how indignantly Caroline Decker's red head and snappy eyes will express her rage at receiving her weapon from the despised enemy?

Yours anyhow,
Lincoln Steffens

To Robert Cantwell

The Getaway,
March 2, 1934

Dear Cantwell:—

Two errors (or sins) I observe. Your letters of apology are so good: so exhaustive, particular and interesting; they must be taking it out of the book. Ella Winter reads them for fun and for revelation! That's No. 1. The second sin (or error) I recognize because I've used it like a vice. You say that some day you are going to write a novel about all this. Terrible! What do you think you are doing now? I think you are writing a novel now. You ought to think not only the same but that you are engaged upon the only work you ever have or ever are going to do. This saying you are some day going, etc., is a sneaking trick to get out of doing what you are doing. It's conscience,

Catholic conscience; an indulgence before the crime. And that's against my principles. I don't stand for it. See?

I'm keeping your wonderful letters. Peter and I are noting great scenes and passages, and, if you leave them out of "our" book, "we" (the editor) will order them in. "The two old men,"—for example. That belongs.

And, generally speaking, "we" are not talking about a modern (fact) novel, we are writing one,—now; not some time. Now.

Funny boy, you are. Ella Winter looks up from your letters to exclaim: "Wonderful!" or "I like, I do like Cantwell," and so do I. But you are not, to me, a promising writer; you are a writer writing. And the Thing you are writing is the great, modern, American novel,—now.

Perhaps it's misleading to call it a novel. Let's call it a book into which everything true, picturesque, sad, funny, wise, tragic, etc., goes, leaving it to the critics to name it. We'll have no traffic with categories like fiction, biography, poetry and such. We are just telling something.

Am I clear? Are you?

Ella Winter is in San Francisco. She has just put over a swell show for the Scottsboro kids and made money; selling MSS., drawings by artists from all over the world. James Cagney was auctioneer. He sold about half of 200 items and took in $1,400.

Jo and Yvonne Davidson are coming down with her today.

Affectionately,
Steffens

To Mrs. Gilbert E. Roe

The Getaway,
March 9, 1934

Dear Mrs. Roe:—

Thank you for a thoughtful letter. Fred wired, and today I have a letter from him. So I have a complete picture of our Marie's quiet,[1] victorious end, the week before, the week after and how Fred and you and all of us take it. And I tell you, as I do Fred, that it's all right. Marie went as she wanted to go. She said so, but I did not need her say-so to know that. I knew her, you know.

I don't want to write more now.

[1] Marie Howe died suddenly March 1, 1934.

Except, of course, to say unnecessarily to you that I appreciate your thought of me at this time.

Affectionately,
Steffens

To E. A. Filene

The Getaway,
March 13, 1934

Dear E. A.,

Do you happen to know who sent Pete an alarm clock which has been going off ever since? It came in a box. Pete opened the fascinating parcel and lifted out the clock with a wild exclamation of, —something; joy, I guess. He examined it with tenderness, made stunning discoveries: "Three Little—!" "The Big, Bad Wolf!" "The Wolf's bites make the ticks!!"—A *succès d'estime!* So far, so good. But Pete discovered also how the alarm worked; he proved it, and then he went off ahead of time to bed. Why? He had set the alarm for 9 P.M., an hour after bed-time, and had to sit up himself because he knew what was coming. And it came, therefore, not when he was asleep. He set it again for getting up time,—7:30 A.M. Since he could not sleep with the event impending, Peter moved it. He slept, sadly, wronged, but it was left set for 7:30 A.M., so he was up and out in the living-room, to see it go. He saw it; he got pretty cold waiting, but it did go. He set it for the hour he had to go to school. It went, so Pete got to school in time. But he set the clock for the hour he'd get home,—4 P.M.; he set it for his music hour; then for his bath hour. All to the good. And again he wanted to sleep with it. There was mighty maneuvering for beds,—to get where he could be wakened by the clock. I helped, so we managed to sleep in range and he set the clock for 6:30 A.M., so as to be sure to be sound asleep when the Wolf called. A kid *does* like to experience the real thing. But doggone it, knowing the clock would explode at 6:30, he woke up at 6 A.M. and sat freezing in its face till—

It's been so ever since that blooming clock got here. And the whole school is excited about it. Pete's class sent a committee of nine down to the house one afternoon to find out if it was true that it would go off at 4 P.M. It did, and Pete is not a liar; he is a proud and exceptional guy. But he isn't very well; hasn't slept well for days; has had his first headache; and has a continuous war with his mother, a war which goes on forever, even through peace, like the one in Europe, Asia and the Americas.

Hence my question: Who sent Pete that Big, Bad Wolf?

Something about it makes me suspect a big guy, a grown-up, who loves toys and actually goes shopping for them.

I have your Washington letter with the good but incomplete report on the state of the N.R.A. and of the country, showing that some business men haven't yet learned even that the A. F. of L. is an employers' organization and that there is no Communist Party or Union.

Yours affectionately,
Stef.

The Getaway,
April 1, 1934.

Dear E. A.

Why don't you send us the bill for that typewriter for Caroline Decker? She has it. She "adores" it, as Pete does his. She won't let anybody else touch it. I guessed that she was keeping it in good shape for the next raid by the Chamber of Commerce and the Law-and-Orderlies.

Jo Davidson has been here with a photo of his Roosevelt, and I sent it to the *Peninsula Herald* with a tip that there was news in the jaw of that bust: It shows much more strength than I had any previous sign of. I challenged it, as an exaggeration. Jo answered me by signing the photo to me inscribed: "He is like that." Well, we'll see. So far the President has tight-roped along between you and Kirstein,[1] balancing, avoiding a decision. And Jo says he's a man of decision. He is taking his time; give him all he wants, but I tell you that I doubt his power to decide, or, if he does, the Kirsteins will win.

I'm going more and more to the Left myself. A class of business men who cannot see that the A. F. of L. is their best weapon, can't run business. They have spies; don't the spies tell them that Green & Co. are enemies of labor? Mine do, and I was with them in their darkest days, too. I have met A. F. of L. leaders who do not forget that I saw them through their degenerating chapter, and they admit that I am still loyal, I am; and that they are not.

[1] L. E. Kirstein, Vice President of William Filene's Sons Co. since 1911.

To Robert Cantwell

Carmel, April 8, 1934

Dear Biographer:—

The impression grows upon me that you are writing this biography out of as much pains, agony and doubt as I put into an autobiography. Each letter of yours piles up stuff to pile on that profound impression. Ella Winter says heartlessly, "Oh, what of it? Suppose there never is another such work of fiction. You are getting some dandy letters." She, however, is one of the unscrupulous kind to which you and I do not belong. We care; we take, and we carry responsibilities, like the Great Man we are to pluck from God's hand to turn into a Work of Art. She, said same Ella Winter, she said she had half a mind to write you herself to lift some of your problems and I didn't want that, so I'll try my hand at easing the burden at one point that I think I eased before. My reasons are better than hers.

She says you need not hurry to rush out here because, she argues, she is just finishing a book as novel as yours; it's all about her own experiences in the agricultural strikes. And, to come to the point, she wants me to be free to edit that. She is not jealous of you, but very tolerant of your devotion to the research out there. Also she seems to know, as I only intend, that I am not going to write the book with you, your book. I'm only going to be the first person to enjoy it. She never thinks that there is any haste to give me enjoyments.

Pete can articulate the principles involved. A teacher in his school says that one day, when she asked him something personal, he replied:

"My daddy, you know, is down on happiness. He forbids anybody to laugh in our house and garden. We are supposed to go to school or some other asylum for anything like that."

No. Take your time. And, I suppose, Ella Winter would add "Don't take our time." In a word: come when you are jolly well ready to come.

It's Sunday afternoon, the sun is out, so is the whole family. I must get out. So long.

Steffens

I'll write to E. A. about his disappointment in Washington.

To E. A. Filene

The Getaway,
April 19, 1934

Dear Captain:

Or, do you hire a skipper to navigate your blooming boat?

Anyhow, it's a success, that boat on your post-card. It makes your friends envy you, if that's what you want. Even I contemplated it a moment with green in my eye. "The son of a gun!" I muttered to my meanest self, "has a helluva good time when he doesn't deserve it." So I thought thoughtlessly and then I read the writing on the card and rewrote my mind thoughtfully, comfortingly. "I see," I said, "he isn't having any fun. He thinks he ought to be navigating the U. S. A., not a mere tug! Thinks his home-crew, conspiring in mutiny, got him off there to let the world enjoy itself."

From my ivory tower here, I can see that this world is going its own fool way, not yours, not Roosevelt's, not Tugwell's, not even mine. And I suspect or expect that said world has more to teach all of us than all of us have to teach the world,—even I. To say nothing of you. F. D. R. has enough of the world in him to teach you,—something. He is going Right; and I don't mean right. I mean wrong. As we would in his spot.

You-all look to me from this distance like a lot of boys on a chip in the river. You are talking more or less,—about which way to go and don't notice that the river is carrying you, all the while, down to the sea. And I laugh. Not a bit sympathetic.

For I know that you won't take the chance you have on that anchored boat to look back at Washington, New York, Roosevelt, Kirstein and A. L. to see and learn and change,—your mind, not the world, but your funny mind, and Roosevelt's and,—I tell you that you can detect a direction. You can't tell what's right and wrong, but you can see where we're going,—if we don't look out. It's difficult to do this on the chip in the river,—but from way off in Canada or Florida or from the bank of the river you can see the stream, the current, even the eddies.

Why don't you come out here with Cantwell, take a nice little house near us, and,—as the Chinese say,—"look see."

I've been put to bed again for a week, but only to catch my breath. Love to all you unlovables.

Stef.

Carmel, April 26, 1934

Dear E. A.

I've just got from the publishers, Farrar & Rinehart, Cantwell's new novel, *The Land of Plenty*. And it's really new, not only *his* new novel, but a new sort of fiction. You must read it. That boy will go far. It's a fiction report of a strike, without a hero and without a villain. Or, let's say, with a lot of heroes,—none very heroic, and a lot of villains, all pretty ordinary. Like his *Laugh and Lie Down* it will be greeted as an event in literature, as a step forward to the kind of fiction we are coming to. That boy is, in his line, what you are in yours: a leader. I am delighted with it and with him.

Tell Mama[1] to be sure to read it right away, and write to me. She is living with some great men and she might as well know it. I wish she'd keep a diary or make some notes. She could write a book some day on, say, "My Sufferings with the Great." I wouldn't mind if she rung me in on it, and, for contrast, Glenn Frank. But, of course, you and your Boswell would be the real Things.

But,—to get back to *The Land of Plenty,*—notice Cantwell's mastery of detail; how he gives you confusion of a mob movement; how he keeps big tragedies down on the level of actuality; shoots your characters without effort,—there's great writing in this plain, unusual book. It makes me sure of the biography, which will be such a different thing.

You needn't tell him; keep him down; but he's a great guy. As you are. Two great guys will certainly make a great book. And, if two can't, we'll add a third, the greatest of all—

Yours affectionately,

Stef.

To Sam Darcy[2]

Carmel, April 28th, 1934

Dear Darcy,

Your letter, reporting the Committee's unexpected conditional decision,[3] was here this morning and I wired for your convenience at

[1] Lillian Schoedler, Filene's private secretary.

[2] District Organizer of the Communist Party in California.

[3] Steffens had been asked to run for the office of U. S. senator by the state party organization, but the circumstances were such that he would have had to run as a member of the Communist Party. See Steffens's statement for the party rally, Appendix VI, p. 1050.

once as follows: "For reasons I am writing I will have to say definitely no with regret and appreciation."

My appreciation is of the judgment that I am fit for party membership. As a lifelong liberal, with liberal instincts and habits of mind, I had not thought I was up to that. And I still doubt it. Too many of my kind and class have had to get out after being in. Party Communism is really a matter of class or of intense discipline over a long period; not of goodwill and fresh insight.

I could quote you something Lenin once said to me along this line, something that has served me ever since as a light in dark places. But I'll stick now to my reason for declining an honor.

As a liberal bourgeois I have come to see not only that the Communist Party is the only organisation in existence that really wants to deal with our situation in *all* its phases, but I see also, as few liberals do, that the workers and peasants, the dispossessed who have no privileges to lose, the proletariat and their very own leaders, must lead, control, and carry through this program. Liberals and all others have and always will rest and compromise before the hard, long job is finished. We liberals must not have power, not ever; we must not be leaders, we must not be allowed to be parties in the leadership. Too much to lose, besides our chains, which we are too used to.

The liberals, all privileged persons, and all the associates of the privileged, belong in the second line,—when their eyes are opened. And this goes for me. See? I am not doubting others; I am doubting me. I think that I am not to be trusted in the party or in the front rank of the struggle that is on. I know it, and that's what I'd like to say conspicuously at this critical stage of our common history; that it's true: we, who have fitted successfully into the old culture, are to the very degree of our education and adjustment,—we are corrupted and unfit for,—the kingdom of heaven.

You Communists say it. I also say it, see it, believe it and,—I am clear,—I must act upon it.

I would take a position from which I can labor this point, and illustrate it, but I will not go into your organised party leadership, not even formally. I will back, I will not pretend to captain Labor. No. Labor must do it. Tell 'em that with my compliments.

Your very humble and obedient comrade,

Lincoln Steffens

To E. A. Filene

Carmel, May 9, 1934

Dear E. A.,

   Your letter of April 30 is here and you ask me in it the question which you are asking yourself: What exactly ought to be done in Washington? You didn't ask me that, did you? I could answer it but you would despise me for undertaking to do what the President himself is only trying to do. As I watch him here from my bed, and you, it seems to me that you are trying to persuade a lot of hogs to eat decently out of the trough, with their snouts, without getting in with all their four feet. And you can't seem to put it over on them. The Chamber of Commerce doesn't know what you're talking about, either of you. Of course not. They have always been in the habit of getting their food in a certain way and they don't understand how otherwise to get it.

   Let's put it this way: The President has devised a plan to save them from themselves and proceed to do business in their long range interests. Voluntarily. He wants them to do it of themselves. He has said that if they cannot do it thus voluntarily of themselves he may have to apply compulsion. Their conduct is such that, viewing it from here, one would think that they wanted him to use force. And I think he'll have to. He dreads it. Evidently he sees that that means Fascism. And it does.

   But, just the same, I think he will have to enforce the codes.

   I think your job is to understand this very sympathetically but with a very wide-open mind which never should forget that the President himself calls it experimenting. So go ahead and experiment but don't let the failure of an experiment break your funny heart. And do not be impatient with us radicals because we hold up the real test of the experiment. We do know, better than you, the power of old business in the executive, legislative, the judicial, the police and the social department of the real government. I, for example, don't believe you can make the old system work at all. But I'm very sympathetic with your experiments, your attempts to make it go.

   What amuses me most, however, is the dramatic situation: The President is trying also to maneuver a revival of business. Every time business gets a little better I observe that business men become a little more cocky and impossible. Every time, in other words, you put a little more feed in the trough, they try to get a few more of their pig's feet into it.

To Frederic C. Howe

Carmel, May 11, 1934

Dear Fred,

Nice long warm letter from you today that struck a note I can sing to: I'd like to have a nice long warm talk with you. A few words, here and there, now and then, will do for a while, but the time comes when friends need a feast. Then they can live long on a few occasional phrases.

Tugwell I have with me always, as I used to have Tom and Bob La Follette and T. R.,—all the comic heroes of my day and yours,— where I could call them out from under my heart for a smile. All wrong, they are, but all right with me. They're in Hell now, but they'll be happy in there. They'd be happy in Soviet Russia now, no other where. But all I wrote you about Tugwell was that I was sorry that he and your brain trust were so innocent of the charges of Mr. Wirt.[1] I wanted them to be guilty. I wanted it to be true that there was conspiracy on to change the very bottom of our system.

Oswald Villard, when he was out there, told me a sad story along this line. He said the President asked his cabinet one day if they knew "what we are up to or if they could see the direction they were taking." When they said no, he said: "No, no, you are too busy, but I, who have time and the duty to look around and see ahead,—I don't see either."

Well, I hope that the brain trust or Tugwell did. That's all. Nothing deep about that, is there? You've got an awful lot of sailors on your ship, but I think that you and we need someone navigating, one. Is that asking too much?

Yes, there is something in my *Moses* for you. When God led Moses to lead the slaves out of Egypt for the Promised Land and they behaved like slaves all the way, God told Moses to let his people wander around in the Desert till all the old ones died off. Forty years. Then he let the new generation, born in the wilderness, go on over in. In a word:

You must keep up the depression till the old guys have had time to die. For I notice that the big business men and bankers, who were

[1] William A. Wirt, who accused the "Brain Trust" of being Communist.

humble and tractable in the depths of the depression, have become cocky and impossible whenever the fog lifted a little. But I've just been writing this to E. A. Filene, who still has hopes and crying spells over his old Chamber of Commerce. I'll send you a copy of it.

It's tough on the rest of us, but we must all suffer till that old crowd is dead. We can't have a boom and a recovery too.

But the cause of our tragedy is a comedy to me: "We produce so much that we can't consume it and so the remedy,—we go hungry." A people whose minds work like that ought to die. If you don't think so ask God or my boy Pete.

Yours affectionately,

Lincoln Steffens

To Rose Isaak

Dear Rose Isaak: Carmel, June 16, 1934

Can't I see Schmitty[1] when he comes out? He's a friend of mine, you know; and I mean friend. I have kept away only because I was told to, by his sister, for him. I understood that all right. But my obedience was for his sake, not mine, and now, when he comes out and goes to Heaven, I'd like to see him, shake his hand and look into his honest, humorous eyes. Also I could make a suggestion or two for his life in Russia. Do ask him if there is any way I can meet him, if only for a moment.

You will, I know. You are always on the spot in an emergency, but then you are on the spot all the time.

Yours affectionately,

Stef.

To Joseph Freeman[2]

Dear Joe Freeman: Carmel, July 5, 1934

Your extraordinary approval of my review of Max Eastman was gratifying to me, of course, and surprising. I never expect to get such things right in the eyes of the Party. But,—for the same liberal reasons,—I do think I can understand the other liberals and their troubles, which amuse me immensely.

---

[1] There was again a possibility that Matthew A. Schmidt, sentenced to life imprisonment in the McNamara case, would be let out on parole. The parole was denied.

[2] An editor of *New Masses;* he had commented on Steffens's review of "Artists in Uniform," published in the *New Republic,* June 20, 1934.

I wish you-all could treat us-all as generously as you have treated me. It's O.K. (as Pete says) to shoot us, but why torture us? Communism, when it is ripe and ready, will be a basis upon which will be erected such liberalism as the world has never seen but always has longed for; naturally.

Yours by stages,
Lincoln Steffens

To the Editor of the New Republic [1]

Carmel, California,
[July, 1934]

Sir:

Max Eastman convicts me of unclearness, certainly. He is puzzled, and he a humorist. Well, so am I—puzzled.

When I hauled off and smote him affectionately on the wrist for enjoying for his own sweet sake—not art's—the misdirected joy and rage I have watched him arousing for about five years, I had no idea that I was delivering a "mortal thrust." Honestly, I didn't. I imagined that I was snuggling in with him on the fun he was having. It makes me feel silly now to have to deny that I intended to hint at "an inside" news story of his "personal degradation." I did not know there was one. My guess was that he had stopped growing back somewhere in our liberal days when the rude revolution went its own narrow way instead of ours. But that my favorite philosopher and friend was making money or going back on the inscription on my gift-book and his tombstone—that I never suspected and cannot yet believe. The only decay my fond eyes can detect is in his once so lively, lovely mirth.

"The elementary routine of the Stalinists" by which he says I was "trotted out" after the equally innocent Matthew Josephson to dispose of the issues of the Revolution, not by debate but by the method of excommunication and personal slander—I can't deal with a charge like that without bursting into tears—or something. And my old beloved Max would not have expected me to. I can tell how I was "trotted out" in review *Artists in Uniform*. Ella Winter was reading the book and, knowing that I was not interested in muckraking in Russia, not incensed at tyrannies and idiocies inevitable in the early

[1] Published *New Republic,* Aug. 1, 1934, answering Max Eastman's letter in the same issue objecting to Steffens's review of his *Artists in Uniform.*

stages of a planned evolution, and did not much mind if our group, the intelligentsia, got some of the medicine they gave other groups and classes, she asked if I could review the book without getting mad? I could. So she suggested to the editors of the *New Republic* my assignment to the pleasant job. That is all Stalin had to do with this particular persecution.

I would like, however, in all earnestness to meet one thrust of his. He says that the Stalinists' (including evidently my) refusal to debate some issues, "has enabled them (the Stalinists) to keep alive those disastrous policies—the splitting of the trade-union movement on grounds of doctrine, the denouncing of socialists as 'social fascists,' the refusal to form with them a genuine united front against a common enemy, the substitution for hooliganism for working-class enlightenment—which are delivering the nations one by one into the hands of fascism."

Now I can't speak for the Stalinists (they wouldn't let me), but I have been watching some Communist leaders of the American working class out in the field and I have found them to be thoughtful, rather silent men and women, terribly overworked but poised in their manifold activities, loyal, uncompromising, daring and very understanding. They do not refuse, they labor incessantly but wisely, to achieve a united front. They are indeed splitting the trade union movement, but they have not gone far enough in that direction; they have not yet chiseled off all the old pacifist, liberal, socialist labor leaders whom the big-business leaders find "reasonable" and can "do business with."

As a mere political observer, I will report to Max Eastman and all my other old friends, that out here on the picket lines of the actual struggle there are Communist party leaders whom I can follow. I can't lead them, Max, but I can follow them with a satisfaction I have never felt before in all my professional career.

Lincoln Steffens.

To Frances M. Perkins [1]

Carmel, July 19, 1934

Dear Miss Perkins,

There is hysteria here, but the terror is white, not red. Business men are doing in this Labor struggle what they would have liked

[1] The longshoremen's and marine strike, called May 9, developed into the San Francisco General Strike, July 16.

to do against the old graft prosecution and other political reform movements, yours included; they are sicking on the mob, which, mark you well, is all theirs. It is the lawless tool of these righteous civic leaders who have always corrupted the law and the government. As an expert on government I tell you that the workers' management of this general strike was better government than that of the City itself.

Appeals to settle the strike recognise that. They are addressed mainly to Labor, just as if it were hopeless to talk to the employers, just as if the strikers had civic virtues and the bosses none. This may be true; business men may be anti-social creatures, but is it tactful now to proclaim it? Our Mayor Rossi and your General Johnson ask the men, first, to call off the general strike. Then they promise to be vaguely fair! I personally would not trust such official promises by any business-like politicians; I did it once and there's a man in the penitentiary now paying with his life for my fool confidence. Our governor is moving you to deport aliens as if—

Let me remind you that this widespread revolt was not caused by aliens. It takes a Chamber of Commerce mentality to believe that these unhappy thousands of American workers on strike against conditions in American shipping and industry are merely misled by foreign Communist agitators. It's the incredibly dumb captains of industry and their demonstrated mismanagement of business that started and will not end this all-American strike and may lead us to Fascism. The cries you hear from them are hypocritical lies, as you probably know but can hardly openly say. Well, I can. Hence this open letter.

Yours sincerely,
Lincoln Steffens

To Louis Oneal

The Getaway,
July 27, 1934

Dear Mr. Oneal,

Will you not do now what you hankered to do last year; send flowers to Caroline Decker? She (and about twenty-five other organisers of migratory workers) was arrested in Sacramento on account of the hysteria of the General Strike in San Francisco. The prisoners were caught red-handed at an open meeting in their headquarters. The charge is vagrancy. No. Don't laugh. They may have been picked up for being so busy. They raised wages,—a little,—last year, but this year the farmers did it voluntarily, all by themselves. At the mere sight of Caroline's agitators coming down the road, the bosses increased the consuming power of their pickers and so beat the pot out of the Revolution and all its workers.

But you can close one eye and see that Caroline Decker, her Union, and our typewriter ought to be in jail for life and it's hard that there isn't some law (besides vagrancy) for her and them to have broken. I too sympathize with the constituted authorities. It's tough to have to hold up our tottering civilisation these days and find the straws as well as the bricks.

So I suggest you send flowers to Caroline; that you contribute to a fund to hire for the whole twenty-six of them some one cheap attorney or/and drop in here and there where it will count, a whispered word, like, for example: "Don't be silly." There must be some wise candidate for office who will understand our homely humour.

By the way, our typewriter wasn't smashed. "They" picked Caroline off the machine, but they didn't molest the property.

I wish I could call on you some day in your office, close the door and not say a word; just laugh, and laugh,—and cry.

Yours solemnly,
Lincoln Steffens

To Mr. and Mrs. Alfred A. Guidotti

Carmel, August 11, 1934

Dear Mr. Guidotti, and equally dear Mrs. Guidotti,

I have a letter from a queer friend of ours named Philip O. Keeney,[1] who with his wife, Mrs. Keeney, went East from the frontier of Montana last summer looking for some enlightened outlookers. They have written to me to report that on that long voyage of exploration they found two; they found you and apparently that's all. But they suggested that I communicate with you, but all they gave me to communicate about is, apparently, the joy of discovery. Well, I can't write much on that basis; it makes a short letter but a high bright light to write that I am glad that there are six of us, the Keeneys, the Guidottis, and the Steffenses.

[1] Librarian at the University of Montana, dismissed for his liberal views, later reinstated.

Will you write to the Keeneys and say that I have done this, with a broad, deep smile.

Yours happily,
Lincoln Steffens

To Sidney Hook [1]

Carmel, [August 1934]

My dear Sidney Hook,

Your long, thoughtful letter deserves a thorough answer but I can't send you one. I haven't the strength. Laid up here in bed, I lack the energy even to contemplate such a job; my doctor says I must not do it. And my spectator's interest in the world, I can see from here, is in history; not in the wrong or right of it, but in the play which I find I cannot direct or act in.

And I find that I can indeed still learn from watching,—if I can keep my mind from thinking out logically its own thoughts. As I said somewhere in my book, which you cite against me, I do better by seeing than by reasoning. True here in the U. S. A., it is truer in Germany, Austria, Italy, Russia. It is shocking to my well-paved mind to see that in all the crimes of change, either Right or Left, the winners turn round and abuse the losers as they, the winners, were once abused. But I can see through these abuses to the conclusion that, at our stage of development, the winners will abuse the losers in the next crisis; in the next General Strike (in Minneapolis) the same violence will occur that we saw in the last General Strike (in San Francisco). I had a talk with Lenin once on this thing and I accept his conclusion: "Don't minimise the Terror. Red or White, it will occur. It's part of the cost, and we must be prepared to pay it. Till we know enough psychology to deal with it."

Three times I have been to Soviet Russia since the Revolution and I saw it with eyes that had seen through the United States and more of our Western Civilisation. Once when I was in there a responsible group came up to me and asked if out of my experience with bribery and corruption here, I could advise them what to do about bribery and corruption there, in Russia.

"Tell me about it," I said, and they catalogued all the bribery they had come upon. It was all so petty, so like tipping in our world, that I laughed.

[1] Associate Professor of Philosophy at New York University.

"Nothing," I exclaimed. "If we had only that to deal with in the United States we'd be happy and honest. It's nothing, your graft, and I would do nothing about it."

But they would not take my view of comparative corruption, and they did do something about it. They punished their tip-takers as you would probably punish bureaucrats, censors and tyrants.

Yours sincerely,
Lincoln Steffens

To Frederic C. Howe

The Getaway,
August 22, 1934

Dear Fred:

We have been pretty busy out here, as you may have heard, read or seen, all of us; even Pete, the kid, who once upon a time p—d in a school yard and twice busted windows just because he couldn't take a dare. Local newspapers exposed Pete, but we, his parents, suspect that the blasts were aimed at his mother, who has been interested in strikes in your department,[1] in the valley crops by migratory workers who have been misled by unconfirmed rumors about a New Deal.

Filene has been here for a week. My impression is that E. A. is surer of the New Deal than the President himself. I have heard the President say that it was an experiment and as that I can look on it with patience, but when a Big Business Man comes all the way out here to tell me that it must succeed I look with impatience upon the other Big Business Men and their chiselling. What this country needs is a Humorist. A few politicians and a humorist would clear the air nicely and, if they failed, I'd add a son-of-a-bitch to explain the joke to his kind and his class, who, you might view with alarm, are recovering from their once profound humility and shame faster than prices, profits and wages. I have met bankers lately who talk like our old bankers, with self-respect, and as for employers—

Well, Fred, all this rigmarole is relative to your inquiry for letters from Marie. We have some. Peter says she has some dandies, but the police have been raising hell out here with private letters so we have been burning and storing ours till now everything is out of reach. She says that if you want Marie's letters, you must get the

---

[1] Mr. Howe was working in the Agricultural Adjustment Administration.

Government to let up on us and somehow guarantee security for private letters (if for nothing else). Even this letter may be opened, you know. Our whole mail, out or in, is noticeably delayed. I don't mind much, but all that awful respect I used to have for law and government is gone.

I am much better in health, Fred. True I am still abed and I can't do much work, but I may get up and move around the place a couple of hours a day and am happy over the state of the world. Peter is more than busy, so that she is satisfied; activity is her one need. And Pete, in spite of all a few enemies of mine say, is a fine boy without many illusions. He is growing up to think that, not the land or capitalism, not Jews or aliens, but grown-ups account for all the evils in the world and the cure is just kids. His problem is to learn to recite what the dumb adults teach without swallowing a word of it. He is polite to these enemies of Man and Life; he does not show them the pity he has for them and his amusement at their Civilization. I think he is nicer to people because they are not his "superiors," because they give him no sense of inferiority.

Affectionately,
Lincoln Steffens

To E. A. Filene

The Getaway, September 5, 1934

Dear E. A.

. . . We were comparing your intellectual integrity with that which I was seeking that time when I inquired in Wall Street for a railroad man who had not forgotten that railroads exist to carry freight and passengers. I found none. You, who never forget that a department store is a machine to distribute goods, are a rare phenomenon, and that's what's rare, Bob says, and now Ella Winter sees it: intellectual integrity. . . .

Meanwhile it is calming down here. I sent for a chief of the Vigilantes and tried to persuade him to send me to the penitentiary as a sort of symbolic end to my *Life* and my life. Showed him I deserved it as much, almost, as Jesus, and promised, if they would draw the indictment to my satisfaction, that I would plead guilty. "If you will allege,—your true complaint,—that I am an exceptionally intelligent citizen," I said, "I will admit it in court under oath." He wouldn't agree to my plan. Too bad. It would have saved me writing my third volume.

Thanks for the thought of me in San Francisco,—the big chair, the bed rest and the dominoes. They have not come yet, but I can see them on the way, with both of you behind them, you and Mama. What a combination! Heart and brain, and nobody but me knowing which is which. No, don't be alarmed; I won't tell.

Enough, now; I'll quit this nonsense and go to work. There's something I want to do in the garden, something important, so—

Lift my hat to Charlie Wood, step gently but decisively upon Mama and shake your head solemnly over E. A. for me. Tell Cromie [1] that Pete, when he saw the spread on you all over the *Sun,* looked up amazed at me and asked: "Say, Daddy, is Mr. Filene as Great as that?" I think Pete thinks that only Jimmy Cagney is as great as that.

To Hugh Jones

The Getaway,
September 6, 1934

Dear Mr. Hugh Jones:

Sinclair is being bitterly attacked as a Communist. There is a fierce hysteria here against Communism, you know. It began with the general strike, when "They" discovered by experimentation that Bridges and some other labor leaders could not be bribed. You can be trusted, I think, to understand how terrifying that discovery can be in real life. If we can't buy a man with real money, how are we to make labor leaders see reason? No, when bribery fails what is left one but,—but violence? It is frightening, and we are indeed frightened. Our hysteria is sincere; and it is widespread. And we can see that, since the symbol of fright is the word "Communist," all we've got to do is to stick it on anybody we fear and hate. It used to be "Hun," now it is Communist. See? Sinclair is a Communist. But he says he isn't and the Communists say he isn't. They are damned liars, of course, so, you see, if I, an honest man, will come out and declare or denounce publicly Upton as no Red but a Fascist I shall embarrass the Republicans, the herd, and I shall at the same time be doing a service to our Socialist Democrats. The Sinclair managers are considering now just how hot they want me to be.

[1] Robert J. Cromie, publisher and editor of the Vancouver *Sun.*

upper: JOHN STEINBECK (photo by Sonia Noskowiak). *lower:* ROBERT
CANTWELL (photo by Sybil Anikeef).

The sight of his party is one of the clearest expositions I have ever seen of the reason why Communists stress the need of building up a disciplined party to take over and exercise power; of the reason why a mere Socialist can't do the trick.

Bob, by the way, has left here. Thought he had to get out of this atmosphere. . . . We are almost as dangerous as the Party; even my little boy, Pete, who is nine years old, was under fire, and as for his mother,—he remarked to her one day: "You have got yourself in Dutch, haven't you, Mama?" It is all very amusing but you must realize that to elect a good, old, safe Republican out here we are going to have a bigger and better hysteria which it will soon appear might as well be made permanent. Certainly it must be developed enough to defeat Sinclair, and I think it will. I expect soon to hear that he will drive, not capitalism, but capital out of California. Why don't you come out here and see for yourself the leading state in the Union; and us warm spots, pretty spotted, but still warm.

Sincerely,
Lincoln Steffens

To Anna Louise Strong

The Getaway,
Sept. 11, 1934

Dear Anna Louise:

I wish I could write you at length about the chapters you have sent me of your book, your autobiography.[1] It is important, it is new and it is very well written. It shows too that the transition, the revolution the Revolution is making in you, is not yet finished. You haven't made the grade, but I think that is all to the good; it makes your story more meaningful to the rest of us who are only on the way. The chapter on the press and on "controls" is typical and the best yet. I feel and sometimes see that you yourself don't "get" what Borodin is trying to give you. To reproduce that impression is beautiful reporting, and it is charming modesty too. Before you let it go, I hope you will clinch it by further talks with Borodin and perhaps some editing by him.

Get the notion of liberty out of your head and out of the heads of your (American) readers. It is false, a hangover from our Western tyranny, and you say so when you show yourselves looking around

[1] *I Change Worlds.*

for a boss or a control. Borodin, who, by the way, sticks up wise, patient and balked by you in the chapter, seems to be trying to tell you and all journalists that the supposed bosses don't want to boss; they want you to find your own consultants, and I guess that he sees how, if you go on searching, you will find the "control" finally in your ever-changing readers. And he seems to be urging you on to develop the machinery by which you can communicate with your readers. Funnily enough, it is the essentials of democracy that you and "we" can't seem to get.

I wished as I read you that I could see and have such talks with Borodin. He has so much to give and I have so much to get,—not merely facts, but sheer wisdom. Sometimes I think that I will close up here and go and live in Russia. Impossible, yes, but it's a lovely dream to dream. And you can get it all. Go through your "civilized" mind and throw out the debris, and then, Anna Louise, write it,—to me. For keep this up front in your head: you can write.

To A. R. McNamara [1]

The Getaway,
September 13, 1934

Dear McNamara:

Laid up in bed here with a stroke that struck me months ago, I cannot go to see Jim, but I'll have someone call and report. I've heard, too, that he is not so well, but I can tell you that in spirit he is O.K. No man ever survived duress as he has. And he has kept pace with the Labor movement. Wonderful.

The story I heard is that, as the attendant on men in the death cells, he smuggled in an extra beef-steak. And I can believe that. And I can see him take on the chin whatever is coming to him.

Yours sincerely,
L. Steffens

To Frederic C. Howe

The Getaway,
September 16, 1934

Dear Fred:

Good letter yours of September 7, inciting to insight, exciting to imagination, but leaving too much to the reader. I feel the same way.

[1] Brother of J. B. and J. J. McNamara.

I too am reluctant to look at things I can see through, kindo' ashamed for the poor things and hoping I will be proved wrong the way I used to seek evidence that I was right. Isn't that it? Isn't that the way you feel? Or are you just afraid of your stenographer?

As I see it from here, the President has failed to induce the business men to agree and coöperate in measures to their interest. The next step is compulsion by him and his Administration, but they, the business men, have beat him to that; theirs is the force. And there is the stalemate. Watching him in the papers and on the screen I get the impression that there is no dictatorship in him. True?

On the other hand I get the soft sense that he will never have his Johnson taken out and shot. Think of a democrat keeping a dictator of the other side! I can "get" Johnson, but I can't get Roosevelt at all. I can see that he would like to save business, but what makes him think that business men will help him? The only ones I ever saw that might swim along and keep from choking a life-saver are Filene and our Tom. I watch them out here, where they prefer Merriam to Upton, who is a perfect Ramsay MacDonald.

Tell me when the next Smash is coming, Fred, and how. That interests me. The Turn doesn't. I know where that is, the very corner. I am glad 'Sconset is safe; may go there some time myself.

Affectionately,
Stef.

To Mrs. A. Winter

Carmel, September 24, 1934

My dear Mother-in-law:

I begin thus because Pete is away at school and has nothing to do with this manuscript, not a thing. He can write his own stuff these days; he has grown, you know. Pete is much older than when he was younger; he has developed naturally and, having the kind of mother I, in my wisdom, found for him, his head is sticking up above the rest of us like a giraffe. He jumped a grade in school last year, is still leader in his present form and is to be jumped ahead again next year. Pete is a credit to his father's family. Besides all which you may have a passing interest in the detail that he is a very happy, self-confident kid.

As to his mother, well, that's a different story. As I look out of the window I see her laboring naked (almost) in the garden, taking in all the sun there is. (She is in her bathing suit, which she uses for all occasions except only swimming.) She looks very settled, but go down to her and she will talk about going to New York or Hollywood or taking on another newspaper (besides the one she has taken on) or, —or,—or any two or three other jobs. Energy, Madam, energy. And we have just come through a White Terror in which she appeared as "that Ella Winter." She has worked it around so that she is blamed for me and the General Strike and everything, instead of vice-versa. I noticed in a letter from Guy Hickok, the ex-Paris correspondent of the Brooklyn *Eagle,* that he gave her a recipe for removing tar and feathers. So I inferred that the papers out East have reported what a terrible woman your daughter has come to be in spite of my good but gentle attention and example. And she is indeed pretty Left; and bold; and clear-spoken. I kinder like her myself; I rather like it all.

Coming now to the interesting point in this letter, I may say that I am better. I have been getting up out of bed more and more, and I believe I shall soon be able to write. When I do I shall work on a postscript to my book, my *Autobiography,* which our publisher has contracted me to deliver. He prefers that to the Pete book. You know about that? A book for kids to tell them about this cock-eyed world they have been born in. I wanted to explain to the fresh, unspoiled, uneducated minds of all learners how absurd it all is and how easy to set right. But the *Autobiography* has circulated so far and wide that the publisher feels that in the fan letters we get there is a ready market in the demand for more of my life. All right, I'll do that next. If I don't Peter will, so—

She started a book on the strikes, you know, and has written a play on one, a play with another fellow. It turned out to be a pageant, so it has to be done all over again.

The weather is fine. We have had our first rain, ending the dry season and putting out the forest fires, cleaning the air and starting up the wild flowers. The hills will soon be in color. Pete will have to wear shoes and Peter will have to put some clothes on. I may go out of the house. Business is reluctantly picking up. Sorry, men had not yet got far in the thinking that was predicted as a fruit of the depression; they had only had some feelings, but thought was in sight; and now that will be stopped. We hear that England is coming to life. Germany is going to Hell. But you know and tell me all about that side. Love to all, all.

To Robert Cantwell

The Getaway,
September 29, 1934

Dear Life-saver:—

I got your account of the cure of E. A. and I rather envied him. For it came, that letter, on a murder-suicide day, something new for me. I've had murder days before, days when I'd like to drop on someone with, very explicitly, a small, very heavy, blunt hammer. And I've had gentler days, which I call suicide days, when I'd like to take poison. But,—the combination days on which I yearn pathetically to kill myself and others too, are a recent development. Your essay, therefore, showing that murder, retail and wholesale, too, is being established as a custom of country, fell on fat ground.

I wish some Marx would come along and make a study of psychology. He should be an American; no alien has the material for the proper understanding of the possibilities of the human mind, its powers, its weaknesses. I'd like to see someone portray a supremely virtuous, law-and-orderly, anti-violence son of a bitch going around with a blunt hammer.

I'm relieved to hear that Upton and the governorship are to be left to Mr. Merriam, who works for The Revolution without any cost to Moscow gold.

Yes, come down. Any day you're not expected will do.

Yours,
Stef.

To Fremont Older

Carmel, Oct. 20, 1934

Dear Fremont:

Your note of yesterday surprised and shocked me. I had not heard of your September attack; nobody told me a word, and I know some of your neighbors. Yesterday Peter went up to the city to call on you and see why you were so silent. She would have told you how dumb and close I am. Perhaps we can agree on a date and go together,— as we always have. Maybe I can get someone to drive me over to your hill. We could look out over the world and see how it is going. From here it is going quite fit to quit. It is going back to its foundations, but the far future is all right. It will be tough on Peter, but will be fine for Pete.

Meanwhile, good heart, do you drive down here if you can make it. I'm sorry you are weak,—where you used to be strongest; at the pump. Peter was going to ask you to write to J. B. McNamara, just to straighten him with the Warden; he is under a cloud, lost his old cell and his job and some prestige. And Peter is getting lots of letters sent to him.

J. B.'s younger brother, Bob, out here for the A. F. of L. convention, called here and stirred us up. Peter may be going over there today. I'll write again, Fremont. Don't feel alone,—I'm with you to the very end. Love to Cora, too.

Affectionately,
Lincoln Steffens

To Anna Louise Strong

Carmel [October, 1934]

Dear Anna Louise:

The last copy of your Life to get here came last night, and I read into it. And I'm convinced. It's just what it should be and it's good; it's very, very good. . . .

You have a big subject, you know. To make and cross a bridge from one age to another, from one whole, new, united philosophy to another, is something that was never done in any other transition in history; not that I know of. You see, I say doing,—for the first time. Your difficulties with Trotzky are the sign of your failure. The great man matters with both you and Max. Certainly you can see, can't you, that under our old culture justice must be done him and that, under the new Soviet culture, justice is for the people. Don't answer that justice is for both. That's a matter of course, but it may come to a choice at this stage of history (and of the writer's psychology). In that case your concern is,—not with Trotzky. You get the sense of the mass moving along the "line" and that's what you once did not have and what your readers over here do not have, and ought to get, from your story. Well, hang onto that glimpse, strengthen it and make us see it. That we *all* have to stick together on that till it is established in our habits. Then we can, and shall, differ on points and details.

Trotzky was a hero to me once too, but when he put "right" above unity and broke our front to be right, I, from here,—I recognized that he was not of the New Day, but of the old. He says to the world what is only fit for the Party. I have things I would like to say or sound the Party on, but I can feel in my bones that I must not say them at this stage to the enemy. As against Labor or even against the millions of Russia, Trotzky does not matter. Get back on the line, Anna Louise, and go back knowingly; and tell that. It's one of the biggest lessons we "Christians," we capitalists, have to learn. The Truth from now on is always dated; never absolute, never eternal.

You can learn that; Max never can. Almost all my liberal friends can't. The right is right, isn't it? they say. My answer is, When? Which seems the height of absurdity to them, and it is,—now, in these United States. But not in Russia. There, now, it is the essence of Right.

Fascism is forcing our minds to see that "free speech" is not an abstract "right." We want liberty for us, but not for Hitler and Mussolini. And the liberals can't make that "right." They can't see that time is a dimension; as it really is; and as the new culture of Soviet Russia can see. Treason to the Tsar wasn't a sin, treason to Communism is. You see that every single thing is changed by the process of history that you are describing your way through. You made the passage that will take us over here decades to go through,—you are speeding through it. Don't leave your mind or even your instincts behind.

Affectionately,

L. Steffens

The Getaway,
Jan. 10, 1935

Dear Anna Louise:

There have been several letters from you but I have not been able to answer. I had a set-back a while ago, and it is very difficult for me to use my hand, even to write with, but I can tell you that I awfully wanted to write to you about your chapters as they come along. It seems to me that you are learning as you write; that this book has made you digest what you know, and the fascinating part of it is that you really do not get the Russian culture. You will. Don't worry. And when you do, I think that you'll want to write another book. They have over there an entirely different culture, more different than the Christian was from the old Greek. Sometimes I think the Russian Communists do not themselves realize it fully. They also are a lot of capitalists who are only learning gradually and with difficulty the implications of what they say. But that is obvious, I think; it explains a lot of their news; and, for our present purpose, it explains you and your book. That's what makes it so extremely interesting.

But the news in your letter that interested me most is that you are coming over here. I have been thinking of going over there, and I would if I thought my health would permit me to be of any use. I have been asked by someone here in authority over there to go over to one of their summer places, settle down in comfort and safety and write interpretations of their news, especially when it shocks our people. The treatment of suspects after the assassination of Kirov is an example. It seems to me that I understood that. I am not sure or proud of it even now. I'll send you a copy of my editorial[1] so that you can see how we are both in the same boat as far as understanding goes. But it is a satisfaction to hear that you are coming out here. We can understand things together and I hope you will get here before it is time for me to make up my mind.

Yours affectionately,

Steffens

To E. A. Filene

The Getaway,
May 18, 1935

Dear E. A.,

A nice, long letter from you yesterday that prompted me to lay it down to wish. You suggested that I go along to Russia; you knew I'd better not, but you considered it. So I,—I knew I couldn't, but I enjoyed the thought of going with you. I always did love to be tempted. And Russia just now is a sort of heaven, where humans have got rid of the great primitive problems of food, clothing and a roof. And therefore of all the other mean problems that go with business for private profit. That leaves the Russians with minds for philosophy, art and science. Now civilization may begin.

After just one more world war which will spare, I trust, the soldiers in the trenches and fly over the fronts to rid the earth of the generals, bankers and nice people in the rear.

The interesting thing for you to notice in Soviet Russia is that everything is in course of evolution; nothing all right and stationary,

[1] In *Pacific Weekly,* Jan. 4, 1935.

as with us. The theory of evolution is recognized and counted upon. They have not got anywhere, but are only on the way. There are no facts to get there, only plans and processes. Whatever you see will be changed to something better next year. If I went with you I'd concentrate on their intentions because, with privileged business out, they can have aims that can be realized. Our observers can't realize that and ask what they have accomplished. The answer to that is, "Nothing: compared to what they propose they have done nothing but clear the ground."

Ask them how they would deal with our dust storms? We can't, they can, fix the top soil. For it's a social, not an individual job.

Affectionately,
Stef.

To Robert Cantwell

Carmel, June 8, 1935

Dear Bob:—

Your stunning article for "us,"—your New York letter,[1] came in last night and I read it as news, which it was to me. It took you to make me believe it. I mean that I wouldn't have accepted it if it had come from somebody like me. And,—excuse me, Bob,—it was so well done. Peter, gone to San Francisco, hasn't seen it. She will be home tonight with stuff for a piece you suggested on the longshoremen, I think. They are using their power, actually wielding the Union! They strike at every little wedge the employers stick in, 129 strikes this year so far. It's exasperating; a man can't run his own business because these workers want to run their own lives.

Your description of the E. A. *Life* reminds me of a story Anton Johannsen, the dynamiter, tells on me. When we were settling up the McNamara case in Los Angeles he says that I wished some guilty labor skate would get himself arrested and go into court to tell in full detail how Labor had to use dynamite, and that I suggested that he do it. And he says that I admitted that it might hang him, but he says I remarked that it would make a great story. Your letter sounded like that. E. A. might suffer and not like it, but it was my part to handle him and, meanwhile, yours would be a wonderful story.

How can you expect to write the truth till after The Revolution,— long time after; Lenin guessed fifty years.

[1] "A Letter from New York," *Pacific Weekly,* June 21, 1935.

Some good liberals were here Sunday. After they left I wrote for liberals a piece on the United Front, which has gone to you in the current number.[1] I have from Upton Sinclair a letter taking exactly the opposite view. I want the Communists to front the U. Front; he wants Upton Sinclair to do it or nobody. Want to comment? It's an issue out here.

To E. A. Filene

The Getaway,
June 19, 1935

Dear E. A.,

This then is my last letter to you before your sailing. . . . Take it easy on this trip, E. A. Of course, you are bound to go on and die in your tracks. Pride, vanity. But you need not wind it all up on this journey. Apply enough of your philosophy to the situation to modify a little your way of life. Enough to laugh through. Be wise, and not for Europe alone, nor for mass production alone. Travel lightly and don't ever hurry. The proud are dropping dead out here on the golf courses daily, and we laugh at them. Don't behave as if you were forty. Play you are eighty; play you have sense; and don't give your enemies the satisfaction of passing out like the N.R.A. (By the way, the Supreme Court was unanimous and the President talks of changing, not the Court, but the Constitution.) Let Mama be your supreme court and let her bow to my wishes.

That's all, for the present. I'll say goodbye and wish you a pleasant, instructive and wise journey. From my heart I wish it you.

Stef.

To Robert Cantwell

The Getaway,
June 28, 1935

Dear Bob:—

I miss you and your letters, your touch. I can see that you are working; I can even read your works; read a review in the *New Republic* last night. But that's as far away as the Bible is from God. An article by you in the *Pacific Weekly* is nearer. Only a letter is near,—enough. In a word: do write to Papa. I'm better. In my mind.

That bank business of mine is near a settlement, and the result is

[1] Reprinted in *Lincoln Steffens Speaking,* p. 207.

thanks to E. A. He saved me my home here. My health too. You don't got to be grateful, but I am.

It will interest you to hear that S. F. B. Morse, the Del Monte properties man, and Byington Ford, the real head of our Vigilantes, have both called. They came to explain "some mistakes" they made, mistakes made in the excitement following the general strike. We told them of some other mistakes that occurred after that spell that they knew not of. I told them I *was* for Communists knowingly and showed them that they were Fascists unknowingly. I believe I convinced Ford he was a Fascist indeed. He was surprised; was *that* Fascism? Yes, when a man joins vigilantes to support the present state of business by force, that was *it*. But what the calls meant was that they had felt a change of public opinion here, and others tell me it is all for us. I have been more and more open and clear in my talk and writings in the *Weekly*, yet I make, I do not lose, friends. We explain or state things the Communists want said all the time. It's a pleasure to do it and it does not hurt us. It helps us, so far as I can see. Don't you think the *Weekly* is fun? Of course it is not always on the line, but some of us don't know the line.

Go ahead, Bob, keep up your New York letter and do turn off a line to me now and then. I, we, appreciate it.

                                                    Fondly,
                                                    Stef.

                                                    The Getaway,
                                                    July 8, 1935

Dear Bob:—

. . . I told Peter when she came home from San Francisco what an interesting letter I had from Bob. She read it after a while and couldn't see it. Said your letters were always as good as that.

She would not be so encouraged as I was that you said you'd all be with me if I wrote my third volume. Of course you won't and I know I'll have to do it alone, as I should, but I got a push out of that. You'd help if I hollered. The idea for the next New York letter was an interest. I'd like to get a picture of the intellectuals from you for the *Weekly:* what they talk about, where they foregather, what they are in doubt about,—how far they have got. Why did Strachey think our highbrows were so far ahead of his and yours?

I want to tell you that a married couple of teachers, whom we talked to half a year ago, came in to see me on the Fourth of July. They wanted to thank me for the mental relief they found in a solution and a decision; their perplexity was all over. But, when I asked them how they, as school-teachers, could get by unhurt, it developed,—they exclaimed that as Communists they had discovered in other teachers, the superintendent of schools and, as they said, "everywhere," there were secret Communists or "Reds." They had joined the party, but the multitude had not; only secretly sympathetic. I did not realize how right Hearst is; do you? Another thing: some reporters on the capitalist papers have very recently been joining the C. P. Asked how they got there, whether they had been reading the *Western Worker,* they explained that they had been seeing the *Pacific Weekly.*

Things are certainly moving out here. You could have more fun writing a Pacific Coast letter to New York.

Keep me informed on the family, and, if it does not disturb, let me feel in touch with the growth of the E. A. book.

Affectionately,
Stef.

To Michael Gold

The Getaway,
August 21, 1935

Dear Mike Gold:

I fell for you first when you got me right and roasted me to a turn for a sentimentalist who liked everybody. When you forgave me, I slowed up, but I went on reading and heeding you. You were wrong, but I forgave you as one weak heart has to allow for another. Now I see you like France [1] as I liked America, and for the same reason which, between you and me, is no reason at all. Marx and Lenin had the right reason; did you know that Lenin had a weak heart? He had to hide his under a hard head, which I see you trying all the time to do. In vain. You are not so great as Lenin; you are only a little greater than I am, than I was when I liked America and la belle France. And Mike Gold. And Mike Gold.

Sincerely,
Lincoln Steffens

[1] "A Love Letter for France," by Michael Gold, *New Masses,* Aug. 13, 1935.

To Joseph R. Boldt, Jr.[1]

Carmel, September 10, 1935

Dear Mr. Boldt:

The fact is that I am laid up in bed here and have been for a year or more. My doctor lets me do my column a week for our *Pacific Weekly* and see some callers; all else is forbidden me. He is trying to get me in shape to write the third volume of my *Life*. Letters like yours and like the one you mention, from John Keller of Texas, land hard upon my conscience and ride there. I do want to answer them, but they call for the book, not a mere letter. The perfect place would be over the beer at one of your graduate evenings. However, that is not what you ask for.

I had come to regard the New Capitalism as an experiment till, in 1929, the whole thing went over the top and slid down to an utter collapse. That was clear to all. I went to New York to hear the semi-scientific captains of industry say in words and facial expressions that they did not know what had happened or what was to be done about it. They did not understand their own experiment. Then—not till then—did I give up, and turned to see what else there was. Well, I had been to Soviet Russia and, as I looked us and the Russians over, I saw this that appealed to me:

The Russian Revolution had abolished all those privileges which, in this country, balked all reforms. Gone! All gone.

So I said out loud and to myself, "The Russians have it." And that, in a word, is about all I have to say today. The Russians have it,—to get, and they can get it all, because they have got rid of the obstacles. No private banks, no railroads run for profit, no business ditto.

I am not a Communist, but I am a follower of the labor movement into that party and into the revolution which the capitalists are making.

There, my duty is done, one letter is written. Will not you send it to all of your crowd who might be interested? Yes, and to the waiter at the Hohokus Inn. Tell them that it is not important what they have done; what is important is what they all will do, they and you. Our old culture is finished, we all have got to turn to welcome the new culture, which covers everything,—the arts, science, business, life.

[1] A Dartmouth graduate (1932) who had written asking for a clarification of Steffens's political position.

Let me compliment you upon your letter to me which expresses a good, clear mind. You can write.

To James Cagney

The Getaway,
Oct. 9, 1935

Dear Cagney:

We thought of you last night; we went to "Top Hat." It is beautiful dancing and I always recall your unprofessional admiration of a rival. We shall soon be getting you direct. "Midsummer Night's Dream" is about due at our theatre and you'll be shining in the kind of part you always wanted to play. Pete, Peter, Petest,—we all want to see you do it, undoubting how you will do it. I have never been so sure of an actor as I am of you. I don't know of any part in literature that would call for all your qualities, none. Do you?

We have a little theatre here that shows seconds and foreign reels. A Russian piece tonight, "Chapayeff." Ever see it, you? It is said to be very good. A true story made for the screen, a hero who has to be prompted by a politician; a general with a shrewd commissar to steer him. I have read the history, now I'll see the fiction; the facts in an art form. I wish Hollywood would dare to do it. Is Hollywood planning to do Ethiopia? I'd give you Mussolini and some dramatic incidents and sayings of his; I had an interview with him once. I'll write you after your Shakespeare.

We have lots of visitors, correspondents and others who know the news, but none like you, Cagney. I wish you'd come up. Pete is away at school, but I know he would second the invitation. He claims you, you know. . . . Bring Mrs. Cagney and come for a day, a week or what you like.

Affectionately yours,
Lincoln Steffens

To the Editor of the "Peninsula Herald"

Carmel, Oct. 11, 1935

When my little family returned home from Europe and the war we brought with us our Anna, who had been a nurse for the boy and soon became a personal friend of mine. Other men and women seemed to recognize her qualities.

The men came with flowers; courting, and I took an interest; Anna let me. We considered these men, seriously; rejecting,—not too seriously, several who were polite and charming and most attentive. We finally took Leslie McCarthy, a solid, silent, electrician, who called frequently, and sat and waited obstinately.

There was something sterling about the big red man. Anna married Leslie, who moved in and began a happy family life that we appreciated out of the corner of our eyes. It was one of the gentlest, happiest unions we knew about, and regular. Leslie was a "regular." Anna's husband became a friend of mine.

When he died yesterday, I too lost a friend, a regular friend. He was a "good Catholic," if you know what that is; a union worker, who always paid his dues; not a Red, never a scab. And a husband! And such a father! For they had a little, pretty girl baby who was to have been Anna's but became Leslie's. She exclaimed to him rapturously the other day: "Oh, Daddy, you are the onliest you I everest had!"

He never said it; never said anything much. A silent beggar, but you knew, as the child knew, and his priest knew, and his pals, the regular guys. Leslie McCarthy, as I have said, a regular guy and all the regulars knew it.

All ended now. Years ago he was smashed up in an automobile crash. His skull was fractured, one eye permanently damaged. He used that fixed eye to chill his charming smile, to keep his rich Irish humor,—regular. Well, the other day he got,—probably from Betty Ann, his little girl,—a throat infection and some otherwise harmless germ crept up through that old fracture, paralyzed his respiration and so,—in a second he died, in the hospital, with the nurse and doctor looking on.

Not Anna McCarthy; Anna is waiting a week or two to go there to have another child that Leslie can't love away from her.

Leslie McCarthy is the man I remember,—Anna and I,—as about the most fit of the survivors, of the victors of our civilization; about the best of us: kind, silent, square, fit.

To E. A. Filene

The Getaway,
October 26, 1935

Dear E. A.,

You are home, no doubt, and probably settling down to work. In your own, dear house. And that will make you realize that you are all well again. I am not so well. About the date of your arrival, I was deep in the dumps. I'm getting tired of this bed, which I can leave only for short spells which I don't enjoy or profit by. I begin to think that my ailment is age, something you don't know a thing about.

I'd like to hear your impressions of the state of the country; I mean your honest first impressions, not what you decide to conclude after a second thought. Your Governor has been out here and I have an impression he got a view, but our Governor and our business men are too interested in their own concerns to have been able to tell him a true thing. We are still fighting any raise of wages, any increase of our purchasing power. Fighting is the word I used. You would think to watch them that they were hired by Moscow to bring on the revolution here. They hate the President for trying to go ahead slowly. They prefer Fascism, and are looking for a Hitler, although they think they are chasing Mussolini. Fortunately, they can't find a man, not even for President. The type they really want is Owen D. Young, and he's a Democrat. Well, they'll get Roosevelt again. And they'll build him up by the terms of their opposition. Hearst is quitting this state and saying so; and his reason is his super-taxes. That will help the President, whom we'll soon see resisting our warmongers, who do not like our neutrality.

I must stop this. My orders are to write only short letters, and they are best, anyhow.

Yours,
Stef.

To Margaret Johannsen [1]

The Getaway,
Dec. 23, 1935

Dear Margaret:

I'm sorry. I don't know what I meant by saying your art was a way out, except that we all seem to be looking for some art or game to put the world aside and have something to work our idealism off into. If you prefer to think of it as a way in, so be it with me. And anyhow it's Christmas; what's the use of arguing? I'd be willing to fight with Jo but not with Margaret. No, not Margaret.

Jim McNamara got for Christmas a transfer from Quentin to

---

[1] The wife of Anton "Jo" Johannsen, the labor leader, had taken up painting at this time.

Folsom which depressed and annoyed him greatly. Some of his pals think it is not so bad. The same reason. He is the oldest, most influential prisoner at Quentin and had a big following. Now he will have a new crowd to work on. I hope he will soon get interested in his fresh field. Maybe we can see him now, as we could not under Holohan. Peter was refused recently. I miss Schmittie; haven't called on him since he sent word, through his sister, to lay off. I was too radical to help.

Things are drooping toward a new year here, in New York, Washington, London, Rome and Ethiopia. How about Chicago? Can you see the revolution from there?

Does it ever occur to you that you always had it in you to paint and you'd have loved it when you were a girl? I thought it was poetry that ailed you; never thought of color till you showed it in light and shade. And what does Netta say about it? She is looking for a way out or in. She too. And others. All the world is looking for a way in or out. Nobody but our Jo is content. I never knew he had so much sense; did you?

Love to the whole gang, Margaret, all of you.

Affectionately,
Steffens

To James Cagney

The Getaway,
Dec. 28, 1935

Dear Mr. Jimmy Cagney:

Speaking of hills, this is a hill and there are others all around here. Do come here. We have evidence to show that you are thinking of it; some one of your staff of attorneys has been sounding here for you and keeping long distance tapping our wire at ten minute intervals. We were eager to say: "Yes, here he is." Unless you are a fugitive from justice! If you are we'll lie and connive, of course, of course.

And I have a warm shoulder for you and your tears and your troubles, if you have any. Come on and let's talk it over. Pete will give you advice; he too has troubles. The magnitude of his problems might make yours look like thirty cents. And you might be able to advise on them. What would you do about a mother, who, just because she has caught him in a few lies, thinks him a liar? And how would you get out of practicing on your violin without busting the thing or giving up learning to play? He and I think you are the friend he needs. Are you? And we know we are the very lawyers you are looking for. Better come and see. Jo Davidson may be coming too, later.

Anyhow, do your best. Get good and tired of art and come to crime and rest. May I be remembered to Mrs. Cagney? And may I mention the Merry Christmas behind us and the Happy New Year ahead?

Yours affectionately,
Stef.

To Sam Darcy

The Getaway,
Jan. 4, 1936

Dear S. and E.

Your letter was a holiday event and though we expressed to each the satisfaction we felt, there was nothing new in the warm goodwill we found in it. I shall not attempt to reply in kind; long distance letters estop me always; I write them with a sense of evaporation; and some other senses too. Let me stick to facts.

The proposition that I go to Russia came from a representative of the Soviet Union after and apparently because of a couple of editorial paragraphs I wrote guessing at explanations of events in Petrograd on the theory that American and Soviet psychology was, not identical, but near enough alike to be mutually comprehensible. I was asked to go live in the soft part of Crimea and report events without authority except as I got it from visiting firemen.

The young editor of that paper puzzles me too. Peter brought him here; he had read and admired my book. In the course of time I said that he could not do on a conservative paper the things he and I would like to do, but he should do some straight reporting of facts and situations, especially in the labor field, that conservatives ought to know to fight their battles. I showed him how, by the way, and by being fair to labor, there was a big circulation to get. He tried it, and he stopped the sneering at the workers, respected their leaders, saw them, reported them, and, true enough, his readers increased as his rivals decreased. In other words it worked. But he is warned and knows that when a crisis arises, he will have to go wrong, he'll shinny on his own side. I think I shall have to quit our paper to write a third volume to my book; there are other excuses but that one is paramount. I did think I might do that on the trip you speak of; the trip would give it point, you know. I could describe the path into the future I see.

I was asked for and have done an article on Lenin as a liberal, as a man of humour.[1] You'll see that and comment on the question raised: is it time yet for such stuff? There is more to write. . . .

Thanks for the Soviet testament you sent us, the little book with a million facts. . . . This sort of writing, this letter, is unaccustomed to me,[2] but I can at least say that I appreciate and rejoice in your wisdom and your warmth.

Sincerely,
L. S.

To Charles Erskine Scott Wood

The Getaway,
Jan. 10, 1936

Dear Erskine:

I have half a mind to write one New Year's letter just to break my rule and, to be sure it does no harm, I'll address it to you and Sara, the last old believers in love and justice left in the whirling world. You two are incorrigible. In spite of all the history we have unrolled at your feet you will not let the light go to your heads. You resist learning. You believe just what you believed when I first met you. War, peace, Ethiopia, Mussolini, England, France, the depression, the recovery and now President Roosevelt and the splitting Republicans have come,—all in vain. You two conservatives have closed your eyes and just stuck. Sometimes I think you have opened your eyes and stuck. Anyhow you have stuck. Liberty and love. Poetry is a terrible business, especially in a period of transition.

I believe that if I now should walk up to your front door, you, Erskine, might be calm and fair, but Sara would somehow express her partisanship for me. Sorry I can't demonstrate my theory, but I assert and I hang right on to it. It is you two, not Wall Street and not only Soviet Russia, which prove that human nature is human nature, that, no matter what you do, flowers will go right on blooming.

---

[1] "The Greatest of Liberals," published in *Soviet Russia Today,* Jan., 1936.
[2] At this period in California there was a general suspicion that letters were opened.

I wish you both a Happy New Year in the wide garden of weeds, —from my heart I do. Never mind how wrong you are, I bless you as all right all right.

Affectionately and tolerantly,
Lincoln Steffens

To Frederic C. Howe

The Getaway,
Jan. 21, 1936

Dear Fred:

Thanks for a good, enlightening letter. But you always consider and supply what the other fellow wants to know. Your situation out in the country fascinates me; that's a way to live; that's a way I'd like to live. But that is the way you always lived when you were free and happy. I wish you'd come and live so around here somewhere. But that's because I can't move. I depend on others coming to me, as they do.

Kyle Crichton was here this last week-end with his wife. A serious humorist, as you probably know. Sam Adams,[1] a cripple, too. Next week-end James Cagney is coming, and Sam Spewack. I wish you could get away. But that would be longer. We have such a lot to trade, you and I.

I like your scheme to write a book on rulership by lawyers; they represent the things, the Things, we all care for. If we cared for our health as much as our privileges, the doctors would rule us. As the preachers did when we prized our blooming souls. We beat the preachers only by abolishing our souls, and so we'll beat the lawyers only by wiping out privileges—as the Soviet Russians have done. I have just been reading for review a book on your subject; it is entitled *Lawless Judges*.

Do you ever see Brandeis these days? Justice Stone, by the way, is my favorite on that doomed bench. Any chance of the President challenging the Supreme Court? A fat field for a fight, that is; all on record. But you know all about that. It's dangerous how I agree with you. About the President being the only man for the transition and the Supreme Court and the conservation being Fascism. The owners of things will force the revolution by blocking Roosevelt or any other

---

[1] Samuel Hopkins Adams, novelist, who had been one of the muckrakers.

"gradualist." Dramatically, I like everything and everybody. And, Fred, I think Tom [1] would like it all and laugh and laugh and laugh. But not in public. Publicly he would cry.

Stef.

To Sam Darcy

The Getaway,
Feb. 25, 1936

Dear Sam:

Your pleasant, gossipy note came in yesterday to warm us after a severe winter of rains and floods. We have had lots of visitors from the East: Robert Forsythe,[2] Sam and Bella Spewack, Dr. Frankwood Williams, the psychiatrist who discovered and announced in his book that they were weak in mental diseases in Russia; and why; Jo Davidson, E. A. Filene, and others are coming. Mr. F. learned a lot this time; I'll enclose an interview in a local paper.

Reports from many sources go to show a shift in public opinion. The social problem is the subject of conversation everywhere.

We have developed a new and promising author in this neighborhood. His name is John Steinbeck. His novel is called *In Dubious Battle,* the story of a strike in an apple orchard. It's a stunning, straight, correct narrative about things as they happen. Steinbeck says it wasn't undertaken as a strike or labor tale and he was interested in some such theme as the psychology of a mob of strikers, but I think it is the best report of a labor struggle that has come out of this valley. It is as we saw last summer. It may not be sympathetic with labor, but it is realistic about the vigilantes. If you haven't had a copy sent you, I'll order you one. It will interest you, especially when I tell you that some of our friends furnished the facts. Steinbeck has been in strikes, but not out here.

I'll be writing again soon, when I make application for a pass, and my health is still a-tremble, but I am pretty sure I can go.

Salutes all around. We miss you, sometimes acutely.

Affectionately,
L. S.

---

[1] Tom L. Johnson (1854-1911), four times "reform" mayor of Cleveland, whose influence remained strong in the lives of both Steffens and Howe.
[2] Satirist on the *New Masses.*

To Frederic C. Howe

The Getaway,
March 11, 1936

Dear Fred:

Thanks for a short, but awfully interesting letter. We all enjoyed it, Ella Winter too. As for me, I cannot see California so cheerfully as you and your friends (who visit us) do. It seems like a dumb, respectable, vigilante state to me, ready with the rope and the righteousness. We have them in this town, too, and we josh and enjoy them, but I can see how dangerous they are. The only way I can keep them from lynching me is to ask them to. A local mayor stands up for me by saying out loud: "No, don't arrest him; he'd like it."

And I would. I am getting strapped, you know, broke. And, laid up an invalid in bed, I can't work. So any haven, like a prison, would provide what liberty hasn't got: security. Still we are thinking seriously of going to Boston (to visit Filene), to France (to see Jo Davidson), and to Soviet Russia (to see Henry George at work). You notice, I suppose, how the Soviets now allow all private property except privilege. You can own a farm as long as you work it, but you can't sell, rent or will it out of your family.

I'd like to have you come out here to get California right, and to be seen by me, but it were better for the cause to see Russia.

Stef.

To E. A. Filene

The Getaway,
March 23, 1936

Dear E. A.:

It must be about time to write again. I haven't kept close tabs but I can guess you are out of the Canal, out on the Atlantic and approaching old Boston towne, where the fur will begin to fly. Well, if it takes the form of reëlecting Roosevelt, it's all right with me, although I am out for Hoover myself.

The editor of the S. F. *Chronicle* called in yesterday; he also and his paper are for the G.O.P., but he makes a wry face when I step up beside him. Earlier in the day, George West, the editor of the S. F. *News,* the Scripps paper, was in and he, of course, is for Roosevelt. But the partisan I count on for Roosevelt is Roosevelt; when he gets talking over the radio you will hear some politics. You should be able to help the President by taking my slant. Why don't you come out for Hoover and the Revolution?

Yes, yes, I know what you want to know and I am reluctant to tell it you; I am not better. The doctor, Kocher, sees no sign of my going to Boston nor do I. Not this summer. Every time I get up and move about, even in the house, my heart beats and skips, and I have to go back to bed for a week.

What do you think of Japan? They have a lot of ideas that don't bother us. Their substitution of a brother-in-law for a marked statesman is worth copying; it finds a use for an in law. And food for thought also is the defeat of the Ethiopians,—if true, and I guess it is. But this country remains the most interesting scene, with the President the most satisfactory hero. You ought to be seeing him soon. Nothing has happened so far that he cannot blast with his radio speeches, he alone; but you can and you do help him. I wonder if he knows that.

Affectionately,
Stef.

To Clinton Hollister

The Getaway, March 23, 1936

Dear Clint:

When your son [1] is old enough to take any name you are wise enough to give him and not lose his temper; when you have reduced him to that degree and made him fit to join the Republican Party; and generally brought him up to bear no resemblance to his father and his paternal family,—when the hard work is done and the boy is fit for human communication,—I wish you would report to me and let me address him on the state of the world he has blundered into. I merely wish to warn him of dangers I see laying for him and tip him on how to circumvent them. I think it is only right to tell a kid about his parents and grandparents and grown-ups generally. In his helpless infancy a fellow is apt to take such inferior people for granted and insult them as they richly deserve. By reminding Pete of certain obvious truths which he had not yet had an opportunity to learn and properly digest, I made him polite to all grown-ups, as you find him today. I told him, and I would be glad to tell your boy, what he will discover for himself too late, that grown-ups cannot help it; that they

---

[1] Clinton Hollister had just had a baby son.

mean well and, in spite of appearances, do the best they can. Pete is polite and kind to us all, because he is so damned sorry for us; and your son can be ditto if I can have a private moment with him before his father et al. finish with the poor little human being. You could do this yourself if you were honest and intelligent like your Uncle

Lincoln

To Jo Davidson

The Getaway, March 30, 1936

Dear Jo:

This may not beat your sailing date, but I'll send it, fast, though it is only to say goodbye or so long. . . . Pete came home the other day and quoted with staring eyes to me a line from his copy book that seemed to have landed on him, something about the way to win a friend is to be one. And I reflected that here was the explanation of your many friends.

You are sailing suddenly, Jo, and maybe I also will sail suddenly. It can't be any other way. I haven't felt lately like getting up and going to Europe. I haven't felt like getting up, and I guess that as long as I deliberate I'll not move. I'll have, as I say, to rise up, suddenly and be there. . . .

Do I get it right from Dr. Suggett that you might consider going to Russia this year? Your plans, as I have them, would seem to preclude such an excursion, but Suggett writes that you said distinctly that we might go together. I am not sure either he or I will go, but if you will I would be mightily tempted. My idea would be to write there the new end of my book and write it as the end of my life-journey, of my search for a way out. I have no doubt that it is the end of all our living, both Russian and European. I was talking to a rich man yesterday who is so convinced that our business world is coming to an end that he is making a farm up north to live on when it is over. A place like Bêcheron that he will make self-sufficient. I have heard of another such man who has picked and bought a ranch high up in mountains that could be easily defended.

But these are just sea-going thoughts that will be wasted unless this letter can be closed up and sent flying off to New York,—in time.

My love to you and your children and grandchildren; and to Bêcheron, Jo.

Affectionately,

Stef.

To Sam Darcy

Carmel, April 12, 1936

Dear Boss and E.,

Just before my birthday when I became of age,[1] I received the most amazing sheaf of cables and I suspect, with my congenital modesty, that one way or another, they are all from you. One, unsigned with a Moscow date, was obviously from you two. A second was from about six Shakespeares,[2] likewise from the capital of the Future. There was one that looked to me like a mistake from Foster and Browder, another from Hathaway[3] and staff, which anyone would prove that I was all right or all left, according to your own place on the line. One signed Stassova[4] nearly bowled me over till I remembered that you were there to spread rumours about me all over the shop. Of course, at my age, no great harm will have been done; it doesn't matter if I do step up into vanity and take a fall to earth, but don't say such things to E. W. or Pete or anyone else that there still is hope for. . . .

I am being urged to go to France for the summer by an artist who offers to go later to Soviet Russia with me. Others want me to go and I have seen that I might go there and finish my *Life* and my life. My sister and her husband are planning to go and we are sorely tempted, but my doctor and, more important, I have my doubts. I don't mean too literally to end my life over there, and I might not have the energy to come back, even if I could get there.

The John Reed book is out; I have read it and I can tell you that the authors, Granville Hicks and John Stuart, have got the poet and playboy, a sunny, happy hero, without suppressing any of the facts; not a detail. It is obvious in this remarkable biography that a poet can through poetry become a revolutionary. The book, by the way, is dedicated to a pal[5] and I am now writing a page review for *New Republic,* with permission to tell anything I wish to about Jack as I knew him. I hope to point out that Granville Hicks has met the propaganda problem by not suppressing but by telling all the facts

[1] April 6th was Steffens's seventieth birthday.

[2] Members of the Union of Russian Writers.

[3] William Z. Foster, Chairman of the Central Committee of the American Communist Party. Earl Browder, Secretary of American Communist Party. Clarence Hathaway, editor of the *Daily Worker.*

[4] President of the Central Committee of the International Workers' Aid in the Soviet Union.

[5] *John Reed: the Making of a Revolutionary* is dedicated to Steffens.

and so finding that there is not only one, the classical or logical, but other roads into revolution; that poetry, romance,—all roads in our day lead to Moscow. It's a very fine piece of criticism, the more impressive to me in that I did not think that Hicks could do it. Hicks, I think, should do other such lives; he should be worked almost to death. Communist propaganda can be left principally to the Capitalists' acts.

Your
Dub

To Fola La Follette

The Getaway,
May 2, 1936

Dear Fola:

A nice, warm family letter from Fola fell on me yesterday right out of "the blue"; all about all the kids, who are not exactly kids now any more, and the work you are all doing; the *Life*,[1] for example. I had forgotten about that. The last I heard was in Washington, where your mother was putting her love and conscience into the task. (By the way, don't let too much conscience leak into the book. Make a story, not a record.) Now you are working on it. And the boys are making it endless, for it's a family history, this life. Your letter gives me a sense of the whole family, even of the little children I don't personally know but who walk right in and belong to the picture, my picture of "the La Follettes." A pleasant intimacy. Marie Howe would love it. (I wonder why I thought of her just at that point, in that connection.)

I must not go on writing like this; not allowed. The doctor will hear of it. I'll close. Scatter my love around the family circle and include Mrs. Roe, who belongs. And write again, Fola.

Affectionately,
Stef.

To Jo Davidson

Dear Jo: The Getaway, June 15, 1936

The last I have heard from you is by way of an article cabled to the N. Y. *Times* from London, a bit of wise propaganda. Very good. But, as I read it, I saw you shining in person there in London. And

[1] Of Robert M. La Follette, Sr.

I envied you. You know enough insiders over there to feel out what the English feel in their decline into error. I would like to get that; I don't care much for Mussolini, but I do like to see that the English are in awe of his vulgar bluffing. Europe is interesting these days, but the centre, the lead, is in France, as you know. You can't bust a mob, of course, but if you could you are out of place. Tell the French that, if they can beat Fascism, we can. What they do, therefore, is important in France, America and in history. We all want the road to fork.

The Revolution is interfering with The War rather humorously, as we can see from over here and no doubt from over there too. I trust you can see that. I wish Blum would go left, but I guess he can't. He knows. Can't you write us an article from France, England, Europe? Writing is your next art, you know; you're not quite up to doing it in music, which would be best. Better write. And, in order to get the benefit of my invaluable editing, you would better stick to news. Write to and for me. See? Yes, I thought you would.

To Robert Cantwell

The Getaway, June 15, 1936

Dear Bob:—

Very deliberately, very solemnly, with no show of envy, I beg leave to welcome the new baby and congratulate the father and, by the way, the mother. Pete and his mother join me in all these activities.

I am glad to see or hear or read that you are back at work. I can see your work count, every review you write convinces one about you, if not about Hearst, for example. I did one on Hearst, pointing what you missed, that the man has but one fault: his riches; and suggesting that, if we would take it away, Hearst would be as good as you or, even, I. The editors did not accept my wisdom. Too Marxian, I suppose.

"We" have "seized" the *Pacific Weekly* in the last three weeks. I am editor-in-chief. I may say that I will be pleased to consider any article from your baby's father which points out anything the world has overlooked anywhere.

Go and lift your hat to the mother and the babies, and say the graceful greeting is from me.

Yours affectionately,
Lincoln Steffens

To Prospective Supporters of Pacific Weekly

Carmel, California,
June 16, 1936

My dear ——

I have found—or been found by—a more or less twinkling group of gamboliers who agree with the observation that there is a big hole out here for a *Pacific Weekly* which, beginning small on our Coast, can become as big as the whole United States. These are crucial, confusing times. The world is in motion, squirming all over as we are out here. Our amiable theory is that there is news, here and there, now and all the time these days, to report and to interpret, that will show dramatically, entertainingly, that all us isolated groups and nations of human beings are buzzing about pretty much the same predicament. We are strung out along one wide road away from one and the same problem to an as yet unknown solution; we don't know where we are going, but WE CAN know. We can learn from one another, if we will understand that France, for example, and Germany; Italy and Spain and England, yes, and Ethiopia and the United States and China are riding the same storm, stopping to try out much the same experiment in different—and yet not so different—ways.

It is possible to watch and relate all these "crises," movements and "news" in such a way that the human race, already on the verge, can be made conscious of what has happened to each of us and lead us all gently, even humorously, to a common solution, both as to method of procedure and to result, which we can become at least aware of.

It will cost some little money, work, art, management, character, but it will be some fun too. I am asking you to join us and to match our efforts with enough cash and credit to carry on, to look around us and mass our world news. Will you gamble on the chances we take and offer? NOW?

Yours anyhow,
Lincoln Steffens
Editor-in-Chief

To Mrs. J. James Hollister

The Getaway,
June 25, 1936

Dear Dot:

Your Gang,—or part of it: the part that called here: Clint's bunch, —spent two happy (for me) days here and left yesterday afternoon.

They are probably with you now and you are having the good time that we had. What a charming crowd they are. Even Pete likes them, —a little. He wants to go down after his next concert which is Saturday night. He is practising his concert pieces now, here, in this room.

It wasn't a very good time for our visitors: too much else going on. We were putting the *Pacific Weekly* to bed, and Peter is up at the office now, finishing that weekly job. The editor-in-chief is here in bed already. We had also the finish of that Sharkey spy story [1] which has agitated Carmel for so long. He didn't find out a thing, but we can't get that said: have to write it ourselves. He told the Legion, who invited him to address them, that he had proved everything he expected to and I guess they believed him, though he did not give his evidence or specify anything. Left it vague for everybody to accept or reject as they wished. We'll probably be suspected and shunned, but not inconvenienced. Absurd!

The *Weekly* is succeeding,—in vain. We have to raise money to get out each number as ever. No advertisers as usual; some new subscribers but not enough.

Give my love to Jim, Dot, and scatter the rest around among all your cowboys and girls.

Affectionately,
Len

To Frederic C. Howe

The Getaway,
July 8, 1936

Dear Fred:

. . . The grand old Republicans are said to be considering accepting and backing Roosevelt, whom they hate, but meanwhile we vague Democrats foresee his election by a decisive majority. That speech of acceptance he made was a corker, a classic. Whether he means and can do it, he has delivered us something said, something accepted, which is a *fait* accomplished all in itself. The drought can't dry that up.

You speak of Pete: he has gone to my sister's ranch near Santa

[1] "Charles Y. Sharkey," or Captain Bakcsy, also known as "Captain X," and by a variety of other aliases, had been sent to Carmel and had set up a paraphernalia of dictaphones, etc., to "discover," for certain employers and patriotic groups of San Francisco, the "Moscow gold" that was, in their belief, financing the waterfront strikes.

Barbara for his long summer vacation and is very busy there, with other kids and a few thousand head of cattle. I will hold your greeting to him till he has time to listen to it and appreciate it.

We here are watching France rather anxiously; if they can beat the Fascists we can. We keep one eye on Soviet Russia, which, having wiped out privileges, can draw a constitution and grant liberty and democracy with some sense of security and permanence. All they've got to beat now is war. They are clear, the rest of the world is confused, like England, or "right," like Germany. Your Scandinavia seems to be genuinely experimenting with privileges kept, though kept down. Has Roosevelt any philosophy? I hear, I judge, not, but I often wonder if some of you democrats are not leading him to learn. When next you write try to find a way to tell me about this.

I like the picture you give of your setting and your interest in it: I can see that you are happy enough to go away somewhere. The book sounds fine. I have one about ready for the Fall too; it's made up out of my column "Lincoln Steffens Speaking."

Professor Counts [1] was in here one day last week, a wide open mind, filling up with ideas and facts to teach. And evidently he is a teacher, both by profession and by instinct. He is going to Russia as you are to Sweden and Austria.

So long, Fred. I gotta quit enjoying myself.

Affectionately,
Stef.

To Pete Steffens

The Getaway,
July 8, 1936

My dear Pete:

Your card came as a relief. We were sure you got there, but it was nice to hear that our theory was correct. All theories are like that: sure till proved, then dropped as commonplace facts. Like this arrival of yours at the ranch.

You did arrive, didn't you? Dot did call for you, didn't she? She does believe you got to Gaviota at seven, now, doesn't she? What did you do while waiting for Dot to believe us and call for you? Did Margaret go on home and leave you? And the calves and other young

[1] George S. Counts, Professor of Education at Teachers College, Columbia University.

things, were they glad to see you, unharmed by your vacation with us? I am so glad to hear all this, and your mother will be. You remember your mother, don't you?

We've got a famous Dutch screen-director [1] coming here in a few minutes with several pictures to show at the Filmarte tonight. Everybody (except Pete) is going. I may send you clippings about it tomorrow or next day. Lots of company too.

A letter from Anna says she'd like to come back here from Wales to live. She might even leave Pat and Betty Ann with her mother in the old country. I would love to have Anna back; wouldn't you? I think I'll write her a love letter and tell her so. You may too, if you have time. Send it to me and I'll forward it.

Give my love to Aunt Dot and Uncle Jim, to all their descendants unto the second and third generation; and to mine, which means you.

Very affectionately,
Your Father,
Pop

The Getaway,
July 13, 1936

Dear Pete:

We have been busy, as busy as you have been, I doubt not, and I think I can put you at your ease by warning you that whenever you are neglected by your parents you may remember that this is the busiest centre of a busy world in all this busy world. Not the ranch, not Gaviota, but Carmel, especially The Getaway. We are making a paper, the *Pacific Weekly*. This last week-end we had a conference of editors and workers here, and we really conferred. True, I slept a couple of hours, but your mother worked and I sympathized with her so that I got tired. You know how it is.

We have had some visitors too, not connected with the paper. The one I liked best was Professor Counts, a man who, with Dr. Beard the historian, is in all wrong with Hearst and the reactionaries. You know, like Mama and me. He is a live man, what we call a live wire. He came West to speak at Stanford and I found him one of the most open and fearless minds I ever met. Stanford is the university where your aunts, Dot and Laura, studied; they don't encourage live minds there, but they invited Counts even against Hearst's objection and

[1] Joris Ivens.

liked him. Your principal, Mr. Bardarson, called here with Counts and stayed with him.

Your neighbor, Sharkey, has not exposed us yet, though he still promises to.

Tell Aunt Dot, with my compliments, that the Republicans haven't decided yet whether to back Landon or the President. Ask her which she prefers, if anything. Roosevelt is going to win anyhow, I guess, but we Republicans can make it certain; or unanimous. Give her my grinning love, give some to Uncle Jim, and spread the rest all over the ranch to all the humans. The cattle and animals generally don't care much. With a little from your mother too.

Affectionately your Father,
Dad

Carmel, July 21, 1936

Dear Pete:

Aunt Dot will be amused to see the check which the *New Republic* paid you for the item they published from you;[1] you are pretty young to begin making money for your writings.

We have been having busy, rather hectic days on the *Pacific Weekly,* but we have had results; we get around sixty subscriptions a day. The circulation is going up and the paper continues to live. It may succeed.

I can tell you, and they can explain, that President Roosevelt is running, like Uncle Jim, for reëlection of himself to be kept in office and for the support of their policy of the New Deal. You don't know it, but you and the other kids are concerned in the result; but we have got to make the grown-ups understand; and that is possible but not so easy. The whole world is in turmoil. Especially Spain and France are fighting even to the death for what we are only voting.

Mum and I enjoyed your last, long letter. It was well done, clear and interesting. We are always eager for your communications.

By the way, that *New Republic* check I spoke of above was sent to you, I think, or will be, and Aunt Dot will tell you how to cash it. She may do it for you the next time she goes in to Santa Barbara if you will endorse it.

Have you begun to use that pony your cousin Joe picked for you

---

[1] An item sent in for the "Bandwagon" column.

upper: KYLE S. CRICHTON (photo by Valentino Sarra). *lower left:* SAM DARCY (photo by Consuelo Kanaga). *lower right:* ANNA LOUISE STRONG (photo by Ossip Garber).

kids? It's a chance to learn to ride. A boy who can swim and ride a horse can always escape in the night. Or in broad daylight.

Keep us forewarned as to when you and Cousin Jane and the others are coming up this way.

Please present my respect to Uncle Jim and Aunt Dot, my love to all the others, including even the baby you say doesn't count.

Lovingly, your father,

Lincoln Steffens

To Anna McCarthy

The Getaway,
July 25, 1936

Dear Anna:

I have got to stop thinking about you so much, and write to you. It is a good day for that. It is wet and rainy. Note the date. Midsummer, when you know it never rains, and Peter has been out in the garden collecting two barrels of snails. Leslie would have gathered four and even Pete would have had one barrel to show. Wonderful! Everything is changed. A revolution in Spain and France, an election on here! A big strike coming in the fall,—you wouldn't recognize your adopted country.

Some things are the same. Anna, for example; she has only changed her residence for a while. And Pete, he has gone away to the ranch for part of the summer. His cousin, Joe, has found a pony on the ranch that is sober enough for kids and is letting Pete break him for the kids who are about as numerous as the chickens or the calves. No. That part,—the ranch is all right. But,—

Our Anna is gone; you know; the backbone of this funny family, the mother of us all, she is not here. And we miss her. I have no one to blame when anything is wrong. No one to be unjust to. It is fierce, Anna. When are you coming back? Your sweet little rooms we let out for a night or two to friends who are not like Anna and Leslie and Betty Ann. Better come back, Anna, and let me abuse you. Stay as long as I do.

Give my respects to your mother, father, sister; remember me to the children and keep my love for my Anna.

Sincerely and affectionately,

"Papa" Lincoln Steffens

To E. A. Filene

Carmel, July 25, 1936

Dear E. A.,

I wrote to Jo Davidson yesterday and that reminded me that I have not noticed you for a long while. I wrote Jo about the revolution which is all around him, but principally it is the country, Spain, where you foresaw it when you were there. Can you foresee it here now? I can, and we have in power the man who can check it,—if anybody can. But I'll bet your ex-class will block him in some way. Why do they hate him so? Like you, Roosevelt told them the truth, told and he tells. They hate *that*. They do out here. They are working and conspiring for a coast-wide struggle with labor which is exactly what they should not want now; labor should, but not the bosses. There's enough on now, what with France and Spain, and the steel strike and the conflict between Lewis and Green over something the rank and file of the workers are aware of and interested in. Craft unions are doomed. And at just this time, when craft unions are failing, the bosses bring up the company union! You'd think Soviet Russia had got into the Chamber of Commerce to steer it to bring on the revolution, to make faces at France and Spain, who are very busy. With history! Can't the college graduates recognize history when they see it?

You are right in your day. You are backing the one and only man who is born to meet his day. Even the Communists realize that he (and his Democratic Party) is all that can save what democracy we have. I wish you were in a position to say a few things briefly to him; your disposition would be to rub it in, repeat, elaborate, prove. The time has come for him and everybody to deal in slogans. The telegraph is our medium these days. I might begin and end with the message in this too long letter: You are right, Mr. President, keep right on. And look out for the labor troubles invited by the Republicans this fall. There's a revolution in every strike.

Are you going abroad this summer? When? Where? I'd suggest that you go to England, and watch and listen. The English have not decided yet which way to turn. Fred Howe and some tourists high up in the Administration are heading right now for Scandinavia. Might go there. That means they are still looking for a third way. There is no third way, but you always hoped for one, the impossible. I have to sit right here in my little bed; no improvement. It takes about all the wind I have to go to the wash-room and back.

Well, I'll close my telegram, wishing you all well.

Affectionately,

Stef.

To Pete Steffens

Carmel, August 2, 1936

Dear Pete:

We have, amongst us, received several letters from you, and we are well pleased, very well pleased. The first to come was the one you sent to your music teacher, who sent it over for us to enjoy. She is a thoughtful neighbor and thinks not only in music. We returned it for her to keep. The other letters were to Mama and to me. They were the best of all; gave us a picture of the fun you are having and of the busyness of the ranch. I liked your notes on Uncle Jim's campaign for the senatorship and on the dehorning of the calves. Lots of people never saw that done; don't know it happens. You are learning about life. As you will realize when you come to write, as you will.

I like too your very courteous reminder that Jane is coming up after August 6. Are you coming with her? Better think of it. It's a good chance to get home. Talk it over with Aunt Dot, Uncle Jim and my niece Jane. And speak to Aunt Dot about this: there was a German scientist and scholar here, who wanted to see you. He had read my book, and was disappointed that you were not here. When we said humorously that he might call on you at the ranch, he thought he might if Dot and Uncle Jim would care to have him call. Tell Aunt Dot that his name is Lederer, Dr. Emil Lederer. He is an economist, he was among the first to leave Germany when the Fascists began to express themselves. He got together with Alvin Johnson in the University in Exile at the New School for Social Research in New York and has been there ever since. Johnson made him read my book for a true picture of the U. S. and he got you and me all mixed up. I think he thinks you won that pony on my miserable, merry Christmas. Anyhow he wants to see the hero of my *Life* and imagines You are it.

We continue to have a procession of visitors. Bill Rogers, the son of Will, called yesterday, so did the correspondent Spike (Frazier) Hunt, his wife and son. The usual run of editors, receivers and friends of *Pacific Weekly* came and went. It was decided that we continue under the same old arrangement for a few weeks more. Most of this that I am telling you will interest Aunt Dot more than it will you, but my letter is addressed to you.

I'd like to hear more about the pony.

Give my love to everybody in a perfectly wasteful way, keeping enough for yourself.

Affectionately, your Dad,

L. Steffens

APPENDIX

Certain letters, interesting as documents, and intended as such, have been printed here rather than in the body of the book. They show Steffens's part in certain historical events and his ways of exercising his personal influence.

I. ON WAR HYSTERIA AND LABOR

Colonel E. M. House,
State Department, Washington, D. C.

The Players, New York City,
Oct. 18, 1917

The war is dividing men along the class line. It is becoming a class war.

This is the conviction I got on my lecture trip across the country.

Business men and the upper class generally are for the war, honestly, but passionately; aggressively. Accused of sordid motives and conscious of making money, they are developing a moblike madness which is understandable but harmful. Officials and the press are catching it.

Labor and the lower classes are not exactly against the war, but they are not for it; not yet; and the attitude of the upper class and the policy (or some acts) of some parts of the government and press are packing the workers back into a suppressed, sullen opposition.

This can be cured. More. I believed that this evil tendency can be turned into a force for good. And the principle to apply is that of good politics as distinguished from good morals.

A democratic government must not only be right; it must appear right.

The Administration is not making a class war. Let it show that it isn't. It's no use resenting the imputation and pointing to scattered acts and facts which will set the Administration right in history. This is no time for argument and controversy. Act.

Accept openly the fact that there is this growing feeling. Say so. Call it by its names: doubt, confusion, suspicion, hate. And don't rebuke it. Understand it, sympathetically, and then—melt it into something akin to love and faith.

Ask the pro-war people to be more patient with the anti-war folk.

Ask the pacifists to be more considerate of the fighters; and to put their minds, not on peace, but the terms of a permanent peace.

Ask the soldiers again, as Baker did once, not to deal with the I.W.W.'s in the I.W.W. spirit. Ask this of the employers also.

Ask all editors, writers and speakers,—all—to remember that the war psychology is a little like a sickness; that it makes men's minds sensitive and sore; and that to say things that give pain to this state of mind is like being rough with the wounded.

Ask official prosecutors of war-time offenses to be fairer; they must do they duty, but they should do it less personally than some of them are doing it now; and more gently, much more justly.

Ask the President to practice mercy, as Lincoln did; only, in this later day, more systematically, on a larger scale. He could pick from among his personal friends some humane spirits (like Fremont Older) to go about for him "visiting them in prison" and calling on the families of the convicted, and recommending pardons, many, many pardons.

I would reverse the policy as to free speech and a free press, but I will not urge this. I have seen Russia, and I learned there to trust "the mob"; to put in "the people" a faith which I did not have before. I know now that liberty works. The final effect of free speech in Petrograd was to make the speakers moderate their tone and consider the feelings of their auditors!

But certainly the President can repeat his assurance now that after the war, the war measures limiting our liberties will be repealed. And he can clinch this by letting us hope that some bad practices (notably in the Post Office) which grew up before the war, may be stopped when we make peace.

All these things should be done in one proclamation; and this also: the most important of all:

Stop the appearance of "war on Labor." Stop or suspend labor prosecutions. Declare an amnesty in the class struggle and pardon all labor convicts in prison for "labor crimes"; all.

Too much? Hear me out.

The President is acting in the Mooney case now, and for Berkman, I hear. That is good, but it's too quiet, too slow. What we need now is an act of clemency so big, so loud, so unmistakable, that all men will get it and feel it. I would have the President and Governors, too, join in a declaration of amnesty and pardon *as an attempt "to win back a faith that Labor had no right ever to lose in their government."* In other words, I would handle it as an emergency; and it is an emergency to be faced as such.

Labor thinks that this is a class war; that capital is getting the better of labor in it; that the employers were using the situation to gain advantages; and I heard groups of workers and one group of business men declaring that the Administration was in the "plot" to "fix" Organized Labor now for good and all!

I tried to reason with this state of mind, and failed. It's that terrible war psychology, which takes a few incidents that have no relation to one another, and darkens them into a conspiracy. Officials are doing the same thing. This is the day of "conspiracies." The prosecution of the I.W.W.'s is for conspiracy; a pro-German plot; and no doubt there are "proofs" which will appeal to a jury in wartime. But I happen to know that Arturo Giovanniti, Gurley Flynn, Tresca, and other Eastern I.W.W.'s quarrelled a year ago with Haywood and the Western I.W.W.'s and not only could not have conspired with them; they "did not speak." And the rank and file of labor know this. And they think that the detectives didn't investigate far enough to learn of it. Nor did the investigator find out, apparently, that Giovanniti, for one reason, and Haywood, for another, are fiercely pro-Allies and anti-German.

If there was a conspiracy in the I.W.W. it was to use the emergency of war, as Labor thinks their bosses have, to raise prices and improve their condition.

And so on the other side: Labor's suspicion that the administration is in a conspiracy with the employers' associations to make war on Labor under cover of the war in Europe! Labor has "proofs." They point to this wholesale indictment of I.W.W. leaders at this time. I happen to know that employers' associations were preparing for this and other labor battles before the war on Germany was declared; and I don't know it, but I am as sure as I am of President Wilson's democracy, that the Administration is not in any such "conspiracy."

But I do see that the Administration seems to think that Mr. Gompers and the Central Organization of the A. F. of L. represent labor. They don't. There are over 100,000 workers in the I.W.W. and a great majority of the A. F. of L. has a silent, but deeply class-conscious sympathy with the I.W.W. and other radical labor groups. I know this from leaders close to Gompers; and I know it from having seen with my own eyes contributions by A. F. of L. unions of moneys for the defence of I.W.W. and other radical cases, which represent to labor "the fight of their class against the Government, the War and Capital."

And so, knowing this and knowing what the "proofs" are that the agitators use, I can see that one flash of lightning might clear the whole atmosphere, disarm the suspicious and inspire all men with the President's spirit. Let me sound Haywood and the I.W.W.'s on an amnesty; and the pacifists; and, yes, the farmers and big employers' associations. All men are capable of great things, if only they are asked for great things. I believe that with half a chance, I could show you that with a generous, candid, kindly democratic proclamation of a labor-peace policy such as the President is always disposed to make, he can mobilize America for what he is after—one last war for an everlasting peace.

Anyhow, get me a hearing. Or, if you can't or won't, please don't scorn my faith. It is good. I got it in the muck.

II. ON MEXICO

The Players,
16 Gramercy Park, New York,
Feb. 21, 1918

Hon. Charles A. Douglas,
University Club, Mexico.

My dear Judge Douglas:

I am sorry I cannot go to Mexico, but I can't, so I shall try to put to you in writing what I wanted to have said, and ask you to present it with my very sincere compliments to President Carranza.

President Wilson's recent peace messages to Congress carry an obvious meaning for Mexico and all the other Latin American Countries. And Mr. Wilson knows it; he intends it. He is declaring for the right of all nations, large and small, to work out for themselves, each its own destiny in its own way and in its own good time. This means, not only Belgium and Finland, Russia and France, India and China; it must mean Mexico, too. And it does. It means Mexico and Cuba,

Porto Rico and the Philippines. It means all the Americas. And I believe President Wilson intends it to.

I wish President Carranza could believe this.

President Wilson is making war on Imperialism. Not only German Imperialism. He is turning the war against German Imperialism into a war against all Imperialism: German, British, Russian, French, Italian *and* American. And I assert that this is not only implied in his messages; it is meant in his mind.

I have reason to think that when peace is in the making, President Wilson will be heard saying that whatever we ask other nations to renounce or agree to do: Germany, France, Italy and Great Britain— that the United States of North America also will do; and that he will be able and willing to pledge the United States to accept as a basis for our policy in both the Americas whatever principle of liberty and self-determination the other powers can be persuaded to adopt for the guidance and the limitation of their conduct in Europe, Asia and Africa.

I would beg President Carranza and his people to believe this. President Carranza sees the implications, of course, but I infer, I feel, that he does not wholly accept the intention. I can understand why. While we point to Germany in Belgium, we are in Hayti, Nicaragua and Santo Domingo. We have "taken" Porto Rico; we let Cuba go, but our Platt Amendment is a gloved fist over her. And then there is our history; Texas and California; there is the constant interference in Mexico and the menace of intervention everywhere. It is bad. I have travelled enough in Latin countries to realize that we, the United States, look to our Latin neighbors very much as Germany looks to Europe and now to the United States. What is more to the present point, I personally believe that we are a peril to the other countries in America—if Imperialism is not killed by this war.

There are other reasons, more intimate, pettier, more annoying, why it is hard for any patriotic Mexican to put faith in what President Wilson or you, Judge Douglas, or I may say. I am thinking now, not of history, but of the current conflict between our words and our official acts. But I need not go into these. You know what they are; we have discussed them between ourselves, and with anger, pain, shame. I call them to your mind only that President Carranza may perceive that I am aware of the whole case against my contention.

But President Wilson knows these things too. He has referred to them twice in conversations with me, once when we were talking about Mexico, again when I was telling him about the Russian revolution. He understood his official fault and his unofficial helplessness. And so, of course, does President Carranza know by experience how a responsible president is not able always to have all things exactly as he would like them.

And there you have the explanation of my old-time wish that the two Presidents could personally meet and have a candid, quiet talk together, man to man. They would arrive thus at an understanding which would spread through the two nations and on through many future years.

President Wilson sees our drift into imperialism. He is an historian, trained to note tendencies, but also he is accustomed as a scholar to recognize the forces which cause such movements. He can't stop American imperialism. He has to yield to it. It seems to me that Mr. Wilson feels as other sound economic observers feel, that, unless *all* imperialism is stopped by the peace which ends this war, all nations will run over (or under) into empires and on to other and greater wars!

That is the New Russian view. I was over there, as you know; I talked much and intimately with the leaders and members of all the groups and parties. And I pointed it out in my introduction to Trotzky's book just published.[1]

When we Americans in Petrograd asked the Russians if they did not fear lest the Germans would conquer and exploit them, they used to answer:

"Yes, but what's the difference? If we are to be taken and exploited and misgoverned, what does it matter whether it's done by Germans or Americans, English or even Russians. No, we must all altogether put a stop to all conquests and all exploitation or go on suffering."

This, by the way, this common experience and feeling of the Russian and the Mexican peoples, was what prompted me to urge upon you and Mr. Bonillas and Mr. De Negri an exchange of Mexican and Russian ministers.

It is against this common experience and universal danger that

[1] *The Bolsheviki and World Peace,* Boni & Liveright, 1918.

President Wilson is pleading, and for a peace that shall be founded upon an understanding among all nations. With what results? When he reasserted the Russian peace terms as his; as ours; as the Allies', he got no full answer from either the German or the Allied governments. Trotzky showed by his peace negotiations that the German reason was that the German Government still clung to the hope of empire. H. G. Wells, the English writer, said in a recent article that the British also hoped still for Empire and more Empire. But there were answers to Mr. Wilson's call for renunciation. One came from British Organized Labor; another from the radical Left of the German and Austrian Socialist parties, a third came from the mutterings of the people and from the debates in the Parliament of Italy. It's the old story; the people heard him gladly. And that's something. That is a great deal.

The war against Imperialism is on. The war is becoming indeed a war for democracy; really; and not only for democracy in Germany. It has reached a point where it can be turned into a war to "make the world safe for democracy," when democracy comes. But only if all the forces interested in this result can learn to understand and believe in one another; Mexico and all Latin America; Russia and the neutrals; Spain, Holland, Norway, Sweden and Denmark; and especially the nations, like China, which feel themselves in danger; these and all the common people of all the world.

Wherefore I suggest first that a Pan-American Congress be called to carry on the policy already broached by President Wilson for a substitution of Pan-Americanism in the stead of the Monroe Doctrine; and that that convention proceed to do now here on the American continents what is to be proposed to be done on the world at large: set up an American League of Nations to deal with international questions in dispute.

Second: that President Carranza and his Cabinet put themselves in the way to ascertain whether my theory as to the deliberate intention of my government is not right, arranging to that end for a meeting of the two presidents; or for a diplomatic test question, such, for example, as:

"Would President Wilson be willing to say now to Mexico or others that he is prepared, if the European Powers gave up annexations and interventions, to bring the United States to do likewise?"

If these should seem for any reason to be inadvisable, I would suggest:

Third, that Mexico get in touch with China, Spain, Norway—the other neutrals; the other Latin countries; and, certainly Russia, with the purpose of an anti-imperialist understanding for joint action at the peace conference. My belief is, as you see, that such a joint commission would find itself working there with President Wilson, the Russians and a powerful, world-wide, democratic public opinion. But that is not my point. I am not now asking help for my country; I do not suggest that Mexico declare war. And neither am I presuming to befriend Mexico.

My interest is that of an anti-imperialist. I would like to see Mexico and all the other nations concerned to defeat imperialism take steps at this favorable moment to inform themselves anew upon the acts and the intentions of the U. S. Government and the other warring governments so as to be ready, both as governments and as peoples, to pick quick their friends early in the peace negotiations. My theory that, in that case, they would come to trust and work with my President and my people, may be set down only as a measure of my faith and of my confidence in my comprehension of the facts.

I am a friend of Mexico, but I am first a patriotic American. Therefore I dread imperialism—not, you understand, not only for the sake of Mexico, but because I know that American Imperialism will corrupt and spoil the United States as it did Spain, and as it is spoiling England, Germany, and the whole bleeding world. Imperialism caused this war; it is the cause of all wars; if it is not killed now, it will cause "the next war." And I invite you, Judge Douglas and President Carranza to imagine what the next war will be like with the further "progress in science," with its enlarged and improved guns, its perfected submarines and flying machines, its deadly gases and liquid fire.

I shall expect no reply to this letter, except your polite acknowledgment of its receipt. But I will ask you to assure President Carranza of my respect and to vouch to him for the sincerity of my plea for his attention. I beg to remain, my dear Judge Douglas,

Faithfully yours,

Lincoln Steffens

III. ON FREE SPEECH

San Francisco, Cal.,
May 11, 1918

W. H. Porterfield,
Editor, *The Sun,*
San Diego, California

My dear Porterfield:

Now that the "trouble" is all over and the public mind of San Diego (so to speak) is pacified, or exhausted, perhaps you will let me speak a few last words. You must. You called me (among other things) a good scout for "standing for" your report of what I said about the mob of Petrograd. Well, do you be a good scout also, and print what I say about you and your report, which amazed me. I could understand why it was hard for you to believe that the Russian mob was (to use my words; not yours) "great, stupid, stinking, conscious, beautiful." It was. It was orderly, just, and very gentle. This is incredible to you because you never saw such a thing. You have seen only the mobs of San Diego, and they are—well, they are not beautiful. No, I know about your mobs. As a member of the Free Speech League, I inquired diligently into each of the several mob manifestations which have put San Diego on the map in our country, and I have noted, and you must remember, that your San Diego mobs have always been better class mobs: "respectable": educated, possessed, righteous. That makes a difference. The upper class mobs of Russia also were violent, fierce, and obscene. But the mob I was describing was illiterate, poor, and very, very humble. It was never sure it was right. It used to make me think of the mobs that followed Jesus around about Jerusalem.

But I could not understand why you called me dangerous and a philosophical anarchist. I'm not dangerous. I'd like to be. I used to try to be dangerous, but only as you want to be: to the grafters, crooks and traitors who undermine our American Government, corrupt our churches, schools, press and business; and debase our American ideals of democracy, liberty and independence.

And then, there was that "something sinister," which you said you detected in my talk; which you yourself described as "the spirit of brotherhood," and which you finally decided was Bolshevikism and philosophical and anarchism! My lecture was on the Russian Revolution; that is now Bolshevik. I had to present Bolshevikism as it is. But the Bolshevik party is not anarchistic. It is the very opposite. The Bolsheviki and the Russian Revolutionists generally are orthodox Marxian socialists; and I read in the news today that in Moscow they are fighting and arresting the anarchists.

But I, you may say, I was the anarchist. That's what Captain Fredericks, the one-time prosecutor of Los Angeles, said to me once in court, and I answered him as I will answer you:

"I am worse than an anarchist; more radical, I mean. I believe in the teachings of Jesus." I believe that it is my job, as a reporter and a citizen, to put into all I write, see or do, not only good faith and hope, but that understanding of others—whether men, mobs or nations, which is my interpretation of "love" or "charity." I don't always practice this, as this letter shows, but as your phrase, "the brotherhood of man" shows, I did get it into my lecture. Isn't it amazing that you and the Christian world should so commonly mistake Christianity for anarchism, and move instinctively and instantly to crucify it?

But you may have been joking. I thought, when I first read your "scare" report, that I detected a sinister note of humour in it. It was subtle, too sinister for these times and for your journalistic followers. People are really deeply suffering just now, and sickly suspicious. They have lost their sense of humor entirely.

And the editor of that other paper: *The Union*—he plainly never had any sense of humour; and no initiative and no independence. If he follows all your leads as he did this one; if he has no reporters of his own and takes your reports as he did in this case; and if he is always as excitable and as uneducated in the use of English, as he proved himself to be in his editorials about me, you should be careful not thus to mislead him. He means well; his simplicity of purpose and of mind is obvious, but the man is dangerous. He is, unconsciously, a most unphilosophical anarchist, and while not pro-German, he is pro-autocracy. Isn't he? Doesn't *The Union* belong to that special interest which has Prussianized San Diego?

But he developed one point which you didn't cover. He convinced me that there are at least two honest men in San Diego. If his paper represents what other newspaper men tell me it represents, then, the passion, the joy with which he sprang from my prostrate reputation upon the upright characters of Messrs. Bard and Johnson, is proof positive to me, an expert "muckraker," that these gentlemen, whom I barely knew before, are good citizens and in some way dangerous to those dark forces which have corrupted San Diego until it has come to be regarded, I find, as one of the three least liberal, most timid of American cities.

No? Yes. The lecture I gave on the Russian Revolution is one I have given in over fifty places in the United States and it has disturbed only two or three of the most reactionary of my auditors. It was twice reported verbatim to the Government, and once when the proper official in Washington showed me the secret service report of it, I asked him whether I should stop it; he said "No, of course not. The President says the Russians still are our allies and anything that helps to an understanding of them is right." And the lecture your new Chief of Police was telephoned to stop was an appeal to our people, and especially to the pacifists, not to oppose this war, but war; and not even war directly, but the causes of war, by standing firm and cool and clear, for what President Wilson is gradually persuading all the allies to fight for: a settlement of this war which shall recognize, describe and remove the underlying economic and political causes of all wars and so achieve, finally, an enduring, democratic, universal peace.

In brief then, my dear Porterfield, the "trouble" was not with me and my lectures, but with you and San Diego.

Hoping to meet you both again some day, I beg to remain,

Yours philosophically,

Lincoln Steffens

IV. ON A GENERAL AMNESTY FOR POLITICAL PRISONERS

Chicago, Ill.,
November 1, 1921

Honorable Will H. Hays,
Postmaster General,
Washington, D. C.

My dear Sir:

I was looking for you in New York last week to urge you to move the Administration to break the hate in this country; to gentle away the last frowns of the old war psychology and bring in an era of good will. It can be done. The President could do it with a stroke, and the chance is coming soon. I heard him say so.

I went in with the reporters to the White House Conference one afternoon. A correspondent asked: "What about Debs?" The President answered that there would be nothing about Debs until peace had been finally, formally and officially established. Good. My suggestion is that, when the peace is thus accomplished, the United States grant not only a pardon to Debs, but a general amnesty; and not only a cautious picked, gingerly amnesty, but the broadest, most generous declaration of pardon that has ever been declared in any country at any time.

The act alone, if sudden and big, would speak the message that needs to be sent all over this land and other lands. But if the President would put out with it a short fine appeal for peace at home and good will among men, he would lift up in the American people, I verily believe, a spirit with which he could work wonders both here and abroad.

And we lack that spirit now. We had it when we went into the war. We had it when we went into the peace, too. President Wilson and the American people were the hope of the world. The peoples of Europe believed he and we would set up peace, permanent peace. And they wanted that. God, how they wanted that! The French peasants knelt beside the track at night when the American president's train passed. Italian peasants put Wilson's picture beside their saint and prayed to him.

Then the disappointment: the peace that is no peace. There were reasons, of course; none that the people could understand. So they sank back into despair, sullen, bitter hopelessness. I was there among them. I saw, I felt it; but all the world knows about it; this tragedy of the masses, this failure of "the American president and the American people." For they lump us, Mr. Postmaster General. We all failed when the American president failed to do the impossible.

And then, the radicals of Europe, jealous for their leadership, afraid of the United States as a world leader,—they took pains to report that we were hard, legalistic, commercial at home, too. We were the only country that had no pardon for our war criminals. And here at home, I a radical, can tell you that the Left is using the apparent government policy of justice without mercy and the outspoken aims of

Business to weaken Organized Labor (they lump you and Business, you know) to prove that the Class War is on; to whip up the normal antagonisms into passion and so drive the worker's Left. And they are succeeding.

I am talking to labor audiences all the time and I read in their faces prejudice, bitterness, feelings. It's hard to reason. It's easy to appeal to passion. It's all wrong. I, personally, would like to have a state of mind which would take my reporter's facts and think about them. And you, the Administration, you need such a state of mind in your business. You need a period of credit, moral credit; time and the willingness to wait and think and work together, free of suspicion, free of ugly misinterpretations.

Wilson could have got this, if, when he came home, he had been generous and willing to play politics; big politics, I mean. Politics can be big and generous. I think politics is nobler than business. But I think you see that. I am writing to you on a matter outside of your department because I have heard you say things which indicate that you understand that politics is the doing of public business with some sense that public opinion, the mute longings and the suppressed spirit of the masses, are elements in the job. And the President has shown this democratic sense, once very clearly, and, I think, beautifully. There's heart somewhere in this Administration.

But Mr. Wilson, in his disappointment or his sickness, was hard. He yielded nothing; he was right and he was righteous. No soft word came from him, no peace. The American People have gone back to work (and to fight) at home, without ever anybody speaking a single kindly word from the heart. And that's not true to us, Mr. Hays; that does not represent us. We, the American People, have a soul.

Express it. Abide your time, wait till all is ready, but then, remember that the Thing I complain of, the hard, just, legal, the righteous political Wrong has gone on so long that no little act will accomplish now any such release of good will as I am pleading for. It will be weak, not strong; a surrender, not a triumph, to let Debs go alone. Let them all go; all the war and Labor prisoners. Call in all the governors of states, yes, and the captains of industry, and altogether, president and governors, and—all, pardon all the men and women who did their crimes for what they thought was—a cause, any cause. In a word, make peace, Mr. Postmaster General, give us peace.

If, Sir, you are disposed to shake your head at this, thinking, as I have, of the difficulties and the risks of it, let me see and talk to you. I can tell you some inside facts. I can tell you what has happened to some of the prisoners of this sort who have come out of jail. The triumph is not theirs, and the triumph will not be for the others either. No. They will not be heroes, pardoned, as they are now. The victory will be the Government's; and I don't mean merely the Administration's; it will be a triumph for the United States of America, and a World Triumph.

Yours very sincerely,
Lincoln Steffens

V. SECOND THOUGHTS ON REFORM

To the Editor of the *Bee* [1]
Sacramento, California

Tahoe City,
July 5, 1927

Sir—When I called upon you the other day it was for the very private purpose of explaining myself, personally, to you, personally. It was not to correct anything.

You have found fault with me, but in the main your criticism has been just. I have been inconsistent. Indeed, I have been consistent only in my inconsistency; in the open-mindedness with which I have followed the facts I have had to report.

But I never could see why you, a newspaper man, were so impatient with a reporter, whose business it is to go out on all sorts of assignments and report the news as he finds it, with all the implications he can comprehend.

The facts I have reported have been often as great a shock to me as to you. The revelations and revolutions I have witnessed have produced revolutions in my theories. For I have believed what I

---

[1] When the *Bee* published this letter on July 27, under the title "How to Treat Criminals," it was prefaced by the following editorial note:

"LINCOLN STEFFENS, whose reputation as a tireless delver into municipal, state and national offenses and crimes is international, was in Sacramento last week.

"In the course of his visit to his old home town, he called upon the Editor of *The Bee,* and dwelt briefly upon his present views as to the best way to treat criminals and general public offenders.

"He was asked to sketch out his ideas and send them in for publication. And here they are."

reported. I have taken in, slowly, painfully, but conscientiously, the meaning of my news, and of course that has changed my mind often.

When I went from city to city, from state to state and to Washington, D. C., and saw with staring eyes that they all were governed, not by the constitutional mayors, governors, presidents and legislatures, but by bosses and rings representing, not The People, but privileged business, I wrote and published; but I also verily believed that our actual government differed from our paper government; that our chartered authorities were subject to an invisible government, which, described, was not only a scandal but in some sort the result of natural as distinguished from man-made laws.

I lost some of the illusions I had learned as a boy at the public schools of Sacramento and Berkeley.

This made of me, not a cynic and a "practical man," but a student. I began to report to the public and to study for myself the reform efforts of those days: Roosevelt and the police of New York; Folk and corporation corruption in Missouri; the young fighters of Chicago; the old fighters in Philadelphia; La Follette of Wisconsin; the graft prosecution of the labor government of San Francisco; Ben Lindsey and the "bad" boys and girls of Denver; and others, many, many others, as you well know.

You saw them all, and you saw that each of those reforms failed; the last one, Ben Lindsey's, only a few days ago. But I saw them all fail. I was struck by a generalization.

The reforms of our day improved, not government, but the methods of the graft system.

I wondered, and I ask you to wonder, why reform fails. The scientific approach to the truth is to set up a theory and then test it out. I formed, cautiously, some tentative explanations to account for the universal state of political corruption and the universal failure of evolutionary reforms.

One fault the reformers made was to blame bad men instead of the bad conditions which mechanically, naturally and necessarily produce the bad men and the bad governments.

There is a standing reward of riches, power and prominence for any men who will go and get and exploit natural resources, like forests, minerals and oil; and public franchises, like water, light and power.

I, too, called those bold bribers villains until I came to listen to them, as I had to to fix my facts and avoid libel. They told me only what you have heard them say: That they could not carry on their business without paying for "protection."

You may not have believed them; I didn't at first. But you are an editor. I am a reporter; and, one by one, year after year, city by city, state by state, many of these able, courageous, imaginative men both in politics and business showed me that you cannot run a privileged business without breaking, making or unmaking laws. I came to understand and like these men; I did not want to see them punished; it seemed to me that they should be used.

My theory was that, if we could take away the privileges which tempt and make them enemies of the common good, the big bad men would indeed become the leaders and servants of The People.

My reformer friends would not accept this theory. Naturally, they were brought up in the classical, not the scientific, culture; they acted upon "liberal principles." They were for punishing and ousting bad men and putting themselves and other good men in power. They did that. Very well. That was an experiment, too, a set of experiments, which failed.

The pressure of the privileges which they did not remove made them, the good men and their good government, bad. What would happen if these privileges were abolished? I wanted, I want still, to know; don't you?

When the war came—a consequence of the competition of the privileged interests of the great powers for imperial privileges; the trade routes, oil and other natural riches in weaker countries—when the world war put a breaking strain upon all the modern states, I followed, not the battles, but the revolutions which, to me, were merely fundamental reform struggles, efforts to change our system, not by punishing individuals, but by removing the privileges of the privileged classes.

The revolutions—Mexican, Russian, German, Italian, but especially the Russian—offered an opportunity to see how far men can get with their attempt to change the foundation instead of the superstructure of society.

You may not share the hopefulness of my interest in Soviet Russia, but you can understand how my close-up reporting of American (and English, French, German and European) reform failures might account for my wish that somehow, somewhere, some people will find the way out.

It is excusable in the mob to call me a Bolshevik, when I report on Soviet Russia's experiment, or a Fascista when I tell what I have seen in Italy under Mussolini; but I submit that it is not good journalism in an editor thus to confuse the reporter with the report.

And meanwhile, here at home, you may not approve, but you might possibly see, that I am consistently following my experience when I appear at the side of "bad" men and women, who, however violently or foolishly, commit against the law acts which I think are an effect upon some temperaments of causes and conditions, conditions which we (the editorial "we") will not even look at, to say nothing of reform.

Science is showing that a large proportion of our criminals, socalled, are sick people. It seems to me to be unscientific to punish sick people. But there are other healthy, so-called responsible offenders—the labor dynamiters, for example, whom also I have interceded for.

Yes, and there are still others—big capitalist bribers, the oil grafters and their bought cabinet officers, whom I would like to defend.

If, instead of threatening them with punishment, we would ask them to tell us why they did what they did, we might find out what the oil man's problem really is and how to solve it without bribery and wars, now absolutely unavoidable.

But, let me take the dynamiters' case, because that illustrates my theory of good and bad men. I was in Europe when I heard that the McNamaras were to be tried for blowing up the Los Angeles *Times* building.

Returning immediately, I got from a group of papers an assignment to report the case. Going back of the evidence, I learned easily that the McNamaras were guilty; but not alone; their labor organization had employed them to blow up non-union steelworks.

What were the conditions of conservative American workers to use dynamite against a large organization of American employers? The court could not ask that question. The rules of evidence excluded it.

The judge, whom I talked with about it, said that he had to handle the case as a simple murder; he could not recognize any "class war." Of course. But that meant that the truth (about the labor conditions which were making toward violence) could not come out in court.

With the permission of Clarence Darrow, the attorney for the defense, I went back of the court to—whom? To the commanding men of Los Angeles. I used my knowledge of other cities in that way.

The actual governors of every city are not the officials thereof, but the big business men who "had to" control the politicians.

I asked a politician who they were and went to them—on a theory. My theory was (and it is) that such men are not only powerful, but courageous and imaginative. They have vision. They have nerve. They never have to go to someone else for a decision; they make up their own minds, and they act off their own bats. They are what I call principals, the opposite of heelers.

I got a list of seventeen in Los Angeles; it was too large. There are not seventeen principals in any city. But the principals of Los Angeles were on my list, and they saw and they acted upon the idea I offered them, viz:

That there was a better way than force to meet their emergency. Labor had struck them. It was their turn to strike back.

"I think you can convict and hang those labor men," I said: and they thought so.

"But don't," I urged. "Let them go free; they are only agents. Let them go; call off the pursuit of their pals. Stop all prosecution in labor cases, then call in the principals of the labor movement and sit down with them on the job of making Los Angeles the best instead of the worst-paid labor town in the United States."

Each one of those men agreed to this startling proposition. Each one that agreed himself opposed an appeal to the others. They also had no faith in their kind.

"Do you mean to imply," I asked, "that you are the only one capable of a big, generous, wise act like this?"

That thought carried them.

So we went on and got, first, ten; then toward the end we had a meeting of some seventeen leading citizens of Los Angeles, including Mr. Harry Chandler and General Otis of the *Times,* with the district attorney, Captain Fredericks.

The district attorney said that he could not let the McNamaras go utterly unpunished; even if they did plead guilty and even though the meeting was for mercy, the Erectors' Association of Indianapolis (the national steel employers' organization) was demanding some sentence.

The present point, however, lies in the fact that those commanding men of Los Angeles, including the owners of the Times Building, blown and fired, assured the district attorney that they would back him in any settlement he might make, and they agreed with me to carry out the rest of the program; to consider anew the labor problem of their city.

I negotiated the exact terms of the settlement. That is to say, I was the medium of communication between the McNamaras and the county authorities, and the agreement made was not kept.

At the last moment, Fredericks told me in court that "Indianapolis" insisted that the sentence the McNamaras had accepted had to be increased; and later the other men indicted, Schmidt and Kaplan, who were to have been not prosecuted, were taken and sent to the penitentiary.

And, in the confusion and outcries over the settlement, the meetings of labor and capitalist principals were never called.

The whole plan to reverse the usual policy of an eye for an eye; force for force; and to make a practical demonstration of the efficacy of scientific (Christian) principles was not carried out.

But my belief that there is another, finer way of dealing with such problems was confirmed, and my theory that big men are as ready and able to do good things as bad things, was proven, as T. R. used to say, "up to the hilt."

When I went East again, I met on Fifth Avenue in New York Mr. Drew, the secretary of the Erectors' Association, which had blunted the Los Angeles settlement so badly. He stopped me to ask, "What the deuce were you trying to do out there?" I told him in a few words.

"Why didn't you let us in on it," he answered. "We would have stood in with that."

The trouble with the Erectors' Association was the trouble with all our big men, I think. They were not—they are not—asked to make sacrifices.

They are asked for money, for charity, for little favors; and these they do generously.

What would they do if they were asked to "hurt business" to help the country or labor or—their enemies?

This is one of the questions I am seeking to report the answers to, and my principals—the big bad men, whether in finance, politics or labor,—understand that and are privately my friends, as I am privately,

Yours,
Lincoln Steffens

VI. ON REFORM AND COMMUNISM [1]

To Sam Darcy,[1]
Nominee of the Communist Party for Governor of California
Chairman of the Communist Party Rally
San Francisco, California.

The Getaway,
Carmel, Cal. [1934]

Comrades:

All my long life—too long—I have been following the stink of the trail of our so-called political corruption back up from the bad politics we deplored to the good business that bought and owns our bad government: to its war and its peace; to our riches, to our poverty, vice, to our college-bred ignorance on down to the world-wide collapse from within of the whole stupid, crooked, mean economic system that we call civilization today. When the panic came in 1929, I struck the trail again to see and listen to some of the big bosses of this big business, the men who had jeered at us muckrakers and—I found that they did not know what had happened to them and us, they did not know what was wrong, what to do about it! They DID not know, they DO not know. Our rulers and masters do not understand the machinery of their business or of our civilization; nor what to do about it; and our schools and colleges—our culture does not know what else to do than to go on and rise and collapse again, and again, and again.

And they want you and me to be patient—they in their comfortable riches, want you and me in our distress to stand still and take poverty and wretchedness on the chin—

Now, all this lifetime of mine when they jeered at me and my colleagues of the muckrake—these makers of the muck in high jest bade me report to them if I came to the end of my trail when, if ever, I found a cause and a cure for us and for them and our evils— And

---

[1] Statement to be read at the Communist Party rally in San Francisco, September, 1934, endorsing the party's candidates for State offices.

I promised many of them and myself that when that day came I would indeed—report.

Well, that day has come.

I can come down to earth, here, on this carefully chosen spot—before this crowd of willing listeners, to the only crowd that *must act*—I can come here and point out to you and to them and to all my fellow-American citizens a scientific cure for all our troubles.

It is Communism. For these United States. I mean *especially* for this great and successful country, at this very time of its distress and confusion, now, when we are shocked to discover that in our dumb blindness we have hit upon machinery and methods by which we can produce so much food, shelter and clothing, that we cannot distribute our abundance at a private profit— Now here, where seventeen million hungry people are creating a fierce demand for all we can produce and more—exactly for America, the American Communist Party proposes a program which meets all our social problems —*all*—graft, ignorance, poverty and over-production, vice and an impending war—exactly.

Communism can solve our problem. Communism does solve our problem—in Soviet Russia— That's my muckraker's proclamation; that the American Communist Party program meets our American capitalist situation precisely and it is the only American party that meets it—head on: all of it: the political corruption, the poverty and plenty, the periodic depressions of business—all our troubles; and proposes to solve them at any cost. The Communist Party offers to do that in California, in the United States; it offered to do it in Germany and it has done it in Soviet Russia, where you can go and see—as I have—where anyone can go and see our horrid old uncivilized economic system lying upside down on its back out on the steppes with its rusty wheels in the air.

There, before our eyes, our searching, unbelieving eyes, there, a leading part of the human race has done the job, brown, that we still have to do. And need to do, and must do. We cannot do it as Upton Sinclair proposes. We cannot any of us go out "as one good man for governor" and do it individually. We must do it as the American Communist Party, taught, fortunately, by the Russian pioneers, proposes to do it, by the building of a trained, highly-disciplined party, all of whose members—*all*—want—at any cost—to do the same one, agreed-upon, fundamental thing.

BIBLIOGRAPHY
OF LINCOLN STEFFENS

Newspaper articles, with a few exceptions, are not included,
nor are some articles in smaller magazines

1. MAGAZINE ARTICLES AND STORIES

The Viking's Boat Song, *The Berkeleyan,* June, 1887
Sweet Punch, *Harper's Weekly,* Dec., 1893
Schloma, the Daughter of Schmuhl, *Chap-Book,* June 15, 1896
The Count and the Baker, *New York Post,* Aug. 12, 1896
The Tanagra of Mulberry Bend, *New York Post,* Nov. 21, 1896
De Howlers an' de Growlers, *New York Post,* June 19, 1897
The Modern Business Building, *Scribner's,* July, 1897
Life in the Klondike Gold Fields, *McClure's,* Sept., 1897
The Business of a Newspaper, *Scribner's,* Oct., 1897
Bloke Murray's Golden Moon, *New York Commercial Advertiser,* Dec. 19,
    1897
Itzig: "A Reporter's Boy," *Youth's Companion* [1]
For the First Edition, *Youth's Companion* [1]
John Howe of Seven Truck, *Youth's Companion* [1]
Yalan Mohamadac [2]
The Pride of Greenwich Village [2]
The Real Roosevelt, *Ainslee's,* Dec., 1898
Theodore Roosevelt, Governor, *McClure's,* May, 1899
The Use of Katie, *Youth's Companion,* June 8, 1899
Old Jim Horse, *McClure's,* May, 1900
The Compliments of the Chief, *Ainslee's,* July, 1900
Governor Roosevelt—as an Experiment, *Ainslee's,* June, 1900
Senator Jerry Watkins, *Ainslee's,* Nov., 1900

[1] Included without dates in a scrapbook of short stories apparently prepared
for publication. Probable year, 1898.
[2] Possibly appeared in a newspaper, the *Post* or *Commercial Advertiser;* included in the scrapbook without date or place of publication.

Dan McCarthy, Captain of Police, *McClure's*, March, 1901

Two Bosses: Platt and Croker, *Ainslee's*, May, 1901 (unsigned)

Politics, *Ainslee's*, Oct., 1901

The Overworked President, *McClure's*, Apr., 1902

Labor Leader of Today: John Mitchell and What He Stands For, *McClure's*, Aug., 1902

Tweed Days in St. Louis, *McClure's*, Oct., 1902 (in collaboration with Claude H. Wetmore)

The Banker's Love Story, *Ainslee's*, Oct., 1902

The American Man on Horseback, *McClure's*, Dec., 1902

The Shame of Minneapolis, *McClure's*, Jan., 1903

The Shamelessness of St. Louis, *McClure's*, March, 1903

Masters of Their Craft, *McClure's*, Apr., 1903 (signed Adrian Kirk)

Pittsburgh, a City Ashamed, *McClure's*, May, 1903

Jacob A. Riis, *McClure's*, Aug., 1903

Chicago, Half Free and Fighting On, *McClure's*, Oct., 1903

The New School of Journalism, *Bookman*, Oct., 1903

New York: Good Government in Danger, *McClure's*, Nov., 1903

Enemies of the Republic, Missouri, *McClure's*, Apr., 1904

Enemies of the Republic, Illinois, *McClure's*, Aug., 1904

Enemies of the Republic, Wisconsin, *McClure's*, Oct., 1904

Rhode Island: a State for Sale, *McClure's*, Feb., 1905

New Jersey: a Traitor State, *McClure's*, Apr., May, 1905

Ohio: a Tale of Two Cities, *McClure's*, June, 1905

The Chief, the Child, and Mickey Sweeney, *Collier's*, Apr. 22, 1905

Philadelphians Are Grafting, *New York World*, May 21, 1905

A Servant of the People, *McClure's*, Jan., 1906

The Gentleman from Essex, *McClure's*, Feb., 1906

Newspaper Syndicate Series (*New York World* and other papers)

   Is "Our" Government Ours?, Jan. 14, 1906

   The President Is President, Jan. 21, 1906

   The Senate as It Sees Itself, Jan. 28, 1906

   Our Dummy Directors in the House, Feb. 4, 1906

   The President as a Boss, Feb. 11, 1906

   The Reign of Public Opinion, Feb. 18, 1906

   Our People Are Helpless, Feb. 25, 1906

   Washington: A Spectacle, Mar. 4, 1906

   Forming New Political Parties, Mar. 11, 1906

   How to Reform Congress, Mar. 18, 1906

   National Bankers' Graft, Mar. 25, 1906

Journalism, Sunday Magazine of the Minneapolis *Journal*, Aug. 5, 1906

Ben B. Lindsey, the Just Judge, *McClure's*, Oct.-Dec., 1906

A Stolen Rescue, *American*, Oct., 1906
Hearst, the Man of Mystery, *American*, Nov., 1906
The Making of a Fighter, *American*, Aug., 1907
The Taming of the West, *American*, Sept.-Oct., 1907
The Mote and the Beam, *American*, Nov., Dec., 1907
Rudolph Spreckels, *American*, Feb., 1908
U'Ren the Law Giver, *American*, Mar., 1908
William J. Burns, Intriguer, *American*, Apr., 1908
Apology for Graft, *American*, June, 1908
Roosevelt, Taft, LaFollette, *Everybody's* June, 1908
Bryan, Johnson, *Everybody's*, July, 1908
Mickey Sweeney, Detective of Detectives, *American*, July, 1908
Mickey's Yaller Dog and the Chief's, *Collier's*, Aug. 29, 1908
Eugene V. Debs, *Everybody's*, Oct., 1908
The Least of These, *Everybody's*, Jan., 1909
The Twice-Told Tale of a Stolen Theater, *Success*, Jan., 1909
The Mind of a State, *LaFollette's Weekly*, Jan. 9, 1909
Sending a State to College, *American*, Feb., 1909
Mickey's Homicide, *Everybody's*, Feb., 1909
Joseph Fels, *American*, Oct., 1910
It: An Exposition of the Sovereign Political Power of Organized Business,
    McClure's
    1. The Boss of All the Bosses, Sept., 1910
    2. Wall Street on Wall Street, Oct., 1910
    3. The Power of the Money Power, Nov., 1910
    4. The Politics of Business, Dec., 1910
    5. A Business Republic, Feb., 1911
    6. A Ring-Robbed Railroad, Apr., 1911
Watch Your Congressman, *Everybody's*, May, 1911
Mary Austin, *American*, June, 1911
The Right of Free Speech, *Everybody's*, Nov., 1911
Free Speech vs. Censorship, *Everybody's*, Dec., 1911
Out of the Muck, *Everybody's*, Dec., 1911
A King for a Queen, *Masses*, Apr., 1913
Why Not Be Interesting?, *Harper's Weekly*, Oct. 11, 1913
Culture and Agriculture, *Harper's Weekly*, Jan. 10, 1914
Police! Police!, *Harper's Weekly*, Feb. 21, 1914
The Case for Inequality (Prize Winning answer to George Bernard Shaw),
    Metropolitan, Feb., 1914
A Cure for Corruption, *Metropolitan*, Feb., 1914
The Failure of Government by Good People, *Metropolitan*, Mar., 1914
Fruits of Good Government in New England, *Metropolitan*, Apr., 1914

News as Is News, *Harper's Weekly,* Apr. 11, 1914
How to Get an Education Even in College, *Harper's Weekly,* Apr. 11, 1914
How College Students Can Educate Themselves, *Harper's Weekly,* Apr. 18, 1914
Free Speech With and Without, *Harper's Weekly,* May 9, 1914
The Dying Boss, *McClure's,* May, 1914
A Way Out for Any City, State, or Nation, *Metropolitan,* May, 1914
Robert Dunn, *Bookman,* June, 1914
The Reluctant Briber, *McClure's,* Mar., 1915
The Sunny Side of Mexico, *Metropolitan,* May, 1915
The Master of Women, *Everybody's,* July, 1915
The Honesty of Honest Tom, *McClure's,* July, 1915
Collusion, *Life,* Aug. 26, 1915
Pop's Ribbon-Thief, *Everybody's,* Sept., 1915
Pop's Place for Sassy Sally, *Everybody's,* Dec., 1915
A Po-lice-man, *Life,* Jan. 13, 1916
Strictly Business, *Life,* Jan. 27, 1916
The Boss Who Was Bossed, *McClure's,* Jan., 1916
The World's Interest in the Mexican Revolution, *Accion Mundial,* Feb. 5, 1916
California and the Japanese, *Collier's,* Mar. 25, 1916
Into Mexico and—Out!, *Everybody's,* May, 1916
A Talk Across the Border, *Masses,* July, 1916
Thirty-Three, *Everybody's,* July, 1916
Making Friends with Mexico, *Collier's,* Nov. 25, 1916
Bunk, *Everybody's,* Feb., 1917
The Great Lost Moment, *Everybody's,* Mar., 1917
What Free Russia Asks of the Allies, *Everybody's,* Aug., 1917
Rasputin—the Real Story, *Everybody's,* Sept., Oct., 1917
Introduction to *The War and the Bolsheviki* by Leon Trotzky (Boni & Liveright), 1918
The Rumor in Russia, *Nation,* Dec. 21, 1918 (signed Christian)
Report of the Bullitt Mission on Russia, *Nation,* Oct. 4, 1919 (later published as a government report)
The White Streak, *Collier's,* Jan. 15, 1921
Tale of Tails, *Century,* Feb., 1922
The Battle of Celayo, *Collier's,* Mar. 11, 1922
The Devil's Own Way, *Century,* June, 1922
Gift from the East, *Century,* Dec., 1922
How Europe Can Help America, *Century,* Aug., 1923
Atlas, a Fable, *Century,* Oct., 1923
Soviet Russians, *The American Weekly,* Dec. 2 and 9, 1923

Moses: a Miracle of Mercy, *Century*, Dec., 1923
N.E.P.'s, *transatlantic review*, No. 2, Feb., 1924
The Pallor of the Yellow Peril, *Century*, Oct., 1924
Knowledge of Trees, *Century*, Dec., 1924
Stop, Look, Listen, *Survey-Graphic*, Mar. 1, 1927
Pull, *Survey-Graphic*, Dec. 1, 1928
A Miserable Merry Christmas, *Pictorial Review*, Dec., 1927
The Light That Failed, *Survey-Graphic*, Jan. 1, 1928
Becoming a Father at Sixty is a Liberal Education, *American*, Aug., 1928
Roosevelt as a Politician, *Plain Talk*, Sept., 1928
Getting Old Bill Devery, *Plain Talk*, Nov., 1928
How I Made a Crime Wave, *Bookman*, Dec., 1928
I'm Teaching My Boy to Defy Me, *North American Review*, May, 1929
Brains, a Fable, *New Freeman*, Dec. 10, 1930
Two Fables, *New Freeman*, Mar. 11, 1931
Don't Say Don't, *New Freeman*, Apr. 8, 1931
As Steffens Sees It (Mussolini the Fascist), *Survey-Graphic*, Oct. 1, 1931
Armenians Are Impossible, *Outlook*, Oct. 14, 1931
Bankrupt Liberalism, *New Republic*, Feb. 17, 1932
Attorney for the Damned, *Saturday Review of Literature*, Feb. 27, 1932
Satan Invents Art, *Saturday Review of Literature*, Feb. 27, 1932
This World Depression of Ours is Chock Full of Good News (republished
    as Youth and Plenty in *Lincoln Steffens Speaking*), *Cosmopolitan*,
    Oct., 1932
But Will It Be All the Same One Hundred Years from Now?, Symposium,
    Cosmopolitan, Feb., 1933
Satan's Version of the Fall of Man, *Scribner's*, Jan., 1934
Introduction to *Fatherland* by Karl Billinger (Farrar & Rinehart), 1933
The Greatest of Liberals, *Soviet Russia To-Day*, Jan., 1936
A Letter About Jack Reed, *New Republic*, May 20, 1936
The Influence of My Father on My Son, *Atlantic*, May, 1937 (written
    1930, published posthumously)

Steffens wrote a regular column, as well as editorials, book reviews and
    articles for local Carmel papers from 1927 to 1936—*The Carmelite*,
    Controversy, and *Pacific Weekly*. Some excerpts from these were re-
    printed in *Lincoln Steffens Speaking* (1936)
Book reviews also appeared in the *Nation*, *New Republic*, and *Saturday
    Review of Literature*.

2. BOOKS

The Shame of the Cities, McClure, Phillips & Co., 1904
The Struggle for Self-Government, McClure, Phillips & Co., 1906
Upbuilders, Doubleday, Page & Co., 1909
The Least of These, Hillacre-Riverside Press, 1910
Out of the Muck, Hillacre-Riverside Press, 1913
Free Speech With and Without, Hillacre-Riverside Press, 1914
John Reed: Under the Kremlin, Introduction by Clarence Darrow, Walden
    Book Shop, 1922
Moses in Red: The Revolt of Israel as a typical Revolution, Philadelphia,
    Dorrance & Co., 1926
The Autobiography of Lincoln Steffens, Harcourt, Brace & Co., 1931
Boy on Horseback, Harcourt, Brace and Company, 1935
Lincoln Steffens Speaking, Harcourt, Brace and Company, 1936

INDEX